DESIGN 1935–1965
WHAT MODERN WAS

DESIGN 1935-1965

EDITED BY MARTIN EIDELBERG

ESSAY BY

Paul Johnson

CONTRIBUTORS

Kate Carmel

Martin Eidelberg

Marilyn B. Fish

David A. Hanks

Frederica Todd Harlow

Christine W. Laidlaw

R. Craig Miller

Lenore Newman

Marc O. Rabun

Gregory Saliola

Penny Sparke

Jennifer Toher Teulié

Christa C. Mayer Thurman

Christopher Wilk

Toni Lesser Wolf

Alice Zrebiec

LE MUSÉE DES ARTS

DÉCORATIFS DE MONTRÉAL

in association with

HARRY N. ABRAMS, INC.,

PUBLISHERS, NEW YORK

WHAT MODERN WAS

SELECTIONS FROM THE LILIANE AND DAVID M. STEWART COLLECTION

Château Dufresne, Musée des Arts Décoratifs de Montréal

Exhibition organized by David A. Hanks & Associates, Inc.,
for Le Musée des Arts Décoratifs de Montréal.

Project Director: Marti Malovany
Editor: Lory Frankel
Designer: Bob McKee

Library of Congress Cataloging-in-Publication Data
Design 1935–1965: what modern was: selections from the Liliane
    and David M. Stewart Collection; Le Musée des arts décoratifs de
    Montréal/edited by Martin Eidelberg.
            p.   cm.
        "Exhibition organized by David A. Hanks & Associates . . ."
        "Exhibition and catalogue have been sponsored by a grant from
    the IBM Corporation."
        ISBN 0–8109–3205–9
        1. Decorative arts—History—20th century—Exhibitions.
    2. Decoration and ornament—International style—Exhibitions.
    3. Postmodernism—Exhibitions.   4. Stewart, David M.—Art
    collections—Exhibitions.   5. Stewart, Liliane—Art collections—
    Exhibitions.   6. Decorative arts—Private collections—Québec
    (Province)—Montréal—Exhibitions.   7. Musée des arts décoratifs de
    Montréal—Exhibitions.   I. Eidelberg, Martin P.   II. Musée des arts
    décoratifs de Montréal.   III. David A. Hanks & Associates.
    IV. International Business Machines Corporation.
    NK1394.D47   1991
    745′.09′0407471428—dc20   90–46962
    ISBN 0–8109–2480–3 (pbk.)

Title page (left to right): Harry Bertoia, coffee service; Alvar
Aalto, armchair; Philip Johnson and Richard Kelly, floor lamp

Table of Contents

Acknowledgments

This exhibition and accompanying publication are the result of the dedicated work of talented people both inside and outside the museum. The conception and organization of this exhibition is due to the efforts of David A. Hanks & Associates, New York, the museum's consulting curatorial team. Overseeing all the philosophical and scholarly complexities of organizing a book of this magnitude was Martin Eidelberg, the editor of this publication. He managed this enormous undertaking with determination, commitment to quality, and perceptive knowledge. As coordinator, Kate Carmel was responsible for many aspects of the publication and exhibition, including the pursuit of acquisitions and meetings with numerous designers and manufacturers. Marc O. Rabun was responsible for coordinating the production of the manuscript and preparing the photograph captions for the book; he also wrote label and wall text for the exhibition. Caroline Stern was responsible for directing photography and photo research and helping prepare objects for exhibition; her long-term commitment to this project has been an indispensable factor to its success. Gordon Frey provided untiring assistance in locating comparative photographic images and securing permission for their inclusion in the catalogue. Mary Dellin assisted in carrying out many special tasks. Of the past and present staff and interns at David A. Hanks & Associates, we would like to thank Jessica Deutsch, Derek Ostergard, Jennifer Toher Teulié, and Sandee Heneson Walker. Ellen Davidson patiently carried out both word processing and proofreading under a rigorous schedule. And most particularly, without the dedication, perseverance, and patience of David A. Hanks, this collection, exhibition, and book would not have been possible.

To acknowledge those who participated in the writing of the catalogue, the entries carry the initials of the authors, whose names are cited in full in the list of contributors. We are greatly indebted to them for their expertise and spirit of cooperation in bringing this publication to fruition. We owe special thanks to our colleagues Christa C. Mayer Thurman, R. Craig Miller, and Christopher Wilk, who were the early enthusiastic supporters of this exhibition effort. Christine W. Laidlaw deserves thanks for accepting additional assignments and her untiring, excellent work.

Many scholars, archivists, and dealers were willing to share research unearthed in their fields of specialized study, as were family and friends of the designers. These include Marco Albini, Mrs. Gunnar Andersen, Yvonne Brunhammer, Elaine Lustig Cohen, Judy Cohen, Priscilla Cunningham, the late Mitchell Cutler, the late Ralph Cutler, Laurence de Lamaestre, Eleana Chiappini di Sorio, Helen Drutt, Lynn Felsher, Vinny Fuller Fish, Barnaba Fornasetti, Barry Friedman, David Gebhard, Harwell Hamilton Harris, Eric Helton, Suzanne Huguenin, Michel Hurst, Mark Isaacson, Mrs. Richard Kelly, Marguerite R. Kimball, Dan Klein, Catherine Kurland, Suzanne Lipschutz, Mark MacDonald, Larry Majewski, Daniel Marchesseau, Nancy McClelland, Greg Nacozy, Mrs. George Nelson, S. Bernard Paré, Mrs. Davis Pratt, Luigi Ricci, Irving Richards, Robert Swope, Mr. and Mrs. George Tanier, Helena Tynell, Alexander von Vegesack, and Gregory M. Wittkopp.

For advice and aid in locating information about objects, we wish to thank numerous designers whose work is represented in this exhibition: Eero Aarnio, Magdalena Abakanowicz, Irena Brynner, Torun Bülow-Hübe, Wendell Castle, Gunnar Cyrén, Lucienne Day, Alexander Girard, Eszter Haraszty, Irving Harper, Sheila Hicks, Grete Jalk, the late Finn Juhl, Ray Komai, Donald Knorr, Jack Lenor Larsen, Ibram Lassaw, Ross Littell, the late George Nelson, Ed Rossbach, Lino Sabattini, Robert Sailors, Ruth Adler Schnee, Ettore Sottsass, Marianne Straub, Marianne Strengell, Toshiko Takaezu, Lenore Tawney, John Van Koert, Hans Wegner, and Edward J. Wormley.

Objects in the collection chosen for the exhibition have frequently required the attention of skilled conservators in Canada and the United States. We would like to thank The Canadian Conservation Institute, Rudy Colban, Judith Eisenberg, Tom Frank, Elayne Grossbard, Paul Hazlett, Ellen Hess, Ellen Howe, Abraham Joel, Hermes Knauer, Christine Krumrine, Susan Schussler, Marjorie Shelley, Dr. George Wheeler, and Polly Willman. For scientific analysis and identification of materials used in the objects in the collection we thank Sharon Blank, assistant objects conservator, Los Angeles County Museum of Art; Donna J. Christensen of Forest Products Laboratory, United States Department of Agriculture; Dr. Brandt A. Rising of Lucius Pitkin

Laboratories; and Martin N. Youngberg. Among the individuals who have lent their time and talents in the transportation and storage of the collection, we would like to mention Daniel Amadée, president of Museo Techni, Montréal, Richard Haase, New York, Betty Teller, Jacques Viens, Museo Techni, and Bill and Doris Zamprelli, Eagle Warehouse, New York.

Manufacturers and retailers of objects in the exhibition have also been of enormous help in the research for this publication. These include: Ahlström-Iittala (Satu Grönstrand), Akari Associates, Akari-Gemini, Arabia Oy (Mirja-Kaisa Hipeli), Bing & Grøndahl, Carl Hansen & Son A/S (Jørgen Gerner Hansen), Edison Price, Inc., Georg Jensen Silversmithy (Michael von Essen), AB Gustavsberg, Heal and Son Ltd. (Jane Taylor), Herman Miller, Inc. (Linda Folland), Knoll International (Carol A. Kim), AB Kosta Glasbruk, Laverne Originals (Erwine and Estelle Laverne), Marimekko Oy, AB Orrefors Glasbruk (Anders Reihnér), Polaroid Corporation, Porzellanfabrik Thomas Rosenthal, Towle International, Venini S.p.A. (Giuliana Tucci), and Warner & Sons, Inc. (Mary Schoeser).

Special photography was carried out for this publication. Over a number of years, Richard P. Goodbody, New York, has brought great sensitivity to the photographic interpretation of objects. We have been fortunate in having the services of the photographers Schecter Lee, New York, Mark Meachem, Teca Cay, South Carolina, and Giles Rivest, Montreal. We are also grateful to Liz Finger, New York, for advice on graphic design over the past years.

The complex task of producing a publication with such a variety of scholarly material has been carried out by an able staff at Harry N. Abrams, Inc., who performed graciously under the pressure of an extremely difficult deadline. Marti Malovany was responsible for bringing the project to Abrams and for coordinating it over the past five years. The handsome design and visual organization of this large body of photographs and text was carried out by Bob McKee, with the assistance of Laura Lovett. Lory Frankel has edited the extensive manuscript written by multiple authors with great clarity, ably assisted by Ellyn Childs Allison and Alexandra Bonfante-Warren.

It is a pleasure to thank the staff of the IBM Gallery of Science and Art. Special thanks also go to the IBM Corporation for its subvention of the research for the catalogue and sponsorship of the exhibition.

We were aided by the skills and experience of our own museum staff: Pascale Champoux, Diane Charbonneau, Sylvia Deschênes, Cheryl François, Louise Giroux, Elizabeth Lewis, Maryse Ménard, Beth Morgan, Jacques Surprenant, Suzanne Taylor, Estelle Thibodeau, and Jean-Michel Tuchscherer. Grants from a variety of Canadian agencies were pivotal to the exhibition's success, and we would like to express thanks to Fernand Tanguay, director of the International Cultural Relations Bureau, Department of External Affairs, Ottawa; The Canada Council; Ministère des Affaires culturelles du Québec; and Communications, Canada.

To the dedicated staff of the Macdonald Stewart Foundation, we owe our gratitude. James Carroll, director of the Foundation, has patiently overseen numerous arrangements for the exhibition and publication from concept to execution. Others at the Foundation to whom we owe thanks are Bruce Bolton, Guy Ducharme, Lucille Riley, and Doug Ross.

The American Friends of Canada made possible the acquisition of many of the objects in the museum's collection selected for this exhibition. Stanley M. Ackert III and Gaetana M. Enders have enthusiastically contributed their time in support of this exhibition.

Roy R. Eddey, deputy director of the Brooklyn Museum, provided advice for the development of the exhibition contract. National publicity for the exhibition was carried out by Debra Greenberg and Anne Edgar, The Kreisberg Group, Ltd., New York.

Above all, we are grateful to Mrs. David M. Stewart and the late David M. Stewart, for forming this collection and supporting the scholarship that has made this exhibition and publication possible.

Luc d'Iberville-Moreau
Director
Le Musée des Arts Décoratifs de Montréal

Foreword

The Château Dufresne opened its doors to the public on June 14, 1979, as Canada's first museum devoted exclusively to the decorative arts. At that time my husband and I, after considering various options, decided to start a collection of twentieth-century decorative arts, concentrating on the postwar years. This decision was based on our feelings that collections of earlier, traditional periods were already well established and that master-pieces were avidly sought by museums and private collectors, thus limiting the possibilities of creating a new collection of international distinction. On the other hand, few institutions had made a serious effort to collect decorative arts of the postwar years. The challenge to create a collection in an area barely researched by scholars and little known to collectors was compelling.

We formed an Advisory Board of persons interested and involved in the decorative arts, gathering together a wide range of expertise. The members were Yvonne Brunhammer, conservateur en chef, Musée des Arts Décoratifs, Paris; R. Craig Miller, associate curator, Twentieth Century Art, The Metropolitan Museum of Art, New York; Eleana Chiappini di Sorio, curator, Museo Correr, Venice; Duke Umberto Pini di San Miniato, interior designer, Montreal; Stephen Bailey, director, Design Museum, London; and Jack Lenor Larsen, president, Jack Lenor Larsen Inc., New York. These and many other specialists who have been consulted over the years have greatly helped us with the collection.

The museum is currently housed in the Château Dufresne, which is an unusual twin residence built in 1914 for the Dufresne brothers. In the 1960s the building was saved from demolition by the City of Montreal, but it remained unused and empty until we took it over in 1976. The acquisition of the original furnishings of the Château Dufresne provided a unique opportunity to return some of the rooms to their original 1914 splendor. Seven rooms have been restored; two salons, a library, a dining room, and a smoking room were completed for the opening, and a bedroom and bathroom were finished seven years later. We wanted to provide space for a collection of decorative arts as well, and thus the rest of the building was converted into offices and exhibition galleries. This juxtaposition provides an interesting comparison between objects in context and objects displayed singly as works of art.

The museum and its collection have been a cooperative undertaking. The historical and modern design collections, owned by the Château Dufresne Inc., the Lake St. Louis Historical Society, and the American Friends of Canada, are on permanent loan to the museum. The museum building is owned by the City of Montreal, and its operation is funded by the Macdonald Stewart Foundation and governmental and other agencies. This unique cooperation has helped contribute to the flourishing of the arts in Montreal.

A program of special exhibitions has always been part of the museum's mission. Space in the mansion is devoted to showing some of the exciting traveling exhibitions that have been organized on both historic and contemporary aspects of twentieth-century design. In addition, the museum itself has organized a number of exhibitions: "Eva Zeisel: Designer for Industry" (1984), which has traveled to museums in North America and Europe; "École du Meuble 1930–1950: Interior Design and Decorative Art in Montreal" (1989); and "Modern Jewelry from the Helen Williams Drutt Collection" (1985), which subsequently traveled to museums in the United States.

This exhibition, "Design 1935–1965: What Modern Was," marks the culmination of ten years of collecting. Initially, our idea was to collect international decorative arts from 1940 to 1960. However, we soon realized that the commencement date of the collection should be pushed back to 1935, closer to the genesis of prewar modern design. The collection was to have terminated with objects produced around 1960, but it became equally clear that the collection should be extended to 1965 because of the dramatic shifts that occurred culturally and aesthetically in the middle of that decade. Although the collection goes up to the present day, our concentration remains on the period from 1935 to 1965.

Since my husband's death in 1984, I have continued to carry out these original goals so dear to his heart. Although at first the collection carried my name, I decided in 1984 to rename it the Liliane and David M. Stewart Collection because of the great enthusiasm shown by my husband while we were collecting together, as well as the tremendous support he gave me.

Our museum has quickly grown into a major repository of objects and important archives, but we find that we have now outgrown our charming first home. At the end of 1988, it was apparent that if we wished to show a reasonable portion of our collection, we would either have to enlarge the museum or move to another location. A museum planning committee is presently studying the specific space requirements of our collections and exhibitions and the demands placed on it by a growing audience. We are making plans for the next twenty years of the museum, and we hope that we will soon have a new facility that will be a marvelous setting for our collections.

Mrs. David M. Stewart
President, Château Dufresne,
Musée des Arts Décoratifs de Montréal

Modern in the Past Tense

Modernity is closely linked with a sense of time. That temporality is normally based in the present, and occasionally it is linked to the future, especially if it carries implications of lasting values. "Modern is . . ." and "modern will be . . ."—those are the standard declensions. "Modern was . . ." is a disquieting conjunction, for it creates a seeming contradiction.

Modern design, in its simplest and most generic form, implies the up-to-date, a current trend, or, better still, a future trend. Many use Modern with a capital M to refer specifically to the period between the early 1920s and the outbreak of World War II: the heroic age of Le Corbusier and L'Esprit Nouveau, the age of Walter Gropius and the Bauhaus. It was the time when the guiding principles of twentieth-century industrial design were forged, the time when an idealistic generation sought to clarify and purify design, to create a language of rational, eternal form. Others might argue that Modern design, even with the capital M, also encompassed the decade and a half after the war, an equally heroic age of artists like Charles and Ray Eames, Eero Saarinen, and Tapio Wirkkala.

From the vantage point of the 1990s, the nomenclature and chronology of Modernism take on a certain irony. Can events of three-quarters of a century or even a half-century ago still be termed *modern? Ars longa, vita brevis,* but can we term designers *modern* when they have been dead for several decades?

The emergence of the term *Post-Modern* has, if anything, emphasized the curious sense of separation that now exists between us today and that age that we designate as Modern. This distance is not merely the syndrome of a past Golden (or Silver or Bronze) Age; it comes from a very real sense of the passage of time and the change in ideas. In fact, the term *Post-Modern* was already being used sporadically in the 1930s and 1950s, as each generation recognized its distance from a previous generation.[1]

Semantics aside, the issue is to understand and chart what really occurred. The decision to form the Stewart Collection and stage this exhibition has afforded an interesting opportunity to look back at the period from 1935 to 1965 and to examine the changing concepts of Modernism. History, however, is elusive. It eludes us, as it happens, because of the magnitude of the data, which can be so great that we do not distinguish the trivial from the ultimately meaningful. Moreover, despite the seeming wealth of documentation, despite the profusion of magazines, books, and exhibition catalogues dealing with art and design, and despite the growth of corporate archives and oral history, it has been distressing to find that so much basic information from our recent past is still lacking. Even with the availability of introductory promotional material and the texts of later scholarship, the verbiage frequently tells us little that is concrete. There are times when events and ideas of forty years ago seem as remote and inscrutable as those of Periclean Greece.

Based on the range of objects in the Stewart Collection, it was decided to arrange this publication as a series of thematic chapters, each dealing with an aspect of Modernism.

Although there is an underlying chronological scheme—one that goes from 1935 to 1965, from Marcel Breuer to Ettore Sottsass—the aim has been to avoid a strictly chronological ordering. As will become evident, there was no single line of development but, rather, a series of different and occasionally overlapping issues. For example, there was a continuity between prewar and postwar ideas and between different stylistic movements. Our aim was not to classify a designer one way or the other but to establish some sense of the growth and flow of ideas. Nor have we felt any compunction about dividing an artist's work among several thematic sections when appropriate, especially if he or she shifted his stance with the passage of time or experimented with different viewpoints concurrently. We have also resisted the common temptation to classify objects by types or mediums; although the specific concerns of seating furniture are different from those of ceramic dinnerware, the more significant concepts are irrespective of category.

A large number of people have spent many years in preparing this study, yet it should be viewed as a modest document. It has been subject to many restrictions, such as the availability of objects, the constraint of time, and the problem of available space within the exhibition and publication. There are prejudices of scholarship and taste that consciously or not have guided us. Nonetheless, we have tried as best we could to gather the various historical threads together and weave them into a meaningful fabric. As we begin this journey, we might consider the inscription commissioned by the French government from Paul Valéry, the national poet, for the Paris 1937 "Exposition Internationale des Arts et Techniques." Though posed in the lofty rhetoric of an earlier generation, it still has value for us today.

IT DEPENDS ON WHO PASSES
WHETHER I AM A TOMB OR A TREASURY
WHETHER I SPEAK OR AM SILENT
THIS DEPENDS ONLY ON YOU
DO NOT ENTER WITHOUT INTEREST . . .

WITHIN THESE WALLS CONSECRATED TO MARVELS
I GREET AND GUARD THE WORKS
FROM THE PRODIGIOUS HAND OF THE ARTIST
THE EQUAL AND RIVAL OF HIS THOUGHTS
THE ONE IS NOTHING WITHOUT THE OTHER

THINGS RARE OR THINGS BEAUTIFUL
HERE ARE WISELY ASSEMBLED
THEY INSTRUCT THE EYE TO LOOK
AT ALL THINGS IN THE WORLD
AS IF NEVER SEEN BEFORE[2]

ME

The Age of the Giant State

The third of a century from 1935 to 1965 marked the climax of state gigantism, which has been one of the central features of the twentieth century. It has left its mark on every aspect of life, not least design. For the state, whether totalitarian or social democrat, whether engaged in power politics or dispensing welfare, needed to impose its authority on reluctant, recalcitrant, or skeptical populations, and one way in which it did so was to increase its visibility. It impressed through the eyes. It designed for itself new sets of regalia that centered around symbols—the fasces, the hammer and sickle, the swastika, the Maoist sun. It staged regular mass public ceremonies. It pushed through vast programs of public works, from workers' housing to government buildings. The state strove for omnipotence and, in order to achieve it, gave the impression that it was ubiquitous; the citizen could not stroll more than a few hundred yards without coming upon some visible evidence of the state's activity.

By 1935 state power in large parts of the world had been expanding steadily for over two decades. Before World War I, the state's activities were relatively limited in most countries, absorbing only between 5 and 10 percent of the gross national product. In 1913 the state's total income (including local government), as a percentage of the gross national product, was as low as 9 percent in the United States. In Germany, which under Bismarck had begun to construct a formidable welfare state, it had risen to 18 percent; in Britain, which had followed the German welfare model from 1906, it amounted to 13 percent. The largest state sector was found in czarist Russia, where the state, in pioneering and accelerating rapid industrialization, had acquired oil fields, gold and coal mines, two-thirds of the railway system, thousands of factories, vast tracts of farmland worked by "state peasants," and control over all the major financial institutions.

World War I saw a fundamental increase in the scale and variety of state activity, much of which was to become permanent. It is true that in democracies like France, Britain, and the United States, the new wartime institutions, such as the United States War Industries Board, were usually disbanded when peace came, although some remained in residual or notional form and would resurface many years later. American wartime statism, for instance, later played a significant role in the New Deal (1933–39), the New Frontier (1961–63), and the Great Society (1963–68) programs. In other countries, the expanded wartime state remained a fixture. Germany, fighting for its existence under the quasi-military dictatorship of General Ludendorff, adopted most of the Russian state innovations and procedures for running the economy. This became known as War Socialism, and its success in raising production so impressed Lenin that after he seized power in Russia in October 1917, he made it the model for his own restructuring of the economy.

Thus, from the early months of 1918 onward, the foundations of the first all-embracing totalitarian state were laid. Lenin was not a man to whom the arts were important; he had, rather, the temperament of a spiritual fanatic—in another incarnation he might have been a missionary, pope, or the founder of a great religious order—but he did have a symbolic vision of his new state. In 1919 he read the newly published book *Der*

Zukunftstaat (The Future State) by Karl Ballod, which described a society run on electricity. It convinced Lenin that electricity was the means whereby all the inefficiencies of the old order would be banished from his new utopia. Hence his slogan: "Communism is Soviet power plus electrification of the whole economy." The electric power station, with its vast size and power enclosed in severely functional lines, became the realized logo of the new state.

Russia was not alone in worshiping the giant power station. In 1930s Britain, the first nation to create a national electricity supply grid embracing the entire country, the modernistic-looking power station, especially the examples brilliantly designed by Sir Edwin Lutyens, became something of a cult building. But in Soviet Russia these new creations acquired ideological and even spiritual significance and became the centerpiece of much of the state propaganda.

Lenin's Russia was the first but soon not the only utopian despotism. In the autumn of 1922, five years after Lenin's putsch, Benito Mussolini staged a "March on Rome" that brought him dictatorial power in Italy. Like Lenin, he was not by nature artistically inclined. Indeed, he often argued that Italy had been seduced by its artistic leanings from its stern duty to rebuild the Roman Empire. He hated art galleries, and when Adolf Hitler paid him a state visit, it was only with the greatest reluctance that Mussolini was persuaded to show him around the Uffizi in Florence. However, as the dictator of the new-style corporate state, which was run not by counting individual votes but by representative bodies of interests, he saw the importance of associating artists, craftsmen, and intellectuals with authority. Much of his political inspiration came from the Italian Futurists. Like them, he saw himself drawing a sleepy, inefficient, almost medieval country into an exciting future of speed and machinery. He adopted the slogan of Futurist poet Emilio Marinetti: "Velocizzare l'Italia" (Make Italy Go Faster). Much of the propaganda-poster art of his new regime was designed by artists of the Futurist school.

3. *Albert Speer. German Pavilion, "Exposition Internationale des Arts et Techniques," Paris, 1937*

4. *City of Paris Pavilion, "Exposition Internationale des Arts et Techniques," Paris, 1937*

Mussolini also took over the fasces and other symbols of imperial Rome, several as they had been "modernized" by the Neoclassical designers of Napoleonic France. It was Mussolini's aim to re-create the power and glory of antiquity in a modern setting, which entailed gigantic building schemes. Just as Pharaonic Egypt, fifth-century B.C. Athens, and imperial Rome had associated the artist with the state to impress a servile populace, so he was determined to rebuild Italy's cities on lines that were simultaneously classical and ultraefficient. The stress was on size. When he visited the Parthenon, Mussolini commented with satisfaction that Rome's Capitol was "much bigger." His own schemes were conceived on a heroic scale. Some were in the nature of public works. He drained the Pontine Marshes near Rome. He set about embanking the Venetian lagoons. He hewed roads through the Apennines and the Alps.

Mussolini also patronized artists on a princely scale. In the 1920s and, even more so, the 1930s, Italian artists received more government patronage than at any time since the High Renaissance. In addition to the commissions, the government awarded lavish annual prizes and bestowed honors, titles, and offices. Like Richelieu and Napoleon, Mussolini set up academies to associate intellectuals of all kinds with the state. His Italian academy included Marinetti, the playwright Luigi Pirandello, the atomic scientist Enrico Fermi, and the opera composer Pietro Mascagni, and it was presided over by the pioneer of radio, Guglielmo Marconi. Sculptors, painters, and designers were well paid. But they were expected to toe the line. Giuseppe Bottai, Mussolini's Minister of Arts, told them to avoid Surrealism, abstraction, Dada, and anything "nostalgic." Their work had to be direct, understandable, and "useful."

In the 1930s, Mussolini set about various building projects on a huge scale, both in Italy and its new African empire. A great Arch of Triumph went up in Libya. A vast modern road, suitable for large-scale military parades, was driven through medieval Rome to link the Capitol with the Colosseum. Scores of medieval and Renaissance buildings were demolished for this purpose. Mussolini had even bigger schemes. He loved skyscrapers, which to him symbolized modern efficiency. He wanted to build a six-hundred-foot clock tower (though in a Gothic mode) next to Milan Cathedral. He also drew up plans for a

5. *Constitution Mall, New York World's Fair, 1939*

6. *Russian Pavilion, New York World's Fair, 1939*

Forum of Mussolini near the Tiber, dominating the Vatican and Saint Peter's. It was to feature a marble obelisk weighing 770 tons and a bronze colossus of Hercules bearing Mussolini's own features. Planned to be some three hundred feet high, it would have been the largest statue in the world, but only one enormous foot had been cast when the war led to the suspension of this and his other grandiose projects.

From the perspective of today, Mussolini appears a preposterous buffoon, comic in life, tragic only in his humiliating death. In the 1930s, however, he was a much admired figure who had modernized and transformed backward Italy and made it a major European and imperial power. His corporate state was studied and imitated in countries like Portugal, Hungary, Poland, and Romania. The sumptuous style of the regime, with its uniforms, flags, symbols, medals, and platform arrangements, became the model for many countries in Europe and Latin America. The Japanese imperial theocracy picked up design ideas from him. Even Joseph Stalin—who succeeded Lenin in 1924, made himself dictator by 1926, inaugurated his Five Year Plans in 1928 and collectivization in 1929, and started his great purges at the end of 1934—took over some of the physical trappings of the corporate state from Mussolini.

By 1935 Stalin was in a position to impose his own artistic concepts on the world's first Communist society. Lenin had not set a style—indeed, he had permitted some degree of artistic freedom and innovation—but he had produced a symbol in the power station. Stalin joined it to the tractor, symbolizing the centerpiece of his own program, agricultural collectivization. The power station and tractor symbolism was broadened to embrace the whole notion of ultramodern machinery, framing and energizing a society in which the individual was nothing and the state everything. The dictator himself had taken a pseudonym that meant *steel*, and his Five Year Plans revolved around expanding steel production. The new Russia was to be powered by Lenin's electricity and made of Stalin's steel, which, as the international scene darkened, would go into tens of thousands of tanks as well as millions of tractors. Visually, then, it was a tank-tractor regime. Also, being totalitarian, it favored monumentality. It was in this respect that Stalin tended to imitate Mussolini.

7. Adolf Hitler at a rally, Nuremberg, in 1934

8. President Truman and family being questioned for the census, Key West, Florida, in 1950

By 1939 Stalin had created an artistic wasteland in Soviet Russia. The two major poets of the October Revolution, Sergei Yesenin and Vladimir Mayakovski, had both committed suicide. Maxim Gorky had died of a broken heart in 1936. The great short-story writer Isaac Babel had vanished into the gulag camps. Musicians like Dmitry Shostakovich were cowed or silenced. Writers and artists were organized in official unions, membership in which was mandatory if they wished to work at all. The writers union and the Ministry of Culture encouraged writers to imitate the turgid and repetitive style of Stalin himself.

Stalin put his imprint on all the arts. In music he favored traditional harmonies and tonalities, and he bullied his composers to oblige him. In the visual arts his tastes were less pronounced, but he favored size and the combination of classicism and modernity that distinguished Fascist architecture. The great apartment blocks, hotels, and ministerial buildings that thus grew up in Moscow in the 1930s, though of much poorer quality than their Italian counterparts, were designed in essentially the same spirit. It was a spirit that persisted into the postwar period and, indeed, until the end of the 1950s. Soviet Russia was a drabber society than Fascist Italy, and this made itself apparent in every aspect of official design. But it was based on the same maxim coined by Mussolini: "Nothing without the state, nothing outside the state, nothing against the state," a sentiment reflected in all its visual apparatus.

When Adolf Hitler was made Reich-Chancellor in January 1933 and proceeded to set up a totalitarian regime as thorough as Stalin's and as vainglorious as Mussolini's, he drew heavily on the experience of both, not least in visual presentation. But there were two important differences between Hitler and the others. First, he could draw on an exceptionally rich depository of artistic talent. Berlin in the 1920s and early 1930s had been the artistic and literary capital of the world, and Weimar Germany had many centers of artistic excellence—Hamburg, Munich, Dresden, Frankfurt, as well as the capital. It is true that Hitler and his Nazis were opposed to what they termed the Jewish cosmopolitanism of Weimar art: many artists fled when the Nazis took over and others were put into concentration camps; galleries and institutes were shut; newspapers and periodicals closed down. Yet the volume and variety of the remaining talent was still formidable, and this gave the new regime's visual presentation a gloss no other government in the world could match at the time.

Second, Hitler himself made a contribution. Whereas Lenin was the religious type of revolutionary, Mussolini the journalistic rabble-rouser, and Stalin the perfect revolutionary bureaucrat, always at his desk with his files, Hitler was the romantic artist-revolutionary. This was recognized by Thomas Mann in his perceptive essay "Brother Hitler" (1939), in which he argued that Hitler, both as a constructive and a destructive force, exhibited an aspect of the artistic character.

Hitler was a failed painter who might have been an architect of considerable power. He tended to be visual in his approach. He first became conscious of what he considered his public mission when he saw a performance of Wagner's *Rienzi*. *Parsifal* remained a model for the Nazi political spectacles he designed. Although Mussolini had staged great marches and gatherings to bolster his regime, and Stalin rearranged Red Square in Moscow as an arena for displays of his power, Hitler's rallies at Nuremberg were of an altogether superior order. The uniforms, flags, and banners he and his staff designed set new standards of excellence in totalitarian regalia. He drew on the experience of Bayreuth, the stage tricks of Max Reinhardt, and the lighting arrangements of Fritz Lang—and other exponents of the despised Weimar culture—to compose his propaganda spectacles. Hitler was the first to appreciate the mesmeric power of loudspeaker amplification and the magic of the searchlight. He seems to have invented *son et lumière*, and he used it to devastating effect at his night mass meetings in Nuremberg and elsewhere.

In his plans of conquest, Hitler thought architecturally. There was always an artistic dimension to his schemes. When, from 1941 through 1943, he gave directions for the political, demographic, and economic transformation of tens of millions of square miles of Europe right up to the Ural Mountains, he did not omit to put in the artistic details, even to the Babylonian gardens that were to adorn the special cities allocated to the German master race. The empire was to radiate from Berlin, which Hitler planned to rebuild completely after the war was won. Detailed plans were made for a series of colossal imperial buildings, and in some cases scale models were constructed. He also intended to rebuild his own hometown, Linz in Austria, on a monumental scale. It is characteristic of Hitler that he put his architect in charge of war production.

Indeed, Hitler himself planned to spend his triumphant retirement supervising his building schemes. Few of them, of course, were realized. It is worth noting, however, that the first *Autobahnen*, or freeways, themselves a masterpiece of utilitarian design, and the beetle-shaped *Volkswagen*, or People's Car, which enabled the German masses to use the new highways, were conceived by Hitler during his spell in Landsberg Prison in the 1920s and were brought into being after he came to power. From the start, the Nazi monster state had distinctive visual characteristics, which were also wholly typical of the midtwentieth century.

It might, in fact, be appropriate to coin the term *totalitarian international* for the visual impress that the growth of state power left on the world from 1935 on. Whether a regime was Communist or Fascist seemed to make little difference. One might go further, and argue that even the democratic states yielded to similar artistic impulses. When General Francisco Franco began a military revolt against Republican Spain in 1936, subsequently becoming dictator of the country for an entire generation, he brought with him some of Mussolini's corporatist notions as well as tricks learned from Hitler. But there is a continuity between his monumental propaganda design and vainglorious official architecture and that of the Communist-dominated republic he overthrew. His *Valley of the Fallen*, a spectacular monument he built to the insurgent war dead, might equally well have been commissioned by the ill-fated President Juan Negrin had the Loyalists won. Indeed, it even carried echoes of the superb monuments with which Lutyens had adorned the British war cemeteries in France in the 1920s. The spirit of the age, which was statist, was greater than the sum of its separate ideological components.

As the 1930s progressed, the democracies felt they had no alternative but to enlarge the state again, both to defend themselves against the totalitarian wave sweeping the world and to save their stricken economies from mass unemployment. In the United States, Herbert Hoover, though with agonizing reluctance, had turned increasingly to state intervention and corporatism even before he was swept away by Franklin D. Roosevelt in the 1932 election. What Hoover did grudgingly, Roosevelt turned into a virtue and christened the New Deal. While it was not the coherent master plan his public-relations men and sympathetic historians presented, it did involve a considerable outlay of federal money, not only to promote economic growth but also—a sure sign of an expanding state—to subsidize the arts. For the first time, actors performed and artists painted by grace of the American taxpayer—a momentous innovation for the United States. The largest, and visually the most spectacular, work of the expanding state was the transformation of the Tennessee Valley by a federal body, the Tennessee Valley Authority. The modernistic lines of the concrete hydroelectric dam became the ocular evidence and symbol of this new development.

Equally, the coming of the Popular Front government in France in 1936, though short-lived in itself, set off a process of large-scale nationalization. Entire industries, like the railroads, were taken into public ownership, which meant in effect that they were administered as the patrimony of the state. A similar restructuring of the economy occurred in Britain in the second half of the 1930s. The state engineered larger industrial groupings and closely monitored them both for reasons of national defense and to reduce the number of people on welfare. Imperial Airways, Imperial Chemical Industries, the Big Four railroads, the national electricity grid, London Transport, and other giant concerns reflected this tendency to concentration, often under state impulsion. There were similar regroupings in the automobile, aircraft, and shipbuilding industries, closely related to the rearmament program and large-scale state purchases. These larger units, overshadowed by the state itself, tended to give a statist impulse to visual forms, ranging from the Supermarine flying boats, soon to evolve into the brilliantly designed Spitfire, victor of the Battle of Britain, to the distinctive stations and posters of the London Underground.

The coming of war, for Britain and Germany in 1939, for Russia and the United States in 1941, carried these tendencies further. The state began to manage not merely parts of the economy but all of it. The statist expedients that had emerged tentatively toward the end of World War I were now wholeheartedly adopted right from the beginning. The great English economist John Maynard Keynes had urged from the early 1930s on that the Great Depression could be ended and full employment achieved by macroeconomic policies conducted by the state, using credit control and deficit budgets to stimulate demand. He had put his views to Roosevelt without any notable response and had then set them out in his major theoretical work, *The General Theory of Employment, Interest and Money* (1936). With the coming of war, macroeconomic management by the state was adopted by the British government almost as a matter of course, as the most efficient way of concentrating national resources on the war effort. It was to continue in Britain throughout the postwar period, right into the 1970s. Keynesian management was also adopted by the United States Treasury in wartime, lapsed in the second half of the 1940s, and was then resumed with the election of John F. Kennedy, whose inauguration in 1961 marked the point at which Keynesianism became quasi-official American policy. Keynesianism impinged on world financial arrangements, since Keynes and the United

States Treasury official Harry Dexter White had in 1944 drawn up the blueprints of the World Bank and the International Monetary Fund, and this structure in turn provided the background and inspiration for the Marshall Plan (1948), whereby the United States government, in a Keynesian-type operation, pumped over ten billion dollars into the ailing economies of twenty-two European states.

There was thus, in most countries, a political and economic continuity among the immediate prewar period of the late 1930s, the war itself, and the postwar period. The most striking aspect of this development was the expansion to an unprecedented size, even in the democracies, of the state, which assumed an astonishing variety of roles. Of course, the war itself marked the largest point of the state's distention. During the war, the state not merely directed production of civil as well as military products, in many cases it also decided how they should be made and even styled. When Italy invaded Ethiopia in 1935, the League of Nations imposed economic sanctions on Italy. This had the effect of putting steel in short supply, which the government directed to essential industries. Noted Florentine shoe designer Salvatore Ferragamo (later of Hollywood), unable to obtain steel for high-heel supports, responded by introducing a wedge heel made of cork—which became a prevailing world fashion. This was a foretaste of the way in which wartime conditions and the continuing postwar shortages influenced design by enforcing simplicity and economy of materials. The Germans pushed the concept of *ersatz* to its logical conclusion. The United States produced standardized "Liberty Ships" by the thousands. The British developed "Utility Products" from clothes to furniture. In many European countries these wartime stringencies continued long after peace came.

There were some flamboyant gestures against austerity. The French fashion industry had been stylistically constrained by the chronic wartime and postwar shortage of textiles. But in August 1947, a new designer, Christian Dior, brought off one of the great coups of design history when he swept aside economies and introduced the "New Look," with its luxurious use of fabric. But for most people in Europe, hard times remained until the Marshall Plan began to take effect. In Britain some forms of rationing lingered on into the 1950s.

In the postwar era, the state continued to play its expanded role, no longer for war-winning purposes but in the name of social justice. The United States alone among the major powers remained committed to an essentially free-enterprise economy in which social insurance and health care were left largely to individual provision. But public welfare began to expand slowly in the 1950s, and then much more rapidly after the victory of the Democrats in the 1960 election. Elsewhere, the welfare state became the norm. In the Scandinavian countries, Norway, Denmark, Sweden, and Finland, the ruling Social Democrat parties steadily expanded both the state sector and the legislative framework of the direction and supervision of daily life. Postwar West Germany, which, when it became politically independent in 1949, opted for conservative Christian Democratic rule and the free-enterprise system—the source of its "Economic Miracle"—nonetheless proceeded to complete the Bismarckian system of welfare "from the cradle to the grave."

In Britain the 1945 election gave the Labour Party, for the first time, an outright, indeed, overwhelming, parliamentary majority. It put into effect welfare socialism, not merely a welfare state, including a free national health service, but also the nationalization of a large part of the economy: railroads and other forms of transportation, coal, utilities, steel, the Bank of England, and many other enterprises. The object was to produce an egalitarian society. What emerged was a grayish one, scarcely relieved by such attempts at national uplift as the 1951 Festival of Britain, which marked the apotheosis of utilitarianist design. Labour fell the same year but the Conservatives, back in office,

9. *London County Council Architects Department. Alton Estates, a postwar housing project near London. 1952–59*

10. *Postwar housing project in Moscow. c. 1950s*

maintained what was seen as a "national consensus" over the welfare state and the expanded public sector.

In France, the social security system had been expanded during the ultra-Catholic wartime government of Marshal Pétain, which saw it as a means of raising the birthrate and bolstering the family. This expansion was maintained in the postwar period. In addition, the public sector was enlarged by the confiscation of many large firms accused of collaboration with the Nazis. France also adopted a national economic planning system designed by Jean Monnet, which was made the basis for the later international Coal-Steel Pool—itself, in turn, the prototype for the European Economic Community. This last, designed to enlarge the free market in European goods, came into existence in 1958. Monnet wanted it operated with the minimum of bureaucracy, using what he called "indicative planning" rather than the Soviet-style command economy. In the end, all these developments inevitably enlarged the role of the state.

The expanding state affected all postwar activities, including developments in the arts. The economy influenced their scope. Important economic differences in the immediate postwar positions of the leading democracies help to explain their relative contributions to international culture in the twenty years from 1945 to 1965. The United States emerged from the war in 1945 with a degree of supremacy in the world economic order never before achieved by a single state, not even Britain in the first half of the nineteenth century. Its industrial economy was considerably larger than that of the next three largest economies combined. It had more than half of the world's export trade. It was the ultimate source of virtually all the world's credit. As the only nuclear power (until 1949) and the custodian of world order on behalf of the democracies, it was filled with a self-confidence that at the time seemed boundless. This was reflected, internally, in the rapid development of the largest market for contemporary art the world had ever seen and, externally, in a global cult of American forms and images—economic, constitutional, and even, thanks to Hollywood, social and artistic. By contrast, the three leading European powers of the interwar era, Britain, France, and Germany, were all exhausted in 1945 and for years afterward. West Germany made a rapid recovery in the late 1950s, but the nation as a whole remained divided, guilt-stricken, and lacking in the self-esteem needed to produce powerful ideas. France did not recover its economic dynamism until the 1960s and Britain not until the 1980s.

Scandinavia was much less ravaged by the war than the rest of Europe. Norway had suffered grievously in 1940. But Denmark, though occupied by the Nazis, was neither fought over nor victimized and remained remarkably untouched by wartime bestialities. It was the first of the belligerents to recover its prewar living standards. Sweden, by its neutrality, actually benefited economically from World War II, as it had from the earlier world war. In 1945 and for the next two decades, Stockholm was the most prosperous capital in Europe and an important symbol of modernity, stability, and rationality. The Scandinavians as a whole were exemplars in the pursuit of civic virtues, including public patronage of the arts.

Italy, too, was an exceptional case. It had certainly suffered in the war: it not only lost its empire, in the years from 1943 to 1945 it was also the theater of a bitterly contested campaign that swept up the peninsula like a rake. But the war did not destroy its immensely tenacious workshop tradition, and the end of an authoritarian (though culturally generous) regime brought a sense of liberation and an unleashing of energies that filled the decades from 1945 to 1965 with excitement and innovation. However, it must be stressed that in Italy and Scandinavia, as well as in the rest of democratic postwar Europe, the ubiquitous operations of the state remained the essential framework of life.

Behind the Iron Curtain that settled over Europe in the late 1940s, the totalitarian system was imposed everywhere. The new governments of Poland, Czechoslovakia, Hungary, and Bulgaria embraced the repressive Soviet model and conformed dutifully to Moscow's directions. Yugoslavia, Albania, and Romania were less docile or broke away completely from the Soviet Union's grip but remained Soviet-style states. East Germany, one of the most servile members of the Soviet bloc, appeared to combine some of the worst features of both the Nazi and the Stalin regimes. It was, however, unusually skillful in exploiting the arts for purposes of political propaganda. It set up a lavishly financed state theater for the German Communist playwright Bertolt Brecht. The vast resources on which he could draw for the spectacular presentation of his plays helped to establish his world fame in the 1950s. Moreover, his genre of political writing for the stage, together with the ensemble acting, design, and direction he made fashionable, was peculiarly well adapted to the new state-subsidized national theaters that emerged all over Europe in the postwar years—one aspect of a vastly increased state patronage of the arts in the West. Hence, the message of collectivism and statism was widely and directly transmitted from the stage, not just behind the Iron Curtain but also in many democratic countries.

How can we sum up this third of a century from 1935 to 1965? I believe that the expansion of the state was the most marked global characteristic of the period. The year 1935 was the apogee of the dictatorships, which used the state as the instrument of their personal, ideological, and national ambitions. By 1965 the state was even more powerful and ubiquitous, but it was presented rather as the benevolent dispenser of social welfare and national prosperity. The world was still in the middle of the long postwar boom, which lasted from 1945 to the end of 1973. These years of easy and seemingly endless prosperity helped to conceal the magnitude of the burden the world was imposing on itself by its varieties of state worship. It was a different matter, of course, in the later 1970s, when darker days came and a new ideological climate began to develop in consequence. But in 1965 the state was still riding high all over the globe, and this was the essential political and social backdrop to the stage on which artists and designers performed.   PJ

The Modernist Canon

The year 1935, despite its lack of a signal event or focus, serves as a convenient starting point for our discussion of Modernism. It had been ten years since the great Paris "Exposition Internationale des Arts Décoratifs et Industriels Modernes," whose very name invoked the two chief concerns of the midcentury: "modern" and "industrial." The drama and the grandeur of the interiors by Émile-Jacques Ruhlmann, the extravagance of Maurice Marinot's and René Lalique's glassware, the splendor of Cartier's jewelry and Jean Puiforcat's silver—all gave undisputed evidence of the supremacy of French taste and the triumph of French luxury. Within that display of costly merchandise ran a variety of stylistic currents, from contemporary versions of the classicism of Louis XVI to Cubism to the exoticism of the Near and Far East. The unifying factors were the richness of costly materials and superb craftsmanship, aptly summed up in the title of one of the leading French design periodicals of the day: *La Renaissance de l'art français et des industries de luxe*. France was indeed the international arbiter of taste and luxury.

But by 1935 this had all drawn to a close. The Great Depression had brought an end to that era of conspicuous consumption. Although the French government tried to maintain the aura of supremacy, as in the state-supported furnishing of the SS *Normandie*, the period of French artistic domination had passed its peak. The 1937 "Exposition Internationale des Arts et Techniques" in Paris was not another triumphant celebration. At its best, it recalled the importance of the fair held twelve years earlier, but it was a spectral reminder, overshadowed by economic depression and the ominous clouds of a new pan-European war.

By the 1930s a new set of principles and a new sense of *modern* had arisen: a rational, architectonic style with a reductivist aesthetic. The importance of the Bauhaus had already been revealed, although it was not then widely recognized, at the 1923 exhibition at Weimar, and the same rationalist principles had been proclaimed at the "Weissenhof Siedlung" exhibition of 1927. In France, Le Corbusier had expressed similar thoughts in his Pavillon de l'Esprit Nouveau at the 1925 exposition, but his work had been greatly overshadowed by the more decorative aspects of the French fair. However, in 1930 the Deutscher Werkbund staged an important exhibition in Paris at the XXe Salon des Artistes Décorateurs; designed by Walter Gropius, Marcel Breuer, László Moholy-Nagy, and Herbert Bayer, it brought home the importance of this new aesthetic. Similar tendencies were revealed in the important exposition held in Stockholm in 1930 as well as at the Monza IV Triennale in 1930.

This shift in taste between 1925 and 1935 involved more than aesthetics; it had a basis in socioeconomic issues. The Great Depression was accompanied by major social changes. It is significant that the 1930 Stockholm exhibition occurred in a period in which Socialists took over the Scandinavian governments: Denmark in 1929, Sweden in 1932, Norway in 1935, and Finland in 1937. It is equally significant that the 1930 Monza Triennale was devoted to the theme of the electric house; Il Duce and the Fascists sought a future in which the engineer was the new savior. Indeed, wherever we turn, it was industrial design rather than handcraftmanship that was being stressed as the new key element of design. Consequently, it was the architect and the industrial designer, rather than the artist or the craftsman, who were promoted as the new heroes.

The establishment of the Museum of Modern Art in New York in 1929 was another significant marker. Its very principle of equating painting and sculpture with architecture and design was derived from Bauhaus pedagogy. Its emphasis on industrial design and low cost was part and parcel of the democratization of art. In 1931 it opened a major exhibition, "Recent European Architecture," which featured the work of Ludwig Mies van der Rohe and Gropius from Germany along with that of Le Corbusier and André Lurçat from France and of J. J. P. Oud and Gerrit Rietveld from the Netherlands—all the major protagonists of the new rationalism. It was organized by Philip Johnson and Henry-Russell Hitchcock, whose book *The International Style: Architecture since 1922* appeared a year later. This book was especially significant because it gave the movement its name: the International Style, a designation that the authors themselves left in lowercase letters but which Alfred Barr, Jr., director of the Museum of Modern Art, capitalized. In this slim volume, Johnson and Hitchcock presented a series of Modernist principles: functionalism, architecture conceived as volume rather than mass, regularity of planning without axial symmetry, and the avoidance of applied decoration. These principles became the new commandments of design.

The new aesthetic and its ethos of design are summarized in a radio script presented in 1935 to the American audience. It encapsulated what *modern* meant to the enlightened individual.[3] This short dialogue registered the demise of a traditional, perhaps Edwardian, interior (fig. 11) as well as the demise of the style that we call Art Deco today but which then was known as Art Moderne or modernistic. It also documented the rise of the new International Style of rational Modernism. In this radio drama, Philip Johnson discussed with a Mrs. Platt how to refurnish her living room.

MR. JOHNSON: *Do you want to modernize it?*

MRS. PLATT: *Not too much. I'm afraid of modernistic things.*

MR. JOHNSON: *So am I.*

MRS. PLATT: *But you're head of the architecture department of the Museum of Modern Art—I thought you'd recommend the modernistic style.*

MR. JOHNSON: *Modern, Mrs. Platt,* not *modernistic.*

MRS. PLATT: *But aren't they the same?*

MR. JOHNSON: *Not at all. The word* modern *means up to date; and to use the modern style means to take advantage of the technical achievements of our age. It means using the new materials and the new ways of construction that have been developed in recent years. It also means to study changes in our way of living and in our taste.*

MRS. PLATT: *But if that is* modern, *what is* modernistic?

MR. JOHNSON: *Oh, just an attempt to disguise old principles with a new surface treatment. For example, a* modernistic *chair is simply an old chair that tries to look modern. Curves are replaced by freakish angles. Geometric zigzags or cubistic designs are used in its upholstery patterns, but in principle it is nothing but an old*

11. *Chandler W. Ireland. Living room of the decorator's residence, New York. 1925*

chair carrying a new burden of ornament. Now take a modern chair. Modern techniques have evolved the steel tube. Its strength makes it unnecessary to use the bulk needed for a wooden frame. The fact that steel is flexible makes box springs unnecessary. There is no make-believe or useless complication in really modern furniture. You see, the modern style is based on two cardinal principles: utility and simplicity.

The changes that Johnson proposed for Mrs. Platt's apartment reveal the new credo of "utility and simplicity." The wallpaper, a copy of an old and supposedly charming French model, was replaced by painted walls. The three separate windows, each with its own set of shades, curtains, drapes, and valance, were given a continuous wall of curtain and drape hung from the ceiling. The picture moldings and most of the pictures were eliminated, the baseboard was simplified, the door paneling was covered by flat plywood. The heavy upholstered furniture was replaced with fewer, less cumbersome pieces. Steel and leather chairs were introduced; five wood tables were replaced with a single coffee table of chromed steel and glass. Mrs. Platt seemed wary but Johnson assured her that she would find her "modern interior restful, beautiful, and above all more enjoyable because it is *sensible.*" Whether his client would have enjoyed this spartan arrangement is moot, but Johnson himself believed in this credo, and his own apartment marks the triumph of this rational functionalism (fig. 12).

No discussion of Modernism and the Modernist canon in the prewar years can stop with reference to the rise of the International Style. By 1935 it was clear that other changes had taken place. The architectonic rigidity and metallic hardness that one associates with the International Style had evolved into or coexisted with a newer mode. The changes and their implications can best be demonstrated through the work of Finnish architect and designer Alvar Aalto. In the early 1930s he began turning away from what has been called "sober Bauhaus realism" and began to take organic nature as his model. The different approach first became manifest in his furniture, particularly in the brilliant solutions he arrived at in his experiments with laminated wood. The results, which employed modern methods, were technologically sound; at the same time, the change to

12. Philip Johnson. Interior of the architect's residence, New York. Before 1935

wood introduced a less mechanistic aesthetic. The supple, curving lines of Aalto's *Paimio* chair (fig. 15) announced a new idiom that, however, remained functionalist. For others, as we shall see, they signaled the starting point of an expressive biomorphism. The same dramatic changes can be seen in the Municipal Library at Viipuri (figs. 13, 14), the Paimio Sanatorium, and the exhibition halls at the Paris and New York world's fairs of 1937 and 1939; the introduction of sweeping open spaces and undulant wooden ceilings and walls suggest Aalto's shift from a hard-edged architecture into another sphere.

Aalto took technology as his means and nature as his model, and in the interplay between the two found not only artistic expression but also a new form of Modernism. This shift in aesthetics is well summarized in the catalogue prepared for an Aalto exhibition in 1938:

> *Like the designs of other men first active in the '30's, Aalto's work, without ceasing in any way to be modern, does not look like the modern work of the '20's. The younger men employ new materials and new methods of construction, of course, but these only partly explain the change. The buildings of men working naturally in an already established style are less assertive of that style's tenets than those earlier and more puristic buildings. . . . Certain materials and forms once renounced because of their association with non-modern work are now used again, in new ways or even in the old ones. To the heritage of pure geometric shapes, the younger men have added free organic curves; to the stylistic analogies with the painters, Mondrian and Léger, they have added Arp. Personal and national qualities are more apparent than a decade ago.[4]*

It would be all too easy to characterize this new direction as an anti-Bauhaus or post-Bauhaus phase, had the Bauhaus been an institution with only a single vision. But the Bauhaus was more than the architecture of the Dessau buildings and Breuer's tubular steel chairs. Its teaching and creative spirit were far more complex and artistically rich. The Dada and Constructivist ideas that permeated its early years had a profound impact on its later development and teaching. This can be seen in the work of Moholy-Nagy, who headed the metal workshop and restructured the basic Bauhaus introductory course. In his book *Von Material zu Architektur* of 1929 (translated as *The New Vision*), Moholy-Nagy

13, 14. *Alvar Aalto. Lecture hall, Municipal Library, Viipuri, Finland. 1934*

15. *Aalto. Paimio chair. 1931–33. Collection, The Museum of Modern Art, New York. Gift of Edgar Kaufmann, jr.*

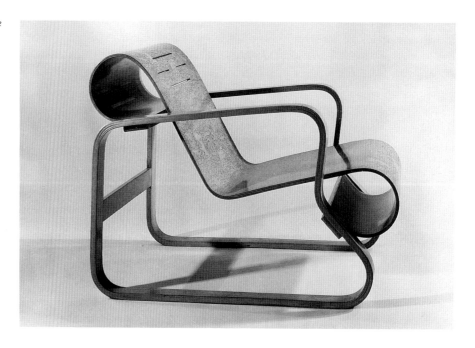

expressed the idea of biotechnology and the concept of the interaction between technology and nature, the interplay between the medium (the material), the tool (the machine), and function, with nature as a guiding principle. He emphasized experimentation, creative play, and the significance of spontaneity. It has been proposed, in fact, that one of the major factors in the shift of Aalto's work in the early 1930s was his friendship with Moholy-Nagy and the exchange of views between the two artists.[5]

The singling out of Aalto and Moholy-Nagy is a useful way of expressing the new course of Modernism in the early 1930s in that these two men are emblematic of the change that occurred throughout Europe and ultimately the United States. Just as the International Style traversed borders quickly, this new development was equally international. In addition to the traditional means of twentieth-century communication — travel, publications, exhibitions (all significantly expanded from the level of thirty years earlier) — the special political circumstances of the later 1930s played a major role.

The growth of the Modernist style did not take place in all countries. Under the consolidation of power by the Nationalist Socialists in 1933, the Bauhaus was closed and progressive design in Germany decisively checked. The Soviet Union might have been a more fertile ground for that development. The architect Sven Markelius and the Swedish Clarté group were working in Russia, as were Le Corbusier and André Lurçat; Hannes Mayer and his Bauhaus students went there in 1930. The Soviet Union, with its social and artistic concerns, seemed to offer great possibilities, but the situation changed dramatically with Stalin's consolidation of power and the beginning of the terror purges. The scheduled meeting of the CIAM (Congrès International d'Architecture Moderne) in Moscow for 1933 and its sudden cancellation by the Russian authorities are symbolic both of hopes for Russian progressivism and the death of those aspirations.

Not surprisingly, France also was not the place for these Modernist developments — but England was. Just as earlier in the century English ideas of reform design had influenced Germany, Austria, and Scandinavia, in the 1920s and 1930s England was receptive to the reverse flow of ideas from the Continent. For example, most of the Aalto furniture sold outside Finland was purchased by the British. England was also a haven for many of the leading artists fleeing political strife. After 1935 it was host to Gropius and Moholy-Nagy, who arrived in 1934, and Breuer, who arrived in 1935. Art historian Nikolaus Pevsner arrived in 1933 and three years later published his *Pioneers of the Modern Movement from William Morris to Walter Gropius*, one of the major early treatises defining the evolution of twentieth-century Modernism.

Ultimately, though, the United States became the haven for these émigré artists and the fertile ground in which the new ideas of Modernism took root. Josef and Anni Albers had already arrived in 1933 and set up a Bauhaus-type program at Black Mountain College in North Carolina; comparable programs were established in the mid-1930s at Pratt Institute and the Design Laboratory, both in New York City. In 1937 Gropius, Breuer, and Moholy-Nagy immigrated to the United States from England, while Mies van der Rohe and Herbert Bayer came directly from Germany. Gropius became director of the Illinois Institute of Technology, and Mies was appointed chairman of the Graduate School of Design at Harvard, with Breuer on his staff. Moholy-Nagy established the New Bauhaus (later the School and then the Institute of Design) in Chicago. Bayer set up practice in New York in 1938. Thus, the spirit of Bauhaus practice and education continued strongly in the United States during the war years. This influx was complemented by many others without a Bauhaus background who also played significant roles in the development of Modernism. For example, Swiss graphic designer Herbert Matter arrived in New York City in 1936, and E. McKnight Kauffer, American-born but based in

London, fled in 1940 with his companion, the celebrated rug designer Marion Dorn, and also sought haven in New York.

Eva Zeisel is an interesting example of an émigré artist whose career encapsulates all of these currents: her early training had been in Budapest and Vienna; she had become involved in the Modernist movement in Germany; and she went to the Soviet Union in 1932 and took part in the great social experiment until she was imprisoned by Stalin. After her return to Hungary, she fled from the Nazis and sought temporary shelter in London; she then immigrated to the United States in 1937 and taught at Pratt Institute in a Bauhaus-type program. Her first major American commission was a dinner service (figs. 55–57) whose style bridged the prewar and postwar periods; it was commissioned about 1942 under the sponsorship of the Museum of Modern Art and was exhibited by the museum in 1946.

Despite the outbreak of World War II and America's entry in late 1941, there was a great deal of continuity between prewar and postwar design in the United States. Notwithstanding the shortages of materials and the effects of military conscription, the war provided a useful period of time in which the innovations of the 1930s could be absorbed. Designers had time to process ideas that once had been startling and revolutionary and now became the foundation stones of an accepted dogma.

Charles Eames and his wife, Ray, are a significant case in point. They trained at the Cranbrook Academy of Art, the institution in Michigan headed by Finnish-born architect Eliel Saarinen. Though Cranbrook had no systematic curriculum, it responded to Modernist developments in Europe, especially in Scandinavia, and the Eameses were particularly receptive to the architecture and design work of Aalto. Important ideas that he had initiated in molded plywood were explored further by them, as in the splints they developed in California during the war as part of research sponsored by the United States Navy and the influential series of chair seats and bases, which, appropriately enough, were celebrated in a major exhibition at the Museum of Modern Art in 1946.

The Eameses' exhibition of 1946 and the commencement of production of some of their designs illustrate the dilemma of separating prewar and postwar design. The Eameses' work can be seen as the culmination of the former, the beginning of the latter, or a convenient marker in a continuum of important but changing ideas regarding the nature of Modernism.

ME

Note on the use of the Catalogue

Each object from the Stewart Collection is illustrated and has its own catalogue entry.

Dimensions are in inches, taken to the nearest sixteenth of an inch, followed by centimeters in parentheses. Height precedes width precedes depth. In measurements of textiles, warp precedes weft. Jewelry is measured across, in closed position.

Marks written in script or printed in italics are rendered here in italics.

An asterisk following a donor's name indicates an object on permanent loan to the museum from the American Friends of Canada.

Individual entries are signed with the initials of the contributors; the full names of all the contributors appear on the title page.

Illustrations with more than one object follow the order in the catalogue entry and read left to right.

Additional caption information for comparative illustrations is given at the end of the book.

Alvar Aalto

Armchair: model no. 379
Designed 1932
Birch-faced plywood and laminated birch;
   25¾ × 24 × 30½ inches (66 × 61.5 × 78.2 cm)
Produced by Huonekalu-ja Rakennustyötehdas
   Oy (Helsinki), 1932–35; by Artek (Helsinki),
   1935 to the present
Impressed under each runner: 379
D85.113.1

Alvar Aalto is widely recognized as a giant of modern architecture. Less well understood is that his furniture was even more influential than his architecture. More than any other furniture de-signer since Michael Thonet, Aalto devoted him-self to laminated wood, resulting in his complete mastery of the material. Through his designs, he established the basic formal vocabulary for mod-ern plywood furniture.

This cantilevered armchair (generally known today as the *Springleaf*) is one of Aalto's most important and influential designs. It is a poetic tribute to the possibilities inherent in bending, gluing, and molding together sheets of thin birch wood. From the beginning, Aalto looked to the abundant birch forests that covered his native Finland for the raw material for his furniture. Although a strong hardwood, birch is easy to cut and work. A light-colored, smooth wood gener-ally without noticeable grains, pores, or rings, birch draws little attention to itself. In it, Aalto found the perfect material with which to create his visually light, delicately curving designs.

Aalto's graceful armchair is made from a pair of continuous, flexible, cantilevered supports, of laminated birch veneers, that form the arm, leg, and base of each side. (While all plywood is made from laminated wood, that is, pieces that have been glued together, not all laminated wood is plywood. True plywood must be made from ve-neers, each of which is laminated with the grain facing perpendicular to the grain of the adjacent

16. *Alvar Aalto. Armchair: model no. 379*

sheet. The arms of this Aalto chair are laminated wood, not plywood.) The chair's seat and back are made from a single piece of very thin plywood fitted into the frame supports with tongue-and-groove joints and then reinforced by a single crosspiece located behind the sitter's calves.

While Aalto's lyrical, flowing design was very much a part of international Modernism of the 1920s and 1930s, it stands apart from the better-known tubular steel furniture of that period. Like the iconic chairs of Marcel Breuer and Mies van der Rohe, Aalto's design demonstrates the architect's interest in the structural and visual possibilities of the cantilever: the chair's seat hovers and flexes, supported not by a second pair of legs but only by the strength of the gently curving frame. Aalto, however, could not accept the machinelike surfaces of chromed or nickeled steel. "Steel and chromium are not satisfactory from the human point of view," he wrote.[6] Instead, Aalto combined his interest in the structural with a traditionally Finnish love and sensitivity for the natural qualities and organic properties of wood.

CW

Alvar Aalto

Stool
Designed c. 1946–47
Birch-faced plywood and cotton webbing;
    16¹⁵⁄₁₆ × 16¼ × 16¼ inches (43 × 41.3 × 41.3 cm)
Produced by Artek (Helsinki), 1947 to the present
Unmarked
D82.109.1

Alvar Aalto's handling of birch wood was both ingenious and masterful, and the joining of member to member, as in this stool, gives proof of his unique, aesthetic sensibility. In Aalto's furniture, the bending and joining together of two pieces of wood took on a profound importance, as is also attested to in the many relief sculptures of laminated wood that he created from the 1930s through the 1950s (fig. 115).

This stool marks a return to a number of formal themes the architect first explored in his furniture of the 1930s. Most important was his search for a standardized leg design. Between 1932 and 1933, Aalto arrived at a solution he considered his most important innovation in furniture design. The leg, which he dubbed the "bent-knee," was first used in a simple yet highly successful stacking stool, which has become one of the most ubiquitous examples of Modernist furniture (fig. 17). It was precisely to the issues

17. *Alvar Aalto. Stacking stool. 1932–33. Collection, The Museum of Modern Art, New York. Phyllis B. Lambert Fund*

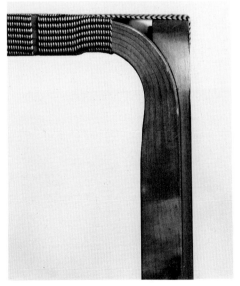

18. *Detail of Aalto's stool, c. 1946–47, showing Y-leg*

raised in that design that Aalto returned in this mid-1940s leg design—referred to as the "Y-leg"—which was used in a table, chair, and the stool presented here. Given its origin, the later stool can only be understood in the context of its predecessor.

In his 1932–33 bent-knee leg, Aalto faced what he described as furniture design's "basic problem from an historical—and practical—point of view . . . the connecting element between the vertical and horizontal pieces."[7] He solved the problem not by bending a solid piece of wood at a ninety-degree angle but by forming a sandwich of thin laminates that could be easily bent. The stool leg was a solid, straight piece of birch; just below where the bend was to be it was backsawn to make it pliable. A piece made of identically wide laminates was then glued onto the solid leg, interlocking layer by layer, with the thin pieces extending from the solid leg. This end of the leg was then bent and attached to the underside of the stool top.

In addressing the same design problem in the mid-1940s, Aalto again found a solution that could be applied to different furniture types. As before, two pieces of wood were joined at the point of the bend by interlocking layers of laminates (fig. 18). However, instead of merely serving as noncontinuous supports for a tabletop or case piece, each of the members was continuously linked with the adjoining one, creating a fully integrated structure capable of standing by itself and clearly revealed to the viewer. The two pieces that form each leg are delicately joined, suggesting an organic structural unity.

CW

19. Aalto. Stool

20. *Bruno Mathsson.* Working Chair

Bruno Mathsson

Chair: *Working Chair*
Designed c. 1933–36
Beech, laminated beech, and jute;
31⅜ × 19⅜ × 28½ inches (79.8 × 49.4 × 72.4 cm)
Produced by Firma Karl Mathsson (Värnamo, Sweden), c. 1936–78; by DUX Industrier, AB (Trelleborg, Sweden), 1978 to the present (this example 1939)

Paper label on underside of seat rail, printed and handwritten within bordered rectangle: Komp./*Bruno Mathsson*/Tillv./*Karl Mathsson*/Värnamo/B[?]M 1936/KM 39
Second paper label on underside of seat rail, printed within bordered rectangle: MADE IN SWEDEN
D83.135.1

Bruno Mathsson was fascinated by the act of sitting and the physiology involved. After designing chairs with webbed seats and conventional frames in the early 1930s (fig. 49), he decided to develop a new kind of chair, one that was adapted to the person sitting in it rather than the other way around. In order to make the seat comfortable without using upholstery, he designed chairs contoured to follow the curves of the human body.[8]

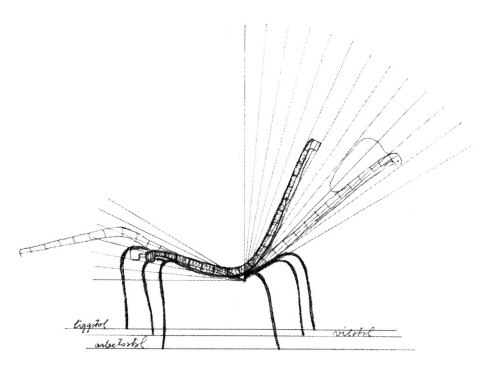

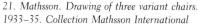

21. Mathsson. Drawing of three variant chairs. 1933–35. Collection Mathsson International

22. Mathsson. Working Chair with arms. 1941

Marcel Breuer

Lounge chair: *Isokon Long Chair*
Designed 1935–36
Birch-faced plywood; 30½ × 24½ × 54 inches
   (78.2 × 62.8 × 138.5 cm)
Produced by Isokon Furniture Company
   (London), 1936–39; intermittently, with
   design changes, through the present
Unmarked
D81.116.1

Marcel Breuer's *Isokon Long Chair*—the name differentiates this model from a shorter lounge version—was not a completely original design but a translation into plywood of an aluminum chair Breuer had designed in 1932–33 (fig. 24). The impetus for the project came from the German architect Walter Gropius, Breuer's mentor and friend.[15]

Gropius had immigrated to England in 1934 and worked on a number of unrealized projects with Jack Pritchard. In November 1935, a month after Breuer's immigration to England, Pritchard established the Isokon Furniture Company, a firm devoted to the promotion of modern architecture and design in England, and shortly thereafter, Gropius suggested that Breuer try a plywood version of his aluminum lounge chair for Isokon.

Plywood was chosen primarily because Pritchard had worked for more than a decade for the Venesta Plywood Company of Estonia and because it was felt that the English public, generally unreceptive to untraditional, avant-garde design, would respond more to the warmer qualities of wood than it would to the coldness of metal. The *Isokon Long Chair* became the first of five Breuer designs produced by Isokon.

Breuer's chair is made from frame elements meant to look as if a single length of plywood had been split lengthwise, one part rising to form the arm and back support, the other continuing straight along the ground to form the base, then curving up to become the front leg. Suspended

Like Alvar Aalto and Marcel Breuer, he experimented with laminated bentwood, since it has more springiness than solid wood.

Between 1933 and 1936 he developed the concept of a chair with two basic components: laminated bentwood supports and a contoured seat with a solid wood frame (fig. 21). For flexibility and comfort, the seat was webbed with leather or a fabric woven from jute or hemp.[9] The chair in the Stewart Collection is one of the first that Mathsson designed using these principles. Originally called *Arbetsstol*—literally a *work* or *working chair*[10]—it demonstrates his belief that one works best when sitting in a relaxed position.

Mathsson exhibited three new chairs—this model, a similar reclining chair, and a lounge chair—at the Röhsska Konstslöjdmuseet in Göteborg, Sweden, in 1936.[11] Although the show was a great success, the Swedish furniture industry was unwilling to manufacture such daring and novel designs. Mathsson was obliged to

have them made in his father's furniture workshop.

In 1941 Mathsson designed a separate bentwood arm that could be attached to any of his chairs, either during production or later. From then on, all his chairs were available with arms (fig. 22) or without.

The innovative design of the *Working Chair* and its graceful, natural curves made it very popular. It was imitated both in Europe and in America by many designers, including Jens Risom, who in 1941–42 designed the model 650 chair for Knoll with a similarly contoured webbed seat.[12] In 1957, it was chosen as one of a hundred noteworthy examples of Swedish furniture by the Swedish Society of Industrial Design and the Swedish Furniture Industry Federation.[13] When DUX took over the production in 1978, it changed the name of the chair to *Eva*.[14] The *Eva* chair is still in production today, over fifty years after Mathsson designed it.   CWL

23. *Marcel Breuer.* Isokon Long Chair

between these frame elements is a long, thin, single sheet of molded plywood intended to be covered with padded upholstery.

The form of the chair, according to an Isokon sales brochure, "is shaped to the human body. It fits you everywhere. It rests ALL your muscles at once. . . ."[16] Whereas Breuer's modern furniture had been promoted in Germany as rational, functional, and logical, the British public was offered a cozy chair expressing "ease, comfort, and well-being. . . . Try it after dinner: ten minutes in an Isokon Long Chair after a meal is as good as any medicine." Its modern appearance and the fact that it was designed by a leading international architect were not emphasized.

The *Isokon Long Chair* represented a decisive point in Breuer's work, marking his turning away from metal, a material he had first worked with in 1925 and with which his most celebrated furniture had been executed. As many of his fellow architects turned away from the purity of early 1920s Modernism, so Breuer gave up metal as his material of choice and concentrated on the or-

ganic shapes of laminated wood. For the next dozen years or so, he devoted much attention to the design of both molded and cutout plywood furniture, but he rarely arrived at design solutions as interesting as his Isokon line.

Although the conception of the *Long Chair* was firmly rooted in another Breuer design, it also showed the unmistakable influence of the furniture of Alvar Aalto, which had created a sensation in England at a 1932 exhibition, and was well known to Breuer. It provided the formal vocabulary: the single sheet of plywood that forms the back and seat and the thick supporting arms and legs. However, it should also be remembered that Breuer's first tubular steel chairs and tables with their continuous frame elements were instrumental in the genesis of Aalto's wooden chairs.

Breuer's *Isokon Long Chair*, although always a favorite of designers and furniture aficionados, was never a commercial success. Structural and manufacturing problems dictated constant changes during the 1930s and even after World War II. Nevertheless, it remains Breuer's most

important and influential design in plywood as well as one of the most significant examples of Modernist furniture produced in England.

CW

24. *Breuer. Lounge chair. 1932–33. Collection, The Museum of Modern Art, New York. Gift of the designer*

Russel Wright

Dinnerware: *American Modern*

Designed c. 1937

Glazed earthenware; pitcher: 10⅝ × 8⅛ × 8⅛
  inches (27 × 20.6 × 20.6 cm)

Produced by the Steubenville Pottery
  Company (Steubenville, Ohio), 1939–59

Creamer, sugar bowl, chop plate, dinner plate,
  dessert plate, celery dish, soup bowl,
  impressed on underside: *Russel*/*Wright*
  /MFG. BY/STEUBENVILLE

Teapot, impressed on underside: *Russel*/
  Wright/MFG. BY/STEUBENVILLE . . .

Pitcher, impressed on underside: *Russel*/
  Wright/STEUBENVILLE/A ·

Other pieces unmarked

D82.105.1, gift of David A. Hanks;
  D87.170.1–3; D88.180.1–10

The product most synonymous with designer Russel Wright's name is his *American Modern* dinnerware. In production for two decades, it reputedly grossed over $150 million in sales.[17] It was claimed to be the best-selling dinnerware ever manufactured.

At first few thought that *American Modern* would prove to be successful. Although already established as a designer, Wright needed several years to find and convince a pottery to put his dinnerware into production. Even then, the Steubenville Pottery agreed only because it desperately needed a surprise success to save itself from imminent bankruptcy and because the designer and his wife agreed to finance the venture through their own firm.

The forms were certainly novel. In contrast with Keith Murray's 1934 designs for Wedgwood or Frederick H. Rhead's *Fiesta* ware of 1937 for Homer McLaughlin, both of which relied on concentric rings and strong angles, *American Modern* emphasized soft curves. This is most evident in the serving pieces. The creamer and teapot are elongated, fluid forms. The sides of the celery dish are gently lapped over, and the sides of the serving bowls are indented. It has become commonplace to designate this dinnerware as Biomorphic.[18] Yet there is nothing specifically Biomorphic in the shapes.[19] In fact, symmetry predominates; for example, the lapped edge on one side of the celery dish is balanced by a lapped edge diagonally opposite.

What inspired Wright to create such fluid forms? Perhaps it was his use of bentwood frames for furniture and his seeming awareness of the innovations of Alvar Aalto and other Scandinavian designers. Also, *American Modern* participated in the Modernist trend of the late 1930s to create forms both organic and functional: the long, curved, distended necks and spouts facilitate the flow of liquids; the indentations on the bowls and the salt and pepper shakers provide convenient handholds. Similar solutions were soon offered by László Moholy-Nagy's students at the Chicago School of Design[20] and by Wilhelm Kåge in his *Soft Forms* for the Gustavsberg factory (fig. 282).

The colors of *American Modern* also announced a change in aesthetics. The dinnerware first came in a choice of four different glazes (developed by the students of Donald Schrenkengost at Alfred University): Chartreuse Curry, Granite Grey, Seafoam Blue, and Bean Brown. Especially when seen in combination, these warm colors evoke the late 1930s. And they were meant to be combined: gray cup with chartreuse saucer, brown teapot with chartreuse sugar bowl. Not only did this add to the set's festive, informal nature, it also allowed greater flexibility for the producer, who could sell place settings and open stock without concern for absolute uniformity.

Perhaps least obvious today are the social changes implied in Wright's dinnerware. While a certain amount of informality had been tolerated in breakfast and luncheon services, dinner had continued to imply formality. *American Modern* was intended for informal living and the middle-class family, which was increasingly servantless and chastened by the effects of the Depression. Wright particularly prided himself on the reduced number of elements in a full set.[21] Emily Post, the arbiter of America's social behavior, railed against the implications of *American Modern* and Wright responded in kind.[22] His dinnerware signaled the democratization of the American table.   ME

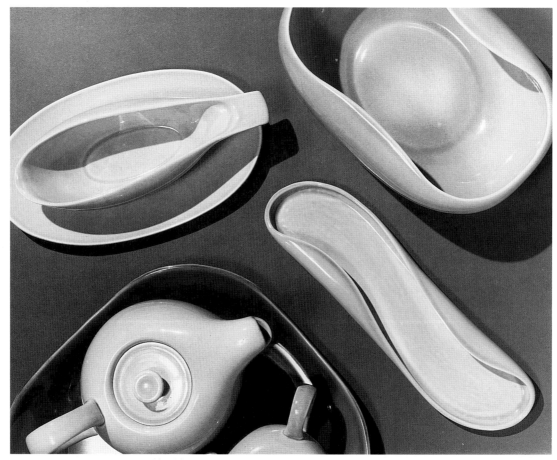

(above and opposite) *25, 26. Russel Wright.* American Modern *dinnerware*

Charles and Ray Eames

Lounge chair: model LCW
Designed 1945–46
Stained laminated ash, stained ash-faced
  plywood, and rubber; 26⅜ × 22 × 21⅞ inches
  (67 × 55.8 × 55.5 cm)
Produced by Molded Plywood Division, Evans
  Products Company (Venice, California),
  1946–49; by Herman Miller Furniture Co.
  (Zeeland, Michigan), 1949–57 (this example
  c. 1947–49)[23]
Remains of rectangular label on underside of
  seat, near the front
D81.152.1, gift of Ann Hatfield Rothschild*

The plywood chairs designed in the Eameses'
studio in the mid-1940s represent one of the great
achievements in modern furniture. As in the
finest examples of industrial design and decorative art, the designers managed to synthesize perfectly the technical and the aesthetic. The chairs
are technically innovative, economical to mass-
produce, and among the most beautiful seating
designs of the post–World War II period. It is
difficult to imagine the excitement and acclaim
that greeted the introduction of this furniture and
the extent to which it became standard furnishing
in the self-consciously modern interiors of the
late 1940s and early 1950s.

The origins of the chair can be found in the
seating furniture designed by Charles Eames and
Eero Saarinen for the Museum of Modern Art's
"Organic Design in Home Furnishings" competition of 1940–41 (fig. 27). With this furniture,
Eames began working with molded plywood and,
in particular, with the notion of a chair that
could be simply and cheaply stamped in a machine from one piece of wood.[24] Although the
Eames-Saarinen designs won the competition,
they proved impossible to manufacture inexpensively from a shell of plywood.

Having moved to California in 1941 with his
new wife, Ray Kaiser, Eames continued to experiment with the molding of plywood through a
commission from the United States Navy to develop plywood stretchers and leg splints (fig. 28).
The development of these urgently required designs allowed the Eameses to refine methods of
molding plywood in three-dimensional forms
and to work out the complicated technical methods of bending, gluing, and molding. The kind of
plywood molding used in this work apparently
was not to be found anywhere else in America.
While they worked on the military contracts—
which also included the nose of an ill-fated plywood glider for the United States Army—the
Eameses designed a number of experimental
chairs (fig. 29), which resulted in the lounge chair
under discussion. Interestingly, all of this work
was accomplished in a small and rather primitive
workshop rather than in a sophisticated factory.[25]

The LCW (for "Lounge Chair Wood"), clearly
constructed and assembled from five separately

(above left) 27. *Charles Eames
and Eero Saarinen. Drawing for
conversation armchair submitted
to "Organic Design in Home
Furnishings" competition of
1940–41. 1940. Collection, The
Museum of Modern Art, New
York*

(above right) 28. *Charles and
Ray Eames. Traction splint for
leg. c. 1941. Liliane and
David M. Stewart Collection.
Gift of Judith Hollander,
D81.115.1*

(left) 29. *Charles and Ray
Eames. Lounge chair (tilt-back).
c. 1944. Collection, The
Museum of Modern Art, New
York. Gift of Charles Eames*

finished elements, represents a refinement of the outstanding features of these experiments. The separateness of the various elements is one of the chair's most distinctive and successful features. Although the Eameses would return to the notion of stamping or molding a chair from a single piece, they seem to have concluded that plywood was not the optimal material for such a feat and decisively abandoned the idea in this chair.

The black rubber shockmounts (as they were called) joining the seat and back to the frame articulate and emphasize the separate elements, while at the same time providing flexibility and resilience, hence comfort, to the seat and back.[26] Comfort, not to mention a pleasing appearance, was supplied primarily by the superbly designed three-dimensional molding of the seat and back. Although it is a chair that does not allow an infinite number of seating positions, it easily accommodates a great variety of body types.

Contrasting with the round-edged, dishlike shape of the seat and back are the thicker, two-dimensionally molded frame elements. These long lengths of plywood are cut in tapering shapes, in a design that gives the chair its deliberate and playful anthropomorphism.

It is arguable which version, the all-plywood or the plywood and metal, represents a more successful solution for design and/or production. Yet it is irrefutable that in both cases the Eameses and their coworkers managed to create chairs of unrivaled harmony, personality, and practicality.

CW

30. Charles and Ray Eames. Lounge chair: model LCW

Charles and Ray Eames

Screen: model FSW
Designed c. 1946
Stained ash-faced plywood and canvas;
   67¾ × 60 × ¼ inches (172.1 × 153.8 × 0.6 cm)
Produced by Molded Plywood Division, Evans
   Products Company (Venice, California),
   1946–49; by Herman Miller Furniture Co.
   (Zeeland, Michigan), 1949–56
Unmarked
D81.134.1

A screen offers a designer unusual freedom in that its program generally requires little more than that it stand up without falling over. It does not have to support a sitter or even an evening's worth of dishes; it is generally not subject to physical wear (including handling); and it tends toward simplicity rather than complexity not only in its function but also in its construction.

The Eameses' screen is remarkable for its undulating, organic shape and the technical ingenuity of its design. It is a bravura demonstration of the sculptural and practical possibilities of molded plywood adapted to the requirements of mass production. The manner in which the screen folds, its method of construction, and the fact that it is made entirely from identical wood pieces demonstrate the Eameses' typically ingenious economy of means and their feeling for form, shape, and surface.

The screen is composed of six identical molded plywood sections joined together by equally tall pieces of canvas sandwiched between the layers of wood. The use of identical elements permitted an economy of scale in production and the manufacture of a variety of screen sizes without requiring additional molds.[27] The soft canvas joining the sections together gives the screen an unusual degree of flexibility and ease of movement. This soft material, rather than the common alternative of metal hinges, determined the pleasing and articulated appearance of the screen and, most important, allowed the fourteen-and-a-half-foot screen to be easily folded into an incredibly small unit of seven inches in depth (fig. 31). Not only was this convenient for use in the domestic interior, it also resulted in significant savings in storage and shipping costs for the manufacturer.

CW

(upper left) 31. *Charles and Ray Eames. Screen in open and folded positions*

(above) 32. *Eames. Screen: model FSW*

33. *Jupp Ernst.* Neues Wohnen

Jupp Ernst

Poster: *Neues Wohnen*
Designed 1949
Offset lithograph; 33 × 23⅛ inches (84 × 59 cm)
Printed by Kölnische Verlagsdruckerei
 (Cologne, West Germany), 1949
Signed in the stone, upper left: *Jupp Ernst*
D85.162.1

Postwar reconstruction afforded new opportunities for the design of home furnishings. The subject of this poster is a 1949 Cologne exhibition, "Neues Wohnen," sponsored by the Deutscher Werkbund. This association was founded in 1907 by designers and craftsmen to promote progress in German industrial design.[28] Suppressed by the Nazis for over a decade, the Werkbund was revived in 1947 to meet postwar needs.

Along with a general return to basics, German postwar designers were encouraged to create inexpensive, functionalist household furniture. In 1949 Jupp Ernst collaborated with Josef Lucas on an exhibition, "Die Wohnung für das Existenszminimum" (Subsistence Housing), that included a model house as a guideline for reconstruction.

Ernst has illustrated in this poster two new examples of chair design. While theoretically based on functionalist precedents, they both make use of current aesthetic forms. The dynamic design of the bentwood armchair in the foreground, possibly one by Axel Larsson,[29] is drawn schematically against a flat background of yellow and white, but the chair's rear leg is cleverly aligned with the juncture of the two color planes and with the orthogonal of the steep perspective system. This in turn draws attention to the background scene of a modern terrace with a striped lounge chair, all rendered in a typical postwar illustrative style. The use of lowercase, sans serif gray type, subtly mixed with capital letters of the same scale, underscores the new design's debt to Bauhaus principles and its later modifications. FTH

Gerrit Rietveld

Armchair
Designed 1950[30]
Birch-faced plywood and chromium-plated
 steel glides; 24³⁄₁₆ × 26 × 23 inches (61.5 ×
 66 × 58.6 cm)
Manufacturer unknown
Unmarked
D84.154.1

This somewhat diminutive armchair presents itself both as an example of the work of an architect who throughout his long career addressed himself to furniture design and as part of the postwar explosion of plywood furniture.

Rietveld's 1950 armchair was designed thirty years after his first known plywood furniture—in particular, the iconic *Red and Blue Chair*—and more than twenty years after his first attempts at three-dimensionally molded plywood or fiberboard chairs. While he returned to molded plywood with this chair, Rietveld used a new vocabulary, that of overlapping sheets of wood treated as flexible and strong yet interdependent elements.

The overlapping sheets of plywood that serve as the structural system for the chair are completely revealed to become an integral part of the chair's aesthetic. What we see are broad, flat sheets of wood, laid over each other like solid pieces of a thin, highly flexible material. The pieces that form the back and arms are raised up and hover in a manner that seems to contradict their actual thinness and pliancy. Yet details where sev-

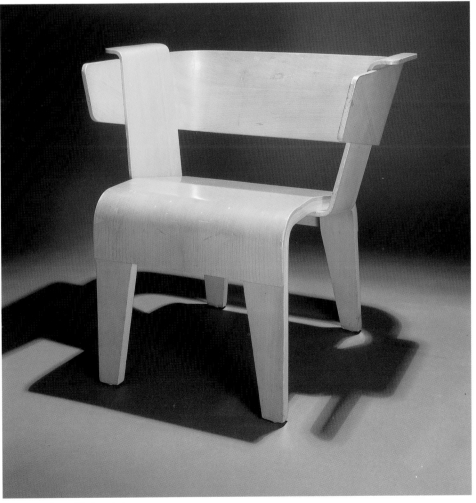

34. *Gerrit Rietveld.* Armchair

eral layers of wood overlap—such as the sides of each seat—show a thick and dense supporting structure.

In its legs and seat, Rietveld's chair recalls the general appearance and detailing of Marcel Breuer's tables and side chairs produced a decade earlier for the Isokon Furniture Company (fig. 23). But the treatment of the material is unmistakably reminiscent of the mid-1940s furniture of Charles and Ray Eames. Despite Rietveld's long experience with plywood and his sen-

iority in the architectural world, he seems to have derived his inspiration from the young Eameses' experimental chairs of around 1944 (fig. 29) and their production furniture from 1946 (fig. 30), apparently the first well-known and published examples to use a vocabulary of overlapping plywood sheets. Rietveld clearly responded to the manner in which the Eameses carefully formed chair seats and backs from several layers of plywood sheets, at the same time disregarding what was initially an even more important design ele-

ment of the Eameses' furniture: their attempt to construct enclosing, volumetric, shell-like forms.

The Rietveld armchair did not offer radically innovative technical or aesthetic solutions to the problem of chair design. However, it merits consideration both as a late example of the work of one of the century's major architect-designers and as an example of the widespread interest in plywood furniture that was so decisively influenced by the work of the Eameses.   CW

35. *Rietveld. Back view of armchair*

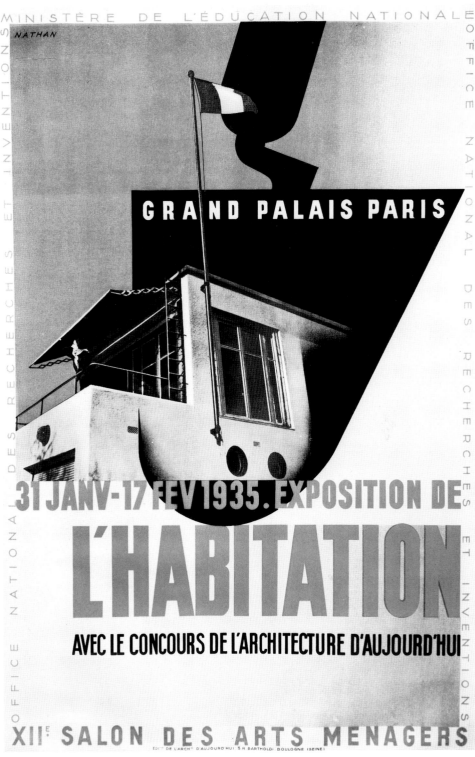

36. *Jacques Nathan-Garamond*. L'Habitation

Jacques Nathan-Garamond

Poster: *L'Habitation*
Designed c. 1935
Offset lithograph; 47½ × 31⅛ inches
    (120.7 × 79.1 cm)
Printed by Édition de L'Architecture
    d'Aujourd'hui (Boulogne [Seine],
    France), 1935
Signed in the stone, upper left corner: NATHAN
D86.151.1, gift of Lynn Brows, by exchange*

This early poster of Nathan's was commissioned for the officially sponsored 1935 "Home Exhibition," the twelfth Salon des Arts Ménagers, held at Paris's Grand Palais.

Nathan used the most up-to-date graphic design techniques in this poster. A Modernist tradition prevails in its tightly constructed geometric composition, which is further emphasized with a border of sans serif type. Airbrush, recently introduced to graphic art, is here used to define a blue sky as well as to set off the exhibition's bold red title. Like Herbert Matter's *All Roads Lead to Switzerland* (fig. 37), also of 1935, *L'Habitation* makes use of a restricted range of primary colors and photomontage, a technique new to graphic design. Nathan wittily placed a modern French house by architect Pierre Sardou[31] in a schematically rendered black trowel. The whimsical sense of fantasy expressed in the juxtaposition of the house and trowel and the Synthetic Cubist way in which they merge are typical of the French school of graphic design. The spatially ambiguous, airbrushed background, against which the type and photomontage appear to float, adds a Surrealist effect. The rich pictorial quality of this work in many ways sums up prewar school of Paris art.

FTH

43

Herbert Matter

Poster: *All Roads Lead to Switzerland*
Designed 1935
Photogravure; 37⅞ × 25½ inches (101.3 ×
 64.1 cm)
Produced by the Swiss National Tourist Office
Printed in red in lower left corner: [device of a
 circle with a winged wheel and SNTO, both
 stripped in in white]
Printed in lower left: fretz/Printed in
 Switzerland *herbert matter*
D87.147.1

After studying painting in Paris, Matter returned
to his native Switzerland. From 1932 to 1936 he
designed this and many other dynamic photomontage posters for the Swiss National Tourist
Office, posters on which his early fame would
rest.

In photomontage, several views are combined
to create a forceful new composition. Herbert
Bayer, the master typographer at the Bauhaus,
had used this experimental convention with great
success at that teaching institution and then in
Berlin, but he generally combined disparate images in a disquietingly Surrealist manner and
added painting or drawing, as in his famous advertisement for Adrianol (fig. 340). While Matter
may have echoed Bayer's signature by writing his
own in lowercase script letters, he used photomontage very differently.

This poster, which was issued in versions for
nine languages (English, French, German, Italian, Dutch, Swedish, Spanish, Czech, and
Hungarian), relies on a few simple images—a
roadway, hills, mountains, and sky—that are dramatically integrated in a visually compelling and
seemingly rational way. The foreground is dominated by a cobblestone road, suggestive of an old
Swiss street. Pitched at an angle, it sweeps the
viewer deep into the pictorial space and, a common feature of Matter's work, gives a textural

37. *Herbert Matter*. All Roads Lead to Switzerland

richness to the composition. Then a horizontal
band of hills and the winding Tremola Road,
which leads to the Gotthard Pass, playfully carry
the eye across the poster horizontally. Finally, the
peaks of the Jungfrau and Mount Silberhörner,
set off against a blue sky, dominate this scene,
which epitomizes the grandeur of the Alps and
the excitement of travel.

For Matter, text was subordinate to the visual
message. A sans serif typographic slogan in red is
canted at the same angle as the road and serves as
the base line of the image. The lettering is more

even and clean-cut than most of Bayer's commercial typography.

Thus word and image, each compelling in
itself, are combined successfully and are united
with a strong, simple color scheme of red and
blue to create an advertisement that is both pic-
torially rich yet straightforwardly simple, that
recognizes technological innovation yet appeals
to human emotion. It is little wonder, then, that
Matter's experimental tourist posters revolutionized the genre and were imitated worldwide in
advertising design.   FTH

EXPERIMENT IN TOTALITY

Moholy=Nagy

THE FABULOUS STORY OF A MODERN GENIUS

A BIOGRAPHY BY SIBYL MOHOLY-NAGY

38. *Herbert Bayer.* Experiment in Totality: Moholy-Nagy

Herbert Bayer

Placard: *Experiment in Totality: Moholy-Nagy*
Designed 1950[32]
Offset lithograph; 21⅛ × 12⅞ inches
  (53.7 × 32.7 cm)
Printed in black in lower left edge: *herbert
  bayer 50*
On reverse, typewritten on white adhesive
  label attached to upper right corner: PLEASE
  RETURN TO HERBERT BAYER[33]
D88.130.1

Bayer's close, longstanding relationship with
Hungarian Constructivist László Moholy-Nagy
made him an appropriate choice of artist to design this placard advertising Moholy-Nagy's biography. Written by his widow and second wife,
Sibyl, it was published in 1950 by Harper and
Brothers of New York.

Experiment in Totality is an image that unites
two important artists who shaped the Bauhaus: it
conveys a visual summation of Moholy-Nagy's
artistic contributions, rendered in the graphic
style of the early Bauhaus by Bayer, that school's
master typographer. Paying homage to his late
friend's position as a founder of the Constructivist
movement, Bayer employed a composition that
recalls Moholy-Nagy's early, Constructivist style
(fig. 39). True to Bauhaus tenets, Bayer used only
primary colors and placed a three-quarter-length
photographic reproduction of the late artist reading against a yellow Constructivist background,
creating a Surrealist effect seen in Bauhaus art of
the 1920s. Intersected by diagonal bands of red
and gray and punctuated with circles of yellow,
red, and blue, the placard's controlled composition is as analytically geometric in Bayer's hands
as it would have been had Moholy-Nagy himself
created it. Acknowledging the latter's interest in
typography, Bayer superimposed blocks of assorted lettering styles, stripped in in white or
printed in black, at contrasting angles in typical
Bauhaus typographic fashion.

This placard testifies to the lingering impact of
the Bauhaus legacy on postwar design.

FTH

39. *László Moholy-Nagy.* Composition
No. 19. 1919. *Busch-Reisinger Museum,
Harvard University, Cambridge, Massachusetts.
Gift of Sibyl Moholy-Nagy*

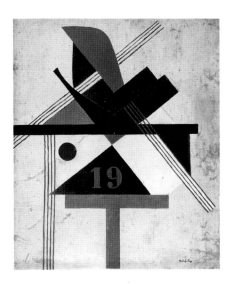

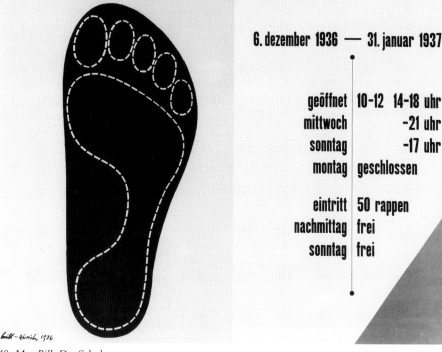

40. Max Bill. Der Schuh

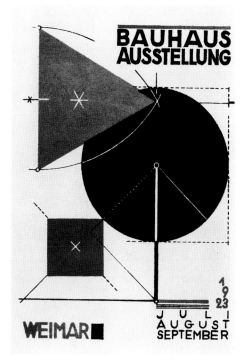

41. Herbert Bayer. Postcard for Bauhaus exhibition. 1923. Busch-Reisinger Museum, Harvard University, Cambridge, Massachusetts

Max Bill

Poster: *Der Schuh*
Designed 1936
Lithograph on two sheets; 50⅜ × 35⅝ inches
  (128 × 90.55 cm)
Printed by the Kunstgewerbeschule Zürich,
  1936
Printed in lower left corner: *bill-Zurich 1936*
On reverse, handwritten: ⅟₁₇₅ [in ink] D/1936
  [in pencil]
D87.172.1

This 1936 poster is from the influential series commissioned by the Zurich Kunstgewerbe-museum, which promulgated the revolutionary graphic designs of the Swiss Constructivists in the late 1920s and 1930s. This series fostered a highly respected Swiss style of graphic design whose tightly composed appearance exemplified Good Design for the following decades.

Der Schuh announced an exhibition on the history of footwear manufacture and fashion using the new Bauhaus principles of layout and typography established by Herbert Bayer. Bill used typography as an art form to convey a spirit of functionalism in design appropriate for the machine age. Purposely antielite, impersonal, and standardized, this Bauhaus-inspired message was expressed typographically in the use of lower-case sans serif type. Three different sizes of the same type provide variety and distinguish the title, subtitle, and times of the exhibition.

Bill's aesthetics were based on architectural and geometric principles. The consistent rationalism and minimalism of his style exceeds even that of the geometrically based compositions of early Bauhaus graphics, like Bayer's post-card of 1923 (fig. 41). In *Der Schuh*, the lettering is arranged as a major compositional element and is complemented by blocks of strong primary colors—bright blue, yellow, red, and black—that do not deviate from the impersonal color scheme of De Stijl and the Bauhaus. A simple rectangle and triangles give directional emphasis and stimulate visual interest, while the dotted outline of a foot inscribed within the shoe sole contributes a topical and whimsical note, somewhat restrained.   FTH

Angelo Testa

Textile: *Sportsmen's Blues*
Designed 1942
Cotton, plain weave, silk-screen printed;
  75 × 51 inches (190 × 129.5 cm)
Produced by Angelo Testa and Company
  (Chicago), c. 1947
Unmarked
D84.148.1, gift of Geoffrey N. Bradfield*

Angelo Testa designed *Sportmen's Blues* while a student at the School of Design in Chicago. Five years later, when he established his own company, he included this design in his collection of abstract-patterned fabrics.

Given the title of this work, one might take it as an abstraction of sports-related elements, such as riding crops and horseshoes, but it can also be read as a totally nonobjective design. Testa appears to have derived his formal means from

his mentor at the School of Design, László Moholy-Nagy. *Sportsmen's Blues* shares with Moholy-Nagy's *Space Modulators* (fig. 43) an emphasis on Constructivist principles and geometric forms as well as visual transparency and a sense of motion. In Testa's pattern, the alternating thin red stripes and thick black bands are printed on a white ground. The abstract "objects" that seem to rise above the surface are actually negative areas—white spaces of the ground. And where one of the shapes overlaps two levels, it creates a refractory shift, one of the effects of the manipulation of space sought by Moholy-Nagy in his *Space Modulators* and by the jewelry designer Margaret de Patta (fig. 224), another graduate of the School of Design.

If patterns in the past were contained rigidly in banded compositions, Testa's *Sportsmen's Blues* frees itself to some extent from such traditional thinking. Although the design is basically banded, the shapes move freely across the planes, so that the pattern can be read both laterally and vertically; where they extend from one band to the next, they help to integrate the pattern.

As one of the earliest silk-screen-printed fabrics in the United States, *Sportsmen's Blues* is of great importance. In Europe, screen-printed fabrics appeared first at the Wiener Werkstätte, and then the Viennese Josef Frank introduced screen-printed fabrics to Sweden in the 1930s through his work for the Swedish store Svenskt Tenn. (In France, Paul Poiret's Atelier Martine used block printing, while at the Bauhaus the emphasis was on woven pattern.)

Directly or indirectly, *Sportsmen's Blues* influenced textile design, not only in the Chicago area but throughout the United States. Testa was looked on as the "guru," as one colleague put it,[34] and the ingenuity and freedom of his patterns inspired colleagues and students alike.

CCMT

(left) 42. *Angelo Testa*. Sportsmen's Blues *textile*

43. *László Moholy-Nagy*. Space Modulator.
*1939–45. Solomon R. Guggenheim Museum,
New York*

Hans Coray

Armchair: *Landi*

Designed 1938

Aluminum and replaced rubber feet; 29⁷⁄₁₆ × 20¼ × 24¼ inches (74.8 × 51.5 × 61.5 cm)

Produced by Blattmann Metallwarenfabrik AG (Wädenswil, Switzerland), 1939 to the present[35] (this example before 1962)

Impressed on front side of seat back: METALLWARENFABRIK WAEDENSWIL

Impressed on rear side of back seat rail: SWITZERLAND

Printed on paper label on front edge of seat: MADE IN AUSTRIA/[device with A][36]

D87.129.1, gift of Galerie Metropol Inc., New York

44. *"Landesaustellung," Zurich, 1939, with* Landi *armchair on grounds*

45. *Hans Coray.* Landi *armchair*

This stacking armchair intended for outdoor use has become so ubiquitous and widely imitated that we are apt to underestimate its ingenuity and technical sophistication. This tendency is compounded by the fact that its designer was not well known outside of Switzerland and that, due to the outbreak of World War II so soon after the chair's introduction, it was unable to establish itself in the prewar marketplace. Only after the early 1950s did it become successful and widely known throughout the design world.

The chair derives its name from the exhibition for which it was designed, the "Landesaustellung" (Swiss National Exhibition) of 1939 held in Zurich (fig. 44). The choice of an aluminum chair to furnish the exhibition grounds—1,500 were produced—was particularly appropriate, as the production of aluminum and aluminum products was important to the Swiss economy and was highlighted at the fair. [37]

The *Landi* chair was manufactured from newly refined aluminum alloys, which were delivered to the factory in a "soft" or highly flexible state before being stretch-stamped and then baked over a prolonged period into a rigid shape. The pair of arm/leg units and the seat were manufactured separately and finished with an alkaline lye bath and a clear lacquer spray before final assembly.

Admirably suited to its purpose as indoor/outdoor furniture, the *Landi* chair weighs little more than six and a half pounds and fits into a genuinely compact stack for storage or moving. Made of a strong but lightweight alloy, the chair is durable enough to stand demanding wear and flexible and resilient enough to create a comfortable seat. The seat perforations, intended to prevent the collection of water or snow, not incidentally add a note of geometric patterning to the surface. Finally, the material is genuinely water- and rustproof, claims left unfulfilled by many outdoor chairs of the period.

Coray's armchair is a remarkable design that participated in the Modernist tradition of metal (mainly steel) furniture while dissenting from the rigid geometry and hard edges associated with that tradition. Unique at the time because of its exploitation of newly developed aluminum technologies, it was subsequently imitated in a wide variety of metals and plastics from the 1950s through the present day.   CW

Jean Carlu

Poster: *Give 'em Both Barrels*
Designed 1941
Offset lithograph; 30 × 40 inches (76.3 × 101.7 cm)
Printed by the United States Government Printing Office, 1941
Signed in the stone, lower left: Jean/Carlu
D84.187.1, gift of Geoffrey N. Bradfield*

Give 'em Both Barrels is a striking example of the posters that Carlu executed for the United States Division of Information Office for Emergency Management in the agency's effort to encourage Americans to produce equipment and supplies for prewar mobilization as well as manpower. [38]

Carlu's image here is a visual pun, which refers to the riveter's barrel as well as the artillery soldier's. The dynamic figures are as one with the tools of their respective trades. By this time, Streamlining had gained a hold in the industrial arts. Its influence is reflected here in the design's smooth, flowing lines and the use of airbrushing, a technique introduced in the 1930s, both of which heighten the mechanized effect of the images. Also, the poster's bold type is canted to simulate forward movement. The two profiled figures are stark against a plain yellow background, with the airbrushed riveter appearing as a ghost of the gunner below him. Profiles and hands, prominent in this poster, are among Carlu's recurring images. Tight, geometric com-

46. *Jean Carlu.* Give 'em Both Barrels

positions, a hallmark of Carlu's work and very evident in this example, reflect his early architectural training. However, his comparatively literal and ornamental approach to subject matter is characteristic of French graphic design.

FTH

Jens Risom

Side chair: model no. 666 WSP
Designed c. 1942, redesigned c. 1946[39]
Birch and plastic (vinylidene chloride and
vinyl chloride copolymer) webbing; 30⁵⁄₁₆ ×
17½ × 20¼ inches (77 × 44.5 × 51.5 cm)
Produced by Hans G. Knoll Furniture Company
(later Knoll Associates, Inc.) (New York),
c. 1943–at least 1954 (this example after 1946)
Unmarked
D84.171.1, gift of Geoffrey N. Bradfield*

While much of Europe was plunged into the horror of World War II, designers living in the United States had the exceptional opportunity not only to continue working but also to design new lines of furniture and accessories for the domestic market. Hans Knoll's furniture company took on its identity as a design-conscious firm precisely at this time through the work of Jens Risom, a free-lance Danish designer who had recently immigrated to the United States.

This side chair was Risom's first design for Knoll and part of a line of fifteen Risom pieces sold by the firm. Responding to government regulations limiting or banning the use of materials needed for the war effort, it contained "no metal, no plywood, no springs, and no accessories."[40] Made of inexpensive cedar—one of a number of "noncritical" softwoods unrestricted by wartime regulation—and army surplus webbing, it filled what proved to be a sizable market demand for relatively inexpensive modern furniture.[41]

Both the sloping angularity of the chair's original design (fig. 48)—characterized by obtuse angles and few ninety-degree angles—as well as the tapering, often triangular shape of its various parts were typical of progressive plywood and solid wood furniture of the late 1930s through the 1950s. In this it went beyond the neoclassicism of modern Scandinavian furniture, from which it derived its form. A particularly relevant comparison is with a Bruno Mathsson side chair of 1932 (fig. 49). The modernity of the shape of the Risom chair was probably somewhat mitigated for American consumers by its plain wood surfaces, certainly more acceptable than metal would have been, and the familiarity of the webbing used for the seat. That modern design should appear in its least threatening guise was particularly important for the American and British markets, as they were traditionally resistant to modern design.

Interestingly, the design of the leg and back support was later modified by Knoll, possibly with the involvement of the designer (in which case before the spring of 1946).[42] As a result, the design became less abruptly angular in appearance. With the relaxation of wartime restrictions, other materials were also introduced, such as a new type of plastic webbing for the seat and newly available beech, birch, and maple for the frames.[43] (The later, modified version is the one in the Stewart Collection.)

Although in retrospect a design of unprepossessing appearance, modest aspirations, and plainspoken modernity, Risom's side chair signaled the successful inroads that Scandinavian-derived Modernism had been making in the United States and the internationalism that would characterize Knoll as one of America's leading makers of modern furniture.

CW

(opposite) 47. Jens Risom. Side chair: model no. 666 WSP

(above) 48. Risom. Drawing of original and later versions of the designer's side chair. 1989. Liliane and David M. Stewart Collection. Gift of Jens Risom

(above right) 49. Bruno Mathsson. Side chair. 1932

50. *E. McKnight Kauffer.* Organic Design in Home Furnishings

51. *McKnight Kauffer.* Power, the Nerve Centre of London's Underground. *1930. Collection, The Museum of Modern Art, New York. Gift of the designer*

52. *McKnight Kauffer.* Magicians Prefer Shell. *1934. Collection, The Museum of Modern Art, New York. Gift of the designer*

E. McKnight Kauffer

Catalogue cover: *Organic Design in Home Furnishings*
Designed 1941
Offset lithograph; 7½ × 10 inches (19 × 25.4 cm)
Printed by William E. Rudge's Sons (New York), 1941
Front cover, printed in white in lower right corner: E McKnight Kauffer
D88.165.1, gift of Mrs. Stanley Hanks

Although born in the United States, E. Mc-Knight Kauffer became one of the leading graphic designers in England in the 1920s and 1930s. When the Museum of Modern Art commissioned him to design this cover for the catalogue of its "Organic Design in Home Furnishings" exhibition of 1941, he was already well known at the museum. He was acquainted with its director, Alfred H. Barr, Jr., and the museum had recently exhibited many of the striking posters he had designed in England.[44] After Kauffer returned to the United States in 1940 as a war refugee, the museum used his cover design for the catalogue of the "Britain at War" exhibition[45] and then asked him to design this cover as well. Kauffer's bold graphic style, Modernist imagery, and reductivist typography were well suited to the museum's aesthetic.

The front cover is a stark contrast of white forms on black, with a red elliptical line adding a strong touch of color. These colors are reversed on the back cover, the background being red and the line black. The word *organic* stands out against the spare design because of its ornamented typeface, curiously archaic for a work published by the Museum of Modern Art. By contrast, the other words are set in a modern sans serif type of the sort that Kauffer had used earlier, and the museum's name at the top is tellingly presented in Bauhaus-style lowercase letters.

The ball on the elliptical line, a motif that also appears in Alexander Calder's works,[46] suggests movement, although the hand is static.

Hands appeared frequently as a motif in Kauffer's works. In *Power, the Nerve Centre of London's Underground* (fig. 51), a heavily muscled arm and fist emerge from the symbol of the Underground, sending out jagged bolts of electricity. This dynamic image reflects the influence of Futurism and Vorticism on Kauffer's early work. He also used stylized hands in *Magicians Prefer Shell* (fig. 52), changing them from dark on light to light on dark, a reversal suggesting the sleight of hand that is the magician's stock-in-trade. In Kauffer's design of 1937 for a prologue curtain for Ninette de Valois's ballet *Checkmate*,[47] two disembodied forearms floating in the evening sky represent the forces that control the game of chess between Love and Death, the theme of the ballet. Again, one arm is light against dark, the other the reverse, echoing the alternation of a chessboard.

For the *Organic Design* cover, Kauffer simplified the elements of these earlier works, creating an image both starker and stronger than its predecessors. Although the imagery bears no apparent relationship to the furnishings in the exhibition, the elliptical line linking the hand to the word *design* seems to emphasize the role of the hand in the creation of all designs.

CWL

Eero Saarinen and Charles Eames

Modular furniture: four cabinets, two benches, and a desk
Designed 1940–41
Mahogany-faced blockboard, yellow poplar, cherry, and elm secondary woods; cabinets: 22 × 18 × 17⅞ inches (55.8 × 45.8 × 45.4 cm); cabinet: 15³⁄₁₆ × 18⅛ × 17⅞ inches (38.6 × 46 × 45.4 cm); benches: 13¹⁄₁₆ × 36 × 17⅞ inches (33.2 × 91.5 × 45.4 cm); desk: 30⁵⁄₁₆ × 49³⁄₁₆ × 21 inches (76.8 × 125.1 × 53.4 cm)
Produced by Red Lion Furniture Company (Red Lion, Pennsylvania), c. 1941
Unmarked
D83.111.1–6; D89.183.1, 2

At the time of its founding in 1929 the Museum of Modern Art in New York assumed the mission of forwarding the cause of Modernism, but it was during the 1940s and early 1950s that its reputation for fostering progressive, mainly domestic, design was made. For its first major competition, "Organic Design in Home Furnishings" in 1940–41, the museum secured the collaboration of twelve major American department stores, which offered sponsorship for the project and the promise of manufacturing contracts for the winners. Eero Saarinen and Charles Eames entered as a team in two categories and won both. While their seating design (fig. 27) has become known

53. *Eero Saarinen and Charles Eames. Possible arrangements of modular furniture*

54. Saarinen and Eames. Modular furniture

due to its seminal role in the development of the Eamses' ubiquitous chairs, their modular case furniture has not. Indeed, in retrospect it may be difficult to comprehend how such seemingly modest designs were said by the exhibition organizers to carry "the principle of standardization farther than any other group yet produced in this country."[48]

Designated as furniture for a living room, these modular units were referred to at the time as "unit furniture." They were seen by the exhibition organizers as American versions of the much admired German *Typenmöbel*, which was described as having been developed for the domestic interior by the Bauhaus architect Marcel Breuer.[49] They thus fit neatly into the precise branch of Modernist design with which the Museum of Modern Art wished to associate itself.

The Saarinen-Eames entries consisted of a series of seven wooden cabinets, based on a module of eighteen inches, which could be combined in a variety of ways, and a group of three four-legged bases (fig. 53). A base could also serve as a bench, flower stand, or desk. The system was completely flexible, as no fixing was required; rubber grips held the case units in place.

While acknowledging that the entry did not pioneer the use of separate base and case units for storage systems, the jury felt that the base design introduced radical innovations through its minimal design and the fact that it was raised above the ground. Not only could the base be used as an independent piece of furniture but, most important, its design allowed the case units to clear baseboards and plugs and to fit closely to the wall, features not shared by units that sat on or close to the floor.

Standardized unit furniture offered the opportunity to produce economically a range of furniture from a small number of constructional elements that could cover a wide variety of needs as well as allow a relatively large number of unit combinations. With America's entry into the war, however, much furniture manufacture was temporarily curtailed, and the Saarinen and Eames unit furniture never had an opportunity to test its market. In 1946 the Eameses revived the idea with a group of updated designs for Herman Miller (fig. 61), which were never put into production. Three years later, they returned to the idea of modular storage units but radically altered their approach (fig. 63).   CW

Eva Zeisel

Dinnerware: *Museum*
Designed c. 1942–43
Glazed porcelain; coffeepot: 10½ × 7⅝ × 5½
   inches (26.9 × 19.5 × 14.1 cm)
Produced by Shenango Pottery (New Castle,
   Pennsylvania), for Castleton China, Inc.
   (New York), 1945–at least 1960
Bowl and coffeepot, transfer printed in black
   on underside: [device of stylized lyre]/MADE
IN U.S.A./CASTLETON/CHINA/REG. U.S.
PAT. OFF.
Plate, transfer printed in black on underside:
   [device of lyre]/CASTLETON CHINA [in
   ribbon]/MADE IN U.S.A.
Handleless creamer, transfer printed in black
   on underside: MADE IN U.S.A./CASTLETON/
   CHINA/REG. U.S. PAT. OFF.
Other pieces unmarked
D85.155.1–3; D83.113.1, 2 and D86.102.1, 2,
gift of Hans Zeisel*

The genesis of this dinnerware service is intimately connected with the Museum of Modern Art's desire to foster Modernist design by entering the marketplace and becoming a mediator between designer and manufacturer.[50] Louis Hellman, the president of Castleton China, reputedly approached the museum after its "Organic Design in Home Furnishings" exhibition, requesting it to recommend a designer to create a modern-style dinner service.[51] Eliot Noyes, director of the museum's design department, pro-

55. *Eva Zeisel*. Museum *dinnerware*

56, 57. *Zeisel*. Museum *dinnerware*

posed Eva Zeisel. The contract that evolved was a novel one: while Zeisel was to be the designer, the museum reserved the right to judge every piece in exchange for its imprimatur.

Formal porcelain dinnerware in the modern style already existed, but it was European, such as Trude Petri's *Urbino* service for the Berlin Staatliche Porzellan Manufaktur. Modernism in American dinnerware had been confined to informal earthenware sets, such as Frederick H. Rhead's *Fiesta* and Russel Wright's *American Modern* (figs. 25, 26). Thus this project responded to a real need, especially since the war had stopped the importation of such wares.

The striving for formality is reflected not only in the choice of the clay body but also in the way that it is used. The walls of the plates are intentionally thick at the bottom, to provide stability, but they rise to thin, elegant edges. In accord with Zeisel's theory of the psychology of forms, the coffeepot has "curves extending into straight lines" and small openings at the spout and lid, to appear "light, graceful, cold." Formality is also reflected in the range of pieces in the set, including individual salts and demitasse cups.

The style of this service exemplifies an important transitional moment. Some pieces use prewar solutions. The covered bowls (fig. 56), shaped like Chinese rice bowls, recall similar vessels in Petri's *Urbino* set. The plates, essentially square but rounded in the corners, recall

those that Russel Wright had introduced in *American Modern*. On the other hand, some pieces suggest postwar designs. Zeisel's open bowls (fig. 57) flare upward in the corners; the handleless creamer and the coffeepot have elegant, fluent forms. The multiplicity of styles is partly due to the designer's tendency to compose a service with a variety of subsets. Yet it is remarkable how harmoniously she integrated them.

Although the major aspects of the service were supposedly established by 1943, wartime conditions prevented production. Not until April 1946 was it presented publicly, but then it was done with great fanfare, in a special exhibition at the Museum of Modern Art. Coming only months after the exhibition of the furniture of Ray and Charles Eames, it was a signal honor for Zeisel, and it certainly helped Castleton to promote its ware.

The museum maintained its purist stance of insisting on a clear glaze over the cream-colored body. Its one concession to the market was to allow some of the smaller plates to be colored maroon or dark or light green to provide accents, but even that experiment was soon abandoned in favor of the monochromatic scheme. However, over the course of the many years in which the product was sold, Castleton added transfer-printed ornament to satisfy the demands of the retail market. Aesthetic idealism and commercial reality were not always in harmony.

ME

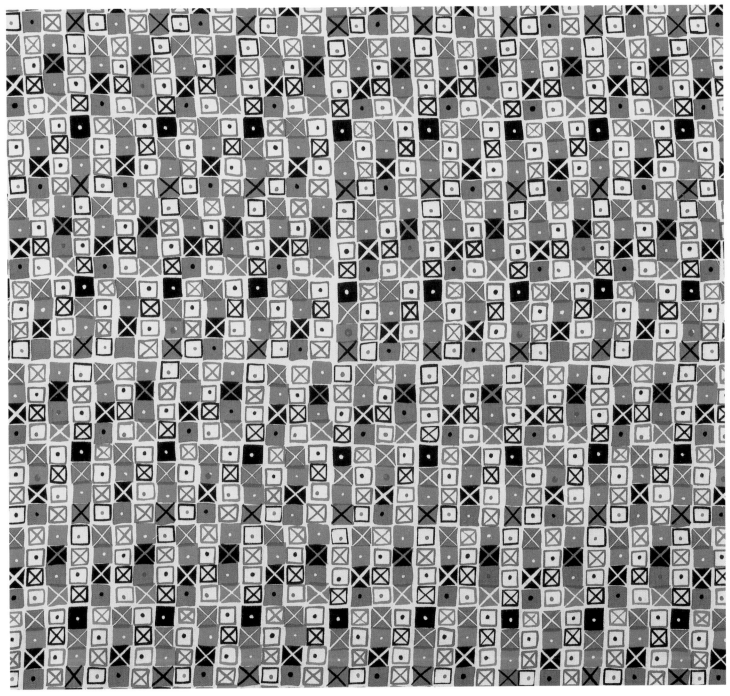

58. *Ray Eames.* Cross Patch *textile*

Ray Eames

Textile: *Cross Patch*
Designed c. 1945[52]
Cotton, plain weave, silk-screen printed;
 38¾ × 50½ inches (98.4 × 128.3 cm)
Produced by Schiffer Prints, Division of Mil-
 Art Company, Inc. (New York), c. 1947–49
Printed twice in black in right selvage: "CROSS
 PATCH" by *ray eames*
Printed twice in black in left selvage:
 © SCHIFFER PRINTS VAT DYE HAND PRINT
D83.117.1, gift of Geoffrey N. Bradfield*

Although Ray Eames had been exposed to textile
designing while at the Cranbrook Academy of
Art, this was not an area in which she had practi-

cal experience, and, in fact, it remained a minor
aspect of her career. In 1945 she designed a number of textiles, including *Cross Patch*, *Sea Things*
(a humorous and freely drawn study of crusta-
cea), and *Dot Pattern* (an interesting geometric
construction). The former two patterns were submitted to the Museum of Modern Art's "Competition for Printed Fabrics" in 1947.[53] *Sea Things*
received an honorable mention and both it
and *Cross Patch* were subsequently included in
Milton Schiffer's Stimulus Collection, a project
of printing new textiles in the modern style.

Cross Patch is an allover pattern of small
squares filled with diagonally crossed lines or
dotted centers. The color scheme is blue, black,

and red against a yellow background. Its basic
geometric configurations and its scheme of primary colors look forward to other of Charles and
Ray Eameses' designs, most notably their house
and the ESU storage units (figs. 62, 63). On the
other hand, the effect of the textile is whimsical
rather than architecturally stable; the squares are
irregular in shape and size and quixotically mis-
aligned. Ultimately, the pattern of dots and x's
suggests not an engineering scheme but the game
of ticktacktoe, which, like the intentional naiveté
of the geometry, is entirely fitting, since *Cross
Patch* was intended to be used in a child's room.[54]
CCMT

Davis Pratt

Chair
Designed 1948 and executed c. 1948
Steel, inflatable rubber tube, rubber, and
  cotton cover; 26¹⁵⁄₁₆ × 31¾ × 26 inches
  (68.6 × 80.7 × 66 cm)
Unmarked
D83.106.1, gift of Davis Pratt

The inflatable chair is a furniture type that is universally associated with the Pop art sensibility of the 1960s. Most of those designs were made from a single piece of inflatable plastic and reflected the period's interest in an informal and self-consciously untraditional life-style. Pratt's chair, a distinctly postwar design, was less con-

cerned with aesthetics or with making a political statement against traditional conventions of seating; in fact, the unorthodox, inflatable seat was completely hidden by a nubby slipcover. Instead, the Pratt chair was designed in response to the Museum of Modern Art's call for entries for its "International Competition for Low-Cost Furniture Design." This example was one of a number of prototypes made by the designer. The program, based on the short supply and small areas of postwar living spaces, called for comfortable, inexpensive, well-designed furniture, "in other words, mass-produced furniture that is integrated to the needs of modern living, production and merchandising."[55]

Pratt's use of an inflated inner tube for the chair's seat and back reflected the interest among American designers during and following World War II in expanding the constructional vocabulary of furniture. Taking a different direction from the European architects of the 1920s and 1930s who used the resilience of a steel- or plywood-framed cantilever to compensate for their stripping away of comfortable upholstery, Pratt arrived at an alternative to covered spring upholstery.[56] Interestingly, the component parts of automobile design provided the inspiration in both instances: cantilevered metal seating had been used in automobiles, and Pratt's comfortable seat is literally made from the inner tube of an automobile tire (fig. 60).

Pratt's chair was awarded a second prize in the competition, which it shared with Charles and Ray Eames' series of fiberglass seating (figs. 309, 310).[57] In awarding a second prize to Pratt's chair, the competition jury singled out its comfort—it was certainly the most comfortable of all the prize-winners—and its collapsibility. The latter was an important issue to designers, manufacturers, and retailers of mass-produced furniture who were concerned with lowering product prices. Collapsibility and the related solution of stacking designs addressed two important and potentially expensive aspects of furniture manufacture and distribution: shipping and storage costs. Both approaches to this problem received considerable attention during the 1920s and 1930s and became even more important during the postwar search for low-cost furniture.

It is interesting to observe the fates of both second-prize winners four decades after the Museum of Modern Art's competition. The Eameses' chairs, distinguished by their sculptural form and durability—though certainly not comfort—have been universally acclaimed, became ubiquitous, were widely imitated, and have remained in continuous production. Pratt's chair, despite its comfort and ingenious use of materials, was never mass-produced and today seems a bit of an anachronism: a dated, if amusing, exercise in the never-ending search for the perfect chair.

CW

59. *Davis Pratt. Chair*

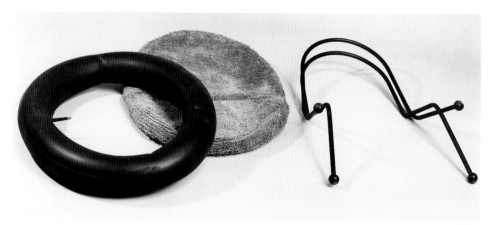

60. *Pratt. Component parts of chair*

58

61. *Charles and Ray Eames. Modular storage units. 1946*

62. *Eames. The designers' residence, Santa Monica, California. 1948–49*

Charles and Ray Eames

Storage unit: model no. ESU 421-C
Designed c. 1949
Zinc-plated steel, birch-faced plywood, plastic-coated plywood, and lacquered Masonite; 58⅝ × 47 × 16¾ inches (148.9 × 119.4 × 42.5 cm)
Produced by Herman Miller Furniture Co. (Zeeland, Michigan), 1950–c. 1955
Unmarked
D83.144.1, gift of Mr. and Mrs. Robert L. Tannenbaum, by exchange*

Modular storage units were yet another object type to which the Eameses applied themselves over a period of years. Like many of their designs, this, too, had its conceptual origins in the Saarinen-Eames collaboration for the Museum of Modern Art's "Organic Design in Home Furnishings" competition of 1940–41. The simple modular system of different-size wood cabinets that could be variously stacked that they developed in 1940–41 (figs. 53, 54) evolved into a related but visually more pleasing series in 1946 that never went into production (fig. 61). Then the Eameses completely rethought the notion of storage furniture and transformed their stackable wooden units into a sophisticated system of steel-frame construction that supported a variety of interchangeable parts.

The ESU (Eames Storage Unit) series was presented as a "modestly priced" response to the need for home or office desks, cabinets, and cases.[58] Basic steel-frame units were made in different sizes, allowing two widths, three heights, and one depth. The frames could be fitted with a large variety of drawer units or open or closed shelving, the latter faced with a choice of wood or plastic sliding doors; the sides and back could be enclosed by wire struts, metal grilles, plywoods, and solid or laminated plastic. The variety of material choices allowed the Eameses to exploit their interest in texture and color to a degree hitherto impossible in their furniture designs.

It is difficult to consider the ESU unit without thinking of it as a miniature version of the house the Eameses were building for themselves (1948–49) in Santa Monica, California (fig. 62). Indeed, not only do the house and the storage units share technical features and aesthetic qualities, but the two aspects, in the canonical Modernist tradition, are one and the same.

In both the furniture and the architecture, the constructional systems were derived from industry: in the case of the storage units, metal shelving of the type used in warehouses and factories; for the house, "light factory framing members."[59] In both instances, the undisguised structural components were used for decorative effect. The appearance was based on a steel structural frame, reinforced by wire struts, whose open spaces could be filled with large panels of various materials in a variety of colors. The effect in both was striking: thin, delicate, and of obvious aesthetic intent, yet sturdy and workmanlike in the choice of materials and the undisguised, unornamented steel structure. The reference to Japanese domestic design was unmistakable and not inappropriate to design in California.

Among the Eameses' furniture, the storage units represent an unusual formal exercise in geometric design. And, although they are functional examples of furniture made from mundane, industrial elements, they possess the beauty, integrity, and delight characteristic of so much of the Eameses' work.   CW

63. Eames. Storage unit: model no. ESU 421-C

Ed Rossbach

Drapery textile

Designed and executed 1947

Cotton, plain weave, with tuberlocking tapestry weave in weft, painted warp and painted design; 86 × 36⅜ inches (218 × 92.4 cm)

Unmarked

D85.164.1, gift of Ed Rossbach

In 1947, prior to graduating from the Cranbrook Academy of Art, Rossbach simultaneously painted and wove this length of fabric. Clearly reminiscent of the paintings of Piet Mondrian, its pattern is a series of rectangles and squares, separated by black lines in both the warp and weft directions, and its color scheme is limited to the primary colors—blue, red, and yellow. Rossbach had been exposed to the De Stijl movement through exhibitions held at the Museum of Modern Art in New York. He conceived his casement fabric in this style because he realized that "the essence of weaving seemed to be horizontal-vertical."[60]

The fabric also reflects his intention to weave something like stained glass with heavy leading. The colored portions of the fabric were designed to let light pass through, while the black lines—the black leading—were meant to be opaque. Although it would have been much simpler to paint or print the design on a woven cloth after completing the weaving, Rossbach resorted to a painstaking process in which he dyed sections of his warp threads while they were on the loom and inserted the weft at the same time. The process he developed has something in common with ancient techniques such as warp painting or ikat dyeing, both unknown to him at the time.[61]

Rossbach was indeed brave to have been so experimental at Cranbrook, for, as he said later, "Cranbrook kept us focused on a very narrow range of weaving possibilities."[62] Marianne Strengell, his instructor and head of the weaving department, did not like his independence. If any coloring was to be done, she wanted it done the traditional way, either in the weaving through the use of different colored yarns or by block or silk-screen printing. Rossbach remembers to this day how "disturbed and eager Marianne Strengell was to get the fabric off the loom and the loom cleaned up—as some of the textile color got smeared onto the breastbeam."[63]

In retrospect and seen within the context of Rossbach's weavings, this casement fabric à la Mondrian represents the artist as an ardent experimenter, a characteristic of his entire career. He did not remain in the De Stijl tradition, nor did the primary-color palette influence his future weaving. The piece shows independence in thinking and practical application, trademarks that have continued to direct Ed Rossbach throughout his creative life.   CCMT

64. Ed Rossbach. Drapery textile

65. *Donald Knorr. Side chairs with and without upholstery*

66. *Knorr. Prototypes of side chair submitted to the "International Competition for Low-Cost Furniture Design," 1948–50. c. 1949*

Donald Knorr

Side chair: model no. 132 U

Designed c. 1949

Painted zinc-plated steel and chrome-plated
    steel; 31⅞ × 21⅛ × 21 inches (81.1 ×
    53.6 × 53.3 cm)

Produced by Knoll Associates, Inc. (New
    York), c. 1950–52

Unmarked

D85.169.1, gift of John and William Minnich,
    by exchange

Encouraged by his mentors at the Cranbrook Academy in Bloomfield Hills, Michigan, Eliel and Eero Saarinen, Knorr entered an inventive chair design in the Museum of Modern Art's famous "International Competition for Low-Cost Furniture Design," held in 1950, and was cowinner of the first prize in the seating category.[64]

Knorr's original presentation model (fig. 66) had been made of quarter-inch-thick thermosetting plastic, a material then under development by the U.S. Rubber Company. In its eagerness to develop the new product, the company set its research department to work with the young designer, who quickly grasped the ease with which this material could be raised from a flat sheet with heat application, thus avoiding the expensive, specially molded die-cut forms required to form sheet metal.

As deceptively simple as a conical paper cup, this design raises a single flat sheet of material to sculptural form. The seat was fitted with a doughnut-shaped pad for comfort, and this also covered the seam at the bottom, which was a bent flange, much like a boat keel. The legs were made from two bent steel rods, one forming the front legs, the other the back legs, and both bolted directly to the flange. Knorr notes that he deliberately minimized the legs, giving them low visibility to point up the sculptural seating form.

In accord with the provisions of the museum's competition, which stipulated that the winning designs were to be produced by a manufacturer and then offered for sale by one of the department stores or retail outlets who were the underwriting sponsors, this chair was put into production by

67. *Knorr. Side chair: model no. 132 U*

Knoll. However, Knoll's production department found in its initial small trial run that such a new technology was not cost-effective, and the company decided to use steel. Knorr participated in the redesigning process. The metal's gauge was half as thin as the plastic, and thus necessitated certain changes. These included the reduction of both the keel and the proportion of the flange, as well as mounting the legs laterally on either side of the keel.

The chair in the Stewart Collection is the new, revised model that was put into production. Its body is painted black, as are almost all examples, though both red and yellow versions were listed in the 1950 Knoll catalogue.[65] Although a relatively simple, straightforward design, it recieved a great deal of praise. The Museum of Modern Art called it "one of the most ingenious structural schemes seen in modern furniture."[66] Such praise notwithstanding, the chair was ultimately not that successful. Ironically, producing this chair in sheet metal raised the costs considerably, leading to a price of $59, which was not considered moderate. Moreover, the government restricted use of this gauge sheet metal in 1952 during the Korean conflict, which curtailed the chair's production. By the time the material was again available, Knoll was moving away from this type of simple, early Modern design to the more sophisticated designs of Ray and Charles Eames and Eero Saarinen, and this chair was dropped from its line.

KC

Dorothy Liebes

Drapery textile: *Bon Bon*
Designed c. 1950
Cotton and metallic (Lurex) yarn, handwoven, twill and plain weave; 107¼ × 48⅜ inches (272.4 × 122.9 cm)
Produced by Dorothy Liebes Design (San Francisco), c. 1950[67]
Printed and handwritten on paper label:
DOROTHY LIEBES/TEXTILES 'Bon Bon'/ #920
Printed and typewritten on second paper label:
DOROTHY LIEBES DESIGN/767 LEXINGTON avenue new york 21/TE8–3791/MEMO *No.* 3 Handwoven drapery. #920 'Bon Bon'./ Cotton & Metallic yarn. C. 1950
D88.129.1, gift of Luc d'Iberville-Moreau

Bon Bon reveals Dorothy Liebes—known throughout her career as "the First Lady of the Loom"[68]—to be a daring and inventive weaver, interior decorator, and stylist, unafraid of introducing novel color and fiber combinations. This handwoven drapery material, with its combination of pink and green highlighted by the shiny silver metallic glint of Lurex yarn, is a striking example of what became known as the "Liebes Look."[69]

Pictorial imagery was never a consideration for Dorothy Liebes or the eight or ten weavers who worked in her studio. Liebes saw her mission as supplying woven yardage like *Bon Bon* to her architectural associates and colleagues, who had relatively little to chose from if they were searching for unusual woven fabrics. Most textile designers of the period had taken up silk-screen printing, a faster and simpler way of decorating cloth. *Bon Bon* is a prime example of the type of custom-designed fabric in which the Liebes studio specialized.

68. *Dorothy Liebes.* Bon Bon *drapery textile*

Dorothy Liebes's emphasis in weaving had little to do with experimentation in structure. She used the traditional weaving vocabulary and reserved her inventiveness for color combinations and yarn selection. *Bon Bon* was conceived in the twill weave, and the treadling required to set up the loom probably did not even need to be drawn out on graph paper. Created spontaneously on the loom and composed of a series of stripes and bands of varying widths, *Bon Bon* made use of a mixed warp of pink and green fibers, as well as silver Lurex of varying diameters, for the vertically running, stationary threads on the loom.

In using different colors in the warp threads—one of Liebes's secrets and trademarks—Liebes went against tradition, which dictated one type of thread, either white, neutral, or a single color.

Liebes used the silver Lurex yarns in the belief that "metals extend the weaver's color palette. They provide tonal qualities peculiar unto themselves and judiciously used, highlight and dramatize the other colors in the cloth."[70] A jingle was sung by all those working at the Liebes studio: "Something dark, something light, something neutral, something bright."[71]

CCMT

Robert Sailors

Textile
Designed 1944
Wool, cotton, linen, and Lurex; 55 × 30 inches
(139.7 × 76.2 cm)
Produced by Contemporary Textiles Weaving
Company (Bitely, Michigan), 1947–60 (this
example 1959)
Unmarked
D89.136.1, gift of Robert D. Sailors

From the time Marianne Strengell took over the
direction of the weaving studios at the Cranbrook
Academy of Art in 1937, emphasis shifted away
from art fabrics and rugs to textile prototypes for
production, a direct legacy of the Bauhaus. Strengell encouraged experimentation with newly invented synthetic fibers, unusual materials, and
uncommon color combinations, and she advocated that her students be able to translate the
artistic quality of the handmade textile into production for the mass market.

In June 1944 one of Strengell's star pupils,
Robert Sailors, was invited to teach in the
Cranbrook weaving department. Shortly afterward, he was sent to the Rhode Island School of
Design in Providence to investigate and train on
power-loom machinery that Cranbrook was soon
to purchase. A power loom was installed at the
Academy in early 1945, and teaching its use became Sailors's responsibility. The acquisition of
the power loom made Cranbrook uncommon
among American art schools in its ability to teach
both craft and industrial weaving.[72]

Sailors first hand wove this herringbone-
striped material in 1944. Interesting weaving
materials were hard to come by during the war
years, and Sailors recalls that the Academy accepted any excess stock that the yarn jobbers could supply. Using an assemblage of very ordinary and dis-

69. *Robert Sailors. Textile*

parate materials in exciting new ways required
considerable inventiveness. Varied weights and
couplings of cotton and linen yarns and threads of
black, blue, beige, brown, red, gray, and chartreuse define the several widths of vertical stripes,
and the weft field is predominantly a golden
yellow. This textile fit the then current taste for
highly textured, richly colored stripes, plaids,
and other geometric patterns. In Sailors's own
estimation, the only exciting new element it offered was the extremely fine-gauge, bright gold
metallic thread woven in horizontally with the
wool weft.

After Sailors set up his own company in 1947,
this pattern became available in both handwoven
form, forty-two inches wide, and power-loom
form, fifty-four inches wide. As it has a fairly
loose weave, it was intended to be primarily a
drapery material, but with the application of latex
to the back it could be employed as upholstery
fabric. (This particular example, made from two
pieces sewn together, once covered a couch
owned by the designer's parents.) It was sought
after by clients who wanted an interestingly textured, richly colored fabric, one that had more
variety than the commercial fabrics then avail-

able. Frank Lloyd Wright, for example, used it in the house he designed for the Albert Adelman family in Fox Point, Wisconsin, in 1947 (fig. 70).[73] Looking for restrained but luxurious materials that met his criteria for quiet elegance and repose in the furnishing of his houses, the architect specified this textile for both drapery and upholstery.

KC

70. Frank Lloyd Wright. *Interior of Adelman house, Fox Point, Wisconsin, in 1948, with Sailors's textile used for drapery and upholstery*

Bernard Rudofsky

Textile: *Fractions*
Designed c. 1948–49
Cotton, twill weave, photo silk-screen printed; 47½ × 50⅜ inches (120.7 × 127.9 cm)
Produced by Schiffer Prints, Division of Mil-Art Company, Inc. (New York), c. 1949
Printed twice in black in right selvage:
SCHIFFER PRINTS . . . . . . VAT DYE HAND PRINT
Printed twice in black in left selvage:
"FRACTIONS" by BERNARD RUDOFSKY
Printed on paper tag: CHRISTIAN MUELLER & ASSOCIATES, INC./1314 Merchandise Mart/ Chicago 11, Illinois.
D85.130.1, gift of Geoffrey N. Bradfield, by exchange*

A clever and unusual design utilizing the typewriter, *Fractions* is composed of seven horizontal rows of typewriter characters stripped in against a black ground. The first line alternates the letters x and o. The second line alternates the fraction ¼ and asterisks, the third the fraction ½ and dashes. Then there follow a row of quotation marks, a row of dots, a row of the capital letter X, and, finally, a row of the capital letter I alternating with paired asterisks. A solid line completes the design, and a slightly thicker line is used for every second repeat.

Rudofsky's *Fractions* is one of several textile designs that he created in this manner, which form part of a still larger oeuvre based on his early fascination with his first typewriter, a portable

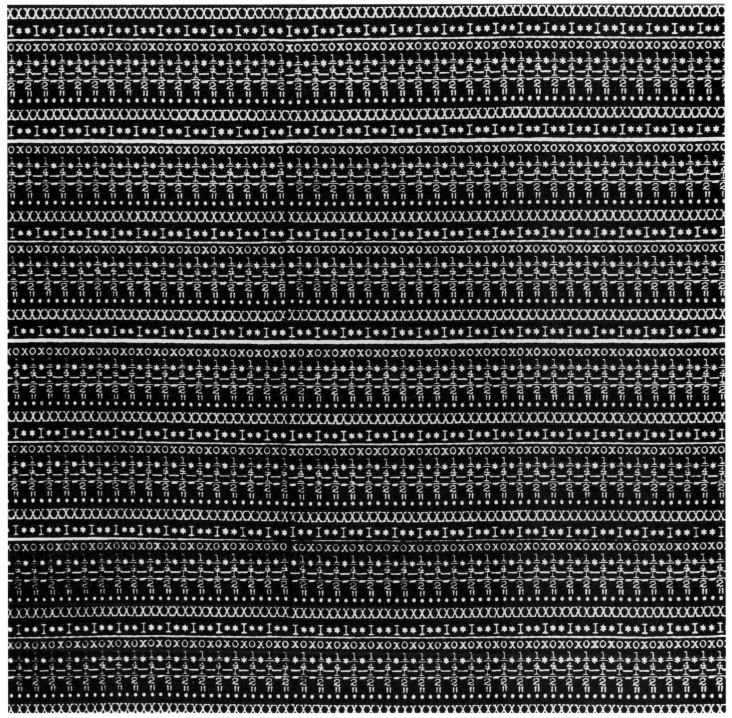

71. *Bernard Rudofsky.* Fractions *textile*

Olivetti. At first Rudofsky had used the typewriter for invitations, then Christmas cards; at some point he began to use a two-color ribbon. Yet, as he once wrote, "my typewriter art was really ignored."[74] When, in about 1948 or 1949, Schiffer Prints invited Rudofsky to design some textiles for curtains and furniture, he applied his typewriter art to textiles.

The commission formed part of what Schiffer called its Stimulus Collection, textiles by six selected artists, none of whom had any training in textiles. The six, who included Salvador Dalí (fig. 422), Ray Eames (fig. 58), George Nelson, Abel Sorensen, and Edward J. Wormley in addition to Rudofsky, were given complete freedom. They worked separately from one another, keep-ing their designs secret until the project was completed. Yet, except for Dalí, they all "showed a tendency of having produced something barely designed and arriving at a minute balance between colors and form."[75]

One of the other textile patterns Rudofsky created for Schiffer used the dollar sign and the percentage symbol arranged on a diagonal axis (fig. 72). Others have cleverly arranged rows of parenthesis signs, dashes, and number signs. Le Corbusier wrote a delightful congratulatory letter to Rudofsky in 1950, shortly after the fabrics had been introduced.[76]

CCMT

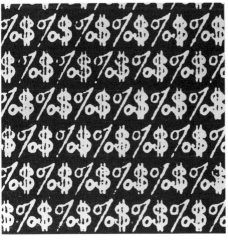

72. *Rudofsky.* Textile. *1949*

73. Andries Copier. Vase: model no. K.O. 1753

Andries Copier

Vase: model no. K.O. 1753
Designed 1936[77]
Glass; 7¾ × 5½ × 5½ inches (19.7 × 14 × 14 cm)
Produced by N.V. Koninklijke Nederlandsche Glasfabriek Leerdam (Leerdam, the Netherlands), 1936–c. 1942 (this example 1939–c. 1942)
Acid stamped on underside: monogram of c with dot inside and reversed L
D88.179.1

The standards of good design set early in the 1930s had specific parameters in terms of both universal concepts and individual materials. Glass was considered a transparent substance whose clarity had to be acknowledged and respected; coloration within the mass of the glass was tolerated but applied decoration rarely was. Whether the glass was hand blown and unique or molded and mass-produced, the criteria did not vary. Among the inevitably selected standard-bearers of good design in glass were petri dishes and chemical flasks (fig. 74), Wilhelm Wagenfeld's storage containers, and the Jena tea service—all rational, functional, colorless, and undecorated geometric vessels. The same canon of good taste was applied to vases and other "ornamental ware," none of which was ornamented in the traditional sense of the word.

Though set in the 1930s, these concepts still held true after the war—at least in some quarters. In his 1950 treatise *What Is Modern Design?*, Edgar Kaufmann, jr., maintained the same canonical truths.[78] His choices of good design in glass included Josef Hoffmann stemware of the 1920s, Czech and Italian tumblers of the 1940s, a bowl by Andries Copier of the 1930s (fig. 75), and a Gunnel Nyman vase from the 1940s—all predictable choices and all expressive of this ascetic aesthetic. Kaufmann provided a separate category of "fantastic forms," which included a Tiffany vase, Alvar Aalto vases (figs. 124, 125), and an Orrefors bowl with internal *Ariel* decoration, but even these supposed fantasies were essentially conservative. Kaufmann bypassed more exuberant forms, such as the extravagances of Paolo Venini and his Murano colleagues. At the end of the decade, when Kaufmann served on the jury of the Corning Museum of Glass's exhibition "Glass 1959," he noted, "Earlier twentieth-century taste pushed transparency and purity of body to the limits"—yet he went on to reiterate the same canonical ideas as before.[79]

The Copier vase in the Stewart Collection demonstrates this asceticism in terms of its formal shape, transparency, and absence of ornament. Despite the taper at the bottom, the hard-edged form is emphasized by the flat plane at the top. Although it is colored a deep green, this was an acceptable and time-honored tradition, as witnessed by the "Bristol green" glassware of the eighteenth century. Moreover, this model had first been introduced in a puritanically clear version. The emphatic thickness of the glass walls was also part of the Modern tradition, for glassware was supposed to be either thin or thick, and was even divided into these two rigid categories.

Looking only at this vase and the bowl by Copier, though, gives a distorted view of his oeuvre. In much of his prewar glassware, for example, he introduced metallic oxides to create variegated though not necessarily rich color effects. In the postwar period he produced bent, asymmetrical forms. Quite naturally, his unique pieces tend to be more elaborate in form and materials, but the same ideas were found in models established for serial production. In short, only certain examples from an artist's work might satisfy the canons of Good Design.

ME

Gunnel Nyman

Vase: model no. GN27
Designed 1947
Glass; 6⅞ × 3¹⁵⁄₁₆ × 3¹⁵⁄₁₆ inches (17.5 × 10 × 10 cm)
Produced by Nuutajärvi-Notsjö (Nuutajärvi, Finland), 1947–51
Acid stamped on underside: G. Nyman/ Nuutájárvi-Notsjo
D85.115.1

In certain ways, this vase summarizes Modernist glass in the years just after World War II. Its fluidity of form, its limpid mass, and its use of internal air bubbles were all distinctive features of the mid-1940s.

Much of the strength and interest in this vase stems from the three dramatically twisted feet that establish the base and then merge into the vessel itself. Indeed, many of Nyman's other vessels rely on baroque, serpentine forms or forms that seem to have been created by folding and overlapping. Such movement-filled shapes, created by twisting the hot, still malleable material, characterized much postwar glass, from the relatively conservative accents used by Steuben to the extravagantly extruded sculptures of the Daum factory.

On the other hand, this vase cannot be characterized as a purely postwar phenomenon, for the antecedents of such fluid forms can be found in the 1930s, especially in certain organic shapes introduced at the Venini and Orrefors factories (fig. 76). Likewise, Nyman's preference for a thick, bubbled glass recalls a tradition that goes back to the prewar period, above all to the French glass master Maurice Marinot, who exerted considerable influence. His flacons of richly striated and bubbled glass were *objets de luxe*, but their truthfulness to their material and their avoidance of applied ornament appealed even to right-minded purists. The possibilities of bubbled glass had also been explored in Scandinavia before the war, as in Edvin Ollers's designs for the Kosta factory and in the work of Arttu Brummer and Nyman at Riihimäen Lasi (fig. 77).[80] As this vase reminds us, the tradition was continued after the war, not only by Nyman and Brummer and their younger countrymen Kaj Franck and Tapio Wirkkala, but also by some of the surviving French practitioners.[81]

Whereas most bubbled glass relied on an irregular distribution of large and small bubbles for interest, Nyman perfected a technique of carefully controlled bubbles, all of the same dimension and laid out in regulated patterns. As difficult as this may seem, it was achieved with relative ease by blowing glass into a pin-studded mold. The glass was then removed and cased with a second layer; the indentations caused by the studs became the trapped bubbles. The mechanical nature of the process allowed it to be extended on a relatively economical basis to functional tableware such as serving pitchers and drinking glasses (fig. 78). This dualism of the artistic and the functional was a goal Scandinavian design frequently sought but did not always achieve.

ME

(top) 76. *Nils Landberg. Vase. c. 1940–45*

(above) 77. *Gunnel Nyman. Carafe. 1933. Suomen Lasimuseo, Riihimäki, Finland*

(right) 78. *Nyman. Pitcher and bowl. 1947*

(opposite) 79. *Nyman. Vase: model no. GN27*

Streamlined Modern

Streamlining was the branch of Modernism that combined the principles of aerodynamic engineering with the functional geometry of the International Style.[82] Quite naturally, it made its first appearance in the field of transportation. The aim, based on observation of test models in experimental wind tunnels, was to create shapes that offered the least resistance to wind. This inevitably meant a bullet- or tear-shaped volume that tapered backward.

Although some of the earliest examples are European—for instance, Count von Zeppelin's work in Friedrichsaften, an important center of experimentation—Streamlining held a particular fascination for American designers. Leading the way was a new breed, the industrial designer. While many of their most extreme plans remained on paper, victims of the Great Depression and industry's lack of vision, still, elements of Streamlining became widespread. The fronts of trains and automobiles were transformed from awkward boxes to bulletlike projectiles (fig. 80). As die-stamping machines became more sophisticated, junctures between parts were rounded to create what was known as fairings. Separate parts, such as the wheel fenders and the body, were visually joined, often by covering the complex machinery with a sleek, smooth sheath. Finally, differentiated sections of color or the application of doubled and trebled ornamental bands emphasized the length of the body and the horizontal thrust of the vehicle. Much of this transformation was effected in the name of aerodynamic technology, but behind it was also the conscious intention of creating a futuristic style.

Architecture soon succumbed to Streamlining. Individual elements could already be found within the canon of the International Style. Henry-Russell Hitchcock and Philip Johnson deemed horizontality "the most conspicuous characteristic of the international style . . . in terms of effect."[83] Horizontality was praised because it supposedly expressed the storied construction of modern buildings—even skyscrapers. Likewise, there occasionally were curved walls and canopies in International Style buildings. One such example is J. J. P. Oud's Hook of Holland project (1924–27), and another is Erich Mendelsohn's Schocken Department Store in Chemnitz (1928–30), where the entire building formed a dramatically curved arc. Yet Hitchcock and Johnson warned that only weak architects would seek horizontality for its own sake; they also warned that curves were only occasionally demanded by function and often introduced unnecessary complications in a building's normal regularity. Their wariness suggests something of the ultimate schism between proponents of the International Style and those favoring Streamlining.

As Streamlining became a popular mode, architects soon diverged from the purist quality that Hitchcock and Johnson so fervently espoused. Norman Bel Geddes's 1931 House of Tomorrow (fig. 81) shows many of its features full-blown. Not only are there dramatic curves in the projecting garage, the canopy over the door, and the front room on the upper story, but also the transition from flat roof to vertical wall is curved on both the front and lateral sides. An equally bold statement is the entrance to the 1931 McGraw-Hill Building, New York, by Raymond Hood and J. André Fouilhoux (fig. 89). The rounded entrance walls of an otherwise rectangular structure are adorned with horizontal bands of aluminum and blue-enameled stripping, an effect carried throughout the upper floors of the skyscraper in modified form and recapitulated in the crowning tower. Even Frank Lloyd Wright's Johnson Wax building has to be considered in this context—and comparable styling could be found in countless commercial buildings, movie theaters, small diners, and gas stations.

Interiors were easily brought into conformity with this new style.[84] The junctures of flat walls were rounded; ceilings were recessed and inset with fluently curved modulations (fig. 82). Even rectangular public halls and commercial spaces could be moderated with undulant counters or partition walls, and this undulation could be emphasized by double or triple lines of applied metal banding. Domestic interiors could be updated through some of the same devices—falsely curved corners, recessed horizontal bands of bookshelves curving around two or more walls, a mantelpiece or sofa with one end rounded

(opposite) *80. Henry Dreyfuss. Locomotive of New York Central's* Mercury. *1936*

81. Norman Bel Geddes. The House of Tomorrow. 1931. Norman Bel Geddes Collection, Hoblitzelle Theatre Arts Library, The Humanities Research Center, University of Texas, Austin

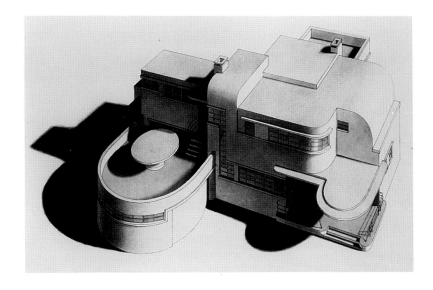

82. *Reinhard Hofmeister. Interior of Chase National Bank, Rockefeller Center, New York. 1937*

83. *Harwell Hamilton Harris. Library of the Cecil J. Birtcher residence, Los Angeles. 1941–42*

(fig. 83). Even rectilinear furniture could give the appearance of Streamlining, provided it was low enough to create a horizontal effect; it was for this reason that one critic praised overly long modular sofas.

The same stylistic elements were quickly transferred to the world of applied arts, from metalwares and ceramics to small calculating machines and cameras. In some cases, already existing forms in the modern taste were updated by a slight transformation of the shape or the addition of appropriate ornament. A good case in point is a tea and coffee set by the English firm of Elkington and Company (fig. 101). The downturned handles and massive finials, while reminiscent of a service exhibited by Puiforcat at the 1925 Paris Exposition Universelle, are offset by much rounder forms than those shown in 1925, and they are encircled by horizontal channeling on the lower half to emphasize the horizontality. Much more dynamic and stylized is Raymond Loewy's pencil sharpener, whose very form is a bulletlike projectile; the whole machine seems to be in dynamic propulsion, even though it is at rest. Often this transference was facilitated by the fact that many of the artists who designed these commercial objects were actually industrial designers—the very same ones who designed train locomotives and automobiles.

Unlike the rationalist version of modern design, whose austerity did not stir a popular response, Streamlining had the glamour and theatricality to make it a popular style. Its ornament conveyed the idea of travel, science, and progress. It is not surprising that Peter Müller-Munk's pitcher (fig. 94) was named for its resemblance to an ocean liner's funnel, and Eva Zeisel's first major set of dinnerware in the United States was called *Stratosphere*. Science was popular because of its positive nature.

Despite our tendency today to view the International Style and Streamlining as compatible aspects of a single Modernist movement, the two were quite distinct and, in fact, often opposed. To many Modernists who promoted the International Style and the Bauhaus, Streamlining was anathema. Hitchcock and Johnson, for example, criticized the rounded corners on most of the International Style buildings they discussed; their reasons varied from example to example, but the cumulative effect was apparent.[85] Streamlining was condemned and excluded from the Museum of Modern Art's 1934 exhibition "Machine Art,"[86] and the museum's staging of a Bauhaus exhibition in 1938 represents a continuation of that aesthetic stance. As Edgar Kaufmann, jr., so aptly remembered, "Streamlining was nearly a four-letter word around 1940, at least in some circles, like the Museum of Modern Art."[87] In his primer for that museum, *What Is Modern Design?*, published in 1950, Kaufmann himself unequivocally ruled, "Streamlining is not good design."[88]

The functionalists opposed Streamlining because they felt that there was no "efficiency" in making a stationary object conform to the laws of aerodynamics. On the other side, the adherents of Streamlining rationalized their aesthetic. Apologists like Sheldon and Martha Cheney countered some of the arguments, contending that smooth shapes gave "plastic order" and provided "no lodgement to dust."[89] Likewise, László Moholy-Nagy recognized some of the faults of Streamlining but argued that there were technological advantages, such as the suitability of rounded curves to stamping and plating.[90]

However, the main driving force behind Streamlining was the desire to create a style, a rhythmic exterior surface that presented a dramatic new silhouette associated with movement, science, and technology, in a way that is almost Futurist in its ideology. Streamlining conveyed the aspirations of both actual technology and the science fiction of the future. The sets for the British-made film version of H. G. Wells's *Things to Come* (1936), Norman Bel Geddes's *City of the Future* for the New York World's Fair of 1939, and visions of interplanetary vehicles conveyed the same image, an image that was shared by adding machines and cameras and jukeboxes.

When Russel Wright reacted against the 1938 Bauhaus exhibition staged by the Museum of Modern Art, he sought to establish the primacy of a non-European, pro-American art. His chauvinism aside, it is interesting to see why he rejected the spartan Bauhaus style and to note the forms of expression he correlated with American design and Streamlining:

> . . . we seem to have our own conception of scale and it is grander than the European conception; our use of form is bolder and more vital; our use of color is distinctly our own.
>
> Why can't someone, a Museum of Modern Art or a New York World's Fair, put on an exhibition in which they would dramatize all design that is American? First, let them parade those unconscious developments free from any aesthetic inferiority complexes. Our bridges. Our roads. Our factory machinery. Our skyscrapers. . . . Roll out our trick cocktail gadgets—our streamlined iceboxes—our streamlined pencil sharpeners. Let them show our electric light bulbs on white velvet like jewels. The work of Frank Lloyd Wright. Our gasoline stations. Our movie theatres. Our cafeterias. . . . Our handsome business machines. . . . Our gleaming fat automobiles. . . .[91]

At the heart of the matter was the unspoken issue of applied ornament. In essence, Streamlining was an imposed style. It did not result from the object's function or its various parts; quite the contrary, it was a sheath put around the object to give it a compact, fluent form and—heresy of heresies—ornament. The bands of blue enamel and aluminum wrapped across the rounded corners of the glamorous entrance to Hood and Fouilhoux's McGraw-Hill Building or the horizontal ridges and rounded corners of a teapot or tape dispenser served only an ornamental function; although a *modern* ornamental style, it was ornament nonetheless.

The heyday of Streamlining was in the 1930s but it remained a strong stylistic current well into the 1940s. Its lessons of compact forms and fluent contours were remembered but were also refined as the postwar period sought a lighter, more elegant style. The jump from Kem Weber's *Airline* chair (fig. 84) to Eero Saarinen's pedestal furniture (fig. 335) may seem a long leap, yet there was a continuum.

However, Streamlining should not be viewed only in terms of what it contributed to postwar design. It needs to be judged in and of itself, and, indeed, today Streamlined objects convey the same wonderful aura of technology and science, of glamour and sophistication, that they evoked over a half-century ago.

ME

84. *Kem Weber.* Airline *armchair*

85, 86. *Unpacking and assembling an*
Airline *armchair*

Kem Weber

Armchair: *Airline*
Designed c. 1934–35
Birch, ash, replaced wool upholstery, and
 cotton batting; 31½ × 25 × 36½ inches
 (80.7 × 64.1 × 93.5 cm)
Produced by Airline Chair Co. (Los Angeles),
 c. 1935[92]
Unmarked
D85.172.1, gift of Geoffrey N. Bradfield*

The large, comfortable lounge or club chair is a design problem that was addressed between 1917 and 1932 with startling clarity, originality, and artistry by early Modernist architects in Europe such as Gerrit Rietveld, Marcel Breuer, Ludwig Mies van der Rohe, and Alvar Aalto. Few American seating designs of the interwar years were able to match the inventiveness or level of inquiry demonstrated in the European work. One of those few was Kem Weber's *Airline* chair.

The name chosen by the designer for his chair signifies little beyond a desire to associate the design with the fastest and most up-to-date product of modern industry. The aesthetic feature shared by airplanes and the armchair was clearly the application of the principles of aerodynamics.

In addition to their emphatically rounded edges, most Streamlined objects were characterized by an attempt at extreme reduction of form, a minimum number of parts, the use of parallel horizontal decoration, and, above all, the packaging of all of these features in a single, integrated mass. Though a distinctly Streamlined design, the *Airline* chair broke nearly all of those conventions. Particularly unusual was the fact that each of the chair's arm/leg units was made from a number of clearly differentiated pieces and that those units were unavoidably contrasted with the separate seat and back. Nonetheless, the chair retains the strong and essential impression of an object whose form has been shaped by the flow of air around it.

Attempting to explain the design of the chair to a magazine editor with language that clearly reflected the functionalist arguments of his Modernist European colleagues, Weber wrote that he was driven by "the desire to make a comfortable, hygienic and beautiful chair inexpensively."[93] Sharing the Modernists' concern with cleanliness, visual transparency, and portability, he described the chair in terms of its suitability to the modern interior:

> It eliminates the dust-catching box upholstery with its accumulation of undesirables well protected on the inside. It is light to move about and has no corners.[94]

To these practical concerns Weber wedded the structural features of a cantilevered seat and a knockdown design. The strength of the chair's frame allowed the designer to dispense with rear legs, thereby offering the sitter a comfortable, resilient seat, one that symbolically reminded the sitter of the structural triumph of the designer over the natural law of gravity. The knockdown design was genuinely functional, unlike most contemporary attempts at such space-saving chairs. The chair came in a flat, square box that was relatively inexpensive for a manufacturer to store and ship, and it was easy for the consumer to assemble (figs. 85, 86).

The *Airline* chair seemed destined to be a great commercial success. It garnered much favorable publicity, all of which highlighted the chair's light weight, portability, and ease of assembly.[95] Orders were received from department and furniture stores as well as from businesses and private individuals. Unfortunately, despite extensive discussions between the designer and a large number of American manufacturers, factory production never became a reality.[96] Although three hundred chairs were ordered by and delivered to Walt Disney Studios for use in its projection rooms, lounges, and offices, they were, ironically, made by a local cabinetmaker rather than a major furniture producer.

CW

Kem Weber

Digital clock: model no. 304-P40, *The Zephyr*
Designed 1934
Brass with partial bronze plating, plastic, and
 enamel; 3⁵⁄₁₆ × 8 × 3¼ inches (9.1 × 20.3 ×
 8.3 cm)
Produced by Lawson Time, Inc. (Alhambra,
 California), 1934–c. 1941(?) (this example
 after 1937)[98]
Impressed on black-and-brass-colored metal
 plaque attached to back: *Lawson* ELECTRIC
 CLOCK/CYC. [above] 60 V. 110   W.4 OR LESS
 STYLE NO. [above] 304/MODEL P 40/PAT. NO.
 1990645/LAWSON TIME INC., PASADENA,
 CALIF.
Printed in black on decal on clock face:
 Lawson
D88.136.1, gift of David A. Hanks in memory
 of David M. Stewart*

This digital clock transposes the Streamlined modernism of architect Kem Weber's buildings and furniture designs into a small, functional object. Where Streamlining in American architecture was often represented only by a token curving wall or pipe railing, the style became an

87. Kem Weber. The Zephyr *digital clock: model no. 304-P40*

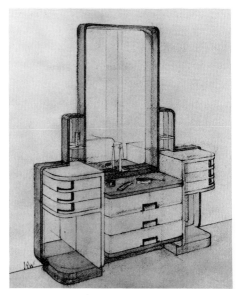

88. *Weber. Drawing for a dressing table (detail). c. 1930. Architectural Drawing Collection, University Art Museum, University of California, Santa Barbara*

aggressive, overall expression in Southern California, where Weber had his practice.

These characteristics are especially notable in Weber's furniture, for example, a dressing table from about 1930 (fig. 88), as well as lamps, vessels, and interiors in general. This digital clock epitomizes the cultivation of the horizontal line and the rounded corner, two definitive motifs of Streamlined styling. A strong tonal and color contrast is also evident in Weber's use of a bronze-finished metal for the body of the clock and shiny brass bands as accents.

Weber designed several clocks, both digital and nondigital, for Lawson Time during 1934 and 1935. The horizontal emphasis of the digital clocks readily lent itself to the effects of Streamlined bands. Beyond the look that was created, digital time and Streamlining lent themselves to

the very *idea* of modern life. Lawson Time advertised its digital clocks, an innovation introduced in 1932, as "modern time . . . *exact* time at a glance. No hands pointing uncertainly . . . masterpieces of precision and design . . . streamlined for instant perception."[98] *Streamlining* became a key word in the company's promotional matters. The very names assigned to the Lawson models—*Manhattan, Fifth Avenue, Vogue*—were meant to conjure up images of urbanism and modernity. Especially significant is the name of this model, *The Zephyr*, which refers to not only the god of winds but also movement; not coincidentally, *Zephyr* was the name used for the new Streamlined stainless steel trains first introduced in 1934 and which likewise epitomized modern progress, technology, and high style.[99]

TLW

Designer unknown

Jukebox: *Penny Phono*
Designed c. 1939
Lacquered plywood, plastic, stainless steel, and
  glass; 42½ × 22 × 18 inches (108 × 55.9 ×
  45.7 cm)
Produced by Cinematone Corporation
  (Hollywood), 1939–42
Impressed on metal label attached to lower
  front center: MANUFACTURED U.S.A.
  BY/CINEMATONE/HOLLYWOOD, CALIF.
  CORPORATION PATENT PENDING
D88.188.1

Although the first coin-operated phonograph was invented in 1889, automatic phonographs were not common until electrically amplified versions were introduced in 1927. The machines, later called jukeboxes, quickly became popular, supplying music at first in speakeasies and then in bars and restaurants.[100]

Like radios and phonographs, jukeboxes were originally made of wood and designed to look like heavy furniture. Then in 1937, Paul Fuller introduced colored, illuminated plastic panels and brightly glowing tubes in his new, Streamlined jukebox, the Wurlitzer model no. 24 (fig. 90).

89. *Raymond Hood and J. André Fouilhoux. Entrance to McGraw-Hill Building, New York. 1931*

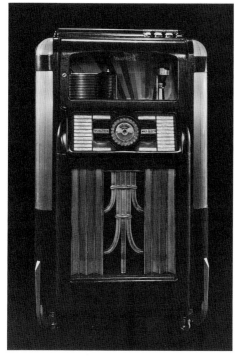

90. *Paul Fuller. Wurlitzer Model 24. 1937*

Despite these flashy innovations, part of the case was still made of fine wood. Most other jukeboxes in the late 1930s and the 1940s also had illuminated plastic panels, bands of Streamlining on the sides, and, often, Art Deco metal grilles as well.

The *Penny Phono* belongs to this trend of Streamlined jukeboxes, but it is also very different. It is smaller and more compact than most jukeboxes. Although the song panel window and the green plastic panels are illuminated, it is far less gaudy. Furthermore, its style is more consistent and architectural. Its rounded corners, streamlined fins, and horizontal banding resemble the entrance of Raymond Hood and J. André Fouilhoux's McGraw-Hill Building (fig. 89) and the work of Kem Weber and other California architects. It also looks something like an appliance, such as Raymond Loewy's Streamlined *Coldspot* refrigerator for Sears (1934). Indeed, this was a time when kitchens and bathrooms were said to be the only modern rooms in American houses.

The mechanism of the *Penny Phono* also was unusual. Most jukeboxes of the time had twenty-four records with one song on a side, requiring an elaborate record-changing mechanism. However, the *Penny Phono* holds a special twelve-inch long-playing record with ten songs on a side, which could be played for only a penny a song,[101] making it as innovative inside as it was outside.

Despite these innovations, the *Penny Phono* did not last long in production. The firm producing it went out of business in 1942, shortly after the United States entered World War II.

CWL

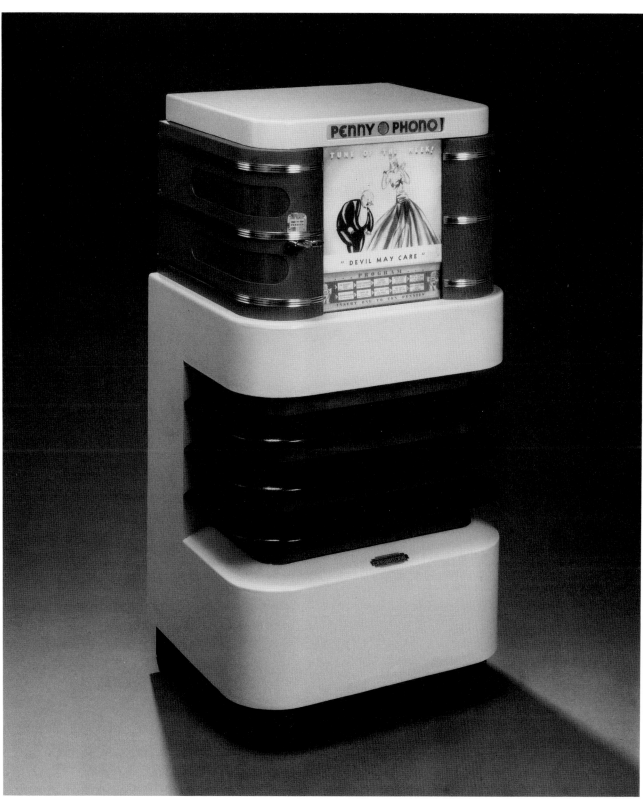

91. Penny Phono *jukebox*

Walter Dorwin Teague

Desk lamp: model no. 114, *Executive*
Designed 1939
Bakelite plastic and aluminum; 13 × 10 × 9
  inches (33.3 × 25.6 × 23.1 cm)
Produced by Polaroid Corporation
  (Cambridge, Massachusetts), 1939–41; by
  Mitchell Manufacturing Company, c. 1941
  (this example 1939–41)
Printed in white on gray paper circular label
  on underside: [device of two overlapping
  circles]/[same device in miniature]/POLAROID
  [same device in miniature]/DESK LAMP
  114/USE 100 WATT FROSTED BULB ONLY./To
  insert bulb, ... [text deleted due to
  length]/POLAROID CORP., CAMBRIDGE,
  MASS./Mfd. under U.S. Pat. Nos. 1,918,848;
  1,951,664;/[text deleted due to length]/[same
  device in miniature] T.M. Reg. U.S. Pat.
  Off. Made in U.S.A./Fm. #149-A Printed
  in U.S.A.
D82.113.1

In 1939, Walter Dorwin Teague, assisted by his son Walter Dorwin Teague, Jr., and Frank Del Giudice, redesigned for the Polaroid Corporation a desk lamp that had been put into manufacture the previous year (fig. 92).[102] The lamp contained a light diffuser of polarized cellulose film that eliminated glare and thus eased eyestrain. Teague's Streamlined design went beyond cosmetic changes; it also improved the function and salability of the product: it resulted in less bulk, was simpler to operate, and cost less than its predecessor, retailing for $9.75. Furthermore, the molded plastic hood greatly increased the area of illumination, covering evenly the surface of an entire newspaper.

The hood is supported by a slanted, conical, aluminum stem attached to a Bakelite, raised, round base, which houses the on-off switch. Cooling vents both in the hood and the stem were integrated into the overall design. The plastic parts of the lamp were available in walnut or black.

The desk lamp was Teague's first assignment for Polaroid, the beginning of a relationship that lasted until the early 1960s. However, because of Polaroid's heavy involvement in the war effort, the manufacture and sale of the Polaroid desk lamp was licensed to the Mitchell Manufacturing Company in 1941.

FTH

(above left) 92. *Clarence Kennedy and Charles Baratelli. Desk lamp. 1937*

(above) 93. *Walter Dorwin Teague*. Executive *desk lamp: model no. 114*

Peter Müller-Munk

Pitcher: *Normandie*
Designed 1935
Chrome-plated brass; 11¹⁵⁄₁₆ × 9⅝ × 3¹⁄₁₆ inches
   (30.4 × 24.4 × 7.7 cm)
Produced by Revere Copper and Brass Incorporated
   (Rome, New York), 1935–c. 1941
Impressed on underside: Revere/Rome/N.Y.
D83.131.1, gift of Geoffrey N. Bradfield*

Peter Müller-Munk's inexpensive, mass-produced pitcher is an undeniably humble, utilitarian object. Yet it possesses an artistic integrity that belies the generally modest aspiration of the object type.

The form of the pitcher, as well as its name, was intended to suggest the smokestacks of the famous French ocean liner whose much publicized maiden voyage took place the same year that the pitcher was introduced (fig. 95). The Revere company catalogue of 1936 stated that the pitcher was "inspired by the leaning streamlined stacks of the famous French liner." Although the pitcher might have evoked the elliptical cylinders that rose from the deck of the SS *Normandie*, it even more boldly embodied the smooth, windswept curves and, in plan, teardrop shape of aerodynamic Streamlining, a style that subjected all objects to the designer's imaginary wind tunnel.

Equally important as its Streamlined form was its manufacture by a company not known for producing consumer products. During the 1930s many of the American companies engaged in the manufacture of metal for commercial use (including the Chase Brass and Copper Company, Kensington Incorporated, and Revere Copper and Brass Incorporated) began to produce specialty or gift lines of decorative accessories aimed at the domestic market. Revere normally manufactured copper, brass, and aluminum to fill industrial and residential needs; it produced copper tubing, shingles, and siding for use in building construction and made cookware for commercial and domestic markets.

New York industrial designer Russel Wright, who designed, produced, and marketed a line of modern metal accessories beginning in 1929, served as a precedent for the sale of American metalware with a distinctly progressive look. The increasing appeal and marketability of self-consciously modern products for the home, as well as newly improved methods of manufacturing, plating, and decorating sheet metal, gave rise to a search for new product lines. Many firms were spurred to find new markets for their products by the economic pressures of the Depression.

The *Normandie* pitcher stands as one of the finest examples of American metalwork of the 1920s and 1930s. It was Müller-Munk's most important and artistically successful design. Although he made the transformation from silversmith to industrial designer during the 1930s and went on to have a successful career as a teacher and industrial designer, he was never again to design a single object that so eloquently embodied the aspirations of its time or so sucessfully combined the design and production processes.

CW

94. Peter Müller-Munk. Normandie *pitcher*

95. French Line's SS Normandie, *c. 1934–35*

Henry Dreyfuss

Thermos pitcher and tray: model no. 539
Designed 1935
Aluminum, enameled steel, glass, and rubber;
  pitcher: 5⅞ × 6⅛ × 4¾ inches (14.9 ×
  15.6 × 12 cm); tray: 9¼ × 6⅝ × ½ inches
  (23.7 × 16.9 × 1.2 cm)
Produced by American Thermos Bottle Company
  (Norwich, Connecticut), c. 1935–after 1946
Pitcher, stamped in relief on base, in outer
  circle: THE AMERICAN THERMOS BOTTLE
  CO./NORWICH, CONN. USA
Pitcher, stamped in inner circle: THE
  ONLY/THERMOS/REG. U.S. PAT. OFFICE/NO
  539/VACUUM BOTTLE/DESIGNED BY/*Henry
  Dreyfuss*.
Tray unmarked
D81.155.1, 2

The 1930s is often referred to as the decade of Streamlining; it could equally be called the era of the industrial designer in America. For it was that decade that saw the professionalization of industrial design, as the burgeoning field made itself an integral part of American product manufacture. Henry Dreyfuss was one of an elite group of designers who managed to convince corporate clients that the improvement of a product's appearance would lead directly to an increase in sales. In an American economy still reeling from the effects of the Depression, this promise raised hopes of economic recovery and expansion, which were largely fulfilled. Their argument that restyling or changing a product's design every few years leads to consumer demand has, for better or worse, shaped the nature of twentieth-century Western consumer society.

An indication of the new status of the industrial designer is be found on the underside of this thermos jug. In addition to all of the usual patent and manufacturer's information are the words "Designed by Henry Dreyfuss," with the designer's name in the form of a facsimile script signature. The appearance of a designer's name in an advertisement, sales brochure, or on an actual product is so commonplace today that it is easy to overlook both the novelty and cultural significance of such an occurrence in 1935. It became accepted, for the first time in American history, that the name of a designer could actually help sell a product. American Thermos went further by using a facsimile of the creator's signature, hoping it would induce consumers to think they were purchasing the sophistication, style, and expertise of the industrial designer himself.

Dreyfuss's thermos is an accomplished example of Streamlined design that can also be appreciated in aesthetic terms. The forms of the handle, jug, and lid are harmoniously integrated into a continuous shape that follows all the canons of Streamlined design. The flat lid, neck, and bottom of the handle, along with the horizontal lines molded into the base, cleverly emphasize horizontality, while the gentle, downward curves of the body, echoed by the perfectly proportioned handle, give the unmistakable feeling of surfaces delicately sculpted by the flow of air around them.

CW

96. *Henry Dreyfuss. Thermos pitcher and tray: model no. 539*

Jean Puiforcat

Tureen
Designed c. 1935
Silver and parcel gilt; $10 \times 10\frac{7}{8} \times 10\frac{7}{8}$ inches
  ($25.4 \times 27.6 \times 27.6$ cm)
Produced by Puiforcat Orfèvre (Paris), 1937 to
  the present
Tureen, impressed on underside: [hexagonal-
  shaped hallmark with the head of Minerva
  facing left in profile]
Tureen, impressed on underside: [diamond-
  shaped hallmark with a knife between E and
  P]/JEAN E. PUIFORCAT/MADE IN FRANCE
Lid, impressed on side: [hexagonal-shaped
  hallmark with the head of Minerva facing
  left in profile]
Lid, impressed on side: [diamond-shaped
  hallmark with a knife between E and P]
D87.239.1

The ancient Greeks and Renaissance Italians believed the golden section—a mathematical principle of proportions based on a ratio of approximately 3:5—to represent a perfection of harmonious design. This tureen by Jean Puiforcat is the golden section incarnate. In a 1933 letter to Count Fleury, Puiforcat stated, "I plunged into mathematics and fell on Plato. . . . From him, I learnt the arithmetic, harmonic and geometrical means, the five famous Platonic bodies, illustrated later by Leonardo. . . ."[103]

Puiforcat's goal was nothing less than to achieve ideal form in objects made from silver. Although he found in mathematics a means to attain this goal, it did not lead him to embrace a dry, coldly calculated style. On the contrary, he was constantly exploring new ways to create visual excitement—for example, through the addition of vermeil, as on this tureen, or exotic woods, or colored stones such as jade, lapis lazuli, and rose quartz. He claimed, "The geometric armature is only a skeleton of a vibrant body to which it is the artist's role to give life."[104]

His earlier output, exemplified by a silver vase from 1925 (fig. 98), manifests a preoccupation with the straight line, which emphasized structural aspects.[105] Puiforcat grew to believe that he was abusing the straight line, using it too often because it was easier to work with than the curve. By contrast, this tureen, designed at the culmination of a period when Puiforcat underwent much introspection, reevaluation, and study of classical logic and theology, demonstrates his later belief that "the circle, which explains the entire world, is the ideal figure, and the curve which approaches it, is more noble than the straight line."[106]

The *Tracé Harmonique* (Harmonic Sketch) of his silver, vermeil, and ivory golfing cup from 1934 (fig. 99) well illustrates the proportions of the golden section and its adaptation to Puiforcat's circular forms. In the tureen, Puiforcat also achieves a sense of speed and circular movement, through the dynamic interplay of curves, light and shadow, and color, all of which sweep one's eye around the vessel. It expresses aerodynamic styling as well as the formal application of Puiforcat's rational design theories.

This tureen was exhibited in 1937 at the "Exposition Internationale des Arts et Techniques" in Paris, where Puiforcat had an entire pavilion devoted to his work.[107]   TLW

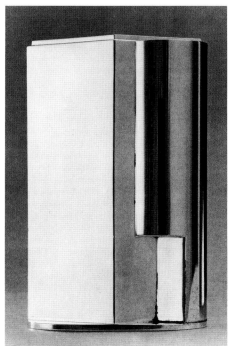

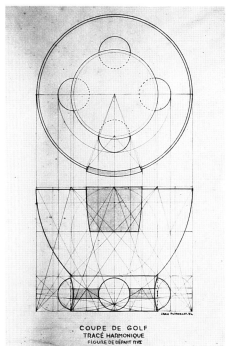

(top) 97. *Jean Puiforcat. Tureen*

(above left) 98. *Puiforcat. Vase. 1925*

(above right) 99. *Puiforcat. Drawing for a golfing trophy. 1934. Collection Puiforcat Orfèvre, Paris*

100. Folke Arström. Cocktail shaker

Folke Arström

Cocktail shaker
Designed 1935[108]
Nickel-plated and silver-plated brass,
    plastic, and cork; 8⅝ × 3⁹⁄₁₆ × 2¾ inches
    (21.9 × 9 × 7 cm)
Produced by GuldsmedsAktieBolaget GAB
    (Stockholm), 1935–after 1942
Impressed on underside: G.A.B. [device of a
    two-handled amphora] N.S. ALR
D87.169.1

This cocktail shaker cleverly blends elements of
Streamlining with functional considerations. It is
a handsome vessel and quite agreeable to use. Its
generally cylindrical shape is created by four con-
traposed, curvilinear surfaces; one pair is concave, the other convex. The convex indentations,
beyond adding an element of stylishness, form
two recesses that comfortably accommodate the
hand and facilitate pouring.

Arström's overall design is dependent on the
rules of Streamlining, most clearly in the parallel
grooves that sleekly wrap around the convex surfaces horizontally (their presence is underscored
by oxidation). A similar emphasis on horizontal
banding can be found elsewhere in European
design, as in an English silver-plated tea and
coffee service (fig. 101). In both instances, the
banding is placed on the lower portion of the
vessel so as to emphasize a low-slung, horizontal
effect. The shaker's cap, also scored horizontally,
is made of black plastic, a status symbol of modernity. In its own small way it emphasizes the
sophistication of this modern implement and the
modish drink it contains.

In the 1920s and 1930s, Neoclassicism and
Modernism were frequently—and skillfully—
blended in European architecture and art, espe-

101. Elkington & Co. Tea and coffee service. c. 1935–40

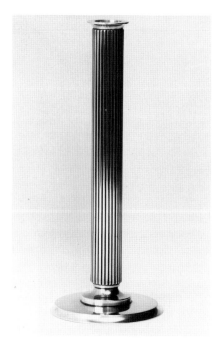

102. Count Sigvard Bernadotte. Candlestick.
1938. Georg Jensen Museum, Copenhagen

cially in Scandinavia.[109] In Sweden this blend could be seen in the early architecture of Erik Gunnar Asplund and the sculpture of Carl Milles. This same stylistic hybridization is apparent in many of the designs Count Sigvard Bernadotte created at this time for the Georg Jensen Silversmithy: the famous *Bernadotte* flatware, in which parallel, linear ridges emphasize clean-line, Modernist forms, and also in candlesticks whose ridges imitate fluted columns (fig. 102). Thus, progressive and conservative Modernism could approach each other in form and even be confounded—because the difference between these objects is essentially the direction of the grooves.

TLW

103. *Harry Bertoia. Coffee service*

Harry Bertoia

Coffee service
Designed and executed c. 1937–43
Pewter and stained wood;[110] coffeepot:
   7 × 7½ × 5⅝ inches (17.8 × 19 × 14.3 cm)
Coffeepot, chiseled on underside: [monogram
   of A inside C]/HB
Other pieces unmarked
D89.192.1, gift of Dr. Luc Martin
D89.192.3, gift of James Barron, by exchange

This coffee service by Harry Bertoia, executed during his tenure at the Cranbrook Academy of Art, Bloomfield Hills, Michigan, and a preliminary drawing (fig. 104)[111] reveal the Cubist and Modernist principles that formed the basis of Bertoia's industrial designs.

The juxtaposition on the coffeepot of a circular body and a rectangular spout links Bertoia's work to that of the French designer Jean Puiforcat, who in 1925 designed a coffeepot as a sphere within a square.[112] The way Bertoia attached the handle to the vessel only tangentially at two points, extending it over the body to form an arc, is also an idea that Puiforcat had previously used (fig. 105). In the drawing, the overlaying of additional circles to establish the size of openings and

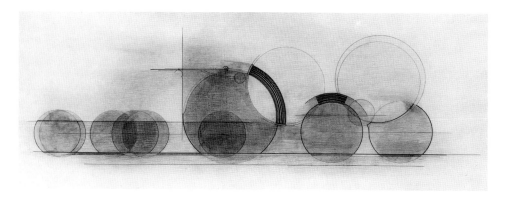

Cartier

Necklace and bracelet
Designed c. 1935–40
Yellow gold, lapis lazuli, and diamonds;
    necklace: 5¾ × 5 inches (14.6 × 12.7 cm);
    bracelet: 3 × 2¾ inches (7.6 × 7 cm)
Produced by Cartier (New York), c. 1935–40
Necklace, incised: *Cartier 14K 1312*
Bracelet, incised: *Cartier 14K 186*[or 0?]3
D89.100.1, 2

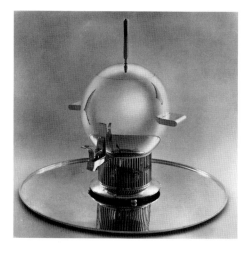

create a rhythmic interplay perhaps owes a debt to Puiforcat's *Harmonic Sketches* (fig. 99), as well as to the paintings of Robert Delaunay and others. Certainly this type of French geometric design was not unknown at Cranbrook, especially since George Booth, founder of that institution, had bought a substantial number of works by French silversmiths over the previous decade.[113] Moreover, this type of strong geometric design showed up in the work of Eliel Saarinen, as in the impressive tea urn that he designed for the academy (fig. 106).

Certain small changes can be discerned between Bertoia's drawing and the executed coffee service. For the sugar bowl, he had originally planned an arc-shaped handle, like that on the coffeepot, but he evidently decided in favor of a vertical one. He may have been following the model of the finial on Saarinen's urn, although Bertoia's is not as thin or disproportionate. The sturdy bases Bertoia created for each of the vessels were barely intimated in his drawing; they were, however, standard to many geometric designs of this period, especially Puiforcat's.

A crucial aspect of Bertoia's coffee service is its strongly Streamlined effect. Whereas the forms in the sketch seem spherical, each piece was made from two shallow, spun segments that were attached at their circumference and thus form ellipses coming to sharp points. The bases, bands of sheet metal, form equally sharp, pointed ellipses. The diagonal at which the creamer is cut, as well as the fact that it is strikingly devoid of handles, also emphasize this sense of thrusting form. Moreover, unlike the smooth, directionless surfaces of Puiforcat's and Saarinen's works, Bertoia's bears insistent concentric rings resulting from the spinning process. The closest parallel is to be found in contemporary American Streamlined objects.[114]

It is important to remember that at the same time that he was creating this type of sleek, machinelike design (albeit executed by hand), Bertoia was also fashioning jewelry in an organic, whimsical, Calder-like mode (fig. 384), demonstrating the contemporaneity and compatability of different forms of modernism even within the work of a single artist.

TLW

This Cartier necklace and bracelet exemplify the voluminous, geometric style of late 1930s jewelry, combining the staunch, machine-age sensibility of that era with lingering characteristics of a 1920s decorative style.

It is clear that the Cartier firm was not committed to a truly Modernist vocabulary. The elaborateness of the design and the apparent luxury make this suite characteristic of the old-line French jewelry houses. Also, the lighthearted combination of colored semiprecious stones (lapis lazuli) and diamonds was popular in the 1920s; specifically, the setting of diamonds at the centers of the lapis lazuli beads recalls a device used by Cartier in the 1920s, as, for example, in a bracelet that displays diamond-mounted rubies in a dense configuration of other stones (fig. 109).

By comparison with the 1920s bracelet, whose bold and jubilant mixture of so many colored stones—rubies, emeralds, and sapphires—has generated the name of "fruit salad" style, the 1930s suite is greatly simplified. In fact, the later pieces show strong affinities with the strict geometry and machine metaphors seen repeatedly in the designs of such individualists as Jean Fouquet (fig. 107), Raymond Templier, and Jean Després, where the number of forms and the range of color have been reduced. While the geometric jewelry of the 1920s tends toward a certain flatness, here the emphasis is on volume. Indeed, the combination of gold balls (*boules d'or*) and lapis lazuli spheres was a Cartier innovation presented about 1937.[115] The typical rounded curves of the period are present as half-cylinders in the gold

(above from top)
104. Bertoia. *Drawing for a coffee service.*
c. 1937–43. Liliane and David M. Stewart Collection. D89.199.1

105. *Jean Puiforcat. Watering can. 1933*

106. *Eliel Saarinen. Tea urn and tray. 1934. Cranbrook Academy of Art Museum, Bloomfield Hills, Michigan*

107. *Jean Fouquet. Bracelet. 1931*

108. Cartier. Necklace and bracelet

mounts of the necklace, and there are truncated cones—elements comparable to the base and finial on the tureen by Jean Puiforcat (fig. 97).

A Cartier bracelet clearly contemporary with these pieces, also of lapis lazuli and diamonds but made by the Paris branch of the firm, transforms the geometric nature of the lapis beads back into what could be considered bunches of grapes. This suggests the ambivalence of such old-line houses toward the new style.[116]

TLW

109. Cartier. Bracelet. 1929

Biomorphic Modern

Biomorphic objects with strangely rounded and pierced shapes epitomize the design of the postwar era for some. Others recognize the place of Biomorphism in the prewar years. Some see it as a momentary blind alley in the evolution of modern design, while others disregard it entirely. At the root of this confusion is a basic problem: the role of Biomorphism in the decorative arts has not been properly charted.[117]

The origins of this movement, which lie in painting and sculpture, are traceable to the years between 1915 and 1917, when Jean Arp was living in Zurich, the cradle of the Dada movement. During that time Arp experimented with automatism, doodling unconsciously on paper. The resultant lines and abstract blobs, which suggested living organisms, led to designs for reliefs composed of jigsawed pieces of wood cut in organic forms, layered over each other and painted. In works such as *Enak's Tear* (or *Terrestrial Form*) (fig. 110), Arp set the standard for what became an integral and significant part of his own oeuvre, and which ultimately made a profound impact on Dada and abstract Surrealism in general.

Arp not only maintained this formal vocabulary but enlarged it by removing the back plane of the relief so that, in effect, he created free-standing sculpture (fig. 111). He then took the final step a few years later by transforming Biomorphism into a fully three-dimensional idiom, sculpting gently undulant surfaces and rounded holes that conveyed his initial sense of abstract, mysterious organisms (fig. 112). By the 1930s, two-dimensional Biomorphic forms were also endemic in the paintings of Salvador Dalí, René Magritte, Joan Miró, and Fernand Léger. Alexander Calder used similar shapes for his mobiles, where they playfully chased each other. Occasionally, artists like Dalí experi-

(this page and opposite)

110. Jean Arp. Enak's Tear. 1917. Collection, The Museum of Modern Art, New York. Benjamin Scharps and David Scharps Fund and purchase

111. Arp. Hand Fruit. 1930. Private collection, Switzerland

112. Arp. Human Concretion. 1935. Collection, The Museum of Modern Art, New York. Gift of the Advisory Committee

mented with the illusion of three-dimensional Biomorphic forms in their paintings, as in his *Birth of Liquid Desires* (1933), but these ideas were more skillfully adopted by English sculptors Henry Moore and Barbara Hepworth, who maintained Arp's language of forms and concavities in a three-dimensional mode.

These undulant forms gradually made their way into the decorative arts. Some of Arp's own designs were woven as early as the teens by his companion and later wife, Sophie Taeuber, but they were not influential on the decorative arts. Biomorphism surfaced occasionally in the 1920s, though still ineffectually. Quite unexpectedly, one of its initial appearances was at the Weimar Bauhaus in the metal shop worktables. Although the design of these tables was perhaps motivated by functional considerations, such as keeping the work stations separate,[118] they also look like transcriptions of Arp's forms, and they were even different from each other, as can be seen in a photograph of them in situ (fig. 113). These tables aside, however, and excepting other precocious appearances, such as a brooch made by the German sculptor Richard Haizmann,[119] Biomorphism did not come into vogue until more than another decade had passed.

The emergence of Biomorphism in the decorative arts in the mid-1930s may seem tardy, but Surrealism was still a vital artistic force—perhaps the most avant-garde—in that decade. In fact, it was at that point that Biomorphism received its name and became an identifiable concept and style.

The transition of Biomorphism from painting to flat, two-dimensional design was an easy one. Posters with a combination of abstract, undulant forms, pictorial images, and text typify the avant-garde graphic language in Europe before World War II. A natural

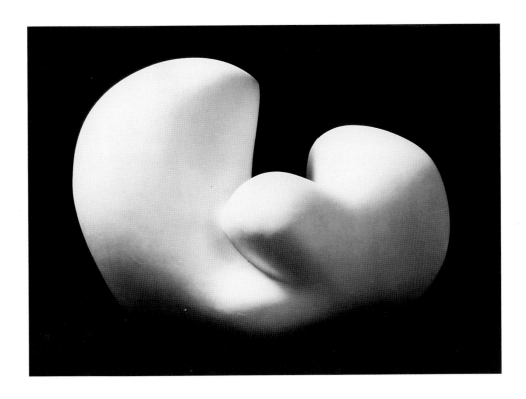

113. *Worktables in the metal shop, Bauhaus, Weimar, in 1923*

form of Biomorphism—white calfskin with black spots—was utilized by Ludwig Mies van der Rohe and Marcel Breuer for their furniture, and Alvar Aalto chose a man-made fabric with a similar effect for his furniture. Biomorphism also was the basis of much camouflage, though few probably thought of this in terms of art or design.[120] Visitors to the Paris 1937 "Exposition Internationale des Arts et Techniques" and the New York World's Fair of 1939 found themselves looking through Biomorphic windows at some of the displays.

The initial introduction of Biomorphism to furniture can perhaps be traced to the early 1930s and the side pieces that Aalto used for his *Paimio* chair (fig. 15), but it was not until the middle of the decade that the style became prevalent. In 1935 Frederick Kiesler in New York designed striking, low cocktail tables with amoeboid tops and chairs with Biomorphic sides (fig. 114). The following year Aalto designed a less fluent but clearly Biomorphic table for the Karhula factory's glassware exhibition in Stockholm (fig. 126). Many designers and architects began experimenting with Biomorphic forms, replete with requisite holes. Breuer, for example, tried this new vocabulary in the plywood chairs he designed in England and the United States, and which he explained in rationalist terms, namely, that the material was not limited by the structural problems of regular wood: "It is therefore possible to cut plywood in free forms or to perforate it without sacrificing its strength."[121] While these high-style items, such as the table Isamu Noguchi created for A. Conger Goodyear, were primarily private commissions, they were also beginning to enter the commercial market, as in the Scandinavian Modern furniture produced by A. Berg, which was promoted at the New York World's Fair of 1939.

The examples cited above register an interesting evolution in approach, going from a two- to a three-dimensional sense of form. In the first works, including the Bauhaus and Kiesler's 1935 tables, the amoeboid tabletops are flat, like Arp's early reliefs, and rest on straight or columnar legs. In the later examples, such as Noguchi's table for Goodyear, the legs are transformed into sculptural, three-dimensional elements, although on a very limited scale. Another significant marker in this evolution is the lounge chair designed by the Brazilian architects Antonio Bonet, Juan Kurchan, and Jorge Ferrari-Hardoy. While based on the principle of a British army folding chair, its shape reflects the new artistic

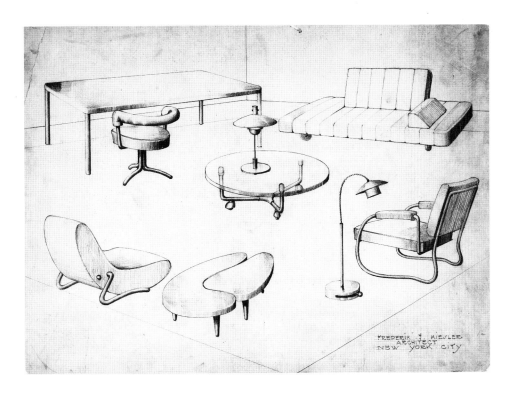

114. Frederick Kiesler. Drawing for furniture. 1935.
Collection Lillian Kiesler/Mrs. Frederick Kiesler

impulses and adumbrates the sculptural possibilities that the postwar generation would use to advantage.

Surprisingly, smaller accessories rarely used the Biomorphic style prior to World War II, and rarely were they three-dimensional. The one major exception is the series of vases that Aalto designed for the Karhula factory in 1936–37 (figs. 124–125). Although they possess volume, they are essentially flat Biomorphic shapes extended on themselves in cylindrical fashion, a form of high relief.

When Biomorphism first flowered in the 1930s, it paralleled Streamlining in certain ways. Each style, in its own fashion, softened the ascetic, rectilinear aspects of the International Style. But Biomorphism's intent and effect were quite different from those of Streamlining. Its analogue was sculpture and painting, not, as in the case of Streamlining, architecture. Its concern was the unexpected and the irrational. It could lay claim to Freudian or Jungian principles, but not, like Streamlining, to engineering or the rational. Each Biomorphic object stood as an independent entity rather than participating in an overall scheme with a unified style. Kiesler's tables, for example, differed from the other furniture that he designed for the very same apartment—they served as sculptural accents.

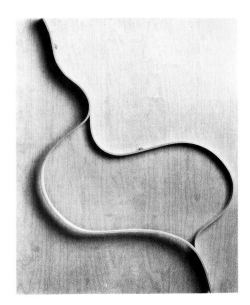

115. Alvar Aalto. Wood relief. c. 1931

Indeed, most of these early examples were by sculptors or designers closely allied with painters and sculptors. Kiesler had been a member of the De Stijl group and had been friendly with the Constructivists, but then he became closely allied with the Surrealists, including Marcel Duchamp, Alexander Calder, and New York City gallery owner Julien Levy. Noguchi, of course, was a sculptor who had studied with Brancusi and was also deeply influenced by abstract Surrealism. Breuer had been exposed to the wide range of modern art during his stay at the Bauhaus and through his close friendship with Herbert Bayer; while in England he had belonged to a vanguard circle that included Henry Moore.[122] Aalto had ties with Calder in the late 1930s, but even earlier in that decade he had made experimental reliefs from plywood that resemble Arp's reliefs (fig. 115).

Biomorphism had made strong inroads by the outbreak of World War II, especially in the United States. A major enterprise was Kiesler's project for Peggy Guggenheim's Art of This Century Gallery in New York (fig. 116), one of the few examples of an entire interior

116. *Frederick Kiesler. Interior of Art of This Century Gallery, New York, 1942*

designed in the Biomorphic mode. Large multifunctional units cut from plywood in Biomorphic forms were used as chairs, tables, and pedestals. Open from 1942 to 1947, this gallery of abstract and Surrealist art became a major attraction. Biomorphism was explored at such design schools as László Moholy-Nagy's Institute of Design in Chicago.[123] There were a few commercial ventures, such as Dan Cooper's designs for Drexel Furniture Company, and some bold schemes from Ralph Rapson and the Eameses, but the war put a damper on most creative enterprises.[124]

Once the war was over, and designers could let loose their imaginations, the creative potential of Biomorphism was unleashed. Noguchi produced a number of striking designs for Knoll (figs. 142, 144), Carlo Mollino pushed Biomorphism to an extreme (fig. 145). Biomorphism touched all mediums: Zeisel's *Town and Country* dinnerware (figs. 140, 141), Henning Koppel's designs for Georg Jensen silver (figs. 133–35, 137, 138), and Vicke Lindstrand's designs for Kosta glassware (fig. 160). There was a universal tendency toward pierced, asymmetric forms that explored all the possibilities of two- and three-dimensional form.

Even a number of buildings were conceived in this style. Significantly, there were few examples of Biomorphic office buildings or public housing. Many, such as Luciano Baldessari's Breda Pavilion in Milan (fig. 118), fit into the category of temporary architecture—advertising graphics on a large scale. The most spectacular and most memorable Biomorphic structure was Eero Saarinen's TWA Terminal at Kennedy Airport (1956–62), where the reinforced concrete shells created sculpture of extraordinary volumes and dimensions, especially on the interior (fig. 117). There were understandably few examples of such sculptural and Biomorphic architecture on this vast scale, despite the possibilities and advantages offered by reinforced concrete.

Regardless of its elitist beginnings, Biomorphism became a popular and democratic style. After World War II it soon descended to a very commercial level. "Boomerang" jewelry, amoeboid tables, lamps with pierced bases, and kidney-shaped swimming pools could be found everywhere. The zoomorphic even entered the world of popular culture, in the form of Al Capp's cartoon character "The Shmoo," which became a national folk

117. *Eero Saarinen. Interior of TWA Terminal, Kennedy Airport, New York. 1956–62*

118. *Luciano Baldessari. Breda Pavilion, Milan. 1952*

hero, and the extraterrestrial amoeba that threatened us in the 1958 science-fiction movie *The Blob*.

Despite its pervasiveness, the Biomorphic became passé by the mid-1950s. In 1961 the critic Willy Rotzler wrote: "From no choice of their own, Arp, Miró, Moore and their contemporaries became the godfathers of battered and holed vessels of glass, earthenware and metal."[125] By this time, Biomorphic forms seemed to belong to a past generation. And, as often happens when a new generation tries to assert itself by refuting the previous generation's style, Biomorphism was judged to have been a folly. Today, with the advantage of several more decades, we can be more generous in our appreciation. With hindsight, we realize that it contributed significantly to the postwar emphasis on curvilinear design. And in itself, Biomorphism was one of the more charming and original attempts to create a modern style. ME

(above left) 119. E. McKnight Kauffer. Rug. 1929. Victoria and Albert Museum, London

(above) 120. McKnight Kauffer. Design for a mural. 1929. Victoria and Albert Museum, London

(left) 121. McKnight Kauffer. Design for the Mars Group "New Architecture Exhibition." 1937

E. McKnight Kauffer

Rug
Designed c. 1935
Wool, handwoven, cut pile; 77 × 58 inches
   (229 × 151 cm)
Produced by The Wilton Royal Carpet Factory
   Ltd. (Wilton, England), c. 1935
Woven monogram in lower right corner:
EMCKK
D89.119.1, gift of Paul Leblanc

Although E. McKnight Kauffer is primarily known for his Cubist-inspired posters and book illustrations, he also created a series of avant-garde designs for rugs in the late 1920s and 1930s, following the example of his companion, the rug designer Marion Dorn.[126]

This is one of Kauffer's later rugs from the mid-1930s, which shows his shift to Surrealist shapes. His earlier rug designs (fig. 119), derived ultimately from Synthetic Cubist paintings, closely resembled the rectilinear-patterned rugs designed in France by Ivan da Silva Bruhns and others. Kauffer was influenced by the organic forms of Surrealist art in France, and, like Henry Moore, Barbara Hepworth, and other members of the British avant-garde, began to move away

from rectangular forms in the late 1920s and 1930s. His 1929 design for a mural panel displays several Biomorphic forms pierced by amoeboid holes (fig. 120). The mural was conceived as a trompe-l'oeil relief, with shapes reminiscent of those used by Jean Arp (figs. 110, 111). Another design by Kauffer, for the "New Architecture Exhibition" organized by the Mars Group in 1937 (fig. 121), has two flat Biomorphic shapes, one filled with bricks and one with wood. The rug in the Stewart Collection is another example of Kauffer's move toward curved forms, and marks the height of Kauffer's Biomorphism.

As a rug designer, Kauffer developed certain precepts, some of which changed over the years. At first, flatness of design was important. In 1929, he said that one should "avoid any sensation of the solid in the modern rug. It must be flat and horizontal."[127] When he came to design this rug, he partly abandoned that idea to create a trompe-l'oeil relief. Still, the apparent relief is limited to two thin, flat planes. He also believed that "a pattern is much more restful and dignified when it is a definite decoration within a fixed area."[128] Thus, the trompe-l'oeil hole in the center of the design can be seen as enhancing the concentric feeling he prized.   CWL

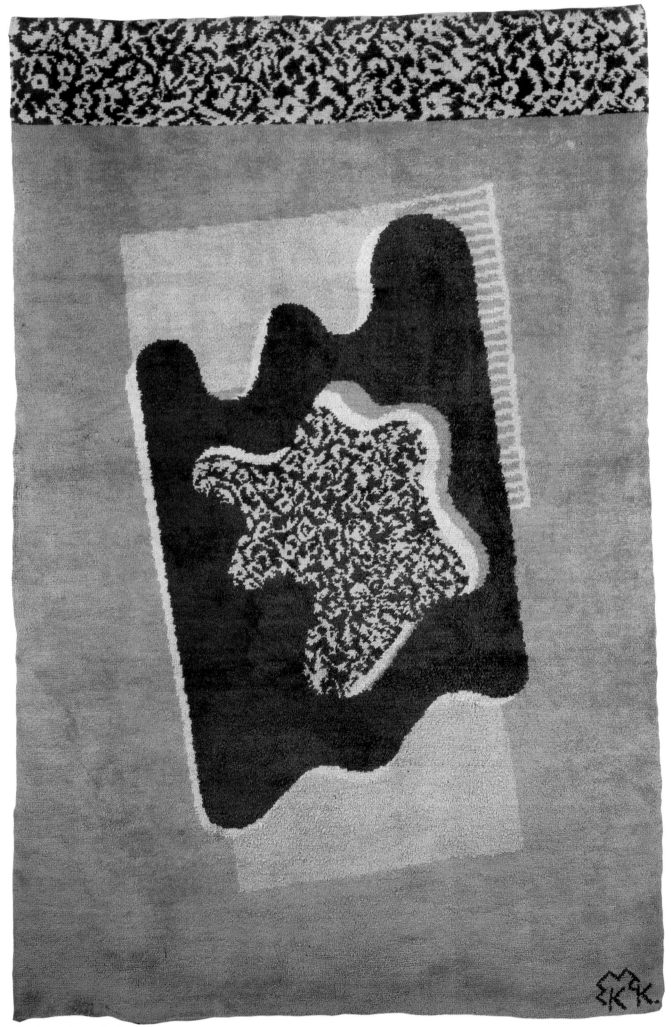

122. *McKnight Kauffer. Rug*

Alvar Aalto

Vase: model no. 9745 (Karhula) or 3035
   (Iittala), *Aalto*
Designed 1936
Glass; 3⅛ × 14¾ × 11¾ inches (8 × 37.5 ×
   30 cm)
Produced by Karhulan Lasitehtaalla (Karhula,
   Finland), 1937–c. 1949; by Iittala Lasitehdas
   (Iittala, Finland), 1954–56 and 1962 to the
   present[129] (this example before 1964)
Unmarked
D88.116.1

Vase: model no. 9744 (Karhula) or 3031
   (Iittala), *Aalto*
Designed 1936
Glass; 11¼ × 11⅝ × 11¼ inches
   (28.5 × 29.5 × 28.5 cm)
Produced by Karhulan Lasitehtaalla (Karhula,
   Finland), 1937–c. 1949; by Iittala Lasitehdas
   (Iittala, Finland), 1954–55, 1962–73 (this
   example probably c. 1954–55)
Engraved on underside: ALVAR AALTO 3030
D87.149.1

In the 1930s, when commissions were scarce and his fame not well established, Aalto frequently participated in design competitions, one of them sponsored by the Karhula glassworks.[130] The architect submitted four freely executed drawings for vases of varying heights and shapes, all with undulant walls (fig. 123). Awarded first prize, his designs were produced and exhibited at the 1937 Paris "Exposition Internationale des Arts et Techniques."

These vases constituted an important opening salvo in the establishment of a Biomorphic style for the decorative arts. Although Aalto is inevitably placed in the forefront of rationalist design, by the early 1930s he had turned away from the hard-edged rigidity associated with the International Style movement. The side section of the *Paimio* chair (fig. 15) and the undulant ceiling of the Viipuri library (figs. 13, 14) register this new vocabulary of pliant wood and rhythmic curvature. An analogy between the *Paimio* chair frame and these glass vases is particularly apt, since Aalto had envisioned shaping the glass with steel

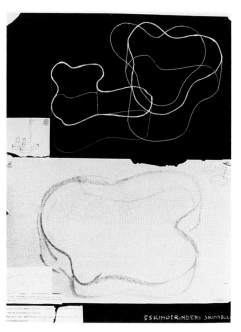

123. Alvar Aalto. *Drawing for vases submitted to Karhula glassworks competition. 1936. Collection Iittala Glassworks, Iittala, Finland*

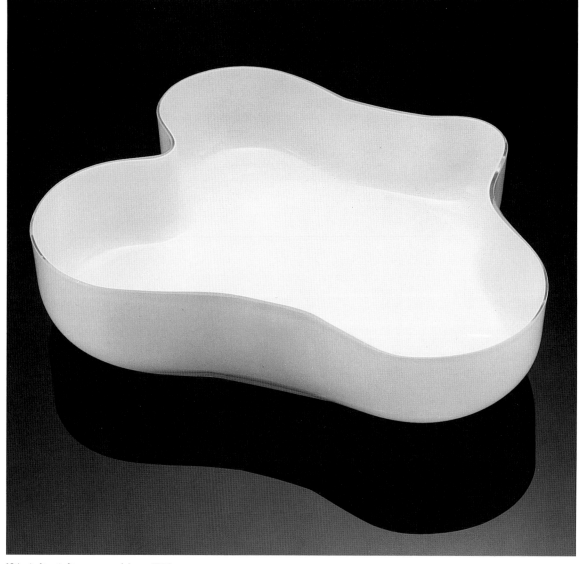

124. *Aalto. Aalto vase: model no. 3035*

125. *Aalto. Aalto vase: model no. 3031*

braces, much the way that his laminated wood was bent. Ultimately, it proved more expedient to use wooden molds. Most important, the folds of the vases are far more complex and irregular than those on the chair; they propel Aalto's language of form into something quite new and distinctive.

An interesting transitional stage is revealed in a drawing made in 1936, supposedly by his wife, Aino, for the stand that Aalto was commissioned to create for an exhibition in Sweden (fig. 126). In addition to a spartan International Style cabinet, Aalto planned a table whose top could be considered Biomorphic and whose contour resembles

that of the side piece of the *Paimio* chair. Most striking of all, though, is the vase that sits on the table. With its series of stepped rings, it recalls the *Bölgeblick* stacking vases that he and his wife had designed earlier for Karhula, except that it substitutes undulantly rhythmic walls for the hard-edged geometry of the *Bölgeblick* series, thus pointing the way to the vases for the Paris exhibition.

Aalto's organic designs may have their origins in several sources. One is the contour lines of hills and lakes—geographical features common in Finland—which Aalto always took into ac-

count in his architectural designs. In fact, Aalto planned a pond with rounded contours for the Paris exhibition hall. Abstract Surrealism is another possible source. Aalto made sculptural reliefs from sections of bent wood (fig. 115) that suggest a knowledge of Arp. Certainly, the close friendship that developed between Aalto and Alexander Calder when the Finn visited Paris in 1937 indicates Aalto's interest in such art.

Finally, we might consider the impact of Japanese art. At this time, Aalto and his wife were quite friendly with the Japanese consul and his wife in Helsinki.[131] Aino even took lessons in

Japanese flower arranging. Early publicity photographs show the tall vase's suitability for holding single branches of flowering blossoms asymmetrically to one side. The shorter vessels recall the proportions of the bowls actually used in Japan for flower arrangements.

The vases in this series have proven immensely popular over the course of the last half-century. Although certain models were made only intermittently or in certain colors, production of the series itself never ceased. They are generally known today as *Savoy* vases, a name introduced in the 1950s and stemming from the fact that some were ordered at the outset for the Savoy Restaurant in Helsinki. Originally, they were referred to as the *Aalto* vases or *Paris Object*. The name *Aalto* was restored in the 1960s,[132] but there is an ironic side to this turn of events, for Aalto never received compensation for this popular product beyond the initial prize money of 1937.   ME

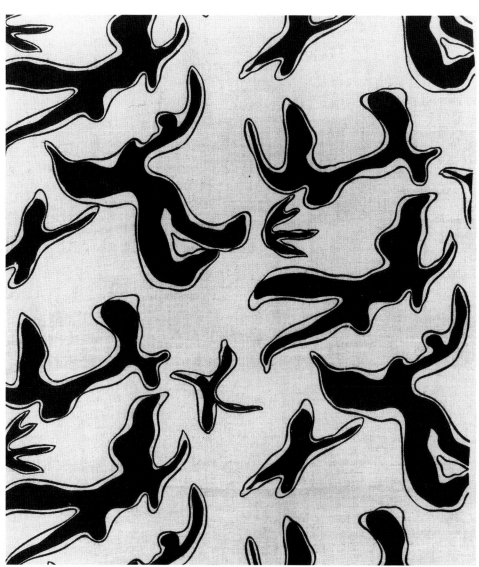

127. *Benjamin Baldwin and William Machado*. Flight *textile*

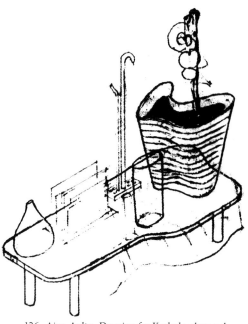

126. Aino Aalto. Drawing for Karhula glassworks exhibition stand (detail). 1936

Benjamin Baldwin and William Machado

Textile: *Flight*
Designed c. 1946–47
Linen, plain weave, silk-screen printed;
    31¾ × 24¾ inches (80.6 × 62.9 cm)
Produced by Arundell Clarke (New York),
    1948–c. 1955
Printed and typewritten on paper tag:
ARUNDELL CLARKE/425 EAST 53 STREET/NEW
YORK 22/PLAZA 3–7368/PHILA OFFICE [struck
through]/NAME FLIGHT/NUMBER/REPEAT
24″/COLOUR NAVY #1 [handwritten] *or to
order*/WIDTH 48″/CONTENT BELGIAN LINEN/
RETAIL/DELIVERY 2–3 WEEKS/[handwritten]
12/10
D87.135.1, gift of Jody Kingrey

Flight is an early example from a successful line of fabrics created between about 1946 and 1950 by the team of Baldwin and Machado under the name of Design Unit New York.[133] The architect and painter collaborated as a team on fully coordinated interiors, in which these exclusive and cooperatively designed textiles formed an integral part. To harmonize with the wood, stone, or brick of the room, the patterns were printed on natural linen or raw silk.[134]

The textiles of Design Unit New York were custom-manufactured by Arundell Clarke, silk-screened to order in the color and fabric of choice, with the name of both firms printed in the selvage. Dorothy Noyes also carried examples in her New York shop, New Design. The patterns proved successful, but when Arundell Clarke eventually omitted the name of the design team, the move provoked legal action and led to the withdrawal of the line from his company.[135]

Although the Biomorphic motifs may seem figurative, appearing to have a life of their own, the designers insist they are nonobjective and were conceived to convey a sense of movement, as the title implies. Characteristic of the more inventive fabrics of the late 1940s, these bold forms are rendered with but one opaque color—here blue, although brown and terra-cotta were also offered—and spaced to give importance to the neutral-colored, textured ground.   AZ

128. *Art Smith*. Lava *bracelet*

129. *Smith*. Modernette *bracelet. 1948. Collection Fifty/50 Gallery, New York*

Art Smith

Bracelet: *Lava*
Designed and executed c. 1946
Silver; 5⅞ × 2¼ × 2⅞ inches (14.9 ×
    5.7 × 7.3 cm)
Unmarked
D87.213.1

Two undulating forms slither, amoebalike, around and about each other in this outsize cuff bracelet. The piece is constructed with two free-form shapes, each cut from flat silver sheet, the smaller piece soldered on top of the larger one. In some areas, the two pieces are relatively congruent in shape. At some points the two surfaces were fitted flush together, while at others the upper surface was hammered to form slight arches. The depths of the hollows that resulted have been intensified by oxidation. Subsequently, the whole piece was forged to curve around a wrist. While the lower piece curves away from the arm at both ends, the upper section seems to strain to free itself from the platform to which it is attached.

There are four distinct aspects to this bracelet. First is Smith's fascination with protozoan imagery, whose roots can be found in the work of Jean Arp, Joan Miró, and Alexander Calder. The areas where the silver curves most deeply contain dramatic negative spaces, waiting to be filled in by a forearm; air is to be replaced by skin.[136]

Secondly, viewed within the context of Smith's black heritage, this bracelet suggests aspects of African tribal culture. There exists a heaviness, a deliberate naiveté or primitivism, in its visual presence and its mode of execution. Smith used the most basic metalworking techniques, comparable to those a native artisan would use. Were it not for its Biomorphic aesthetic, this bracelet could be taken for one created by a primitive metalsmith. In another Smith bracelet, one that shares similar techniques (fig. 129), explicit tribal references can be seen in the allusions to the human skeletal structure—a popular image in primitive jewelry—and perhaps also to the *mbira* or *sanza* (African finger piano).

A third aspect of Smith's work is its strong sense of drama and theatricality, which is especially evident in the scale of this bracelet. Smith actually made costumes and jewelry for the Pearl Primus and Talley Beatty black dance companies. He learned from experience that stage jewelry must be on a grand scale to create a dramatic impact but, at the same time, the effect must be one of grace, strength, and simplicity, so as to accentuate, not detract from, the visual drama of the dancers.

Lastly, Smith believed that jewelry was not fully expressed until it was worn. The human body acted as an armature for jewelry to embrace and modify, and jewelry was unresolved sculptural expression until it was related to human structure. "Like line, form, and color, the body is a material to work with. It is one of the basic inspirations in creating form." He asked "not how do bracelets go, but what can I do with an arm?"[137]

TLW

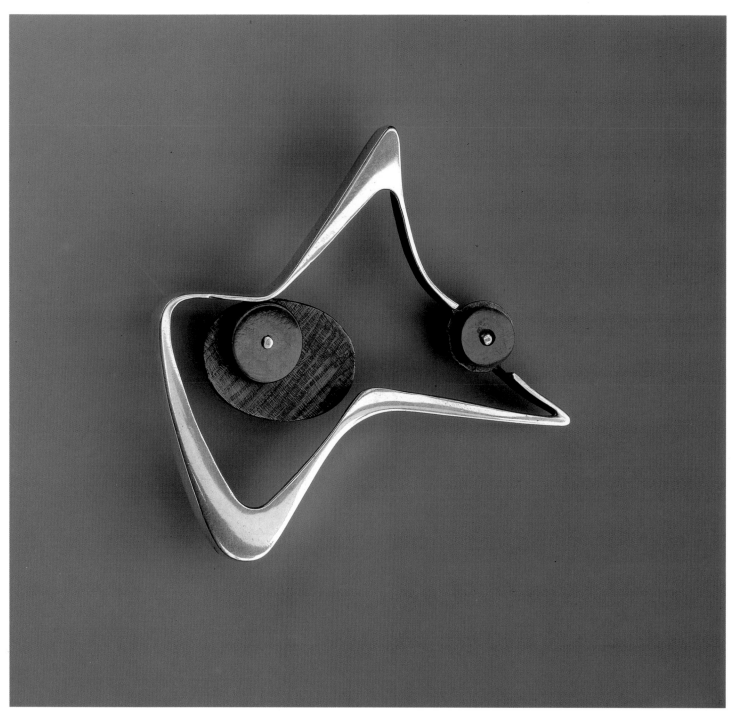

130. *Margaret de Patta. Brooch*

Margaret de Patta

Brooch

Designed c. 1946–50

Silver, malachite, and jasper; 3 × 3 inches (7.7 × 7.7 cm)

Executed c. 1946–58; assembled c. 1985 under the supervision of Eugene Bielawski[138]

Impressed on reverse: STERLING/ [insignia of a stylized M]

D86.160.1

Margaret de Patta's stated aim was to express, in jewelry, principles of modern design derived from nonobjective abstract painting and sculpture. The greatest influence on her work was the Constructivist aesthetic of László Moholy-Nagy, the former Bauhaus instructor with whom she studied in 1940–41 at the School of Design in Chicago. He emphasized the rigorous structuring of space through the use of line, light, and color.[139]

The positioning and mounting of the malachite and jasper elements in this pin illustrate one of de Patta's solutions to Moholy-Nagy's recommendation, "Catch your stones in the air. . . . Make them float in space. Don't enclose them."[140] In order to display the stones as small masses frozen in space, de Patta anchored the stone disks not by bezels or prongs but by a single silver wire passed through each of the centers. In addition, when de Patta's jewelry rests on fabric, the negative spaces read as texture as well as color.

This pin manifests a combination of both Constructivist and Biomorphic vocabularies. Organic form was not a primary focus of de Patta's oeuvre, yet it played a certain role, just as it had at the Chicago School of Design. Some of the early graphic designs she did at school (fig. 131), clearly derived from Moholy-Nagy's experimental art

(fig. 43), show how she, like her mentor, successfully united artistic disciplines that are normally considered opposites: the thoroughly planned structuring of Constructivism and the unconscious, organic fantasy of Surrealism.

As early as 1946, de Patta and her husband, Eugene Bielawaski, began exploring the possibilities of limited production. She felt socially and philosophically committed to maintaining the highest standards of design and craftsmanship while making her jewelry available at lower cost to the public at large. The general consumer, the very segment of society that her conscience wished to reach, could not afford her meticulously wrought designs. Imbued with the Bauhaus tenets that she had absorbed under Moholy-Nagy's tutelage, de Patta espoused the synthesis of art, craftsmanship, and machine production. This pin, although produced in limited quantities, is virtually indistinguishable in quality from her unique pieces; it differs only in its less complicated composition.

For example, in comparison with a similar but one-of-a-kind example done around the same period (fig. 132), the latter piece reveals a more intricate structure. A simple Biomorphic shape is cut from sheet metal and a second, somewhat larger shape is drawn in wire, thus creating a more complex arrangement of positive and negative images. The solid shape also has surface embellishment, which adds to its richness. In addition to a malachite disk attached by a pin, it carries a disk of oxidized silver and a coral cylinder at different levels. As the upper silver shape pivots, it hides the malachite and exposes the coral, thereby creating different color and compositional choices. Production pieces did not offer such mobility of parts and flexibility of design.

TLW

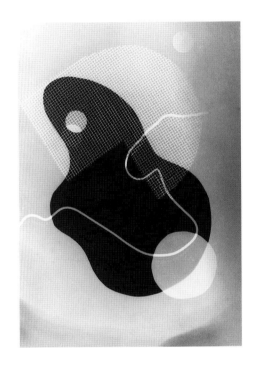

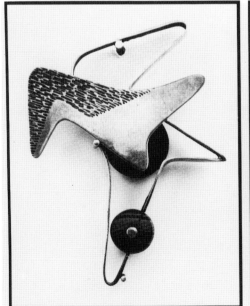

(above) 131. de Patta. Photogram. 1939. Collection Fifty/50 Gallery, New York

(left) 132. de Patta. Brooch, in two positions. c. 1946–50. Eugene Bielawski Collection, Berkeley, California

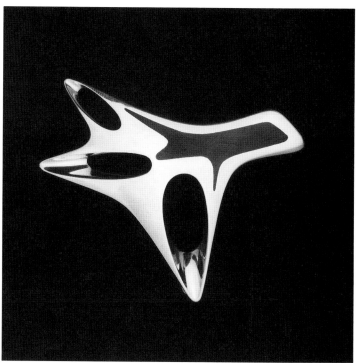

133. Henning Koppel. Brooch: model no. 307

134. Koppel. Brooch: model no. 323

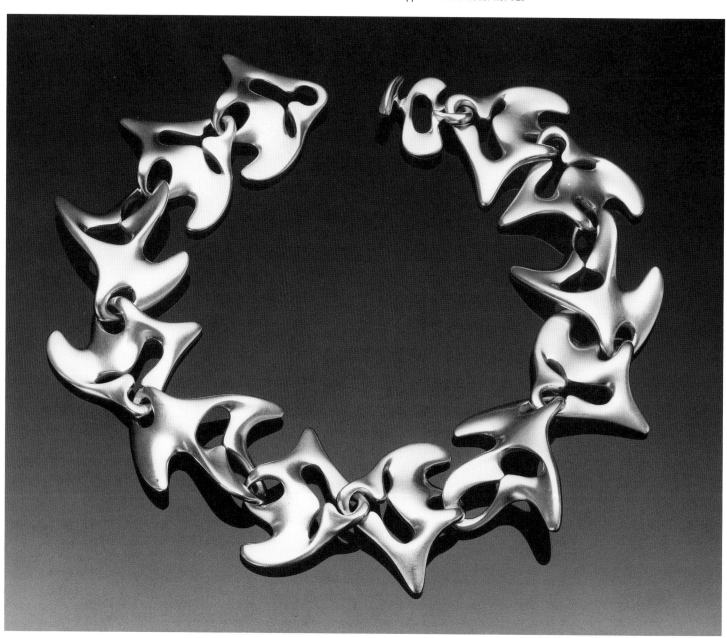

135. Koppel. Necklace: model no. 89

Henning Koppel

Brooch: model no. 307
Designed 1947
Silver and enamel; 1⅝ × 2½ inches
(4.2 × 6.4 cm)
Produced by Georg Jensen Silversmithy
(Copenhagen), 1947–c. 1982 (this example
before 1975)
Impressed on underside: HK/GEORG JENSEN/925
S/DENMARK/307
D86.184.1, gift of Lynn Brows, by exchange*

Brooch: model no. 323
Designed 1956
Silver and enamel; 2¼ × 2½ inches
(5.7 × 6.3 cm)
Produced by Georg Jensen Silversmithy
(Copenhagen), intermittently from 1956 to
the present
Impressed on underside: GEORG JENSEN [in
oval]/STERLING/DENMARK/323
D87.220.1

Necklace: model no. 89
Designed 1947
Silver; 1¾ × 17½ inches (4.5 × 44.5 cm)
Produced by Georg Jensen Silversmithy
(Copenhagen), intermittently from 1947 to
the present
Impressed on underside: GEORG JENSEN [in
oval]/925 S/DENMARK/89
D88.121.1

In 1945, after War World II ended, Henning
Koppel left the sanctuary of neutral Sweden and
returned to Denmark, where he began working
for the Georg Jensen Silversmithy. Although he
had been trained as a sculptor, he opted for a
career in applied art, which was much more lucrative in Denmark. At first, due to the low supply of silver in Europe, he designed mostly
jewelry.

Koppel's jewelry manifests a radical departure
from the early-twentieth-century style of Georg
Jensen, the company's founder (fig. 136). While
still retaining an organic approach to form, he
made no attempt to adapt Jensen's fruit or floral

motifs to a modern idiom. At the same time, he
repudiated the Modernist trend at Georg Jensen,
represented by Henning Seidelin's functionalism
and Count Bernadotte's geometric modernism,
both introduced in the early 1930s (fig. 102).

Instead, Koppel drew inspiration from the
antigeometric vocabulary of Biomorphism, perhaps influenced by the work of Alvar Aalto. The
fluid curves of Koppel's brooches bear an unmistakable resemblance to the shapes of Aalto's
glass vases and his *Paimio* chair (figs. 124, 125, 15).

Rather than literally translating natural forms,
Koppel adopted a "characterful physiognomy" in
his jewelry forms.[141] He alluded to a quasi-facial
character in brooch no. 307—one with distinct
tribal or primitive associations—contained within the purple enamel silhouette.[142] Koppel's
brooch no. 323, created almost a decade later, is
treated as an abstract image of a tree. Each
"branch," however, contains an oval that is
pierced obliquely. These three negative shapes
serve to increase the sense of depth and under-
score the Biomorphic quality.

Necklace no. 89 displays the same remarkable
sense of fluid forms. The silver links, their shape
evocative of dinosaur bones, appear to grow organically from one another, like vertebrae, and
create a continuous, undulating whole. This was
an ingenious innovation, transcending more traditional chains composed of links connected by
separate rings or hinges. The flux of the necklace's contours creates subtle shadings, a chiaro-
scuro that intensifies both the visual undulation
of the surface and its tactile sensibility.

This necklace evolved out of a similar one
designed a year earlier, which, although it presented a comparable silhouette, had an openness
in its design that did not permit the same sort of
complexly contoured surfaces. A fascinating
three-armed candelabra Koppel designed that
first year at Jensen (fig. 137) displays complex
surface modulations and contrasts of solids and
voids as vibrant and successful as those of necklace no. 89.

One might overemphasize the sculptural and
aesthetic values of Koppel's jewelry. However,
when the brooch is pinned onto a dress or the
interlocking chain of his necklace encircles the
neck, they reveal Koppel's ability to extract function out of form.   TLW

136. *Georg Jensen. Brooch: model no. 22. 1905–6.
Georg Jensen Museum, Copenhagen*

137. *Koppel. Candelabra: model no. 956. 1946.
Georg Jensen Museum, Copenhagen*

Henning Koppel

Wine pitcher: model no. 978
Designed 1948
Silver; 13⅞ × 7⁹⁄₁₆ × 6⅛ inches (35.3 × 19.2 × 15.4 cm)
Produced by Georg Jensen Silversmithy (Copenhagen), 1948 to the present
Impressed on underside: DESSIN/HK [in oval]/ DENMARK GEORG JENSEN [in beaded oval]/STERLING/978
D86.244.1

This wine pitcher was one of the first in a series of characterful jugs.[143] Like the jewelry that he began designing for Jensen, Koppel's Biomorphically conceived hollowware marked a radical departure in the company's style. For example, Johan Rohde's pitcher model no. 432 (fig. 139), designed for Georg Jensen in 1920, was also conceived as an organic design, the handle seeming to grow outward from the body. Rohde's example, however, has a more architectonic form and clearly states its function: to contain and pour liquid. By contrast, Koppel's pitcher presents itself as sculpture, its visual presence having very little to do with its function. The rounded, low-slung, pregnant belly most certainly could hold liquid, but the undulating curves of the neck and the backward arch of the spout seem to deny a pouring capability. As a matter of fact, when this jug was first introduced, it was simultaneously considered to be both balanced and graceful and "full of tension," leaving the viewer with a sense of unrest.[144] While Koppel's pitcher is eminently usable, its functional aspect remains secondary to aesthetic considerations.

Since formal subtleties were of paramount importance to him, Koppel, like Danish furniture designer Finn Juhl, conceived of each object in the round. After first sketching the object to be crafted, he modeled the prototype in clay, continually refining the contours and perfecting the silhouette from every angle.

Silver, when it remains without ornamentation, as in this pitcher, demands meticulous raising to absorb and break up the light.[145] While Rohde's pitcher retained the hammer marks, which fragment and scatter the light, Koppel's smooth surface reflection has only form to rely on; the manner in which the contours guide the eye around the vessel, thereby defining the shape, must control the movement of light and prevent visual distortion.

Koppel's wine jug is witty and humorous: it suggests some fantasy fowl. All his designs from this period have a comparable character. His famous fish server of 1954 exploits a visual pun in the manner by which the cover meets the platter: each end forms a pair of fish lips, and these actually also facilitate the removal of the lid. His pitcher is the epitome of his sculptural approach to utilitarian design. Understandably, its sensuous, radical configuration won a gold medal at the Milan IX Triennale in 1951.

TLW

(opposite) 138. Henning Koppel. Wine pitcher: model no. 978

139. Johan Rohde. Pitcher: model no. 432. 1920. Georg Jensen Museum, Copenhagen

Eva Zeisel

Dinnerware: *Town and Country*
Designed c. 1945–46
Glazed earthenware; teapot: 5⅛ × 11⅝ × 7⅛ inches (13 × 29.5 × 18.1 cm)
Produced by Red Wing Potteries, Inc. (Red Wing, Minnesota), 1947–c. 1950
Unmarked
D88.133.1–5, gift of Mr. and Mrs. Charles D. O'Kieffe, Jr., in memory of Mr. and Mrs. Charles DeWitt O'Kieffe, by exchange*

The organic Biomorphic designs of Zeisel's *Town and Country* dinnerware mark an interesting turn in the designer's development.[146] Her previous commercial work—in Germany, the Soviet Union, and then the United States—had been hard-edged and geometric, with only occasional examples, such as the handleless creamer in the Castleton *Museum* service (fig. 55), displaying elegantly extended arcs. The most organic of her previous designs had remained experimental teaching exercises devised for her classes at Pratt Institute, Brooklyn. The marked change represented by this dinnerware supposedly owes something to the president of Red Wing Potteries, who asked her to make something "Greenwich Villagey," that is, bohemian and artistically eccentric. The specific eccentricity of this service reflects the type of Biomorphic design that had incubated in New York City during the war years and had begun to emerge in painting, sculpture, and, also, in the world of design.

The most striking and most Biomorphic elements in the service are the salt and pepper shakers. Their organic shapes and the placement of the openings create the impression of creatures with eyes and noses; the designer often photographed them to suggest a mother and child or a whole family of friendly creatures. They strongly suggest the influence of Jean Arp's free-form

140. Eva Zeisel. Town and Country *dinnerware*

141. Zeisel. Town and Country *dinnerware*

sculpture. (It should be mentioned that Zeisel staunchly disclaimed such an influence, maintaining as late as 1983 that she had never even heard of Arp, despite his prominence in publications on modern art. She claimed that if an outside influence were to be cited, it should be the melting watches of Salvador Dalí.)

To a degree, a similar type of undulant, sculptural form can be seen in the handles of the pitchers and the stacked set of serving platters. Even the dinner plates and saucers depart from the norm of symmetry: the central depressions are off center, and one side is higher than the other, creating a gently sloped shape. Other elements in the service—the teapot, the casserole dishes, the cups—are more routine in design, with only an

occasional accent—the canted lid on the sugar bowl, the rounded stump handle of the bean pot—registering this new trend in design.

In certain ways this service was a natural outgrowth and response to Russel Wright's *American Modern.* It, too, was in earthenware, and thus calculated for an informal and middle-class market. Like *American Modern,* it was offered in a comparable color range: soft blue and chartreuse, sand and peach, dark brown and a gun-metal black, all of which could be combined in a variety of ways. Also, like Wright's service, Zeisel's was intended for a young, forward-looking audience. The *Town and Country* service—like the magazine of the same name—emphasized a democratic, servantless life-style with casual etiquette,

family meals, and buffet parties (this is reflected especially in the inclusion of two sizes of casserole dishes and coffee mugs).

It is an interesting barometer of taste that much of Arp's sculpture, including early models, was actually cast in the postwar period. At the same time, although on a very different socioeconomic level, Zeisel's salt and pepper shakers found acceptance in domestic interiors. Even more fascinating, only a few years later the cartoonist Al Capp used these very shapes for his famous "Shmoo" characters, Arp-like creatures that delighted Americans' imaginations and flooded the toy industry. In this restricted sense, intellectual and popular culture briefly shared a common meeting ground. ME

142. *Isamu Noguchi. Chess table: model no. IN 61*

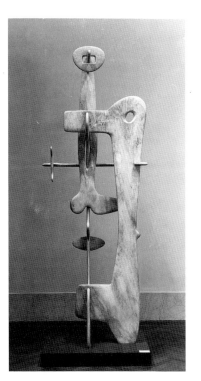

143. *Noguchi. Kouros. 1944–45. The Metropolitan Museum of Art, New York. Fletcher Fund, 1953*

Isamu Noguchi

Chess table: model no. IN 61
Designed c. 1947
Ebonized plywood, aluminum, and plastic;
   19¼ × 33⅞ × 30⁹⁄₁₆ inches (48.8 × 86 × 77.6 cm)
Produced by the Herman Miller Furniture Co.
   (Zeeland, Michigan), 1950–51
Unmarked
D85.132.1, gift of Jay Spectre, by exchange*

When discussing the Biomorphic impulse in furniture and objects, it is usually necessary to speak of abstract, Biomorphic painting and sculpture and their influence on the designers of useful objects. In the case of Isamu Noguchi's furniture, however, the three-dimensional, curvilinear shapes that suggest the surge and pulse of organic life in their lines and mass were very much present in the full range of the artist's work (fig. 143). His chess table cannot be separated from the rest

144. Noguchi. Chess table: model no. IN 61

of his art; instead, it should be seen as an example of functional sculpture.

The table consists of an irregularly shaped, four-legged base, a thin plywood top into which have been set red and yellow dots to signify the spaces of a chessboard, and an undulating component supporting the top whose cavities function as storage space for the chessmen. All of the table's elements are dynamic; they curve and swell as if possessed with powerful, organic life forces. Yet the table is not necessarily infused with the solemnity or mystery that is often evoked by three-dimensional Biomorphic forms.

Although Noguchi's furniture and industrial designs were limited to a mere decade or so[147] and

form a body of work that the artist did not much care to discuss, his attitude during the time was all-inclusive and fun-loving. His openness to nontraditional sculptural forms and materials was suggested in much of his writing. Discussing his sculpture, Noguchi asked:

But then why did it have to be fine art? Why not objects of use and popularity? By use I meant enjoyment—things for everybody's enjoyment. I thought that a really new creation (invention) could rise above the demeaning categories of applied art and the like. Originality might survive mass production.[148]

In the case of Noguchi's chess table, the conception did indeed survive production—but it did not survive the demands of the commercial marketplace. According to the artist, the table was designed and made for an exhibition at the Julien Levy Gallery held around 1947, although the actual date may have been 1945.[149] It was offered for sale in the Herman Miller catalogue of 1950 but not in the subsequent edition of 1952.[150] Apparently, although recommended for use as either a chess or coffee table, its uncompromising Biomorphic aesthetic proved too emphatic to stimulate sufficient demand.

CW

Carlo Mollino

Table: *Arabesco*
Designed 1950
Maple-faced plywood, brass, and replaced
 glass; 19¾ × 48 × 19½ inches (50.2 × 122 ×
 49.5 cm)
Produced by Apelli & Varesio (Turin, Italy),
 1951
Unmarked
D88.128.1

The *Arabesco* table is one of Mollino's en-
chanting and imaginative Biomorphic designs.
The undulating plywood base with its curved cutouts resembles some sort of strange creature, with
the two brass fasteners as its eyes. The table, fully
three dimensional like Baroque sculpture, demands that the viewer walk around it to fully
appreciate it.

To make the base of the table, Mollino used a
sheet of plywood bent into a series of curves, like
the seat and back of Alvar Aalto's *Paimio* chair of
the early 1930s (fig. 15). The forms of the table are
in the same vein as the extravagant flowing curves
and circular cutout of Charles and Ray Eames'
experimental chaise longue of 1948. However,
Mollino's table is more whimsical and playful
than either Aalto's or the Eameses' chairs.

All these organic curves were inspired by the
Surrealists. Indeed, Mollino called himself a
"streamlined Surrealist." The base of the table,
with its irregular, curved cutouts, copies the flowing lines and Biomorphic shapes of Jean Arp's
wooden reliefs (figs. 110, 111). Another Surrealist
aspect is Mollino's taking a form and employing it
in an unusual context. He played a game with the
Arabesco table, using the outlines of a woman's
torso traced from a drawing by the Italian Surrealist Leonor Fini (fig. 146) to establish the shape of
the tabletop.[151]

Most of Mollino's furniture was commissioned
for specific interiors. This *Arabesco* table was
made as part of a large commission for the office
of the Lattes publishing firm in Turin.[152] Among

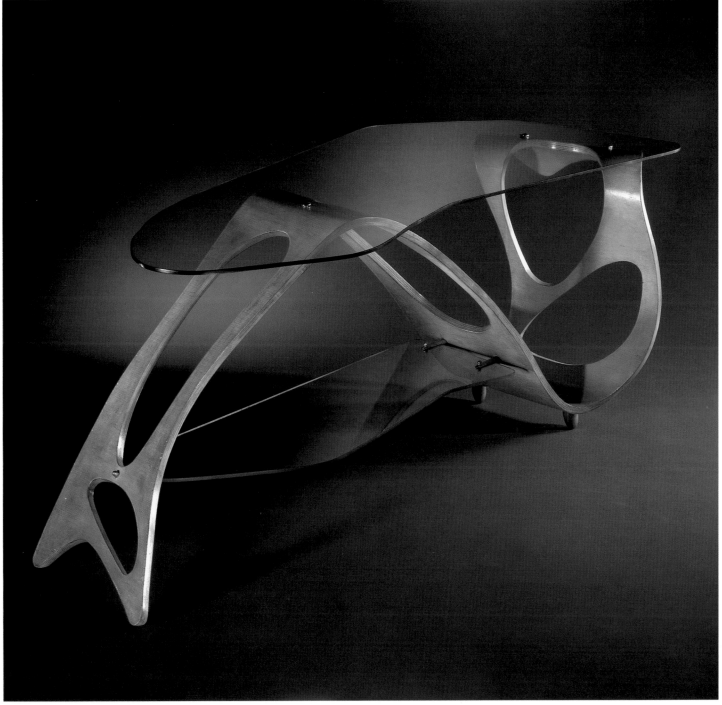

145. *Carlo Mollino.* Arabesco *table*

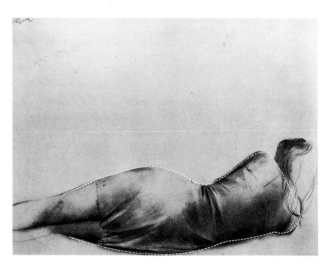

Mollino's other inventive pieces for this office was a *Vertebrae* table, whose elaborately cut and bent base resembles a spine with ribs and vertebrae. These elaborate tour-de-force tables in plywood and glass reveal an expressiveness that was essentially restricted to Italian postwar design.

Mollino's first *Arabesco* table was designed for the living room of the Casa Orengo in Turin in 1949,[153] where it was used as a piece of sculpture in a clean-line, Modernist environment (fig. 147). That version was higher and less lengthy than all the later ones. In a contemporary photograph of the same room in the Casa Orengo, one can see a copy of Peggy Guggenheim's *Art of This Century* on a writing table. Much of that book is concerned with Surrealist art, and its presence attests to the artistic currents in Mollino's circle.[154]

CWL

(above left) *146. Leonor Fini. Study of Reclining Female. Outline is by Carlo Mollino. c. 1950*

(left) *147. Mollino. Living room of Casa Orengo, Turin, in 1949*

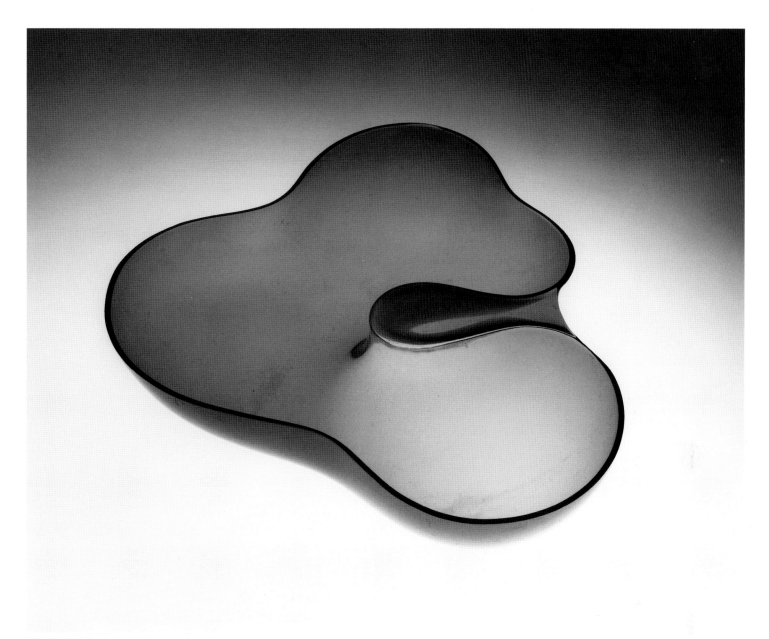

148. *Eva Zeisel*. Cloverware *serving platter*

Eva Zeisel

Serving platter: *Cloverware*
Designed c. 1947
Plexiglas; 2½ × 12⅞ × 10⅞ inches (6.3 ×
    32.7 × 27.7 cm)
Produced by the Clover Box and Manu-
    facturing Company (New York), c. 1947
Unmarked
D88.123.1, gift of Eva Zeisel

Among the most Biomorphic of Eva Zeisel's designs is this compartmented serving dish, created
as part of a fifteen-piece line of tabletop accessories. The walls are boldly undulant in cross section, as in Alvar Aalto's vases of a decade earlier
(figs. 124, 125), but Zeisel's bowl shows a slightly
more complex handling of form. She established
an interesting fluctuation, for the heights of the
walls and also sculpted the bottom as a series of
gently rising and falling concavities. The resultant Biomorphic shape is more truly three di-

mensional, similar to the storage pockets on
Noguchi's chess table (figs. 142, 144). In fact, it
became such a common type of postwar solution
for commercial products that nowadays we may
not recognize its originality.

When her *Cloverware* products were released,
it was emphasized that the shapes were the result
of both aesthetic intent and the technological
means of production: "lines both functional and
artistic," as it was phrased.[155] Publicity releases
made much of the fact that they were "hand-
blown forms . . . modeled by pressure of air."
Yet, despite such attempts at material determin-
ism, the material was, in essence, immaterial.
Zeisel's turn to a Biomorphic idiom was not restricted to plastic; it had already been advanced in
her favorite medium of ceramic, in the *Town and
Country* dinnerware (figs. 140, 141), and she explored it later in her chair of steel tubing (figs.
149–51), a design that she vaunted because no two
lines were parallel.

Despite the importance of plastics in the 1930s,
when radios, jewelry, and small, often Streamlined objects were created in Bakelite, many designers displayed a reluctance to use plastic for
high-style design in the years immediately after
the war. Zeisel's own words betrayed this defen-
siveness, as she explained that "the disappoint-
ment we often feel in handling an item made of
plastic . . . is partly the reason for the antipathy
we sometimes feel for the material." Moreover,
plastics such as Plexiglas had serious technological disadvantages, such as a tendency to scratch.
It is significant that the *Cloverware* line was only
for occasional accessories, such as serving trays,
salad bowls, nut and relish dishes—objects that
receive less use than regular dinnerware. Although more serviceable plastics such as melamine soon came into use, plastic remained a
lowly material, shunned by leading designers for
another decade or so, until it became a vehicle for
high-style design, especially among the Italians.
                                                            ME

(opposite) *149. Eva Zeisel. Chair*

(right) *150, 151. Zeisel. Chair frame, assembled and disassembled*

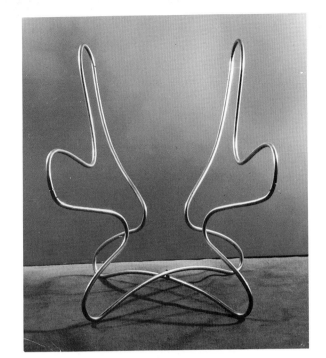

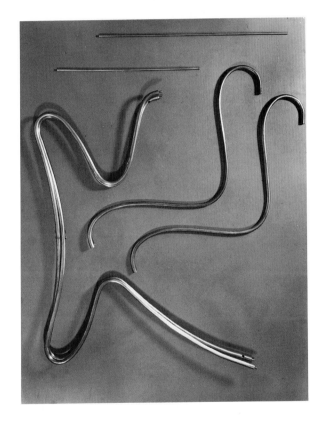

Eva Zeisel

Chair
Designed 1948–49
Chrome-plated tubular steel and replaced
    cotton cover; 28¹⁵⁄₁₆ × 25 × 25⅝ inches
    (73.5 × 63.5 × 65 cm)
Produced by Hudson Fixtures (New York),
    c. 1949
Unmarked
D86.179.1, gift of Eva Zeisel

Although best known as a designer of mass-produced ceramic tableware (figs. 55–57, 140, 141), Eva Zeisel became enthralled with the idea of designing a chair. She financed its development through the prototype stage, at a cost of seven thousand dollars, using the income from a line of General Mills metal cookware on which she was then working.[156]

Zeisel began with an image of a typical cantilevered chair of tubular steel, concerning herself particularly with its springy quality. However, she was thinking not of the European, architect-designed cantilevered chair of the 1920s but, instead, of the typical "dinette set" chair that became a common feature of American kitchens both before and after World War II. Zeisel intended the chair to be used in domestic interiors, and she designed it as a knockdown so that it could be taken camping and picnicking as well. Accordingly, it belongs by conception and design to the nineteenth-century tradition of folding camp chairs.[157] Her ambition was to create a particularly comfortable and portable chair based on the notion that "you sit on a whole spring, not just a seat with a spring."

The chair that fulfilled Zeisel's ambition was made of four lengths of unusually thin-walled bent tubular steel. These were braced with two straight crosspieces to which was fitted a single-piece fabric cover forming seat and back. Critical to the chair's design was the shaping of the frame elements. It took Zeisel some time to work them out, joining them together and fitting the cover so that the chair would move and flex in all directions while still maintaining its structural integrity and providing the sitter with comfort. The chair that resulted from this careful planning of subtly bent curves can only be fully appreciated through use; photographs necessarily make it appear static, whereas, in fact, it is a design geared to movement, in which its flexibility and exuberant flow of line come into play.

Following small-scale manufacture in New York and the refining of a die for the manufacture of the chair parts, Zeisel contracted with a company in Iowa to mass-produce the chair.[158] The firm destroyed Zeisel's die but could not duplicate the original, and production never began. Nearly fifteen years later, in 1964, the chair was shown in the American section at the Milan XIII Triennale, where it featured a knit cover by Mary Walker Phillips. Although another American firm entered into negotiation for production rights, the chair was never manufactured. In retrospect, Zeisel says of the chair:

> It really is one of the things that hurts me most because it was so charming and I know exactly how it should be done. [The design] cannot be altered. . . . My ambition was not to add another chair to the happiness of chair makers. It was the idea of springiness, it was the wire.

CW

152. *Marianne Straub.* Surrey *drapery textile*

Marianne Straub

Drapery textile: *Surrey*[159]

Designed 1951

Wool, rayon, and cotton, jacquard-woven twill
  weave; 37½ × 23½ inches (95.3 × 59.7 cm)

Produced by Warner & Sons Limited
  (London), 1951

Paper label, printed within a rectangular box:
  WARNER [device of a circle, within which
  there is a W, a tree with fruit, and an S,
  and, below the circle, REGD TRADE MARK]
  FABRICS/No. P. 736.C [handwritten]/Mtrs.
  _____ /Width Cms. _____ /Description
  SURREY [handwritten]/Made in _____

Handwritten in margin of paper label: 193
  [arrow] TOP

D87.204.1, gift of Warner & Sons Limited

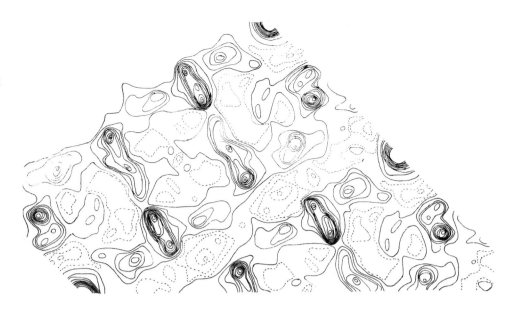

In 1949 Mark Hartland Thomas, director of the
Council of Industrial Design, established the Festival Pattern Group with a mandate to search for
fresh ideas for products and designs for the up-
coming Festival of Britain. Twenty-six leading
manufacturers, with Warner & Sons represented
by Marianne Straub and Alec Hunter, were invited to develop designs—not only for fabrics but
also for furniture, floor coverings, wallpapers,
cutlery, ceramics, and glass—utilizing diagrams
of crystal structures.[160] Hartland Thomas had
selected the leitmotiv of crystallography after
hearing a paper read by Professor Kathleen Lons-
dale at a weekend course at Ashridge, and after he
explored the idea further with Dr. Helen Megan
of Girton College, Cambridge, who became the
group's scientific advisor. She arranged for models and dye lines of the crystal structures to be
supplied to the group by scientific laboratories.
Seemingly a fresh idea, this linkage of design
with science had been earlier "in the air," but it
had never before been explored so system-
atically.[161]

In *Surrey*, Straub chose to enlarge and emphasize the naturally repeating Biomorphic shapes
she saw in diagrams of the crystals of afwillite
(figs. 153, 154), a hydrous calcium silicate. She
skillfully used contrasting colors and the varied
textures of the jacquard weave to introduce a
heightened sense of movement to the sinuous,
amoeboid forms and concentric formations.

Straub's design was seen to great advantage
because it was used prominently by Misha Black
for curtaining in the Festival's Regatta Restaurant. Through this promotion and visibility, *Surrey* became perhaps the best known of Straub's
many designs—a truly ironic situation, as the
fabric was not typical of her work of the period,
and it was never mass-produced.[162]

AZ

153, 154. *Dye lines of afwillite crystals. Collection
Warner Archives, London*

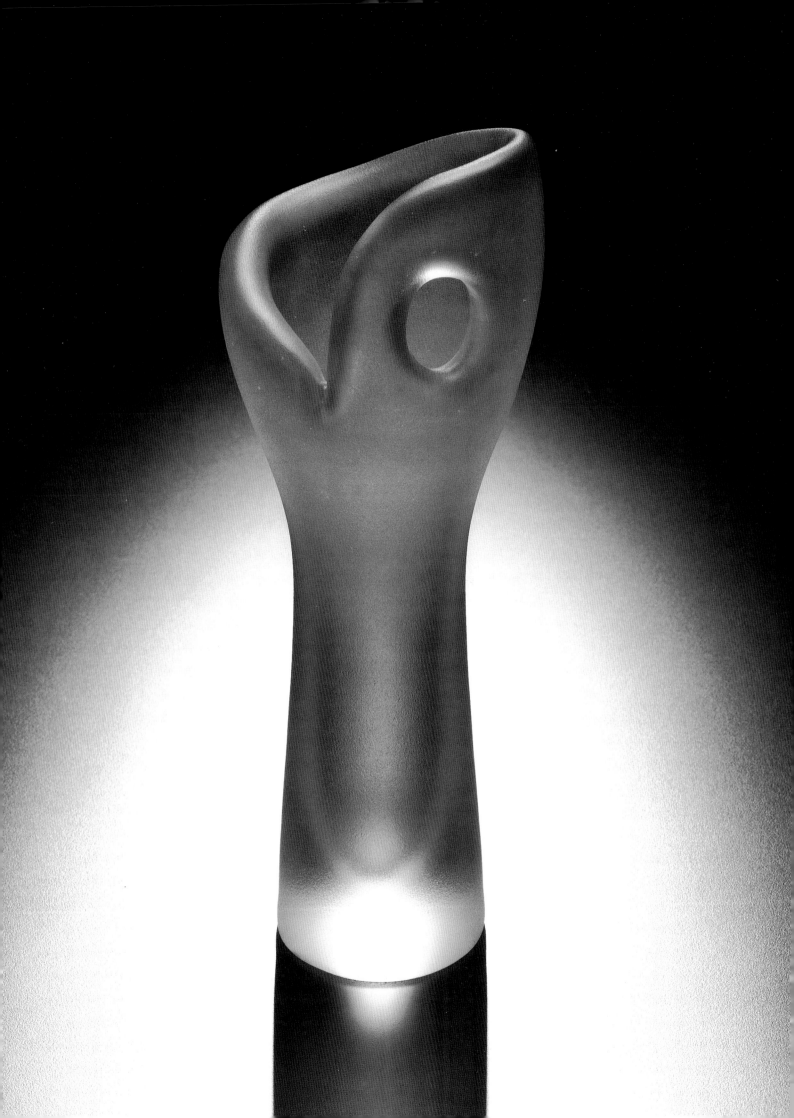

Timo Sarpaneva

Vase: model no. 3530, *Devil's Churn*
Designed c. 1950–51
Glass; 11⅜ × 4¾ × 4⁵⁄₁₆ inches (29 × 12 × 11 cm)
Produced by Iittala Lasitehdas (Iittala,
    Finland), c. 1952–59[163] (this example 1954)
Engraved on underside: TIMO SARPANEVA —
    IITTALA — 54
D86.159.1

The *Devil's Churn* was one of a series of related forms Sarpaneva created soon after he joined the Iittala staff (fig. 156). Their strongly sculptural, asymmetrical shapes and pierced walls mark the apogee of his Biomorphic style. This vase, although conceived as an abstract form, was given its name to accord with the romantic naturalism that pervaded Finnish postwar design. *Devil's Churn* (*Hiidenkirnu* in Finnish, sometimes translated as *Pot Hole*) refers to a natural cavity in a boulder caused by the eroding effects of water and a smaller, trapped stone.

Several decades afterward, when writing about the style of postwar ceramics and glass, Sarpaneva described it as a "union of free forms and abstract masses." He placed its origin in the architecture of Charles Eames and Eero Saarinen, as well as in Frank Lloyd Wright's Guggenheim Museum in New York City.[164] He also cited three examples from the fine arts: "Salvador Dali's fluid objects, Joan Miró's flowing rhythms, and Barbara Hepworth's spatially innovative wood sculptures." When discussing the glass of Vicke Lindstrand, Sarpaneva again cited the influence of Hepworth as well as Henry Moore. His focus on Hepworth and Moore is illuminating, especially since the impact of their sculpture can be perceived in his own work—including the *Devil's Churn*.

Indeed, Sarpaneva's approach to design was rather like that of a sculptor. After its initial forming, the glass was cut and pierced with shears; its surface was blasted with sand and treated with acid to reduce its transparency, giving it a stonelike appearance. However, Sarpaneva did not fully achieve the three-dimensional, sculptural qualities of Hepworth or Moore. His vase is still cylindrical and relatively symmetrical in its volume. Although the wall is pierced, the shallow hole does not have the cavernous depth of the British sculptors' work and does not generate the same type of interplay between negative and positive space. In short, bold as it is, the *Devil's Churn* also reveals restraints.

ME

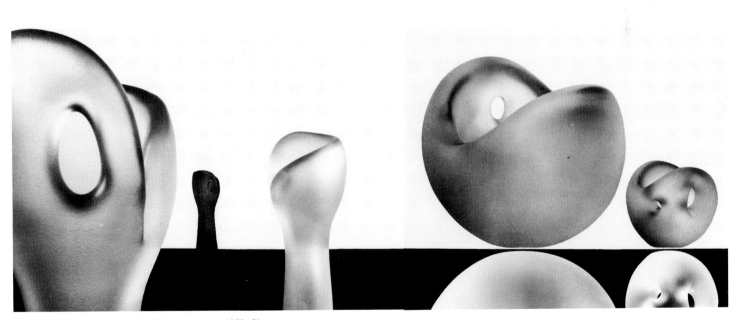

(above) *156. Sarpaneva.* Devil's Churn *series. c. 1950–51*

(opposite) *155. Timo Sarpaneva.* Devil's Churn *vase: model no. 3530*

Vicke Lindstrand

Vase: model no. LH 1181
Designed c. 1953
Glass; 11 × 6½ × 3⅛ inches (28.2 × 16.7 × 8 cm)
Produced by AB Kosta Glasbruk (Kosta, Sweden), c. 1953–c. 1963
Engraved on underside: LH 1181
D88.196.1, gift of Mr. and Mrs. I. Wistar Morris III*

Vase: model no. LH 1175
Designed c. 1953
Glass; 10¹⁵⁄₁₆ × 4¼ × 2⅜ inches (27.9 × 10.8 × 6 cm)
Produced by AB Kosta Glasbruk (Kosta, Sweden), c. 1953–63[165]
Engraved on underside: Kosta LH 1175
D85.136.1

157. *Kosta Glasbruk advertisement for Lindstrand vases, c. 1953*

158. *Vicke Lindstrand. Torso vase. 1937. Collection Orrefors Glassworks, Orrefors, Sweden*

159. *Fulvio Bianconi. Vases. c. 1951*

From the moment Lindstrand joined the Kosta staff in 1950, he showed a marked preference for fluent forms. To overcome the traditional globular shapes inherent in the glassblowing process, Lindstrand resorted to simple expedients. Perforce, the vessel was still blown as a symmetrical form, but while it was still warm and malleable, it was "deformed." Sometimes it was cut at an angle, or, as in these two vases, the walls were pierced with shears. The black vase was also paddled to create ends of different thicknesses. Company photographs (fig. 157) reveal the endless and equally witty possibilities: long-necked or wide, pierced centrally or off center, single or double holes, clear or dark or clear with a dark filament. Variety could be produced with ease and only moderate expense, important factors when producing artistic glass at a factory that had to heed the economics of the marketplace.

Much of Lindstrand's fluidity of design is adumbrated in his prewar creations for Orrefors (fig. 158). The rhythmic, Matisse-like females and the playful contrast between long arcs and circular disks offer striking analogies to his later work. But his early designs were two dimensional and confined to symmetrical vessels. Such Scandinavian postwar designers as Timo Sarpaneva took an important step toward greater fluidity, but even in Sarpaneva's sophisticated *Devil's Churn* vase (fig. 155), the irregular form is still basically cylindrical and the hole is merely a shallow opening in one wall.

Somewhat bolder solutions were introduced in Fulvio Bianconi's work (fig. 159). The volumes of his vessels are handled more sculpturally, and the apertures are emphatically three dimensional. Since Venini's vases were exhibited, widely published, and sold in Sweden, they form a readily available and provocative prelude to Lindstrand's work.[166] On the other hand, it is just as useful to consider the difference between the two temperaments. Whereas the Italian shows a preference for eccentric, occasionally anthropomorphic, and even ungainly shapes, the Scandinavian displays a more tempered balance. Likewise, the choice of colors is telling. The intensely bright range of Venini's colors contrasts markedly with Kosta's somber palette. Despite the international character of postwar design, national differences can be discerned.

ME

(opposite) 160. Lindstrand. Vases: model nos. LH 1181 and LH 1175

Modern Historicism

Within the canon of pure Modernism, progressive design and a dependence on historical styles of the past have generally been considered antithetical. As Edgar Kaufmann, jr., expressed it in his primer *What Is Modern Design?*,

> *Designs made now in mimicry of past periods or remote ways of life ('authentic Chippendale reproductions,' or 'Chinese modern'), cannot be considered as anything more than embarrassing indications of a lack of faith in our own values.* [167]

Kaufmann's view, the predominant one of the time, was that the present age was unique, distinct from the past because of its form of government (democracy) and the advances of technology (new materials and means of production). Modern design was morally obliged to express those new conditions and the new spirit of its time in a new language, unfettered by references to the past.

The nineteenth century, in apparent contrast, had reveled in borrowing both from the past and from remote cultures; it was the very core of Romanticism. The list of revival styles seems endless: Gothic, Renaissance, Rococo, Islamic, Egyptian, Japanese. Yet there was an ambivalence between historicism and Modernism even during the heyday of the former's existence. The Gothic Revivalist Augustus Welby Pugin warned against a superficial borrowing of crockets and spires, and he urged the sensible adaptation of Gothic architectural principles. Owen Jones, whose *The Grammar of Ornament* was the most frequently used source book for nineteenth-century plagiarists, warned against the outright adoption of other cultures' patterns and urged instead that the designer study the underlying principles governing those patterns.

Notwithstanding the increasing movement toward an antihistoricizing stance in the first quarter of the twentieth century, when the early Modernist canon was evolving, references to past historical styles were a major part of modern design. Siegfried Bing, propagandist for the Art Nouveau style, denounced a Renaissance chair as being identical in form to a Gothic chair save for the change in ornament, yet his atelier relied heavily on Louis XV forms to lure a French clientele. Richard Riemerschmid and his German colleagues often looked to the medieval past. By 1910, with the waning of Art Nouveau, designers turned to classicizing styles, following either the ancient model or Neoclassicism. The glass of François Decorchemont, the furniture of Paul Follot, and the architecture of Josef Hoffmann all reveal a curious blend of Modernist and classical solutions. A comparable mixture of contemporary and historicizing elements held true in the 1920s. A modern form of classicism was evident in the sculpture of Aristide Maillol and Carl Milles, the furniture of Émile-Jacques Ruhlmann, and the glassware of the Orrefors factory in Sweden. Moreover, Orientalism still had a pervasive hold, as in the ceramics of Émile Decoeur and Émile Lenoble, the jewelry of Cartier, and the lacquer of Jean Dunand.

One might be tempted to analyze the ambiguous relationship between Modernism and historicism as a gap between theory and practice, but that does not provide the whole answer. As the theory of Modernism developed in the 1920s, it, too, accepted the usefulness of historical models. For example, in Germany in the early 1930s an important exhibition compared archetypal designs culled from the past with contemporary works and found that certain simple forms had eternal values of beauty and function.[168] Unornamented Sung bowls and Roman works of pure form were singled out because, of course, they corresponded to the then prevalent code of Modernist design. The emphasis changed in terms of which cultures or periods were considered and what particular aspects were selected, but this has always been true. Each generation finds corroboration from the past in terms of its own specific needs.

Echoes of this type of Modernist historicism can be found in Kaufmann's *What Is Modern Design?*:

> Modern design makes use of good ideas out of the past. . . . We use certain articles constantly whose forms have scarcely changed for two hundred years. Most of them have to do with eating—flatware, china and glass. Until modern designers develop fundamental improvements on them we shall pay tribute to the competence of the past in this field.[169]

Hidden in this apparent catholicity, though, is a continued Modernist bias. Kaufmann acknowledged issues of form but disregarded decoration and other factors. Secondly, by limiting the discussion to tabletop elements, generally viewed as minor areas within the already "minor arts," he did not consider the importance of the past for jewelry, textiles, glass, and, on a larger scale, furniture as well.

A less prejudiced view than Kaufmann's reveals that throughout the midcentury there were many cross-cultural exchanges. Oriental, African, and vernacular art were all used for inspiration. Hans Wegner's *Y Chair* (fig. 161) and Gio Ponti's *Superleggera* chair (fig. 188), Jens Quistgaard's ice bucket (fig. 177), and Gertrud Vasegaard's tea set (fig. 175), as well as Isamu Noguchi's lamps (figs. 166, 170) and Archimede Seguso's bowl (fig. 184), show that modern industrial design borrowed freely to create new works. Historicism ranged from the smallest to the largest of objects and embraced all materials. As a phenomenon it was as international an idea as its very sources. In the craft world it was as pervasive as in industrial design or even more so, and it often encompassed not only form and decorative schemes but also technical issues such as types of glazes and ways of working glass. Most important of all, this creative adaptation could be and was indeed inventive. One could look back to the past in order to create for the present and the future.

To a certain degree the prewar idea of eternal forms held true—as witness the Ponti chair and the Vasegaard tea service—but for the greater part, there was no attempt to find lasting values. Rather, the idea of change and novelty seems to have been an equally important issue. In fact, it may go some way to explain why historicism played such an important role: it provided a novel outlook and a different code, and this helped combat the ennui of established forms. Despite the optimistic rationalism of prewar theory, variety and change in the postwar world have proven to be factors as important in marketing as the design itself.   ME

Hans Wegner

Side chair: model no. CH-24, *Y Chair*
Designed 1949–50
Beech and rush; 28½ × 21⅛ × 20½ inches
  (72.4 × 53.6 × 52.1 cm)
Produced by Carl Hansen & Son (Odense,
  Denmark), 1950 to the present
Branded into center of rear seat rail: MADE IN
  DENMARK
Stamped on right of rear seat rail: 11
In pencil on left of rear seat rail: KM
D82.119.2, gift of Sherman Emery*

Hans Wegner's *Y Chair* is emblematic of an important line of development in Scandinavian furniture in the second and third quarters of this century. Faced with the challenge of the Modernist industrial style, designers searched for historical precedents that manifested simple, functional forms. Two popular sources were vernacular furniture, including Shaker designs, Windsor chairs, and patent furniture, and Chinese furniture. Kaare Klint, one of the early leaders of this movement in Denmark, was very much attracted to eighteenth-century English design, especially Thomas Chippendale's *chinoiserie* chairs with Marlborough legs.

Wegner's *Y Chair* is the last in a series of five designs inspired by sixteenth- and seventeenth-century Chinese chairs.[170] In about 1940, Wegner had produced a prototypical armchair for Johannes Hansen loosely based on Chinese Chippendale forms: the chair featured a serpentine crest rail, curved splat, and upholstered seat. Wegner is alleged to have spent time in the local Århus library studying historical furniture during the war years, in particular between 1943 and 1944, with the virtual cessation of private work.[171] He designed three Chinese-inspired armchairs. The first model, produced for Fritz Hansen in 1943–44, took off from round-backed Chinese forms; it featured a continuous U-shaped arm and crest rail, curved splat, loose, tufted cushion, and no stretchers. Two other chairs that were variants on this initial design followed in 1944. The next year Wegner designed for Fritz Hansen a fourth model, with a beech frame and plaited sea grass seat (fig. 162); it had lost much of its historicizing detail and looked decidedly more Scandinavian.

With his characteristic tendency to refine a form continually, Wegner produced, five years later, yet another variation: the *Y Chair*. By this point, the design had become Wegner's own, with barely any trace of Chinese precedent discernible. He retained the continuous U-shaped arm and crest rail, but here kept it in one plane, paying equal homage to the famous Thonet model no. B9 armchair of about 1904 (fig. 196). A solid, more traditional splat has been replaced with a splayed, Y-shaped element. Most important, the rear stiles have been dramatically twisted forward in two dimensions, thus eliminating the need for a front post and at the same time achieving a bold, cantilevered armrest. The juncture of seat rails and stretchers to the legs shows Wegner's mastery of detailing and his ability to unite the decorative and the constructive. Tenons are exposed only on the front legs at the juncture of the seat rail and front stretcher, where they are more visible, thus providing a subtle ornamental detail. Likewise, an elegant play of line is developed between the canted seat rails and tapered stretchers on the two sides. In short, the *Y Chair* stands as one of Wegner's most accomplished integrations of historical form and traditional construction.   RCM

(opposite) *161. Hans Wegner.*
Y Chair: model no. CH-24

162. Wegner. Chinese armchair. 1945

Carl-Harry Stålhane

Vase
Designed c. 1948
Glazed stoneware; 7⁷⁄₁₆ × 5³⁄₁₆ × 5³⁄₁₆ inches
  (18 × 13.2 × 13.2 cm)
Produced by AB Rörstrands Porslinfabriker
  (Lidköping, Sweden), c. 1948–c. 1960
Scratched through slip on underside: [device of
  R surrounded by three crowns]/SWEDEN/CHS
D86.139.1, gift of Geoffrey N. Bradfield*

Western connoisseurs and potters alike have always found Oriental ceramics worthy of both admiration and imitation. Throughout the first half of the twentieth century, they were particularly attracted to wares with simple forms and monochromatic glazes (fig. 163), especially those of the Sung dynasty. Their purity of form, justness of proportions, and subtle nuances of color and texture satisfied the Modernists' desires. It is as self-revealing an interest as the eighteenth century's admiration for brightly decorated *kakiemon* wares and the Victorian preference for elaborate *satsuma*. Inevitably, each generation seeks out models appropriate to its own age.

It was often remarked that stoneware such as this vase by Stålhane had been deeply influenced by Swedish archaeological explorations of Chinese kiln sites in the 1930s and the collection of Chinese wares that had been brought back for King Gustav Adolf.[172] This may have been an important stimulus but, in fact, the tradition of looking to the East in just this manner had already become a part of Scandinavian tradition, beginning earlier in the century with the imitation of Japanese stoneware and Franco-Japanese pottery.

Moreover, a comparison of Stålhane's vase with the type of Chinese vessels he is supposed to have imitated reveals that there is much more interpretation than imitation. While the curved foot ring, globular body, narrow neck, and flared lip of Stålhane's vase are elements of Chinese ceramics, the pronounced cyma curves differ greatly from the gentler slopes of Chinese vessels. Stålhane's globular sphere is exaggeratedly wide for the small foot, and the neck is exaggeratedly thin in relation to the broad shoulders. The resultant fluency of line, of course, is typical of the

lyricism of postwar design. (Not surprisingly, Western versions of Oriental pottery dating from the 1930s tend to be more hard-edged, with more strongly demarcated transitions and the overall shapes of a more regular geometry.)

Stålhane's work, as well as that of Berndt Friberg at the Gustavsberg factory, typified the then current desire to find a "classical" statement of the potter's art. These simple forms and mat glazes, because of their understated nature, accorded well with reductivist principles and seemed to establish a universal standard of good taste. However, it was ultimately a short-lived goal, for by the end of the 1950s many of the potters, Stålhane included, had moved in more expressive directions. Stålhane turned to raku, aggressive forms, and bold calligraphy—still, ironically, under the spell of Oriental prototypes.[173]   ME

163. *Vase. Chinese, Sung dynasty, 10th century*

164. *Carl-Harry Stålhane. Vase*

Isamu Noguchi

Table lamp
Designed c. 1945
Cherrywood, fiberglass-reinforced polyvinyl
    chloride, and steel; 15¾ × 7 × 7 inches
    (40.4 × 17.8 × 17.8 cm)
Produced by Knoll Associates, Inc. (New
    York), c. 1945–at least 1954
Unmarked
D86.135.1

The roots of Isamu Noguchi's lighting designs lay in his "light sculptures" of the early 1940s—sculptures containing an internal light source. The notion of a sculpture producing its own light seems to have seized Noguchi's imagination when he realized that much of his work was being displayed not outdoors, as intended, but indoors. Noguchi was inevitably confronted with the displeasing sight of an artificial light illuminating his work. His response to this challenge was his series of *Lunars* (fig. 165):

> *I thought of a luminous object as a source of delight in itself—like fire it attracts and protects us from the beasts of the night. The self-contained luminous object was sculpture, so far as I was concerned, but I could arouse no interest in either critics or dealers.*[174]

He decided that "Lunars should be available to all," and proceeded to make a lamp for his sister, an aluminum cylinder with legs attached. He then tried variations in plastic and paper, which caught the interest of Hans Knoll, who agreed to

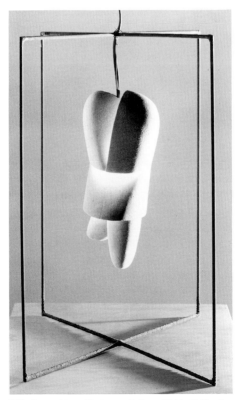

165. *Isamu Noguchi. Lunar Infant. 1944. Collection Isamu Noguchi Foundation, Inc., Long Island City, New York*

166. *Noguchi. Table lamp*

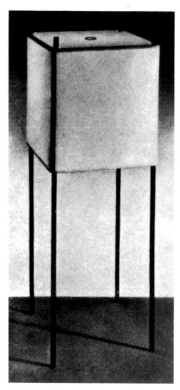

167. Noguchi. Table lamp. c. 1952

manufacture what Noguchi described as "a small version."[175]

The production version of Noguchi's small table lamp is an exercise in simplicity, elegance, and utility. The translucent plastic strip—which at first sight looks like paper—wrapped around the delicately shaped uprights turns the lamp into a luminescent object, mysterious and practical at the same time. The design eschews the Western convention of a lamp base with attached shade and instead refers to the Japanese tradition of paper lanterns. What makes this lamp so exceptional is the complete integration of shade and base, a notion that Noguchi expanded on in his lamps of the 1950s (fig. 167).

Noguchi's table lamp was so well received and so utterly simple in design that cheaper imitations started appearing at once, causing Knoll eventually to cease production. More than forty years after its first production, and after hundreds of lamp designs conceived in similarly abstract terms (including those by Noguchi), we are likely to underestimate the originality and inventiveness of this design.   CW

168. Japanese woodblock print illustrating a variety of Japanese lanterns

Isamu Noguchi

Floor lamp; shade: model *H*
Shade designed c. 1954,[176] base designed 1962
Mulberry-bark paper, bamboo, cast iron, and
    steel; 74½ × 22½ × 22½ inches (191 ×
    57.7 × 57.7 cm)
Produced by Ozeki & Co. (Gifu, Japan), for
    Akari Associates (Long Island City, New
    York), 1962–c. 1966
Impressed in ballast box: GENERAL [device of
    GE within a circle] ELECTRIC/[device of UL
    within a circle] RAPID START BALLAST/CAT.
    6G1070/SA/FOR ONE 40 WATT/RS LAMP/
    SOUND RATED A/120 VOLTS 70 AMP 60 CY./
    DANVILLE, ILL. MADE IN U.S.A. VV./
    [remainder of text deleted due to length]
D86.245.1

In 1951 Isamu Noguchi traveled to Japan, where his interest in light sculptures found resonance in the Japanese tradition of folding paper lanterns, specifically the *chochin* lanterns of Gifu, which were constructed of a framework made from a single, spiraling length of bamboo covered with paper (fig. 168). He had been invited to Gifu by the city's mayor, who apparently hoped that Noguchi could bring renewed vitality to the important local craft.[177] The traditional *chochins* were unornamented and diffused candlelight; however, in recent times they had become covered with common painted scenes and were brought out only on festive occasions.

Inspired by their beauty, Noguchi banished the degrading decoration and adapted them to electric light for daily use. His first paper lanterns, designed his very first night in Gifu, reflected the shape of the new light source (fig. 169).

> . . . I think that candles are more humanly attractive than electric lights; but there must be change, without which lanterns too must go, whatever their sentimental appeal. And to survive only as festive decorations is to deny lanterns a very real part of their intrinsic beauty, as well as their honorable tradition as a source of light.[178]

Like the *chochin*, Noguchi's lamps were designed to be collapsible, packed in flat envelopes or, with their thin, rodlike bases, in boxes. Although the mulberry-bark paper *(mino)* he chose for the material was finer than that used in the traditional lanterns, it still allowed for easy collapsibility. The packaging was ingeniously simple and typically Japanese.

He called his new paper lanterns *Akari*, which, he explained,

> . . . in Japanese means light as illumination just as our word light does. It also suggests lightness as opposed to weight. The ideograph combines that of the sun and moon. The ideal of akari is therein exemplified with lightness (as essence), and light (for awareness). The quality is poetic, ephemeral, and tentative.[179]

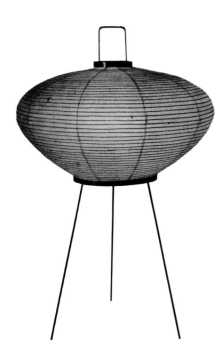

(below) *169. Isamu Noguchi. Lamp. 1951*

(right) *170. Noguchi. Floor lamp*

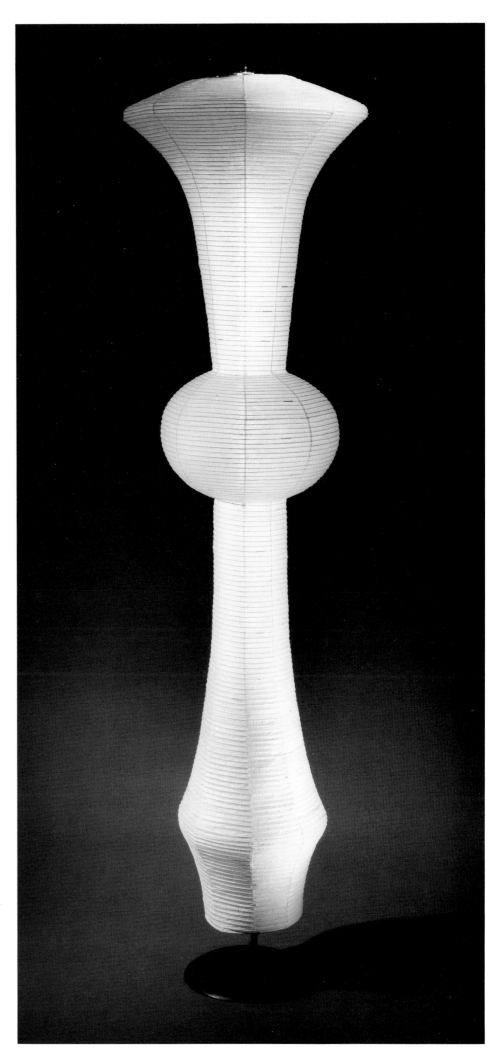

Noguchi continued to design *Akaris* for at least another twenty-five years, creating shades more complicated and angular and introducing notes of both playfulness and complexity.[180]

In 1962 Noguchi introduced fluorescent tubes as the source of light and created a new type of standing lamp by using flat metal bases and metal rods to carry the shade. A fluorescent tube gave off a more diffused light than a small incandescent bulb, eliminating the noticeably bright "hot spot" that incandescent bulbs always created. However, Noguchi felt that the fluorescent bulbs were too bright, and as dimmers for such fixtures were not available, the fluorescent base units were dropped from the line during the 1960s.

Noguchi constantly refined and developed the *Akari*, not only because of its sculptural possibilities but also because he was haunted by cheap imitations. He felt that by innovating continually he would leave the imitators behind. The marketplace, he observed, "is based on standardization. Stores do not want continual change."[181] In 1969 he introduced thirty new designs as signed, more expensive, limited editions.

In his *Akari* lamps Noguchi achieved his ideal of creating floating luminescent sculptures out of a venerable craft tradition. They are virtuoso examples of art as design, as well as reminders of the powerful sway that Japanese traditions have held for Western, and specifically Modernist, design during the last century.   CW

Friedl Holzer-Kjellberg

Bowl: model no. FK/5, decoration:
  Kukka (Flower)
Designed c. 1942[182]
Glazed porcelain; $3^{7}/_{16} \times 6^{1}/_{8} \times 6^{1}/_{8}$ inches
  (8.7 × 15.5 × 15.5 cm)
Produced by Arabia (Helsinki), c. 1942–74
Incised on underside: ARABIA/-FHKJ-/MADE/IN/
FINLAND
D87.178.1

Vase: model no. FK/10, decoration:
  Oksa (Branch)
Designed c. 1942
Glazed porcelain; $6^{5}/_{8} \times 6^{1}/_{4} \times 6^{1}/_{8}$ inches
  (16.8 × 15.8 × 15.5 cm)
Produced by Arabia (Helsinki), c. 1942–74
Incised on underside: ARABIA/F.H.K./ 7 [?]
D87.177.1

In the 1930s, simple Chinese porcelain and stoneware bowls were singled out for their purity of form and their truthfulness to materials. Friedl Kjellberg herself made such bowls (fig. 172), and they fit directly into that particular branch of Modernism that saw itself as the inheritor of "eternal forms" from both the East and West.[183]

During the war years, she perforated the walls of some porcelain bowls, still in emulation of Chinese models, with small lozengelike incisions that resemble grains of rice—hence the name "rice grain porcelain." This technique had originated in China in the eighteenth century and was a staple of commercial export ware by the twentieth century.[184] The Chinese had exploited it to produce some tour-de-force examples, but the most common form, known from import shops and restaurants, has simple rows of openings.

Some of Kjellberg's designs were geometric, but for the greater part she chose patterns suggestive of flowers and leaves. The patterns correspond in many ways to the lighthearted, naive designs that became so much a part of the Scandinavian textile industry as well. Despite the historic references, Kjellberg fashioned a work responsive to modern taste. She endowed the vase with a fluency of movement, clearly visible in the curving pattern of leaves, and also present on the bowl in the way that the small flower heads are staggered, with a greater concentration at the bottom and wider

171. *Friedl Holzer-Kjellberg. Bowl and vase: model nos. FK/5 and FK/10*

spacing near the top. Another modern characteristic is the way in which she paddled the vase from a symmetrical circular form into a rectangular one with rounded corners.

In the postwar years, when Finland's trade with the West was resumed, the Finnish used their ceramic and glass industries to generate badly needed cash. Kjellberg's rice grain porcelains found great commercial favor because of their charm and delicacy (as well as their conservatism). Thus, a special department was set up in the Arabia factory, with Kjellberg in charge. Typical of the Scandinavian approach to crafts, the work, while produced in a factory, continued to be done by hand.   ME

172. Holzer-Kjellberg. Porcelain bowl and vase. c. 1939

Bernard Leach

Vase
Designed c. 1931 and executed c. 1962
Glazed stoneware; 15⅜ × 6⁵⁄₁₆ × 6⁵⁄₁₆ inches
    (39 × 16 × 16 cm)
Impressed on lower side in a vertical column:
    [obscured circular mark of reversed s with
    horizontal cross bar and two diagonally
    posed dots] [obscured rectangular mark of
    B . . .] [obscured horizontal rectangular
    mark]
D84.169.1, gift of Jay Spectre*

In trying to bridge the gap between Eastern and Western cultures and in promoting handicraft in an industrial age, Bernard Leach set himself herculean tasks. Yet his goals were not uncommon ones in the early twentieth century, and they were especially appropriate to English culture, whose colonial interests helped to focus attention on Eastern civilization and which cultivated an Anglo-Japanese aesthetic.

This vase with its carp and banded lines is a late descendant of a model Leach established first about 1931 (fig. 173). He regarded it as a favorite and repeated it many times over in his long career. Like Eastern potters, he emphasized repetition, as can be seen in looking over his immense personal oeuvre, which the potter himself estimated to be over one hundred thousand pieces. One soon realizes that he used a comparatively small range of models with frequent repetition and minor variations.

While Leach proclaimed a goal of bridging Eastern and Western culture, he succumbed almost entirely to the former. The motif of the joyful, leaping carp and the rapidly brushed calligraphy are decidedly Eastern. The form of the bottle vase also owes more to the East than the West. The ash glaze he used is based on a formula from a Chinese manual that he had had translated when he first studied in Japan. The climbing kiln in which he fired his wares was Eastern and, in fact, had been built by Japanese colleagues. Though the clay was from a local source, the ash glaze was made with local bracken, and the fuel was gathered locally, the result displays very little of Cornwall or an English tradition.

Yet one cannot stress sufficiently the importance that Leach's work had in the development of Western ceramics, especially after World War II. Leach's influence was inescapable. His *Potter's Book*, first published in 1940, and *A Potter's Portfolio* of 1951 provided not only practical information but also the spiritual and philosophical basis for his art. Leach traveled and lectured extensively, and he and his British students taught many of the next generation of potters.

Vessels such as the one in the Stewart Collection became icons of devotion and emulation for other potters—at least through the 1950s and into the 1960s. Since then, times and taste have changed, and Leach's conservatism and his strong Eastern aesthetic have been seriously challenged and even repudiated.[185] But for many decades it represented modern good taste.

ME

173. Bernard Leach. Vase. c. 1931. Victoria and Albert Museum, London

174. Leach. Vase

175. *Gertrud Vasegaard. Tea service*

Gertrud Vasegaard

Tea service
Designed 1955–57
Glazed porcelain and bamboo; teapot:
  8⅛ × 6¼ × 4⅜ inches (20.6 × 15.9 × 11.1 cm)
Produced by Bing & Grøndahl (Copenhagen),
  c. 1957–87
Teapot, printed in blue on underside:
  COPENHAGEN PORCELAIN MADE IN DENMARK
  [encircling device of a three-turreted
  building]/B&G/654/[monogram of
  G inside U]
Saucer, printed in blue on underside: [device
  of a three-turreted building]/B&G/
  KJOBENHAVN/DENMARK/[monogram of
  G inside U]
Cup, printed in blue on underside:
  COPENHAGEN PORCELAIN BING & GRONDAHL
  [encircling device of a three-turreted
  building]/B&G/DENMARK/473/[monogram of
  G inside U]
Cake plate, printed in blue on underside:
  COPENHAGEN PORCELAIN MADE IN DENMARK
  [encircling device of a three-turreted
  building]/B&G/304/[monogram of
  G inside U]
D89.105.1–4, gift of Royal Copenhagen/Bing
  & Grøndahl

In the realm of functional ceramics, the teapot often stands as a paradigm of culture. It can be as emblematic of taste as the chair. It offers a balance between the restrictions imposed through functional requirements and the freedom allowed for artistic exploration. Its requirements are simple: a vessel of specific volume, openings for filling and pouring, and a handle. Each era has come up with breathtakingly wonderful design solutions. One need only think of the Suprematist design of Kazimir Malevich, the Bauhaus variations of Theodore Bogler, or the recent fantasies of Dorothy Hafner to recognize the wide range of possibilities.

In the middle of this century there was a resurgence of interest in the design of teapots. They became the hallmark and economic mainstay of many serious studio potters, as is witnessed by the output of Lucie Rie in England and the Scheiers in the United States. Remarkably, these works do not seem as distinctive as those other examples mentioned above. But these midcentury examples share an underlying unity among themselves in their reliance on ideas borrowed from Chinese and Japanese models in terms of form, material, and color.

It is in this light that we should approach Gertrud Vasegaard's tea service for Bing & Grøndahl. The hexagonal shape of the teapot and its bamboo handle are openly derived from a standard Chinese type. The Orientalizing quality can also be discerned in the handleless, broad cup. It was suggested at the time that the outturned rim allowed the cup to be held by the fingers, and the cups were made large so that they would not have to be completely filled, thus avoiding the finger hold.[186] A muted gray glaze and a stain of iron oxide at the edges also contributed to the Orientalizing style.[187]

In its day, Vasegaard's tea service was highly acclaimed. It was awarded a gold medal at the Milan XI Triennale in 1957 and has been consistently selected to represent modern Scandinavian design.[188] This is perhaps ironic for a design that, at least in terms of Western art of the last hundred years, is without overt personality and that betrays little of its designer. In fact, it might even be misclassified as non-Western. Yet it is just these very features that tell us much about postwar culture and the standards of Good Design. Good Design implied a median position that generally denied personality. It demanded refinement of contour and volume, crispness of edge, and subtlety of color. It was produced industrially and thus was cost-conscious. It responded to the demands of a conservative, intellectual elite whose consumerism was geared to this Eastern aesthetic of understated elegance and tranquillity.   ME

Jens Quistgaard

Ice bucket
Designed before 1958[189]
Teak and plastic; 15¼ × 7½ × 7½ inches
  (38.5 × 19 × 19 cm)[190]
Produced by Dansk International Designs Ltd.
  (Mount Kisco, New York), before 1958–73;
  1983 to the present (this example c. 1970)
Branded on underside: [device of a mature
  duck/a wave/two ducklings/a wave/a
  duckling/a wave]/DANSK DESIGNS/DENMARK/
  I H Q/©
D87.184.1, gift of Geoffrey N. Bradfield*

This ice bucket, typical of the fluid, sculptural approach that characterizes the work of Quistgaard, is one of his most popular designs for the Dansk firm. Considered one of the company's premier designers, Quistgaard has worked for the enterprise since its founding in 1954.

Like other Dansk craftsmen/designers, Quistgaard is steeped in the craft tradition of Scandinavia. Wood carving was one of the first craft disciplines he learned, probably from his sculptor father. The ice bucket's staved construction owes its inspiration to his study of the wooden hulls of Viking ships[191] and shows the designer's organic sense of form as well as his respect for the material. "I like my work to flow," he acknowledged.[192] This ice bucket also recalls Japanese ceramic prototypes in its overall shape and the handle that bridges the bucket's all-in-one construction (fig. 176).

For all its derivation from traditional forms and construction, the bucket relies on modern technology—a plastic liner on the interior—to make it truly functional.

FTH

176. Vessel. Japanese, 18–19th century.
Rijksmuseum, Amsterdam

177. Jens Quistgaard. Ice bucket

Ercole Barovier

Plaque
Designed c. 1958
Glass; 14⅜ × 14⅜ inches (36 × 36 cm)
Produced by Barovier & Toso (Murano,
    Italy), c. 1958–60
Engraved around pontil: Barovier/&
    Toso/Murano
D83.132.1

In the 1950s the ever-inventive Murano glass workshops began producing a new type of glass called *pezzato* (pieced). It was made by slicing and flattening canes of glass, assembling them side by side, and fusing them onto a gather of hot, clear glass. From this material bowls, vases, and plaques were made.

When these works were first exhibited, especially by Venini in 1951 at the Milan IX Triennale, they were greeted with enthusiasm, and their novel technique was praised. In fact, *pezzato* was one of the many Murano innovations that were derived from studies of older glass. The basic technique of piecing can be seen in Roman examples, such as a coupe made in the first century A.D. (fig. 179). In the late nineteenth century, a period concerned with historic revivalism, the important Venetian glassblower Antonio Salviati was stimulated to revive this technique (fig. 180).[193] A half-century later, in the late 1920s and 1930s, the firms of Barovier & Toso and Venini created bowls and vases formed from fused canes in imitation of ancient Roman glass.[194] These can be seen as important forerunners of the postwar work in *pezzato*. Indeed, one small bowl made by Ercole Barovier in 1942 can be seen as a transition to the *pezzato* work.[195]

In contrast to the Venini firm's rather flamboyant vessels employing this technique (figs. 283, 284), Barovier & Toso took a more conservative approach.[196] It chose relatively plain cylinders or restrained classical balusters as vessel forms and employed the *pezzato* technique in an equally controlled manner, often using a pattern that imitated a basket weave, like that used by Salviati three-quarters of a century earlier. In 1958 it introduced a variant called *a spina* (spinelike), in which the sections were laid in a type of herringbone pattern.[197] Occasionally, as in this plaque, the cane sections were manipulated as curving arcs to create a charming starlike or flowerlike configuration. Even Barovier & Toso's range of colors was muted—pale browns, yellows, purples—and looks very restrained in comparison with Venini's intensely bright palette. Yet the conservative nature of this work did not detract from its critical success and popularity— quite the contrary. Through the next decades, Barovier & Toso continued to produce modern variants on this millennium-old process.

ME

178. Ercole Barovier. Plaque

179. Footed bowl. Alexandrian, 1st century A.D. *Victoria and Albert Museum, London*

180. Antonio Salviati. Bowl. c. 1880. *Trustees of The National Museums of Scotland*

Archimede Seguso

Footed bowl
Designed c. 1949–50
Glass; 5¾ × 8⅞ × 8⅞ inches (14.7 × 22.7 × 22.7 cm)
Produced by Vetreria Archimede Seguso S.a.S. (Murano, Italy), c. 1950
Unmarked
D82.116.1

Given its formal balance and harmony of proportions—its classic sense of beauty—it is easy to understand why this coupe was so frequently cited in publications dealing with Good Design and modern glass, and why it was selected for "Italy at Work," a traveling exhibition that circulated through the United States in 1950 to promote postwar trade and Italy's "renaissance in design."[198]

At the heart of Seguso's design is a centuries-old tradition of Venetian glassblowing, a tradition that, decade after decade, keeps offering ideas to be revived and reinterpreted. The form of this footed bowl and of the other vessels in the series (fig. 181) recalls the honored examples of Venetian Renaissance and Baroque glassblowing (fig. 182). The technique used, *vetro a reticello* (glass with a small network), also pays homage to the past.[199] An internal decoration of delicate filaments of white glass that are crossed in a diamond pattern, it is one of the variations of the centuries-old latticino work in which Venice specialized. In accordance with custom, in both Seguso's work and the sixteenth-century example, the finesse of technique is emphasized by the placement of a trapped air bubble at the center of each diamond-shaped field.

As retrospective as Seguso's work may be, it presents a selective, modern interpretation, eliminating the elaborate knops and fussy handles that had become the trademark of *façon de Venise* ware, which then dominated the tourist market. The simplicity of Seguso's contours and the large volumes of his vessels contribute to a sparse, elegant Modernism. In this sense, Seguso's work recalls an earlier stage in the "renaissance in design": in the mid-1920s Paolo Venini and Giacomo Cappelin produced glassware whose forms were derived from vessels depicted in Old Master paintings by Titian, Veronese, Holbein, and Caravaggio, among others (fig. 183). Those objects were highly touted in their day for their purity of form and their purgative effect on the Venetian glass industry, both when they were first introduced and later in the postwar years.

It is often overlooked that the Venini firm continued making the Old Master forms (*soffiati classici*) in the postwar years, at the same time that it was executing bolder, more innovative pieces.[200] The stylistic range of Seguso's output was more restricted, since he specialized in the filligraine technique and preferred symmetrical forms, but even he occasionally proved susceptible to the charms of the tapered asymmetrical shapes that became popular in the 1950s. Conservatism and Modernism could be juxtaposed or harmonized, but both remained viable currents.

ME

181. Archimede Seguso. Vases and bowls. c. 1949–50

182. Footed bowl. Venetian, 16th century. Seattle Art Museum. Gift of Mrs. John C. Atwood, Jr.

183. Vittorio Zecchin. Soffiati classici *vases.* 1921–24

184. Seguso. Footed bowl

Gio Ponti

Side chair: model no. 699, *Superleggera*
Designed 1955[201]
Ash, rush, and steel glides; 32⅝ × 15⅞ ×
 17⁷⁄₁₆ inches (82.6 × 40.3 × 44.3 cm)
Produced by Figli di Amedeo Cassina (Meda,
 Italy), 1957–at least 1978[202]
Unmarked
D83.115.1

185. *Chiavari chairs illustrated in* Domus, *1948*

Ponti's chair, the *Superleggera* (extralight), is important as a Modernist updating of a traditional kind of light wooden chair made in the fishing village of Chiavari, one version of which was called the *Leggera*. Photographs of various versions of these chairs had appeared in *Domus*, Ponti's own magazine, in the years preceding Ponti's version (fig. 185). He even had praised the lightness of several older Chiavari models on the very same page that he published two modern Scandinavian chairs, one by Finn Juhl.[203]

As simple as the *Superleggera* chair may be, it took several steps to develop. In 1949 Ponti designed a side chair that, in its simplicity and light weight, followed in the Chiavari tradition (fig. 186) but that was definitely modern in the use of pale wood, the way the back is bent to fit the curve of the spine, and the triangular flaring of the legs. A variation of this chair was made by Cassina around 1951 (model 601).[204]

In 1951, Ponti designed another chair for Cassina (model 646), for the Milan IX Triennale (fig. 187). In this model, he hovered between the modern and the vernacular tradition, by combining the modern bent back of his earlier design with the traditional lines of a Chiavari chair and also by using a seat of green, blue, or yellow cellophane woven as if it were traditional rush. The result is a chair of classic simplicity with modern elegance.

Ponti described it thus:

A chair-chair, modestly, without adjectives . . . (rational chair, "modern" chair, prefabricated chair, organic chair and so on). . . . It must be light, slim and convenient. . . . this modest and reliable chair,

this Cinderella chair . . . has been progressively admitted . . . as the true "traditional chair. . . ."[205]

In 1955 Ponti designed a new version of the chair: the *Superleggera*.[206] This version is two centimeters narrower and shallower than the original, and its legs are slightly thinner. Ponti wrote that in designing this chair he had

followed the perennial process of technology, which moves from heavy to light. Look at the triangular section of the legs—inert material and weight have been removed, identifying, wisely and without virtuosity, "the limits" of the structural form, while keeping the usefulness and "exact solidity."[207]

This version was shown at the XI Triennale in 1957 and won a Compasso d'Oro prize that same year.[208]

By 1967, Ponti's model 646 and *Superleggera* chairs were available in natural ash, aniline-stained, ebonized, or lacquered and came with a choice of cellophane, woven cane, or upholstered foam-rubber seats.[209] Those versions with a lacquer finish and rush seats look traditional, very much like the Chiavari prototype, while those with a light-colored ash frame and colored cellophane seat have a more modern appearance. All the models were extremely popular, because their lightness made them versatile and especially suitable for small postwar apartments, where space was at a premium.[210]

CWL

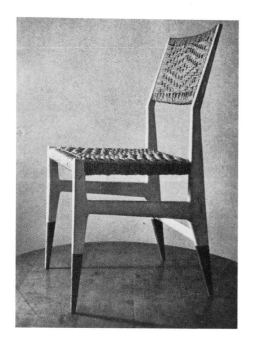

(far left) 186. *Gio Ponti. Side chair. 1949*

(left) 187. *Ponti. Side chair: model no. 646. c. 1951*

188. Ponti. Superleggera *side chair: model no. 699*

189. Hans Bellmann. Table

Hans Bellmann

Table
Designed c. 1945
Painted ash, painted birch-faced plywood, and
    steel; 20 × 23¾ × 23¾ inches (50.8 × 60.3 ×
    60.3 cm)
Produced by Hans G. Knoll Furniture Company
    (later Knoll Associates, Inc.) (New York),
    1946–after 1959
Unmarked
D85.114.1

The postwar search for functional and inexpensive furniture often led to archetypal concepts. The Swiss architect Hans Bellmann turned to the idea of a tripod table. Folding stools and collapsible tripod tables were commonly found in ancient Greek and Roman domestic interiors and in turn served as models for military campaign furniture throughout history. Also, light, portable furniture of simple design has always been a feature of African nomadic life.

Bellmann's table has a striking simplicity, achieved with an extreme economy of design. Its knockdown design features three tapered birch legs converging at a central fulcrum and held together by a metal screw. The legs impale the perimeter of a round birch plywood top at the points of an equilateral triangle. By relying on elegance of proportion and fluidity of line that is undisturbed by ornamentation, Bellmann improved on an ancient design to create a modern classic.

Attesting to the flexibility and popularity of Bellmann's design, the table was produced in three sizes.[211] This example is the smallest; the others measure 22 by 36 inches and 28 by 48 inches. The plywood top was painted white, while the legs were available either ebonized, as in this example, or in a natural finish.

FTH

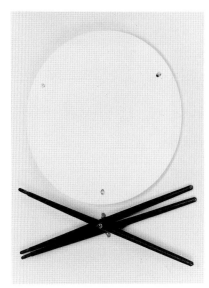

190. Bellmann. Table disassembled

Franco Albini

Armchair: *Margherita*
Designed 1950[212]
Malacca and Indian cane, viscose rayon, and
    foam rubber; 39 × 31 × 31 inches (99.1 ×
    78.8 × 78.8 cm)
Produced by Vittorio Bonacina & C. (Lurago
    d'Erba, Italy), 1951 to the present
Unmarked
D84.177.1, gift of Jay Spectre*

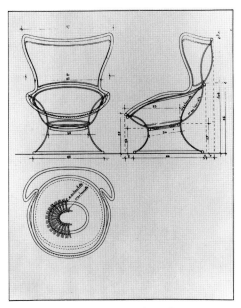

191. *Franco Albini. Drawing of* Margherita
armchair. c. 1950

192. *Albini*. Margherita armchair

193. *Albini. Suspended staircase at Villa Neuffer, Ispra, Italy. 1940*

The chair is atypical of Albini's work in terms of its material, shape, and structure. Although he designed several other rattan pieces, he generally preferred wood, metal, and glass. Most of Albini's furniture from the 1930s through the 1950s is spartan and rationalist. Much of it, like the *Luisa* chair of 1955 (designed with Franca Helg), has stark, angular lines. According to Vittorio Bonacina, Albini first designed the *Margherita* with a square seat.[216] However, the version that went into production has a circular geometry, with full circles for the pedestal and curves of the back and seat. For all the geometric quality of this design, the chair is named after the daisy, the cushion forming a center and the loops of cane serving as petals.

Whereas Albini's other chair designs have a four-legged frame separated from the seat and the back, the structure of the *Margherita* resembles a suspension bridge with a roadway hung from cables. The seat is both supported from below and suspended from above by the crossed pieces of cane (fig. 191). The shapes and the construction here, both modern elements, derive from Albini's architecture, for one of his specialties was the use of open spiral stairs supported from below and suspended from above (fig. 193).

Initially unpopular, the chair eventually made the manufacturer's fortune. Although it was designed for a terrace, it usually was placed indoors, and over the next decade a number of architects selected the chair to provide a circular note in their rectilinear interiors.[217]

CWL

The *Margherita* armchair was designed for the La Rinascente store's exhibit at the Milan IX Triennale in 1951, where it won a gold medal.[213] Since it was made for a terrace in the La Rinascente model home, Albini used rattan, a traditional material for garden furniture.[214] This turn to vernacular materials was common right after World War II, when Italy was struggling to rebuild its manufacturing capability. Throughout Europe at this time, manufactured materials were expensive, while labor was cheap. So Italian furniture makers turned to traditional materials to make light furniture, largely by hand. In fact, Albini originally designed this chair with only very thin cane before discovering that thicker elements were necessary to provide enough support.[215] Nearly forty years later, the *Margherita* chair is still mostly handmade.

Hans Wegner

Armchair: model no. J.H. 500
Designed 1947
Lacquered ash, teak, and Kraft manila paper twine; 42½ × 30 × 28¼ inches (107.9 × 76.3 × 71.7 cm)
Produced by Johannes Hansen (Copenhagen), 1948 to the present
Branded on underside of seat: JOHANNES HANSEN/COPENHAGEN/[conjoined initials H and J]
D88.137.1

The *Peacock* chair, as it is widely known,[218] was one of the first of Hans Wegner's great chairs. An updated version of an early-nineteenth-century hoop-back Windsor chair (fig. 195), it was designed at a time when Danish designers were using earlier, vernacular furniture as models. Wegner himself had already designed several chairs that looked to the past, including a version of an English Chippendale chair and a series of *Chinese* chairs (fig. 162). Many years later he wrote that during the 1940s

> . . . the architects built on and were inspired by the experiences and traditions of the past; they did not want to copy specific styles, but

194. Hans Wegner. Armchair: model no. J.H. 500

195. Windsor chair. English, c. 1800. Wycombe Chair Museum, Wycombe, England

on the other hand, they thought it would be absurd not to learn from what had existed for generations. Many younger architects were especially attracted to the simple rusticity of Danish furniture, to the structural elegance of Windsor chairs, to the honest and restrained expression of Shaker chairs, and to the brilliance of Thonet's bentwood chairs from the middle of the last century.[219]

Wegner says that his idea was to make a new interpretation of the Windsor chair, one with a back that would be more comfortable to lean against than the round sticks of the originals.[220] He took the simple lines and "structural ele-gance" of the Windsor chair and exaggerated them rhythmically. The back of his chair rises dramatically in a forceful curve that is both higher and wider than that on the vernacular originals. The top rail, sharing the rounded quality found in Wegner's *Chinese* chair, extends further forward than in the Windsor chair, swooping down and around on both sides to meet the seat rail halfway along the sides. Wegner also flattened sections of the spindles for the sitter to rest against. These flat areas are lined up in a swelling curve that echoes that of the top rail. They resemble the eyes of a spread peacock's tail, hence the chair's nickname *Peacock*.[221]

The first example of this chair was built for the Copenhagen Cabinetmakers' Guild exhibition in 1947. The sketching process and the building of the first model took place simultaneously. But the final drawings for construction had not been completed when the only existing model was sold by mistake at an exhibition in the Netherlands. Without the model, it took another year to finish the final drawings, so that the chair was not put into production until 1948.[222] Once introduced, it proved to be a popular design; for example, it was used in the Delegates Lounge at the United Nations Building in New York in 1948.

CWL

George Nelson Associates

Armchair
Designed 1952
Laminated birch, wool upholstery, and cotton
   batting[223]; 31¼ × 23⁷⁄₁₆ × 19³⁄₁₆ inches
   (79.4 × 59.6 × 48.7 cm)
Produced by Herman Miller Furniture Co.
   (Zeeland, Michigan), c. 1955–c. 1960
Unmarked
D84.174.1, gift of George Nelson

George Nelson has stated that the genesis of this design lay in his desire to produce an exceptionally strong and light chair in the tradition of Gio Ponti's *Leggera* chair (figs. 186, 187): "something you could lift with two fingers."[224] Nelson settled on laminated wood as the appropriate material and curvilinear, rather than rectilinear, design as the appropriate formal vocabulary. It

was then John Pile, head of furniture design in the Nelson office, who produced the sketch that determined the chair's appearance.[225]

The Nelson firm's chair belongs to the modern tradition of bent and molded laminated furniture. Its overall form clearly derives from the Thonet company's famous bentwood armchair, model no. B9 (fig. 196), a chair designed around 1904 that gained new popularity when it was used extensively by Le Corbusier during the 1920s. The use of laminated rather than solid bentwood and the treatment of the material in the Nelson chair owe a considerable debt to Alvar Aalto's well-known and influential laminated furniture of the 1930s as well as that of Charles and Ray Eames of the 1940s.

Yet, while belonging to that recent tradition of laminated furniture, the Nelson chair, with its

attention to detail and proportion, especially its subtle handling of the laminates, has an identity all its own. A single piece forms the arms and back curves, bending like a solid ribbon filled with air. None of the lengths of wood are of a uniform width or depth from one end to the other; their fluctuations of size seem to represent the various degrees of structural support they offer. The seat and back sections are perched on delicate legs that gently bend and taper to narrow, thin points. The inner laminates of these legs (and of the uprights that rise from the seat to support the back) are of a dark color and are sandwiched between matching lighter-colored veneers. Even these dark interior veneers taper from fat to thin, echoing the overall shape of the leg.

Although the Nelson firm produced a design of remarkable lightness and fluidity of line, the Her-

*196. Gebrüder Thonet. Armchair: model
no. B9. c. 1904*

197. George Nelson Associates. Armchair

man Miller Furniture Company, with whom Nelson had a close working relationship, was unable to manufacture a satisfactory version of the chair. The present chair is probably one of twelve prototypes that were produced. The very element that gave the chair its exceptionally delicate form—the thin, laminated members—rendered the chair too difficult to produce economically in a factory setting and insufficiently strong to support long-term use. The Miller company attempted to subcontract manufacture to the Plycraft Company of Lawrence, Massachusetts. Although production and marketing lasted only briefly, Plycraft itself eventually sold a version of the chair redesigned by Norman Cherner in 1958. That version, with a single-piece seat and back, bears little resemblance to the original. Much closer to the Nelson design, but sapped of the original's lightness of form and careful detailing, is a version introduced by the ICF firm of Italy in 1986.

The Nelson chair presents the historian with a problem that surfaces time and again in the history of functional design: how do we reconcile the obvious aesthetic merit of an object with its failure as a practical industrial product? Can we praise a form that does not achieve its goal, to be affordably mass-produced? When a chair is a unique or limited-production piece without pretension to large-scale manufacture, this is not an issue. The answer to reconciling the contradiction may be merely that there are occasions when the aesthetic or technical solutions offered in a finished product are so impressive that we admire and even extol a design despite its practical failure.   CW

198. Richard Riemerschmid. Music room, "Deutsche Kunstaustellung Dresden," 1899

Edward J. Wormley

Armchair: model no. 4797, *Riemerschmid*
Designed c. 1946
Mahogany, rayon, linen, and wool
    reupholstery;[226] 30⅞ × 22⅞ × 22¼ inches
    (78.5 × 58 × 56.5 cm)
Produced by the Dunbar Furniture
    Corporation of Indiana (Berne, Indiana),
    1947–81 (this example 1947)[227]
In pencil on underside of seat: 4797/24244#
    105/Dunbar L.A./Batten Side/#2#2
D82.107.1, gift of Edward J. Wormley

This armchair is an interpretation of a much publicized chair by Richard Riemerschmid that the German architect placed in the music room he designed for the "Deutsche Kunstausstelung Dresden" of 1899 (fig. 198). Wormley saw an illustration of the Dresden music room in a magazine and found it interesting that a chair designed fifty years earlier still lent itself so well to contemporary design.[228] The simplicity of the design and the strong thrust of the rear stiles supporting the back were particularly appealing aspects. Wormley's admiration for the Riemerschmid chair was shared by his friend Edgar Kaufmann, jr., who praised the chair's "exceptionally graceful, strong triangular bracing" and noted that the "modulated shapes of this chair are not unlike those used half a century later, by Juhl. . . ."[229]

143

Wormley had only a poor photograph of Riemerschmid's chair for reference, and his differs from the prototype in several aspects: its simplification, the elimination of Riemerschmid's carved ornament, the tapering of the front legs, and its altered proportions, with a higher placement of the seat. After learning that the turn-of-the-century designer was still alive, Wormley wrote to him. Riemerschmid sent the original sketch of the Dresden chair, and the Dunbar company offered him financial remuneration for using both his design and his name.[230]

The new chair represented a softening of the current geometry of Modernism, a trend that had begun even earlier, in 1937, when a visit to Sweden had inspired Wormley to create a new line of "Swedish Modern" for Dunbar.[231] Before that, Wormley became interested in American turn-of-the-century design through the influence of Edgar Kaufmann, jr., who had begun collecting the work of Louis Comfort Tiffany. After the war, Wormley used Tiffany's iridescent glass tiles in one line of furniture designs and incorporated Tiffany lamps and vases in his interiors.[232] Likewise, when Wormley traveled to California in 1939, he saw turn-of-the-century houses designed by Greene and Greene. He later adapted their furniture for his 1957 *Janus* line, maintaining that good design from the past was suitable for and could be successfully adapted to a contemporary market. Indeed, the *Riemerschmid* chair was among Dunbar's best-selling designs.

DAH

199. *Edward J. Wormley. Riemerschmid armchair: model no. 4797*

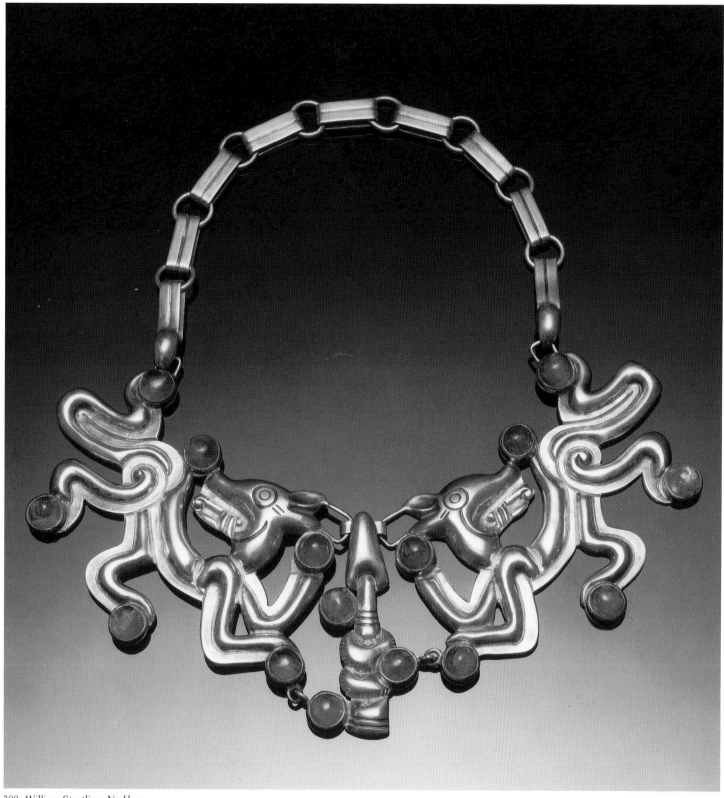

200. *William Spratling. Necklace*

William Spratling

Necklace

Designed and executed c. 1940[233]

Silver and amethyst; 3½ × 8 inches
　(8.9 × 20.3 cm)

Impressed on reverse of left dog's paws:
　[in oval] SPRATLING/SILVER [in circle]
　SPRATLING/[monogram of WS in
　center]/MADE IN MEXICO

D88.182.1, gift of Vivian and David M.
　Campbell

This necklace by William Spratling typifies the ethnic revivalism of the 1940s. Many of Spratling's early designs, like this necklace, were inspired by the archaeological artifacts he collected. Among his interests were masks and pre-Columbian clay stamps (fig. 201), all enriched with animal motifs that once held religious significance for the Aztec and Mayan Indians of Mexico.

Spratling was a well-educated American architect who possessed a sophisticated sense of design and was influenced by the prevailing Modernist vocabulary. This necklace, in fact, is a cunning combination of tribal and modern styles. The animals are certainly Indian in imagery yet possess a decidedly ordered silhouette. The overall effect is a mannered, rhythmic study, appearing more as the asymmetric arrangement of strong, curvilinear lines than the spontaneously naive rendering of animals that is evident in the clay seals.

Spratling's jewelry was truly innovative within the cultural milieu of Mexico. It seems strongly ethnic in flavor—especially when compared to Modernist geometric or Biomorphic designs from Berlin, Paris, or New York—yet this appearance is misleading. Spratling's silver and amethyst necklace is without precedent in pre-Columbian jewelry, which was almost always fabricated from gold and was sometimes decorated with paint or flat mosaics of turquoise or shell rather than single, bezel-set stones. Spratling's work is also at a far remove from another local and ethnic style, the jewelry from Iguala (fig. 202), the town from which he recruited his original workers. Artisans of Iguala made filigree goldwork in traditional Spanish patterns from the eighteenth and nineteenth centuries. Spratling's intent was to create jewelry that had local color, borrowed from Aztec sculpture, and that also carried the strength of modern design.

TLW

201. Stamp. Mexican, c. 1250–1521. Collection The Josef Albers Foundation, Orange, Connecticut

202. Woman wearing a gold filigree necklace from Iguala, Mexico, in c. 1963

Coral Stephens

Textile: *Swazi Drapery*
Designed 1951
Mohair and cotton, plain weave; 143½ × 57⅜ inches (364.5 × 145.8 cm)
Produced by Coral Stephens Ltd. (Piggs Peak, Swaziland), 1951 to the present
Unmarked
D86.115.1, gift of Jack Lenor Larsen

Animated by a belief in the democratic distribution of good design, Jack Lenor Larsen found early commercial success by adapting the essence of handwoven textiles to machine-woven production. Such effects, even in industrial production, could not be achieved inexpensively, but Larsen felt the necessity to re-create the irregular surfaces and brilliant colors of handwoven textiles in order to humanize the contemporary interior.

The conformity of available yarn stock spurred Larsen to investigate the remnants of hand production left in various pockets of the third world.

The tragic loss to the Industrial Revolution was not handweaving but handspun yarns. Their random profile and modulating color best compensate for natural organic surfaces missing in our indoor world.[234]

Larsen sought out fibers and sources for production in thirty different industrial plants and small-scale workshops around the world.

An architectural tour of the villages of Nigeria and South Africa in 1960 resulted in his introduction to Coral Stephens, an Englishwoman who had established a studio workshop on her forestry plantation in the remote mountainous north of Swaziland, a former British protectorate in southeastern Africa, bordered by South Africa and Mozambique, which became independent in 1968.[235] She employed local Fosa tribeswomen to prepare the mohair wool and weave fabrics (fig. 203). Larsen selected three of Stephens's horizontally banded designs for his African Collection, *Swazi Lace, Swazi Casement,* and *Swazi Drapery. Swazi Drapery* was offered originally in five colorways; the soft brown of this example, rich amber, coppery orange, ivory, and denim blue. Colorfast aniline dyes were imported from Europe and used in open-fire dyeing vats on the plantation.

This part of Africa had no weaving tradition at all. Coral Stephens notes that in the mid-nineteenth century the natives had gone from wearing skins to wearing brilliantly colored cot-

203. Fosa tribeswoman weaving for Coral Stephens Ltd.

204. *Coral Stephens.* Swazi Drapery *textile*

tons printed in England. She had to instruct her employees in the skills of spinning, dyeing, and weaving. The colors chosen by herself and Larsen had no relation to the bright colors favored by her workers but responded to European and American taste. And, while the geometric pattern might seem African in style, it was not based on indigenous ethnographic traditions. Stephens's approach was to produce textiles in a preindustrial, handcrafted fashion and to recall the eccentricities of a certain primitiveness. The hand-spun, ungraded mohair fiber is characterized by interesting irregularities of thickness and color variation. Moreover, while there is a repeat in the pattern approximately every two feet, the hand weaver's personal style is evident, making pattern matching difficult. As Larsen himself explained:

> *We started out as revolutionaries, wanting only to make brave new designs for a contemporary society. Today our mission is to maintain the great tradition for luxurious quality as a buffer against mass production.*[236]

KC

Ray Komai

Textile: model no. L-420, *Masks*
Designed 1948
Fiberglass, plain weave, silk-screen printed;
   23⅝ × 24¹³⁄₁₆ inches (60 × 63 cm)
Produced by Laverne Originals (New York),
   c. 1948
Printed on paper label: [diamond-shaped
   device, with white running horse and star]/
   LAVERNE
Printed on reverse of paper label: LAVERNE
   . . . Fabric & Wallcovering Division/160
   East 57th Street, New York 22, N.Y. PLaza
   9–5455 . . . DESIGN NAME/width-48″ approx.
   MASKS [typewritten]/ITEM NO. L-420–5-B
   [typewritten]/COLOR PERSIMMON, BLACK
   [typewritten]/REPEAT—approx. 17¾″
   [typewritten] . . . . . FABRIC—price per yard
   8.25 [handwritten] . . . . . [remainder of
   text deleted due to length]
D88.114.1, gift of Helen Fioratti, by exchange

The directness and vitality of the irregular lines in
Ray Komai's cover illustration for the May 1948
issue of *Interiors* (fig. 205) caught the attention of
Erwine Laverne, who was looking for new design
directions for Laverne's Contempora Series.[237]
He asked Komai, a graphic designer, to provide
textile designs with a similar character, which
resulted in the fabrics called *Masks* and *The Big*
Catch. Together with Alvin Lustig's *Incantation*
(fig. 367), also made for this series, they were
chosen as Museum of Modern Art Good Design
selections.

Just as Picasso had been captivated by the vigor
of African art earlier in the century, so, too,
Komai had long admired African masks that he
had seen in various museum collections. In his
textile design he reduced the masks to ellipses and
squat circles articulated by energized lines, and
he rhythmically arranged them within compartments. To achieve the uneven, textured appearance of the containing boundary lines, Komai
used the technique he employed for the cover of
Interiors: he dipped a stick in ink and then laid it
on the paper, in the manner of printing with a
rubber stamp. The built-in imperfections seen in
the intentional irregularity of the lines of the
grid, the rough shapes of the masks themselves,
and the uneven coloring of the motifs produced
a design evocative of primitive block printing
rather than sophisticated silk-screening, an effect
further heightened by the nubby surface of the
ground fabric. The same design took on a totally
different decorator look, however, when it was
printed on drapable, textured rayon woven with
gold and silver lamé[238] or when it was produced as
a wallpaper.

AZ

205. *Ray Komai. Cover of* Interiors, *May 1948*

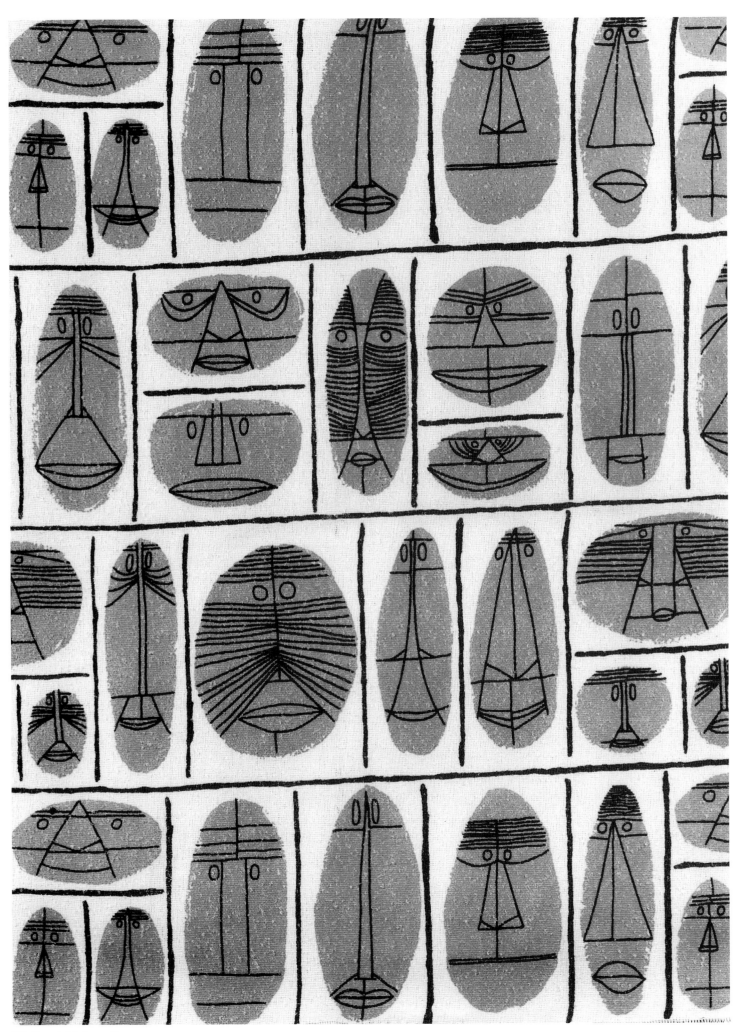

206. Komai. Masks *textile*

Postwar Modernism

The political and artistic repercussions of World War II were manifold. France, though technically a victor, never recuperated its former artistic supremacy, except perhaps in the field of couture. England, also a technical victor, faltered and fell in the world of design. Its system of rationing, the Utility Scheme, extended aspects of prewar functionalism into the most common strata to create rational but uninspired designs. By the time of the 1951 Festival of Britain, which claimed that "Britain Can Make It," it was evident that England, like France, was at best following the lead of other countries. Germany, despite its remarkable economic recovery, had lost its artistic leaders before the war, and it, too, followed in the wake of other countries' achievements.

One of the surprises is that defeated Italy experienced a burst of artistic energy. Its creativity had been held in check and people in the art world persecuted during the Fascist regime of Mussolini. Yet, because its design sector was based on small-scale artisanal shops, it was relatively easy to start up again without much capital investment. By 1950, when the traveling exhibition "Italy at Work" circulated, the new sense of creativity was already apparent in many mediums, and especially in the fields of furniture, ceramics, glass, and enamels. Moreover, its Milan Triennales resumed in 1947 and became the leading design show in the world. It afforded Italians direct access to the most recent trends and, at the same time, gave them an advantage in showcasing their own work. *Domus*, Italy's leading design periodical, took on a new, anti-Fascist editor and reassumed its prewar importance. By 1954 it was joined by *Stile Industria*, and the Milanese department store La Rinascente instituted its influential annual Compasso d'Oro awards for design[239]—all of which set in place a strong support system for Italian design.

After the war Scandinavia quickly assumed an ascendant position in the field of design. It has been argued that Sweden's success was due to its neutrality during the war, which resulted in a period of sustained industrial and financial well-being. But art had not been nurtured in the other Scandinavian countries during the war. Denmark had been occupied by the Germans, and its artists had suffered or fled, yet it, too, emerged triumphant. And what of Finland, where the political situation had been grievous? It had been defeated by the Soviet Union in the Winter War, had then sided with Germany in World War II, and was forced to pay a devastating indemnity after the war. Nonetheless, it assumed a dominant position, not only through the work of Alvar Aalto but also through that of the younger generation headed by Tapio Wirkkala. The year 1951 was one of major triumph for Wirkkala and Finnish design. Both were celebrated at a display Wirkkala created for an exhibition at the Zurich Kunstgewerbemuseum and then at the Milan IX Triennale, where Finland garnered twenty-five prizes, including three grand prizes for Wirkkala. In the same year, Wirkkala and Danish furniture designer Hans Wegner were awarded the first Lunning Prize, a prize that boosted Scandinavian design's reputation over the next two decades.[240] Scandinavia became synonymous with the forward-looking aspects of postwar design and craft, as was stressed by the many propagandistic publications and exhibits that emanated from these Northern countries. Design became an exportable Scandinavian commodity.

The United States emerged from the war as a world leader, both politically and artistically. In the world of design, its émigré artists and the young generation led by the Eameses had worked through the war, creating a relatively seamless transition between prewar and postwar productivity. The strong economy, the abundance of materials, and the GI Bill of Rights, which raised attendance at art schools by subsidizing returning veterans—all these contributed to a flowering of culture. As in the fields of painting and sculpture, design in the United States took a more independent course, although European ideas remained influential.

In the postwar years, the battle for the Modernist cause was fought with unabated energy. The principles promulgated by the leaders of design some twenty years earlier— acknowledgment of technology, mass production, reductivism of elements, absence of applied ornament—were still being enunciated, perhaps with even greater force. And they became institutionalized. The Museum of Modern Art kept the sacred flame burning, especially at its "Good Design" shows, which designated meritorious products at the Chicago Merchandise Mart. Other museums, including the Walker Art Institute, Minneapolis, and the Detroit Institute of Arts, took up the crusade as well. The terms *Design* and *Good Design* became part of a new international language.

It is not easy to define postwar style, for there were a number of concurrent tendencies. Nor should this be surprising, since this was true in 1900 and again in 1925. The postwar

207. Le Corbusier. Notre Dame du Haut, Ronchamp. 1951–55

151

208. *Le Corbusier. Philips Pavilion, Brussels World's Fair. 1958*

period saw the juxtaposition of opposites, of some designers working in a curvilinear and others in a rectilinear mode, some avant-garde and others conservative or retrospective.

Certainly one of the most distinctive stylistic currents was an emphasis on the long, flowing curve. The search for a flexible and organic idiom had been initiated by Aalto, was maintained by Bruno Mathsson and other Scandinavians, and had entered the repertoire of Bauhaus masters, including Marcel Breuer and even Mies van der Rohe. Also, Streamlining continued to play a significant part in postwar design. Even as its distinctive details, such as the banded horizontal lines, gradually disappeared, the spirit of 1930s Streamlining remained strong, contributing to the organic nature of postwar design not only its emphasis on rounded corners but also, more important, its masking of disparate parts beneath a smoothly sculpted outer skin. With hindsight we can recognize how the formal vocabulary of aviation—the shapes of wings and tails and the way they joined the fuselage—adumbrated the shapes of Eva Zeisel's dinnerware (fig. 286) and Finn Juhl's chairs (fig. 269), not to mention the ubiquitous fins of America's luxurious cars. The numerous attempts to fold plywood, ceramics, and glass, as in Stig Lindberg's series of *Veckla* vases (fig. 280) and James Prestini's bowl (fig. 285), reveal how designers exploited materials to create such flaring forms.

Biomorphism also played a role in determining postwar design, helping to establish an aesthetic of rounded forms. It flourished after the war, expanding from an elitist to a popular mode, but it was relatively short-lived. Between the years right after the war and the mid-1950s there was a noticeable shift: designers who began by exploring the repertoire of Biomorphism gradually turned to a more restrained vocabulary of curved forms. For example, there is a clear difference between Timo Sarpaneva's earlier, Biomorphic *Devil's Churn* (fig. 155) and his slightly later *Orchid* vase (fig. 250). This shift is also visible in the differences between the Biomorphic furniture Isamu Noguchi designed just before and after the war (figs. 142, 144) and his much simpler work from the later 1950s (figs. 316, 317). Similarly, we might compare Eero Saarinen's Biomorphic TWA Terminal at New York's Kennedy Airport of 1956–62 (fig. 117) and his slightly later, elegant Dulles Airport, near Washington, D.C., of 1958–63; the former is an eccentric exaggeration that became an artistic cul-de-sac, while the latter building, with its graceful sense of lift and buoyancy, was often imitated.

The overall impression given by many postwar objects, be they chairs or pitchers, is a sense of organic unity. Zeisel, for example, quite rightly wrote of the new "lyrical" style and the "poetry of communicative line."[241] A sense of rhythmic unity could be expressed in the entire object, as in Fulvio Bianconi's *Pezzato* vase (fig. 283) or Lino Sabattini's *Como* service (fig. 232). More often it was found in the small elements of the design, such as the beautifully sculpted junction of post and arm in Hans Wegner's *Round* chair, where the two parts flow together in one unbroken rhythm (fig. 265). It was also evident in the union of the handle and lip of Zeisel's *Tomorrow's Classic* pitcher, the two parts merging together as a continous surface (fig. 286).

While sometimes the curve of postwar design was truly spherical, more often it was a parabolic arc or it rose to a gentle peak, as in Tapio Wirkkala's *Kanttarelli* vase (fig. 211) and Finn Juhl's bowl (fig. 271). In the realm of architecture, the curve was featured in Le Corbusier's remarkable church at Ronchamp (fig. 207) and the Philips Pavilion at the 1959 Brussels World Fair (fig. 208), as well as in the soaring arcs of Danish architect Jörn Luxton's Sydney Opera House.

There was yet another alternative in postwar design: the oblique angle. Whether on a monumental scale, as in Pier Luigi Nervi's forceful piers of precast concrete for the Palazzetto dello Sport in Rome (fig. 209) or on the intimate scale of Raymond Loewy's 2000 dinnerware for Rosenthal (fig. 259) and Gio Ponti's flatware (fig. 229), these thrusting

(above) 210. *Ludwig Mies van der Rohe. Lake Shore Apartments, Chicago. 1951*

(left) 209. *Pier Luigi Nervi and Annibali Vitellozzi. Palazzetto dello Sport, Rome. 1957*

lines are indicative of the 1950s desire to create powerful forms. Straight-edged or curved, these long lines and unornamented forms carry on the legacy of Modernism.

Indeed, one of the restraining elements in postwar design was the remaining presence of the early Modernist tradition, with its emphasis on simplicity. Mies van der Rohe's 1950 Farnsworth House and his 1951 Lake Shore Apartments (fig. 210) are reminders of the unbroken link between prewar and postwar worlds, and the continued vitality of a minimalist sobriety. This was the basis of most architecture and most industrial design. It can be seen, for example, in Sarpaneva's series of *i* decanters (fig. 251), Achille and Pier Giacomo Castiglioni's lamp (fig. 320), Marianne Strengell's *Taj Mahal* fabric (fig. 300), and Walter Ballmer's poster (fig. 295). All share the traditional Modernist respect for the rectilinear grid and a simplicity of volume and line, but they have less flair than the newer type of "lyrical" postwar design.

Lightweight structure is another important aspect of postwar design. If the prewar period favored flat sheet metal and tubular steel for the legs of Modernist chairs and tables, the postwar period favored steel rods and wire. In the Eameses' DAR chair (fig. 309) and Isamu Noguchi's table (fig. 316), the legs resemble Constructivist sculptures—cages of wire that encompass space, creating volume without mass. The entire structure might be a cage of wire, as in Harry Bertoia's *Diamond* chair (fig. 313) and Earl Pardon's necklace (fig. 326), or it might be coupled with a flat plane or a curvaceously sculpted shell, as in the Eameses' ETR table (fig. 312) and DAR chair. The interest in wiry construction helps to explain the proliferation of patterns structured with diamond shapes and other crisscrossing, such as Ross Littell's *Criss Cross* (fig. 325) and Sven Markelius's *Pythagoras* (fig. 323).

There are some who would argue that the essence of postwar design was its scientific, industrial basis. Just as the prewar innovations of cellophane, Bakelite, and fiberglass conjured up an image of sophistication in the early years, so, too, the postwar synthetics seemed to offer greater and greater proof of the triumph of science and industry. The postwar period also offered a wealth of new technology: better wood lamination, more complex molding processes, greater sophistication of die stamping, arc welding, and so on. Certainly these considerations were an important aspect of design.

Yet, interestingly, design ideas often were in advance of technology. For example, Eero Saarinen's *Womb* chair (fig. 307) could be presented only in an upholstered version because the bonding agent required to stiffen the fiberglass shell was too unsightly, and his *Pedestal* chair (fig. 335) had to have an aluminum base because a sufficiently strong plastic did not yet exist. In many such instances, artistic desire preceded the reality of technology, though technology often caught up.

The imperatives of design were not only technology and rationalism but also aesthetics. A number of outstanding works often considered to epitomize a utilitarian point of view, such as Kaj Franck's *Kremlin Bells* decanter (fig. 254) and Nils Landberg's *Tulip* goblets (fig. 337), served no true function but, rather, were conceived for display. Likewise, Prestini's bowl (fig. 285) was meant primarily as sculpture, and Sarpaneva's *Orchid* vase (fig. 250), though it could conceivably hold a single bud, was aptly titled *Art Object*. As Henning Koppel admitted about one of his beautiful silver pitchers for Georg Jensen, it took twenty-five days of handwork to produce, and it cost at that time over a thousand dollars: "no one buys it exclusively to use for water or milk; silver work of this kind must have an independent artistic value that raises it above ordinary utility wares."[242] Likewise, careful distinction must be made between, say, functional furniture that was industrially produced in large, inexpensive series and furniture that was carefully hand-crafted from costly woods. Arne Jacobsen's simple *Ant* chairs of plywood (fig. 273) show a refined design appropriate to its targeted market, while Wegner's and Juhl's handsome teak chairs (figs. 265, 269) reveal a richer sculptural treatment. Despite the democratization of industrial design and many designers' professed goal of such democratization, there was a fair amount of self-indulgence in the design world, and many of the objects presented here were relatively costly and deluxe.

With the passage of time, many of these postwar designs may seem to be commonplace or outmoded clichés. The startling vitality that they once offered has often been obscured by the countless and debased imitations that industry quickly set loose on the commercial market, and these have substantially dulled our senses. Many of the objects presented here are already a half-century old, and many of the designers have since died or retired. The wheel of fortune has already begun to turn full cycle again, bringing with it the inevitable round of nostalgia and revival. This may help us realize the heroic nature of that generation of designers who in their time tried to define what modern was.

ME

Tapio Wirkkala

Vase: model no. 3280, *Kanttarelli*[243]
Designed 1947[244]
Glass, machine engraved; 8¾ × 6½ × 6⅞ inches
  (22 × 16.6 × 17.5 cm)
Produced by Iittala Lasitehdas (Iittala,
  Finland), c. 1948–c. 1961[245]
Engraved on underside: TAPIO WIRKKALA—
  IITTALA
D85.134.1

Vase: model no. 3551, *Varsanjalka*
Designed c. 1950
Glass, machine engraved; 15 × 4⅝ × 4¼ inches
  (38.1 × 11.7 × 10.8 cm)
Produced by Iittala Lasitehdas (Iittala,
  Finland), c. 1950–c. 1960 (this example
  1955)
Engraved on underside: TAPIO WIRKKALA—
  IITTALA—55
D88.164.1

211. Tapio Wirkkala. Kanttarelli *vase: model no. 3280 and* Varsanjalka *vase: model no. 3551*

The *Kanttarelli* vase is the second in a series
whose name and forms were derived from the
chanterelle mushroom, an edible wild species
with a distinctive shape: its stem and cap flow
together in one continuous curve and its edge is
curled (fig. 212). The mushroom also has chan-
neled ridges, which Wirkkala has suggested with
engraved lines on the exterior surface of the glass.

Wirkkala's first *Kanttarelli* vase (fig. 213) was
part of his prize-winning entry in a contest sponsored in 1946 by the Iittala firm. The design was

212. *Chanterelle mushrooms*

213. *Wirkkala*. Kanttarelli *vase. 1946. Iittala Glass Museum, Iittala, Finland*

214. *Gunnel Nyman.* Calla *vase. 1946. Suomen Lasimuseo, Riihimäki, Finland*

Tapio Wirkkala

Platter
Designed c. 1950
Birch plywood; 1⅝ × 23 × 3½ inches
  (4 × 58.5 × 8.9 cm)
Produced by Soinne et Kni (Helsinki),
  c. 1951–c. 1954[247]
Incised on underside: [monogram of TW]
D87.108.1

reputedly so revolutionary that the Iittala glass-blowers feared that the model would be impossible to blow or market. Neither fear proved correct. In fact, Wirkkala's design was not all that revolutionary. It was closely aligned with the tradition of modern Finnish glass design, beginning with the pre–World War II designs of Tyra Lundgren. Chronologically closer at hand are certain models produced in 1946 at Riihimäki: Helena Tynell's *Kaulus* and Gunnel Nyman's *Calla* (fig. 214). These vases signal an important shift in Finnish design toward an abstract, organic-based style. In many ways, Wirkkala's design is the most graceful, with a complex, waisted silhouette. The engraved lines, rather than stopping abruptly as Nyman's do, rise the entire height of the vase and expand outward as an organic part of the design. It is little wonder that the *Kanttarelli* became Wirkkala's first international success.

The creation of the second version of the *Kanttarelli* sheds interesting light on the relationship between art and commerce. The first model was issued as art glass in a limited edition of fifty exemplars (and later was reissued in a second edition of the same amount). A decision was apparently made to create a different, less expensive version to be produced in unlimited quantities. In order to facilitate its production, Wirkkala substantially changed the contour by eliminating the curled lip (which had necessitated hand engraving the underside) and by using a simpler, stockier, more cylindrical form. Something of the difference between the two versions

is also registered in their prices: the second model sold for one-fifth the cost of the limited edition.[246]

Although much emphasis was put on the organic, nature-oriented basis of such Finnish designs, another strong component is the taut geometry of their structure and decoration. The form of the *Kanttarelli* shows the influence of Brancusi's sculpture, and its linear decoration suggests analogies with the stringed constructions of Antoine Pevsner and Naum Gabo (fig. 222), and even with Alvar Aalto's contemporary *fan* leg. The geometric underpinnings of Wirkkala's art are clearly revealed in the second vase in the Stewart Collection, model 3551. Here, the column of glass is waisted toward the middle, and the engraved lines emphasize the Constructivist torsion of this abstract sculpture.

Although Wirkkala had an immense success with his abstract *Kanttarelli* vases—the second *Kanttarelli* was awarded a grand prize at the Milan IX Triennale of 1951—he continued to use figurative imagery for much of his work in the late 1940s. It was not until the beginning of the 1950s that the abstract element dominated in his oeuvre, and it was those objects—whether executed in glass, wood, or metal—that signaled the triumph of postwar Finnish design. Yet, even then, the publicity about his pieces inevitably emphasized the designer's references to natural forms and a Nordic mystique of nature, allowing the public a safety net, so that it did not have to grapple with the difficulties of art that was too abstract or nonobjective.

ME

In the early 1950s, Wirkkala created a series of wooden platters and bowls in plywood. Although Alvar Aalto and Bruno Mathsson had already developed a Scandinavian tradition of making plywood furniture, Wirkkala used the material in an entirely new way. He took a piece of plywood and turned it around ninety degrees, converting what is normally an ugly edge into the decorative surface.

This idea came to him in the late 1940s while he was visiting Soinne et Kni, a company owned by one of his friends, which made a special type of laminated wood for airplane propellers. The alternating layers of light wood and dark glue in the laminate reminded Wirkkala of the growth rings of a tree. He realized that cutting the laminates vertically produced narrow stripes while cutting at an angle made wider ones, and that cutting a round shape made the straight layers seem to curve. Even though these differences could be calculated mathematically, Wirkkala recognized that the laminate had to be cut by hand to bring out the full beauty of the material. In Wirkkala's first experiments, he cut the material himself. Then he moved on to drawing the

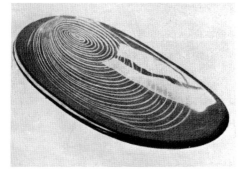

215. *Gunnel Nyman.* Näkki *(Mussel) bowl. 1946*

156

design and left the actual carving to a skilled craftsman, Martti Lindqvist.[248]

Wirkkala had perceived a visual relationship between nature and this half-natural and half–man-made material, and he expressed it in his plywood platters by giving them the shapes of shells or leaves. His use of abstract natural forms followed the example of designers such as Gunnel Nyman; his shell-shaped bowls, like her mussel-shaped glass bowl of 1946 (fig. 215), have concentric rings. He had already used natural forms in his *Kanttarelli* vases of 1946–47 (figs. 211, 213) and in a series of glass bowls shaped like shells and leaves (fig. 217). Although his glass shells preceded his wooden ones, his leaf-shaped pieces were developed in the two materials at about the same time, both being put into production in 1951.[249]

Wirkkala's laminated bowls and platters created a sensation at the Milan IX Triennale of 1951. He won three grand prizes, one of them for his wooden pieces. These pieces were widely published in Europe and America, and one platter was chosen as the most beautiful object of 1951 by *House Beautiful*.[250]

Wirkkala soon branched out into larger and more three-dimensional pieces in laminated wood. By 1953 he had designed several sculptural tables, one with concentric rings centered over a leg carved out of the same laminate (fig. 218). The table can be read as spiraling down to a point or as twisting up to the top and expanding out in all directions. Wirkkala went on to create large, complex plywood sculptures, such as his *Pyörre (Whirlpool)* of 1954, an elaborately curved spiral form.[251]　　　　　　　　　CWL

216. *Tapio Wirkkala. Platter*

217. *Wirkkala. Bowl. 1951*

218. *Wirkkala. Table. c. 1952*

Tapio Wirkkala

Vase: model no. TW2
Designed 1954[252]
Silver-plated alpacca; 9¹⁄₁₆ × 2⅞ × 2⅛ inches
   (23 × 7.2 × 5.4 cm)
Produced by Kultakeskus Oy (Hämeenlinna,
   Finland), 1954–75
Impressed on lower side, near bottom: ALP
   MADE IN FINLAND
D86.163.1

After Wirkkala's triumph at the Milan IX Triennale in 1951, Kultakeskus Oy, the Gold Center Company of Finland, invited him to work in silver. He designed bowls and vases inspired by natural forms as well as practical pieces—a coffeepot, a thermos bottle, and flatware. By the end of 1954, thirty-four of his designs were being produced in sterling silver.[253] Some models, including the one in the Stewart Collection, were also produced in alpacca.

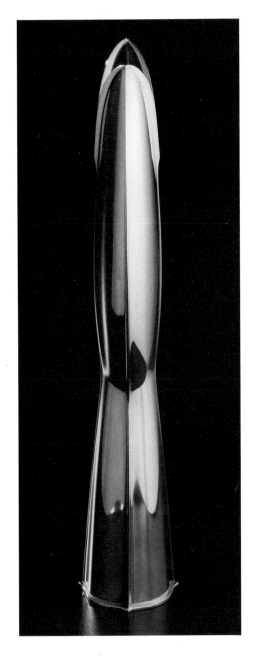

219, 220. *Tapio Wirkkala. Vase: model no. TW2*

Several of the silver vases were displayed at the Milan X Triennale in 1954 (fig. 221), where they attracted worldwide attention.[254] Some of them were in shapes of stylized flowers, as in the case of this model. The form rises out of the base, tapers in at the waist, and then swells out in a graceful curve to form the two petals. The flower is flattened into an oval, and as a result the side of this vase, with its elegantly elongated lines (fig. 219), looks very different from the rounded front.

Wirkkala made the construction of this vase an important part of the design. He used the soldered joints at the sides to advantage by creating flanges that form points at the base, turning the essentially circular base into a compressed quatrefoil. These flanges then taper in toward the top

and, along with those at the rim, define the form of the vase, giving it a sense of crispness.

Wirkkala had made use of plant forms before this, as in his glass vases of the late 1940s and early 1950s, including the famous *Kanttarelli* glass vase (figs. 211, 213). When Wirkkala designed the metal vases, though, he gave them a somewhat tauter geometry. He used similar shapes in some of the porcelain vases he designed for Rosenthal beginning in 1956.[255] Like the metal vases, the porcelain ones have columnar tapering stems, small waists, and vaguely organic tops. The extension of ideas and forms from one medium to another is typical of Wirkkala's work throughout his career.

CWL

221. Wirkkala. Vases. 1954

Irena Brynner

Brooch
Designed and executed 1952–53
Silver and turquoise;[256] 4⅜ × 1 × ⅞ inches
 (11.1 × 2.4 × 2.2 cm)
Unmarked
D88.150.1

Irena Brynner's brooch underscores her approach to jewelry as sculpture in miniature. It exists almost as a model for a Constructivist structure; indeed, "the Constructivists often referred to their modest-sized sculptures as 'laboratory models,' suggesting both objects resulting from research and projects for monumental structures. . . ."[257]

The brooch is especially reminiscent of Naum Gabo's linear, spiral constructions of the 1940s

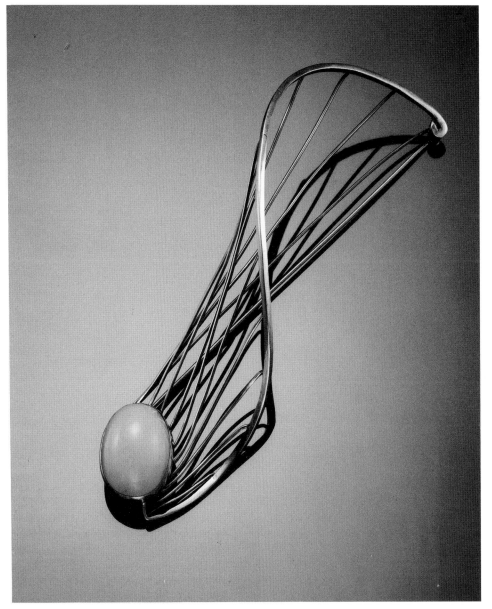

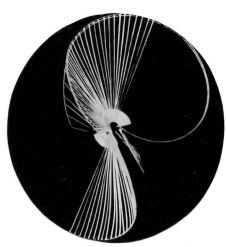

222. Naum Gabo. Relief. 1937.
Collection Wallace K. Harrison

223. Irena Brynner. Brooch

224. *Margaret de Patta. Pendant. 1948. Eugene Bielawski Collection, Berkeley, California*

and 1950s, which were fabricated from plastic sheet and cord. In fact, Brynner acknowledged these constructions as the source of her inspiration. This type of sculpture, which stems from Vladimir Tatlin's *Monument to the Third International* (1919–20) and which could be seen as well in the string constructions of Naum Gabo (fig. 222) and the works of Antoine Pevsner, Henry Moore, and Barbara Hepworth, was an important influence on midcentury design.

Curvature became a major element in the work of Gabo and Pevsner from the 1930s onward. It was during this period that the overall tendency of Constructivist work was to create regularity through simplifying and repeating shapes and rhythms.[258] Furthermore, the linear motif indicated dynamic "force" — the Constructivist ideal of a perfect union of form and meaning. Brynner's brooch derives its graceful power

from this spiraling linearity and light and airy structure. Space becomes an element of the total design, no distinction being made between its inside and outside.

Although both Brynner and Margaret de Patta were affected by Constructivism, they took very different approaches. De Patta manipulated space through light and translucent form; in one of her pendants, she presented internal spatial structuring through the faceting and striations of a rutilated quartz stone (fig. 224). Brynner enveloped open space in a gentle, three-dimensional S curve that makes up the structural system of the brooch. The turquoise stone serves as the base of the piece, but it is dominated by the vertical wires radiating outward from it, whereas de Patta's stone is the primary focus. De Patta's pendant is about the stone, while Brynner's is concerned with the metal.

TLW

Arne Jacobsen

Flatware: model no. 660, AJ
Designed 1957
Stainless steel; knife: 7¹⁵/₁₆ × ¹¹/₁₆ inches
    (20.1 × 1.8 cm)
Produced by A. Michelsen (Copenhagen),
    1957 to the present
Each piece except dinner knife impressed: A. MICHELSEN/STAINLESS/DENMARK/[monogram of AJ to the right]
D85.125.1–7

The AJ flatware pattern by Arne Jacobsen is a prime example of a functionalist, albeit sculpturally inclined, architect's conception of cutlery, appropriate in shape and material for industrial mass production. Designed to coordinate with the furniture and other objects — as well as the entire exterior edifice and interior space — of the Scandinavian Airlines System (SAS) Royal Hotel in Copenhagen, all by Jacobsen, these stainless steel utensils are entirely devoid of ornament, emphasizing instead a tapering silhouette and refined sculptural presence.

Jacobsen's design reflects other contemporary flatware patterns. The butter knife recalls the knife in Gio Ponti's 1951 stainless flatware (fig. 229), and a similar attenuation of the handles is characteristic of Henning Koppel's *Caravel* pattern, also designed in 1957 (fig. 226). Jacobsen's design, however, is far more exaggerated than the others. Indeed, it looked so extreme and untraditional that the flatware was misunderstood by the hotel management and was supposedly poorly received by hotel guests. The hotel soon replaced

it with a more conventional flatware, neither designed by Jacobsen nor manufactured by Michelsen.[259]

When one tries to eat with the utensils, it is easy to understand the adverse reaction the flatware caused. Though Jacobsen, ever the functionalist, provided a special bouillon spoon for the left-handed diner, the bowls of the teaspoons are too shallow to hold much liquid. The fork tines are extremely short and the bowl is flat, so that although the fork can pierce anything solid, it does not lend itself to scooping loose food. Although the knife and butter spreader are very comfortable in the hand, the implements, in general, are diminutive and thin. The public was accustomed to handling weightier utensils. Also, it may have seemed easier to accept modernism in a chair or lamp, but forks, knives, and spoons are intimate items that are held in one's hand and go into one's mouth. Apparently wanting its eating utensils comfortable and familiar, the public was not yet ready for such a futuristic statement in flatware. As a matter of fact, AJ was the very cutlery chosen to be used on board the spacecraft in Stanley Kubrick's 1968 science-fiction film epic *2001: A Space Odyssey.*

Public rejection notwithstanding, Jacobsen's flatware achieved critical success and was consequently exhibited at the Milan XI Triennale of 1957 (fig. 227). Put on the open market and sold through Georg Jensen, it eventually became quite successful commercially. The design needed to be given time to achieve a rapport with the consuming public.

TLW

225. *Arne Jacobsen.* AJ *flatware: model no. 660*

226. *Henning Koppel.* Caravel *flatware. 1957*

227. AJ *flatware displayed at the Milan XI Triennale, 1957*

Arne Jacobsen

Desk lamp: model no. 5744160052 *Visor*
Designed c. 1956
Zinc-plated steel and lacquer; 21½ × 13½ × 6½
  inches (54.6 × 34.3 × 16.5 cm)
Produced by Louis Poulsen & Co. A/S
  (Copenhagen), 1957 to the present
Impressed on underside: LP 253 M
Printed on paper label: Louis Poulsen and
  Company
D81.106.1

As part of his commission for the SAS Royal
Hotel in Copenhagen, Jacobsen created a lamp
that, with minor variations, could be placed on a
table, attached to the wall, or stood on the
floor.[260] An important aspect of this lamp is the
concealed hinge that makes the visor-shaped
hood movable, thus allowing the user to control
the light source. In the bedrooms, one guest
could use the table lamp without disturbing a
roommate; similarly, wall-mounted lamps in the
telephone booths focused the light within the
limited space. It proved to be an elegant and
flexible solution.

The aesthetic impact of the lamp is derived
from the visual tension and play between the
mass of the shaped hood and the circular cutout
of the base. Similar contrasting relationships can
be seen in the architecture of the SAS Royal
Hotel, as, for example, in the undulant stairway
that contrasts with the rectilinear space of the
lobby. If the geometric severity of this lamp har-
monizes with the stark lines of this International
Style building, its sculptural form also parallels
the softening effect of the *Swan* and *Egg* chairs
(figs. 277, 278), designed for this hotel as well.

DAH & JTT

228. Arne Jacobsen. Visor *desk lamp*

229. *Gio Ponti. Flatware*

Gio Ponti

Flatware
Designed c. 1951
Stainless steel; knife: 7⁷⁄₁₆ × 1¼ inches
  (18.9 × 3.1 cm)
Produced by Argenteria Krupp (Milan),
  c. 1951–at least 1957[261]
Each piece stamped on back of handle: PONTI
  [pentagon surrounding image of a bear
  above KRUPP]/FRASER's/ITALY[262]
D84.101.1–5

In his flatware, architect Gio Ponti exercised an instinctual awareness of the most basic forms possible for tableware; at the same time, he pursued his functionalist aesthetic. Furthermore, the relatively linear profile of each utensil reveals the designer's architectural roots.[263]

Quite simple and straightforward, particularly in the elongated triangular handles, this flatware represents a major departure from both the concurrent stainless steel flatware in traditional

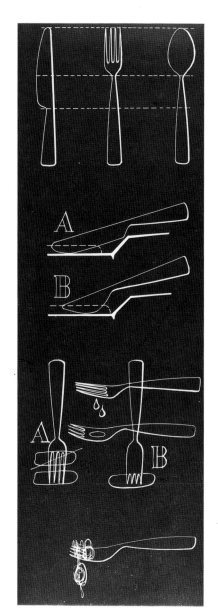

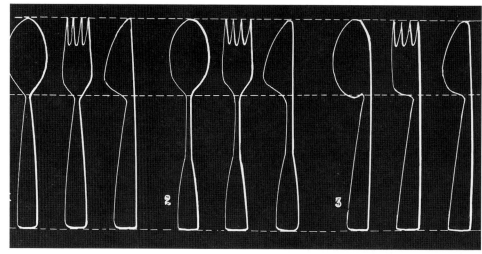

designs and the more avant-garde offerings from Scandinavia, America, Germany, and the Netherlands.

The fork—actually a *forchetta-cucchiaio*, or fork-spoon—is one of Ponti's innovations. Its tines have been shortened and its bowl deepened to create a cavity to catch sauce, such an essential part of Italian cuisine. Also innovatory is the knife, with its drastically reduced and wedgelike blade; this shape was prompted by Ponti's belief that the protracted length of conventional cutlery was helpful only for cutting meat.[264] Ponti's sketch (fig. 230) diagrams the impediments of the traditional knife, fork, and spoon and his alleviation of the problems.

(left) 230. Ponti. *Diagram of traditional (A) and redesigned (B) flatware. c. 1951*

(above) 231. Ponti. *Drawing of three sets of flatware. c. 1951*

Ponti designed two additional sets of flatware (fig. 231). In one, the triangle of the handle digresses into a slender central band before resolving into the spoon or blade forms, while the other repeats an asymmetrical silhouette in each piece. All three cutlery patterns were exhibited at the Milan IX Triennale in 1951.   TLW

Lino Sabattini

Tea and coffee service: model no. M464,
   Como
Designed 1957
Silver-plated brass, plastic cord, and raffia;
   coffeepot: 8⁷⁄₈ × 6⁵⁄₁₆ × 2⁷⁄₁₆ inches (22.6 ×
   17.6 × 6.1 cm)
Produced by L'Orfèvrerie Christofle (Paris),
   1959–70
Teapot and creamer, impressed on underside:
   [polygonal hallmark enclosing device of a
   rooster facing left] GALLIA/FRANCE/[square
   hallmark enclosing O, device of a pawn
   facing left, C]/PROD./CHRISTOFLE
Sugar bowl, impressed on underside: SABATTINI
Tray, impressed on long side: [square box,

enclosing circular device with two horizontal, heraldically reversed clublike motifs, SABATTINI/ITALY] *Lino Sabattini* 1957/1989[265]
D86.164.1–4; D89.174.1, gift of Sabattini Argenteria, S.p.A.

Sabattini's *Como* tea and coffee service is a dramatic example of Italian postwar forays into an expressionist style in hollowware. Its distinctive, protuberant forms reflect tendencies typical of concurrent Italian glass, such as Fulvio Bianconi's *Pezzato* vase (fig. 283), and ceramics. Similar ideas can also be seen in the designs of Henning Koppel (fig. 138). But an even closer

parallel is the tea service designed around 1955 by another Danish designer, Karl Gustav Hansen (fig. 233). While Hansen's sugar bowl and creamer are somewhat different in appearance from those of the *Como* set, the teapot displays a similar stretched-out form.

For the *Como* service, Sabattini took sculpture rather than architecture as his inspirational model, consistent with the prevailing antirationalist philosophy of Gio Ponti and his influential magazine, *Domus*.[266] The whimsical fantasy of *Como*'s curves illustrates the overriding desire

(opposite) 232. *Lino Sabattini*. Como *tea and coffee service: model no. M464*

of post-Mussolini Italian designers to create a wholly new philosophy of the utilitarian object. Founded on an American model, it was antifunctionalist, antigeometric, and antihistorical. Italians wanted to forget the oppression and consequent austerity of the immediate Fascist past and to reconstruct their postwar world with new symbols, based on romanticism, youth, and vivacity.[267] Sabattini conceived of forms inspired by the energy rather than the shapes of nature. This vitality further masked the function of the object.

Sabattini prized the tradition of Italian craftsmanship. Although the prevailing ideal was to gear output toward a powerful new domestic industry, Sabattini maintained the supremacy of individually handwrought objects. He sought to humanize technology or, as Bruno Munari wrote, to create "forms which are an example of perfect fusion between the two components of design considered by many to oppose one another: fantasy and technology."[268] The *Como* service was shaped by cold-bending and turning brass, which was then electroplated with silver—

233. *Karl Gustav Hansen. Tea service. c. 1954*

techniques not inconsistent with Christofle's usual manufacturing methods. (A more costly sterling silver version was offered as well.)

Como won a prize at the exhibition "Formes et Idées d'Italie," held in Paris in 1957. It remains to this day one of the most eccentric and idiosyncratic examples of 1950s Italian style.

TLW

Lino Sabattini

Bud vase: model no. M46, *Cardinale*
Designed 1957
Silver-plated brass; 8⅜ × 1⅝ × 1⅝ inches
  (21.3 × 4.1 × 4.1 cm)
Produced by L'Orfèvrerie Christofle (Paris),
  1959–84
Stamped on underside: CHRISTOFLE/
  FRANCE/[square hallmark enclosing O,
  device of a pawn facing left, C]/COLL.
  GALLIA
D86.180.1, gift of Geoffrey N. Bradfield*

Sabattini's *Cardinale* vase, as its name implies, was inspired by the configuration of a Roman Catholic cardinal dressed in his ecclesiastical robe and miter (fig. 236). In theme and form, the vase resembles Giacomo Manzù's many poetic statues of cardinals.

It can also be interpreted as a homage to the female figure; the attenuated hourglass shape is discerned in much of Italian product design of the mid-1950s. An important stylistic prototype was Conradino D'Ascanio's *Vespa* motor scooter (*vespa* is Italian for *wasp* and refers to the scooter's wasp waist), designed for Piaggio in 1946. Sabattini also meant to suggest symbolically a hand grasping a bouquet of flowers (fig. 234).[269]

The pinched waist that joins two enclosing, tapered forms of different sizes is a motif that repeatedly appears in a great many 1950s designs, in Scandinavia as well as in Italy. Especially germane are the designs of Tapio Wirkkala, an artist whom Sabattini admired. In this light we might well compare the Finn's vases (figs. 211, 220) with the *Cardinale*. Sabattini's vase stretches the idea of tapering cones even further, both literally and figuratively. Graceful elongation is the overriding principle, the protracted length being characteristically Italian, as in the vase by Fausto Melotti (fig. 237). In addition, the top portion of Sabattini's vase is scalloped on two sides to create a duality of opposing points, which extend the upper form even more.

Cardinale was conceived while Sabattini was design director of Christofle's Formes Nouvelles line; it was exhibited at the Milan XI Triennale in 1957 and was produced in two sizes, this example being the smaller.

TLW

234. *Guido A. Niest. Drawing of* Cardinale *vase. 1989. Liliane and David M. Stewart Collection. Gift of Guido A. Niest*

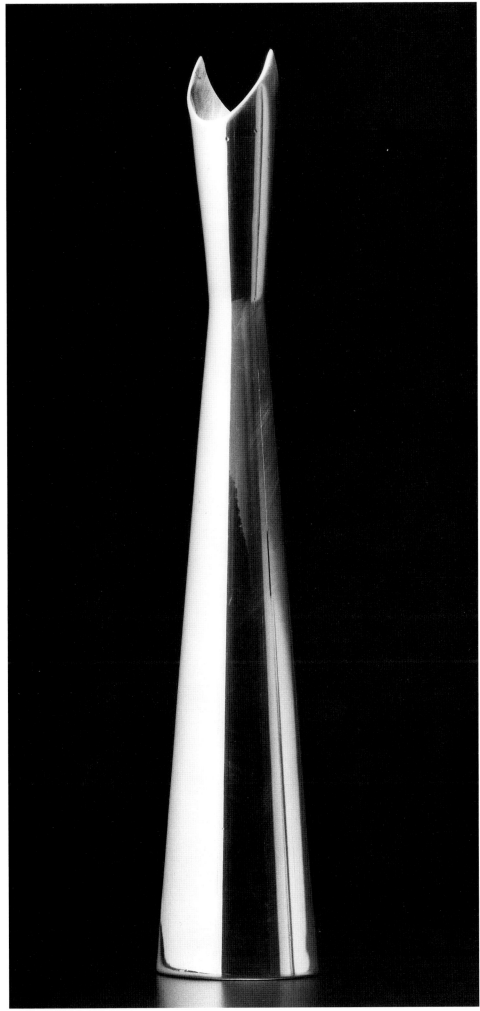

235. *Sabattini.* Cardinale *bud vase: model no.* M46

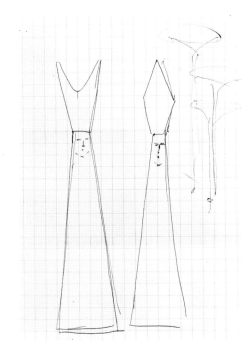

236. *Sabattini. Drawing of* Cardinale *vase. n.d. Liliane and David M. Stewart Collection. Gift of Lino Sabattini*

237. *Fausto Melotti. Vase.* 1955

Carlo Scarpa

Vase: model no. 524.02, *Tessuto*
Designed 1939[270]
Glass; 13⅛ × 5½ × 5½ inches (33.3 ×
    14 × 14 cm)
Produced by Venini (Murano, Italy),
    intermittently from c. 1940 to the present
    (this example c. 1950–c. 1970)
Acid-stamped on underside: *venini/*
    *murano/*ITALIA
D88.109.1

Gio Ponti

Stoppered bottle: model no. 526.19,
    Morandiane
Designed c. 1950
Glass; 15 × 3¼ × 3¼ inches (38.1 × 8.3 × 8.3 cm)
Produced by Venini (Murano, Italy),
    intermittently from c. 1950 to the present
    (this example c. 1950–c. 1970)
Acid-stamped on underside: *venini/*
    *murano/*ITALIA
D88.112.1

Gio Ponti

Stoppered bottle: model no. 526.20,
  Morandiane
Designed c. 1946–50
Glass; 13½ × 4¹¹⁄₁₆ × 4¹¹⁄₁₆ inches
  (34.3 × 11.9 × 11.9 cm)
Produced by Venini (Murano, Italy),
  intermittently from c. 1950 to the present
  (this example c. 1950–c. 1970)
Acid-stamped on underside: *venini/
  murano*/ITALIA
Handwritten on paper label on underside:
  TM1596A/PONTI I
D83.134.1, gift of Mr. and Mrs. Anthony W.
  Roberts*

Paolo Venini and Fulvio Bianconi

Stoppered bottle: model no. 526.15,
  Morandiane
Designed c. 1950–55
Glass; 19⅜ × 2⅞ × 2⅞ inches (49.2 × 7.3 × 7.3 cm)
Produced by Venini (Murano, Italy),
  intermittently from c. 1955 to the present
  (this example c. 1950–c. 1970)
Acid-stamped on underside (partially obscure):
  . . . *ini/* . . . *ano/* . . . LIA
Printed on paper label on underside: VENINI/
  MURANO/NEW YORK/ . . . h/N. 458 [in ink]/
  MADE IN IT . . .
D88.111.1

Toni Zuccheri

Stoppered bottle: model no. 720.03, *Giade*
Designed 1964
Glass and copper filaments; 12¼ × 3½ × 3½
  inches (31.1 × 8.9 × 8.9 cm)
Produced by Venini (Murano, Italy),
  intermittently from 1964 to the present
  (this example c. 1964–c. 1970)
Acid-stamped on underside: *venini/
  murano*/[obscured]
Printed on paper label on underside: VENINI/
  MURANO VENEZIA/N 8666 [in ink]/MADE IN
  ITALY
D88.110.1

In 1956 at the Venice XXVIII Biennale, the Venini firm introduced a new series of elongated forms named *Morandiane*, in honor of Amadeo Morandi. The latter's still life paintings (fig. 239), with their assemblages of long bottles, funnels, and other household paraphernalia, had been held in high esteem since the late 1910s and remained popular in the ensuing decades for both artistic and political reasons. In the postwar years, Morandi's nationality and his figurative imagery provided a welcome alternative to those who feared the double threats of American artistic domination and abstract art. Others were swayed solely by the charm of Morandi's enigmatic, metaphysical art. It is significant that in 1956, the very year that Venini introduced its *Morandiane* series, Gio Ponti's *Domus* magazine featured a visit to the sixty-six-year-old artist.[271]

In a certain sense, the aesthetic of the *Morandiane* series began in the years immediately before and after the war. The tear-shaped vase at the far left, designed in 1939, is unlike most of Carlo Scarpa's prewar models (fig. 240) because here the designer forsook his rectangular forms and sharp corners—a geometric solution typical of prewar taste—for a more lyrical shape. After the war Venini introduced a series of stoppered decanters designed by Gio Ponti (fig. 241).[272] Long-necked and with gently sloped shoulders, these elegant vessels recall the silent guardians of Morandi's still life paintings. It is not that farfetched to

speak of some of these bottles in animate terms as personages—recalling the mannequins seen in Giorgio De Chirico's haunting landscapes.

The *Morandiane* series that was formally introduced at the Venice XXVIII Biennale included a number of tall stoppered bottles in a direct line with those created by Ponti, though with slight modifications. The anthropomorphic decanter (fig. 238, second from the left) looks identical to the one designed by Ponti a decade earlier, but it incorporates minor changes: the neck has been extended in length, the height of the stopper has been increased, and the horizon-

(opposite) 238. *Left to right: Carlo Scarpa, Tessuto vase: model no. 524.02; Gio Ponti,* Morandiane *stoppered bottles: model nos. 526.19 and 526.20; Paolo Venini and Fulvio Bianconi,* Morandiane *stoppered bottle: model no. 526.15; Toni Zuccheri,* Giade *stoppered bottle: model no. 720.03*

(above right) 239. *Amadeo Morandi. Still Life. 1941*

(right) 240. *Carlo Scarpa. Tessuto vases. c. 1938*

241. Gio Ponti. Decanters. c. 1950

tal stripes around the lower portion of the body have been eliminated. Likewise, the central decanter shows slight changes in the shape of the body and the foot, as well as in the overall proportion, when compared to the Ponti model of a decade earlier. The bottle at the far right, conceived almost a decade after the *Morandiane* series was first introduced, shows the continuity of forms and ideas within the Venini workshop.

This group of allied works encompasses a diversity of glassmaking techniques, which suggests the inventive genius of Venini and his associates. The vase at the left shows great control; it was made with a demanding technique called *tessuto* (textile), because of its resemblance to a woven material. It is composed of flattened, fused groups of canes, which are drawn, marvered, rolled over a metal surface, fused, and then blown into shape. Adding to the complexity, half the vessel is made from one set of colored canes, the other half from a contrasting set of colored canes. The anthropomorphic decanter and the one next to it are the result of a difficult process called *incalmo*, which involves blowing the differently colored sections separately, manipulating them in the parison of the kiln until the others are blown, controlling the measurements so that the parts fit exactly, then fusing the different blows of colored glass while they are still in a molten state. The decanter second from the right is of the *fasce* series, with a bold stripe of yellow superimposed over white. Last, the decanter at the right is *vetro groviglio* and is made of cased glass; the inner green core has long filaments of copper embedded within it.[273]

The Venini workshop struck an interesting balance between, on the one hand, very bright color and innovative techniques and, on the other hand, an elegant but restrained sense of form. Although the other Murano firms frequently imitated Venini's innovations, they rarely used them as well or as tastefully. ME

Massimo Vignelli

Hanging light fixtures: model no. 4035L
Designed c. 1953[274]
Glass; 19⅜ × 7¼ × 7¼ inches (49.2 × 18.4 × 18.4 cm)
Produced by Venini (Murano, Italy), c. 1954– c. 1970, 1986
Unmarked
D85.151.1–3

The hanging lamps that Massimo Vignelli designed for the Venini manufactory suggest something of the complex relationship among the designer, the patron, and the artisanal workshop in postwar Italy.[275]

Although Paolo Venini's celebrated glassworks had produced lamps with glass standards and fabric shades, it offered no interesting, modern-style lamps—certainly none to equal the quality and ingenuity of its vases. Then, in the early 1950s, Venini was asked to fabricate a number of hanging shades designed by Studio Architetti BBPR for the Olivetti store in New York City (fig. 242).[276] They were waisted, conical forms with brightly colored stripes derived from Venini's *fasce* vases. With their large-scale, unusual shapes and intense color, the lamps were as dazzling as the rest of this store's ensemble.

Venini then decided to capitalize on the concept and produce his own line of lighting fixtures. He turned to a social acquaintance, the twenty-two-year-old Massimo Vignelli, who was then studying architecture at the University of Venice, and hired him on a part-time basis.

Vignelli worked within the boundaries of Venini's already established concepts of color and decorative techniques. He very much liked the project for, as he saw it, it combined the best of two worlds. He was interested in design but did not want to work for industrial production; he liked handicraft but did not want to work in an idiom that was too craftsy. The shapes were blown in molds, allowing the designer close control over the form, but the decoration was worked more freely, allowing for the possibility of surprise within fixed boundaries.

These lamps are among the earliest models Vignelli established. To reduce the glare of the bulb, the greater part of the shade was left opaque and monochromatic. The initial lamp was white, but then colors were introduced. Here, one shade is blue, one yellow, and one green, creating a vivacious triad. The stripes of additional colors add to the polychromatic effect.

Vignelli created other lamps by inverting Venini vase forms or utilizing the factory's various other glass techniques. The designer recalls that there was much genial discussion between himself and his patron. Sometimes, however, the relationship took a different turn. When Vignelli reported that a British television program was going to promote his designs, Venini became upset that the company's name had not been sufficiently emphasized. He promptly fired Vignelli—an action the designer carefully disregarded. It is noteworthy that while at first Vignelli's name was mentioned in conjunction with this project, by the end of the 1950s it was omitted more and more, until only Venini's remained.[277] ME

242. Studio Architetti BBPR. Olivetti Corporation showroom, New York, c. 1954

243. Massimo Vignelli. Hanging light fixtures: model no. 4035L

Osvaldo Borsani

Lounge chair: model no. P40

Designed 1954[278]

Steel, partly painted or brass-plated, rubber, polyfoam, and cotton upholstery; 34⅛ × 28⅝ × 45¼ inches (86.7 × 72.7 × 115 cm)

Produced by Tecno S.p.A. (Milan), 1955 to the present (this example probably 1959–60)

Printed in red on circular gold label on each side: T

Printed in gold on rectangular transparent label on left leg: TECNO [in red]/mobili e forniture per arredamento/Milano Via bigli 22 tel. 705736

Illegible circular transparent label on right leg D83.116.1

In the mid-1950s Osvaldo Borsani turned away from designing traditional wooden furniture to make remarkably adjustable pieces with metal frames and polyfoam upholstery. The first was the divan-bed D70 of 1954, with an identical seat and back, in the elongated curves popular in Italy around 1950 (fig. 245). It can be arranged with one side down as a seat, or with both sides down as a bed, or even folded up like a jackknife for storage.

Next he designed the P40 lounge chair (P stands for *poltrona*, or armchair), which is, if anything, even more versatile. All the parts move: the seat and back fold up, the footrest extends out or swings up under the seat, and the armrests turn up for use or down to be out of the way (fig. 247). Furthermore, the chair can be turned around and the back used to sit on.[279] Not only is the P40 chair more adjustable than the D70, its curves are more complex as well.

Although the D70 and P40 are mechanical in their adjustability, their organically curved upholstery keeps them from looking machinelike. This mix of mechanical function and organic curves is found in other innovative works of the time, such as Marco Zanuso's adjustable bedsettee for Arflex of 1955.[280]

The P40 chair has twice been modified slightly. Originally, the back had small wings, and the upholstery of the back and the side covering of the back were each made in one piece (fig. 246). The flaring contours suggested the

244. *Osvaldo Borsani. Lounge chair: model no. P40*

more extravagant nature of postwar Italian design. Indeed, the concave back of the original version of the P40 resembles that of Carlo Mollino's more restrained pieces, such as his reclining chair of 1947 for the Casa del Sole in Cervinia.[281] Then the back was straightened and the wings removed, as in this example. Finally, sometime before the 1960s, the cushions and side pieces were changed.[282] The P40 has removable covers, originally offered in black (as here), red, blue, and gray, while the metal center and legs came originally in black or yellow.

Both the D70 and the P40 were exhibited at Milan Triennales, the former in 1954 and the latter in 1957.

CWL

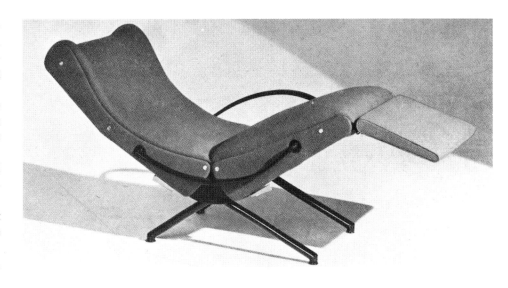

245. Borsani. Divan-bed: model no. D70. 1954

(above right) 246. Borsani. Lounge chair: model no. P40, original version. 1954

(right) 247. Borsani. Lounge chair: model no. P40, in three positions

248. *Jean Prouvé.* Table Bureau *desk*

Jean Prouvé

Desk: *Table Bureau*
Designed 1948
Formica-faced blockboard and steel; 28½ ×
   63¼ × 31½ inches (73 × 162.2 × 80.7 cm)
Produced by Ateliers Jean Prouvé (Maxéville,
   France, and Paris), 1948–60[283]
Unmarked
D86.232.1, gift of Barry Friedman and Patricia
   Pastor

Prouvé's *Table Bureau* is popularly known as the *Compass* desk because of its thin, compasslike metal legs, which are soldered to a transverse tube. From the beginning of his career, Prouvé "industrialized" his furniture designs by utilizing new materials such as sheet metal and steel tubing. Like his architectural projects, his radically functional furniture makes use of prefabricated elements and interchangeable components. He had already begun making prefabricated metal desks with interchangeable compartments and

tops for the Compagnie Parisienne d'électricité in 1926. His later designs, such as this "table desk," are sleeker and even more minimalist.

This version of the *Compass* desk is the most minimal. Alternatively, three steel drawers painted light gray with polished aluminum handles fit into a holder on one side. For more flexibility, another option was a lighter-weight black holder for three colored plastic drawers. The desk was available in laminated coreboard of black or white mat satin finish or mat varnished wood. Along with all its other options, the desk had an alternative curved top, which allowed for greater surface area.

Emphasizing maximum flexibility and cantilevered sweep, this desk exemplifies postwar design at its best and it reminds us that France, even if no longer a design leader, could suavely follow international currents. Steph Simon, a Parisian gallery that specialized in avant-garde furniture design, distributed the desk.

FTH

Timo Sarpaneva

Bud vase: *Orchid*
Designed c. 1953[284]
Glass; 10¾ × 3¼ × 3¼ inches (27.5 ×
    8.2 × 8.2 cm)
Produced by Iittala Lasitehdas (Iittala,
    Finland), c. 1954–72, 1983 to the present
    (this example 1955)
Engraved on underside: TIMO SARPANEVA
    IITTALA 55
D85.112.1, gift of Geoffrey N. Bradfield*

Timo Sarpaneva worked directly with the glass medium and with the glassblowers at the Iittala factory, thereby facilitating a rich interchange of ideas. One important series of experiments involved a method called stick blocking. Glass shapes were formed and cooled to approximately 600° to 800° C, then a branch of an apple tree was inserted. The heat of the glass turned the wood's moisture into a cloud of steam, which, since it was trapped within the mass of the glass, caused an air bubble to form. From these experiments emerged the *Lancet*, *Tear*, and *Orchid* vases, all with interesting interior cavities. (When the vases were put into industrial production, a wet iron rod was used, a less romantic but equally effective instrument.)

These vases mark a significant shift in Sarpaneva's oeuvre. Unlike his earlier *Devil's Churn*, with its sculptural eccentricities and pronounced Biomorphism (fig. 155), here the silhouettes are closed, and the forms, though still organic, are sleeker. To make an analogy with sculpture, the parallel here seems closer to Constantin Brancusi than to Henry Moore or Barbara Hepworth.

This vase is often referred to—and with good reason—as the *Orchid* vase, since its form, espe-

250. *Timo Sarpaneva*. Orchid *bud vase*

249. *Iittala Lasitehdas publicity photograph of*
Orchid *vase, c. 1954*

cially its inner sack, resembles the configuration of an orchid; indeed, an early publicity photograph shows the vase judiciously holding a single wild orchid (fig. 249). In practice, the Iittala factory generally referred to its products by model numbers only, and if a name was used for this model, it was "Art Object" or "Most Beautiful Object"—paying homage to the fact that in 1954 it had been designated "The Most Beautiful De-

sign Object of the Year" by *House Beautiful*. That same year it was also awarded a grand prize at the Milan X Triennale.[285] A measure of its popular success is suggested by the nineteen years it remained in production. In fact, it was returned to production once again in 1983, an indication of the 1980s' renewed interest in midcentury design and an affirmation of the persuasive elegance of Sarpaneva's vase. ME

251. Timo Sarpaneva. Decanters: model nos. i-401 and i-403

Timo Sarpaneva

Decanter: model no. i-401[286]
Designed c. 1955
Glass; 6⁵/₁₆ × 4⁵/₁₆ × 4⁵/₁₆ inches (16 × 11 × 11 cm)
Produced by Iittala Lasitehdas (Iittala,
    Finland), c. 1956–66[287] (this example 1958)
Engraved on underside: TIMO SARPANEVA—
    IITTALA—58
D86.137.1, gift of Geoffrey N. Bradfield*

Decanter: model no. i-403
Designed c. 1956
Glass; 11³/₁₆ × 3¾ × 3¾ inches (28.5 ×
    9.5 × 9.5 cm)
Produced by Iittala Lasitehdas (Iittala,
    Finland), c. 1957–64[288] (this example 1958)
Engraved on underside: TIMO SARPANEVA—
    IITTALA—58
D81.110.1

Sarpaneva's series of *i* decanters speaks eloquently
to the often promulgated idea that Scandinavian
·design is the reflection of a rational, aesthetic-
minded society. Meant to occupy an intermedi-
ary position between expensive, hand-finished
goods and inexpensive, serially produced wares,
this series comprised four carafes with different
liquid capacities (fifty, seventy-five, and one
hundred centiliters) and came in shapes ranging
from round and relatively squat to tall and thin.
Unifying links between the four models are their
distinctive, small spouts and, less obvious, the
inverted conical intrusions at the pontil. They
could be had in four different colors—lilac, a
cool blue, green, gray—or in a clear version.

There were also four different shapes of tumblers
corresponding to the carafes. In addition to their
visual appeal, they function well as utilitarian
objects. The carafes pour smoothly, and the
glasses are pleasant to drink from because Sarpaneva insisted that they have "a rim as thin as
the blade of a knife."[289]

These modern designs strike a curious resonance with eighteenth- and early-nineteenth-
century glass in terms of their simplicity of form
and even their general range of color. But other
aspects remind us of their contemporaneity. The
geometry of their minimalist forms, especially
the broken plane of the tall carafe, accord with
the restraint noticeable by the middle of the
1950s. The exaggerated small spout and the absence of handles likewise became distinctive features of Scandinavian design at this time, evident
in a handleless, cylindrical decanter for Nuutajärvi-Notsjö by Kaj Franck (it was awarded a
grand prize at the Milan XI Triennale in 1957); a
very similar one by Sarpaneva for Iittala; a ceramic decanter by Carl-Harry Stålhane for
Rörstrand; and another ceramic example by Henning Koppel for Bing and Grøndahl.[290]

At times these design elements became mannered. Perhaps the most extreme example is a
series designed by Sarpaneva himself in which
the vessels have striking, elongated proportions
and diminutive spouts (fig. 252). Despite their
advertised *raison d'être* as "vases or decanters,"
they are best seen as sleek, sophisticated sculpture.[291]   ME

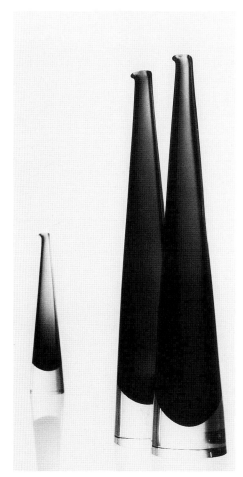

252. *Sarpaneva. Decanters. c. 1958. Collection
Iittala Glassworks, Iittala, Finland*

253. *Kaj Franck. Double decanters. c. 1957*

Kaj Franck

Decanter: model no. 1500, *Kremlin Bells*[292]
Designed c. 1957
Glass; 15¹¹/₁₆ × 5¹¹/₁₆ × 5¹¹/₁₆ inches (39.9 ×
    14.5 × 14.5 cm)
Produced by Nuutajärvi-Notsjö (Nuutajärvi,
    Finland), 1957–67
Etched on underside: Nuutajarvi-Notsjö
Printed on metallic paper label on underside:
    NUUTAJARVI/NOTSJÖ/1793/MADE IN FINLAND
D82.111.1

Kaj Franck conceived this colorful decanter and a
second, closely related model for display at the
Milan XI Triennale in 1957 (fig. 253).[293] The
other decanter uses the same upper vessel and
stopper but has a cylindrical lower section. The
separate parts of these two carafes came in a
variety of colors—olive, gray, blue, purple, pink,
amber—but all were of a grayish cast, as favored
by Scandinavian glassmakers. (This example has
a gray lower section, an amethyst middle section,
and a blue stopper.)

Although not originally intended for serial production, the decanters received such a favorable

reception that they were put into commercial manufacture. This model became known as *Kremlin Bells* because it recalls the fanciful, ogee-shaped towers of the Russian capital.[294] Although marketed as "bottles for water or fruit juice,"[295] there is no specific drink in Finland or elsewhere that requires dual vessels, and, as might be noticed, the upper vessel has no pouring spout. Thus, the appearance of clean-line functionalism, however convincing, is misleading.

But the *Kremlin Bells* decanter has a pleasing style, and it is a decidedly Scandinavian one. Sarpaneva's contemporary series of *i* decanters (fig. 251) shows a remarkable formal relationship to Franck's. Both share a preference for geometric forms and muted colors. Likewise, Sarpaneva's slightly later stacking bottles of 1959[296] have the same qualities of geometric form, varied colors, and multiplicity of units as Franck's massed decanters, and they also pose the question of appearance versus function, for there is no explanation of how the consumer would use such stacking bottles other than as decoration. Nonetheless, these minimalist objects became emblematic of Scandinavian rationalist design.

ME

254. *Franck.* Kremlin Bells *decanter: model no. 1500*

Adolf Matura

Carafe and drinking glasses
Designed c. 1959[297]
Glass; carafe: 11⅛ × 2¾ × 2¾ inches
  (28.3 × 6.9 × 6.9 cm); drinking glass:
  2¾ × 2⅝ × 2⅝ inches (6.9 × 6.7 × 6.7 cm)
Produced by the Borské Sklo Glassworks,
  National Corp. (Nový Bor, Czechoslovakia),
  c. 1960
Unmarked
D83.122.1–3

Matura was concerned primarily with functional household glass, intending his designs to be an integral part of daily life. In keeping with the simple spaces of modern interiors from the 1950s, Matura wrote, "Mass products, freed from their often senseless conservative adornments, should thus become objects of modern significance."[298] The beauty of this ensemble lies in the purity of the forms and their geometric proportions; it was recognized at the Milan XII Triennale in 1961 with a gold prize.[299]

This set, referred to as both a lemonade and a water set,[300] is similar in style to glass designed in other countries during the late 1950s and early 1960s. For example, the simplicity of the colored glass, the minimalism of the refined design, and the small lip of the carafe are comparable to elements in Scandinavian designs, such as Kaj Franck's *Kremlin Bells* of about 1957 (fig. 254) and Timo Sarpaneva's *i* series of about 1955–56 (fig. 251).

Matura's drinking glasses are distinguished from the carafe by color: the glasses are clear while the carafe is light green. Yet the indented base in each of the pieces provides a motif that unifies the ensemble. An interesting aspect of this design is the dual purpose of the glasses. In addition to functioning as drinking vessels, they also serve as lids for the carafe. Each has a deeply indented base, rising to a point in the interior, which fits into the opening of the carafe when the glass is turned upside down. A similar idea had been expressed in Floris Meydam's *Granada* liqueur set of 1954 manufactured by Leerdam (fig. 255).   JTT

(left) 255. *Floris Meydam. Granada liqueur set. 1954. National Glasmuseum, Leerdam, the Netherlands*

256. *Adolf Matura. Carafe and drinking glasses*

Raymond Loewy
Associates

Dinnerware: model 2000, pattern: *Patina*
Designed c. 1952–53[301]
Porcelain; coffeepot: 10 × 8¾ × 4⅞ inches
    (25.4 × 22.3 × 12.5 cm)
Produced by Rosenthal Porzellan AG (Selb,
    West Germany), 1954–78
Coffeepot, impressed on underside: 3
Coffeepot, printed in green on underside:
    Rosen [device of crossed lines surmounted
    by a crown] thal/SELB-GERMANY/V
Coffeepot, printed in black on underside:
    DESIGNED BY/*Raymond loewy* PATINA
Coffeepot, printed on paper label on
    underside: U.S. PAT PEND./©/The
    Rosenthal. Block/China Corp.
Creamer, impressed on underside: 2 K
Creamer and sugar bowl, printed on underside:
    [same green and black marks as above]
D85.197.1–3

The collaboration between Rosenthal, one of
Europe's most important producers of porcelain
tableware, and the offices of Raymond Loewy,
one of the most influential American midcentury
industrial designers, was a logical outgrowth of
commercial reality. Rosenthal depended on the
international sales of its wares and, according to
one account, when its share of sales to the United
States fell way below that of its European competitors, the company decided to hire American
designers to recapture the American market.[302]
According to that account, Rosenthal flew to

New York the following day and initiated talks
with Raymond Loewy.

While certain aspects of this narrative are open
to scrutiny, it expresses some basic truths. Rosenthal's own publicity emphasized that Loewy's
dinnerware was aimed at capturing the American
market, which to a war-ravaged Germany was
certainly a very important commercial prospect.
The speed with which the project was carried out
also attests to the commercial reality. By February 1952 Loewy had completed three different
services (fig. 257), and Rosenthal was issuing
them with twenty different patterns.[303] Moreover, a newly formed commercial venture,
Block-Rosenthal, was created to promote and distribute the wares throughout the United States.

The 2000 dinner service is yet a fourth design
in this series. It was not released until 1954, but,
according to Rosenthal records, it took two years
to complete the design process, which means that
it must have been begun at the same time as the
other sets or soon thereafter.[304] Responsibility for
this design has always been credited to Richard
Latham, one of the chief product designers
within the Loewy office.

Unlike the earlier designs, such as *Continental*, which are related to the generously
rounded, heavy forms of the late 1930s and 1940s,
model 2000 is taut and angular, with two conical
sections that intersect either near the top, as on
the coffeepot and creamer, or near the bottom, as
on the sugar bowl and cups. This type of sharply

waisted vessel is a form frequently encountered in
midcentury design, as we have already seen in
Tapio Wirkkala's glass and metal vases (figs. 211,
213, 219–21) and Lino Sabattini's *Cardinale* vase
(fig. 235).

Although conceived "to express the American
taste," the closest parallels to the 2000 dinnerware
are found in European design. Indeed, one of the
closest parallels—if not its stimulus—is the *Crocus* mocha service designed by the Bauhaus associate Hubert Griemert and manufactured by the
Staatliche Porzellan Manufaktur of Berlin about
1952–53 (fig. 258). After the Loewy-Latham design was released, Griemert wryly commented on
how Rosenthal gratifyingly understood and
helped spread this "form-type."[305] The angular
finial used in the 2000 service is another element
closely related to a solution used by a Bauhaus
disciple, Wilhelm Wagenfeld, for his *Gloriana*
dinnerware issued in 1953 by Rosenthal.

The point is not merely one of Bauhaus or
German influence, though it is apropos to remember that Latham himself had been a student
of Mies van der Rohe. Rather, the emphasis
should be on the international character of much
commercial design that was marketed around the
world. Moreover, this internationalism was furthered by the use of decorative schemes supplied
by Loewy's office, by Rosenthal's German staff of
designers, and by many others, including the
British textile designer Lucienne Day.[306]

ME

(far left) 257. *Raymond Loewy.* Continental
dinnerware. 1952

(left) 258. *Hubert Griemert.* Crocus *mocha service.*
1952–53

(opposite) 259. *Raymond Loewy Associates.*
Dinnerware: model no. 2000

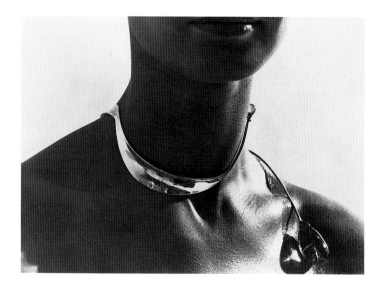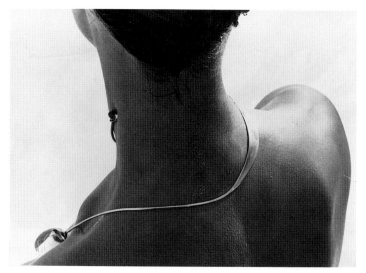

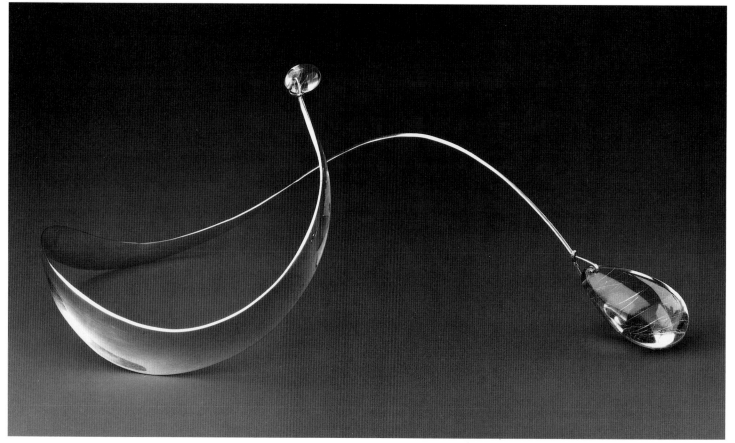

260, 261. *Torun Bülow-Hübe. Necklace*

Torun Bülow-Hübe

Necklace

Designed and executed c. 1954–58

Silver and rutilated quartz; 8¾ × 4⅝ × 6 inches
 (23.5 × 11.6 × 15.2 cm)

Impressed hallmarks: [in a shield, profile of
 Minerva facing right] [in a diamond-shaped
 field, two infinity signs arranged
 horizontally to the left of a vertical line,
 one infinity sign arranged vertically to the
 right]

D89.139.1

This necklace by Torun Bülow-Hübe proposes a revolutionary solution to the practice of encircling the female neck with jewelry. No precedent exists for this asymmetrical torque. With a lifestyle in the 1950s that revolved around constant travel between Sweden and France, Torun was forced to develop a technique that was portable. She set up makeshift workshops in hotel rooms. Unable to employ adequate welding or soldering apparatus, she developed her ability to express herself through hammering metal. In this way, she created a series of springy necklaces, each forged from a continuous piece of silver.

The design of this necklace evolved over a long period of time.[307] Torun had begun establishing the basic idea in her Stockholm studio as early as 1951, and this necklace was started there as well. She took it with her when she moved to France in 1956, and it was not completed until 1958 in the studio she established in Biot on the French Riviera. The open atmosphere of the artists' colony there informed her direction, and the necklace's spiraling rhythm reflects this freedom.

Torun's earlier necklaces from the late 1940s, symmetrical collars occasionally set with a pendant stone, are far more traditional in form (fig. 262). This necklace heralds Torun's reaction against sole frontality. She wanted to enhance the woman's back as well as her front: "Jewelry must marry the contours of a woman's body, in a word be sensuous."[308]

The necklace reflects Torun's admiration for Brancusi, whom she visited in his Montparnasse atelier in 1948. The reductivist sculpture of the Romanian-born artist exemplified a philosophy of universal harmony revealed through sweeping forms—the visual interpretation of an entity's movement. Of Brancusi's sculpture, Torun said:

It changed my whole conception of being and I started making sculptures around the body of the woman, herself a living sculpture—to try to enhance her movements, light in her eyes—her laughter.[309]

Torun has always been fascinated by the swirling line; to her it symbolizes eternal movement, the motion from which the entire cosmos emanates. The spiral represents life, togetherness, two becoming one, and the design of this necklace epitomizes that meaningful curvaceous form.

TLW

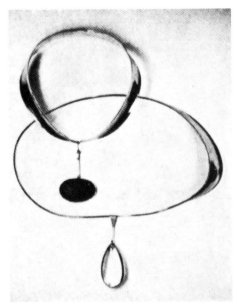

262. *Torun. Necklaces. c. 1948*

Gunnar Nylund

Vase
Designed c. 1950
Glazed stoneware; 11⅞ × 5⅛ × 3¼ inches
(30 × 13 × 8.2 cm)
Produced by Rörstrands Porslinfabrik AB
(Lidköping, Sweden), c. 1950–c. 1960
Incised on underside: [device of R surrounded by three crowns]/SWEDEN/GN/ARZ
D86.138.1, gift of Geoffrey N. Bradfield*

Carl-Harry Stålhane

Vase
Designed c. 1947
Glazed stoneware; 13¾ × 3½ × 3½ inches
(35 × 8.9 × 8.9 cm)
Produced by Rörstrands Porslinfabrik AB
(Lidköping, Sweden), c. 1947–c. 1960
Incised on underside: [device of R surrounded by three crowns]/SWEDEN/CHS
D86.140.1, gift of Geoffrey N. Bradfield*

Carl-Harry Stålhane

Vase
Designed c. 1950
Glazed stoneware; 10 × 4⅝ × 4⅝ inches
(25.3 × 11.7 × 11.7 cm)
Produced by Rörstrands Porslinfabrik AB
(Lidköping, Sweden), c. 1950–c. 1960
Incised on underside: [device of R surrounded by three crowns]/SWEDEN/CHS
D89.182.1

This trio of ceramic vases strikes a distinctive note. Their graceful, attenuated forms, mat surfaces, and subdued colors evoke the sense of simplicity and control characteristic of the 1950s, though their roots lie in the earlier mainstream of twentieth-century Modernism. As mentioned earlier, apropos of another Stålhane vase (fig. 164), experiments emulating Oriental glazes and forms had continued unabated into the 1930s and through the war years, and the specific type of mat crystalline glaze seen on the vase at the right was established at Rörstrand by Patrick Nordstrom as far back as the 1910s.[310] Also, the way the vessel rests directly on the ground, essentially baseless, and the absence of a separate lip at the mouth suggest the kind of clean-line design typical of the International Style. Indeed, the vase at center recalls those glass chemical flasks that were often shown in the 1930s as examples of machine-age technology and good taste.[311]

When these ceramics were first introduced after the war, they were perceived and promoted as representing specifically Scandinavian aesthetic. A writer in *Domus*, Italy's leading design magazine, commented on the abstract quality of Swedish design as exemplifying Swedish purity and broached the notion that that country was cold in aesthetics as well as in climate.[312] When these vases were introduced in the pages of Sweden's leading design magazine, *Form*, they were shown in clusters like organ pipes and labeled "frozen music."[313] The coolness of their palette—the vase at the left is a harmonic blending of browns and grays, the vase at center a periwinkle blue, the vase at the right an icy white—supports this notion. The same types of understated forms and colors are seen in Scandinavian glassware (figs. 251, 254, 337). They are all quite different from the vivacious, hot colors and irregular forms of Italian vases.

At the time of their creation, these Rörstrand vases were deemed to represent a moment of classical balance and to hold the promise of eternal validity. Today it can be seen more clearly that they bear the marks of their age. The exaggeratedly long proportions and mannered, small, thin neck of the central vase; the waisted effect of the vase at the right, with its very wide mouth; the gentle paddling into an oval of the vase at the left and the way that it has been trimmed to form two soaring arcs—all are characteristics of the period. They are part and parcel of an international postwar idea of Modernism, visible as well in Tapio Wirkkala's and Lino Sabattini's designs (figs. 211, 213, 232, 235). They are as specific indications of a moment in time as those of any other age or culture.   ME

263. *Gunnar Nylund, vase (left); Carl-Harry Stålhane, vases*

265. Hans Wegner. Round *armchair: model no. JH 501*

264. Finn Juhl. Armchair. 1944

Hans Wegner

Armchair: model no. JH 501, *Round*
Designed 1949
Teak and alum caning; 29⅞ × 22⅞ × 20¾
   inches (75.9 × 58.2 × 52.7 cm)
Produced by Johannes Hansen (Copenhagen),
   1949 to the present (this example
   c. 1949–50)
Impressed on front side of central stretcher:
   MADE IN DENMARK
Impressed on back side of central stretcher:
   JOHANNES HANSEN/COPENHAGEN
D85.156.1

The *Round* chair is perhaps the clearest state-ment of Hans Wegner's assiduous design process. His is an aesthetic that draws on traditional forms, that perfects details expressive of the con-struction, and that deftly derives an inherent dec-oration from the materials themselves.

The basic concept of an armchair with a con-tinuous, U-shaped armrest and crest rail has a number of historical precedents: Kaare Klint's *Fåborg* chair of 1914, Wegner's own *Chinese* chairs of 1943–45 (fig. 162), and, above all, an early design by Finn Juhl in 1944 for Niels Vodder

(fig. 264), which is remarkably similar in form. However, over a period of some seven years Wegner transformed the motif into a highly per-sonal configuration.[314] This is clearest in the top rail, which evidences his search for sculptural unity. A fluid movement is established between elements, and straight lengths of wood are han-dled with a surprising plasticity. The frame is not laminated or bent but, rather, laboriously crafted by hand. There is no exposed cross-stretcher, though there is a "bow" underneath joining the front and back seat rails. The design of the lower

266. Wegner. Side chair: model no. JH 505. 1952. Study Collection, The Museum of Modern Art, New York

frame—seat rails, legs, and stretchers—shows Wegner's attempt to articulate the construction. He achieved a subtle composition in which gently curved and canted angles are joined in finely wrought details.

The materials and finishes employed by Wegner are further indicative of his design approach. Oak or teak frames are given "natural" wax or oil finishes respectively. The caning is woven in an open, decorative pattern around the rails, creating a play of solid and void as well as residual shadow.[315] The treatment of the backrest also illustrates Wegner's search for a unity between the decorative and the constructive. Early versions of the chair had mortise and tenon joints between the armrest and crest rail, and Wegner employed rattan to cover the "unsightly" joint. In 1950 he perfected a sawtooth or "W" joint, which could be exposed without visually interrupting the rail.[316]

Characteristically, Wegner continued to adapt and modify the *Round* chair over the next two decades, in both side and armchair versions. Among the most notable was a side chair, model JH 505, of 1952 (fig. 266), which featured a cantilevered rail.[317] Evidence as all these later designs are of Wegner's deliberative concern for sculptural form and constructive decoration, his original effort of 1949 stands as perhaps his most important design.   RCM

Finn Juhl

Armchair: model no. P4–107, *Chieftain*
Designed 1949
Teak and leather; 36½ × 39⅝ × 34¾ inches
   (92.8 × 100.6 × 88.2 cm)
Produced by Niels Vodder (Allerød, Denmark), 1949–80; upholstery by Ivan Schlechter (Gilleleje, Denmark)
Impressed on back side of front seat rail: NIELS VODDER CABINETMAKER/COPENHAGEN DENMARK/DESIGN FINN JUHL
D85.122.1

Among Finn Juhl's work of the 1940s, the *Chieftain* armchair stands as perhaps the best synthesis of his concept of form, structure, and upholstery. Its evolution may be traced in a series of three designs from that decade.

Juhl's early attempts at furniture design during the war years took the form of rather massive upholstered pieces for the cabinetmaker Niels Vodder. His sofas (fig. 267) featured high backs, multiple-colored or patterned fabrics, and, most important, strong, curved shapes.

An armchair of 1944 was perhaps the first clear indication of his mature direction, especially because of his preoccupation with the sculptural treatment of the wooden frame. Here Juhl took an unconventional approach, minimizing the upholstery and exposing the dark structural frame. The chair was made of mahogany, rosewood, or walnut. (After the war, Danish design-

267. Finn Juhl. Sofa. 1941

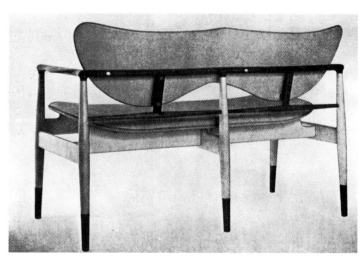

268. Juhl. Settee. 1948

269. *Juhl. Chieftain armchair: model no. P4-107*

ers, including Juhl, Hans Wegner, and Arne Jacobsen, switched to lighter-colored woods, such as beech and teak.) For the first time, Juhl used diagonal stretchers and a soft, flowing profile to unify the upper elements of the frame.

It was, however, in a settee (fig. 268) and armchair some four years later that Juhl was able to integrate completely these ideas. He emphasized the importance of the frame by employing light and dark woods to articulate elements, and, as the major innovation, he introduced a new kind of upholstery: thin, sculptural shells that float on recessed seat rails.

In the *Chieftain* chair designed the following year, Juhl developed these ideas of the shell and frame to their fullest. In an exhibition at the Museum of Modern Art in 1946, Charles Eames had shown similar molded plywood shells, but the American had eliminated seat rails and stretchers altogether. Juhl, on the other hand, chose to make these traditional elements an integral part of a sculptural framework. He thus achieved in his own idiom and in a handmade object the Modernist ideal of the separation of frame and upholstery—that delicate balance between "the *bearing* and the *borne*."[318]

The *Chieftain* chair is, in fact, a masterful example of such a form in a tripartite composition: the blade-shaped armrests are powerful, three-dimensional upholstered shells that float on subtly sculpted wooden bases; the modified oval seat is supported on straight, diagonal stretchers with chamfered edges; and the canted back panel is suspended from tapered stiles by bow-shaped, diagonal wooden elements. This armchair is Juhl's most exuberant example of an organic aesthetic from the 1940s and, some four decades later, may assuredly be acclaimed as one of the masterworks of this century.　　RCM

Finn Juhl

Bowl
Designed c. 1950[319]
Teak; 6⅞ × 13⅝ × 14⅝ inches (17.6 ×
    34.6 × 37.2 cm)
Produced by Magne Monsen for Kay Bojesen
    (Copenhagen), 1951–73 (this example
    before c. 1965)
Impressed on underside: DESIGN/FINN JUHL/
    TEAK/KAY BOJESEN/DENMARK
D85.149.1

Like Finn Juhl's furniture, this bowl conveys grace and beauty while remaining fully utilitarian. It is made of teak, a material that became synonymous with postwar Scandinavian design. Not only is its grain aesthetically pleasing, but also its resinous nature is well suited to a finish of rubbed oil rather than varnish. It can thus be subjected to steady use without damage or the need for periodic refinishing.

According to Juhl, the bowl was originally designed for Just Lunning, then general manager of the New York branch of Georg Jensen Inc.[320] It was hand-turned on a lathe by Magne Monsen for Kay Bojesen, and Juhl supervised the execution. Since ancient times, lathe turning has been the essential method employed for making wooden objects. It was continued in the 1940s and 1950s by craftsmen such as Kay Bojesen and James Prestini. Juhl's bowl, however, is different from theirs in that its top edge is shaped to form a subtle curve terminating in crests. Also, the base is thick, providing strength and stability, while the sides become increasingly slender as they rise upward, creating a graceful and buoyant form. This subtle, sculptural aesthetic is consistent with Juhl's oeuvre, which avoids angularity and relies on curved elements, as can be seen in the back of a chair he designed for Niels Vodder in 1949 (fig. 269).

Four variant designs, each a different size, were made, though always in limited quantities. At first they were made from solid blocks of teak, as is this example in the Stewart Collection. In the 1960s, as teak became scarce, two pieces were glued together in order to create the large size bowls. In 1973, when teak had become too scarce and expensive, production was stopped altogether.[321]

DAH & JTT

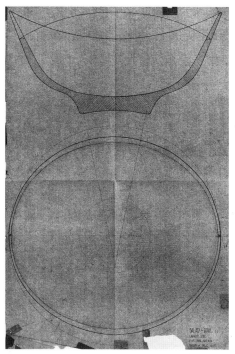

270. Finn Juhl. Drawing for bowl. c. 1950. Liliane and David M. Stewart Collection. Gift of Finn Juhl

271. Juhl. Bowl

272. Arne Jacobsen. *Variants of the* Ant *side chair.* 1952–55

Arne Jacobsen

Side chair: model no. 3100, *Ant*
Designed 1952
Teak-faced beech plywood, steel, plastic
    sheathing, and rubber; 29⅞ × 21¹/₁₆ × 23
    inches (75.8 × 53.5 × 58.4 cm)
Produced by Fritz Hansens Eft. A/S
    (Allerød, Denmark), 1952 to the present[322]
    (this example 1952–55)
Impressed on metal plate on underside of seat:
    FH [in circle]/DANMARK
D83.124.1, gift of Geoffrey N. Bradfield*

While Arne Jacobsen designed a number of custom furnishings for his buildings in the prewar
years, it was not until the 1950s that he began to
think of the industrial manufacture of his designs. Jacobsen's first major attempt to deal with
metal frames and molded shells was about 1952,
while putting together an office series for the
American-Scandinavian Foundation in New
York.[323] One three-legged chair with separate
seat and back panels shows the direct influence of
Charles and Ray Eames' experimental designs,
exhibited in 1946 at the Museum of Modern Art.
Another chair, with a continuous seat and
back unit, was an important variant in Jacobsen's development of the *Ant* chair for mass
production.[324]

The *Ant* chair was, in fact, Jacobsen's first
mature furniture design. A diminutive side chair,
it was originally designed for the canteen of the
Novo Pharmaceutical Co. in Copenhagen and
was mass-produced by Fritz Hansen at about the
same time, in the early 1950s. The profile consists
of an oval seat joined by a slender neck to an ovoid
back, the resultant organic form earning the
name *ant*. It was constructed as a plywood shell
subtly molded in three dimensions. The three-
legged tubular base was attached by rubber
mounts and a metal plate; however, it lacked the
finesse of the construction seen in the Eameses'
DCM chair (1946). The example in the Stewart
Collection has a plastic sheathing over its legs, an
early option available from 1952 to 1955.

273. *Jacobsen.* Ant *side chair: model no.* 3100

274. Carlo Mollino. Side chair. Before 1949

275. Jacobsen. Side chair: model no. 4130. 1955

The *Ant* chair was instantly acclaimed, earning Jacobsen considerable fame. Many have called it the first chair with a continuous seat and back made of one piece of molded, laminated wood—which it most certainly was not. Alvar Aalto, Marcel Breuer, and the Saarinen/Eames team had all achieved such chairs before the war as both two- and three-dimensional forms and with a variety of frames.[325] Even Jacobsen's distinctive back profile has historical antecedents: the ovoid back can be seen in Viennese Biedermeier side chairs, and a more contemporary example was a three-legged molded shell design by Carlo Mollino (fig. 274).[326]

The *Ant* chair was, however, an elegant solution for a lightweight, inexpensive side chair that could be stacked. Jacobsen continued to develop it through the late 1960s with variant shells, bases, and attachments (fig. 272). Perhaps the most notable model was his no. 4130 side chair of 1955 (fig. 275), whose sculpted wooden base was more fully integrated with its shell.

RCM

Arne Jacobsen

Armchair: model no. 3320, *Swan*
Designed 1957
Leather, plastic shell with foam rubber,
    aluminum, painted steel, chromed steel,
    and plastic glides; 29½ × 28½ × 27 inches
    (74.9 × 72.3 × 68.5 cm)
Produced by Fritz Hansens Eft. A/S (Allerød,
    Denmark), 1958 to the present (this example
    1960)[327]
Stenciled in white on underside of shell: FH [in
    a circle inside a square]/MADE IN DENMARK
    D87.244.1

In designing the furnishings for the Scandinavian Airlines System (SAS) Royal Hotel in Copenhagen, Arne Jacobsen produced four chairs that featured upholstered plastic shells. The two most successful were pedestal forms: the *Swan* armchair and the *Egg* lounge chair (fig. 278). This chair series was clearly derived from Eero Saarinen's revolutionary experiments in the late 1940s with three-dimensionally molded plastic shells (fig. 307) and in the 1950s with sculptural pedestal forms (fig. 335). Jacobsen's subsequent designs are elegant—though not original—extensions of this search for a comfortable chair that was lightweight, fluid in form to fit the human body, and required a minimum of padding and no springs.

Although considerably smaller in scale than the *Egg* chair, the *Swan* chair is perhaps the most interesting design in the series. The interaction between the sculptural back and arms creates a positive/negative spatial play, giving it an overall profile that is more successful than the closed form of the *Egg* chair. Although its almost petal-like form is indebted to Saarinen's *Tulip* pedestal chair (fig. 335), Jacobsen's design is still more fluid.

The *Swan* shell lent itself to a number of variants. In addition to a settee (1959), the *Swan* chair was available with a fixed or adjustable aluminum pedestal as well as a four-legged, teak-veneered base (fig. 276).[328] The X-shaped wooden base also appears to be derived from a Saarinen design: the nos. 71 and 72 chair series of about 1950 for the General Motors Technical Center. Jacobsen's wooden base provides a sculptural unity missing in the somewhat truncated metal pedestal, although the designer handled the aluminum base with considerable dexterity in the junction of four tapered feet to a concave shaft.

A most notable feature of the *Swan* chair is the superb detailing employed for the leather upholstery. (The chair also came with vinyl or fabric upholstery.) The back side of this example is covered with a single piece of material applied directly to the shell with a thin layer of padding.

276. Arne Jacobsen. Swan *armchair with wooden base.* 1957

(opposite) 277. Jacobsen. Swan *armchair: model no. 3320*

The juncture to the pedestal is covered by a circular piece of leather, which is glued rather than sewn, and the steel ring that joins the shell and the shaft is painted brown to match the leather. The inside of the shell is likewise covered with a single piece of leather over subtly sculpted foam padding, which is "feathered" to the edge of the shell. The two pieces of leather are joined in a meticulously sewn, taut welt with blind stitching. In all, it is a tour de force of handcraftmanship on an industrially made object, reflecting Jacobsen's concern for fine detailing, not to mention the noted quality control of the Danish furniture industry.

In spite of their lack of originality, both the *Swan* and *Egg* chairs have proven popular over the years. In continuous production since the mid-1950s, they may rightfully be considered among the most influential Danish designs of the postwar era.   RCM

278. Jacobsen. Egg lounge chair, 1957; ottoman, 1959

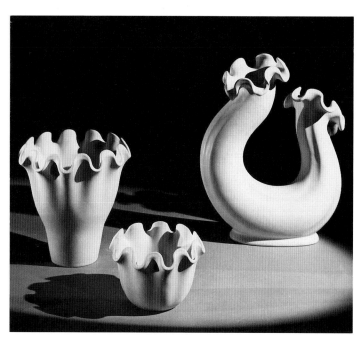

279. Wilhelm Kåge. Vaga vases. c. 1940

(opposite) *280. Stig Lindberg. Veckla vases: model nos. 243, 245, and 236*

Stig Lindberg

Vase: model no. 243, *Veckla*
Designed c. 1949
Glazed porcelain; 4¾ × 5⁵⁄₁₆ × 2¾ inches
 (12 × 13.5 × 7 cm)
Produced by AB Gustavsberg (Gustavsberg,
 Sweden), 1950–c. 1960[329]
Impressed on underside: GUSTAVSBERG SWEDEN
D85.158.1

Vase: model no. 245, *Veckla*
Designed c. 1949
Glazed porcelain; 1⅞ × 5¹¹⁄₁₆ × 3¾ inches
 (4.8 × 14.5 × 9.5 cm)
Produced by AB Gustavsberg (Gustavsberg,
 Sweden), 1950–c. 1960
Unmarked
D85.159.1

Vase: model no. 236, *Veckla*
Designed c. 1949
Glazed porcelain; 14 × 6⅞ × 3¼ inches
 (35.5 × 17.4 × 8.3 cm)
Produced by AB Gustavsberg (Gustavsberg,
 Sweden), 1950–c. 1960
Impressed on underside: GUSTAVSBERG SWEDEN
 [around device of an anchor]/236
Printed on gold metallic paper label on
 underside: [device of a stylized hand and
 G]/STUDIO/VECKLA/CARRARA/236
D86.144.1, gift of Geoffrey N. Bradfield*

281. *Lindberg. Vase. 1938. Statens Konstmuseet, Stockholm*

282. *Kåge.* Soft Forms *dinnerware. 1940*

While ceramics had traditionally been dominated by a circular symmetry engendered by the potter's wheel, designers of the new, postwar mode sought complex curves and asymmetry. The *Veckla* line exemplifies a direct and frequently employed solution, namely, manipulating the vessel while it was still in a pliant stage prior to the first firing. These three eccentric-looking ceramics were cast as simple bowls and cylindrical vessels and gained their distinctive look by then being deftly pinched and folded. *Veckla*, in fact, is Swedish for *folded*. This technique not only solved issues of aesthetics, it also allowed for the production of complex shapes on an inexpensive, industrial basis.

Lindberg had already shown his predisposition for such asymmetry in vases from the late 1930s (fig. 281), and the concept of folding also dates to those critical years in the Gustavsberg factory. An important turning point was the *Soft Forms* dinnerware of 1940 (fig. 282), designed by Lindberg's teacher, Wilhelm Kåge. The walls of the *Soft Forms* serving bowls gently cave in, although this innovation was offset by the traditional symmetry of the dinner service as a whole.[330] Kåge's *Vaga* series of about 1940 (fig. 279) offers a second important precedent, both in the whiteness of the body and in the prominent, ruffled mouths of the vases.[331] The bent, tubular *Vaga* vase at the right uncannily presages the two-horned *Veckla* vase,

but the *Vaga* series was still merely a transitional stage. The essentially static bodies are not rhythmically integrated with the ruffled edges, and the overall impression is of a heavy awkwardness that one often finds in prewar work.

The continued interest in undulant forms at the Gustavsberg factory from the late 1930s onward provided an important tradition that Lindberg could draw on. However, the *Veckla* series evinces a freedom and verve that set it apart from its precedents. These strikingly exaggerated and dynamic vases make a strong, sculptural statement—as strong as can be expected from small containers for flowers.

ME

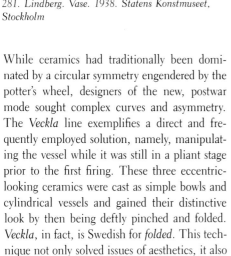

Fulvio Bianconi

Vase: *Pezzato*
Designed c. 1950
Glass; 6⅞ × 8³⁄₁₆ × 4¾ inches (17.5 × 20.8 × 12.1 cm)
Produced by Venini (Murano, Italy), intermittently from 1950 to the present
Acid-stamped on underside: *venini*/murano/ ITALIA
D86.162.1, gift of Bombardier Inc.

The introduction of Bianconi's *Pezzato* vases for Venini at the Venice XXV Biennale in 1950 and then at the Milan IX Triennale the following year (fig. 284) generated a great deal of critical acclaim.[332] Made from fused pieces of glass cut in

squares, diamonds, or long strips, these vessels struck a note of novelty and surprise.[333] Yet the technique itself was an old one, traceable to Roman times (fig. 179), reintroduced in the nineteenth century (fig. 180), and, most germane of all, reestablished in the Venini workshop by Carlo Scarpa in the 1930s.

Bianconi's designs, unlike those produced by Barovier & Toso (fig. 178), expressed a lyrical freedom. Rather than emphasizing the geometric regularity possible in *pezzato* work, Bianconi stressed the fluidity of the medium. In the reheating and shaping of the vessel, the sections of colored glass were distended to varied shapes of different dimensions. The lower portion was

283. *Fulvio Bianconi. Pezzato* vase

pulled outward and the mouth was raised into two peaks separated by gentle curves, which establishes a rhythmic fluidity in the overall design. Not least of all, the boldness of the colors and their exuberant juxtapositions add a carnival quality. Appropriately, this model gained the popular name of *Arlecchino* (Harlequin) in honor of that commedia dell'arte character's patchwork costume.[334] In one sense, the diamond pattern is like Sven Markelius's *Pythagoras* textile (fig. 323) and Earl Pardon's necklace (fig. 326), but the pulsing form recalls Stig Lindberg's *Veckla* vases (fig. 280). The changing rhythms of color and form in all these works are emblematic of the joyous nature of postwar design.   ME

284. Pezzato *vases displayed at the Venice XXV Biennale, 1950*

James Prestini

Bowl

Designed and executed 1954

Mahogany-faced plywood; 4⅝ × 15¾ ×
    8⅞ inches (11.7 × 40 × 22.5 cm)

On label taped to underside, printed and
    handwritten: CRAFTSMAN James Prestini/
    DESCRIPTION bowl 16″ × 8½″ × 4½″/MATERIAL
    Mahogany Plywood/Eligible for purchase?
    Yes X No l/ATTACH SECURELY TO OBJECT

On same label, printed sideways over five red
    lines: 500/A/No. 1141 84 [handwritten in
    ink] 545 [handwritten in pencil]

D85.161.1

Between 1933 and 1953, Prestini made a series of lathe-turned bowls that were highly praised by the critics of the day. Made following the tradition of using solid blocks of wood, these bowls are noteworthy for their beautiful, functional forms and the natural richness of the wood. [335] No templates or mechanical guides were used, and each object became unique through differences in the grain or the character of the wood. Prestini's passion for the Modernist movement was manifested in his reduction of objects to minimal forms.

Prestini experimented with plywood while he was a student and then instructor at László Moholy-Nagy's Chicago School (and later Institute) of Design. From 1939 to 1946, Prestini taught the foundation course at the school, where students were given plywood as an experimental material with which to explore two-dimensional forms and to learn its technological limitations.

Prestini himself began to use plywood for his own art while living in his father's birthplace of Besano, Italy, from 1953 to 1956. In turning to bent plywood, he hoped to achieve greater freedom and asymmetry. He shaped this bowl by cutting an asymmetrical, elliptical form of plywood and bending it around a heated cylindrical mandrel. Its undulating contour has parallels with the experiments of the Eameses' (fig. 30), whose work in plywood he certainly knew. Prestini's plywood bowl belongs to a small series of related pieces, which were honored in their day, receiving an honorable mention at the Milan X Triennale in 1954. [336]

Although this object and similar ones created during his Italian period are frequently referred to as bowls, the designer himself has affirmed that they were "not designed and executed as practical household objects. They were conceived and developed as sculptural forms." [337] As such, they can be considered a prelude to Prestini's sculpture in steel, which afforded him the complete three dimensionality he sought in order to express pure form.

DAH & JTT

285. *James Prestini. Bowl*

286. *Eva Zeisel.* Tomorrow's Classic *dinnerware*

Eva Zeisel

Dinnerware: *Tomorrow's Classic*
Designed c. 1949–50
Glazed earthenware; pitcher: 6⅝ × 7⅜ × 5
inches (16.7 × 18.7 × 12.7 cm)
Produced by the Hall China Company (East
Liverpool, Ohio), 1951–c.1960
Transfer printed in blue: HALLCRAFT/BY/
[monogram of white letters H over C in a
gray rectangular box with rounded corners]
Eva Zeisel/MADE IN U.S.A. BY HALL
CHINA CO.
D82.120.1–6, 9, 15, 16, 19, gift of Sherman
Emery*

In its succession of changing styles, Zeisel's first
decade of work in the United States, from 1939 to
1950, can be said to mirror its time. One can also
perceive an emerging emphasis on emotive expression and lyricism of line, a development that
culminated in the dinnerware known as *Tomorrow's Classic.*[338]

A comparison between the coffeepots from her
earlier *Museum* service and from *Tomorrow's
Classic* (fig. 287) is instructive to establish both
the continuity and the changes in her approach to
form. Although the two pouring spouts are quite
similar in shape, their relationships to the vessels

287. *Zeisel.* Museum (1942–43) *and* Tomorrow's
Classic (c. 1949–50) *coffeepots*

are tellingly different: the *Museum* spout is a
separate unit, clearly demarcated from the body,
while the later spout is subtly sculpted into the
form. A similar distinction is registered by the
two handles: separate from the body on the earlier
vessel, the handle is rhythmically fused into the
surging, upper contour of the later pot. A comparable change is registered in the lids as well: the
geometric, spooled form in the *Museum* series is
replaced by a flared element whose rhythm corresponds with the contour in *Tomorrow's Classic.*

To a certain degree, this sense of fusion and
rhythmic emphasis had already been explored in
parts of the *Town and Country* line, especially in
the pitchers and serving platters (fig. 140), but
here it is used more consistently, as a major note
throughout the whole set, and with greater control. The serving platters and casseroles rise in
soaring arcs, the cereal bowls flare upward on one
end, the dinner plate is distended gently to an
oval. The traditional geometry of static circle and
rectangle is nowhere to be seen. With its sense of
rhythm and pliancy, *Tomorrow's Classic*, like Stig

Lindberg's *Veckla* vases (fig. 280) and Fulvio Bianconi's *Pezzato* vase (fig. 283), all contemporary to one another, has the fluency of form that became one of the benchmarks of postwar style.

Zeisel developed *Tomorrow's Classic* without a commission, and it languished for several years in the office of her agent, Richards Morgenthau. It finally found a sponsor in Charles Seliger of Commercial Decal, a firm specializing in decals for china. His company needed a modern dinnerware service for its own commercial ends, and Seliger arranged for it to be produced by Hall China, a well-established firm that customarily produced decal-decorated ware.[339] The contract required that Zeisel supply the forms and nine

designs for decals for the first year, plus three additional patterns in each subsequent year. These ornaments were designed by her studio assistants, often drawn from the ranks of her students at Pratt Institute, Brooklyn. Among those that were first released were *Frost Flower* by Irene Haas and *Fantasy*, a more architectural, Naum Gabo–type of configuration, by the team of William Katavolos, Ross Littell, and Douglas Kelley. The most popular of the patterns was *Bouquet*, supposedly designed by Seliger but in fact a close imitation of a pattern by Stig Lindberg, once again reminding us of the internationalism of postwar design—and the frequency with which designs were pirated.[340]

ME

288. *Tapio Wirkkala*. Finlandia *dinnerware*

Tapio Wirkkala

Dinnerware: *Finlandia*, pattern: *Majestic*
Designed c. 1954–56[341]
Porcelain; dinner plate: diameter 9½ inches
   (24.2 cm)
Produced by Rosenthal Porzellan AG (Selb,
   West Germany), 1956–73 (this set before
   1960)[342]
Dinner and luncheon plate, transfer printed in
   gray on underside: Thomas [within device
   resembling a lidded casserole]/GERMANY
Dinner and luncheon plate, transfer printed in
   gold on underside: *finlandia*—EIN
   ENTWURF/VON TAPIO WIRKKALA DER MIT
   6/GRAND PRIX AUF DEN TRIENNALEN/DER
   MEIST AUSGEZEICHNETE EURO-/PÄISCHE
   GESTALTER IST. SEIN/GESTALTUNGSPRINZIP:
   KÜNSTLER-/ISCHE AUSDRUCKSKRAFT MUSS
   MIT/GESTEIGERTEM GEBRAUCHSWERT/
   SCHRITT HALTEN./QUALITÄT-THOMAS/MIT
   DEM GOLDSTEMPEL
Dinner and luncheon plate, transfer printed in
   orange on underside: 61
Salad plate and cup, transfer printed on
   underside: Thomas [in gray, within device]
   GERMANY [in gray]
Saucer, transfer printed on underside: Thomas
   [in gray, within device] 61 [in orange]
Soup bowl unmarked
D83.145.1–5

The genesis of this dinnerware can be traced to
Wirkkala's six-month stay in the New York office
of Raymond Loewy in 1954. Although Wirkkala
had already established an international reputation through his designs for Iittala, like many
Scandinavians he wished to study American
methods of mass production. One project in
Loewy's office on which he worked was the dinnerware commissioned by Rosenthal, and it was
sufficiently complete to have gained Rosenthal's
approval before he left. Rosenthal then agreed to
have the Finn complete the project on his own.

A comparison of Wirkkala's dinnerware with
one of the sets that Richard Latham of Loewy's
office developed for Rosenthal (fig. 259) is instructive. Latham and Loewy's design depends
on a hard-edged geometry, while Wirkkala's is
more organic. This is especially noticeable in the
coffeepots, teapots, and pitchers. Latham and
Loewy's finials are triangular while Wirkkala's are
flanges that seem to have been modeled by the
pressure of fingers squeezing the clay. A telling
detail is the cup handle: Latham and Loewy's is a
plain, looped strap while Wirkkala's (fig. 289) is a
series of finely sculpted curves, recalling Art
Nouveau design.

In turning to renowned international designers
such as Wirkkala and Loewy, Rosenthal hoped to
capitalize on their reputations to gain wider markets. Indeed, the long and belabored inscription
on the underside of the dinner plate enumerates
the number of prizes that Wirkkala won at the
Milan Triennales, assuring the potential cus-
tomer of its artistry as well as its utility. Yet,
despite the firm's proclaimed interest in good
design, its idealism often clashed with the realities of commerce. Wirkkala's forms are seen at
their best when left undecorated or, as here, enhanced by simple bands of soft gray, a company-
designed pattern called *Majestic*. However, for
greater commercial viability, Rosenthal also offered the *Finlandia* service with various floral and
geometric patterns designed by the Rosenthal
staff, with results that are far from satisfactory
(fig. 290).[343]

ME

290. *Wirkkala*. Finlandia *service with* Blue Rose *pattern. 1957*

289. *Wirkkala. Detail of* Finlandia *cup handle*

John Van Koert

Coffeepot: *Contour*
Designed c. 1948–50
Silver and melamine: 9⅝ × 7⅝ × 4⅜ inches
   (24.5 × 19.4 × 11.5 cm)
Produced by Towle Manufacturing Co.
   Silversmiths (Newburyport, Massachusetts),
   c. 1951–60
Coffeepot, impressed on underside:
   TOWLE/STERLING/32/[device of a rampant
   lion facing right in a shield-shaped
   cartouche]/350
Lid, impressed on back: 6
D89.126.1, gift of John Van Koert*

Salt and pepper shakers: *Contour*
Designed 1948–50
Silver and replaced plastic stoppers;
   3⅝ × 2 × 1¾ inches (9.2 × 5 × 4.4 cm)
Produced by Towle Manufacturing Co.
   Silversmiths (Newburyport, Massachusetts),
   c. 1951–60
Impressed on underside: TOWLE/STERLING/380
D89.104.1, 2

291. *John Van Koert.* Contour *coffeepot*

These salt and pepper shakers and coffeepot are part of the *Contour* line manufactured by Towle Silversmiths. The line was presented for the first time in 1951 at "Knife/Fork/Spoon," a traveling exhibition of the history of flatware sponsored by Towle for the Walker Art Center, Minneapolis. The entire line was composed of flatware (which was introduced first) and hollowware, including a coffee and tea service, hot and cold beverage servers, candlesticks, and even "Baby's First Toothbrush."

Contour was developed between 1948 and 1950 by John Van Koert, who was then product design director of the company and who had been hired by John Withers, Towle's general manager, to create an intentionally modern style line.[344] *Contour* was born amid some controversy, since

Towle was a company steeped in traditionalism (although it did experiment with new styles periodically). It generated excellent sales initially, but after a few months its popularity waned.

The undulating silhouettes of the vessels are consistent in style with many contemporary works. The salt and pepper shakers are reminiscent of Eva Zeisel's *Town and Country* "Shmoo" salt and pepper shakers (fig. 141), and, in fact, Van Koert has referred to his conception as "shmoo-like." His shakers suggest perhaps a pair of strutting birds. The two vessels seem to interact with one another, their visual dynamics changing as their relative placement is altered. Furthermore, the five cleverly concealed holes, which allow the seasonings to flow out of the receptacles, can be interpreted as facial features.

The asymmetrical contours, sensuous silhouettes, and minimalist approach also suggest analogies with Scandinavian silver of the period. While the coffeepot is a generalized reflection of Scandinavian ideas, the salt and pepper shakers suggest more specific comparisons. Van Koert's work shows an especially strong affinity with the "characterful physiognomy" of Henning Koppel's wine pitcher (fig. 138). Swedish silversmith Sigurd Persson utilized a similar physiognomy in his vase from about the same time (fig. 293). We might also compare *Contour* to a condiment set by Søren Georg Jensen from 1951 (fig. 294). Jensen's forms curve sensuously, yet they also reveal a definite crispness, a sense of hard-edged geometry—of the type that Van Koert employed.

TLW

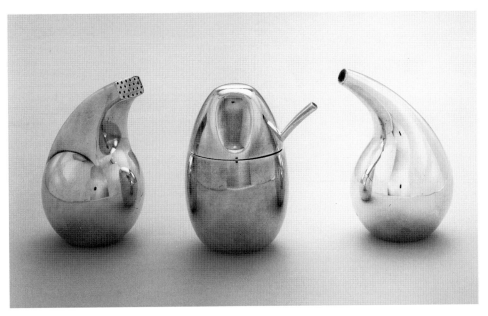

Walter Ballmer

Poster: *Stile Olivetti*
Designed 1961
Offset lithograph; 50⁵⁄₁₆ × 37 inches (127.9 × 94 cm)
Printed by Lithographie & Cartonnage A.G. (Zurich), 1961
Printed in lower left corner: Druck: Lithographie & Cartonnage A.G. Zürich
D84.190.1

This poster was done for an exhibition at Zurich's Kunstgewerbemuseum from April 8 through May 20, 1961, on Olivetti's history and its considerable stylistic contributions to industry. As staff designer for Olivetti from 1956 to 1981, Ballmer was instrumental in shaping that corporation's design image. Excelling in designing trademarks and symbols for corporate identity, he designed much promotional material for Olivetti. He was also the designer of the exhibition itself.

Ballmer's design approach owes much to his training at Basel's Kunstgewerbeschule, and this poster embodies the characteristics of his graphic work. He used an extreme economy of means to achieve a basic clarity and order, making his designs a suitable expression for an industrial product of the space age. This poster's image, dominated by a white O from Olivetti's logotype, is sufficiently allusive to symbolize the exhibition itself. The white O stands out against a brilliant orange-red background, which also sets off the blocks of simple, Helvetica type aligned vertically at the right for maximum clarity and legibility. Arranged in varying sizes, the blocks of type present the viewer with the exhibition's pertinent information regarding the title, dates, and times of admission.

295. *Walter Ballmer.* Stile Olivetti

This poster attests to the survival of Bauhaus-inspired design. Ballmer, however, has tempered the rigid geometry and palette of prewar design by using a generously rounded and squared O and a nonprimary color—evidence of the typically postwar lyrical tendency.

FTH

296. *Armin Hofmann.* Theater Bau von der Antike bis zur Moderne

Armin Hofmann

Poster: *Theater Bau von der Antike bis zur Moderne*
Designed 1955
Linocut; 50¼ × 35½ inches (128 × 90.3 cm)
Printed by Buchdruckerei Verband Schweizerischer Konsumvereine (Basel, Switzerland),³⁴⁵ 1955
Printed in black inside the design, at right center edge: Entwurf und Schnitt: A Hofmann—Druck: Buchdruckerei VSK Basel
D84.184.1, gift of Geoffrey N. Bradfield*

This striking poster announced an exhibition devoted to theaters from ancient to modern times that was held at Zurich's Helmhaus, a municipal gallery for temporary exhibitions, in August and September 1955.

The simple and direct linocut technique was Hofmann's medium of choice to create bold forms and stark outlines. The severe effect is further heightened by the restriction to black and white, a color scheme Hofmann favored in his poster work.

The curved forms embraced by the tight composition echo the rounded shapes found elsewhere in international postwar decorative arts: glassware by Tapio Wirkkala, dishes by Eva Zeisel, furniture by Arne Jacobsen and Eero Saarinen. Here, the two shapes specifically suggest the ancient amphitheater and the modern theater in the round. The starkly geometric, uppercase lettering of the exhibition's title plays upon its resemblance to the lettering of classical Greek inscriptions while offering the sparseness of a modern aesthetic. It contrasts with the serif type within the lower circle, giving the exhibition's hours.

Spare, powerful forms that can be seen at a distance are a trademark of Hofmann's style. The Minimalist movement of the 1970s owes much to such designs, which contain a wealth of information using little formal imagery.

FTH

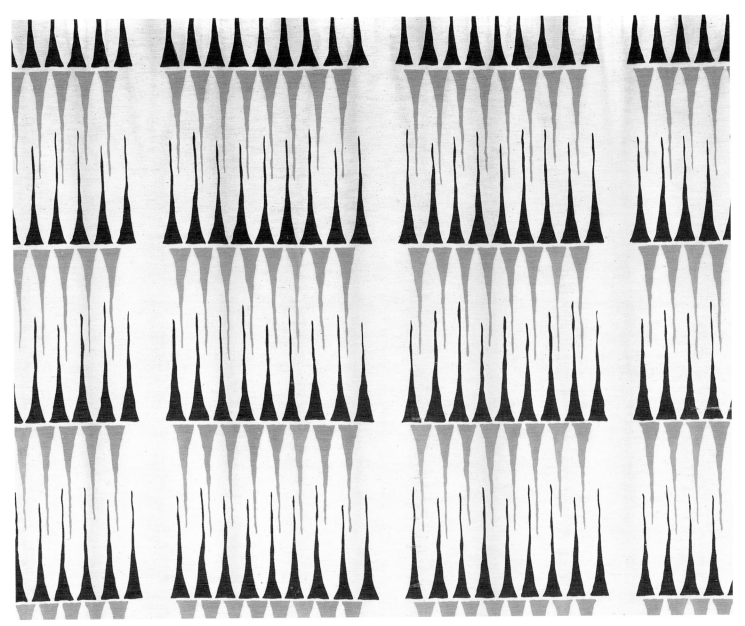

297. *Pipsan Swanson.* Spelunking *textile*

Pipsan Swanson

Textile: *Spelunking*
Designed c. 1952
Cotton, linen, and acetate, weft face of warp-
  float-faced satin weave, silk-screen printed;
  54 × 49½ inches (137.2 × 125.8 cm)
Produced by Edwin Raphael Company, Inc.
  (Holland, Michigan), c. 1952–62
Unmarked
D87.117.1, gift of Lynn Brows, by exchange*

Pipsan Swanson was the designer responsible for interiors in a variety of partnerships formed with her architect husband Robert and her father and brother, the architects Eliel and Eero Saarinen. As part of the celebrated Cranbrook colony, she was frequently approached by manufacturers to supply furniture, furnishings, and other ingredients appropriate to the modern interior.

Spelunking, the name of this fabric, refers to the exploring of caves—no doubt those filled with stalagmites and stalactites. The abstract motif of interrelated shapes is produced by reversing the single screen and printing it in a simple two-color combination. The unprinted ground then becomes the space of the cave interior. In the early 1950s, artist-designed contemporary prints were almost all silk-screened by hand on commercially woven cloth in relatively small quantities. Screen-printing was still a rather novel printing method, bearing all the prestige of the designer-craftsman tradition and relatively little of the expense required for machine-printing for mass market volume.[346]

Postwar architecture provided much of the *raison d'être* for the interest in patterned textiles. As broad expanses of window became increasingly common, full walls of patterned, straight-hanging curtains with designs like *Spelunking* became a means of providing interest in rooms with little architectural detail. According to a contemporary description of display rooms of the Saarinen-Swanson group:

> There is a human quality to these interiors; nothing is overweighted or pretentious. Nei-
> ther the colors nor the furnishings will ever
> dominate the people who live with them. . . .
> Here are backgrounds for living, not stage
> sets.[347]

This concept of "backgrounds for living" keeps alive a traditional principle of Modernism, one enunciated by Philip Johnson in 1935 when he redesigned Mrs. Platt's living room[348] and maintained by exponents of Good Design throughout the postwar years. They generally did not permit themselves or their clients to indulge in figurative or flashy patterns.

KC

Philip Johnson and Richard Kelly

Floor lamp

Designed c. 1953[349]

Bronze and painted aluminum; 38⁵⁄₁₆ × 25 × 25 inches (97.3 × 63.5 × 63.5 cm)

Produced by Edison Price, Inc. (New York), c. 1953; modified c. 1954 and produced until after 1967

Unmarked except for electrical fittings

D88.138.1, gift of Mr. and Mrs. Charles D. O'Kieffe, Jr., in memory of Mr. and Mrs. Charles DeWitt O'Kieffe, by exchange*

The New Canaan, Connecticut, house that Philip Johnson designed for his own use in 1948 is a glass cube set down upon a green carpet of lawn in a carefully landscaped site. His exercise in ideological purity went far in confounding the visual and spatial distinctions between interior and exterior, the glass walls sealing but not separating the house from the landscape.

This glass pavilion posed extraordinarily difficult lighting problems. For a solution, Johnson called on the skills of lighting consultant Richard Kelly.

> He was my guru—the man who taught me the importance of lighting. When I first moved into the glass house, there was no light—other than the sun. You can imagine the problem with reflections. If you had one bulb, you saw six. When it got dark outside, there wasn't anything a lighting man could do, or so I thought. Richard founded the art of residential lighting the day he designed the lighting for the glass house. He realized there was no place to put the lights but the floor. . . .[350]

This lamp was designed by Johnson and Kelly to replace a tall, candelabra lamp used when the house was first completed in 1949.[351] With its low, aluminum cone shade supported by delicate

299. Philip Johnson and Richard Kelly. Floor lamp

298. Philip Johnson. Living room of the architect's residence, New Canaan, Connecticut, in c. 1953

bronze legs, it suggests a Japanese influence, and, certainly, the simplicity of Japanese design appealed to minimalist sensibilities of the late 1940s and 1950s. However, the form is above all the expression of the particular function that this lamp was intended to fulfill.

A bronze cannister is fitted inside with fins that limit the glare from the bulb hidden deep within, a form created for theatrical use. The reflector bulb projects a powerful beam of light (maximum 600 watts) up into the underside of the shade, which is painted white. In turn, the shade deflects the light down toward the floor to create a warm pool of indirect light. The electrical cord

was fitted with a heavy rheostat, a very early use of dimming equipment adapted to nontheatrical use.

Johnson and Kelly together developed the lamp's concept and form, and Edison Price worked out the details for production. It was initially designed with three legs, as seen in this example.[352] That proved unstable, and a four-legged version was developed shortly thereafter. This later form appears in photographs of the Johnson living room (fig. 298). Johnson used this design in other interiors, and it remained in commercial production by Edison Price, Inc., probably until after 1967.[353]   KC

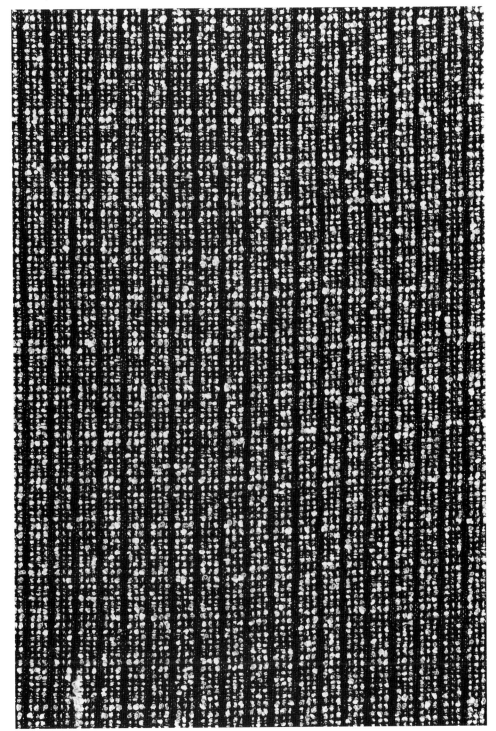

300. *Marianne Strengell.* Taj Mahal *upholstery fabric*

Marianne Strengell

Upholstery fabric: *Taj Mahal*
Designed c. 1957
Rayon, cotton, and metal strips encased in
   polyester film, broken, combined twill
   weave;[354] 29½ × 61¼ inches (75 × 156 cm)
Produced by Chatham Manufacturing
   Company (Elkin, North Carolina), 1959
Handwritten (by artist) on paper label:
   1./Automobile fabric for Lincoln
   Continental/1959/Woven by The
   Chatham/Manufacturing Company,/Elkin,
   N.C./All synthetic. cotton warp.
D85.131.1, gift of Marianne Strengell

From 1954 to 1960, Marianne Strengell was a
consultant and designer for the Chatham Manufacturing Company. This assignment came about
through her connection with the Getsinger-Fox
Company of Detroit, representatives of the automobile industry.[355] She designed for them several
fabrics for automobile interiors. *Taj Mahal*, made
for the Lincoln Continental, was the most prestigious and widely publicized. "When I started it
was all synthetic, ghastly, shiny and discouraging. I feel I managed to turn this trend around
and come up with some pretty good 'stuff.'"[356]

And indeed she did. She used a black rayon
warp and added black cotton and gray, white and
gold synthetic fibers in her weft. Despite its complexity of natural and synthetic fibers, the fabric
is striking in its simplicity. It shows groupings of
three white yarns, nubby in nature. The inclusion of gold metal strips turned this textile into an
elegant yet still functional fabric. Although produced on a power loom, it gives the feeling of a
handwoven fabric.

Strengell first sketched her design concept on
paper. Then, working closely with her colleague
Gerda Nyberg, she produced samples on a hand
loom.[357] The yarns used in the sample were
identical to those used for the mass-produced
yardage. The development process by the firm
took two years; only then was the upholstery fabric ready for use.

In addition to working with the Ford Motor
Company, Strengell developed fabrics for Chrysler and American Motors during those years. In
all instances, Strengell worked closely with the
companies' design studios. The requirements for
such fabrics, called "transportation cloth," addressed such issues as resistance to abrasion,
stretchability, strength, color fastness, ease of
cleaning, and affordability.[358] These were the
very same rules of functionalism that Strengell
had developed in connection with her teaching at
the Cranbrook Academy of Art in Bloomfield
Hills, Michigan.

CCMT

301. *Jack Lenor Larsen*. Remoulade *textile*

Jack Lenor Larsen

Textile: *Remoulade*
Designed 1954–55
Wool, cotton, rayon, linen, Mylar,
   polyethylene, silk, jute, and metallic yarns,
   warp-faced plain weave; 54 × 48 inches
   (138.5 × 128.1 cm)
Produced by Jack Lenor Larsen, incorporated
   (New York), 1956–67
Unmarked
D81.136.1, gift of Kelvyn Grant Lilley*

By the time Jack Lenor Larsen put *Remoulade* into power-loom production in 1956, he had operated a studio in New York for five years and had proven the feasibility of designing for mass production—the subject of his 1951 master of fine arts thesis.[359] He sought a handwoven, hand-colored, and hand-printed appearance, which he wanted to translate through power-driven machinery into custom-designed and, later, mass-produced lengths of fabrics. To accomplish this, Larsen became familiar with all aspects of textile manufacturing, and his technical ability allowed him to maintain the creative spark that had been established in his initial handwoven work.

Remoulade is recognized as one of Larsen's most important fabrics. While at the Haystack Mountain School of Crafts in Maine in the summer of 1954, he created a red wall hanging in weft-faced plain weave. His associates admired the piece and asked him to make it as an upholstery fabric. He complied, weaving the prototype on a hand loom but changing its structure from a weft-faced to a warp-faced plain weave, to allow for easier pattern control on a power loom.[360] The pattern was basically a plaid, elaborately developed in terms of its coloration and its complex mixture of almost thirty natural and artificial fibers. Larsen used these many yarns in different weights and varied the fiber combination compositions, hence the name *Remoulade*, after a piquant sauce with a great many spicy ingredients. The result was a sturdy upholstery fabric constructed in plain weave with supplementary patterning warps, which, through their ratio of floats, skip over a span of three wefts. Thus, a sense of three dimensionality was introduced into an otherwise flat fabric.

To utilize a floating weave structure for a utilitarian, mass-produced fabric was revolutionary and a departure from the straightforward structures to which the public had grown accustomed. The multitude of colors was also technically challenging. *Remoulade* was produced in several color ways: blue, as in the example in the Stewart Collection, olive, turquoise, yellow, and red.

In looking at the panel, one is reminded of architecture, of rows of windows that become alive, through the ingenious use of colored yarns that intersect at right angles. The parallel to architecture is not accidental, as Larsen initially intended to pursue a career as an architect. He once stated that his task became that of "putting together the aesthetics of architecture, the color of painting and the techniques of weaving."[361] Certainly *Remoulade* offset the monotonous rhythm created by the omnipresent glass and steel interiors of the period.   CCMT

Frank Lloyd Wright

Textile: *Design 104*

Designed 1954

Silk and rayon (Fortisan), plain weave, silk-screen printed; 39 × 49⅞ inches (101.4 × 126.7 cm)

Produced by F. Schumacher & Company (New York), 1955–61

Printed in left selvage: "DESIGN 104" AN EXCLUSIVE SCHUMACHER HAND PRINT [in orange] top [in beige]

Printed in right selvage: [in red, square monogram composed of FLW] THE TALIESIN LINE OF FRANK LLOYD WRIGHT [in orange]

D89.115.1

Design 104 was part of a collection of Frank Lloyd Wright textiles and wallpapers that F. Schumacher & Company issued in the fall of 1955 under the name of the Taliesin Line. (Taliesin was the name Wright gave to his homes in Wisconsin and Arizona.) It consisted of six printed and seven woven fabrics, as well as four wallpapers, all in a variety of color ways. It was publicized in a striking portfolio, which included actual samples of the textiles and wallpapers juxtaposed with abundant photographs and drawings of well-known Wright buildings. They, as well as the text, emphasized the close relationship between the architect's structures and the adapted designs.

Design 104 was featured with views of the homes designed by the architect for two of his sons—the Robert Llewellyn Wright home in Bethesda, Maryland, and the David Wright home in Phoenix, Arizona (fig. 302)—houses that use oval and rounded shapes, like those in the textile design.[362]

The Taliesin Line began in 1954 in the office of Elizabeth Gordon, editor of *House Beautiful*, when she was putting together an issue devoted to Wright.[363] After looking at a number of theatrical costumes that had been worn at a performance of the Taliesin Fellowship in Chicago in November 1953,[364] Gordon contacted René Carrillo, director of merchandising at Schumacher, to see if the company would be interested in adapting some of the patterns. Carrillo found them unsuitable, but the idea of a collection of Wright fabrics and wallpapers intrigued him. Extensive correspondence and numerous meetings between Carrillo and Wright followed.[365] In a March 22, 1954, letter, Carrillo outlined the program:

> I was delighted to receive your signed contract and I approve heartily of using the name 'The Taliesin Line.' As a method of procedure, it might be wise to have you send us rough sketches of anything you have in mind. We would then have these rough designs put into the finished state as we would have to have them for either our looms or our various printing processes. These designs could then be returned to you for your final approval and your color suggestions.[366]

The inclusion of gold in this harmony of browns makes *Design 104* one of the most sophisticated designs in the Taliesin Line. It came in six other color ways and could be used as either curtain or upholstery material. Reasonably priced at $6.75 a yard in 1955, the fabric was intended both for those who owned a Wright house and middle-income Americans interested in modern design.[367]   CCMT

302. *Frank Lloyd Wright. David Wright house, Phoenix, Arizona. c. 1952*

303. *Wright. Design 104 textile*

Ernest Race

Armchair: *Antelope*
Designed 1950
Enameled steel and painted plywood;
   31⅛ × 20½ × 20 inches (79 × 52.1 × 50.9 cm)
Produced by Ernest Race Ltd. (London),
   intermittently from 1951 to the present
Unmarked
D88.195.1, gift of Barbara Jakobson*

In international terms, British furniture since World War I has not been particularly important or influential. One notable design, however, was Ernest Race's *Antelope* chair, one of the two Race designs selected by the organizers of the Festival of Britain to furnish the Festival's buildings and grounds on London's South Bank (fig. 306).

The Festival of Britain was a fervently nationalistic celebration of British achievements in science, technology, the arts, and industrial design. It had little to do with its taking place on the one-hundredth anniversary of the Great Exhibition of 1851. Colorful and lighthearted, it offered visitors a welcome diversion from the austerity and unfulfilled promise of the postwar period.

During the years preceding the Festival, Race established a company to develop furniture based on new materials and technologies. At a time when materials, including hardwood, were still rationed or in short supply, he turned to other materials, including steel and aluminum. The two designs for the Festival, the *Antelope* and *Springbok* chairs, were chosen by the Council of Industrial Design, a quasi-governmental agency established to raise the standards of design in Britain, because they projected the sort of bold and forward-looking image the council sought for the Festival.[368]

The *Antelope* chair was intended for both indoor and outdoor use, which—keeping the moist British climate in mind—helps explain the minimal amount of surface area and the holes drilled through the plywood seat. It was solidly constructed of bent, solid metal rods welded together and designed to stack. The splayed feet—which allowed the chair to stack—were capped with wooden balls that were part and parcel of the atomic imagery fostered by the Council of Industrial Design for the Festival.[369] The combination of the enameled white frame and feet with the seat brightly painted red, yellow, gray, or, as in this example, blue, made the chair an object that called attention to itself.

It was a bold, modern design, which perhaps gained a certain acceptance because, at least in outline and perhaps unconsciously, it reminded observers of the familiar form of an upholstered chair. The comparison with an upholstered chair is not a fanciful one. For, while the *Antelope* chair certainly grew out of the international, postwar interest in all manner of thin, metal furniture, Race's chair is, in fact, a version of the designer's earlier upholstered furniture, but with the upholstery stripped away from the frame (fig. 305).[370] The *Antelope* chair could thus be described as a design of 1949 awaiting exposure. Yet it should be clear that the impetus for showing this naked steel frame as an independent design came from the acceptance of metal rod or wire in the years leading up to the Festival.

It is important to remember that in 1951 the British furniture industry was still governed by the wartime regulations of the Utility Furniture Scheme, which rationed the production and consumption of furniture. Race's *Antelope* chair, with its bright colors and free-flowing curves, added a significant note of grace, lightheartedness, and, ultimately, optimism to an England accustomed to the heavy, sober forms of both traditional and Utility furniture.

CW

(opposite) 304. *Ernest Race.* Antelope *armchair*

(above) 305. *Race. Armchair: model no. DA2, sectional view. 1949*

(right) 306. *Regatta Restaurant, Festival of Britain, London, 1951, with* Antelope *chairs*

Eero Saarinen

Armchair: model no. 70, *Womb*
Designed c. 1946
Steel, compound of fiberglass, plastic, and
   wood particle, and unborn calf's skin;
   36 × 40 × 35½ inches (92.3 × 102.6 × 91 cm)
Produced by Knoll Associates, Inc. (New
   York), 1948 to the present (this example
   c. 1950)[371]
Unmarked
D83.109.1, gift of Muriel Kalis Newman*

An enveloping, three-dimensionally molded
shell, cradled in a metal armature, the no. 70
lounge chair—popularly known as the *Womb*
chair—is one of the masterworks of twentieth-
century design. It remains perhaps Eero Saarinen's most successful synthesis of new materials, innovative structure, and arresting form.

The design was an outgrowth of the entries by
Charles Eames and Saarinen for the "Organic
Design in Home Furnishings" competition
(1940–41),[372] their earliest experiments with
three-dimensionally molded plywood shells
mounted on four-legged bases (fig. 27). Eames
later perfected the design in plywood—in a now
classic chair series first shown in 1946—by separating the seat and back panels and mounting
them on a molded wood or an articulated metal
base (fig. 30).[373]

Concurrent with this interest in shell forms in
the 1940s was the advent of plastics in the furniture industry.[374] These two factors were, in fact,
integral to Saarinen's developments from the
"Organic Design" chairs. The first evidence may
be seen in the sketches done for the Case Study
House series (1943), which show variations of the
no. 70 lounge chair and a sofa version, though
there is no mention of material.[375] This was
followed by further sketches published in 1946
showing a further development of the *Womb*
chair, as well as a single-pedestal armchair; both
were envisioned as being made of "paper
plastic."[376]

Saarinen's final design for Knoll Associates,
dating from about 1946, required two years for
production. Photographs of the various prototypes (fig. 308) show the architect's struggle to
achieve a successful base both structurally and
aesthetically.[377] While the no. 70 chair was the
first fiberglass design to be mass-produced in
America, it could technically only be achieved in
an upholstered version at that time.[378] The series
was expanded by the addition of the no. 74 ottoman (c. 1950) and the no. 73 settee (c. 1948),
Saarinen's only mass-produced sofa. The no. 70
lounge chair has remained in continuous production by Knoll for almost four decades, making it
one of the most popular seating designs of this
century.

RCM

307. Eero Saarinen. Womb *armchair: model no. 70*

308. *Saarinen. Prototype of* Womb *armchair. c. 1946*

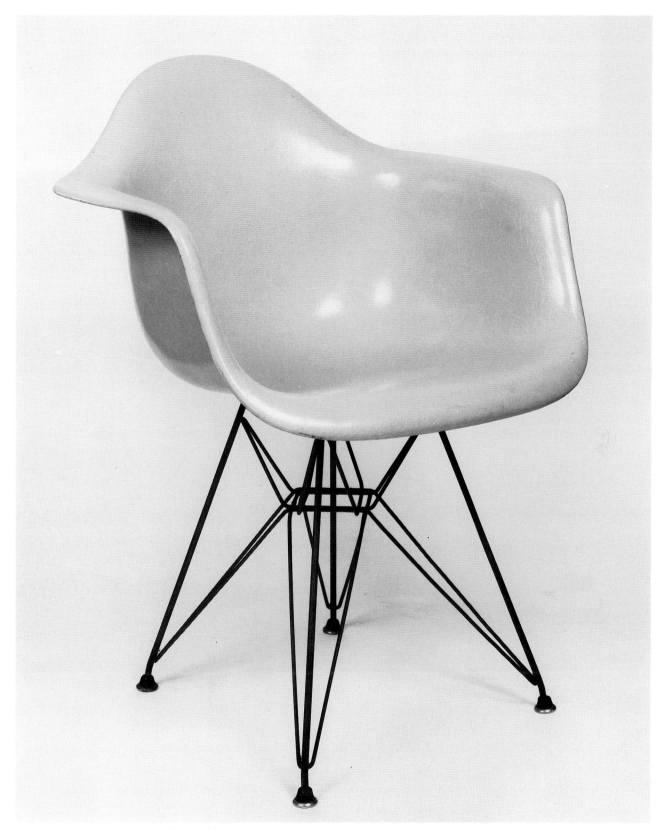

309. *Charles and Ray Eames. Armchair: model DAR*

Charles and Ray Eames,
with members of the Engineering
Department, University of California,
Los Angeles

Armchair: model DAR
Designed c. 1948–50
Polyester fiberglass composite, zinc-plated
   steel, and rubber; 31⅛ × 25 × 23¼ inches
   (79 × 63.5 × 59 cm)
Produced by Herman Miller Furniture Co.
   (Zeeland, Michigan), 1950–c. 1972 (this
   example c. 1955–60)
Printed on partially torn paper label glued to
   underside of seat: This product manufactured

under one or/more of the following patents:/
D 155 273   2 813 528 [remainder of text
deleted due to length]
Impressed on underside of seat: [s within a
circle]/[device of stylized, inverted M]/
HERMAN MILLER
Stamped in ink on underside of seat: SUM . . .
[illegible] PRIME [within a circle] 50 . . .
[illegible] 01
D81.100.1

211

In 1948 Charles Eames was one of six designers awarded a grant from the Museum of Modern Art as part of its "International Competition for Low-Cost Furniture Design." These grants were to foster the application of recently developed technologies to furniture manufacture, recognizing that neither furniture designers nor manufacturers had the resources to do so on their own.[379]

Eames and the team from his office were paired with members of the Engineering Department at the University of California, Los Angeles. The problem they tackled was precisely the one that Eames and Eero Saarinen had attempted in their entries to the Museum of Modern Art's "Organic Design in Home Furnishings" competition almost a decade earlier (fig. 27): how to design and manufacture economically a compact chair made from the smallest possible number of parts.

This time the material chosen was metal, which, due to its malleability under heat and pressure, was far cheaper to manufacture than plywood. In order to make the material tactilely acceptable to the user and to add comfort, the metal surface was sprayed with neoprene, a synthetic rubber (fig. 310).[380] The group of chairs designed by the Eames team was awarded a joint second prize when the judges met in November 1948.

By the time the exhibition was held in 1950, the Herman Miller Furniture Company was able to manufacture the designs (or at least prototypes) in polyester plastic embedded with reinforcing strands of fiberglass.[381] The highly malleable nature of the plastic material made it far more suitable than the heavier metal or the relatively

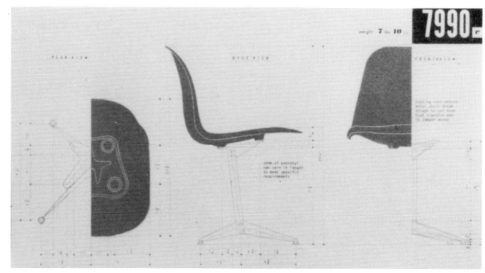

310. Eames. Drawing for DAR armchair submitted to "International Competition for Low-Cost Furniture Design," 1948–50 (detail). 1950

rigid plywood that the Eameses had previously employed. Above all, it made possible the relatively simple three-dimensional molding of a full-size, enveloping shell, a bucket-type seat and back, which the Eameses had sought for nearly a decade.

The DAR's extraordinary light weight, durability, ease with which it could be colored, and remarkable sculptural plasticity were all unprecedented. The light weight of this particular model was enhanced by the thin steel wire base employed, one of a seemingly endless number of leg options devised by the designers during a period in which they experimented with bent and welded metal wire (fig. 311).

The molded plastic chair series—which eventually included a stacking chair—became one of the most ubiquitous lines of American seating furniture. Used more in institutional and commercial rather than domestic interiors, it fulfilled a strong demand for durable, modern furniture. Indeed, few American children growing up in the postwar period can have avoided sitting in the new Eames plastic furniture, so common was it in schools and universities across the land. It was one of the earliest mass-produced plastic chairs, preceding by more than a decade the boom in plastic furniture of the 1960s.

CW

311. Herman Miller publicity photograph showing versions of the DAR chair, 1952

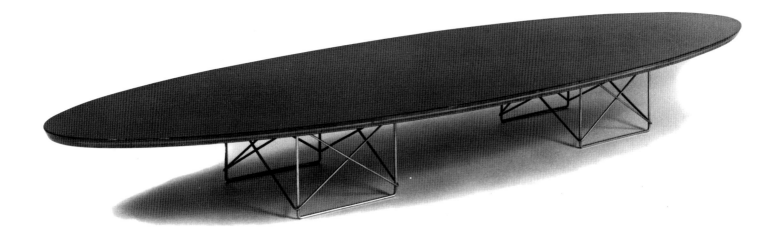

312. *Charles and Ray Eames. Coffee table: model ETR*

Charles and Ray Eames

Coffee table: model ETR
Designed 1950–51
Formica on plywood, steel; $10 \times 89^{9}/_{16} \times 29$
 inches ($25.5 \times 225 \times 73.6$ cm)
Produced by Herman Miller Furniture Co.
 (Zeeland, Michigan), 1951–64
Printed on circular metal label glued to
 underside: [device of a stylized M at
 center]/[around perimeter] DESIGNED BY
 GEORGE NELSON [manufacturing
 error]/HERMAN MILLER ZEELAND, MICH.
D84.182.1

Until the 1960s, humor was an unusual charac-teristic to impart through furniture; however, the qualities of wit, playfulness, and joy are to be found in the life and work of the Eameses. Though it is more commonly revealed in their films, photographs, and toys rather than in their furniture, it manages to come through in this oversize, seven-and-a-half-foot-long coffee table.

The form of the table is a symbolic and literal meeting of East and West, specifically of Japa-nese and West Coast American design. The Japa-nese aesthetic of a table, low to the ground at a height appropriate for a person seated on the floor, is combined with the unmistakable form of a Southern California surfboard—an object well known to the Eameses, who lived and worked along the majestic surfers' paradise of the Pacific Ocean.

The aesthetics of Japan, of course, had been well integrated into West Coast architecture and interiors to a much greater extent than in other parts of the country. The turn-of-the-century furniture and interiors of the Greene brothers, the work of R. M. Schindler and Richard Neutra in the 1920s and 1930s, and—World War II notwithstanding—much domestic work of the postwar period were infused with the vocabulary of Japanese design. The Eameses' own house of 1948–49 (fig. 62) was a prime example: it embod-ied a clarity, simplicity, and spareness typical of Japanese architecture, employing steel and glass to the same effect as wood and paper. Much of the Eameses' seating furniture was unusually low to the ground, which not only suggested Japanese seating conventions but also was in keeping with the relaxed, informal life-style of California.

The ETR table was part of a series of new designs, including tables and chairs, that em-ployed a structurally complex and visually engag-ing steel wire base that contrasted, rather than being continuous, with the form being sup-ported. In the ETR table a pair of thin, cagelike constructions lift the enormous top and allow it to hover above the ground—albeit a mere ten inches. The top is constructed of an elongated oval of plywood covered with a layer of plastic laminate; as was always the case in the Eameses' plywood designs, the laminations are clearly vis-ible and even emphasized on all the edges, as are all the various materials, with their contrasting colors and finishes.

The ETR table, idiosyncratic and amusing, reminds us that despite the gradual homogeni-zation of American culture and the increasing uniformity of the international design world, regionalism remained an important aspect of midcentury design. CW

(opposite and right) 313, 314. Harry Bertoia. Diamond *armchair: model no. 421-1*

Harry Bertoia

Armchair: model no. 421-1, *Diamond*
Designed 1950–52
Vinyl-coated (cellulose acetate butyrate) steel
and cotton upholstery; 30½ × 33¾ × 27½
inches (77.5 × 85.7 × 69.7 cm)
Produced by Knoll Associates, Inc. (New
York), c. 1953 to the present
Printed in black on paper label attached to
cushion: KNOLL/KNOLL ASSOCIATES INC./320
PARK AVE, N.Y. [device of a stylized K
printed in red]
Printed in black on cloth label attached to
cushion: This article is made in compliance
with an act of: Dist. of Col. approved July
3, 1926; Kansas approved . . . . . [text
deleted due to length]/Distributed by KNOLL
ASSOCIATES INC. 320 Park Ave. New York,
N.Y.
D85.154.1

It is sometimes argued that to describe a chair as a work of sculpture is to ignore willfully that designed objects are not aesthetic objects but commodities. Harry Bertoia's chairs, however, were conceived first and last as functional sculptures. "When you get right down to it," he told an interviewer, "the chairs are studies in space, form and metal. . . ."[382]

Bertoia began designing furniture while employed at the Eames studio, where he worked from approximately 1943 until 1946. In addition

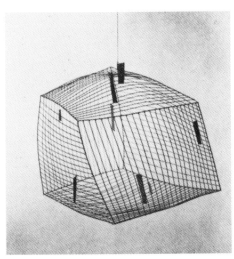

315. Bertoia. Hanging sculpture. 1952

to working on the Eameses' designs, Bertoia experimented on his own with chairs in metal wire; these were never manufactured nor, apparently, photographed.[383]

Following an acrimonious parting from the Eames office and a stint at the United States Navy Electronics Laboratory, Bertoia was lured from the climate and scenery of California by an offer of a job from Hans and Florence Knoll. Bertoia subsequently moved to Pennsylvania, where Knoll had a small factory, and he worked on developing metal furniture while assisting with the production of other Knoll products.[384]

From 1950 to 1952 Bertoia worked on his new metal wire furniture, which he conceived as visually transparent forms floating in space—a network of small diamond patterns within one large diamond. Visual transparency was a characteristic of his sculptures (fig. 315) and his paintings on tracing paper (in which he left unpainted areas), and it accorded with his belief that furniture should be as minimal as possible. The combination of thin metal rods and a surface area made up mainly of space allowed his furniture, as well as his sculpture, to float and interact with the surrounding space. Geometric patterning was also well established in his prints, painting, and sculpture; in the chairs it became expressive of what he convincingly described as an "organic principle, like a cellular structure."[385]

If there is anything in the chair that does not seem organic, it is the relationship of seat to base and the use of upholstery, which hides the pattern of diamond shapes. Bertoia did not, however, see the base as problematic. He felt that the supporting structure of the chair must be distinguished from the seat for the sake of clarity.[386] Although he did not speak about the upholstery, it can be assumed that without it, the chair would not offer sufficient comfort for extended use. Ultimately, the upholstered seat not only mitigates against the effect of transparency, it changes entirely the chair's visual aspect, suggesting a solid but pliable form that has been molded in one piece. In fact, the Bertoia wire furniture was anything but molded in one piece. Each chair was made by hand and Bertoia required considerable assistance from Knoll in working out a proper production method.

Although Harry Bertoia is often described as a sculptor/furniture designer, he actually designed very little furniture. His chairs for Knoll were his final furniture designs. In retrospect he stated, perhaps with posterity in mind: "Furniture is nothing to me—it was a means of eating."[387] Yet his brief foray created one of the most memorable of modern chairs, distinguished by its clarity of design and its beauty as an object.

CW

316. *Isamu Noguchi. Dining table: model no. 311*

Isamu Noguchi

317. *Noguchi. Rocking stool, in 1956*

Dining table: model no. 311
Designed c. 1953, redesigned c. 1957
Formica, plywood, beaverboard, cast iron, and
steel; 34½ × 47⁷⁄₁₆ × 47⁷⁄₁₆ inches (87.5 ×
120.5 × 120.5 cm)
Produced by Knoll Associates, Inc. (New
York), c. 1957 to the present
Printed on paper label on underside of
tabletop: KNOLL/[rectangular device
quartered diagonally] KNOLL ASSOCIATES,
INC.,/575 MADISON AVE, NY 22
D81.102.1

Noguchi's dining table for Knoll was adapted
from a nearly identical rocking stool the artist
designed around 1953 (fig. 317). The origins of
the stool, however, are much less clear, with two
different accounts claiming authority. The first,
and earlier, story related that Noguchi was inspired by an African stool owned by friend and
Life photographer Eliot Elisofon.[388] Inspired by

its form but vexed by its inability to tip backward,
Noguchi created his own steel and wire version.

The second account, provided by Noguchi late
in his life, credits manufacturer Hans Knoll with
the idea of a steel and wire stool.[389] According to
Noguchi, Knoll saw a plastic stool the artist had
designed following a trip to Japan in 1951, said to
have been hourglass in shape and resilient to the
sitter; no photographs of the stool survive. With
Harry Bertoia's steel chairs (figs. 313, 314) just
coming on the market, Knoll may well have
wanted products to complement that line, hence
his request to Noguchi to design a stool in metal
wire. While designers sometimes have the luxury
of being their own clients, at least in the development stage of an object, most manufactured
goods are commissioned by a client hoping to fuel
consumer demand.

Whatever the origins of the stool, it was a
diminutive, playful object that suggested informality. The design juxtaposed the stained finish
of the horizontal wood base and seat with shiny,

V-shaped metal uprights that, when assembled, gave the impression of having been twisted or coiled into a taut structure.

In 1954 Knoll introduced two sizes of the rocking stool as well as a nearly identical children's table. The table was clearly intended to go with the Bertoia child's chair, as the table and chairs were illustrated in the firm's catalogue as an ensemble (fig. 318).[390] Apparently pleased, the Knoll firm then scaled the children's table to full size.[391] Noguchi claimed he was not involved in its redesign—a phenomenon common in the world of furniture manufacture.

Noguchi's stool and the subsequent table clearly had their roots in the postwar vogue for metal wire furniture that saw major designers such as Bertoia and Eames, as well as manufacturers in the middle and lower ends of the market, turn furniture into small-scale feats of engineering, with the emphasis on abstract patterning

created by the structures. The use of iron rods and steel struts exploited both the strength and decorative possibilities of the materials. Interestingly, wire played no part in Noguchi's sculpture of the period, nor was it a material he ever worked with much.

Years later, Noguchi claimed that he was dissatisfied with the design. However, it should be recognized that, like other architects and artists, he feared that attention given to his earlier work as a designer of functional objects would detract from his reputation as a sculptor; in his youth he was quite proud of such projects. He seemed to regard with particular disdain the notion that the idea for the table came from the manufacturer. With the exception of a glass-topped coffee table for Herman Miller, Noguchi viewed his attempts "to comply with industrial design . . . essentially a failure."[392] That judgment is one with which posterity is unlikely to agree.

CW

318. *Knoll publicity photograph of Noguchi's children's table and Harry Bertoia's child's chair, 1954*

Achille and Pier Giacomo Castiglioni

Floor lamp: model no. B9, *Luminator*
Designed 1955
Steel; 71 × 19 × 16 inches (180.3 × 48.3 × 40.6 cm)
Produced by Gilardi e Barzaghi (Milan), 1955, 1957
Printed on white paper label: MADE IN ITALY
D85.171.1

The Castiglioni brothers' stunningly minimal and aggressively modern floor lamp reflects their shared interest in combining the principles of structure, function, and aesthetics in a single composition. In the *Luminator* they achieved this combination through the use of a simple, vertical steel tube—whose diameter is determined by that of the base of the light bulb that fits into it—supported on a tripod made from three even slimmer steel tubes. The only additional features are the wire that flows from the base of the vertical tube and a control switch positioned on the tube near this point.

In this object, aesthetic minimalism has been determined by basic functional and structural demands. Such a rigorous approach characterized the Castiglionis' work from this period. They brought the prewar idea of functionalism into a new era, combining it with a strong interest

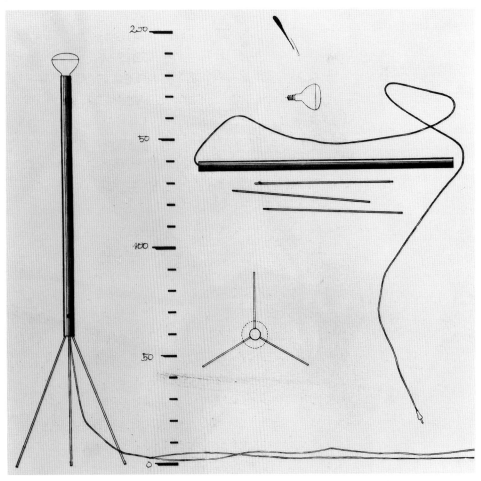

319. *Achille and Pier Giacomo Castiglioni. Drawing of the B9 Luminator floor lamp, with its component parts. c. 1955*

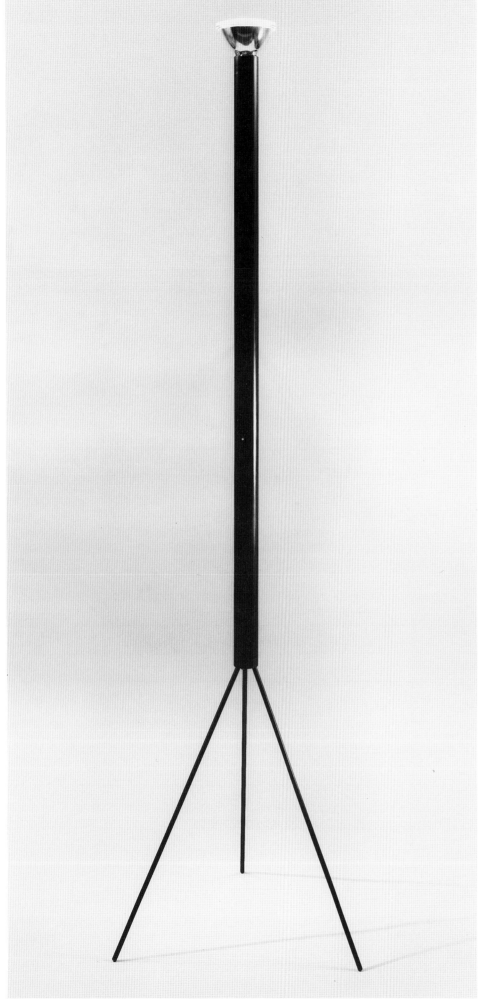

320. *Castiglioni.* B9 Luminator *floor lamp*

in technological innovation. With the exception of an earlier light by Pietro Chiesa—also called *Luminator* (fig. 321)—the idea of projecting light directly onto the ceiling, from there to be diffused into the entire room, had, until this date, been reserved for photographers' studio equipment.

The Castiglionis' *Luminator* does not, however, operate simply on the rational level of technological·determinism. It performs, in the end, the role of an expressive, sculptural object within the modern interior, a strong symbolic presence silently watching over its neighboring objects.

PS

321. Pietro Chiesa. Luminator *floor lamp*

Sven Markelius

Textile: *Pythagoras*

Designed 1952

Cotton, plain weave, silk-screen printed;
132 × 50½ inches (335.4 × 128.3 cm)

Printed by Ljungbergs Textiltryck (Floda, Sweden), for Nordiska Kompaniet (Stockholm), 1952, 1965, and 1984 (this example 1952)

Printed twice in beige in right selvage: NK "PYTHAGORAS" SVEN MARKELIUS DESIGN: KNOLL TEXTILES, INC. MADE IN SWEDEN

D88.184.1, gift of Louise Armstrong in memory of Harris Armstrong

Pythagoras was originally designed by Sven Markelius as a stage curtain for the Folhets Hus (People's House) in Linköping (fig. 322).[393] Thereafter it became one of the fabrics available from Nordiska Kompaniet, and it was distributed as well by Knoll.

The title of the design refers to the theorem involving the right triangle, developed by the Greek philosopher and mathematician who lived in the sixth century B.C. This striking pattern, quite naturally, uses the triangle as its main motif. Symmetry and asymmetry interact in alternating bands, further enhanced by a brilliant color scheme. The design, executed first in a crayon drawing and then in a paper collage, required eighteen screens.[394] It came in three color ways: red, yellow, and, as here, blue. Astrid Sampe, director of Nordiska Kompaniet Textilkammare, calls herself the "textile translator" of this complex design.

Pythagoras, a multifaceted surface composition, calls to mind other Swedish geometric patterns of the late 1950s: Olle Eksell's *Margaret Rose*, Viola Gråsten's *Festive*, The Svedberg's *Atomics* and *Genetics*, Johan Lindström's *Cho-*

rus.[395] Could Markelius's design be the direct or indirect reason for this very popular type of geometric pattern? *Pythagoras* still remains in vogue today. As recently as the fall of 1988 a special order, this time printed on cotton velvet, was made for replacement curtains to hang in the Economic and Social Council Chamber of the United Nations Building, a chamber that Markelius himself designed.   CCMT

(above left) 322. *Sven Markelius. Interior of Folhets Hus, Linköping, Sweden, c. 1952*

(above) 323. *Markelius.* Pythagoras *textile*

Ross Littell

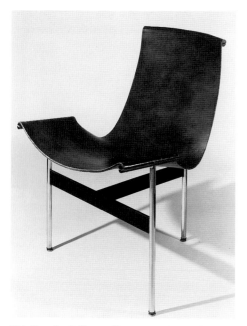

324. *Douglas Kelley, William Katavolos, and Ross Littell. T chair. c. 1950. Liliane and David M. Stewart Collection. D81.101.1*

Textile: *Criss Cross*
Designed c. 1959
Linen, silk-screen printed; 71½ × 50⅞ inches (181.6 × 129.2 cm)
Produced by Knoll Associates, Inc. (New York), c. 1959
Printed one and a half times in tan in selvage: "CRISS CROSS" DESIGNED BY ROSS LITTELL FOR KNOLL TEXTILES © 1959 UP [sideways]
D87.121.1, gift of Ben Short*

The elegantly expressed cerebral sophistication of *Criss Cross* stems from, in the words of the artist, "a series of visual adventures, an exploitation of texture, pattern and form based on visualogies or systems incorporating arithmetic or geometric fundamentals or progressions."[396] Working with self-imposed restrictions of form—the triangle and, by extension, the diamond—and color—tan and natural—Littell created a complex design. Although it appears symmetrical, it shows subtle variations as the pattern progresses from the solid tan center through bicolor geometrics to crisp, pale edges. Inventive and stylishly thoughtful, *Criss Cross* is a natural development from the *T* chair that Littell designed with associates William Katavolos and Douglas Kelley for Laverne Originals (fig. 324), all of whose component parts are variations on the shape of the letter T.[397]

The muted color ways of *Criss Cross*—tan and natural, as here, or charcoal and natural—indicated a change in Knoll's palette to earth tones.[398] In addition to linen, *Criss Cross* was printed on fiberglass, in which form it won a 1959 American Institute of Decorators Citation of Merit Award.[399]

AZ

325. *Littell.* Criss Cross *textile*

326. *Earl Pardon. Necklace*

327. *R. Buckminster Fuller. Pentagonal structure.*
c. 1949. Black Mountain College, North Carolina

Earl Pardon

Necklace
Designed and executed c. 1954
Silver and enamel; 6⅝ × 7⅛ × ½ inches (17 × 18 × 1.2 cm)
Impressed on shaped plate attached to base of one tetrahedron: PARDON/STERLING
D87.243.1

A study in multidimensional structure in which the design "came about through the structure itself,"[400] this necklace by Earl Pardon brings to mind the light, airy, architectural sculptures of Richard Lippold as well as earlier architectural experiments such as R. Buckminster Fuller's geodesic domes (fig. 327). A similar interplay between space and rodlike metal elements is seen in the work of Harry Bertoia, which Pardon claims to have admired particularly.[401] Bertoia's *Diamond* chair (figs. 313, 314), constructed from welded steel latticework, and the Pardon necklace are alike in that they seem composed mostly of air trapped in a cagelike, metal grid. When the necklace is worn it forms a collar around the neck, seemingly without density or weight. It rests on the shoulders and chest, pointing—almost floating—toward the face.

Pardon states that "underlying all my art is a structural attitude shaped by . . . studies of periods and masters in history. Cezanne and Picasso were mentors for me in recent European painting . . . [and] investigations into the work of Zen painters helped form this attitude and spatial philosophy. . . ."[402] The necklace combines the rigid geometry of Cubism with the openness of Oriental compositions. The very choice of the tetrahedron (a pyramid with a triangular base) implies Pardon's Eastern philosophical bent, for it symbolizes an intuitive sense of spatial order.[403] Pardon also signals the Zen rejection of absolutes by using different-size units: of the fifteen tetrahedrons in the piece, no two are identical. This denies symmetry to the necklace and introduces subtle irregularities.

At the end point of each tetrahedron was soldered a ball of silver, which was flattened and then elaborated with an enamel dot, each a different color. These multicolored enamel periods serve to anchor the eye temporarily, thus creating the effect of a jagged edge.[404]

TLW

Perspective of living and dining area in Paris studio

Eszter Haraszty

Rendering: Knoll Paris Studio living and
   dining room
Designed c. 1954 and executed c. 1955
Fabric and mixed mediums on paper; two
   panels, each 18¼ × 26¼ inches (46.5 × 66.7
   cm)
Typewritten in white on black label at upper
   left: Perspective of living and dining area in
   Paris studio.
Typewritten in black on white label at upper
   right: Perspective of living and dining area
   in Paris studio.
D88.178.1, 24, 25, gift of Eszter Haraszty

Rendering: Knoll exhibition in Dallas
Designed c. 1953 and executed c. 1955
Fabric and mixed mediums on paper;
   18¼ × 26¼ inches (46.5 × 66.7 cm)
Typewritten in white on black label at upper
   right: Perspective of Dallas exhibition.
D88.178.1, 11, gift of Eszter Haraszty

Rendering: Den in Fort Worth house
Designed and executed c. 1955
Fabric and mixed mediums on paper;
   18¼ × 26¼ inches (46.5 × 66.7 cm)
Typewritten in white on black label at upper
   left: Perspective of den.
D88.178.1, 32, gift of Eszter Haraszty

(above) 328. *Eszter
Haraszty. Rendering of
Knoll Paris Studio (living
and dining room)*

(left) 329. *Haraszty.
Rendering of Knoll Paris
Studio. 1954*

330. *Photograph of Knoll
Paris Studio in c. 1956*

After leaving her position as head of the textiles department and color planner at Knoll Associates, Eszter Haraszty made repetitions of several of the interiors she had previously designed. Bound in a porfolio, they were to serve as samples of her work for future clients.[405] These renderings are valuable documents of modern interiors from one of the most important American design firms and suggest as well the charm of Haraszty's work as a colorist.

While at Knoll, it had been her custom to work out the design of a room and have a draftsman

from the Knoll Planning Unit make renderings. She then painted them in the chosen colors and pasted in pieces of the actual fabrics that were to be used. She made not only a rendering at normal eye level but also a corresponding bird's-eye view known as a color plan, which received the same elaboration of colors and fabric textures.

For these special portfolios she worked from photographs and memory. As can be seen by comparing her original rendering of the Knoll studio in Paris (fig. 329) with its later copy (fig. 328), the latter is a faithful record except for

minor variations in the house plants, accessories, and the painting on the left wall (each shows a different detail from Duccio's *Maestà*). After her own draftsman drew the rendering, she put in the color scheme and fabrics as before. In these renderings, which are like collages, we see the actual fabric that was used for each piece of upholstered furniture. She said she loved doing these, that it was "like playing dollhouse."

These drawings show Haraszty to be a brilliant colorist. She deliberately employed very little color, but she made that color clear and intense,

Perspective of Dallas exhibition.

Perspective of den.

331. *Haraszty. Rendering of Knoll exhibition in Dallas*

332. *Haraszty. Rendering of house in Fort Worth (den)*

Saarinen or the dry furniture designed by Florence Knoll but the color that makes this interior so dramatic. A contemporary photograph shows that the red chaise longue by Belgiojoso, Peresutti, and Rogers vibrated against the black walls.[406] In the rendering, the white pieces also stand out sharply from the black walls, while bright-colored pillows glow on the white couch. Haraszty said this room caused great excitement, because no one in Dallas had ever seen anything like it.

The most charming of the interiors, and certainly the most widely published at the time, is the Knoll studio in Paris (fig. 328).[407] Here in a small apartment on the top floor of an old building, Haraszty blended old and new. She used some Knoll furniture: Bonet, Kurchan, and Ferrari-Hardoy *Butterfly* chairs and Saarinen dining chairs. These were supplemented with two seventeenth-century chandeliers and a turn-of-the-century Thonet chaise she bought at the Paris Marché aux Puces. The extravagant curving lines of the chaise make it the most interesting form in the room.

Haraszty chose light, airy colors, with patches of blue on the ceiling, giving this top-floor apartment the feeling of being open to the sky. Color photographs show that these blue patches gave the whole room a bluish cast. However, in her rendering and color plan, most of the room is white or neutral. She used black and white fabric for the Saarinen dining chairs and bright, vibrant fabrics for the built-in couch. These vivid colors run through most of the spectrum: yellow and orange for the backrest, blue purple, blue, teal, green, and yellow for the cushions. The few added color touches, such as the couch cushions, were so vivid that they made the whole room seem full of color.[408]

The Fort Worth house (fig. 332) was a private house designed by Edward Larrabee Barnes for which Haraszty planned the interiors.[409] She filled the rooms with light, sandy colors, as was thought suitable for a house in the Southwest. But they were furnished with the standard repertoire of Knoll pieces, including, as we see here, a Saarinen *Womb* chair, other Saarinen chairs, a Hans Bellmann tripod table, and sofas and desks by Florence Knoll. Thus, regardless of whether the interior was situated in the Northeast, the Southwest, or Paris, there was a uniform international code of good taste.   CWL

so that, as she put it, it would sparkle. Her color combinations were revolutionary. At the time no one else used cerise and orange together, or green and blue, as she did here.

Although these interiors differ in purpose and in color, they have several elements in common. Haraszty treated space in a way typical of the Knoll firm's designs. The rooms are open, large spaces, divided into separate areas by rugs and by the arrangement of the furniture in geometric islands, either parallel to the wall or at a forty-five degree angle to it. In fact, one particularly no-

ticeable aspect of Haraszty's drawings is that the space is greatly emphasized. When one compares her rendering of the Paris studio (fig. 328) with a photograph of the actual room (fig. 330), it is evident that the rooms were quite small, even cramped, but in the rendering the perspective was distorted to create a modern sense of flowing space and freedom of movement.

The Dallas exhibition was an installation at the Dallas Museum of Fine Arts, showing the type of corporate interior for which Knoll was famous (fig. 331). It is not the *Womb* chair by Eero

Eszter Haraszty

Textile: *Fibra*
Designed c. 1953
Linen, plain weave, silk-screen printed;
   80¼ × 142 inches (205.8 × 364.1 cm)
Produced by Knoll Textiles (New York),
   1953–at least 1965[410]
Unmarked
D83.141.1, gift of Lita Solis-Cohen*

Fibra is one of several patterns that Eszter Haraszty designed while she was head of textiles at Knoll in the early 1950s. It was a great success at the time: it received the Museum of Modern Art's Good Design Award in 1953 and won a first prize in the American Institute of Decorators 1953 Home Furnishings Design Competition.

Linear patterns like *Fibra* were popular both in this country and in Europe in the early 1950s. The gently flowing lines of *Fibra* were actually based on the weaving process itself. The long lines were inspired by the heddles of a loom, the vertical wires through which the warp is threaded (fig. 333). Haraszty had done hand weaving herself, and at the time she was in charge of the hand weaving as well as the printed textiles at Knoll.

For this design, she photographed the heddles of a loom and then "edited" the photograph to create this pattern.[411] Ironically, this design based on the weaving process is not woven but printed on the fabric.

Haraszty has always believed that color is most effective when small areas of vivid colors are used against black or white,[412] and she followed that idea here. The background is beige, and on it she arranged the heddles in irregular groups of colors: white, black, then light blue followed by orange.[413] Haraszty designed *Fibra* as a drapery fabric, and it was printed on casement cloth as well as on solid linen. One reason for the wide spacing between the stripes of color is that she liked to make casement cloths as transparent as possible so they would not block the view. Therefore, she wanted the pattern suggested rather than printed solidly across the fabric.[414]

When Florence Knoll designed the executive offices of the CBS Building in New York a few years later, she used *Fibra* for the curtains. But Haraszty herself put the pattern to an entirely different use. At the urging of Hans Knoll, she designed three collections for clothes manufac-

turer B. H. Wragge. One of these included a coat with a white on yellow *Fibra* fabric. Haraszty wanted the prototype of this coat for herself, but Diana Vreeland of *Vogue* got it.[415]

CWL

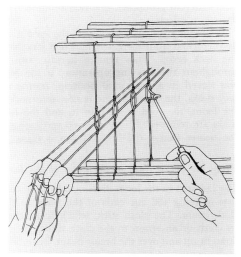

333. *Heddles on a hand loom*

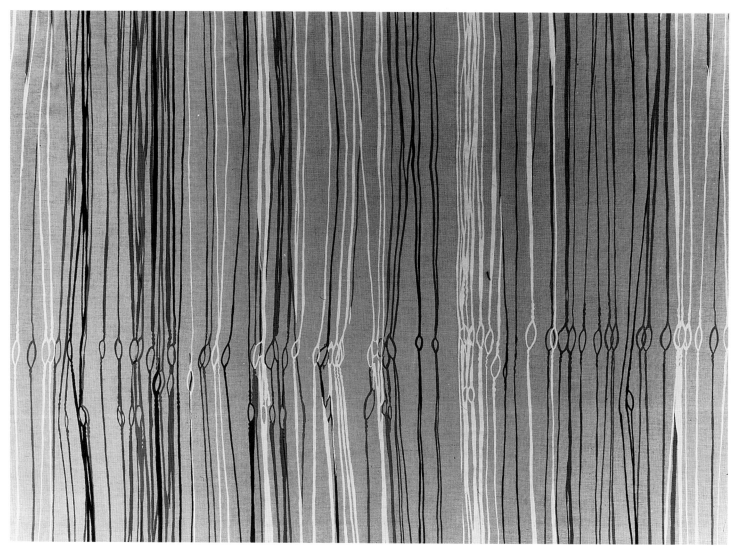

334. *Eszter Haraszty.* Fibra *textile*

Eero Saarinen

Armchair: model no. 150, *Pedestal*
Designed c. 1955
Aluminum with fused plastic finish, fiberglass,
   and nylon upholstery; $31^{13}/_{16} \times 26^{9}/_{16} \times 23^{11}/_{16}$
   inches (80.8 × 67.5 × 60.2 cm)
Produced by Knoll Associates, Inc. (New
   York), 1956 to the present
Impressed on underside of base: BR 50
Printed on label attached to underside of seat:
   KNOLL/KNOLL ASSOCIATES, INC./320 PARK
   AVE. N.Y.
D87.127.1

335. Eero Saarinen.
Pedestal *armchair*

The design of molded shells had preoccupied Eero Saarinen since 1940, starting with his and Charles Eames's award-winning entry for the "Organic Design in Home Furnishings" competition (fig. 27). His large, fiberglass-shell *Womb* chair, which Knoll Associates manufactured beginning in 1948 (fig. 307), serves as a more immediate precedent for this pedestal armchair.

Saarinen typically preferred to eliminate extraneous parts. The elimination of the traditional four chair legs—a standard of all traditional and most modern seating—was highly innovative, though its roots can be found in the cantilevered chairs that mark the Modernist tradition from the 1920s onward. As the architect himself ex-

plained, "The undercarriage of chairs and tables in a typical interior makes an ugly, confusing, unrestful world. I wanted to clear up the slum of legs."[416] In this armchair, he reduced the structure to just three elements: the seat, the stem, and the bolt.

Saarinen remained frustrated, however, with the necessity of a metal support, which is found in the earlier *Womb* chair as well as in this model:

> I wanted to make the chair all one thing again. . . . As now manufactured, the pedestal furniture is half-plastic, half-metal. I look forward to the day when the plastic industry has advanced to the point where the chair will be one material as designed.[417]

With its graceful line and elegant, flowerlike shape, this model came to be known as the *Tulip* pedestal armchair. Its fluid lines reflect Saarinen's early sculptural training and echo the rhythms of his architectural work. He developed the chair's innovative shape with the assistance of Donald Pettit, a model maker from Knoll.

There were many imitations of Saarinen's pedestal armchair manufactured in the 1950s and 1960s, attesting to its revolutionary style and instant popularity. However, they failed to achieve the perfect proportions of Saarinen's design. Saarinen also designed side chairs and tables in the pedestal line, which Knoll continues to produce at its plant in East Greenville, Pennsylvania.

FTH

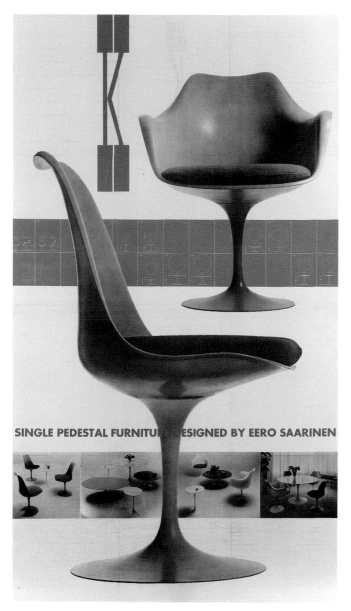

336. *Herbert Matter.* Single Pedestal Furniture Designed by Eero Saarinen

Herbert Matter

Advertising flyer: *Single Pedestal Furniture Designed by Eero Saarinen*
Designed c. 1957
Offset lithograph; 45 × 26 inches (114.4. × 65.8 cm)
Produced by Knoll Associates, Inc. (New York), c. 1957
Unmarked
D87.192.1, gift of Jay Spectre, by exchange*

Matter's geometrically based graphic designs for Knoll were the perfect vehicle for promoting the firm's lean, modern furniture. Matter, who in 1945 was working for Charles Eames in California, was approached by Hans Knoll to design for the latter's seven-year-old New York firm, which was committed, like Matter himself, to a Bauhaus ideal. Matter went to New York in 1946 and devoted the next two decades of his career to Knoll Associates. He was given free rein, first designing the Knoll trademark—which evolved into the red K seen in the upper left corner of this poster—and then some promotional material. Eventually, his technique of photomontage be-

came synonymous with Knoll's visual merchandising, and the resulting projects constitute some of Matter's best work.

This flyer, sent as a folded mailer, features Eero Saarinen's *Pedestal* chairs, designed some two years earlier (fig. 335). Matter gives a frontal view of the armchair and a profile view of the side chair, both of them superimposed against a horizontal band of schematic diagrams printed in red and, below, a comparable horizontal strip of four black-and-white photographs showing groupings of *Pedestal* chairs and tables. These rectangular elements provide information and also anchor the chairs in Matter's typically clean, tight composition. He created visual interest by varying the scale of his images. It is ultimately the pictorial elements, rather than the copy, that convey the product's message. The single line of red sans serif type functions as a compositional repeat of the red strip of plans above. This dramatic poster conveys a great deal of information in a simple fashion while at the same time satisfying many interests.

FTH

Nils Landberg

Goblet
Designed 1956
Glass; 18¹⁵⁄₁₆ × 4¾ × 4¾ inches (46.5 × 12.1 × 12.1 cm)
Produced by AB Orrefors Glasbruk (Orrefors, Sweden), 1957–82
Engraved on underside: ORREFORS Expo NU 312-57
D82.100.1

Vase
Designed 1961
Glass; 15 × 3½ × 3½ inches (38.1 × 8.9 × 8.9 cm)
Produced by AB Orrefors Glasbruck (Orrefors, Sweden), c. 1961 (this example 1961)
Engraved on underside: ORREFORS/EXPO NU/ 629-61/NILS LANDBERG
D88.108.1

Goblet
Designed 1956
Glass; 19⁹⁄₁₆ × 5⅜ × 5⅜ inches (49.7 × 13.6 × 13.6 cm)
Produced by AB Orrefors Glasbruk (Orrefors, Sweden), 1957–82 (this example before 1971)
Engraved on underside: ORREFORS Expo 312-57 Nils Landberg[418]
D84.157.1, gift of Susan A. Chalom*

Like Scandinavian design itself, Landberg's so-called *Tulip* goblets embody those principles of clean line and refined form that dominated so much of postwar thinking. In their day, they were widely publicized and celebrated, and their success was crowned with a gold medal at the 1957 Milan XI Triennale.[419] Even today they are still praised for their elegance and technical virtuosity, and they are often selected to represent Scandinavian design of this period.[420]

Landberg's technique demonstrates an extraordinary mastery of the glass medium. Rather than being assembled from separate pieces, the bowl and stem of the goblet are made from a single pull of glass; the bowl is blown and the stem is then drawn from the pontil. The delicate thinness of the walls and the attenuation of the stem create a severe strain on the material at the moment of creation but ultimately impart an airy buoyancy. Because the glass is cased, with the colored layer inside, the working of the glass results in subtle gradations and a concentration of color at the gathering. The color palette is cool—a dulled red, purples, grays, and greens—and this heightens the ethereal effect.

The one unspoken aspect of Landberg's goblets is that they serve no real purpose. This is especially ironic since Scandinavian design was (and still frequently is) praised as the expression of a functionalist-minded, democratic society. Yet these delicate tours de force were expensive and beyond the means of the middle class. Although sometimes discussed as though they were meant

337. Nils Landberg. Goblets and vase

for drinking—and, indeed, their shapes are related to established types of glasses[421]—these oversize goblets were never intended for human lips. Likewise, they are too tall, too fragile, and too delicately balanced to hold bouquets of flowers. Factory photographs show them in only one context: as *objets d'art* on exhibition. Ultimately, though, all this changed. Their success brought imitations, generally of an inferior quality, from glasshouses on both sides of the Atlantic.[422] Technical virtuosity was replaced by clumsily

simplified forms, and objects for aesthetic delectation became containers for candy. It was in these debased forms that the reverberations of modern design became ubiquitous.

On the other hand, Landberg himself went on to explore comparable forms while maintaining the same excellence of bravura glassblowing. By the end of the decade he had produced a series of vases, like the one here, that have exceedingly thin necks and terminate in mouths with extremely wide, flat flanges.[423] They resemble, in

effect, an inverted *Tulip* goblet, displaying the same sophisticated mannerisms of attenuated form. The vase in the Stewart Collection rests directly on the ground, but some in the series have diminutive foot rings—which emphasize all the more the perilous delicacy of these objects. Although such vases might appear more functional than the *Tulip* goblets, in fact, they belie that appearance: the extreme narrowness of the neck denies any function whatsoever.

ME

Modern Pattern and Ornament

Throughout the 1930s and 1940s, and well into the 1950s, the evangelists of Good Design maintained their opposition to ornament and pattern. The origins of this stance have been often traced to the beginning of the century and Adolf Loos's dictum, "Ornament is a crime." That revelation was confirmed by Mies van der Rohe's pronouncement, "Less is more"—*less* inevitably denoting the absence of man-made pattern. Le Corbusier declared, "Modern decorative art has no decoration." The 1924 exhibition of the German Werkbund was devoted to the theme "Form without Ornament."[424] When Philip Johnson modernized Mrs. Platt's living room in 1935, one of the first things he eliminated was the reproduction of a charming French *patterned* wallpaper (the emphasis is Johnson's).[425] For him, pattern was obtrusive and "a burden" that objects were forced to bear. He tried to assuage his wary client by assuring her that she still had a great deal of ornament: the grain of the wood furniture, the raw silk material of the drapery, even the seams of the leather upholstery on the sofa—all these figured in the new concept of acceptable ornament. Other natural materials, such as pony- and zebra-skin upholstery, were favored in those years, and after the war grass cloth became another common solution. None of these materials, of course, had pattern in the traditional sense of the word.

It is significant that in Edgar Kaufmann, jr.'s *What Is Modern Design?*, that bible of good taste for the 1950s, almost none of the works he designated as representative of Good Design were ornamented. The ceramics he chose all lacked patterns, and he also disdained engraved glass, which he later likened to butter and ice sculpture. The single example of patterned glass he offered was a simple Orrefors bowl with a plain geometric pattern. He claimed that "printed fabrics are a playground for modern designers," but the five examples he put forward to represent "the range of expression" of modern pattern are all rather dry geometrics.[426]

Kaufmann's treatise, which expressed a viewpoint still heavily informed by the precepts of the International Style, exemplifies much of postwar design theory. Yet his conception of Good Design did not represent many designers' work, nor the general public's taste—quite the contrary. Pattern was not merely restricted to a popular consumer level and a lower level of taste, for it existed at very high levels. Artists whom Kaufmann represented with geometric patterns could equally well have been represented by figurative patterns. Had he done so, then his "playground for modern designers" would have looked more playful.

An illuminating confrontation occurred in 1953 when Kaufmann and the Good Design committee came under attack from a trade publication, the *Crockery and Glass Journal*.[427] Among its objections, the journal noted that the committee had never chosen patterned dinnerware, only white or glazed ware. Kaufmann himself replied that the committee wanted to see "surface patterns not imitative of the past," and the following spring it actually selected three patterns. Moreover, in the autumn of 1953 Kaufmann and the Museum of Modern Art held a panel discussion on the topic "Is Ornament Good

Design?"[428] Such conciliatory gestures aside, however, the marked aversion to ornament held true for many design theorists.

The opportunity to show how ornament could be modern and that it need not imitate the past had presented itself some years earlier. In 1949 Robert Goldwater, the noted historian of modern art, in conjunction with René d'Harnoncourt, staged an exhibition at the Museum of Modern Art entitled "Modern Art in Your Life."[429] Its aim was to demonstrate that modern art, rather than being elitist, as was often claimed, had infiltrated and changed the visual language of people's daily experiences. The first section showed the influence of De Stijl painting and International Style architecture. Other sections demonstrated the influence of Synthetic Cubism, the impact of Jean Arp's and Joan Miró's abstract and stylized organic forms, and the influence of Surrealist and fantastic art.

As germane as this exhibition could have been, it fell short because of the museum's basic rejection of pattern and applied ornament. Although Goldwater and d'Harnoncourt chose abundant examples from the world of graphic arts—book jackets, posters, packaging—and from store display, they considered only a few woven or printed textiles with pattern, and they disregarded almost entirely the notion of decorated glass, ceramics, jewelry, and metalwork. They acknowledged, for example, "Pottery and rugs are occasionally ornamented with what is in effect a cubist painting, stylistically unchanged, executed in another physical medium," but they were clearly unsympathetic to such work and did not include any. Had they been willing to cast their net further and consider the vases, textiles, and jewelry of the type that are presented here, they would have found abundant evidence of how modern art had created a new language of ornament, and they would have realized that it was not merely a geometric but a figurative idiom as well.

Among the decorative objects presented here are several created by celebrated artists: the Dufy tapestry (fig. 338), the Matisse rug (fig. 355), the Picasso plate (fig. 346), and the Dalí brooch, tiles, and textile (figs. 412, 414, 422), among others. In some instances, commercial designers took the artists' works and transformed them. For example, the Fuller textile firm contracted with various artists of the Paris school to allow their art to be turned into patterns by Fuller's staff designers (figs. 356, 359).[430] Such collaboration between artists and commerce has an interesting tradition; it has been a recurrent phenomenon since the middle of the nineteenth century and Felix Summerly's Art Manufactory. It continued with such projects as the tapestries and stained glass designed by Edward Burne-Jones, as well as the ceramics of Gauguin. It remained a popular idea well into the 1920s and 1930s, as represented by the fabrics and ceramics of Raoul Dufy and the designs of Matisse, André Derain, and Georgia O'Keeffe for the Steuben glass factory. These types of projects very often have been held suspect in the art world because by their very material they were judged to be lesser works by great artists. Even within Roger Fry's Omega group, a pivotal project of this type, a distinction was made between the levels of performance expected from the artists in terms of salon work and decorative objects. Within the world of the decorative arts, such projects have been greeted with equal suspicion and resentment, often because designers and craftsmen resented the intrusion of outsiders considered by others to be of a higher order. Regardless of all such prejudices, these projects were influential. The celebrity status of the artists attracted public attention and engendered excitement.

Robert Goldwater recognized that often "the artist has given form to a vision which the designer then makes his own," but then he curiously proceeded to assert, ". . . often these resemblances connote a common point of view adopted independently by artist, architect, and designer alike—similar needs provoking similar aesthetic discoveries—and it is incorrect to speak of source and derivation."[431] To the contrary, the fine arts had a decided influence on forming a modern decorative vocabulary. Time after time, designers have admitted to having had their taste formed by exposure to famous works of art. The influence was usually indirect, a conscious or unconscious absorption of basic elements of modern art, the amorphous but omnipresent Zeitgeist. Personal relationships between designers and well-known artists were rare. Likewise, it is difficult to point to a single specific source. Erwine Laverne reports that his wife's textile *Fun to Run* (fig. 378) was based on Matisse's *Dance*, but could one not see the figures as being more analogous to the famous running figures in Picasso's curtain for *L'Oiseau Bleu?* And are not the stars, arrows, and other decorative accents in the background of that textile suggestive of Miró or Paul Klee? Modern art itself is a complex interweaving of overlapping ideas. When we see the open, loose drawing style characteristic of postwar ornament, are we witnessing the effects of Klee's wandering line or Arp's doodle or the calligraphic grace of Matisse? Even if we cannot disentangle all the threads of modern art's Gordian knot, we must recognize that its influence was pervasive, and, as in all periods of the past, it gave rise to an ornamental language of great appeal and vivacity.

ME

Raoul Dufy

Tapestry: *Hommage à Mozart*
Designed 1934
Wool, silk, and cotton, tapestry weave;
  54½ × 44½ inches (138.5 × 113 cm)
Produced at Aubusson, France, 1934
Woven at bottom center: *Raoul Dufy/1934*
D87.189.1

Hommage à Mozart was introduced in April 1936 at the Bignou Gallery in New York City, the initial venue for an international traveling exhibition that created quite a stir in the artistic world.[432] The cause of the excitement was the viewing of sixteen modern French tapestries woven at Aubusson and Beauvais after designs commissioned by Marie Cuttoli of Paris from some of the most prominent artists of the day: Georges Braque, Raoul Dufy, Fernand Léger, Jean Lurçat, Henri Matisse, Pablo Picasso, and Georges Rouault.

All the artists included in this exhibition, with the notable exception of Lurçat, supplied paintings to be faithfully copied by the weavers. Dufy's tapestry is directly based on a model painted in 1934, although its ultimate source is the 1915 composition *Mozart's House in Salzburg* (fig. 339).[433] The one concession that Dufy made to its adaptation into tapestry was the addition of a decorative border.

The consummate skill with which the weavers reproduced exactly the character of each design, including every nuance of color, texture, and brushstroke, was a source of amazement and admiration, but the tapestries themselves had their critics as well as supporters. The latter heralded the creation of a new art form: "easel tapestries"—uncanny duplications of the art of the best modern masters. Noted connoisseur Albert C. Barnes, who termed this project "an epoch in art history," purchased three examples. Critics, however, questioned whether these works represented progress or regression. They viewed the replication of paintings in tapestry as continuing the aesthetic principles and working traditions of the eighteenth century as well as the Victorian era. They suggested that the art of tapestry would be better served if artists designed for the medium instead of requesting tour-de-force copies of paintings.[434]

Pros and cons aside, Marie Cuttoli achieved her aims of the project: it saved the failing French tapestry manufacture through the intervention of painters, and, at the same time, it introduced a modern style that revitalized an age-old craft. *Hommage à Mozart* and the other works generated a new interest in the possibilities of tapestry weaving, raised questions about the interaction between artist and weaver, and paved the way for further developments later in the century, most specifically the renaissance of tapestry through the work of Jean Lurçat.

AZ

338. *Raoul Dufy.* Hommage à Mozart *tapestry*

339. *Dufy.* Mozart's House in Salzburg. *1915*

Herbert Bayer

Magazine tear sheet: *Adrianol*

Designed 1935

Offset printing; 11⅝ × 8¼ inches (29.6 ×
   20.9 cm)

Printed in 1935

Printed in white in lower left corner: [device of
   a rectangle enclosing a Y flanked by two
   pairs of diamonds]

D88.127.1

While living in Berlin from 1928 to 1939, Herbert
Bayer worked as design and art director at the
Dorland Studio, where he was given free rein to
experiment. As a result, the lessons of the Bauhaus entered the world of commercial art through
his work.

This advertisement typifies Bayer's Surrealistic
style of the mid-1930s, in which a rich mixture
of images, textures, and contrasts is achieved
through photographic collage. When Bayer conceived this advertisement, impressions of the
classical world were still strong in his mind from a
trip to Greece he had taken with Marcel Breuer
the previous summer. The marble head of the
"consumer" in this advertisement is taken from
the fourth-century B.C. statue of Hermes by Prax-
iteles, which Bayer had photographed at Olym-
pia. The sinus passages, shown diagrammatically
in red and chrome yellow, are receiving a benefi-
cial dose of the advertiser's product from a drop-
per held by a flesh-tinted human hand. A
photomontage of the packaged product with its
blue label is prominently featured in the upper
right, against a halftone photographic reproduction of a rainswept, cobbled pavement. This startling juxtaposition of images, as well as the
selective use of bright color, not only call attention to the product but heighten the advertisement's overall surreal effect.

Bayer had begun to explore the artistic use of
photomontage, using disquieting juxtapositions
of the animate and the inanimate, in the early
1930s, as seen in *Hands Act* of 1932 (fig. 341). He
had also begun to introduce classical sculpture,
although in a more subtle, painterly way, as in his
1931 advertisement for Lange Radio, where the
ear of Polyclitus' *Doryphorus* is made prominent
in response to the product's aural sensations
(fig. 308). In the later *Adrianol* advertisement,
the same effects are presented in a bold manner.

FTH

340. *Herbert Bayer.* Adrianol

(right) 341. *Bayer.* Hands Act. 1932. *Bayer
Archives, Denver Art Museum*

(far right) 342. *Bayer. Advertisement for Lange
Radio. 1931. Bayer Archives, Denver Art Museum*

A. M. Cassandre

Poster: *Italia*
Designed 1935
Offset lithograph; 39 × 24 inches (99 × 61 cm)
Printed by Officina Grafica Coen (Milan), 1936
Printed in black in upper right: [crownlike device with wavy lines and monogram AMC]
Printed in blue gray in lower left: [circular device enclosing a garland, shield with cross, crown, and monogram ENIT]
Printed in lower right: [circular device enclosing monogram FS]
Printed in lower left margin: OFF. GRAF. COEN & C. - MILANO
Printed in lower right margin: PRINTED IN ITALY BY THE ENIT
Handwritten in ink in lower right: *A. M. Cassandre*
On reverse, handwritten in ink on paper label: . . . Dorothy + Churchill Lathrop/ Dartmouth College/Hanover, N.H.
D87.171.1

In the late 1920s Cassandre revolutionized the poster aimed at the tourism industry. In 1935, despite legislation passed by the Mussolini regime forbidding Italian companies to commission French artists, Italian publisher Augusto Coen invited the celebrated graphic artist to spend the summer at Ghiffa on the shores of Lago Maggiore. There Cassandre and his assistant, Raymond Savignac, designed three posters promoting Italian tourism, one emphasizing sports, one emphasizing travel by ship, and this one, which emphasizes the arts. All three, which are

(below left) 343. *Neroccio de' Landi.* Madonna and Child with Saints. *c. 1475. Pinacoteca, Siena*

(below) 344. *A. M. Cassandre.* Italia

OFF. GRAF. COEN & C. - MILANO   PRINTED IN ITALY BY THE ENIT

233

345. *Giorgio De Chirico.* The Enigma of a Day. *1914. Collection, The Museum of Modern Art, New York. James Thrall Soby Bequest*

among Cassandre's last posters, were published the following year, signed only with the monogram AMC, in order to disguise the French artist's name.[435]

Typical of Cassandre's graphic style of the 1930s, *Italia* reflects a variety of interests, executed with the artist's usual economy of means. He was sympathetic to the Constructivist compositions of the Bauhaus, and his work shows awareness of the importance of geometric placement. Architecture, Cassandre's preferred discipline, accounts for the monumentality of his forms and perhaps also the way in which the architectonic elements anchor the poster's composition. He used typography as an important compositional element. Unlike most Bauhaus-inspired typographers, Cassandre varied his typefaces and preferred uppercase letters. "Italia," written in the alternating red and green colors of the Italian flag, forms the ground line for the poster's composition. Cassandre preferred to place the text of his posters as close to the center of the composition as possible. He believed that the design should be based on the text and not vice

versa, stating, "A poster is above all a *word* . . . but there must be created around that word a series of associations of simple ideas."[436]

A new softness and lyricism of pictorial expression appear in this poster, and his composition is suffused with an experimental, Surrealist spirit. Noted for his borrowings from the fine arts, Cassandre here refers to Giorgio De Chirico's highly personal metaphysical landscapes (fig. 345). *Italia* shares the Italian artist's Surrealistic rendering of space and surprising juxtaposition of images to attract the viewer's attention. The way in which the Quattrocento Madonna and Child, based on a painting by Neroccio de' Landi (fig. 343), dissolve away and the manner in which the balustrade reverses from one color to the other and from solid to void also lend an air of Surrealist mystery. Even the bold, three-dimensional border (Cassandre bordered many of his posters) in orange, violet, and pink suggests ancient Roman illusionistic patterns, thus evoking the poetry and grandeur of Italy's past and promoting Italian tourism.

FTH

Pablo Picasso

Plate
Designed 1949[437]
Glazed earthenware; 15 × 12⅜ × 1⅜ inches
   (38 × 31.5 × 3.5 cm)
Produced by Potterie Madoura (Vallauris, France), c. 1949
Painted on underside: EDITION/PICASSO/
   98/200/MADOURA
Impressed on underside: MADOURA/PLEIN/FEU
D89.191.1, gift of Mrs. David M. Stewart

Picasso's work in ceramics supposedly stemmed from a chance visit in 1946 to Georges and Suzanne Ramié's Potterie Madoura. He modeled three figures and left. As the story goes, he happily discovered these fired pieces on a second trip made exactly one year later, and the joy of his discovery sparked almost three decades of intense

activity in this medium. While some of his work, especially the sculpture, consisted of unique creations, the bulk was conceived for serial production issued in either limited or unlimited runs.

The plate in the Stewart Collection is one of his early designs for limited production; as the number on the underside indicates, it was the ninety-eighth in a series of two hundred examples. The numbering system is like that used for fine prints, and to a certain degree there is a valid analogy between the two mediums, especially since Picasso had already produced an enormous body of etchings and lithographs. In both instances, the artist is able to create a work that can be duplicated and sold commercially at much lower cost than a unique drawing or painting.

When he began work at the Potterie Madoura, one of his favored forms was this oval platter. The shape seems to have suggested itself as a mirror for endless variations on the theme of a face, as the arena of bullfighting scenes, or as a plate to be adorned with fruits or fish. He also created a substantial number with birds—his favored owl or, as is the case here, the dove. At first one might accept the dove for its value as a charming image, but also we might recall the rather pointed symbolism that the peace dove carried in this bleak period after the war. Picasso's political activity was often controversial in those days; an avowed Communist and pacifist, he had used this symbol just a year earlier on a poster for a peace movement conference.[438] For the plate, Picasso modified an earlier design to include a burst of light,

346. Pablo Picasso. Plate. 1949

presumably an element of hope, that streams down from the upper right side.[439]

Working with colored slips, Picasso wielded the brush with the same bravura directness that he displayed on canvas. Then he picked out the dove's feathers by scratching through the slip. An analogy was made above between ceramics in series and prints, yet there is a very provocative difference between the mediums. When an etching or lithograph is made, the design is established on the printing plate, and provided that the process is properly supervised, a substantial number of prints can be pulled with little difference among them. On the other hand, after Picasso made a master ceramic, each exemplar was hand-painted. As carefully as the master was followed—and frequently guides were established in

the mold—each copy was bound to be slightly different. As can be seen by comparing the plate in the Stewart Collection with another in the series (fig. 347), there are abundant differences: the drawing of the bird's eye, the pattern of the masonry border, and, not least of all, the brush-work itself. Still, despite such minutiae these ceramic works convincingly convey the wit and spontaneity of Picasso's art. From the moment they were first exhibited they were hailed as a success. Their impact then and over the next decades should not be minimized. They were not solely a commercial commodity but a significant artistic achievement, whose importance we are only now beginning to grasp.

ME

347. Picasso. Plate. 1949

Pablo Picasso

Vase
Designed c. 1950–54
Glass; 17½ × 11⅝ × 10¼ inches (44.5 ×
   29.5 × 26 cm)
Produced by IVR di Mazzega (Murano, Italy),
   c. 1954
Unmarked
D85.135.1

(right) 348. *Pablo Picasso. Vase (ceramic). 1961*

(below) 349. *Picasso. Vase*

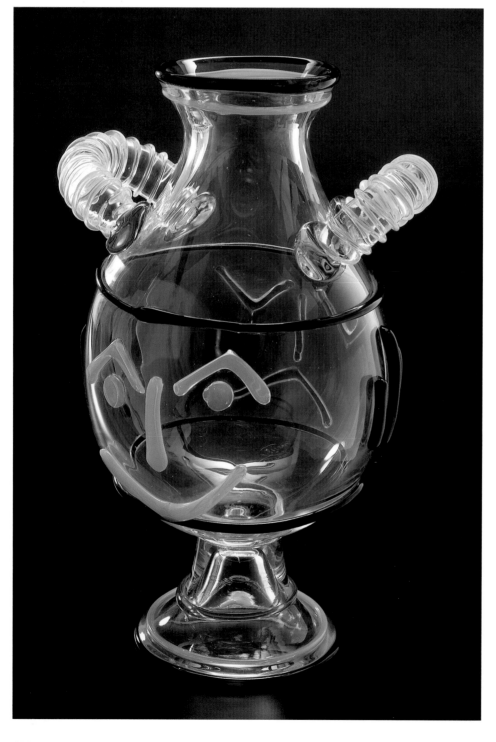

As part of the postwar attempt to revive the glass industry of Murano, Egidio Constantini created the Centro Studio Pittori nell'Arte del Vetro with the financial support of Peggy Guggenheim, flamboyant patron of the arts.[440] As its name implies, the group's function was to seek designs from studio painters that could be translated into glass.[441] Most of the Italian artists, save for contributors like Gino Severini, were unknown outside their native country, but the foreigners were internationally renowned masters of an older generation, including Pablo Picasso, Georges Braque, Fernand Léger, Le Corbusier, Marc Chagall, Alexander Calder, Henry Moore, and Oskar Kokoschka.

That Picasso should have been included in this project is understandable, given the considerable role he played in postwar art. From the moment his ceramics were introduced in 1947, they were greeted with enthusiasm by *Domus* and other Italian publications; special examples were donated by the artist himself to the ceramic museum at Faenza.[442] Moreover, an extremely important retrospective of the artist's work was held in Rome in 1953. Like Michelangelo some four hundred years earlier, Picasso was viewed as the divine creator.

Despite publicity photographs that showed Picasso with these glass vases, it seems that he did not visit Murano, and there was no direct interchange between artist and artisan. In fact, some — if not most — of the Picasso glass vases had first been executed in pottery at Vallauris.[443] This vase is not known to have a specific ceramic prototype, but its general features have a great deal in common with Picasso's designs for that medium (fig. 348).[444] As is frequently the case, the form of the vessel is relatively classical: high-footed, double-handled, and symmetrical. The decoration, however, expressed Picasso's bold, spontaneous draftsmanship in the brash bandings around the handles and the simplistic, schematized smiling and sad faces. The humorous result is typical of Picasso's creations as well as of much postwar design.

Constantini's venture received a fair amount of publicity at the time, and there was even an exhibition that traveled to Switzerland.[445] Yet it had little impact on the Murano glasshouses themselves; they preferred to explore the more intrinsic problems of glass technique. If Picasso and his contemporaries had an impact in Italy, it is among the ceramists, who proved more receptive to such bold imagery.   ME

Salvatore Meli

Ewer
Designed and executed 1956
Glazed terra-cotta; 37⅞ × 28¾ × 9¾ inches
   (96.3 × 73 × 24.7 cm)
Painted in glaze on the rim of the spout: *Meli*
   56 Roma
D88.101.1, gift in memory of Mrs. Daniel
   Barnard Fuller*

Ceramics was one of the Italian artisanal indus-tries that flourished in the postwar years.[446] Small traditional workshops using low-cost raw materials produced exportable wares in large quantities. Leading the way were Guido Gam-bone of Florence, Lucio Fontana of Albisola, Pietro Melandri of Faenza, Fausto Melotti of Milan, and Salvatore Meli of Rome. They set the standard for Italy's boldly patterned and brightly glazed ceramics.

As spontaneous and dynamic as Meli's ewer may look, his normal practice was surprisingly deliberate.[447] He first designed the work on paper and then built up the form, coil by coil.[448] He even drew with charcoal on the finished form before decorating it. However, he also worked with sufficient freedom so that, as one visitor remarked, "The finished form may or may not have any relationship to the original drawing."[449]

As is often the case, there is a discrepancy between what the artist claimed for his work and what the ceramics themselves suggest. Meli maintained that because he grew up in Sicily, the past seemed more meaningful to him than the present, and that he had been inspired by the dignity and richness of Etruscan and Greek pot-tery.[450] Yet the language of his zoomorphic

forms, the bold calligraphy of his patterns, and his stylized figurative elements are aligned with modern European painting rather than the art of the classical past. When asked about the ceramics of Picasso, Meli did not acknowledge the for-mative effect that that painter's work evidently had on him. To the contrary, he criticized Pi-casso for not creating a unity between the decora-tion and the form of the vessel—a synthesis that Meli felt was at the core of his own work.[451]

Meli aspired to escape the limitations of deco-rative art. This ewer, for example, is over three feet tall and weighs some 18½ pounds. Its shape is not functional; it cannot be lifted easily, espe-cially if it is filled with liquid, and its immense scale prevents it from being an *objet d'art* to be displayed in a cabinet or on the omnipresent shelving unit of the 1950s. Its true domain is sculpture, posed on the floor, as the original owners of this ewer displayed it, or on a pedestal. This denial of function and the emphasis on expressive force and increased scale mark a direc-tion that became increasingly important in the late 1950s and 1960s as ceramics and other craft mediums sought to be taken seriously as "high" art.   ME

350. Salvatore Meli. Ewer

Gilbert Portanier

Vase
Designed and executed c. 1958[452]
Glazed terra-cotta; 25⅝ × 7 × 7 inches
   (65 × 17.5 × 17.5 cm)
Unmarked
D87.161.1

From the very beginning of Portanier's career in 1952, critics inevitably paired his name with other ceramists active in Vallauris, a Mediterra-nean town long celebrated for its ceramic tradi-tion. Inevitably, one name loomed larger than all the others—that of Picasso, whose work had re-established Vallauris's reputation and had given French ceramics a new artistic impetus after the war.

Certainly the wiry and impromptu style of Portanier's draftsmanship recalls Picasso's. Also, the themes Portanier favored, such as the nymph and sprightly satyr on this vase or the acrobats and nudes on others, were the sort that Picasso also enjoyed. Is it any surprise that when Portanier and his friends were first beginning to experiment

with ceramics, they sought the counsel of Picasso? Portanier recalls that Picasso "kindly, though somewhat mischievously" told them that their work was very good.[453]

But after such comparisons are made, it is just as informative to consider how different the two artists were. In contrast to Picasso, Portanier became a potter in the fullest sense of the profession, learning to throw and glaze. As a result, the forms, unlike the heavier, molded forms used by Picasso, are subtler and lighter in shape, with volumes that swell in response to the potter's hand. The throwing rings and slight fluctuations of form on Portanier's vase testify to his active participation in the creation of this vessel. Portanier also used banded borders, here and throughout his work of the period, to define the neck and foot of the vase in a way that evokes millennia-old pottery traditions of the Mediterranean, whereas Picasso treated his ceramic forms more as blank canvases or sculptural forms.

Ultimately, it could be said that Portanier was a ceramist who responded more to classical traditions of pottery, while Picasso was essentially a painter who had turned to ceramics. This is not to say that one is better than the other but, rather, to recognize their differences in approach. And, of course, others, such as Salvatore Meli (fig. 350), responded in still different ways to the powerful stimulus of Picasso's work.

ME

351, 352. *Gilbert Portanier. Vase*

Henri Matisse

Rug: *Mimosa*
Designed 1949
Wool, machine-woven pile, Axminster
    construction; 57⅞ × 36¼ inches (147 ×
    92 cm)
Produced by Alexander Smith and Sons
    (Yonkers, New York), 1951
Woven in lower left corner: HM
On reverse, printed in blue and black on cloth
    label glued to lower right corner: This rug
    designed by H. Matisse and named
    "Mimosa" by him, has been woven by
    Alexander Smith in a limited edition of 500
    of which this is number 163 [device of blue
    leaf and yellow bar]
D85.111.1

Henri Matisse was approached in the late 1940s by William F. Cochran Ewing, president of Alexander Smith and Sons. Besides being president of this prominent carpet manufacturing company, Ewing was a painter, and he had the idea to ask Matisse to provide a design that could be made into a hearth rug.[454] This was intended to commemorate the one-hundredth anniversary of the company in 1945, but Matisse's design, a maquette executed as a paper cutout (fig. 353), was not made until 1949.[455] According to one of the artist's biographers, Matisse did not approve the factory's first attempt at translating his design into a rug, causing an entire edition to be scrapped.[456] A second attempt was more to the artist's satisfaction.

During this period of his life, Matisse occupied himself extensively with paper cutouts. He was eighty years old and greatly affected by ill health. Compared to painting, paper cutouts were simpler to do, and they could be executed while sitting in bed or in a wheelchair. He had just worked on a series of large, silk-screened linen panels for A. Ascher, Inc., of London that had been prepared as cutouts, as well as two maquettes for woven tapestries for the Manufacture de Beauvais. Moreover, in early 1948 he had

created his first cut-paper design for the apse window of the Chapel of the Rosary of the Dominican Nuns in Vence and was beginning the celebrated series of designs for vestments.

The composition of *Mimosa* was created through a series of intricately shaped mimosa leaves, a plant closely identified with the Côte d'Azur, placed on top of one another. The dense concentration of leaves at the center is balanced by less densely placed leaf motifs in the four corners of the composition. The leaves vary in size and proportions, and their brilliant coloration of yellow, blue, black, and gray stands out against the background of three different reds.

Mimosa was Matisse's first and probably only pattern specifically designed to be made into a carpet. It is to the credit of Alexander Smith and Sons that the angularity of design normally associated with paper cutouts was not lost in translation. An edition of five hundred was produced by the firm in 1951 and sold for one hundred dollars each.[457]   CCMT

(upper left) 353. *Henri Matisse. Maquette for* Mimosa *rug. 1949. Ikeda Museum of 20th Century Art, Itoh City, Japan*

(above left) 354. *Transferring Matisse's design to a cartoon at Alexander Smith & Sons, Yonkers, New York, c. 1949*

(above) 355. *Matisse.* Mimosa *rug*

356. *Joan Miró*. Femme Ecoutant *textile*

Joan Miró

Textile: *Femme Ecoutant*
Designed c. 1955
Cotton, plain weave, roller printed; 80⅝ × 39½
  inches (203.2 × 97.8 cm)
Produced by Fuller Fabrics (New York),
  c. 1955–56
Printed in red in selvage: *Fuller Fabrics,*
  "FEMME ECOUTANT" BY MIRO. A MODERN
  MASTER ORIGINAL. D.B. FULLER & CO ©
D88.149.1

Textile: *Textures*
Designed c. 1955
Cotton, plain weave, roller printed; 23 × 39
  inches (59.4 × 100.2 cm)
Produced by Fuller Fabrics (New York),
  c. 1955–56
Unmarked
D88.104.1, gift in memory of Mrs. Daniel
  Barnard Fuller*

Perhaps the ultimate "name" collection, Fuller
Fabrics's Modern Master Print series was based on
the works of the most celebrated painters of the
Paris school. Miró, like Pablo Picasso, Marc
Chagall, Raoul Dufy (as represented by his
widow), and Fernand Léger, agreed to let their
works serve as inspiration for Fuller's design studio. The subsequent adaptations were submitted
to the artists for their approval, which was given
in each instance, and then printed at the mill in
Northampton, Massachusetts.

Fuller's designs after Miró accurately evoke the
painter's world of fantasy. His humorously ambiguous people, animals, and objects populate
Femme Ecoutant. The abstract, quasi-calligra-
phic patterns seen in *Textures* are another aspect
of the painter's oeuvre. In the case of *Textures*,
the Fuller studio transcribed one of Miró's lithographs literally (fig. 360) and cleverly turned it
into a repetitive pattern. *Femme Ecoutant*, on
the other hand, required significant changes from
Miró's original painted images. This can be seen
by comparing the textile to its source, *Woman
Listening to Music* (fig. 357), a large oil painting

357. Miró. Woman Listening to Music. 1945. *Private collection, New York*

358. *Miró in his Barcelona studio with model wearing a Claire McCardell ensemble utilizing one of his Modern Master Print fabrics, 1955*

that then was owned by Evelyn Sharp and which decorated the bar of the Stanhope Hotel in New York City.[458] Miró's individual motifs of a woman, a star, and animated abstract figures within aureoles were copied with relative fidelity. However, they have been multiplied, some rendered in mirror image or turned at angles in order to create an overall design that is multidirectional. The color contrast was maintained, but the background was changed from black to café au lait. As evidenced by these two examples, the quality of the printing was superb; it captured painterly nuances of brushstrokes and texture.

Imaginatively promoted across the country through a line of resort wear by American designers, most notably Claire McCardell, the Modern Master Print series enjoyed coverage in both trade magazines and publications intended for a wider audience.[459] These articles emphasized the relation of the designs to their well-known originators (fig. 358) and also suggested how these boldly patterned modern fabrics, sold retail, could be used by the general populace.

AZ

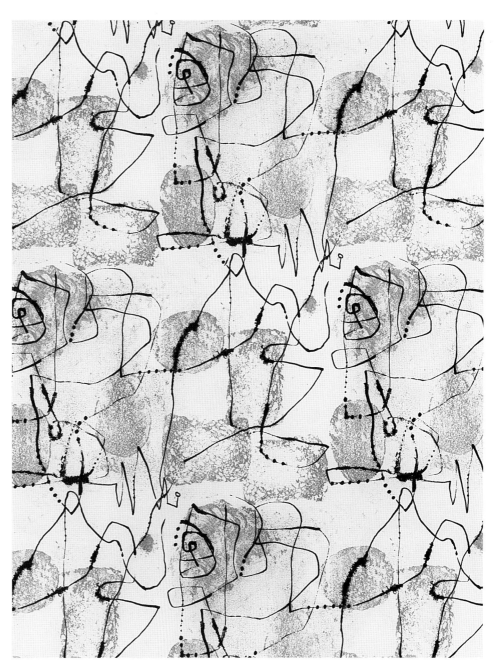

359. *Miró.* Textures *textile*

360. *Miró.* Derrière le miroir. *1953*

Alexander Calder

Textile: model no. L-145, *Calder #1*
Designed 1949
Rayon and fiberglass, plain weave with
   irregular, uncut looping, silk-screen printed;
   33¼ × 49⅝ inches (84 × 126 cm)
Produced by Laverne Originals (New York),
   1949–c. 1965
Printed near the selvage: [device of two
   conjoined arcs, each with a dot in the
   center]
D83.140.1

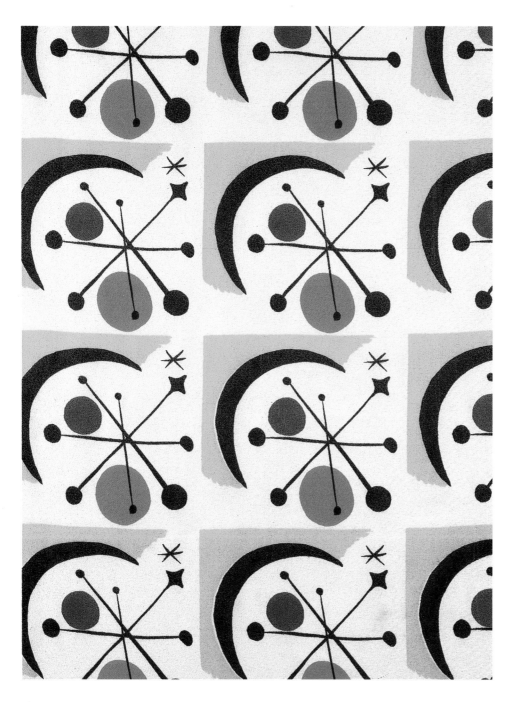

"I'd like to try my hand at doing some wallpapers too," Calder was quoted as having said in 1949 while installing a mobile in the Laverne design studio in New York.[460] This wish was easily fulfilled, and *Calder #1* and *Splotchy* were soon available as part of the Contempora Series of textiles and wallpapers issued by Laverne Originals.

Calder #1 features an abstract composition of stars, moons, and suns conceived in primary colors—yellow, red, blue, and black on white. The pattern is reminiscent of Calder's earlier designs on paper and of his mobiles and stabiles, especially his *Praying Mantis* (1936) and *Constellation* (1943–45).[461] It echoes the artist's preoccupation with and interpretation of the solar system and imaginary universes that he began working on during the 1930s. He once stated that "the underlying sense of form in my work has been the system of the universe."[462] It was the system of the universe that had led Calder ultimately to abstraction.

It is interesting to note that preceding the two Laverne designs by one year is A *Piece of My Workshop*, a silk-screened mural on canvas that Calder created in 1948 for the New York wallpaper firm Katzenbach and Warren, Inc. (fig. 361).[463] A *Piece of My Workshop* depicts in a literal way a mobile with balancing wires, while *Calder #1* gives more of the sense and the proportions of a pattern with an intentional repetitive motif.

CCMT

(above) 361. *Alexander Calder.* A Piece of My Workshop. *1948*

(left) 362. *Calder.* Calder #1 *textile: model no. L-145*

Paul Rand

Poster: *Subway Posters Score*
Designed 1947
Offset lithograph; 45⅛ × 29⅜ inches
 (114.6 × 74.6 cm)
Produced by the New York Subways
 Advertising Company (New York), 1947
Signed in the stone, lower left: *Paul Rand*
Printed in lower center: [circular logo of
 stylized subway train, tracks, tunnel] NYSA
D87.152.1, gift of Mr. and Mrs. Charles D.
 O'Kieffe, Jr., in memory of Mr. and Mrs.
 Charles DeWitt O'Kieffe, by exchange*

This poster for the New York Subways Advertising Company encapsulates Rand's design philosophy that the visual symbol is the most effective means of modern communication. Rand's simple stick figure-cum-target reduces the human figure to a humorous but cogent emblem indicating that the subway rider is a good target for advertising posters.[464]

The apparent playfulness of Rand's image belies a strict adherence to the Modernist principle of basing compositions on geometry. The seemingly random dots of strong color at the bottom of the image form a triangle to stabilize the top-heavy stick figure. And, like the Bauhaus-inspired European typographers of the 1920s and 1930s, Rand used type as a design element. This poster's message, written in the familiar lower-case of Bauhaus typography, is given new life and interest by being superimposed at angles across the stick figure. The subordinate second message, in smaller-point type, extends from the figure's left hand, almost as if it were being held.

For Rand, visual symbols express specific meaning:

> *The circle as opposed to the square. . . as a pure form evokes a specific aesthetic sensation; ideologically it is the sign of eternity, without beginning or end. A red circle may be interpreted as the sign of the sun, the Japanese flag, a stop sign, an ice-skating rink, or a special brand of coffee. . . depending on its context.*[465]

Throughout his career, Rand has been committed to the alliance between fine and commercial art. This poster borrows much from the spontaneous style of Joan Miró (fig. 357), whose work enjoyed great popularity in the 1940s. The Surrealist Spanish artist constructed his playful, vigorous images in bold colors, and he associated incongruous elements to arrest attention, devices Rand successfully used here to convey information.

FTH

363. *Paul Rand*. Subway Posters Score

Alvin Lustig

Book dust jacket: *Anatomy for Interior Designers*

Designed 1946[466]

Offset lithography; 10¼ × 18¾ inches (26 × 47.6 cm)

Published by Whitney Publishing Co. (New York), 1948, 1951

Printed in upper right corner: *lustig*

D86.153.1, gift of Elaine Lustig Cohen

In the United States, Alvin Lustig led the way in creating a modern tradition for book design. He firmly believed in mass communication through visual symbols. By the 1940s those devised by artists such as Joan Miró, Paul Klee, Pablo Picasso, and Henri Matisse had transcended the world of fine arts to enter the public domain. Influenced by the works of those artists, some of which he had seen in the New York galleries of Curt Valentin and Samuel M. Kootz in the 1940s, Lustig similarly sought expression of content through a visual shorthand.

As Lustig was frequently featured in the pages of *Interiors* magazine, it is not surprising that he was selected by the parent corporation, Whitney Publishing Co., to design the cover for a book on graphic standards for interior designers. The book was written by Francis de N. Schroeder, former editor of *Interiors*, and illustrated in stylized black-and-white drawings by Nino Ripetto.

Lustig created a visual pun on the title, using dismembered anatomical sections, silhouetted shapes reminiscent of the bold forms in Miró's paintings (fig. 364). Stylized and monumental, these metaphorical symbols stand out in a bright and surprising palette of blue, yellow, black, white, and gray. Although divided into quadrants, the book cover's composition has a wraparound unity. The front cover is distinguished by the title, self-consciously laid out in a decorative script, the hallmark of 1950s type, while the subtitle below is in a contrasting sans serif Bauhaus-style type. In its aesthetic approach, this book jacket relates to the series Lustig did for New Classics books, for which he devised striking visual symbols on the covers that suggested the books' contents.

There have been three editions of *Anatomy for Interior Designers*.[467] Now much enlarged, it is still in print. Attesting to the success of Lustig's book jacket, the design of the present cover is directly based on his composition of nearly thirty years earlier.   FTH

364. Joan Miró. Composition. 1933. Washington University Gallery of Art, Saint Louis. University Purchase Kende Sale Fund, 1945

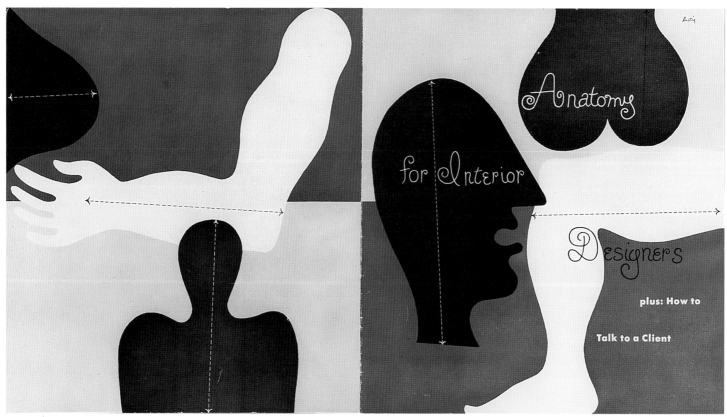

365. *Alvin Lustig.* Anatomy for Interior Designers

Alvin Lustig

Textile: model no. L-335, *Incantation*
Designed c. 1946–47
Linen, plain weave, silk-screen printed;
 40 × 46½ inches (101.6 × 118.1 cm)
Produced by Laverne Originals (New York),
 1948–at least 1951
Unmarked
D86.152.1, gift of Elaine Lustig Cohen

Like Ray Komai's *Masks* (fig. 206), Lustig's *Incantation* was among the first patterns for Laverne Originals's Contempora Series, a line of coordinated fabrics and wallpapers intended to promote new design concepts from artists other than the Lavernes themselves.[468] *Incantation* reveals the influence of artists like Paul Klee and Joan Miró in the use of abstract anthropomorphic and animated geometric shapes. Lustig, an acclaimed graphic designer, was particularly interested in signs and thus, like many modern painters, sought designs with the power and communicative ability of pictographs.[469] Here, he couples motifs suggestive of figures, faces, birds, and animals with an evocative title suggestive of an unknown ritual.

One of the Museum of Modern Art's Good Design Selections for 1948, *Incantation* was frequently illustrated and praised. The pattern was available printed on Peruvian linen or textured rayon with gold or silver lamé, in black on white, as in this example, or the reverse (fig. 366).[470]

AZ

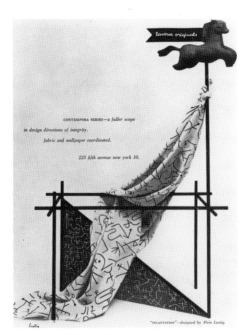

366. *Laverne Originals advertisement for* Incantation *textile, 1950*

367. *Alvin Lustig.* Incantation *textile*

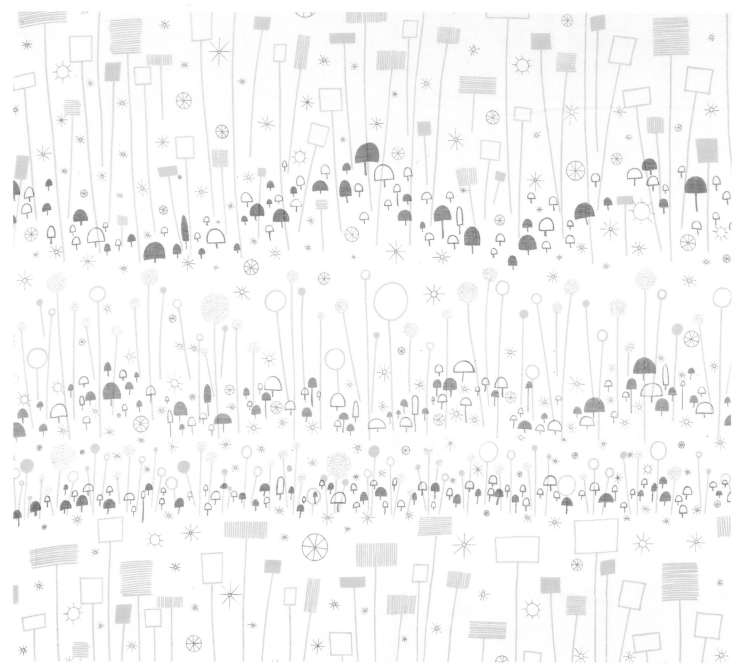

368. *Ruth Adler Schnee.* Seedy Weeds *textile*

Ruth Adler Schnee

Textile: *Seedy Weeds*
Designed c. 1953
Cotton, plain weave, silk-screen printed;
  55⅝ × 52 inches (141.3 × 132.1 cm)
Produced by Adler-Schnee Associates, Inc.
  (Detroit), c. 1953–65
Unmarked
D85.148.1, gift of Mrs. Stanley Hanks

Seedy Weeds won a Good Design Award from the Museum of Modern Art in 1954.[471] It was originally available in three different color ways on either cotton or a mixture of cotton and rayon with a pronounced texture.[472] This example is on the all-cotton fabric, in colors the manufacturer labeled "orange and olive," although the latter is more of a brown. Its pattern is arranged in horizontal rows of stylized mushrooms and floral motifs, interspersed with dandelion puffs on tall

stems. The third row of each repeat shows the tallest stems, which terminate in squares or rectangles. The linear treatment and gentle humor of this pattern recall the work of Adler Schnee's early mentor, Paul Klee, such as his *Pastorale* (fig. 369).

Although the pattern is presented horizontally, the variations in height also allow the eye to move up and down, from the tallest dandelion balls to the lowest of the mushrooms, reinforcing a continuous sense of rhythm. Thus, the pattern is cleverly devised to be read vertically when the fabric is pleated and hung as a curtain.

The title of the pattern, *Seedy Weeds*, is typical of Ruth Adler Schnee's frequent plays on words to identify her textile designs. Others, such as *Fission Chips*, *Slits and Slats*, and *Strings and Things*, suggest her cunning humor.

CCMT

369. *Paul Klee.* Pastorale. *1927. Collection, The Museum of Modern Art, New York. Abby Aldrich Rockefeller Fund and exchange*

Lucienne Day

Textile: *Calyx*
Designed 1951
Cotton and viscose rayon, plain weave,
 silk-screen printed; 144⅜ × 49⅝ inches
 (366.7 × 126 cm)
Produced by Heal and Son Ltd. (London),
 1951–56; by Greeff Fabrics, Inc. (New York)[473]
Printed five times in selvage: Guaranteed to be
 Vat Colors
D88.119.1, gift of Mr. and Mrs. Charles D.
 O'Kieffe, Jr., in memory of Mr. and Mrs.
 Charles DeWitt O'Kieffe, by exchange*

Textile: *Spectators*
Designed 1953
Cotton, plain weave, silk-screen printed;
 53 × 50 inches (134.6 × 127 cm)
Produced by Heal and Son Ltd. (London),
 c. 1953
Printed in black three times in left selvage:
 "HEALS SPECTATORS" *by Lucienne Day*
Printed three times in right selvage: MADE IN
 UNITED KINGDOM TOP [arrow]
D87.195.1, gift of Lucienne Day

Lucienne Day is often credited with introducing
to British textile design an abstract style, which is
ideally illustrated by both *Calyx* and *Spectators*.
The style was introduced by *Calyx*, which was
first shown at the Festival of Britain in 1951. It was

370. *Lucienne Day.* Calyx *textile*

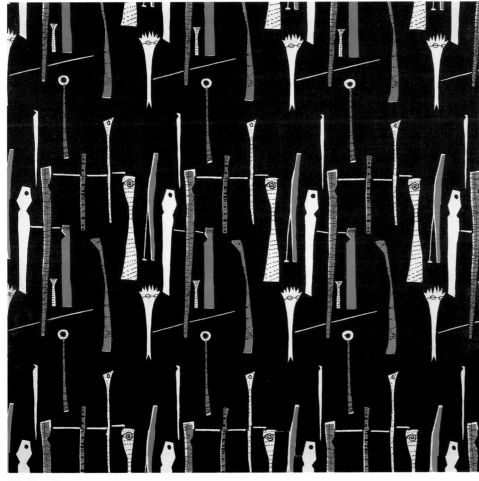

371. *Day.* Spectators *textile*

one of the major alternatives to designs based on
crystalline structures, such as Marianne Straub's
Surrey (fig. 152), which represented the official
style of the Festival. The main motif of *Calyx*
is simplified flowers on slender stalks, with
blossoms and leaves assuming the calyx shapes
indicated by the title. Rhythmically arranged
against a textured brown ground, the forms are
rendered in red, black, beige, and (that very period color) chartreuse.[474]

The inventiveness of the design made it immediately popular. *Calyx* secured a gold medal at the
Milan IX Triennale in 1951 and the American
Institute of Decorators International Award as the
best textile on the United States market the following year. Its fame as one of the most celebrated designs of the 1950s has persisted to the
present. Today, seen through the haze of the
many imitations it sired and the plethora of illustrations of *Calyx* itself, perhaps it is difficult to
appreciate the freshness of the design, although it
is easy to acknowledge its impact.

The appeal of *Spectators*, which won a grand
prize at the 1954 Milan X Triennale, is more
apparent to a later eye. Quixotic and quirky, the
design represents people by their salient characteristics: spiky hair, ties, spectacles. These stylized forms, depicted with a sense of humor in a
bold palette of red, white, and black, are reminiscent of Paul Klee's and Joan Miró's fantasy worlds
(figs. 357, 364) and are as enduring.   AZ

Edvin Öhrström

Vase
Designed c. 1947
Glass; 6¼ × 6½ × 6½ inches (15.3 × 16.5 × 16.5 cm)
Produced by AB Orrefors Glasbruk (Orrefors, Sweden), c. 1947 (this example 1947)
Engraved on underside: orrefors Sweden Ariel nr: 375/E. ohrstrom
D87.111.1

Vase
Designed c. 1950
Glass; 7¼ × 3⅜ × 3⅜ inches (18.4 × 8.6 × 8.6 cm)
Produced by AB Orrefors Glasbruk (Orrefors, Sweden), c. 1950–c. 1960 (this example 1956)
Engraved on underside: ORREFORS/Ariel Nº 325F/Edvin Ohrstrom
Gray rectangular label on side, near bottom, printed within a blue border: SVENKST GLAS/STOCKHOLM
D89.193.1, gift of Dr. Luc Martin

372. Vicke Lindstrand. Vase. 1930. Smålands Stiftelsen Museum, Växjö, Sweden

373. Edvin Öhrström. Vase

The Orrefors factory has maintained a position of artistic leadership in Scandinavian twentieth-century glass because of its innovatory techniques and decoration, both of which are evident in these vases.

The decoration is achieved through a bravura technique known as *Ariel*, which, as the name implies, is a process involving bubbles of air. The design is created through a controlled sequence of steps. First, the decoration is worked out on paper.[475] A sphere of molten glass is blown and cooled in the traditional way, and the pattern is carved away by fine sandblasting. The glass is then slowly reheated and a new casing of molten glass is added. The two layers fuse smoothly where there is no decoration, but where the design was carved away, trapped pockets of air are formed, and they create a silvery pattern that lies elusively under the surface.

These processes are slow and labor-intensive. Moreover, the technique is fraught with difficulties due to the stresses of the repeated expansion and contraction of the glass, a problem that when compounded by the density and weight of the material can result in internal cracks. Thus, these elaborately worked *Ariel* vases are costly *objets d'art*.

When the technique was invented around 1936, it was a timely one that responded to the changed aesthetics of the period. The heaviness of the glass and the use of trapped air bubbles suggested contemporary developments elsewhere, most notably the work of the great French glassmaker Maurice Marinot.[476] Also contributing to the contemporaneity of the *Ariel* glass was the style of its decoration, which at first was heavily indebted to the art of Henri Matisse, Georges Braque, and Fernand Léger. This influence was a natural one, since Öhrström had studied with Léger, and Paris was still the arbiter of taste.

By the late 1930s Orrefors's designers had introduced a fresh repertoire of zoomorphic forms, which suggested perhaps the art of Joan Miró.[477] Not incidentally, they were related to the nascent Biomorphism then emerging in Scandinavia. The decoration of the spherical vase, created just after World War II, reflects this trend. Its theme of fish and cavorting mermaids was already part of the Orrefors repertoire in the 1930s, as is evident in an engraved vase with marine motifs by Vicke Lindstrand (fig. 372). But whereas Lindstrand's vase, both in its distinctively geometric shape and its Moderne classicism, speaks of the 1930s, the distended, rhythmic configurations on Öhrström's vase suggest the Miró-like imagery of the postwar years.

The enigmatic figures on the smaller, cylindrical vase, also water sprites, suggest a somewhat different source of inspiration—the paintings of Salvador Dalí (fig. 375). The skeletal structures of the bodies, the flaming hair, the fleeing, harplike personages—all these elements link Öhrström with Dalí and with much of European postwar decorative arts, such as the comparable figures in Jean Lurçat's tapestries (fig. 395).

ME

374. Öhrström. Vase

375. *Salvador Dalí. Cover for* Vogue, *June 1939*

Jean Colin

Poster: *La Vie Collective*

Designed 1956

Offset lithograph; 64⁹⁄₁₆ × 48⅜ inches (164 × 123 cm)

Printed by Bedos & Cie. (Paris), 1956

Signed in the stone, lower left: *Jean Colin*

D87.201.1, gift of Mr. and Mrs. Charles D. O'Kieffe, Jr., in memory of Mr. and Mrs. Charles DeWitt O'Kieffe, by exchange*

This poster was designed for the first Salon de la Vie Collective, a series of exhibitions devoted to the latest products for a life-style that had changed so dramatically since World War II. Held at Paris's Grand Palais under the auspices of France's Centre National de la Recherche Scientifique, these trade exhibitions were organized by the Salon des Arts Ménagers.[478] The Salons de la Vie Collective contained both foreign and domestic exhibits related to household furnishings, kitchen and laundry equipment, the preparation and consumption of food, and other subjects pertinent to modern home economics.

Colin's poster clearly states the exhibition's theme in visual terms. A white humanoid figure, whose free-form, Biomorphic shape resembles Le Corbusier's *Modular Man* (fig. 377), stands out as the central motif. Superimposed on this shape are a cluster of similar yellow figures, who are visiting the exhibition's various displays. Colin has indicated the exhibition in schematic, blueprint style to form the poster's background. There is a fitting justness in the use of the organic-looking white figure set against the architectural background and the stark sans serif typefaces: Le Corbusier had designed the *Modular Man* as a dimensional unit based on the proportions of the human body as well as the golden ratio, and he intended it to serve as a universal standard for building components and industrial products.[479]　　　　　FTH

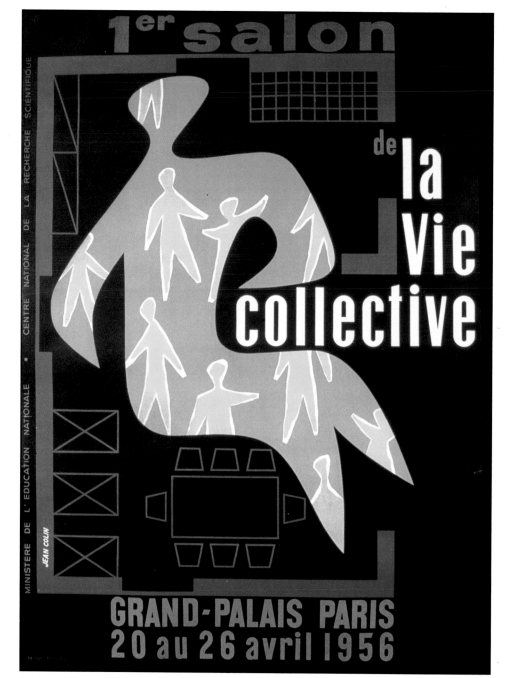

376. *Jean Colin.* La Vie Collective

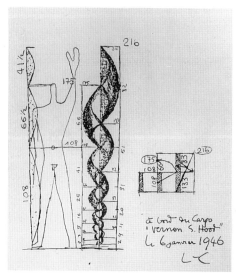

377. *Le Corbusier.* Modular Man. *1946*

Estelle Laverne

Textile: model no. L-265, *Fun to Run*
Designed c. 1947–48
Rayon and gold foil, twill weave, silk-screen
    printed; 83½ × 46¼ inches (212 × 117.5 cm)
Produced by Laverne Originals (New York),
    1948–c. 1965
Printed in brown five times in right selvage:
    An exclusive handprint [device of a star]
    coordinated/*laverne Originals* [surmounted
    by a star]/NEW YORK 10, N.Y. CONTEMPORA
    SERIES/FUN TO RUN
D85.145.1, gift of Alan Moss

Fun to Run won the 1948 American Fabrics
award and was shown in the exhibition "Fabrics of
1948," held at the Metropolitan Museum of Art,
New York, that year.[480] It was very well received
and became part of Laverne Originals's Contempora Series of wallpapers and textiles, a series that
featured not only the Lavernes' own work but also
that of major artists and designers, such as Alexander Calder (fig. 362), Ray Komai (fig. 206), and
Alvin Lustig (fig. 367). At the same time that *Fun
to Run* was introduced, the Contempora Series
was lauded for giving "design directions of integrity."[481]

The inspiration for this pattern was taken from
Henri Matisse's painting *Dance* (fig. 379).[482] *Fun
to Run* exemplifies the Lavernes' practice of
applying fine art to handicraft and machine-
produced objects.[483]

The design was most unusual in using human
shapes in an allover repeating pattern, one of the
few textile compositions of that period to do so.
In addition, amusingly placed arrows, stars, and
dots are integrated at random and with great freedom throughout the pattern. *Fun to Run* shows
Estelle Laverne at her best; it exhibits a refresh-
ing freeness, a fluidity of line, rhythm, and
spontaneity.   CCMT

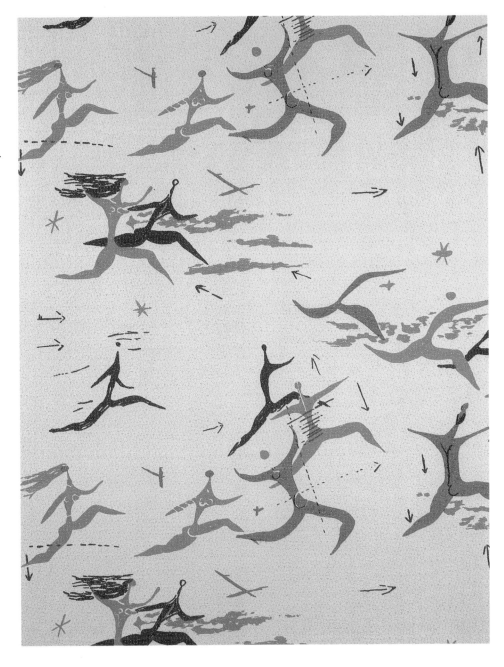

(above) 378. *Estelle Laverne.* Fun to Run *textile:
model no. L-265*

379. *Henri Matisse.* Dance *(first version). 1909.
Collection, The Museum of Modern Art, New York.
Gift of Nelson A. Rockefeller*

Ed Wiener

Brooch: *The Dancer*
Designed and executed c. 1948
Silver; 2⅝ × 1¾ inches (6.7 × 4.1 cm)
Impressed on reverse: ED WIENER/STERLING
D87.242.1

The Dancer is unique in its encouragement of visual associations between two distinct art forms: dance and modern jewelry. It exemplifies one of jewelry's traditional functions: to serve as emblem—a communicative tool designating the wearer as one sympathetic to a particular philosophy or social cause. The subject of this pin announced that the person who wore it championed the modern dance movement, and its bold design proclaimed that the wearer also advocated modern art. Approximately one hundred copies of this design were produced, and the first people who purchased the brooch were actually dancers.

The basic configuration was suggested by a 1941 photograph of Martha Graham by Barbara Morgan that captured a similar gesture (fig. 380).[484] Dance is a transitory medium—a fleeting moment when concept and consummation occur. Therefore, the only permanent record of a dancer's art is in other forms of visual expression. Martha Graham's philosophy of dance as an organic structure in which form and content are functions of each other is conveyed by both the Barbara Morgan photograph and the Ed Wiener brooch. Each offers the impression of a gestural continuum by reliance on the gracefully curving line.

The success of the piece lies in Wiener's use of a free-flowing silhouette. The brooch is constructed from three elements: a Biomorphic shape cut from sheet silver defining the body, dress, and right arm; a calligraphic wire suggesting the dancer's head and left arm; and another wire delineating the skirt ruffle. As the designer stated, "Even in doing literal translations it was important to move it into abstraction and evolve a secondary level of recognition."[485]

Wiener's style in the late 1940s and the early 1950s was heavily influenced by the Cubist/Constructivist sculpture of Alexander Archipenko and Rudolf Belling, yet *The Dancer* brooch is relatively flat, confined closely to the picture plane. Wiener was very careful to distinguish between jewelry and sculpture. He felt that he achieved this differentiation by using oxidation sparingly—only along the shoulder and around the ruffle. The emphasis on the silver surface enhanced the jewellike quality of the pin. "I did not deny the medium," stated Wiener, "and [in so doing] affirmed that I was a jeweler and not a sculptor."[486]

TLW

380. *Barbara Morgan. Martha Graham performing in* Letters to the World. *1941*

381. *Ed Wiener.* The Dancer *brooch*

Harry Bertoia

Brooch
Designed and executed 1942[487]
Brass; 5⅞ × 4½ inches (14.9 × 11.4 cm)
Unmarked
D86.175.1

From 1938 to 1943, when Bertoia ran the metal-working studio at the Cranbrook Academy of Art in Bloomfield Hills, Michigan, he designed primitivistic jewelry such as this brooch, which is defined by meandering lines and textured surfaces. At the same time he created hollowware in a sleek, Streamlined style (fig. 103).

Bertoia's jewelry bears a strong stylistic connection to that of Alexander Calder (fig. 382), with whom he often exhibited in the early 1940s, both at the Alexander Girard Gallery in Detroit and at the Nierendorf Gallery in New York. The two artists employed the technique of directly forging (i.e., hammering) the metal. The main difference between them can be seen in the manner in which each artist connected the various elements: Calder joined them by wires, which he twisted around each other,[488] while Bertoia riveted or fused them. The twelve "legs" or "leaves" of this brooch are formed from six narrow sheets of brass and are joined twice at the center by rivets.

Another difference can be seen in the handling of surface pattern. Bertoia explored the potential of rough and irregular textures, achieved through finishing cloths of varied degrees of roughness and through the application of heat, which results in torch texture or reticulation. Calder was satisfied with simple planishing. In this brooch, Bertoia created a subtle contrast of light and shadow by the slight folding of each leaf; the light breaks as it hits the crease, thereby creating depth and shadow that emphasize the sculptural effect.

Bertoia often exhibited his jewelry with his monoprints (fig. 383), which is fitting in that they use similar formal and experimental devices and share a playful whimsicality.[489] Like the delicate art of Paul Klee, the light, floating shapes of Bertoia's brooch hint of secret life forms. The brooch displays, furthermore, a deliberate ambiguity: Is it animal or vegetable? A crawling insect or a plant whose leaves flutter in the breeze?

Bertoia also addressed the issue of representing movement in space. The center of this brooch combines six relatively straight lines. However, the brass units twist slightly beyond each connection and fan away in diverse directions. Like so many caterpillar legs, they chase each other around the surface, creating a strong sense of movement. The edge formed by the creasing of each metal leg serves to control the feeling of motion. Ultimately, the brooch's configuration can be likened to a "flipbook," where each page implies a movement in a continuum. Thus, in a sense, this concern with movement and its control heralded Bertoia's forays into kinetic sculpture in the 1960s.   TLW

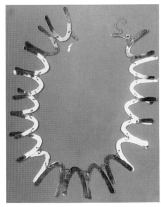

382. *Alexander Calder. Necklace.*
c. 1940. Private collection, New York

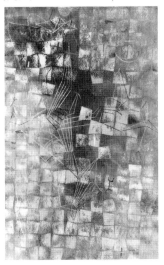

383. *Harry Bertoia. Monoprint.*
c. 1940. Collection Brigitta Bertoia

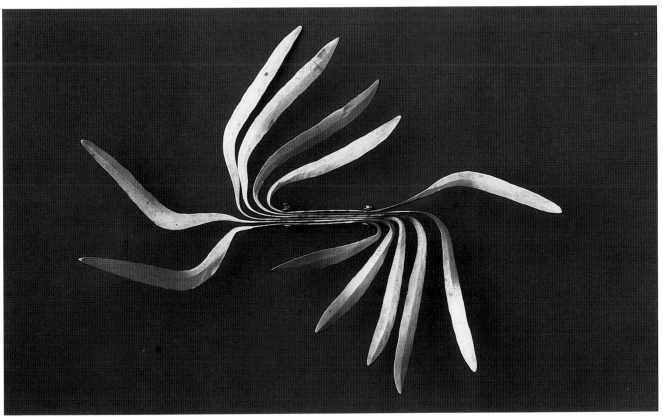

384. *Bertoia. Brooch*

George Nelson Associates

385. Alexander Calder. Constellation. 1943. Collection Jean Lipman

Wall clock: model no. 4755, *Ball*[490]
Designed 1947
Painted birch, steel, brass; 14 × 14 × 2¼ inches
   (35.5 × 35.5 × 5.7 cm)
Produced by Howard Miller Clock Company
   (Zeeland, Michigan), c. 1948–69
Printed on transparent rectangular label glued
   to back: chronopak [surrounded by two
   arches, all within a circle]/*howard miller
   clock company*/ZEELAND, MICHIGAN/115 V.
   60 CY. 2 WATTS PATTERN NO.
D86.150.1, gift of Dr. Arthur Cooperberg

Wall clock: model no. 4756[491]
Designed 1947
Brass and painted steel: 12 × 12 × 4⅜ inches
   (30.5 × 30.5 × 11 cm)
Produced by Howard Miller Clock Company
   (Zeeland, Michigan), c. 1948–c. 1964
Impressed below on back: 04756/HOWARD
   MILLER CLOCK CO./ZEELAND, MICH.
Printed on transparent rectangular label glued
   to back: chronopak [surrounded by two
   arches, all within a circle]/*howard miller
   clock company*/ZEELAND, MICHIGAN/115 V.
   60 CY. 3 WATTS/PATTERN NO.
D87.209.1

386. George Nelson Associates. Ball *wall clock: model no. 4755*

387. George Nelson Associates. Wall clock: model no. 4756

388. George Nelson Associates. Asterisk *wall clock: model no. 2213*

389. George Nelson Associates. Spider Web *wall clock: model no. 2214*

Wall clock: model no. 2213, *Asterisk*[492]
Designed 1950
Painted zinc-plated steel; 10 × 10 × 2¼ inches
    (25.2 × 25.2 × 5.9 cm)
Produced by Howard Miller Clock Company
    (Zeeland, Michigan), 1950–c. 1964
Impressed on back: 2213/HOWARD MILLER
    CLOCK, CO./ZEELAND, MICH.
Printed on transparent rectangular label glued
    to back: CHRONOPAK [surrounded by two
    arches, all within a circle]/*howard miller
    clock company*/ZEELAND, MICHIGAN/115 V.
    60 CY. 3 WATTS/PATTERN NO.
Printed and handwritten on yellow paper label
    on back: 93R 0/11 MO./[logo of a globe and
    a clock]/CALIFORNIA/TIME/SERVICE/
    "SPECIALISTS IN THE WORLD OF TIME"/LONG
    BEACH   SANTA ANA
D87.174.1, gift of Fifty/50 Gallery, New York

Wall clock: model no. 2214, *Spider Web*[493]
Designed 1954
Birch, cord, plastic, painted steel; 19 × 19 × 3½
    inches (48.2 × 48.2 × 8.9 cm)
Produced by Howard Miller Clock Company
    (Zeeland, Michigan), c. 1954–c. 1964
Printed on transparent rectangular label glued
    to back: CHRONOPAK [surrounded by two
    arches, all within a circle]/*howard miller
    clock company*/ZEELAND, MICHIGAN/115 V.
    60 CY. 3 WATTS/PATTERN NO.
D87.237.1

Wall clock: model no. 2201, *Kite*[494]
Designed 1953
Painted steel and wood; 16½ × 21⅝ × 4 inches
    (42 × 55 × 10 cm)
Produced by Howard Miller Clock Company
    (Zeeland, Michigan), c. 1954–c. 1964
Printed on transparent rectangular label glued
    to back: CHRONOPAK [surrounded by two
    arches, all within a circle]/*howard miller
    clock company*/ZEELAND, MICHIGAN/115 V.
    60 CY. 3 WATTS/PATTERN NO.
D87.238.1

Beginning in 1947, the Nelson design office developed a series of new clocks for Howard Miller, whose account it had acquired the previous year. According to Irving Harper, one of two designers on staff, he was assigned the Miller account and "designed all of the Howard Miller clocks, in addition to several other lines . . . until the late 1950's when a small number of clocks were designed by others."[495] Another account, based on an interview with George Nelson, makes Noguchi a member of the design team:

> While Nelson, *his associate Irving Harper, and Isamu Noguchi were discussing the problem, someone asked, "What is a clock, anyway?" and to illustrate the concept drew a diagram of six lines intersecting each other at midpoint. And so the Miller clock is a diagram of time's measurement. Harper, responsible for the clocks' final development, kept it as close to its abstract beginning as possible.*[496]

Although frequently discussed in terms of postwar industrial design, the series has a whimsical quality that can be linked to American sculpture of the period. Indeed, Harper recalls that the wall clocks, unlike other product design objects, were seen as lending themselves to treatment as works of sculptural art. Both the *Ball* and *Asterisk* clocks are reminiscent of Alexander Calder's sculpture of the 1930s and 1940s (fig. 385),

not only in terms of their formal vocabulary, but also because of the interesting contrasts in materials (metal and painted wood), color, and movement. The same spokes with spherical terminals on the *Ball* clock, the most popular in the series, are seen in a textile Calder designed in 1949 for Laverne Originals (fig. 362). Calder's work was well known in the world of designers; in fact, the featured article for the December 1949 issue of *Interiors* included Calder's work in sculpture and the decorative arts.[497] Likewise, the *Spider Web* clock recalls the string compositions of Naum Gabo (fig. 222) and Barbara Hepworth.

The clocks were considered radically modern because they have no traditional clock face with numbers. The wall was the ground, and the clock could be part of the architecture rather than an unrelated hanging object. Numbers were deemed unnecessary as the time was clear from the positions of the hands in relation to the spokes.

Since the clock movements were made by other manufacturers, the Miller firm provided only the finishing and assembly for the case. Therefore, the new line was conceived with a minimum of tooling in order to compete with manufacturers who could produce both works and cases. The Nelson designs helped compensate for the higher price Miller had to charge.[498]

DAH

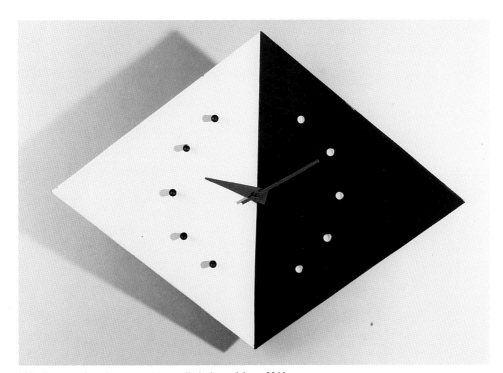

390. *George Nelson Associates.* Kite *wall clock: model no. 2201*

Paavo Tynell

Chandelier
Designed 1948
Brass; 42 × 33 × 33 inches (106.8 × 83.8 ×
  83.8 cm)
Produced by Taito Oy (Helsinki), 1948–c. 1953
Unmarked
D88.152.1

This brass chandelier by Paavo Tynell emphasizes aesthetics over function. It echoes Calder's
mobiles in structure with its pendants cut from
brass wire cascading freely from wire arcs that are
attached to the central post. In form these pendants suggest the patterns seen in Matisse's paintings and textiles (fig. 355). The only part of this
chandelier with a functional element is the bowl
of perforated sheet brass at the bottom of the
central post: it contains the concealed bulbs.

The brass snowflakes cast shadows on the
ceiling and walls, joining the lighting fixture to
its architectural environment. The effect of art-
ful shadows is further intensified by the use of
light-transmitting mesh and pierced brass sheets,
Tynell's signatures at the time. The spectral
images created by the indirect light and cast
shadows also recall the sparkle and romance of
candle- and gaslight. Tynell was fully cognizant
of antique lighting fixtures, having fabricated reproductions of eighteenth- and nineteenth-
century chandeliers for historical buildings. His
intention here was to create a modern-style version of an eighteenth-century crystal chandelier
(fig. 392). Another important inspiration came
from *himmeli*, the traditional straw mobiles
made at Christmas in Finland (fig. 393). Hung by
a single thread of cotton or wool, the delicate
pendants move with the slightest breeze, just as
Tynell's brass pendants gyrate with the air
currents.

The model became a permanent part of
Tynell's lighting-fixture collection for the United
States, distributed by Finland House, a Finnish-
owned company in New York City. Tynell designed several variations in assorted sizes. Since
each chandelier was handmade by metal artisans,
they were very expensive to fabricate, and thus
production was limited to only a few examples of
each.[499]

TLW

391. *Paavo Tynell. Chandelier*

(right) 392. *Chandelier. Swedish, late 18th
century. Röhsska Museum of Arts and Crafts,
Göteborg, Sweden*

(far right) 393. *Finnish himmeli*

Jean Lurçat

Tapestry: *Le Lion*

Designed 1962

Wool, tapestry weave; 42¾ × 67¾ inches
   (108.6 × 172.1 cm)

Produced by Tabard Frères & Soeurs
   (Aubusson, France), 1962

On reverse, printed in black on white cloth
   label sewn to lower left corner, three marks
   in a vertical column at left: [within a
   bordered square, two abstract devices
   surrounded by a motto in a circle]
   "Antimite définitif" MITIN/[device of T
   overlaid with A and ABD]/[device of shield
   with stylized tree (?)]

On same label, printed and handwritten to
   right of three marks: "LE LION" *Carton
   1029*/H: 1 m 09 L: 1 m 73 = _____ /
   CARTON DE JEAN LURÇAT/ÉDITÉ PAR TABARD
   FRÈRES & SOEURS = AUBUSSON = N° 3496

On same label, within a bordered rectangle
   below: SIGNATURE AUTOGRAPHE DE
   L'ARTISTE/*Jean lurcat*

D88.115.1

Le Lion embodies the basic principles of tapestry as defined by Jean Lurçat: the design was created specifically to be executed as a tapestry, and the imagery is powerful and monumental, an effect enhanced by the limited range of colors and the coarse gauge of the weaving. In association with François Tabard, head of Tabard Frères & Soeurs, Lurçat developed an approach to designing tapestry that sought to reconcile both the artist with

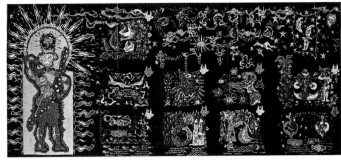

394. *Jean Lurçat.* La Poësie *from* Le Chant du monde. 1957–62

the weaver as well as contemporary art with weaving principles of the Middle Ages. Instead of providing a small easel painting for the weaving atelier to replicate, Lurçat, thinking of tapestry as mural decoration, prepared a full-size cartoon. This was not elaborately colored but, rather, marked with numbers corresponding to the limited shades of the wools the weaver was to use. The design was conceived in terms of the texture of the fiber and palette of the dyes rather than in terms of a painter's pigments, and the cartoon allowed the weaver freedom to interpret color passages in the tradition of the loom rather than the painted canvas.

Lurçat's style, which developed from Cubism to a more personal idiom, allowed him to evoke his universe in a pictorial vocabulary infused with poetic allusions. Certain stylized yet animated images—particularly the sun, the rooster, and the lion—appear frequently in his tapestries. Presented in two dimensions and strong colors, they are meant to evoke layers of meaning and

express Lurçat's Surrealist vision. He explored the iconography of the four elements and the zodiac, and the lion depicted here conjures up references to both as well as to the seasons.

The composition of *Le Lion* is based on the scene representing Leo in the much larger tapestry *La Poësie* (fig. 394) from *Le Chant du Monde*, Lurçat's magnum opus, woven between 1957 and 1962 and composed of nine panels that illustrate the horrors of war and celebrate the idea of world peace. *Le Lion* is also related to other weavings, both earlier and later in date, that have a leonine theme and imagery. Here, with his mane and body rendered like the rays of the sun and surrounded by flaming stars and ambiguous spectral faces, the lion is endowed with energy and mystery. In his work, Lurçat reconciled the old with the new, forging a dynamic harmony among poetic subject matter, modern style, and sound weaving techniques to set a standard emulated by scores of successive tapestry designers.

AZ

395. *Lurçat.* Le Lion *tapestry*

396, 397. Stig Lindberg. Vase

Stig Lindberg

Vase
Designed c. 1951
Terra-cotta with painted faience decoration;
15¾ × 13¼ × 13¼ inches
(40.4 × 34 × 34 cm)
Produced by AB Gustavsberg (Gustavsberg,
Sweden), c. 1951[500]
Painted in blue on underside:
GUSTAVSBERG/SWEDEN Stig L./[device of a
stylized hand imposed over G]
D83.102.1

Lindberg, who had a reputation as a gamin, was known for his exuberant, whimsical decoration. On one side of this vase, the artist painted a lyrical scene of a garlanded flutist who pipes as he emerges from a tree—a pastoral motif that he used a few years earlier for a textile called *Pleasure Garden* (fig. 398).[501] Joining in this serenade is a bird at the top of the tree. On the other side of the vase and admirably suited to its spherical volume is the wistful face of a young woman. She, too, is linked to the bucolic narrative, not only by the leaves in her hair and the flower on her cheek but also by the way she cups her hand to her ear, as though listening to the music offered on the opposite side.[502]

It was Wilhelm Kåge, Lindberg's teacher and predecessor at Gustavsberg, who reinvigorated the tradition of painted faience at Gustavsberg in the late 1930s (fig. 399). As might be expected, there is a discernible difference between the two generations of artists, even in the treatment of comparable subjects. Kåge's heavier, brooding faces and stylized coiffures are reminiscent of Fernand Léger and Georges Braque and are typical of prewar taste, while Lindberg's figures are closer to the lighthearted fantasy of Marc Chagall

that was favored in the postwar world. As was noted at the time:

> . . . [Lindberg] began as a free artist, and as such he evidences a definite literary flavour related to surrealism and above all its predecessor Marc Chagall and his airy, smiling spirit. For Lindberg, anything is possible; arms become branches, hair turns into foliage, hands grow forth instead of horns. . . .[503]

Vases such as this one were created on an individual basis within the Gustavsberg Studio, an atelier set aside for its artists. More commercially oriented faience was produced in the Studio as well (fig. 400); made under Lindberg's direction, these ceramics had forms and decoration designed by the master, but they were conceived for serial production and were painted by assistants. Inevitably, the motifs, still whimsical, were converted into patterns that could be readily duplicated. In this manner Gustavsberg maintained an admirable dualism, balancing handicraft and artistry against modern technology and commercial viability.

ME

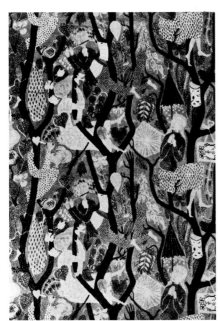

398. *Lindberg.* Pleasure Garden *textile.* 1947

399. *Wilhelm Kåge. Vase and plaque.* 1942

400. *Lindberg. Decorated faience. c.* 1953. *Gustavsberg Museum, Sweden*

Stig Lindberg

Textile: *Pottery*

Designed c. 1947

Linen, plain weave, silk-screen printed;
31½ × 101½ inches (80 × 258 cm)

Printed by Ljungbergs Textiltryck (Floda,
Sweden), for Nordiska Kompaniet
(Stockholm), c. 1947–62

Printed almost six complete times in maroon
in left selvage: "POTTERY" KOMP. AV STIG
LINDBERG. [device of G overlaid with a
stylized hand] NK.'S TEXTILKAMMARE.

D86.143.1, gift of Geoffrey N. Bradfield*

It is appropriate that Stig Lindberg conceived of a
textile entitled *Pottery*, for it was as a ceramist
that he achieved world recognition. The design
was based on actual Lindberg ceramics of varied
shapes, dimensions, and patterns (fig. 400), all
placed next to one another as if on a shelf.[504]
Every so often an isolated hand holding a small
branch appears, while yet another hand, supporting a face, is worked into each repeat. The linear,
two-dimensional treatment and complex patterning produce a visually rich density. The pattern repeat consists of three horizontal rows
balanced by the vertical elongation of undulant
pottery motifs. The humor, the straightforward,
almost naive presentation, and the dense arrangement of the pattern are in keeping with
Scandinavian textile design of the period.

The style of *Pottery* is typical of Lindberg's
oeuvre in the late 1940s. In character, it also
relates closely to a wrapping paper that Lindberg
designed for the Gustavsberg ceramics factory.[505]

About his many interests, Lindberg once stated:

*I myself have, besides my great interest in the
ceramic materials, been working with many
other branches. This is not very common in
Sweden when as a rule there is a specialization and a ceramic artist concentrates not
only on his material but moreover on a particular group of materials in the ceramic
branch, for instance often only earthenware
or faience. My motives have then been the
most subjective. I have been in need of a glass
service and so I have drawn one satisfying
myself. I have needed textile goods and could
not find on the market what I was looking
for—consequently I have designed a new one.
This is really the way of my ancestors to
gratify their wants for things of use.*[506]

CCMT

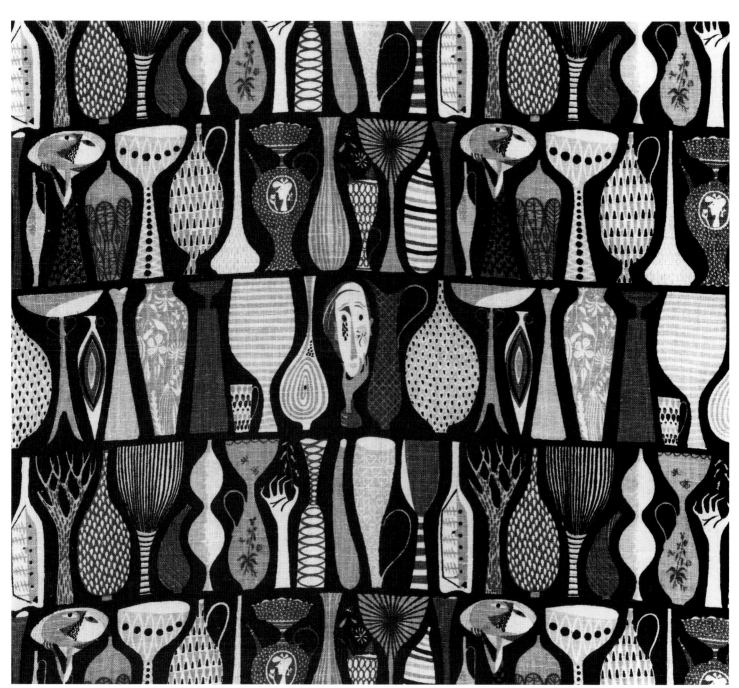

401. Stig Lindberg. Pottery *textile*

Mirko Basaldella

Coffee table
Designed and executed 1955
Pigmented marble dust, wire-reinforced
    plaster, bronze, and painted steel;
    16¼ × 63 × 48 inches (41.3 × 160 × 122 cm)
Painted at lower right of table top: *Mirko* 55
D88.148.1, gift of Adele and Willard Gidwitz*

Mirko, a much celebrated Italian sculptor of the postwar period, had experimented with various mediums in the 1950s. This led him to try his hand at a few examples of painted furniture, which were then shown at Rome's Galleria Scheider in 1954. After making initial pastel sketches, the artist prepared a full-scale cartoon and laid it over a sheet of glass. He transferred the basic lines of his design to the glass, removed the cartoon, and began painting directly on the glass, using a medium of pigment mixed with marble dust. The tabletop's thickness was built up in plaster over a wire armature. The work was then inverted and the glass removed, revealing a painted, marblelike surface. The table's design is of geometric configurations in a palette of rose, tan, and blue, softly outlined in black, thus resembling the paintings of Georges Rouault, such as his 1946 *Flowers and Fruit* (fig. 402), which is executed in the same palette.

The structure of the table is as indicative of the date of creation as is the style of the painting. The composition is framed by a narrow band of bronze, and this, in turn, has been set into a steel frame of minimalist design, painted black.[507] Thus, it served two goals: it was extremely decorative, which is typical of much Italian decorative art of the period, and at the same time, it responded to the international canon of postwar Good Design. It was used by the donors in the living room of their home in a suburb of Chicago, surrounded by and in harmony with significant paintings and sculpture of the twentieth century. FTH

402. Georges Rouault. Flowers and Fruit.
1946. Private collection, Paris

403, 404. Mirko Basaldella. Coffee table

Stanislav Libensky

Vase

Designed and executed 1954

Enameled glass; 13 × 4 × 4 inches (33 × 10 × 10 cm)

Etched on underside: s LIBENSKY 1954 274/62

D83.118.1

The area of Zelezny Brod in Czechoslovakia had a strong tradition in enameled glass, but it tended to be conservative. Libensky, in the 1940s, was the first to take the art in a new direction. His approach to enameling stemmed not from the native tradition but from his training in painting, at the glassmaking schools in Nový Bor and Zelezny Brod, where he made this vase. Because the decoration of his vases from the 1940s and early 1950s was primarily figurative, requiring a great deal of attention to detail, the designer began to use a variety of colors, thinly applied with the subtlety of a watercolorist to accentuate his pictorial images. Libensky scarcely used the traditional colors black and gold, preferring a broader spectrum.[508] In this vase, for example, he combined irregular geometric shapes in red, blue, purple, and other colors, producing a kaleidoscope of color.

Libensky's work in the 1950s consisted primarily of a Cubist-derived figurative art using color in a naturalistic way (fig. 405), though in this vase, the figurative elements—apparently a scene of Venice with an Ionic capital and the prow of a gondola—are minimized, and the artist has emphasized color and abstract forms.

405. *Stanislav Libensky.* Birds with Cherries

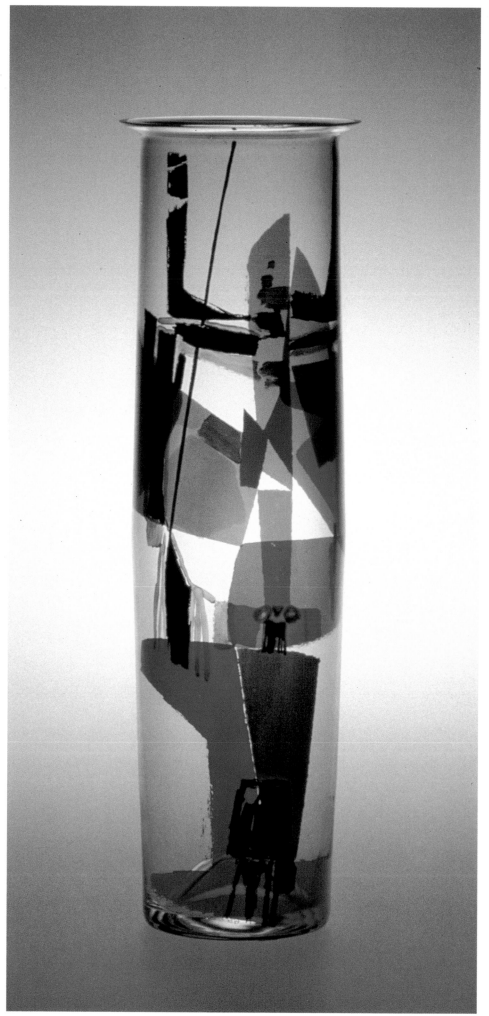

406. *Libensky. Vase*

Vaguely reminiscent of Czechoslovakian Cubism of the 1910s and 1920s,[509] Libensky's sense of color and his compromise between figurative and abstract elements are directly aligned with postwar European modern painting.

Although quite traditional in form, function, and style, this glass vase of 1954 is concerned with ideas that Libensky developed in his later career. His use of colored forms here foreshadows the way he employed large fragments of glass arranged in a decorative manner in his stairway lattice for the International Hotel in Brno of 1961–62 (fig. 407). His use of color to modulate light would be further explored in his large-scale sculpture of the 1970s and 1980s.

JTT

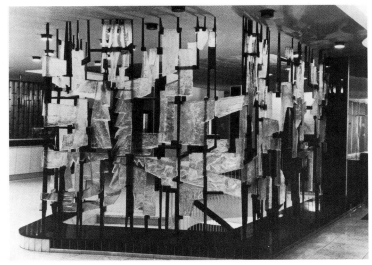

407. Libensky. Stairway lattice for the International Hotel, Brno, Czechoslovakia. 1961–62

Fernand Léger

Textile
Designed c. 1950
Cotton, plain weave, silk-screen printed;
    34½ × 54⅝ inches (87.6 × 138.6 cm)
Produced by Bossi, S.p.A. (Cameri, Italy),
    1950–51[510]
Printed within the design: *F Leger*
D88.166.1, gift of Barbara Jakobson*

During the late 1940s and 1950s Fernand Léger had designed ceramics, mosaics, murals, windows, tapestries, and rugs—all in addition to making paintings. At the request of Enrico Gregotti of the Bossi textile firm, Léger also created two textile designs. In July 1950 the artist authorized Gregotti to produce one of them.[511] Léger worked in two basic styles simultaneously, using a figurative style for his paintings and a more abstract style for most of his decorative work. Léger said at the time that abstraction was "weakish" for easel painting, but could be used to advantage for murals, mosaics, and ceramics.[512]

With its stylized but recognizable butterflies and its crescents, this fabric has elements of both styles. The butterflies are like those in *Big Julie* of

408. Fernand Léger. Textile

1945 (fig. 409), one of Léger's paintings with a bicycling theme. They have similarly shaped wings and the same odd antennae at both ends. On the other hand, the crescents resemble those in the abstract mural Léger later designed for the first-class dining room of the SS *Lucania* (fig. 410). The architect, Giancarlo De Carlo, requested a mural to open the wall visually and make the room seem larger,[513] so the arcs are set against a light ground, as in this textile. Although in both the mural and the fabric the crescents are abstract and turn in all directions, they derive from Léger's earlier depictions of flowers and leaves. One of the petals in the flower held by Julie in the painting is curved in a similar way, as are the leaves of a tree in another picture with a bicycling theme, *Homage to Louis David* (1948–49).[514] This suggests that the crescents in the textile are also abstract renderings of flowers and foliage, a suitable setting for butterflies, while the mural could then be read as an abstract garden scene.

Léger used bright colors here—red, blue, yellow, and orange—and outlined the forms with black lines. This was his normal way of working at the time, which can be seen both in his figurative paintings like *Big Julie* and in his abstract decorative work such as the *Lucania* mural. Léger has said that in painting *Big Julie* he was inspired by the "bad taste [and] glaring colors" he had seen while in the United States during World War II.[515]

It is instructive to compare Léger's design for this textile with three fabrics that Fuller Fabrics produced a few years later, in 1955. The latter were created by Fuller staff designers after already existing works by Léger, such as a drawing of the circus and a stained-glass window showing the instruments of Christ's passion.[516] Léger's own textile design is far more abstract and appropriate to flat pattern than the derivative Fuller textiles (especially the one after the stained-glass window), but they all share bright colors and black outlines. And all of these commissions remind us how esteemed Léger still was at the end of his career.

CWL

(top) 409. *Léger.* La Grande Julie. *1945. Collection, The Museum of Modern Art, New York. Acquired through the Lillie P. Bliss Bequest*

(above) 410. *Léger. Mural for the SS* Lucania. *c. 1951–52*

Salvador Dalí

Brooch: *The Persistence of Memory*
Designed c. 1949–50
Gold, platinum, and diamonds; 2⅜ × 2⅜ × ¾ inches (6 × 6 × 1.9 cm)
Produced by Alemany & Ertman, Inc. (New York), c. 1950–60
Engraved on front: *Dalí*
Engraved on reverse on a raised rectangular field: COP. ALEMANY/ERTMAN INC.
D89.109.1

Eric Ertman, a Finnish shipping magnate, in about 1948 commissioned Salvador Dalí to design a collection of jewelry.[517] The pieces were manufactured by Alemany & Ertman, a New York firm of diamond merchants. A group of twenty-one examples of this jewelry was acquired by the Catherwood Foundation in 1953, which it exhibited in Italy, Spain, and France with the express purpose of dispelling the common belief in Europe that all American products were mass-

411. *Salvador Dalí.* The Persistence of Memory.
*1931. Collection, The Museum of Modern Art,
New York*

412. *Dalí.* The Persistence of Memory *brooch*

413. *Dalí.* The Persistence of Memory *brooch
(original version). c. 1948–49*

produced and of proving that, in fact, there was a great deal of American handwork to be appreciated.

Like other jewelry designs of Salvador Dalí, *The Persistence of Memory* brooch reflects an image taken from one of his paintings, and it must be considered within that context. The motif of a melted watch hanging limply from a tree branch appears in one of his most evocative works, *The Persistence of Memory* (fig. 411), in which it symbolizes a dreamlike world where time has been abolished. As the artist himself later explained:

Awareness of the colligation of time and space entered my consciousness in childhood. Yet my invention of the "melted watch"— first in oil and later in 1950, in gold and precious stones—evoked divided opinion; approval and understanding; skepticism and disbelief. . . . Today [1959], in American schools, my "melted watch" is presented as a prophetic expression of the fluidity of time . . . the indivisibility of time and space. The speed of modern travel—space travel— confirms this conviction. Time is fluid; not rigid.[518]

Oddly enough, Dalí's jewels, although functional, originally were intended not for wear but for exhibition. In addition to the already cited program of the Catherwood Foundation, a number of Dalí jewels from the original collection were exhibited at the Milan X Triennale in 1954.

Their success led Alemany & Company at an unconfirmed date to create six or seven examples of each model, some with variations from Dalí's design, which were sold to the public. The brooch in the Stewart Collection is one of these later versions. While following Dalí's basic scheme, it has prong-set diamonds sprinkled around the tree trunk, whereas the original brooch (fig. 413) incorporates pavé diamonds on the watch face. Otherwise, the two are almost identical.   TLW

414. Salvador Dalí. Tiles

Salvador Dalí

Tiles
Designed c. 1954
Glazed earthenware; 7⅞ × 7⅞ in. (20 × 20 cm)
Produced by MPG (Onda, Spain), 1954
Painted in black on front of all six tiles: *Dalí*
Stamped on back of one tile in black ink: 1954
  Maurice Duchin/all rights reserved
Molded on back of one tile:
MPG-ONDA-ESPANA/MADE IN SPAIN
Both marks on back of four tiles
D87.110.1–6

415. Dalí. Photomontage for Click, *September 1942*

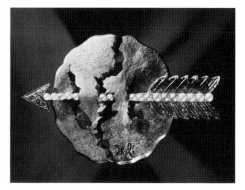

416. Dalí. The Bleeding World *brooch. c. 1948–49*

417. Dalí. Dance of the Flower Maidens *plate.*
1942. *Private collection, New York*

Not one to let either a lucrative commission or an idea go to waste, Salvador Dalí regularly reused themes from his paintings for his decorative projects, often employing the same motif for a variety of different situations. This set of tiles shows his way of reworking earlier material.

The red lips on one tile recall the famous lip-shaped *Mae West* sofa designed by Dalí and executed by Jean-Michel Frank in 1936. Dalí used this motif again in *Ruby Lips* (1949), a brooch that puns on common poetic similes by using real rubies for the lips and pearls for the teeth. The eyes at the ends of the loops on this tile are another motif beloved by Dalí. He had used it in a cover design for the magazine *Click* in 1942 (fig. 415), where flies crawl on one eye while twelve eyelike breasts float in the background. Another example is his *Eye of Time* jewel (1949), which has a watch serving as the iris and pupil.[519]

The converging arrows and cracked surface on a second tile are another conceit that Dalí had used earlier. A similar arrow pierces a cracked egg in his drawing *The Broken Egg* (1943). In a brooch called *The Bleeding World* (fig. 416), a jeweled arrow holds the broken and bleeding globe together; according to the artist, the arrow symbolizes both the love of Christ and the hope for peace in a world torn by war and chaos.[520]

The flying birds of another tile appear in a number of designs. Dalí grouped several birds in flight to create a woman's face in a design for a plate produced by Castleton China (fig. 417), and he repeated this motif in several works—among them a mural for Helena Rubenstein's dining room (1942–43), a cover for *Vogue* (April 1, 1944), and yet again in *Le Roi Soleil*, a Schiaparelli perfume bottle (1949).[521] Unlike those examples, the birds in this tile are more abstract, and they form a nondirectional pattern, giving them a resemblance to Matisse's cutout *Polynesia, the Sky* (1946).

Another tile shows a solar face with leafy branches and birds. The face in the sun resembles a sculpted sunburst head with tangled locks in Dalí's living room (fig. 418), while the branches that extend from the sun recall those growing from Gala's head in his painting *Automatic Beginning of a Portrait of Gala* (1932), as well as those spreading out from a face made partly of acorns in his design for a *Tree of Life* necklace (1949).[522]

The starfish in one of the tiles may be the first to appear in Dalí's work; he had previously used marine life as motifs, but he generally preferred lobsters as a subject.[523] While the starfish looks natural, it has only four arms instead of five,

presumably to fit neatly into a square. The trompe-l'oeil effect caused by the sharp forms and the cast shadows resembles that found in Dalí's Surrealist works of the 1930s, such as *The Persistence of Memory* (fig. 411), and remained a prominent element in his later works, such as his *Afternoon Stones* textile for Schiffer Prints (fig. 421).

The last tile is the least representative of Dalí's work. It was inspired by Picasso's Synthetic Cubism, which Dalí had imitated as a young artist, as in his painting *Harlequin and Small Bottle of Rum* of 1925 (fig. 419). Although Dalí satirized Picasso's works in several later paintings, in this tile he returned to his earlier emulation of his compatriot.[524]

In designing this set of six tiles, Dalí used several disparate motifs and different styles, which he then tied together by the repeated use of the same colors—blue, yellow, brick red, and white. This juxtaposition of unrelated and unexpected subjects forms the basis of much of his work, creating a sense of Surrealist disequilibrium.

CWL

418. Photomontage of Dalí in his living room, in Click, *September 1942*

419. Dalí. Harlequin and Small Bottle of Rum. *1925. Private collection, Paris*

(below) 420. *Salvador Dalí. Drawing for cigarette case (detail).* 1949

(right) 421. *Schiffer Prints advertisement for textiles by Dalí,* 1949

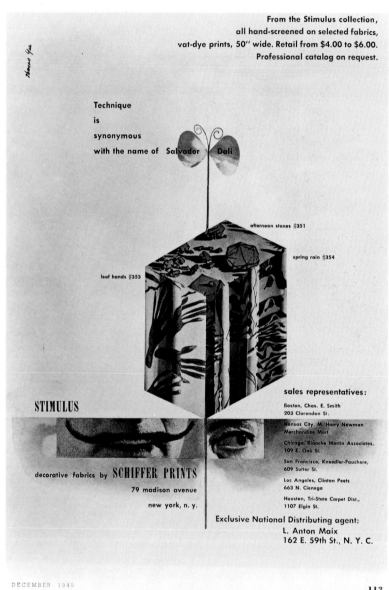

Salvador Dalí

Textile: model no. 353, *Leaf Hands*
Designed c. 1949
Cotton, plain weave, silk-screen printed;
　25½ × 27½ inches (64.8 × 69.8 cm)
Produced by Schiffer Prints, Division of Mil-
　Art Company, Inc. (New York), 1949
Unmarked[525]
D86.170.1a, gift of Jeffrey Stone, by
　exchange*

Leaf Hands is one of the textiles in Schiffer Prints's well-received Stimulus Collection, intended "to bring for the first time to the decorative textile field the fresh, forward-thinking viewpoints of top flight personalities in the related arts."[526] Although other American companies had adapted paintings for their needs,[527] the Stimulus Collection is remarkable in that the manufacturer gave carte blanche to six prestigious artists and designers, none of whom were profes-

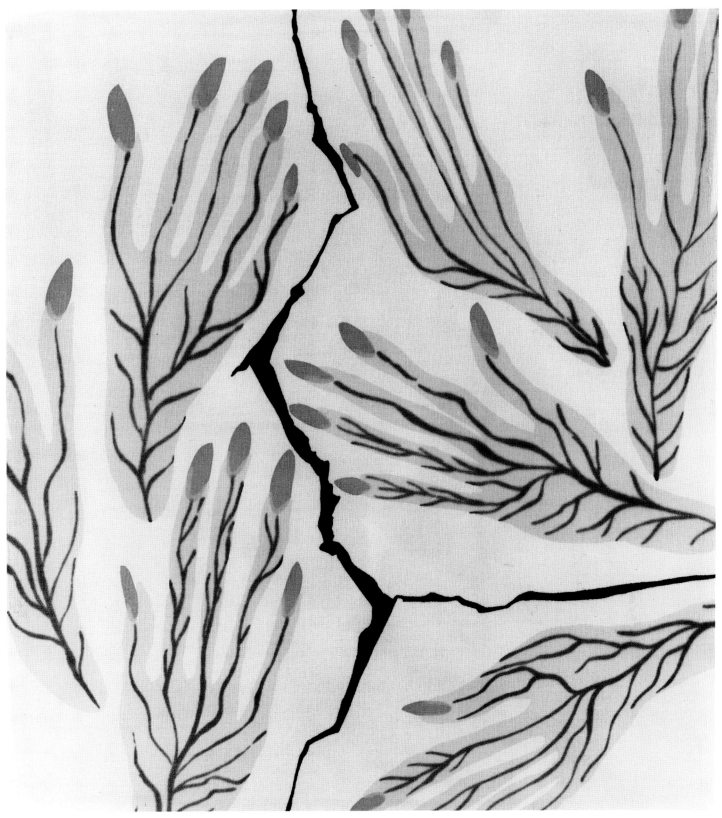

422. Dalí. Leaf Hands *textile: model no. 353*

sional textile designers, to choose their subjects and colors. Working independently, the artists executed each pattern in three color ways.

Dalí's five or more designs are exceptional for the line. While most of the other contributors, including Ray Eames, George Nelson, and Bernard Rudofsky, used small-scale patterns in cool, subdued colors (figs. 58, 71, 72), Dalí conceived large-scale designs in bright and bold pastels.[528] The humor (and sometimes terror) of the unex-

pected, as well as the macabre imagination that characterize many of Dalí's Surrealist paintings, maintain their edge in this printed textile. The uneasy wit imparted by the metamorphosis of long, elegant fingers with brilliantly painted nails into the veined segments of a leaf is an idea Dalí also explored in his jewelry at the very same time (fig. 420). He described this imagery as "transmutational" and a "vegetal vision."[529] His offbeat quality additionally influenced the adver-

tisements for the line and emphasized the unorthodox nature of his contributions to the Stimulus Collection (fig. 421).

Initially the fabrics were available only to architects and interior decorators. Later in 1949, the collection's debut year, eighteen patterns were offered on the retail market. Although designed and advertised for drapery and upholstery, some of these textiles, including Dalí's, were also used for women's sportswear and dresses.[530]   AZ

(above and opposite) 423, 424. *Piero Fornasetti. Screen*

Piero Fornasetti

Screen
Designed c. 1952
Hand-colored lithographs on wood panels,
  brass-plated steel, steel, and rubber;
  79 × 315 × 1⅛ inches (212 × 800 × 3 cm)
Produced by Piero Fornasetti (Milan),
  intermittently from c. 1952 to the present
  (this example c. 1952)
Handwritten in ink on partially torn paper
  label on lateral edge of terminal leaf:
  [P]ARAVENTO 2 × 2/[DU]OMO SOMMERSO/
  [D]ETRO:/[obliterated letters]GIA DOMESTICA
D89.178.1

It may be an anomaly to describe Piero Fornasetti as a designer. Although he created literally thousands of objects—screens, cabinets, tables, lamps, umbrella stands, ashtrays, plates, trays, fabrics—it was their decoration, not their form, that occupied his attention and that was the source of their diversity. In fact, many of the most interesting objects decorated by Fornasetti were designed by others, especially his furniture of the 1940s and early 1950s, much of which was by Gio Ponti.

Like many of Fornasetti's screens, this one has two sides, with no apparent connection with each other. Subject matter, iconography, color, even drawing styles seem strangely unrelated, in a manner calculated to draw the viewer into active consideration of the object. One side depicts Milan with its great cathedral at the center, submerged under blue water; the other is a typical Fornasettiesque trompe l'oeil of an interior complete with bookshelves, drapery, and open door leading into another space. The relationship between the two sides is ultimately a classic Surrealist one, intentionally provocative and unanswerable. They are two illustrations, two stories existing in two different spaces; they can have nothing to do with one another.

In the interior scene, as in Fornasetti's many trompe-l'oeil objects, the confusion between the real and the unreal is a key subject. It is based on the Renaissance use of trompe l'oeil in intarsia furniture and wall paneling, while the confusing disjuncture comes out of the Italian Mannerist tradition, where the bizarre and imaginary exist as separate from the rationality of everyday life.

Although Fornasetti always kept his production techniques secret in an attempt to thwart imitators, the method for making the screen can be described.[531] An experienced printer, Fornasetti created lithographs of his design, one for each panel, which were printed onto transfer sheets and then applied to each section. Once the ink dried, color was painted on, and the panels were later coated with varnish (explaining the yellowed surface of this and other early examples of his furniture).

Because Fornasetti's work stood outside of the Modernist design tradition, it has rarely received the attention it deserves. His objects were never conceived as pure art or, in the language of today, "art furniture." He considered them vital components of the domestic interior, necessary for the pleasure and enjoyment of daily life. As a fantasy-laden object intended for everyday use, this screen typifies his carefully conceived decorations, created with an inventive blending of a Surrealist sensibility and an eye attuned to the traditions of Italian painting and decorative art.

CW

Piero Fornasetti

Plate
Designed c. 1950–55
Porcelain, transfer printed; 10¼ × 10¼ inches
  (26 × 26 cm)
Produced by Piero Fornasetti (Milan),
  intermittently from c. 1952 to the present
Printed in black on underside: [device of an
  eye within a rectangle]/TEMA E/VARIAZONI/
  74 [device of a hand holding a paintbrush]/
  FORNASETTI • MILANO/MADE IN ITALY
D88.155.1

Plate
Designed c. 1950–55
Porcelain, transfer printed; 10¼ × 10¼ inches
  (26 × 26 cm)
Produced by Piero Fornasetti (Milan),
  intermittently from c. 1952 to the present
Printed in black on underside: [device of an
  eye within a rectangle]/TEMA E/VARIAZONI/
  218 [device of a hand holding a paintbrush]/
  FORNASETTI • MILANO/MADE IN ITALY
Printed in green: [device of a rampant lion in
  an oval]/1814/HUTSCHENREUTHER/GERMANY
D88.156.1

Plate
Designed c. 1950–55
Porcelain, transfer printed; 10¼ × 10¼ inches
  (26 × 26 cm)
Produced by Piero Fornasetti (Milan),
  intermittently from c. 1952 to the present
  (this example c. 1952–55)
Printed in black on underside: [device of an
  eye within a rectangle]/TEMA E/VARIAZONI/
  492/[painted] 63/[device of a hand holding a
  paintbrush]/FORNASETTI • MILANO/MADE IN
  ITALY
D89.180.1, gift of Fornasetti S.r.l.

425–28. Piero Fornasetti. Plates

Plate
Designed c. 1950–55
Porcelain, transfer printed; 10¼ × 10¼ inches
   (26 × 26 cm)
Produced by Piero Fornasetti (Milan),
   intermittently from c. 1952 to the present
   (this example c. 1952–55)
Printed in black on underside: [device of an
   eye within a rectangle]/TEMA E/VARIAZONI/
   [painted] 72/[stamped] 382/ [device of a
   hand holding a paintbrush]/FORNASETTI •
   MILANO/MADE IN ITALY
D89.184.1, gift of Fornasetti S.r.l.

In 1951 at the Milan IX Triennale, Fornasetti introduced porcelain plates with transfer-printed designs.[532] As in most of his work, his role was restricted to that of decorator. He did not create the porcelain forms; rather, he relied on relatively simple commercial blanks, which served as canvases for his fertile imagination. His dinnerware proved successful, and he quickly expanded the thematic range of his imagery: besides the expectable fruits and vegetables appropriate to dining, there were suns, shells, classical motifs, and astrological emblems—all apparently borrowed from old prints (a natural source for Fornasetti, who was primarily a graphic artist). The most intriguing images are the most outspokenly Surrealist. One of his most popular series was based on the theme of a dreamy, vacuous female face, which he then spun into endless variations, either by fragmenting the motif or by juxtaposing it against incongruous objects, such as the clock face and fruits here.[533] In some instances the face is mischievously repeated over breasts and buttocks in a highly erotic game of surprise (fig. 429).

Fornasetti's contemporaries often described his work in relation to the great traditions of Italian art. Certainly much of his work in theme and style recalls that of Piranesi and other eighteenth-century view painters. Some of the steep vistas recall the paintings of Giorgio De Chirico and Carlo Carrà. And it is true that he designed plates with faces composed of fruits and vegetables in the Mannerist tradition of Giuseppe Arcimboldo. Actually, though, much of Fornasetti's work is closer to non-Italian traditions. The four plates here suggest strong analogies with the Surrealist collages of Max Ernst (fig. 430). Both artists enjoyed the jarring juxtaposition of innocent, virginal faces with menacing elements to create a highly charged atmosphere redolent of sexual tension. They also delighted in emphasizing elements of old printing techniques—the graphic artist's stocks-in-trade of engraved hachures and dots—to intensify the disparity of the mediums and instill a sense of nostalgia.

While plates generally form part of large sets of dinnerware, Fornasetti rarely provided such sets.

Although one of his early ideas was a setting in which the plates, table linens, drinking glasses, and flatware were printed with a design of newspaper collages,[534] he did not normally think in terms of functional ensembles. He occasionally created full tea sets, but, for the greater part, he provided only plates or cups. Moreover, though his plates might come in sets of twelve, the normal sense of a set was negated by the infinite number of pictorial variations that allowed one set to merge easily into the next.

The ultimate irony is that Fornasetti may not have used his own plates. A visitor to his country home on Lake Como reported that it offered abundant testimony to the artist's love of decoration: each tile of the bathroom, for instance, bore a different sun motif, and even the toilet paper was emblazoned with suns. Yet, much to the visitor's amazement, he found that Fornasetti's table was set with unadorned white china from Limoges.[535]   ME

429. Fornasetti. Plate. Liliane and David M. Stewart Collection. D88.157.1

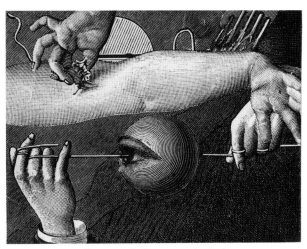

430. Max Ernst. Illustration for Répétitions by Paul Éluard. 1922

Sam Kramer

Cuff bracelet
Designed and executed c. 1960–61
Silver and glass taxidermy eye; 2⅝ × 2¾ × 2⅛
    inches (6.7 × 7 × 5.4 cm)
Unmarked
D87.214.1

Working in New York City's Greenwich Village, "Mushroom Sam" Kramer developed a Surrealist imagery in the medium of "Fantastic Jewelry for People Who Are Slightly Mad."[536] Creatures conjured up by unconscious fantasy were Kramer's favorite motif. He deployed humanoid forms (or parts thereof) like those seen in the paintings of Joan Miró and Paul Klee, displacing the body parts in the manner of Pablo Picasso.

Kramer spurned the Bauhaus-inspired handmade jewelry of the period which, to him, reflected only the rigid geometry of Cubism, "the design [being] in the construction and the construction [being] reduced to a minimum . . . simple forms somewhat mechanical in implication."[537] He considered such jewelry no more imaginative than machine-made examples. Rejecting Constructivism's order and predictability and believing that linear structuring was antimetal because it worked against the fluid possibilities inherent in the medium, he experimented with new technical approaches to jewelry based on random explosions of form, as in the use of molten metal blobs to create the hands and feet of his *Roc* pendant (fig. 432).

Kramer's pendants, brooches, and bracelets, like collages, incorporated a variety of materials, usually semiprecious stones and minerals, to add mystery and magic. He used these to counteract the sterility of the Modernism he saw in coldly calculated geometric jewelry. His use of glass eyes was certainly consistent with his sense of humor

431. Sam Kramer. Cuff bracelet

and his desire to shock, and it linked his jewelry to the tenets of Surrealism. The red taxidermy glass eye in this cuff bracelet moves as the wearer moves, following the viewer's movement and eerily watching spectators. Kramer was also innovative in his use of stones, employing atypical cuts or incorporating stones with odd inclusions.

In the cuff bracelet Kramer also expresses the Surrealists' philosophy of the object "which sets out to be sumptuous while using the simplest means and to exalt the nuances of analogical thought."[538] By incorporating a false but seemingly real eye and by placing it in a fantastic context, Kramer perplexes the viewer, just as Meret Oppenheim did with her *Cup, Saucer and Spoon in Fur* of 1936. This bracelet is in the spirit of a *dreamt object*, something which, according to André Breton, "corresponds to the need, inherent in the dream, to magnify and dramatize." It is a humble, familiar object, that by some caprice of desire is given a sumptuous appearance.[539]

The work was commissioned in 1960 for Geraldine Pogocar by the Helen Drutt Gallery of Philadelphia. Typical of Kramer's later work, it displays a simpler configuration than his earlier pieces. Those produced in the late 1950s, up to his death in 1964, are more economical, both in the number of elements used and in their complexity when assembled. In comparison to this cuff bracelet, an earlier work, *Lovers* of 1949 (fig. 433), shows greater complexity. Its three metal planes are riveted together to create a brooch a full inch deep. But even in the simplicity of his late works, Kramer's is far from a rational and mechanical aesthetic. His jewelry remained only for those who were "slightly mad."

TLW

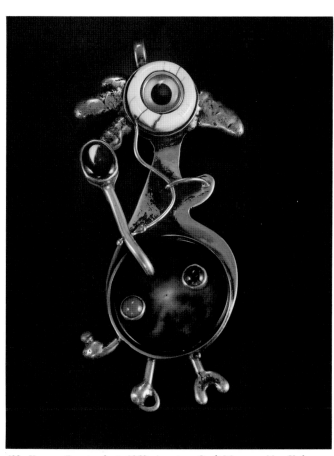

432. *Kramer. Roc pendant. 1958. American Craft Museum, New York*

433. *Kramer. Lovers brooch. 1949. Collection Karen Sebiri*

Peter Todd Mitchell

Design for wallpaper
Designed c. 1950–60
Gouache and pencil on paper; 21⅞ × 13⅞
    inches (55.6 × 35.3 cm)
Unmarked
D89.111.1, gift of Priscilla Cunningham

Design for wallpaper
Designed c. 1950–60
Gouache and pencil on paper; 19⅝ × 15¾
    inches (49.8 × 40 cm)
Unmarked
D89.111.2, gift of Priscilla Cunningham

Design for wallpaper
Designed c. 1950–60
Gouache and pencil on paper; 17¹³⁄₁₆ × 11¹³⁄₁₆
    inches (45.3 × 30 cm)
Unmarked
D89.111.3, gift of Priscilla Cunningham

(above and opposite) 435–37. *Peter Todd Mitchell. Designs for wallpaper*

434. Eugene Berman. Setting for *Italian Symphony. 1940. Collection, The Museum of Modern Art, New York. Gift of Paul Magriel*

One of the more curious aspects of mid-twentieth-century design was the polarization of taste between forward-looking interiors related to the spare aesthetic of contemporary architecture and the emergence of a decorating style created to temper the sparseness and anonymity of the modern interior. Depending on the side chosen, the opposing camps were considered either "serious and important" or "decorative and whimsical."

Reaction to the austerity of Modernism had been made fashionable in the early 1930s by the circle of avant-garde artists surrounding the poet and painter Jean Cocteau. Despite the harsh economic realities of the Depression, Cocteau, acting as cultural impresario, had been able to assist this new generation of talent by promoting their employment as designers for the theater, fashion,

and interiors. This circle included the Neoromantic painters Christian Bérard, Pavel Tchelitchev, and the brothers Eugene and Leonid Berman (fig. 434); the decorator Jean-Michel Frank and the English dandies Cecil Beaton, Rex Whistler, and Oliver Messel were also associated. They investigated Baroque trompe-l'oeil illusionism and architectural fantasy; employed a lighthearted Rococo, Regency, and Victorian revivalism to evoke the charm of the past; and placed architectural fragments and curious objects in irrational juxtaposition. Such Surrealist fantasies became the chic taste of the Parisian elite and had a significant influence on fashionable decorators at the *grand luxe* level, such as Syrie Maugham and Elsie de Wolfe. The publicity this generated brought them to the attention of the public, and

they became accepted into a broad segment of popular taste.[540]

Elements of fantasy and whimsical historicism continued to characterize much of interior decorating of the late 1940s and 1950s. The American Peter Todd Mitchell, who proclaimed himself the heir of Bérard, settled in Paris in 1947 to work in the Neoromantic style that he favored throughout his life. The free-lance designing of textiles and wallpaper enabled him to pursue his career as a painter, and he frequently adapted architectural elements and details from his paintings to his design work.

These three designs for wallpaper employ a vocabulary of highly evocative and playful images that served Mitchell well in the decorators' market. Their poetic and even playful motifs are

redolent with Surrealist decay and fragmentation. The crumbling walls, shards of black-figured Attic pottery, and swagged drapery lyrically evoke a vaguely antique period and the disintegration of ancient monuments and civilizations.

Mitchell's Neoromantic wallpapers and furnishing fabrics were produced by many major American manufacturers, including Katzenbach and Warren, Van Luit, and Scalamandre.

KC

Paul Colin

Poster: *Pour un Meilleur Réseau de Distribution*
Designed c. 1950
Offset lithograph; 30¾ × 22⅝ inches (77 × 57.5 cm)
Printed by Editions Dubelier (Paris), c. 1950
Signed in the stone, lower right: Paul Colin
Printed in rectangle in lower left: EDITIONS
  DUBELIER
D85.116.1

Aside from his better-known music hall and the-ater posters, Colin designed a body of public-service-appeal posters. This example, one of a series done for Electricité de France, advertised prime lending rates and compound interest to stimulate public demand for bonds for a better electrical network.[541]

Colin's typically clever and humorous image capitalizes on electricity's power of illumination. Colin used a black background against which he illuminated a figure with a light bulb head on an electric-cord body. The electric wire also forms the figure's hands, one holding a card repeating the poster's message, the other supporting a clus-ter of sparks suggesting live electricity. Colin's image suggests analogies with Jean Cocteau's contemporary whimsical linear figures (fig. 439) as well as the new wire-frame furniture that ap-peared in the 1950s (figs. 304, 309, 313, 316). True to the French graphic tradition of rich, ornamen-tal lettering, Colin mixed typefaces, using both serif and sans serif styles and different sizes, weights, and colors to create a highly decorative, playful effect.

FTH

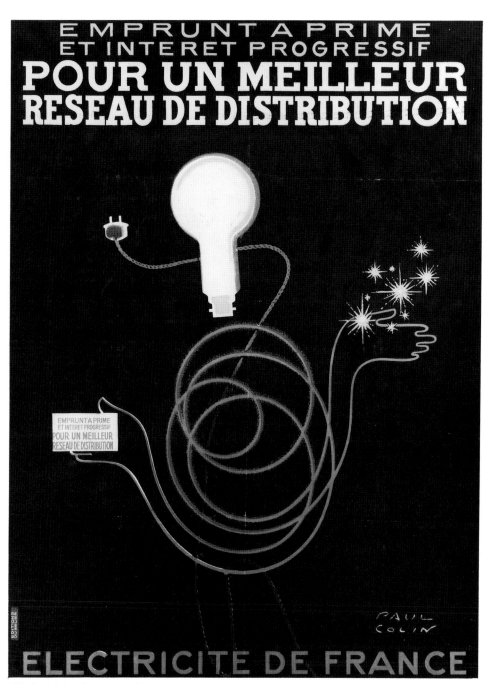

438. *Paul Colin*. Pour un Meilleur Réseau de Distribution

439. *Jean Cocteau. Cover for* Harper's Bazaar, *November 1946*

Giò Pomodoro

Necklace
Designed and executed 1963
Pink and white gold, rubies, emeralds, and chalcedony concretion (agate); extended: 16½ inches (41.9 cm); pendant: 3 × 2⅛ × ¾ inches (7.6 × 5.4 × 1.9 cm)
Etched on reverse of shaft: *Gio Pomodoro*
D88.124.1

The necklace by sculptor Giò Pomodoro illus-trates his preoccupation with the visual signs and symbols of human sexuality, his use of assem-blage, and the early influence of the Surrealists.

Surrealism finds a place in my roots and in a certain way I don't deny that I should like to achieve a sculpture that had a "magic-

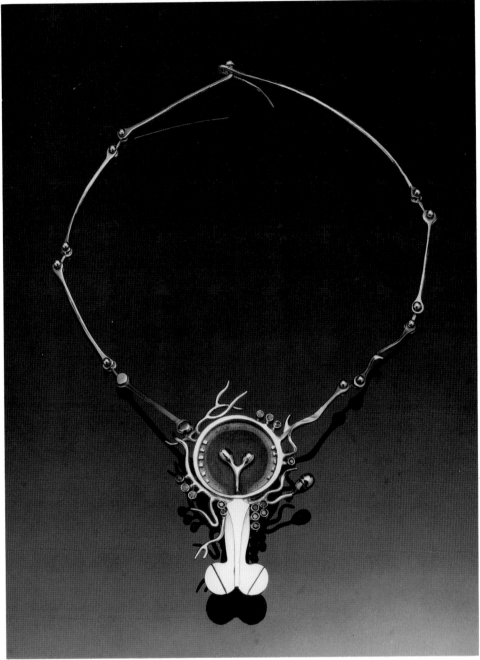

440. Giò Pomodoro. Necklace

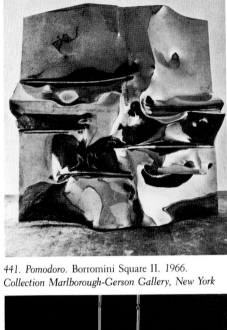

441. Pomodoro. Borromini Square II. 1966.
Collection Marlborough-Gerson Gallery, New York

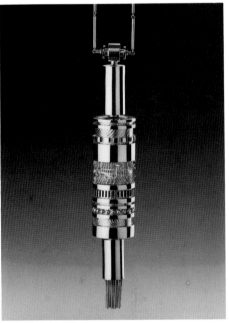

442. Arnaldo Pomodoro. Pendant. 1966–68.
Schmuckmuseum, Pforzheim, Germany

value". . . not as an end, rather as a determining psychic means to be understood more in the meaning of the Latin "monstrum" — an amazing thing to see. . . .[542]

Pomodoro's early silver reliefs and jewelry of 1950 are related to ancient Mediterranean, primitive, Byzantine, and Renaissance models. Practically unwearable bas-reliefs or assemblages done in a variety of materials, they are rich with fantasy figures reflective of Paul Klee, Wassily Kandinsky, Joan Miró, and Max Ernst, as well as the spontaneity of Jackson Pollock and, especially, Franz Kline.[543] In the late 1950s, after he had mastered the techniques of metalwork, Pomodoro began to use precious metals and mounted gemstones, the mediums from which he created this symbolically ambiguous necklace.

In his bronze reliefs and then in his later stone sculpture, Pomodoro has habitually explored a sensuous continuum of forms, the phenomenon of growth and multiplication (fig. 441). This can be seen, as well, in the implied vegetation of the branches (or arms) around the metamorphic tree/human of this necklace. The ambiguous configuration might also suggest reproduction and the implication of intercourse: the female internal sexual organs, the round womb seen in cross section and the looping symmetrical Fallopian tubes leading to it, or, alternatively, the female organs awaiting the approaching male penis. As Pomodoro himself wrote:

> *. . . I would . . . like to achieve the utmost "feminine" quality in my work, which contains this magic substance, an interior fertility, proliferous like Hindu sculpture or the sculpture of Matisse, and this has nothing to do with eroticism.*[544]

It is instructive to compare Pomodoro's necklace with Salvador Dalí's *The Persistence of Memory* brooch (fig. 412). Dalí's tree and flaccid watch are easily recognizable through their realism. Pomodoro's art, by contrast, works on several interpretive levels, using abstract symbols.[545]

Arnaldo Pomodoro, Giò's brother, who was originally trained as an architect, also made jewelry and often exhibited with Giò. However, Arnaldo's imagery (fig. 442) is predominately masculine and mechanistic; hard phallic aggression supersedes gentle, open acceptance. Arnaldo's pendant reflects penetrative precision, while Giò's indicates warm receptivity and reproductive growth.

TLW

Expressionist Modern

The shift of political and economic power to the United States after World War II was accompanied by the country's ascendancy in the visual arts. If Paris had been the undisputed art capital prior to the war, New York now could claim that title. The emergence of such luminaries as the painters Jackson Pollock, Franz Kline, and Willem de Kooning, as well as the sculptors Theodore Roszak and Ibram Lassaw, gave credence to the notion of a New York school. Their work was generally referred to as Abstract Expressionism or, alternatively, Gestural art or Action Painting, names that convey something of the nature of the art.

Whether it was paint that was brushed, flung, and dripped onto the canvas or metal that was welded, the accidental and random spatterings and rivulets vividly attested to the impetuous process of creation, which was the new focus of attention. The means became as important or more important than the end product. The philosophical underpinnings of this art were provided by Zen and Existentialism. Jean-Paul Sartre's thesis that "being is doing" displaced the traditional Cartesian coupling of existence with rational thought.

Much of this new art, with its emphasis on the subconscious and automatism, was based on prior European art, and it is not coincidence that Abstract Expressionism arose in New York, where a number of important Dada and Surrealist artists, including André Breton, Max Ernst, André Masson, Matta, and the city's habitual resident, Marcel Duchamp, had found refuge during the war. (And, indeed, there were movements corresponding to Abstract Expressionism that arose in postwar Europe, especially L'Art Informel and Tachisme, involving artists like Hans Hartung and Georges Mathieu.)

The decorative arts were quickly affected by all these currents, and they reacted by developing a new expressive language. This can be seen in the ceramic vases of Peter Voulkos (fig. 458); the irregular forms of Harvey Littleton's glass vessels (fig. 465); the bundled fibers of Sheila Hicks (figs. 471–73); and the spiky branches of Wendell Castle's furniture (figs. 453, 454). The change was not merely in the external appearance but extended to the mode of creation and the ultimate function of the object.

Previously, control had been the norm; industrial perfection had emphasized flawless surfaces and seamless junctures just as handicrafts had emphasized traditional expertise. Now control gave way to experimentation and energy: simple, fluid forms became irregular and even tortured; smooth surfaces became rumpled and even battered. Despite the difference in mediums, Irena Brynner's jewelry, Littleton's glass, and Magdalena Abakanowicz's tapestry share the same extravagances of surface treatment, which reflect an emphasis on process rather than on the perfected object itself. This tendency was accompanied by changes in scale, as objects became increasingly large, even superscale. The Voulkos pot in the Stewart Collection measures a substantial one and a half feet across, and many of his vases reach a height of eight feet. Hicks's *Banisteriopsis* weighs over 230 pounds.

There was a concurrent decrease in the functional aspects of the object. Although it is possible to sit on the Castle stool and to use the Voulkos jar as a lidded container, their functional qualities are vestigial. It is not without significance that Castle entered his stool in an exhibition of sculpture. The border that separated the decorative and the fine arts became increasingly hard to define.

An instructive parallel can be made between the ceramics of Peter Voulkos and the work of the New York Abstract Expressionist painters. The irregularly shaped slabs of clay that are affixed to the walls of his vases as if they were collages have drips and spatterings of glaze like many New York paintings. The photographs of Voulkos at work (fig. 443), grimacing as he pounds the surface, assembling pieces into structures larger than himself, recall the photographs of Pollock at work (fig. 444), walking in and around his painting, his face contorted as he coaxes and flings paint onto a canvas larger than himself.[546] Voulkos's art, like Pollock's, is concerned with the act of creation, and its improvisational nature is manifest both in the way that the artist worked and in the stresses visible on the finished object, the fissures and cracks that developed during firing and the peeled glazes.

(above) 443. *Peter Voulkos at work, c. 1956*

(left) 444. *Hans Namuth. Jackson Pollock at work. 1950*

In this comparison, the parallels extend beyond work habits and visual appearance, for there was a specific historical relationship between Voulkos and the Abstract Expressionist artists. The turning point in the ceramist's career was a summer spent at the experimental Black Mountain College and a subsequent trip to New York City, during which time he came into contact with Robert Rauschenberg, Franz Kline, and other avant-garde painters and sculptors.

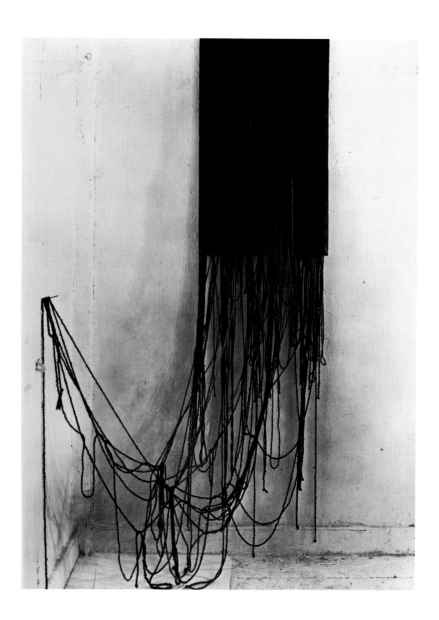

Similar correspondences emerge in comparing the work of Sheila Hicks and Eva Hesse, both painters who turned to working with fiber.[547] Although the two artists emerged from the same educational program at Yale University, they came to related artistic expressions quite independently of each other. Hicks's *Banisteriopsis* (figs. 471–73) and Hesse's fiber constructions (fig. 445) have much in common. Caught between the passing of Abstract Expressionism and the emergence of Pop art, Hesse became absorbed by the conflict between spontaneity and structure. In a seminal essay of the period, the sculptor Robert Morris discussed soft sculpture and the concept of "anti form."[548] He signaled the importance of hanging, random piling, and loose stacking to give passing form to limp material; chance was accepted and indeterminacy was implied, since any movement or replacement created a different configuration.[548] Very much the same experience and description apply to both Hesse's and Hicks's work. *Banisteriopsis* is composed of a variable number of separate lengths of dyed and bundled linen and wool; neither its size nor its formation are predetermined. As with Hesse's *Ennead*, composed of papier-mâché and dyed string, chance is accepted and indeterminacy implied.

Although it is generally presumed that the decorative arts follow developments in the fine arts, it is not so in this case. Hicks's work generally has precedence. More to the point is that both women belong to a larger movement in the development of modern sculpture, one that includes Claes Oldenburg's soft sculptures and Robert Morris's felt sculptures. In fact, one could well ask why Hicks and her work are still classified as decorative art. *Banisteriopsis* is not traditional weaving in terms of technique, nor does it correspond to any traditional function of fiber as textile or tapestry. Its function and most appropriate classification would seem to be sculpture.

It is noteworthy that a substantial number of the artists considered here—Voulkos, Littleton, Abakanowicz, Lenore Tawney—turned to sculpture. Ceramics, glass, and fiber merged into the world of high art, just as painting and sculpture increasingly incorporated these materials into the more standard mediums of paint, marble, and bronze. Academic distinctions of genres have become progressively less clear or meaningful.

As revolutionary as these objects may seem, they also can be linked with established aspects of postwar design, specifically those previously discussed in relation to pattern and ornament. For example, it is worth considering Voulkos's jar in relation to Salvatore Meli's ewer (fig. 350). Both are concerned with boldness of form and texture, drama of scale, and an aggressive expressionism of style. The link between the two artists' works is centered in their common indebtedness to artists like Picasso, whose late creations were very influential.[549] (Voulkos hung Picasso prints around his studio in defiant response to a colleague who had found nothing of merit in Picasso's work; some of Voulkos's early ceramics even had Picasso-like faces and bullfighting scenes.) In the same manner, the revolutionary nature of Harvey Littleton's and other American studio glass is indebted to the freedom and painterly expression introduced by the Venini firm and more flamboyant designers such as Dino Martens at the Aureliano Toso glasshouse.

Given such precedents within the decorative arts and also the persuasive examples of modern painting and sculpture, it was small wonder that this Abstract Expressionist movement became so pervasive and international in scope. Certainly it appealed to the younger generation, but it attracted many established masters as well. The jeweler Irena Brynner went from tight, geometric structures to roughly textured sheets of gold; she turned from a traditional system of assembling and soldering wire to using an acetylene torch and centrifugal casting. The ceramist Carl-Harry Stålhane left behind his sleek vessels and subtle glazes (figs. 164, 263) for heavily grogged and textured clay bodies with bold shapes (fig. 446). Timo Sarpaneva, who had produced some of the most elegant and lyrical forms of the postwar period (figs. 249–52), began designing glass with roughened, irregular surfaces (fig. 447). His shift in style supposedly was prompted by his chance discovery of charred wooden molds that workmen had discarded, but would he have discovered and used these molds had the Abstract Expressionist movement not already turned his mind in that direction?

446. Carl-Harry Stalhåne. Vågen (Wall). c. 1964

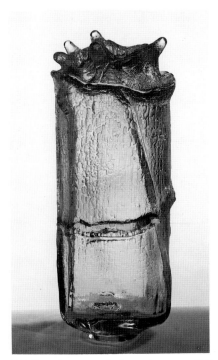

447. *Timo Sarpaneva. Purkaus (Eruption). 1964. Victoria and Albert Museum, London*

As pervasive and universal as this new mode was, though, it was essentially rooted in the world of handicraft and small studios. Its means of production and its surface effects did not easily transfer to the world of industrial design, as can be seen in Gunnar Andersen's poured polyurethane chairs (fig. 461). As was noted about one of these:

> Design is . . . probably the wrong word to use in relation to this chair, certainly insofar as design implies a predetermination of form. Chemistry and gravity were the form-givers here, Andersen their collaborator, trying to hold them in check, to stop short of confusion, to impose order on accident.[550]

Indeed, design and mass production were diametrically opposed to the spontaneity and uniqueness of experience at the core of Abstract Expressionism. Some of the surface effects could be transferred to factory-produced goods. Roughened surfaces could be molded in glass and ceramics, textiles could be given shaggier weaves and highly looped pile, cast jewelry could simulate molten rivulets. The essence of Abstract Expressionism, though, could not be duplicated either as surface or, much less, as experience. The resulting schism that arose between handicraft and industrial design had profound implications for the next decades, as the craft mediums increasingly abandoned their traditional alliance with function and object design and, instead, sought a position aligned with painting and sculpture.

ME

Ibram Lassaw

Necklace
Designed and executed 1956–57
Gilt bronze, amethysts, and emerald;
   10¼ × 11 inches (26 × 28 cm)
Unmarked
D87.219.1

Jewelry is perhaps the most intimate expression of the crafts. A painter or sculptor will often create a piece of jewelry as a gift for a family member or friend. For some it is only a brief experiment limited to, at most, a few examples. For the sculptor Ibram Lassaw, who made this necklace as a gift for his daughter Denise, it was not an isolated event; indeed, Lassaw estimates that over the course of his career he has created more than one thousand pieces of jewelry.[551]

To Lassaw, jewelry represents an integral part of his work. He views it as a way of gaining greater access to the public. Collectors unable to afford a sculpture can purchase his small pendants at a fraction of the cost, giving them the opportunity to own an original work. This is an essential by-product of artist-made jewelry.

The very nature of Lassaw's sculptural technique, working directly in metal, lends itself to jewelry-making. He heats bronze rods with the flame of an oxyacetylene torch to form molten droplets. The size of the clusters is controlled by the gauge of the rods and the size of the torch's tip, which can be compared to a painter's brushes. Although his sculptures are colored primarily by applying chemicals, some include minerals or semiprecious stones (fig. 448), just as this necklace incorporates nine amethysts and one large, opaque, light green emerald for color accents.

Lassaw was one of the first American sculptors who, rejecting the orderliness of Constructivism, embraced the spontaneous idiom of Abstract Expressionism. Utilizing the nonobjective, infinite patterning of New York Abstract Expressionist painting, he abandoned solid mass for forays into space, incorporating air into his compositions in a way that seems to express organic forms and growth. The fused droplets that compose the floral forms of the necklace suggest a molecular structure. One of Lassaw's strongest influences is Zen philosophy, which emphasizes the interrelatedness of all organic and inorganic matter, the microcosm implied in all material substance.

Lassaw's jewelry mirrors the development of his sculpture. His pendants are like miniature sketches, used to explore new ideas in calligraphic configurations and spatial solutions. Lassaw has said, "For me the desire to make jewelry arises from leisurely, even playful, experimentation with forms and the flow of molten metals; sometimes it is probably an unconscious preparation for larger works."[552] He calls his jewelry "bosom sculptures" and treats them in the same manner as his monumental works.

TLW

448. *Ibram Lassaw.* Amethyst Moment. 1957. Collection Mr. and Mrs. B. Sumner Gruzen, Easthampton, New York

449. *Lassaw. Necklace*

Irena Brynner

Rings

Designed and executed c. 1959–62

Gold; 2⅝ × 1½ × 1⅛ inches (6.7 × 3.8 × 2.9 cm); 2⅛ × 1¼ × 1⅛ inches (5.4 × 3.2 × 2.9 cm)

Impressed inside each ring: 18K [diamond-shaped device enclosing 750]   *IB* [in circle]

Impressed on plaque attached inside each ring:
I. BRYNNER

D88.151.1, 2

The idea of two or more units of rings meant to be worn either on separate fingers or together on one finger has precedents in cultures as old as Persia in the eighth century B.C. The Romans in the fourth century A.D. constructed three-ring sets (fig. 451) whose units were soldered together; their use was most probably funerary, since wearing them rendered the hand virtually immobile.

Irena Brynner's aim in her design was just the opposite; she wished it to emphasize mobility. Despite the large scale of her rings, the fingers can move freely, because each unit only goes the length of one finger joint. The wearer may select one of several combinations of rings on different fingers, thus creating a degree of variability. In a certain sense, these rings are a reaction to the designer's earlier, Constructivist-inspired geometric work, such as the brooch from 1952–53 (fig. 223). That piece relates to space architecturally and exists as a somewhat independent object from the body-base. The rings, by contrast, use the fingers as armatures and were conceived with the hand as an integral part of the sculpture.

Brynner had been stimulated by an exhibition in 1957 at the Museum of Modern Art showing photographs of Antonio Gaudí's architecture (fig. 452).[553] Gaudí believed in natural forms as a spiritual basis for an architecture that, to him, was a living organism growing out of its natural environment. The Spanish architect's organic approach transformed Brynner's thinking, and eventually she moved away from the constructed pieces of the early 1950s. The irregular, gently ruffled planes that compose each ring are suggestive of vegetal shapes. Not coincidentally, it was during this period that Brynner began photo-

450. *Irena Brynner. Rings*

graphing vegetation close up, mostly, she explained, as a reaction to all the stone and concrete that surrounded her in New York City.

These rings are excellent examples of Brynner's work in wax. One can perceive the manner in which the wax was melted and then cooled, the way it was pulled, twisted, and indented, the way the heat caused the edges to roll. All this could be captured by centrifugal casting in the lost-wax technique. (This was accomplished at the commercial facilities of Billanti Jewelry Casting in New York City.) The process allowed the jeweler much more freedom than did forging and soldering, and because it facilitated a sculptural expressiveness, many jewelers availed themselves of it in the late 1950s and 1960s.   TLW

451. *Triple ring. Roman, 4th century. Benaki Museum, Athens*

452. *Antonio Gaudí. Turrets of Casa Batlló, Barcelona. 1904–6*

Wendell Castle

Chair: *Scribe's Stool*
Designed and executed 1959–62
Walnut and ebony; 54 × 26 × 26 inches
   (137.2 × 66 × 66 cm)
Incised on underside of seat: *Castle 61–62*
D88.131.1, gift of Vivian and David M.
   Campbell

Floor lamp: *Serpentine*
Designed and executed 1965
Mahogany; 88 × 28 × 28 inches
   (223.5 × 71.1 × 71.1 cm)
Incised on underside of base: Wendell Castle,
   1965
Incised on side, near base: W.C. 65
D88.198.1, gift of Vivian and David M.
   Campbell

Wendell Castle's early furniture, such as these examples, was influenced by the work of Wharton Esherick, a leading American furniture craftsman of the 1950s, and Finn Juhl, one of the period's most prominent furniture designers (figs. 264, 269). Castle's early furniture also reflects the general revived interest in the sensuous forms of Art Nouveau. Castle achieves the fluidity of line shared by these sources of inspiration by using the lamination process, which allows wood to be bent and shaped while retaining its strength.

Scribe's Stool is one of a small series conceived as sculpture that Castle made between 1958 and 1962.[554] Basically linear and flowing with a continuous line, this chair is constructed of carved, laminated walnut sections assembled into a complex, asymmetrical shape. This elegant work relates to open-form sculpture as then practiced by Henry Moore and Alberto Giacometti, two artists whom Castle admired. Its high seat is perched on slender, attenuated legs, which, in the front, support a canted footrest. Extending from the right armrest is a writing surface, which rotates into position.

The artist brought this piece with him in a half-completed state to New York City in 1961. Seeking to distinguish himself from the many sculptors on the New York art scene, he entered this furniture-cum-sculpture in the American

Craft Museum's 1962 competition and exhibition "Young Americans."[555] *Scribe's Stool* attracted considerable attention, launching Castle nationally as an artist and leading to his invitation to become head of the woodworking department at the Rochester Institute of Technology in upstate New York.

Serpentine, an enormous, sinuous floor lamp, was inspired by Castle's bending a paper clip into a three-legged form. Constructed of both laminated and solid mahogany, *Serpentine* has a tail-like support that meanders on the floor and then shoots up into a tall, treelike shaft, terminating in a splayed, notched cone, which conceals the lamp's bulb. Intrigued with exaggerated scale, Castle created a dominant lamp form with a life of its own. The lamp is virtually nonfunctional, of a size that forces it to be treated as sculpture. Castle has always maximized the grain in his woodworking, and in *Serpentine* he further heightened the lamp's texture with a subtle pattern of chisel marks that emphasizes both its handcrafted origin and its expressive power.

FTH

453. *Wendell Castle*. Scribe's Stool *chair*

454. Castle. Serpentine *floor lamp*

Magdalena Abakanowicz

Tapestry: *Abakan biz*
Designed and executed 1965
Sisal; 73 × 71 × 12 inches (185.5 × 180.4 ×
    30.5 cm)
Handwritten in black ink on leather patch
    stitched on the reverse: MAGDALENA
    ABAKANOWICZ/"ABAKAN BIZ"/150 × 180 cm
    1965/M. *Abakanowicz*
D88.258.1, gift of Paul Leblanc

Magdalena Abakanowicz belonged to the intellectual and artistic community in Poland that in the late 1950s and early 1960s began to foment the first important break with the academic style of socialist realism imposed after World War II on the artists in the Communist countries of Eastern Europe. Abakanowicz initiated a revolutionary approach to the use of fiber as a vehicle of serious artistic expression. She used sisal and other fibers in totally new ways, both technically and formally. Employing weaving techniques associated over the centuries with crafts, she created bold sculptural statements far removed from weavers' work of the past.[556]

Abakanowicz's first important works, which she called *Abakans*, were monumental, coarsely woven forms. They include tubular or abstract circular shapes woven on the loom and sewn together into shaggy, three-dimensional forms and incorporate a variety of holes and apertures.[557] This example has a comparatively flat, rectangular shape and was intended for hanging on the wall in the tradition of tapestries. A circle defined by a shaggy weft fringe is raised above the ground of flat Gobelin weave. The hairy circle is split with a vertical slit, embellished by a separately woven flap that is sewn on as well as by an open-ended, tubular protrusion extending twelve inches from the tapestry face. Assorted rope-wrapped hanging elements are also lodged in the dense bush. As the artist explained:

My particular aim is to create possibilities for complete communion with an object whose structure is complex and soft. Through cracks and openings I try to get the viewer to pene-

455. *Magdalena Abakanowicz.* Abakan biz *tapestry*

trate into the deepest reaches of the composition. I am interested in the scale of tensions that intervene between the woven form, rich and fleshy, and the surroundings.[558]

Though notable, the reference to vaginal forms is somewhat discreet and hidden in the brown-black sisal used here. By 1966 the *Abakans* moved off the wall and into the room and assumed large-scale, often aggressively female shapes, frequently colored vibrant violets and reds. Abakanowicz had found in fiber a natural, pliable material well suited to the organic concepts of her sculptural vision. Her manifest need to obliterate accepted categories, to fabricate aggressive objects, and to present subjects tabooed

by accepted standards set her within analogous antirational tendencies developing concurrently in Western art.

From the 1960s onward, Abakanowicz's innovative woven sculptures were on frequent view in the sphere of crafts. Her move around 1973 to ready-made cloth extended her reputation into the realm of fine arts, since the distinction between handmade and ready-made materials has often been used as a criterion to distinguish craft from art.[559]

KC

Peter Voulkos

Jar
Designed and executed 1956
Glazed stoneware; 18¾ × 17½ × 17½ inches
  (47.6 × 44.5 × 44.5 cm)
Painted in slip on underside: *Voulkos 56*
D88.201.1

Peter Voulkos's work symbolizes the expressive force and enlarged scale that entered the ceramic medium in the second half of the century. This jar is a foot and a half high and almost equally wide—the result of heroic throwing. The surface was then hammered with a meat tenderizer or similar instrument, which left an aggressive field of tooth marks. Small slabs of clay were added over this aggressively textured surface to create a low relief, and then brown and black slips were brushed on with power and abandon. Voulkos's disdain for the traditional concerns of workmanship is evidenced by the large number of fissures that developed during the drying and firing of the vessel.

Only a few years earlier, Voulkos's work had been in a different vein. A lidded jar from 1953 (fig. 456) has an elegant form, neat throwing marks, and spooled finial, all of which suggest the calming influence of Scandinavian ceramics. The figurative decoration, derived from the ideograms of Picasso, was delicately drawn in a complex process of wax resist and applied slip that Voulkos invented.[560] Control and artistry were the hallmarks of Voulkos's early work. The large scale, however (the jar is seventeen inches tall), gives an indication of the work to come.

In the interval between these two stages of his career, certain major changes transpired. In the summer of 1953, Voulkos taught at the renowned Black Mountain College with ceramists Karen Karnes and David Weinrib, painters Jack Twor-

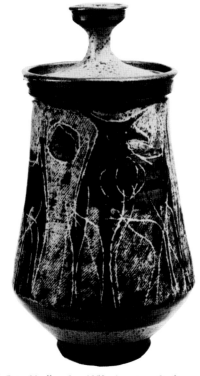

456. *Peter Voulkos. Jar. 1953. American Craft Museum, New York. Gift of Aileen Osborn Webb*

457. *Voulkos. Pot. 1956. American Craft Museum, New York. Gift of Mr. and Mrs. Adam Gostomski*

kov and Robert Rauschenberg, composer John Cage, dancer Merce Cunningham, and other members of the New York avant-garde. Through these artists, he became involved with an art that stressed the process of creation. His experience at Black Mountain was intensified by a trip to New York City, where he met Franz Kline, David Smith, and other members of the Abstract Ex-

pressionist movement. He then went through a period of gestation, in part occasioned by his move from Montana to Los Angeles. By 1955 the impact of this new art, combined with his love of jazz and his interest in Zen (both of which also stressed the importance of process and spontaneity), propelled him forward with his experiments in ceramics.

458. *Voulkos. Jar*

Seen in the light of these biographical circumstances, the lidded jar in the Stewart Collection becomes meaningful in terms of painting and sculpture. Its scale, its bursts of painted slip, its collagelike relief, its cracks and fissures—all are elements that can be compared, for example, to the paintings of Hans Hofmann and the collages of Conrad Marca-Relli.[561] In other works from the crucial years of 1954 to 1959, Voulkos extended the assemblage process by joining pot to pot, stacking them vertically and side by side, and by adding spouts and slabs to his rough-hewn constructions (fig. 457). By the end of the decade, Voulkos was making ceramic sculptures that reached eight feet in height. His work became progressively charged with tension and dynamism, and the origins of that expressive art are already registered in this lidded jar.

ME

Toshiko Takaezu

Vase
Designed and executed c. 1953
Glazed stoneware; 13¾ × 8¾ × 8⁹⁄₁₆ inches
    (35 × 22.2 × 21.7 cm)
Unmarked
D87.101.1

Vase: *Tamarind*
Designed and executed c. 1958
Glazed stoneware; 32⅞ × 9¼ × 8 inches
    (83.5 × 23.2 × 20.3 cm)
Painted on underside: [circle inset with a
    monogram of two TS set at 180° to each
    other]
D88.190.1, gift of Lenore Tawney

Like so many ceramists emerging in the late 1950s, Toshiko Takaezu liberated her medium from the restraint imposed by the potter's wheel. It began in a serendipitous way when she upended a teapot that she was making and used the spout as a long neck for a vase.[562] This initiated a series of vases with multiple spouts, like the one in the Stewart Collection. Though the vessel was still a thrown, spherical form, it was paddled out of symmetry, and the spouts were sculpted into the form. Similarly, the later *Tamarind* series has thrown forms that were paddled and stacked one upon the other, in a somewhat erratic alignment and without any progression in size, yet the separate forms have been sculpted into an organic whole. The important change in this chronological progression is the increasing three dimensionality of form and aggrandizement of scale, creating, in effect, a sculptural presence.

While the impetus for the new direction in Takaezu's art cannot be pinpointed specifically, her work was definitely responsive to the dominant trends emerging in studio pottery during this period. The long-necked forms, the stock-in-trade of most American studio potters, have their roots in European and especially Scandinavian pottery. The ash glazes and the calligraphic brushwork are suggestive of Japanese traditions—not only part of the artist's own Japanese-Hawaiian heritage but also encouraged through the work of Bernard Leach and his followers.

Most important, Takaezu's manipulations—the use of multiple spouts, the paddling and assembling of forms, and the exploitation of the accidental—all partook of American avant-garde ceramics of the 1950s. Both Takaezu and Peter Voulkos (fig. 458) shared experimental attitudes; both manipulated form, increased scale, and used bold calligraphy and glaze to enhance their sculptural forms—yet their results were quite opposite. Voulkos worked with an aggressive energy; he juxtaposed and often set in opposition the parts of his vessels. His contours are accordingly interruptive. Takaezu's work reveals a gentler vision; she sought unity, sculpting smooth transitions between the parts and establishing round-

459. Toshiko Takaezu. Vase

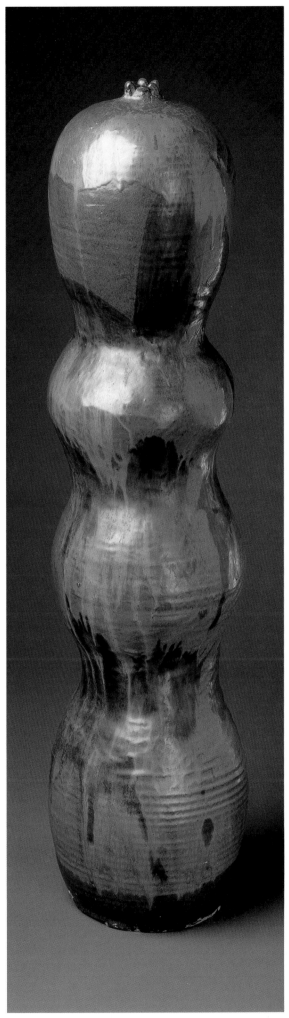

ed, continuous contours.[563] Whereas Voulkos's vessels are obviously man-made concretions, Takaezu's works have an organic quality; she described her multispouted vases as being birdlike, and the *Tamarind* vases, as the name implies, suggest comparison with the irregular fruit pod of the tamarind tree. Voulkos occasionally added jarring notes of harsh red or blue, whereas Takaezu tended toward luminously glowing colors, which can already be perceived in the warm yellows and browns of the *Tamarind* vase. As Abstract Expressionism could encompass both the violent strength of Franz Kline and the poetry of Mark Rothko, so, too, Voulkos's and Takaezu's work display comparable polarities of expression.

ME

460. Takaezu. Tamarind vase

Gunnar Andersen

Armchair
Designed and executed 1964–65
Urethane foam; 27½ × 43½ × 43½ inches
   (69.8 × 100.5 × 100.5 cm)
Unmarked
D87.182.1

Throughout the twentieth century, designers have produced furniture—often chairs—that is more polemical than practical. Gunnar An-

dersen's foam chair belongs very much to that tradition. What makes it a particularly 1960s object is its attempt to question, even turn upside down, not only notions of beauty but also the very idea of design.

The Andersen chair can be seen as part of the vogue for plastic, specifically foam, furniture that swept the design world during the 1960s. Such furniture catered to a youthful audience—or those who identified with the young—who

461. Gunnar Andersen. Armchair

wanted informal, unconventional, even outlandish furniture. Yet the Andersen chair was clearly not a cheerful, brightly colored Pop object intended as mere furnishing for a hip interior. Its method of manufacture and what might be termed its inorganic organicity made it quite unlike any other chair of the period.

The manufacturing process employed by Andersen involved creating a highly toxic blend of urethane mixed with water or Freon, which, when exposed to air, expanded from a liquid mass into a solid piece of foam; this was done at the Dansk Polyther Industri at Frederikssund. This material, rather than being poured into a mold, was either sprayed or poured from a bucket onto the floor, where it grew like an oozing, sludgelike organism out of a 1950s science-fiction film.[564] The chair was built up in stages, as liquid was poured onto layers of the solidified foam, and thus was described by the designer, not without irony, as possessing "a structure similar to the year rings of a tree."[565]

The Andersen chair questions many of the most basic assumptions of design. First, since the chair is unlikely to strike anyone as beautiful—most would find it determinedly ugly—its reason for being becomes an issue of challenge. Second, the production process confronts us with another unorthodoxy: a man-made object whose shape and details are willfully unpredictable. It thus becomes the antithesis of a designed object. That the chair is actually comfortable comes as an additional confusion—that is, if one is brave enough to sit in it.

The Andersen chair clearly had limited appeal, and the use of brown coloring rather than the natural light color of the foam only served to narrow even further its appeal. Despite the novel way it was made, the chair could have been, if so desired, adapted to large-scale manufacture. Yet few were made, and the designer surely realized that the foam would easily decay through use and age. In addition to furniture trade fairs at which it was exhibited, the chair gained notoriety outside of Denmark in no small part because one was acquired in 1966 by the Museum of Modern Art, New York.[566] Perhaps that is another peculiarity of this strange object: few were made, it was not given extensive press coverage, yet it became well known throughout the design world—albeit never imitated.

CW

*462–64. Manufacturing Andersen's armchair
at the Dansk Polyther Industri,
Frederikssund, Denmark, c. 1964–65*

465. Harvey Littleton. Vases

Harvey Littleton

Vase
Designed and executed 1964
Glass; 4⅛ × 11 × 4⁷⁄₁₆ inches (10.5 × 28 × 11.3 cm)
Engraved on underside: *Littleton 1964*
D87.180.1

Vase
Designed and executed 1964
Glass; 12³⁄₁₆ × 5¾ × 3¹⁵⁄₁₆ inches (31 × 14.7 × 10 cm)
Engraved on side, near bottom: *Littleton 1964*
D87.181.1

If credit for today's studio glass movement had to be assigned to a single person, it could be given to Harvey Littleton. Although he trained as a ceramist under Nora Braden and Maija Grotell, and although as such he achieved national prominence, his thoughts often turned to glass. Perhaps it was predestination, for he had been born in Corning, New York, the home of America's finest glass factory, where his father had worked and where Littleton had held summer jobs. In 1957, when already established as a ceramist, Littleton spent several months in Jean Sala's glass workshop in Paris and various glasshouses in Murano. He returned home with glassblowing pipes, and his initial experiments began. After Littleton and Dominick Labino held two workshops at the Toledo Museum of Art in 1962, and Littleton met with the German glassblower Erwin Eisch, all significant turning points, a summer grant in 1963 gave Littleton "the freedom for real work," and the glass revolution began in earnest.[567]

Vessels like those in the Stewart Collection were the fruits of this first significant work. Typical of that stage of development, the emphasis was on the liquidity of the material. The artist blew bubbles of glass shaped more like footballs than spheres and then enriched the forms by the addition of prunts (blobs of molten glass) and by trailings of the hot metal. Curiously, Littleton's ceramics reveal none of these manipulations (fig. 466). Their forms had been symmetrical, and only in the glazes had Littleton allowed happy accidents of chance. It might be tempting to assign his expressiveness in glass to his newness to the medium. In fact, such experimentation in the malleability of glass had precedents in the work of the Murano artisans whom Littleton had visited and, even more germane, in that of Eisch (fig. 467), whom Littleton had praised for his elevation of glass from the "circle of good form" to a "world of poetical possibilities."[568]

Moreover, Littleton saw liquidity as the very nature of glass and claimed that glass was more plastic than clay (although Voulkos and many other American ceramists were also proving the plasticity of clay at that very moment).[569] As Littleton saw it, the chief characteristic of molten glass was its pliancy: it could be pulled to points, cut into shapes, or spun flat. Glass had the additional quality of transparency, and Littleton preferred pieces with wide variations in thickness so as to intensify the play of the light passing through.

Although Littleton initially made his own lead-glass composition, he warned beginners to use a few basic formulas and to avoid complex technological problems. In fact, by the time he made the vases in the Stewart Collection, he was melting glass marbles, thus avoiding the problem of stress in the initial melt.[570] He either left the glass uncolored or, as in the instance of the tall vase, added colorants such as manganese carbonate. At this point in Littleton's career, though, form and expressive energy were the artist's chief concerns.

ME

(top) 466. *Littleton. Vase. c. 1959*

(above) 467. *Erwin Eisch. Bottle. c. 1960–62*

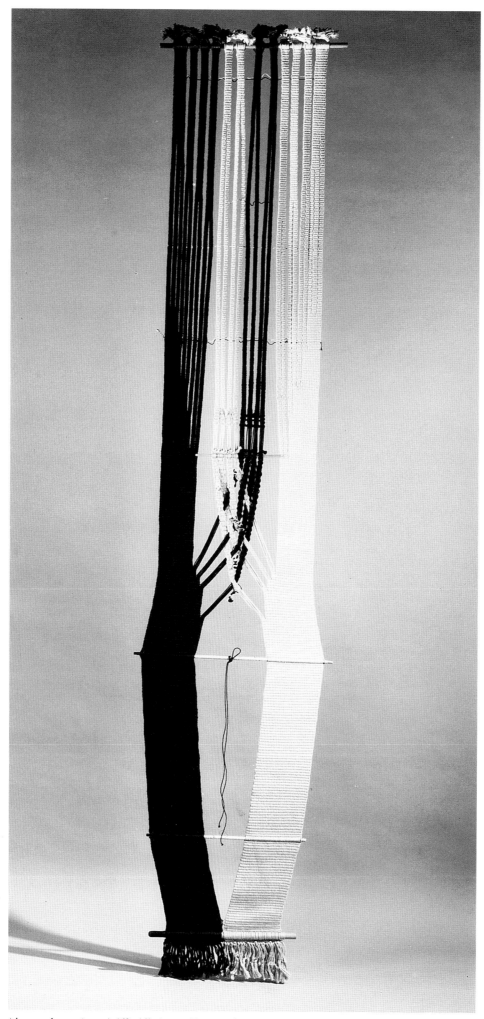

(above and opposite top) 468, 469. *Lenore Tawney.* The King II

Lenore Tawney

Hanging: *The King II*
Designed and executed 1962–65
Linen and maple; 88 × 28 inches (230.5 ×
  71.1 cm)
Unmarked
D89.101.1

The King II belongs to a series of tall, narrow, powerful weavings of the early 1960s that represents a break with Tawney's earlier works. Prior to the new series, her weavings had been rectangular in format, executed on a loom, and manifested a pictorial approach. Tawney then developed a weaving device with an open-top reed, which allowed her to shape some examples and create three-dimensional woven fiber sculpture, whose openness of form depended on her creation of solids and voids.

Tawney eliminated her customary textural mixtures in favor of custom-woven five-strand cables of plied and polished linen yarn, which she ordered in natural, black, and the primary colors. Although a fetishistic tassel dangles below the figure's torso, designating it as a "male" sculpture, Tawney used the black and white palette to symbolize the integration of male/female polarities within herself. Black and white fibers, used in equal amounts in *The King II*, intertwine and overlap midway in this giant, hieratic form. The wood dowels, which anchor the weaving at strategic points and shape it, are painted black where they connect with black linen fibers.

About this new series, whose individual works were named by Agnes Martin, Tawney said:

> . . . *all the pieces are constructed as expanding, contracting, aspiring forms—sometimes expanding at the edges while contracting in the center. The work takes its form through its own inner necessity.*[571]

No longer reliant on a loom nor intended to be hung on a wall, this freely suspended, highly expressive monumental fiber form owes little to traditional textile art of the past.

FTH

470. *Sheila Hicks. Module of* Banisteriopsis

Sheila Hicks

Banisteriopsis
Designed and executed 1964–65
Linen and wool
Unmarked
D89.102.1

Banisteriopsis breaks all boundaries with traditional textile art.[572] Since 1959, Hicks had been working with large volumes of thread wrapped into cords and spools. Having dispensed with the loom, the artist here tied hundreds of yellow fiber "ponytails," cut at one end and looped at the other and made into modules of varying size (fig. 470). There are forty-seven modules in all, one with twenty-five ponytails, two with twenty-six, five with twelve, and the rest with twenty-four. These flexible bundles are piled on the floor to create a monumental "evolving" sculpture of color, texture, and dimension, which can be perpetually rearranged by both artist and spectator (figs. 472, 473).

(above and opposite) *471–73. Hicks.* Banisteriopsis

The work's title refers to the name of a hallucinogenic plant, called the "visionary vine," used by the Jivaro Indians of Amazonia. It is the primary ingredient in an inebriating drink that produces visions in bright yellow-green, among other colors. From the 1950s on, Hicks, who believed her own work to have magical properties, was interested in creative figures such as Antonin Artaud who were known users of mind-expanding substances. The artist envisioned the effects of this plant in the "pure energy of psychedelic color" used in her linen and wool bundles.

Hicks was also inspired by the vegetable displays she saw in Parisian open-air markets—piles of leeks, celery, and cucumbers arranged so as not to topple but conveying the tension of a fragile structure that can be easily undone. In this respect, Hicks's work is aligned with one of the interesting issues of modern sculpture—tension and support.

A rich palette characterizes Hicks's work. The linen fiber used in *Banisteriopsis* was grown, spun, and dyed in northern France and sent to Hicks's Paris studio to be assembled into bundles.

Here, the bundles are composed of fibers of saffron, chartreuse, and chrome yellow, with subtle irregularities of color throughout. The artist chose such bold colors with the conscious desire to create a distinctive form of fiber sculpture.

There are three other suites, in tones of robin's-egg blue, brown, and white, that, together with *Banisteriopsis*, comprise the Evolving Tapestry series. [573] In their triumph over a dependency on the loom and their rejection of fixed form, they epitomize the freedom and self-expression of the 1960s.

FTH

Beyond Modern

Seen in a certain light and with the perspective of time, the decade and a half after World War II appears as an age weighed down by the effects of the war and the ensuing Cold War, a period that had begun in the cold grayness of a devastated Europe and the fear of Communist takeover. It was the age of the conservative businessman in the gray flannel suit, installed in the Knoll corporate office in the anonymous office building, who went home to a suburban tract house with a Formica efficiency kitchen. Good Design, with its functional, rational ethos, had fit in with that orthodoxy.

Signs of changes became visible in the late 1950s and early 1960s. There appeared a new tendency toward flamboyance rather than conservatism, of political activism rather than apathy. It was the Beatles and the Rolling Stones rather than Doris Day and Pat Boone, Carnaby Street rather than Brooks Brothers, Mary Quant and the miniskirt rather than Christian Dior and the crinoline. The order of the day was permissiveness and the Pill. It was the time of Timothy Leary and Bob Dylan, psychedelic drugs, meditation, and gurus rather than Sunday church, and Dr. Norman Vincent Peale.

By the late 1950s, Abstract Expressionism was played out, and instead of providing an art form to correspond to these new circumstances, it served as the foil against which the younger generation reacted. The energy-filled abstract paintings of Jackson Pollock and Franz Kline were supplanted by Andy Warhol's depictions of soup cans and Roy Lichtenstein's homage to the comic strip (fig. 474). In a very different way, the intensely colored, hard-edged geometric constructions of Frank Stella (fig. 475) and Kenneth Noland challenged the drips and spatters of Franz Kline's paintings and the softly blurred edges of Mark Rothko's.

474. Roy Lichtenstein. Engagement Ring. *1961. Collection Gagosian Gallery, New York*

The term *Pop* had been formulated in the early 1950s in England, in the circle of the critic Lawrence Alloway, but it was in the New York area in the 1950s and early 1960s that it took its major form.[574] With hindsight we can recognize the signposts of this shift, in, for example, Willem de Kooning's incorporation of figurative imagery and Jasper Johns's and Robert Rauschenberg's inclusion of words and actual objects. The art that emerged was not merely representational, it was also brash and sardonic. Its subjects were pointedly vulgar and banal. Although it acknowledged the twentieth-century drive to two-dimensionality, it was equally indebted to the effects of commercial printing and photography. By making a cult of the ordinary and the banal, it broke with accepted norms of high art. Pop art was supposedly populist since it drew on objective reality and common means of communication. Yet, though of the people, it was not necessarily for the people—at least not at first.

The alternate reaction—toward geometric abstraction—can be viewed as a complementary movement.[575] It, too, found an important moment of transition in Jasper Johns's targets and flags, but it rejected imagery, finding its roots in the Neoplasticism of Mondrian and his followers. Like Pop art, it was flat and hard-edged as well as frontal and planar, and its color was intense. Unlike Abstract Expressionism, with its emotionalism and personal involvement, it was often described as "cool" or, less flatteringly, "boring"—just as Pop art was sardonic and removed.

As inevitably happens, these changes in painting and sculpture were reflected in the world of architecture and design, and helped bring the era of Good Design to an end. The architect Robert Venturi was one of the chief propagandists for the appreciation of popular

475. Frank Stella. Pagosa Springs. 1960. Hirshhorn Museum and Sculpture Garden, Smithsonian Institution, Washington, D.C. Gift of Joseph H. Hirshhorn, 1972.

culture.[576] He rejected the purist and reductivist attitudes of Modernism and instead extolled the values of Las Vegas's gaudy neon signs and emblematic architecture (fig. 476). His Guild House, an apartment house for the elderly (fig. 477), is emblematic of the direction that anti-Modernist architecture took in the early 1960s.[577] It pointedly rejected the Miesian idiom of steel beam and glass curtain wall, and it also rejected the heroic monumentality of younger Modernists. As Venturi explained, his concern was to create a building that was ordinary—ordinary in its constructional system and program and also, supposedly, ordinary in appearance. It was built of old-fashioned brick, which was of a darker than usual color so as to make the building blend in with its old, dirtied-brick neighbors. The double-hung windows were, according to the architect, intentionally old-fashioned: "Like the subject matter of Pop Art, they are commonplace elements made uncommon through distortion in shape [and] change in scale (they are much bigger than normal double-hung windows). . . ."

Signs and symbols are an important part of Venturi's language, and the fact that Guild House has an emphatic front facade is in itself a significant indicator. Over the door is the disproportionately large name of the building, a reminder of the architect's fascination with American advertising. The entrance is emphasized through the use of white-glazed brick and a rotund column on the central axis—Venturi's ironic comment on the luxurious entrances and lobbies that many ordinary commercial buildings have to make them seem deluxe to potential clients. The final "flourish," as the architect put it, is at the summit: a symbolic, unconnected gilt television antenna, which he intended as "both an imitation of an abstract Lippold sculpture and symbol for the elderly."

476. Sign for Caesars Palace, Las Vegas, in 1968

477. Venturi and Rauch, Cope and Lippincott, Associates. Guild House, Philadelphia. 1960–63

478. Ettore Sottsass. Interior. c. 1959

Guild House is both structure and ideological symbol that has embedded within it a new visual code. As in Pop art, which Venturi repeatedly acknowledged, the "ugly and ordinary" was here elevated to cult status—not, however without irony. The overly emphatic central section, culminating in a fan window, was tellingly likened by the architect to a "giant order (or classic juke box front)." Although there are six equal stories, their uniformity is belied by the large panel of white bricks at the bottom and a supposedly decorative white frieze near the top. In a Mannerist fashion, the bottom section impinges on the second floor, and the upper border cuts through the windows on the fifth level; this establishes an artificial, tripartite division of unwieldy disproportion. The alternating central windows and balconies further challenge our visual understanding of the structure. Thus, through distortion, the purported "ordinary" was transformed into an antirational Pop emblem.

Across the Atlantic, Ettore Sottsass, Jr., was also reacting against the traditional sense of Modernism.[578] His early designs had shown an awareness of postwar Good Design; they share a rational system of disposition, a clarity of construction, and sparse forms. A trip to New York in 1955 proved to be a turning point. It caused him to move from architecture to design and brought him into contact with the second generation of

Abstract Expressionists and the emerging Pop artists. The intensity of their color and the brashness of their imagery greatly stimulated him.

Toward the end of the 1950s Sottsass began to evolve a more personal vocabulary. For example, his installation of the glassware display at the Milan XI Triennale in 1957 employed a spritely profusion of posts and an irregularly spaced, Secessionist-like grid work. The interiors that he designed (fig. 478) reveal a bewildering display of geometric patterns juxtaposed against each other. The same playful energy can be seen in his *ELEA* computer system for Olivetti, a series of freestanding machines of boldly geometric forms that use mass and space in a sculptural way. Most important, he employed a bright palette: color-keyed controls in mauve, turquoise, and yellow were set within a red and white case.

In 1961 Sottsass traveled to India and was profoundly affected by its culture, especially its ritualistic approach to life and the way in which "love and attention take the place of manipulation and use." A second journey to New York in 1962 reaffirmed his interest in

479. Marcel Breuer. Whitney Museum of American Art, New York. 1963

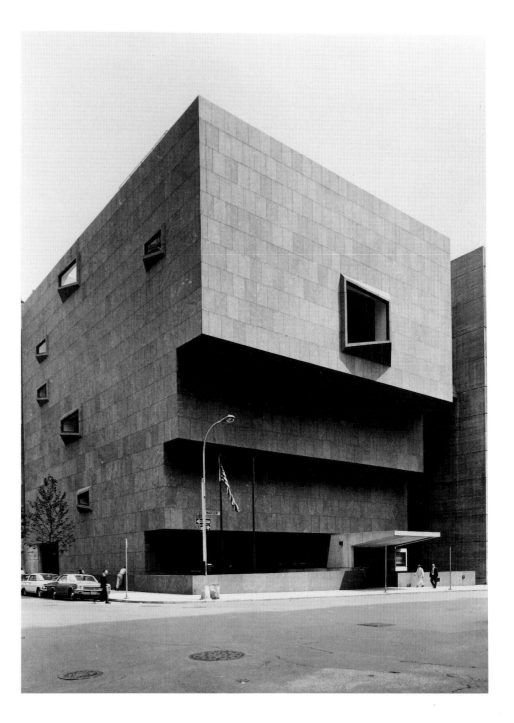

American art, especially its bright, geometric painting. The works he produced at this time—ceramic vases (fig. 503), carpets, and furniture—are marked by increased contrasts of geometric forms and bold color schemes. His geometric designs were supposed to represent his interest in street signs and emblems of urban life such as traffic lights.

Though very different, Venturi and Sottsass were working with similar ideas. Both men, in effect, rejected the rationalist tradition of Good Design. They found inspiration and pleasure in the arena of popular taste or in non-Western culture: Venturi embraced the crassest form of corporate culture itself to signal his rejection of it, while Sottsass embraced Indian culture and the offbeat world of Lawrence Ferlinghetti and Bob Dylan in order to reject what he considered the bourgeois nature of industrial design. Both were also extremely concerned with design as sign and emblem, a not-so-surprising turn in an age concerned with semiotics. Venturi may have turned to the neon language of Las Vegas and Sottsass may have looked to India, but both were swayed by comparable forces. There is even an underlying similarity in their designs. Venturi's Guild House and Sottsass's ceramic vases are built from simplistic, disjunctive, and overscaled geometric forms. Both artists stressed ornament. Both sought to engender a sense of fun, to leave the sphere of serious design and enter that of popular entertainment.

There is a certain irony in the fact that much of this new aesthetic arose in Europe, especially Italy, as a response to the Americanization of culture. It was in reaction to an idealization of American life established in films and on television—an affluent consumer culture seemingly unfettered by tradition, one that apotheosized mechanical innovations and synthetic substances.

It is appropriate that much of the most innovative furniture was made in plastic—a medium that apotheosized mechanical innovations and synthetic substances, a medium that was antibourgeois and antielitist, and by its relatively low price was associated with the popular market. Often such designs—for example, Joe Colombo's stacking chairs (fig. 487) and Verner Panton's single-piece chairs (fig. 489)—were developed despite the limitations of the material, demonstrating once again that the essential driving force was artistic desire rather than technological necessity.

Even when traditional materials were used, as in the Castiglioni brothers' metal and marble *Arco* lamp (fig. 483), Maija Isola's fabrics for Marimekko (fig. 519), and Gunnar Cyrén's *Pop* goblets for Orrefors (fig. 521), the objects have a sense of overblown scale and brashness that marked a new era of design. Whereas the previous generation had tried to create fluent melding of forms and sleek silhouettes, the aim was now reversed. Mario Bellini's lamp of folded sheet steel (fig. 509) and Greta Jalk's chair of bent plywood (fig. 515) have boldly turned angles. Like Sottsass's ceramic vases (fig. 503) and bookcase (fig. 506), these objects derive from an aesthetic of broken silhouette and opposed geometric forms. The same could be said of Marcel Breuer's Whitney Museum of American Art (fig. 479) and Philip Johnson's Pennzoil Building. These two architects, central protagonists in the cause of early Modernism and the International Style, had also progressed—or at least changed—to this newer style.

Design had gone beyond Modern and was on the verge of what would soon be called Post-Modern. There is an irony in these twists and turns of terminology, but they are the same twists and turns that design itself had taken in the ceaseless struggle to define what Modern is and was.

ME

George Nelson Associates

Sofa: *Marshmallow*[579]
Designed 1954–55[580]
Painted steel, latex foam, and vinyl upholstery;
  34¼ × 52⅜ × 33¾ inches (87 × 133 ×
  85.9 cm)
Produced by Herman Miller Furniture Co.
  (Zeeland, Michigan), c. 1955–c. 1965
Unmarked
D81.138.1, gift of George Nelson

This prefabricated sofa developed by Irving Harper in the Nelson office is based on an unusual concept in assembly: attaching a series of eighteen separate circular upholstered cushion units to an exposed frame. This system was very different from the traditional upholstered sofa, which, in addition to a frame, requires springs, foam rubber for padding, fabric covering, and webbing. In the Nelson design, each cushion and its support make up a separate unit. The padded units could be molded, stamped out in an efficient production process, and clipped to the frame. Although chairs were manufactured this way, the idea that one could sit comfortably on independent units rather than on a solid surface was a novel one for larger upholstered pieces.[581]

During the course of design, several changes were made. An early drawing (fig. 481) shows four-pronged supports for each "marshmallow," but they were later replaced by single-rod supports. The frame, initially envisioned with square beams, was constructed with tubes, because such a frame was sturdier and easier to fabricate. The exemplar in the Stewart Collection, originally owned by George Nelson, was the final version prior to production. Painted white rather than the black enamel finish used on those that were mass-produced, it was placed in the living room of the designer's Long Island country house.[582]

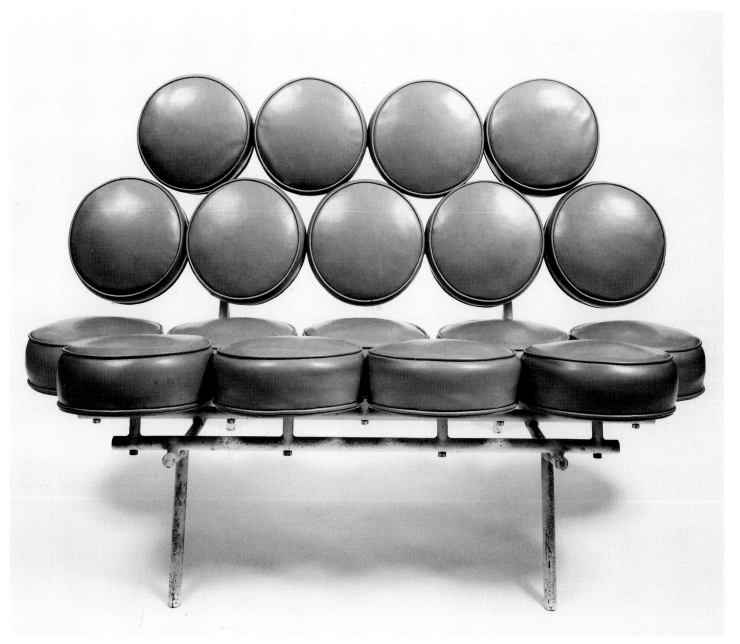

480. George Nelson Associates. Marshmallow sofa

According to Irving Harper, the production process proved costly because it required a great deal of handwork—the very concept of its design made it impossible to mass-produce efficiently. Furthermore, because it was a maverick design in its day and did not relate to conventional modern designs, no one took it seriously, and it remained in production for only a brief period.[583]

Harper does not recall any specific inspiration, but repeated circular shapes are seen in other designs from the Nelson office, such as the *Pavement* textile designed for Schiffer Prints. This design anticipates the strong geometry that emerged in the 1960s, a type of geometry that was to become an important part of the aesthetic of another creative designer who worked in the Nelson office—Ettore Sottsass.

This sofa was available with numerous Herman Miller fabrics. Although the upholstery was generally monochromatic, several examples with original upholstery have a polychromatic scheme, with very bright-colored vinyl cushions.

DAH

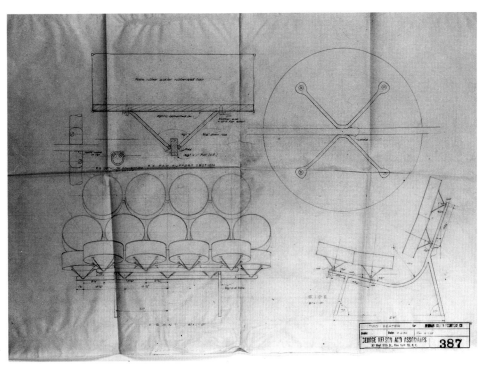

481. *George Nelson Associates. Drawing for* Marshmallow *sofa. 1954–55. Liliane and David M. Stewart Collection. Gift of Irving Harper*

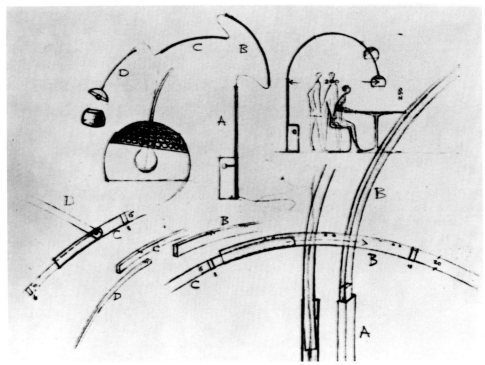

482. *Achille and Pier Giacomo Castiglioni. Drawing of the* Arco *floor lamp, with its component parts*

Achille and Pier Giacomo Castiglioni

Floor lamp: *Arco*
Designed 1962
Marble, stainless steel, and aluminum;
96 × 74 × 12 inches (243.8 × 188 × 30.6 cm)
Produced by Flos (Nave, Italy), 1962 to the present (this example 1962–66)[584]
Unmarked
D82.104.1, gift of Barbara Jakobson*

The early 1960s marked the moment in which Italian design, only effectively constituted as a distinct concept in the years since 1945, began to make its full impact on the rest of the world. This coincided with the period of the "economic miracle" during which Italy also began to establish itself as a modern, consumer society on a par with other industrialized nations.

The Castiglioni brothers' *Arco* lamp is, in many ways, the perfect symbol of this moment. Its high stylishness reflects an approach to the modern interior that stresses affluence and conspicuous consumption, characteristics of what was perceived as the Italian style of the 1960s. The use of marble—a traditional luxury material—combined with aggressively modern metals, steel and aluminum, helped provide a bridge between Italy's design heritage and its incursion into the world of modernity, between an aristocratic past and a democratic present.

From 1945 on, the Castiglionis had worked together on a number of designs for interior objects that helped redefine the meaning of the modern interior. Often borrowing "ready-made" items, such as the tractor seat and the car headlight, and always pushing the boundaries of technological possibilities further forward, they evolved a particular aesthetic, referred to by critics as techno-functionalism, which respected the rules of the prewar Modernists but extended them into the new, postwar context.

Arco stands as a testimony to the brothers' joint concerns in these years. Visually, it seems a cumbersome object, but as it could light a table surface without having to be suspended from the ceiling or fixed to a nearby power point, it introduced a new freedom into the dining or sitting area of the interior. Structurally, it exhibits a great economy of means, consisting as it does of a marble base with two holes (one for the vertical shaft and one as a holding point for moving the lamp); a telescopic steel arc, which contains the

electric wire; and an adjustable aluminum hood, perforated at the top to cool the bulb. Perhaps most important of all, symbolically, it conveys an enormous dignity, strength, and elegance, single-handedly transforming an everyday interior into a remarkable one. It is perhaps the most lasting of all the designs by the Castiglioni brothers, and it remains one of the most powerful icons from the era in which it was born.

PS

483. *Castiglioni.* Arco *floor lamp*

Friedrich Becker

Necklace
Designed 1962 (this example executed 1989)
White gold and rubies; extended: 20³⁄₁₆ inches
    (51.3 cm); pendant: 2½ × 2³⁄₁₆ inches
    (6.5 × 5.7 cm)
Impressed: [B in a circle] 750
D89.121.1

Friedrich Becker is best known today for his kinetic jewelry, and the genesis of that work can be found in his "variable jewels," of which this necklace is a prime example.[585] By manipulating the jointed sections, the wearer can control the configuration. Such jewelry releases the individual elements from the rigidity of fixed composition; three of the many possible variations of the composition are illustrated here.

484. *Friedrich Becker. Necklace*

Becker uses white gold and cabochon rubies as metaphors for industrial machinery; the white metal represents steel and the rounded stones stand for joints or ball bearings. This flawlessly constructed necklace celebrates technology and embodies the machine's capacity for perfection, yet, by its function as jewelry, softens their impact.

After seeing his jewelry, one can appreciate and view a complex piece of machinery in an entirely different light, as a magnificent piece of moving sculpture, rather than as a cold, mechanical, functional necessity . . . .[586]

Becker's jewelry is a logical outgrowth of its antecedents—the late 1930s and early 1940s static, machine-inspired, geometrically styled jewelry. There were already strong allusions to machine parts in Jean Fouquet's bracelet of 1931 (fig. 107) and the Cartier necklace and bracelet of about 1935–40 (fig. 108). However, by the late 1940s, sensuous curves became increasingly prevalent in jewelry; in fact, Biomorphism was a predominant trend of the 1950s. Becker's necklace illustrates a resurgence of hard-edged geometry in the early 1960s. However, his necklace surpasses the machine-age examples because of its emphasis on changeability and an implied symbiosis between the necklace and the wearer, who ultimately controls its configuration. This necklace thus achieves the ultimate closeness with the human body that is the first principle in all jewelry design.   TLW

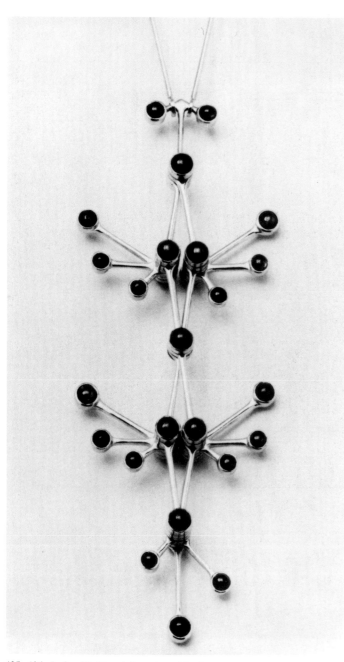

485, 486. *Becker. Necklace (alternate positions)*

487. *Joe Colombo. Side chairs: model no. 4860*

Joe Colombo

Side chairs: model no. 4860
Designed 1965
Injection-molded ABS plastic; 28⅛ × 16⁹⁄₁₆ ×
  19⅛ inches (71.4 × 42.1 × 48.5 cm)
Produced by Kartell (Easley, South Carolina),
  1966 to the present
Impressed on underside of seat: KARTELL®/
  designer: JOE COLOMBO/made in U.S.A. by/
  BEYLERIAN L.T.D.
D87.164.1, 2

Side chair: model no. 4860
Designed 1965
Injection-molded ABS plastic; 28⅜ × 17 × 19¾
  inches (72.1 × 43.4 × 50.2 cm)
Produced by Kartell S.p.A. (Milan), 1966 to
  the present
Impressed on underside of seat: Kartell,
  BINASCO (Milano)/860 e 861 1 5 [within a
  circle] MADE IN ITALY/DESIGN Prof. Joe
  Colombo.
D87.141.1

The Kartell company, established in Binasco just
outside Milan in 1949, was among the first Italian
manufacturers to experiment with the use of plastics in household items. Due to the limitations of
manufacturing technology at the time, its first
products from the early 1950s (designed by the in-
house designer, Gino Columbini) were small domestic objects, such as lemon squeezers, buckets,
dustpans, and brushes. From the outset, Kartell
evolved an approach to the design of its plastic
products that stressed quality and attention to

visual detail—a quite different philosophy from that expressed by the goods then being manufactured by parallel companies in the United States and Britain.

The high aesthetic quality of Kartell's plastic products remained a characteristic of its work in the 1950s and 1960s, during which time plastics technology advanced to the point at which it became possible to manufacture large household goods, such as chairs. While the company's first venture into this new area—Marco Zanuso's stacking child's chair—was still limited in scale, Colombo's plastic chair for Kartell a year or so later was a full-size dining model. Along with Vico Magistretti, who was working along similar lines with Artemide at this time, Colombo put an enormous amount of thought and energy into evolving a plastic chair that not only looked good but was also a viable manufacturing proposition.

Colombo's no. 4860 chair was the first of its kind to be injection molded in one piece (with the exception of the feet). The curves of the backrest of the seat are easy to extricate from the mold, as well as attractive; the small rectangular cutout in the base of the back was included primarily to facilitate the removal of the chair body from the mold. Trying various alternatives (fig. 488), Colombo allowed the manufacturing process to suggest an aesthetic that was sympathetic to it and, as a result, produced a chair with a highly rational reason behind it.

Other functional attributes of this little side chair include its ability to stack and to be linked to one beside it, in addition to the possibility of adding feet of varying heights to fulfill different needs. It can be manufactured at relatively low

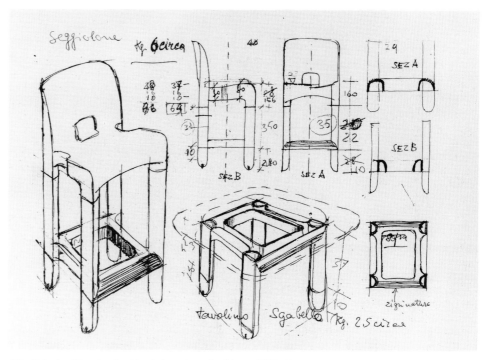

488. Colombo. Drawing for side chair and small table. c. 1965–66

cost and is available in a variety of colors, including green, white, and red.

While Colombo's chair is highly innovative technologically, as well as extremely pleasing visually, it remains both simple and unassuming, representing the democratic face of Italian design from this period and demonstrating that it is possible to combine low cost and mass availability with quality.

PS

Verner Panton

Side chair
Designed c. 1960–67
Luran-S thermoplastic; 32¹⁵/₁₆ × 19½ × 22¼
    inches (83.7 × 49.5 × 56.6 cm)
Produced by Vitra GmbH (Basel), for Herman
    Miller International (New York), 1968–79[587]
    (this example September 1974)
Stamped in relief on underside of seat:
    [horizontal rectangle enclosing device of
    stylized M and herman miller]/[numbers 1
    through 12 arranged inside a circle, arrow
    pointing to 9] 1974 [in inner concentric ring
    inside circle of numbers]
D87.200.1, gift of Luc d'Iberville-Moreau

Throughout the twentieth century, designers dreamed of mass-producing a chair made from a single piece of material that would require no assembly of any kind. The notion of a chair stamped or cast into a single, finished unit was a potent one because of the possibility for large-scale, economical production. Making use of plastic technologies developed mainly for the airplane industry, designers inched their way toward a single-piece chair.[588]

Around 1960 several designs, including Panton's, were in development or had reached prototype stage, but all would have to wait at least six years before production.[589] In the case of Pan-

489. *Verner Panton. Side chair*

ton's chair—the only cantilevered design of the period—the delay was caused by a lack of interest in plastic furniture on the part of manufacturers, the lack of a material that could meet the requirements of the design, and the high cost of the development work necessary for mass production.[590] Nonetheless, Panton's chair still represented a remarkable achievement when first introduced. It is ironic that a designer from Denmark, a country known best for producing handcrafted wood furniture, was the one to create the first single-piece plastic chair.

The origins of Panton's chair can be traced to factory visits during the 1950s that introduced

him to the manufacture of fiberglass crash helmets and plastic buckets. The low cost of the bucket especially spurred him to work on several projects, including laminated wood furniture and the plastic chair. The laminated chair (fig. 490) was designed first and entered in a competition. Though it did not win, it eventually found a manufacturer.[591] Bearing a resemblance to Gerrit Rietveld's famous Z chair of 1934 (fig. 491), it pointed the way toward the form of the far more sophisticated plastic version.

Around 1960 Panton had completed the design of his plastic chair and made the first mold in Denmark. But the technical problems were

deemed insurmountable until 1967, when he collaborated with the Vitra company's technical staff and representatives of plastic manufacturers.[592] The plastic material employed had to accommodate the manufacture of a relatively large object subject to considerable stress. The problem was most acute in the section supporting the seat, which had to leave enough room for the sitter's legs and feet. At the same time, the shape of the chair had to allow stacking, implying a reduction in mass, specifically of the thickness of the chair wall, yet be strong enough to stand up to use. Finally, coloring the material and giving it a smooth, glossy surface also necessitated consider-

able experimentation. The final product was indeed strong and durable, due above all to the variations in thickness of the material, a characteristic that could be achieved only in plastic. The chair even stood up to prolonged outdoor use.

The Panton chair became an icon of Pop design, the most important plastic chair of the 1960s produced outside of Italy. If anything, though, the innovative nature of the Panton chair was somewhat downplayed by the appearance, in the same year, of several plastic chairs manufactured in Italy. These designs, by Vico Magistretti, Joe Colombo, and Marco Zanuso and Richard Sapper, were similarly brightly colored, and some were stacking chairs. Yet none was as structurally daring; in fact, all were four-legged chairs.[593] However, Panton's chair, with its bold and dynamic cantilevered shape, its fully realized exploitation of new materials, and the bright and unusual colors it sported (violet, turquoise, and beige in addition to red, orange, black, and white), has a unique identity.

CW

(above left) 490. *Panton. Chair. c. 1955. The Vitra Design Museum, Weil am Rhein, Switzerland*

(above) 491. *Gerrit Rietveld. Z chair. 1934. Collection Barry Friedman Ltd., New York*

Eero Aarnio

Chair: *Ball* or *Globe*
Designed 1963–65
Fiberglass, aluminum, synthetic foam, and
 wool upholstery; 47 × 40¾ × 37½ inches
 (119.5 × 103.5 × 85 cm)
Produced by Asko Finnternational (Helsinki),
 1966–80, c. 1983–87
Unmarked
D87.254.1, gift of Nannette and Eric Brill*

Table: *Kantarelli*
Designed 1965
Fiberglass; 17¼ × 28 × 28 inches
 (43.8 × 71.1 × 71.1 cm)
Produced by Asko Finnternational (Helsinki),
 1968–c. 1978
Unmarked
D87.246.1, gift of Nannette and Eric Brill*

Although Eero Aarnio was steeped in the handicraft tradition of his native Finland when he launched his career, his best-known furniture designs look forward to the space age. Aarnio has been a leader in the exploration of new materials, especially plastics, and their application to innovative furniture design. His *Ball* chair and *Kantarelli* table were both produced by Asko Finnternational, Finland's most innovative furniture manufacturer.

The *Ball* chair is a response to the quest for a self-contained environment, a post-Freudian upholstered "womb" with optional telephone or stereo speakers. The chair's playful design is reduced to a sum of its parts: an aluminum pedestal supports a fiberglass ball, which is cut in section and padded internally. The chair was available in the bold 1960s colors of white, red, black, or

492. *Eero Aarnio.* Ball or Globe *chair*

493. *Aarnio*. Kantarelli *table*

orange, with either matching or optional two-tone base.

Aarnio's molded plastic *Kantarelli* table shares its name and motif with the famous glass vases of 1946–47 by fellow Finnish designer Tapio Wirk-kala (figs. 211, 213). Both mushroom-based designs flow in an unbroken line from their rounded tops to their indented center stem supports, which pool out at the base. Yet the effect is quite different. Unlike the gracefully attenuated arcs of Wirkkala's designs, or even the fluid lines of Eero Saarinen's *Pedestal* furniture, Aarnio's geometry is of a simpler, more rudimentary type.

When these two items were bought for a London apartment, they were complemented by a third element: a spherical television designed about 1969 by Arthur D. Bracegirdle for Ker-acolor (fig. 494).[594] As an ensemble, all three pieces of ball furniture reflect a more playful attitude toward furniture design than that of the decades immediately after the war.

FTH

494. *Arthur D. Bracegirdle. Television console.*
c. 1969. Liliane and David M. Stewart Collection.
Gift of Nannette and Eric Brill, D87.247.1

318

Vico Magistretti

Table lamp: *Eclipse*

Designed 1965–66[595]

Lacquered aluminum and plastic; 7 × 4⅞ × 4⅞
   inches (17.8 × 12.3 × 12.3 cm)

Produced by Artemide S.p.A. (Milan), 1966 to
   the present

Impressed on underside of base: studio
   ARTEMIDE-MILANO/max. 25 Watt/modello
   ECLIPSE/design VICO MAGISTRETTI/patent
   5278–914551–73865/made in ITALY

D87.217.1

495. Vico Magistretti. Eclipse *table lamp*

This small spherical lamp won a Compasso
d'Oro award for design in 1967. Like Aarnio's *Ball*
chair (fig. 492), which is also basically a sphere on
a circular pedestal, Magistretti's lamp is typical of
the reawakened interest in geometric shapes seen
in the 1960s.

Magistretti had explored the idea of spherical
lamps before this. Around 1960, for example, he
designed purple glass globes that seemed to orbit
around a dark red hall column.[596] Two or three
years later, he designed *Mania*, a circular wall
lamp with a large upper hemisphere of opaline
white glass overlapping a smaller one below.[597]
Magistretti repeated the concept of one circular
form enclosing another in the *Eclipse* lamp, but

496. Artemide publicity photograph of Eclipse *table lamps, in different positions, 1966*

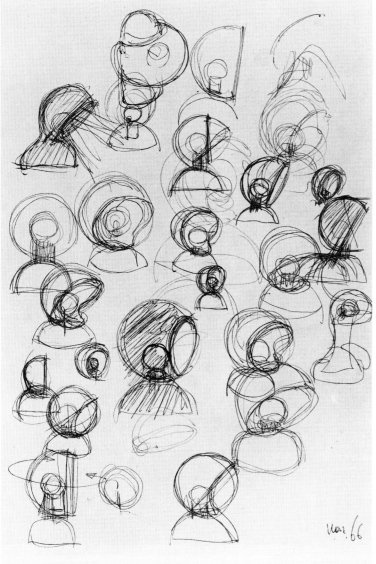

497. *Magistretti.* *Drawing for* Eclipse *lamp.* 1966

498. *Magistretti.* Giunone *(Juno)*
floor lamp. 1969

this time he added the possibility of move-ment.[598] The inner white hemisphere rotates in such a way that in different positions it lets all the light shine out, blocks some of the light, or blocks it entirely—all very much like an eclipse of the sun in miniature (fig. 496). A preliminary sketch (fig. 497) shows that at one point Magistretti con-sidered having parts of the lamp turn vertically as well as horizontally.[599] He later elaborated still further on the possibility of movement in his

Giunone (Juno) floor lamp of 1969, which has not one but four rotating spherical metal shades (fig. 498).

Not only are the circular shapes of the *Eclipse* lamp typical of the art of the 1960s, so, too, are its colors, which are as bright as those used by the American Pop artists. This example is lacquered a bright red. Other colors available at the time were orange, yellow, blue, gray, or white.[600]

CWL

Roy Lichtenstein

Poster: *CRAK!*
Designed 1963
Offset lithograph; 21 × 28½ inches
  (53.3 × 72.5 cm)
Printed 1963
Unmarked
D86.136.1, gift of David A. Hanks*

Primarily a painter inspired by printed images, Lichtenstein developed a style of flat painting that successfully translates to printing techniques. This poster of 1963 advertises an exhibition of Lichtenstein's paintings at Manhattan's Leo Castelli Gallery, the gallery that had launched the Pop art movement two years earlier, claiming Lichtenstein as one of the movement's founders.

Lichtenstein's repeated references to mass media—television, advertising, and, above all, the comic strip—dominate his work of the 1960s. However, he isolated his media-derived images from a coherent context—a basic tenet of the Pop art movement and one of the foundations of Lichtenstein's work. The benday process, which uses dots to replicate halftones in newspaper printing, and the balloon that contains the "text" of the image have a startling, surreal effect when taken from their familiar settings and enlarged.

Lichtenstein introduced humor by using an accepted design convention from comic strips, yet this poster's subject, increasingly a theme of the 1960s in the United States, is violence. Using such contradictions allowed Lichtenstein simultaneously to express his views and demystify "high art," an implicit goal of the Pop art movement.

FTH

499. *Roy Lichtenstein*. CRAK!

The sound is WOR-FM 98.7

500. *Milton Glaser.* The Sound Is WOR-FM 98.7

501. *Glaser.* Mahalia Jackson. 1967.
Collection, The Museum of
Modern Art, New York.
Gift of the designer

Milton Glaser

Poster: *The Sound Is WOR-FM* 98.7
Designed 1966
Offset lithograph; 29¾ × 35¾ inches
   (75.7 × 90.8 cm)
Printed 1966
Printed in black in lower right corner: *Milton Glaser*
D84.191.1

Milton Glaser's witty, colorful style lent itself well to depicting images of rock musicians, and he illustrated many record album covers and posters for this youth-oriented branch of the entertainment business.

In 1966, when Glaser designed this poster advertising the New York radio station WOR-FM, then a rock music station, the Beatles were at the height of their fame. Glaser used the stylized figures of five rock musicians with shaggy, Beatle-style haircuts standing out against a strong, abstract background of radiating red and yellow stripes. The figures are rendered in a semiabstract style achieved by using high-contrast colors, a device borrowed from modern photographic techniques.

Psychedelic color, pattern, and contrast are key ingredients in Glaser's style of the 1960s. Like other graphic artists of the decade, Glaser borrowed from many sources to create his visual message. The sharp contrasts and rhythmic lines of English Art Nouveau illustrator Aubrey Beardsley find their counterparts in Glaser's designs. The flat, patterned effects of Glaser's stylized images also recall techniques achieved in nineteenth-century Japanese woodcuts. Not surprisingly, nostalgia for representational art became an element in the popular imagery of the 1960s, triumphing over the Modernist adherence to simplicity, flatness, and an antidecorative approach to design. Glaser pointedly allowed the guitar fret at the top and the legs of the guitarist at the right to escape from the image's confines to create visual tension by suggesting three dimensionality. On the other hand, while Glaser frequently embellished his graphic designs with highly decorative lettering, as in his double poster for a Mahalia Jackson concert (fig. 501), here his client's message is set in simple, sans serif Helvetica type.

FTH

Ettore Sottsass

Vase
Designed 1958
Enameled copper and satinwood;
   18¾ × 3¹¹⁄₁₆ × 3¹¹⁄₁₆ (47.5 × 9.4 × 9.4 cm)
Produced by Bucci (Pesaro, Italy), 1958
Impressed on underside: IL SESTANTE
D87.158.1

Sottsass, in addition to acting as the chief consultant for Olivetti's new Electronics Division, dedicated much of his energies in the late 1950s to designing decorative objects for the interior environment. Many of them, such as this vase, were manufactured in small series by artisanal firms. Commissioned by the Il Sestante gallery in Milan, an important venue for exhibitions of decorative objects, this vase was part of a series of enameled objects made by the Bucci workshop.

While his interest in craft manufacturing and materials expanded at this time, Sottsass was uninterested in the aesthetic values traditionally associated with craft objects. He sought, instead, ways of linking together domestic artifacts with quite disparate craft roots through the creation of a uniform visual language that could be applied to all of them, irrespective of their materials. In imitation of the European Gesture painters and the American Abstract Expressionists, Sottsass evolved a sophisticated sign language for his objects, a vocabulary of vivid colors and bold marks, which were often geometric and always abstract. This vase, with its brightly colored enamel surface and its wooden base, should be seen, therefore, as an element within a domestic composition rather than as an object in isolation.

Multiple drawings, all executed with a childlike simplicity, preceded the manufacture of each piece. In each case the aim was to create an object that resembled as nearly as possible the original sketch, whatever the material used. Thus, the black, white, and red bands on this vase could have been achieved in wood or ceramic with equal effectiveness and with only slightly different results.

If the aesthetic of the materials used in this period was of only minimal significance to Sottsass, the cultural implications of natural materials were all-important. He found it vital to link traditional techniques with modern images—a synthesis that motivated much of his later work—and his concentration on simple, utilitarian objects such as vases and bowls represented a search for what he considered to be "archetypal shapes."[601] Sottsass was able to explore the modern qualities of vibrant colors juxtaposed against each other while still showing his respect for objects and techniques that go back centuries.

PS

502. *Ettore Sottsass. Vase*

503. Ettore Sottsass. Vases

Ettore Sottsass

Vase
Designed 1959
Glazed earthenware; 18⅜ × 7 × 7 inches
(46.8 × 17.8 × 17.8 cm)
Produced by Cav. G. Bitossi & Figli
(Montelupo, Italy), 1959
Painted in black on underside: *Sottsass*
Printed on partial remains of torn paper label:
LES DECO . . .
D87.240.1

Vase
Designed 1957
Glazed and unglazed earthenware;
5¼ × 6⅝ × 6⅝ inches (13.4 × 16.8 × 16.8 cm)
Produced by Cav. G. Bitossi & Figli
(Montelupo, Italy), 1957
Painted in black on underside: *919[?]/ITALY*
D87.160.1

Vase
Designed 1957
Glazed and unglazed earthenware;
12⅞ × 4⅛ × 4⅛ inches (32.7 × 10.4 ×
10.4 cm)
Produced by Cav. G. Bitossi & Figli
(Montelupo, Italy), 1957
Painted in black on underside: *SOTTSASS/57*
D87.159.1

Ettore Sottsass's first experience with ceramics came in response to a commission in 1956 from Irving Richards, the owner of the New York firm Raymor's, who wanted examples of modern European design for his collection. In 1957, 1958, and 1959, Sottsass designed three ranges of ceramic objects—vases, jars, plates, bowls, and ashtrays—which were executed at the Bitossi factory in Montelupo, near Florence, in collaboration with the firm's technical and artistic director, Aldo Londi. The pieces represent an important stage in the creative career of the architect-designer, who had already applied his skills to a wide range of small domestic products in different materials. They served both to consolidate and communicate many of his concerns up to that date.

Sottsass approached ceramic design from two different angles. First, he was interested in the Italian tradition and the everyday qualities of materials such as terra-cotta and earthenware, as opposed to Eastern ceramics, which were tied up with religious thought: "I think it [ceramic] was always kept in a popular area of non-religious gestures . . . rather than in the area of the temple," and thus ceramic artifacts had an "established position as tools of society."[602] Second, he believed in the decorative role of ceramics within the contemporary interior, alongside other artifacts, such as furniture, mirrors, trays, and fabrics. With this latter function in mind, Sottsass gave many of his pieces, these vases included, an architectonic form and decorated their surfaces with motifs and colors related to many other elements that made up his interiors in these years. He derived much inspiration at this time from the work of the Scottish architect Charles Rennie Mackintosh and from the Wiener Werkstätte. The rectilinear motifs he used repeatedly—squares, rectangles, stripes, circles, and grids—were highly reminiscent of these turn-of-the-century styles, and they also echo traditional Japanese decorative arts.

Another important source for these ceramic experiments came from Sottsass's sojourn in the United States in 1956. There he encountered the work of the American Abstract Expressionists and Color Field painters, which stimulated his growing interest in the concept of pure sensation and the immediate, "sensorial" impact of color and pattern. With their vibrant colors and strong horizontal stripes, all three of these ceramics mirror Sottsass's trans-Atlantic experience.

As in so many of Sottsass's designs, this sense of aggressive contemporaneity is sharply contrasted against a respect for traditional materials and a love of primitive societies. While the vases' aesthetic impact is much more graphic and chromatic than it is tactile, the pieces bearing no trace of the overt language of craft epitomized by so many contemporary Scandinavian artifacts, the use of ceramic was vitally important in a conceptual sense. These designs represent for the artist a marriage between the past and the present, as well as a moment in which he found a medium that was both powerful and flexible enough to express his current preoccupations.

PS

504. Ettore Sottsass. Desk/cabinet/bookcase, Tchou apartment, Milan. 1960

Ettore Sottsass

Cabinet
Designed 1964
Walnut, cherry veneer, and lacquer;
  99 × 60 × 24 inches (251.5 × 152.5 × 61 cm)
Produced by Renzo Brugola (Milan), 1988
Unmarked
D88.132.1, gift of Vivian and David M.
  Campbell

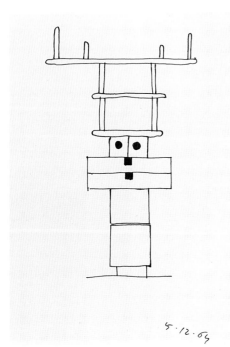

505. Sottsass. Drawing for cabinet. 1964. Centro studi e archivio della comunicazione dell' Università di Parma

In this piece of "tower furniture" (*mobile di torre*), Sottsass created an extravagant assemblage of shapes and colors. It is typical of his work in its exaggeration of scale—it is over eight feet high—and in the way its parts extend up and outward rather than being enclosed within a simple, blocklike contour.

Sottsass was interested in many forms of abstract art: the geometric works of Piet Mondrian and Theo van Doesburg, the Biomorphic Surrealism of Jean Arp, and the spontaneity of American Abstract Expressionism.[603] In the late 1950s, he began to mix an astonishing array of shapes, patterns, and bright colors in his interiors.[604] One room (fig. 478) has a long, vertical painting by Sottsass himself, with geometric shapes ar-

ranged in horizontal stripes, a vertically striped cabinet, squares on the floor, and a mirror frame with stripes and circles. The mix of patterns and colors is reminiscent of the prewar geometric abstract art Sottsass loved, although the designer says he was more immediately inspired by Far Eastern and European popular cultures.[605]

Sottsass designed his first piece of tower furniture in 1960 (fig. 504).[606] It is a freestanding, room-high desk/cabinet/bookcase for the Tchou apartment in Milan, and it contains shelves, doors, and drawers in different colors. In this single piece he achieved the complexity of shapes and colors found in his earlier interiors.

By the early 1960s, Sottsass's work paralleled that of painters like Frank Stella and Ellsworth

506. Sottsass. Cabinet

Kelly, but he felt especially close to American Pop art because of its ephemeral quality and popular imagery.[607] Indeed, Sottsass said he was not looking for a Platonic ideal of Good Design that would suit all times but for something that would express its own moment in time and no other:

If a society plans obsolescence, the only possible enduring design is one . . . that comes to terms with it. . . . The only design that does not endure is the one that . . . looks for the absolute, for eternity. And then I don't understand why enduring design is better than disappearing design. . . . I must admit that obsolescence for me is just the sugar of life.[608]

During and after a long hospital stay in California in 1962, Sottsass designed jewelry for women in love and furniture for the young women of Paris. He commented:

I looked about me, with my hair going grey, and the worst thing about it was not so much that my hair was grey, as that the young women had wrong-footed me with their aggressiveness: they had beaten me to the mark, because what I wanted to do with furniture they had already done with their white canvas boots, with their multicoloured fancy stockings, decorated with stripes, coloured squares and dots.[609]

One of the drawings that Sottsass made soon thereafter, in 1964, was of a whimsical cabinet resembling a creature with large, round eyes and a strange rectangular set of antlers (fig. 505). Some of his other furniture designs of that time were made up by Poltronova and exhibited in Milan in 1965.[610] But this design was not executed until almost twenty-five years after its creation, as a special commission to record an important moment in the history of modern Italian design.

CWL

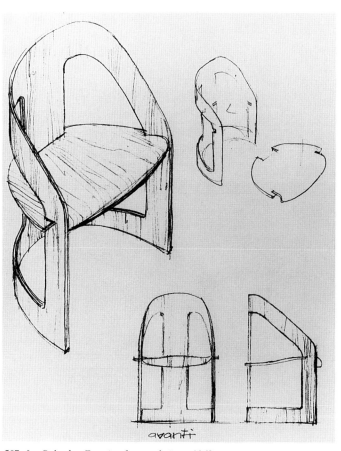

507. *Joe Colombo. Drawing for armchair. c. 1963*

Joe Colombo

Armchair: model no. 4801
Designed c. 1963
Plywood and polyester lacquer; 23¼ × 26 × 27¹⁵⁄₁₆ inches (59 × 66 × 71 cm)
Produced by Kartell S.p.A. (Milan), 1964–75
Unmarked
D83.133.1

An infatuation with new materials represented one aspect of the Italian foray into modern design in the years following 1945. Learning much from Charles Eames, a number of Italian designers explored the sculptural possibilities of the new metals, processed woods, and, eventually, plastics in their designs for furniture. Joe Colombo's armchair grew out of this interest, as well as the abiding twentieth-century search for fabricating furniture from the fewest possible number of visible elements.

The chair is constructed, in jigsaw-puzzle fashion, from three pieces of plywood, which form the seat, the arms and base, and the backrest (fig. 507). Where the curves move into three dimensions, as in the seat, the molding process

508. Colombo. Armchair: model no. 4801

was used instead of the simpler one of bending the wood, which was sufficient to create the smooth contour of the backrest.

Visually, the chair is a composition of curves that flow gently into each other, the spaces between them emphasizing the sculptural play of the wooden masses. This is no mere exercise in form, however, for the chair's real significance lies in the way in which its organic appearance has emerged directly from the processes of bending and molding plywood. Nothing is hidden, and the simple system of interlocking the three

elements avoids complex or concealed fixing or jointing.

Colombo's 4801 armchair was first shown at the Milan Furniture Salon of 1965. In addition to the white version here, it was available in orange, green, and black. Although it was only manufactured in limited numbers, it remains one of the key designs to emerge from Italy at this time, anticipating Colombo's work in plastics for the same company (fig. 487).

PS

(opposite) 509. *Mario Bellini.* Chiara *floor lamp*

(below) 510. *Bellini.* Chiara *floor lamp with* Ciprea *armchair by Afra and Tobia Scarpa*

(right) 511. *Bellini.* Chiara *lamp assembled and disassembled*

Mario Bellini

Floor lamp: *Chiara*
Designed 1964
Stainless steel; 57 × 28⅞ × 20¾ inches
  (144.8 × 73.2 × 52.7 cm)
Produced by Flos S.p.A. (Nave, Italy),
  c. 1964–78[611]
Printed on a rectangular silver paper label
  inside lamp near the top: FLOS [in pink on a
  purple rectangle]/MADE IN ITALY [in white]
Typewritten on paper label attached on
  exterior of lamp near the base: MADE IN
  ITALY
D87.207.1

Bellini's lamp takes its name from its light (in Italian, *chiara*), which wells up from the bulb deep inside the base. Some of it spills out through the slits at the bottom, while the rest strikes the hood and is reflected out.

This lamp is typical of Bellini's use of extravagant and dramatic shapes. The designer began with geometric forms—a cylinder for the base and a circular arc for the shade—and exaggerated them. Both parts are outsize: the base is exceptionally wide for a floor lamp, while the huge hood flares out in three directions. The whole lamp is out of normal scale. The proportions—more suitable for a table lamp—have been enlarged in much the same way that Claes Oldenburg enlarged ordinary objects into monumental

sculptures. Bellini's lamp looms over any chair placed next to it (fig. 510) and dominates the room with a shape whose eccentricity can be found elsewhere in Italian design at this time.

The construction of this lamp also is unusual. A single sheet of steel is wrapped around to form both the base of the lamp and the hooded shade. Ettore Sottsass had made a series of lamp shades a few years before by wrapping a single piece of material around itself,[612] but Bellini went a step further by making the whole lamp in one piece. Even more novel was the fact that the lamp was shipped flat (fig. 511). Ironically, it was the client and not the manufacturer who assembled this seemingly high-tech lamp, by bending the sheet of steel and fastening it into position.

CWL

Grete Jalk

Side chair
Designed 1963
Beech-faced plywood and steel bolts;
  29 × 28¼ × 24¾ inches (73.6 × 71.7 ×
  62.9 cm)
Produced by P. Jeppesen (Stor Heddinge,
  Denmark), 1963
Unmarked
D89.103.1

Periodically, designers have developed plywood products of such ingenuity that it seemed unlikely that the material could be further exploited. Such was the case immediately following the production of furniture by Thonet, then by Alvar Aalto, and then by Charles and Ray Eames. But once the imitators and plagiarizers had completely exploited or debased the original ideas, the material was, in a sense, available, to be considered anew. This does not necessarily lead to new modes of furniture design, but it is part of the process of design experimentation, and it often yields interesting results. Jalk's chair is such an example.

The series of laminated furniture that Jalk began in 1962 continued a collaboration with manufacturer Poul Jeppesen dating back to 1955. That period saw the manufacture of a number of Jalk designs for traditionally handcrafted seat and case furniture. Later, aware of Jalk's interest in less expensive furniture that could be industrially produced and her desire to work with laminated wood, Jeppesen suggested that she experiment along those lines.[613] The first result was a delicately shaped nest of tables, each table made from a single piece of laminated wood (fig. 512). In the following year she designed the chair under discussion and in 1964 a large coffee table.

The chair was made from only two pieces of wood. Although unusually shaped and bent to a remarkable degree, these were bent on only one plane, or in one direction. It was therefore relatively uncomplicated to mold and easier to produce than the type of three-dimensionally molded plywood furniture designed by the Eameses. Yet Jalk certainly had Eames or Eames-

derived designs very much in mind, as is demonstrated by a chair she had designed the previous year (fig. 513).[614]

In the 1962 chair, the relationship of the cutout frame to the simply molded seat and back is decidedly awkward and inorganic. It was a recurring formal (rather than technical) problem that not many designers managed to solve decisively. Jalk's new chair of 1963 manages to combine the emphatically undulant surfaces of the seat and back with the harder, geometric shape of the base with considerable ingenuity, though the result is still slightly discordant. The delicate, ribbonlike curves of the plywood belie the actual solidity and weight of the chair.

By the time Jalk's chair was manufactured, the vogue for plywood furniture that had been so strong in the 1950s was, at least temporarily, waning. Although some plywood furniture by well-known designers continued to find its way into the marketplace, by and large it had become a staple of the lower end of the market. Also, plywood was not the type of furniture that consumers generally sought when looking for Scandinavian furniture, modern or otherwise. As a result, Jeppesen produced only about three hundred chairs, offering them in a variety of surface veneers, including teak, beech, rosewood, Oregon pine, walnut, and oak.   CW

512. *Grete Jalk. Prototype for nest of tables. c. 1962. Collection Grete Jalk*

513. *Jalk. Upholstered plywood chair. 1962. Collection Grete Jalk*

514, 515. *Jalk. Side chair*

516. *Roberto Sebastian Matta.* Malitte *seating system*

Roberto Sebastian Matta

Seating system: *Malitte*[615]
Designed 1966
Polyurethane foam and stretch wool
 upholstery; 63 × 63 × 24¾ inches
 (160 × 160 × 63 cm)
Produced by Gavina (Foligno, Italy), 1966–68;
 by Knoll International (New York), 1968–74
Unmarked
D89.137.1

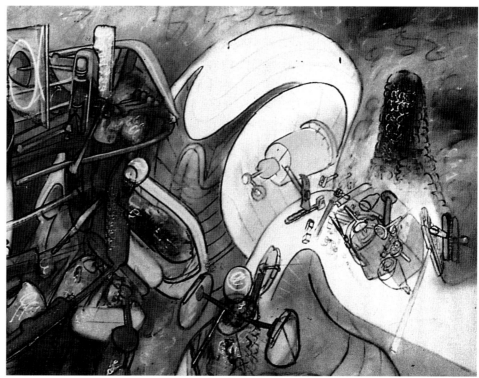

517. *Matta.* Les Puissances du désordre *(detail). 1964–65. Musée National d'Art Moderne, Centre Georges Pompidou, Paris. Gift of M. Alexandre Iolas, 1979*

Matta is best known as a Surrealist painter who in the 1940s became a disciple of Marcel Duchamp, the quintessential Dadaist. The avant-garde furniture maker Dino Gavina, another follower of Duchamp, commissioned from Matta this innovative seating system, which is as unconventional as Duchamp's art. This unusual system is conceived for a generation that was living in bare, minimally furnished rooms and was no longer sitting upright in traditional chairs. The owner can spread the pieces around the room to create

an environment reminiscent of the Minimalist sculptures of artists like Robert Morris or can stack them together vertically into a square jigsaw puzzle (fig. 518).

Matta said he was given a large block of polyurethane foam, a new material at the time, and that he tried to create shapes that would use all the material.[616] He designed four seats cut from the edge of the block and then rounded the remaining center section to be used as an ottoman. Even the construction is novel. There is no frame

of any kind, since the blocks are firm enough to hold their own shape. Each piece was upholstered, the seats in one color and the central ottoman in a contrasting color.[617]

The *Malitte* system accords better conceptually than stylistically with Matta's work. Although elongated curves are found in many of the artist's paintings, such as *Les Puissances du désordre* of 1964–65 (fig. 517),[618] these pieces have a solidity unmatched by the partly transparent forms that Matta generally painted. Nor is this

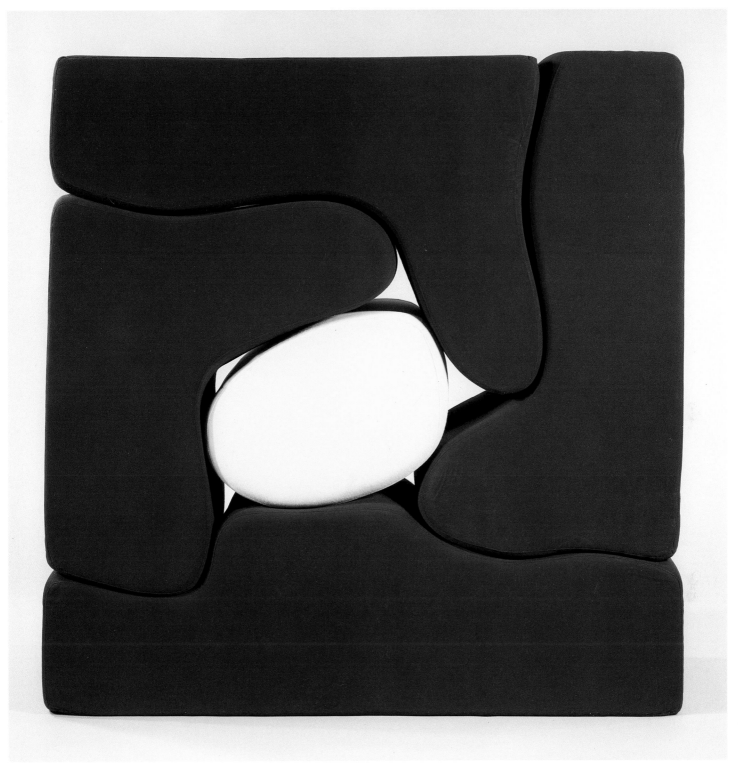

518. *Matta*. Malitte *seating system assembled*

solidity found in his sculpture. In the early 1960s Matta was creating thin, wiry, welded metal sculptures, reminiscent of Picasso's and Juan Gonzalez's work from the late 1920s and early 1930s. Ironically, the forms here are closer to the organic *Navel* reliefs of Jean Arp, a colleague from Matta's Surrealist days.

Although the bulk and the sense of depth found in the *Malitte* system were partly determined by the material, *Malitte* is also an example of the large, blocky forms popular in Italian fur-

niture in the mid-1960s. In fact, several other designers were working with upholstered blocks of expanded polyurethane in those years. Mario Bellini's 932/2 chair for Cassina (1965) is a frameless set of foam blocks that are leather-upholstered and belted together to form an armchair. Closer to the antifurniture spirit of the *Malitte* system is *Sofo*, a set of stackable chairs and sofas of polyurethane made by Design Center (c. 1969).[619]

CWL

519. *Maija Isola*. Kaivo *textile*

Maija Isola

Textile: *Kaivo*
Designed c. 1964
Cotton, plain weave, silk-screen printed;
   108 × 54⅜ inches (275 × 138.2 cm)
Produced by Marimekko Oy (Helsinki),
   1964–79
Printed three times in selvage: MAIJA ISOLA
   DESIGN "KAIVO" © MARIMEKKO OY SUOMI
   FINLAND 1965
D87.167.1

Although Marimekko has produced a variety of printed textiles, it is perhaps those examples from the mid-1960s that have come to symbolize to the public *the* Marimekko style. Many of them were based on the designs of painter Maija Isola, as is the case of this textile. *Kaivo* (a well) is representative of these oversize patterns of bold, simple shapes with dynamic graphics rendered in clear, strong colors that attract or challenge the viewer.

520. *Marimekko dress made from* Cock and Hen *textile by Isola, 1965*

As textile designs, these innovative supergraphics are purely Finnish creations, breaking with a more reserved, conservative tradition and necessitating a fresh approach to interior decoration and fashion to make them work. Conceived independently, they nonetheless reflect contemporary trends in the art world at large, such as the work of American Color Field painters.

This combination of red, white, and blue is one of the 35 color ways in which *Kaivo* was printed and but one of the 145 proposed by Isola for this pattern. *Kaivo* enjoyed a long popularity, primarily as a home-furnishing fabric, for curtains and tablecloths; however, it was also used as a work of art in its own right, in lengths that were stretched, framed, and hung as paintings.[620] While *Kaivo* was not promoted for clothing, similar Marimekko designs were employed to make a new fashion statement (fig. 520).

AZ

Gunnar Cyrén

Goblet: *Pop*
Designed c. 1965–66[621]
Glass; 8¹⁄₁₆ × 4½ × 4½ inches (20.5 × 11.5 ×
   11.5 cm)
Produced by AB Orrefors Glasbruk (Orrefors,
   Sweden), 1966–c. 1976 (this example
   c. 1967)
Etched on underside: ORREFORS EXPO B.548-67
   Gunnar Cyren
D84.156.1, gift of Susan A. Chalom*

In their own way, the small, brightly colored *Pop* goblets have become an emblem of the new direction that Scandinavian design took after the mid-1960s. Rather than marking a sudden break with the past, they are the result of a gradual evolution within the work of one designer. Among the innovations that the twenty-eight-year-old Cyrén introduced when he arrived at the Orrefors plant in 1959 was the use of bright, opaque colors. Sometimes he overlaid successive bands of color with enameled designs, but in this

series of goblets, he let the cacophony of colors stand forth boldly on their own. The designer claims that he was inspired by the vivacious colors of exotic tropical fish[622] but also admits to having been receptive to the new wave of English design, such as the fashions of Mary Quant and Carnaby Street. The irregularities of width and the arbitrary changes from one band to another suggest the brashness of the new taste. The very name, *Pop*, is equally germane; though it was conferred by a journalist, Cyrén accepted it as appropriate after others began using it.

The forms of the goblets might seem subordinate to the issue of color; indeed, the *Pop* goblets imitated Cyrén's *Rundhock* or *Column* drinking glasses that Orrefors had introduced shortly before, in 1965. Yet the shapes also reflect this new direction in aesthetics. The stems are relatively short and thick; the bowls are blocky and straightwalled. These abrupt forms are at a far remove from Nils Landberg's elegantly tapered goblets of a decade earlier (fig. 337).

521. *Gunnar Cyrén. Pop goblet*

522. Cyrén. Pop *goblets*. 1966

When the first *Pop* glasses were shown in 1966, they were presented in a variety of sizes and shapes traditionally associated with drinking glasses for liqueurs, brandies, wine, and other spirits (fig. 522). However, they were not intended as functional objects; they did not come in sets of six or twelve. They were art objects, not intended even for serial production.

The *Pop* glasses were acclaimed for their vitality and "Continental freshness."[623] A selection was included in the Montreal Expo of 1967, and the glasses continued in production for several years thereafter, with constant variety but no major changes, save that the colored foot (present here) was replaced by a clear one. Cyrén worked directly with the glassblowers, and decisions were made on an ad hoc basis. Variations were introduced as one color of pot metal was exhausted, but there were few repetitions of the layered colors. A few goblets may have been made after Cyrén left Orrefors in 1970, but production was definitively stopped in 1976 when the designer returned, for they already represented a past phase of "modernism."

ME

Kaj Franck

Plaque
Designed c. 1965
Glass; 17⅛ × 17⅛ × 1⅜ inches (43.6 × 43.6 × 3.5 cm)
Produced by Nuutajärvi-Notsjo (Nuutajärvi, Finland), c. 1965–76
Engraved on underside: Kaj Franck Nuutajarvi Notsjo
Printed on silver paper label on front:
NUUTAJARVI/NOTSJO-1793/MADE IN FINLAND
D85.100.1

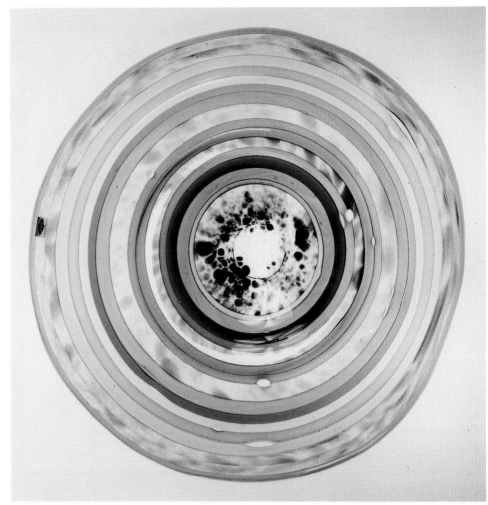

523. *Kaj Franck. Plaque*

Kaj Franck's name is a familiar one in the history of postwar design, but those designs of his that are inevitably cited are from the late 1940s and 1950s (fig. 254), admittedly the most important portion of his career. Although works from the latter part of his career, such as this decorative plaque, are occasionally included in surveys of Finnish design and modern glass,[624] curiously little attention is given to the changes in his style.

The explosion of color in this plaque might have been expected, since the Nuutajärvi factory tended to work with colored glass (unlike the Iittala factory, which worked mostly in clear), and many of Kaj Franck's earlier designs, such as the *Kremlin Bells*, were polychromatic. But the intensity of these colored concentric rings suggests a shift of taste. For those acquainted with modern painting, especially that emanating from New York, one might think of Jasper Johns's target series or Frank Stella's and Kenneth Noland's paintings. But the same stylistic tendency was soon registered throughout European design of the period. The initial impetus for this emphasis on bold colored stripes and the use of assembled laminated pieces can be traced to Venini (figs. 283, 284),[625] but there are other examples closer at hand, such as Gunnar Cyrén's *Pop* goblets (fig. 521). Though the muted, earth tones of this plaque—soft pinks, tortoiseshell, and mossy greens—continue Franck's earlier, gentler palette, other plaques in this series juxtapose intense reds and bright greens and blues, and thus approach more closely the bold graphic system of the 1960s.[626]

ME

Alexander Girard

Drapery textile: model no. 65002, *Mikado*
Designed 1954
Cotton and polyester, plain weave, silk-screen
  printed; 24½ × 24⅞ inches (62 × 63 cm)
Printed by American Art Textile Printing
  Company, Inc., for Herman Miller, Inc.
  (Zeeland, Michigan), 1954–70
Printed in yellow in left selvage: [device of
  stylized M] herman miller fabrics "mikado"
  designed by alexander girard ©
Printed and handwritten in black on paper tag:
  [device of stylized M] herman miller/
  Herman Miller, Inc./Zeeland, Michigan
  49464/telephone 616 772 2161/fabrics/[within
  box: No. 65002 A-1/Yds. 2]/Important/No
  allowances after material is cut.
D84.116.1, gift of Herman Miller, Inc.

Mikado, like Girard's other textiles, was intended to provide an accent and a "soft dimension" in interiors that otherwise could turn into mechanical environments. As the name of the pattern suggests, Girard's inspiration on this occasion was the art of Japan. The sixteen-petaled blossom is presumably a stylized representation of a chrysanthemum, the emblem of the mikado, or emperor. The flower often appears in such stylized form in Japanese textiles, and the way in which Girard has used a square element in the center of each blossom recalls another form of Japanese art, the ornamental sword guard, or *tsuba*, which of necessity includes a square or rectangular opening to accommodate the sword.

As in the case of his *Palio* series (figs. 527–30), Girard here turned to another culture for inspiration, and he transformed his prototype into a very distinct, colorfully abstract, and geometrically bold configuration. The pattern is unremittingly flat and crisp, especially because the squares are as dominant an element as the blossoms. Since each square is six inches, the pattern is by no means diminutive. There was a still larger version, known as *Giant Mikado*, in which the scale was doubled. Girard believed that realism was to be avoided in patterns, that simple, abstract designs in bold colors were the basis of proper design. The combination of pink and crimson seen here was one favored by Girard; these colors dominated the interior of his home and studio in Santa Fe, New Mexico, where this textile was designed. A small yellow square in every other blossom gives a piquant accent to the hot palette.[627]

Girard was also concerned with the practical aspect of how this fabric would be used. The size of the repeat took into account the effect of pleating, which is a basic issue for all curtain material, and it also is indicative of the bolder scale of design established by the mid-1960s.

CCMT

524. *Alexander Girard.* Mikado *drapery textile: model no. 65002*

525. *Palio banner of the Unicorno district, Siena, Italy*

526. *Standard-bearer of the Tartuca district, Siena, Italy*

Alexander Girard

Drapery textile: model no. 1691, *Palio*
Designed c. 1964
Linen, plain weave, silk-screen printed;
 23¾ × 23¾ inches (60.9 × 60.9 cm)
Produced by Herman Miller, Inc. (Zeeland,
 Michigan), 1964–after 1970[628]
Printed in black in selvage: S-1691 "PALIO"
 DESIGNED BY ALEXANDER GIRARD COPYRIGHT
 1964 HERMAN MILLER INC. [device of stylized
 M]
D84.118.1, gift of Herman Miller, Inc.

Drapery textile: model no. 1674, *Palio 2*
Designed c. 1964
Rayon and Verel synthetic, plain weave,
 silk-screen printed; 24 × 24¾ inches
 (61 × 62.8 cm)
Produced by Herman Miller, Inc. (Zeeland,
 Michigan), 1964–after 1970
Printed in yellow in selvage: BY ALEXANDER
 GIRARD COPYRIGHT 1964 HERMAN MILLER
 INC. [device of stylized M]
Printed and handwritten in black on paper tag:
 [device of stylized M] herman miller/
 Herman Miller, Inc./Zeeland, Michigan
 49464/telephone 616 772 2161/fabrics/[within
 box: No. 1674 A-1/Yds. 2.92]/Important/No
 allowances after material is cut.
In pencil on reverse of tag: (10)/PALIO/60 × 62
 cm.
D84.111.1, gift of Herman Miller, Inc.

Drapery textile: model no. 1801, *Palio 6*
Designed c. 1964
Cotton and linen, plain weave, silk-screen
 printed; 24½ × 32½ inches (62.2 × 83.3 cm)
Produced by Herman Miller, Inc. (Zeeland,
 Michigan), 1964–after 1970
Printed in mustard in selvage: S-1692 "PALIO"
 DESIGNED BY ALEXANDER GIRARD COPYRIGHT
 1964 HERMAN MILLER INC. [device of stylized
 M]
Printed and handwritten on paper tag: [device
 of stylized M] herman miller/Herman
 Miller, Inc./Zeeland, Michigan 49464/
 telephone 616 772 2161/fabric/[within box:
 No. 1801 A-1/Yds. 2]/Important/No
 allowances after material is cut.
In pencil on reverse of tag: (14)/32½ ×
 24½/82 × 62 cm
D84.115.1, gift of Herman Miller, Inc.

Alexander Girard, who collected folk art from
around the world, also loved bright colors and
bold patterns, as photographs of his own house
show.[629] In designing this series of textiles, he
was inspired by the colorful patterns of the Palio,
a centuries-old horse race held twice a year in
Siena, Italy, in the medieval town square. There
are elaborate ceremonies before the race, including a long procession with representatives of the
old guilds and members of the various districts,

all wearing brightly colored Renaissance costumes. Two skilled standard-bearers from each district carry the traditional banners of the districts (fig. 526) and toss them gracefully into the air. These banners have an animal emblem in the center set against a brightly colored background.[630] Similar flags fly from buildings in the Piazza del Campo and in the various districts themselves. Girard, who grew up in Florence and had an architectural office there in the early 1930s, had been to the Palio several times, and loved the colors and the excitement.[631]

For the *Palio* series, Girard designed eight different patterns of vertical stripes, adding a ninth textile which combined the other eight designs (fig. 530).[632] Each stripe contains a reverse pattern, the dark and light shapes being mirror images of each other. Girard adapted this feature from the backgrounds of many of the Palio banners. For example, he took the interlocking shapes from the Unicorno banner (fig. 525) and simplified them into an orange and white stripe (in fig. 530, the fifth from the left).

Some of the other textiles are freer adaptations of patterns seen in Siena. For example, the yellow and ivory diagonal lines in Girard's *Palio* 2 resemble the diagonal stripes on the flag of the Tartuca district (fig. 526) and on one of the standard-bearer's leggings.

Presumably, Girard intended these *Palio* textiles as drapery material. Because of the folded pleats that are a normal part of drapery construction, he felt that vertically oriented designs such as these were especially well suited for drapes. For the same reason, he preferred geometric to figurative patterns.[633] On the other hand, he did not approve of large-scale patterns on upholstery material, since, to his mind, they tended to destroy the form of the furniture.

Girard had been designing bold, simple patterns for a number of years, such as his *Mikado* design of 1954 (fig. 524). The *Palio* fabrics, which are even more abstract, suggest analogies with contemporary paintings by Color Field artists of the New York school (fig. 475) because of their hard-edged geometric shapes and incessant repetition. This makes the *Palio* designs, even though they were based on old, traditional forms, look very modern indeed.

CWL

527. *Alexander Girard.* Palio *drapery textile*

528. *Girard.* Palio 2 *drapery textile*

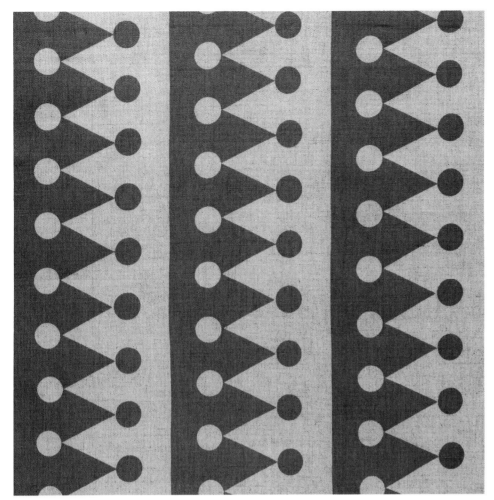

529. *Girard*. Palio 6 *drapery textile*

530. *Girard*. Palio *drapery textile*. 1964

Notes

Modern in the Past Tense

1. E.g., Dorothy Dudley, "Four Post-Moderns," *American Magazine of Art*, 28 (September 1935), 539–47, 572; Joseph A. Barry, "Is Modern Dead?," *House Beautiful*, 96 (May 1954), 152–57, 210.

2. "IL DEPEND DE CELUI QUI PASSE/QUE JE SOIS UNE TOMBE OU UN TRESOR/QUE JE PARLE OU ME TAISE/CECI NE TIENT QU'A TOI/N'ENTRE PAS SANS DESIR . . . /DANS CES MURS VOUES AUX MERVEILLES/J'ACCUEILLE ET GARDE LES OU-VRAGES/DE LA MAIN PRODIGIEUSE DE L'AR-TISTE/EGALE ET RIVALE DE SA PENSEE/L'UNE N'EST RIEN SANS L'AUTRE/CHOSES RARES OU CHOSES BELLES/ICI SAVAMMENT ASSEMBLEES/INTRUISENT L'OEIL A REGARDER/COMME JAMAIS ENCORE VUES/TOUTES CHOSES QUI SONT AU MONDE," quoted in *Revue de l'art ancien et moderne*, 71 (1937), 101.

The Modernist Canon

3. "Drama of Decoration," *Arts and Decoration*, 42 (February 1935), 47–49.

4. *Architecture and Furniture, Aalto* (New York: Museum of Modern Art, 1938), 3.

5. Göran Schildt, *Alvar Aalto: The Decisive Years* (New York: Rizzoli, 1986), 70–78, 216–23.

6. Alvar Aalto, "The Humanizing of Architecture" (1940; reprinted in Göran Schildt, ed., *Alvar Aalto Sketches* [Cambridge, Massachusetts: The MIT Press, 1978]), 77.

7. From Alvar Aalto's introduction to the catalogue of an exhibition at the department store Nordiska Kompaniet, Stockholm, in 1954, reprinted in Museum of Finnish Architecture, *Alvar Aalto Furniture* (Cambridge, Massachusetts: The MIT Press, 1985), 9.

8. Carl E. Christiansson, "Bruno Mathsson: Furniture, Structures, Ideas," *Design Quarterly*, 65 (1965), 11, 13; Erik Zahle, ed., *A Treasury of Scandinavian Design* (New York: Golden Press, 1961), 75.

9. Elias Cornell, "Bruno Mathsson och Tiden," *Arkitektur*, 3 (March 1967), 108. In 1952 the chair was available in black or natural leather, natural jute, and hemp left natural or colored green, white, red, yellow, or tan; see the Bonniers advertisement in *Furniture Forum*, 3 (1952) section, 1, 4.

10. *Form*, 34, no. 4 (1938), 40.

11. Uno Ahrém, "Bruno Mathssons möbler," *Form*, 32, no. 5 (1936), 138–40.

12. For the Risom chair, see Eric Larrabee and Massimo Vignelli, *Knoll Design* (New York: Harry N. Abrams, 1981), 40–41.

13. *Form*, 53, no. 9 (1957), 233.

14. *Form*, 74, no. 8 (1978), 36.

15. Christopher Wilk, *Marcel Breuer: Furniture and Interiors* (New York: Museum of Modern Art, 1981), 126–30.

16. "Isokon Furniture" (London: Isokon Furniture Company, c. 1938).

17. On this service, see Ann Kerr, *Russel Wright Dinnerware* (Paducah, Kentucky: Collectors Books, 1985), 34–44.

18. Rosemarie Haag Bletter, "The World of Tomorrow: The Future with a Past," in *High Styles: Twentieth-Century American Design* (New York: Whitney Museum of American Art in association with Summit Books, 1985), 113: " . . . the work of Jean Arp comes to mind most readily. . . . The unconventional, frequently biomorphic shapes of these pieces . . . create a style of exquisite but willful quirkiness." See also William J. Hennessey, *Russel Wright, American Designer* (Cambridge, Massachusetts: The MIT Press, 1983), 37–38; he also links the dinnerware with Arp and claims that it has "a soft, vaguely organic sexuality that is reassuring rather than ominous or hostile."

19. On occasion Wright did use shapes that were decidedly Biomorphic, as for some of the *Oceana* wooden objects (meant to be used with *American Modern*) and for the windows of the "Focal Foods" display he created at the 1939 World's Fair; see Hennessey, *Russel Wright*, 44–45.

20. László Moholy-Nagy, *Vision in Motion* (Chicago: Paul Theobold, 1969), 67, 73–75, 92.

21. See the designer's comments in "Here Are Fall's Design-Trends," *Crockery and Glass Journal*, 145 (July 1951), 98, 126; also Mary and Russel Wright, *Mary and Russel Wright's Guide to Easier Living* (New York: Simon and Schuster, 1950), 34–36, 164–90.

22. Hennessey, *Russel Wright*, 43.

23. The size of the missing label matches those used in 1947–49, the years in which Evans Products Company still manufactured the chair and Herman Miller Furniture Co. acted as distributor. The black-stained version of the chair was apparently manufactured by Herman Miller until 1954, but it was no longer offered in the firm's March 1955 catalogue, "The Herman Miller Collection."

24. Eliot Noyes, "Charles Eames," *Arts and Architecture*, 63 (September 1946), 36.

25. The earliest published record of the United States Navy commission may be "Artist in Industry," *Fortune*, 30 (October 1944), 243–45, which also contains an evocative description of the circumstances of production.

26. The shockmounts were said to have been joined to the wooden (and, in other versions, metal) parts by use of the Cycleweld process, which used synthetic resin to bond rubber to wood or metal. An early description of the process is given in Noyes, "Charles Eames," 44. Although Eames, Noyes, and certain later writers made much of the designer's use of the Cycleweld process in his early furniture, others have suggested that the process was not perfected for years and that during the first years of production the rubber pieces were glued on in a conventional manner; interview between John and Marilyn Neuhart and Christopher Wilk, September 21, 1987.

27. The original manufacturer, Evans Products Company, made the screen in one size only—68 inches high by 60 inches wide; see the company's 1947 catalogue, "The Collection of Molded Plywood Furniture Designed by Charles Eames"; see also the Herman Miller Furniture Company's 1948 catalogue, "The Herman Miller Collection." By 1950, Herman Miller was offering the screen in two heights—68 or 34 inches—and three widths—60, 80, and 100 inches (6, 8, and 10 sections); see its 1950 catalogue, "The Herman Miller Collection: Furniture Designed by George Nelson, Charles Eames, Isamu Noguchi, Paul Laszlo."

28. Lucius Burckhardt, *The Werkbund: History and Ideology, 1907–1933* (New York: Barron's, 1980); also Joan Campbell, *The German Werkbund: The Politics of Reform in the Applied Arts* (Princeton, New Jersey: Princeton University Press, 1978).

29. For the Larsson chair, see *Form*, 34, no. 1 (1938), 17.

30. The date was assigned by Theodore M. Brown in his authoritative *The Work of G. Rietveld, Architect* (Utrecht: A. W. Bruna & Zoon, 1958). He cites an article on the armchair published in a Danish magazine two years later: *Dansk Kunsthaanvaerk*, 25 (April 1952), 53–68.

31. The identity of the architect of the villa was disclosed by Jacques Nathan himself, as Christophe Zagrodski, of the Musée de la Publicité, Paris, notes in a letter to Frederica T. Harlow, June 9, 1989.

32. Arthur A. Cohen, *Herbert Bayer: The Complete Work* (Cambridge, Massachusetts: The MIT Press, 1984), 233, dates the placard to 1948; however, the signature is accompanied by the date "50," and the biography advertised in the placard was not published until 1950.

33. This placard came from Herbert Bayer's studio and was sold by his widow.

34. Conversation between textile designer Ben Rose and Christa C. Mayer Thurman, April 22, 1987.

35. According to both the publication *Hans Coray—Künstler und Entwerfer* (Zurich: Museum für Gestaltung/Kunstgewerbemuseum, 1986), 19, and the manufacturer (a letter from Blattmann Metallwarenfabrik AG to Christopher Wilk, August 7, 1989), the chair was produced without interruption, beginning in 1939. In 1962 the manufacturer modified its design to include six (rather than the original seven) holes across the width and height of the chair back. However, because the manufacturer occasionally used photographs of the older, seven-hole version in promotional material, post-1962 advertisements and recent exhibition catalogues still sometimes show the earlier version.

36. Like all other examples of the *Landi* chair, this one was made in Switzerland. Then it was exported to Austria, and from there, later, it was sent to the United States. At that point a

label specifying the "country of origin" was affixed to comply with a United States Customs regulation.

37. *Hans Coray—Künstler und Entwerfer*, 19, 36–41.

38. For a survey of his work during World War II, see W. H. Allner, "Jean Carlu," *Graphis*, 3 (1947), 24–29.

39. The chair was probably designed between September 1941 (when Jens Risom and Hans Knoll returned from a cross-country trip to investigate the demand for modern furniture) and mid-1942 (when the first "Hans Knoll Furniture" catalogue was published); letter from Jens Risom to Christopher Wilk, March 6, 1989, and interview between Risom and Wilk, June 5, 1989. Larrabee and Vignelli, *Knoll Design*, 42–43, give contradictory dates for the publication of the catalogue: April 1942 and August 1942.

40. "This First-Rate Medium Priced Modern Furniture Is a Wartime Product," *Architectural Forum*, 75 (June 1943), 2.

41. Letter from Risom to Wilk, March 6, 1989, in which the designer also explains that they were able to obtain webbing that had been "discarded [because it] did not meet, apparently, the strength tests for parachute use." Knoll catalogues of the period include photographs of the furniture in use in airports, USO clubs, and other military installations.

42. Risom ended his association with Knoll in the spring of 1946; interview between Jens Risom and Christopher Wilk, June 5, 1989. The modified version of the chair had been published by the end of 1947; see *Everyday Art Quarterly*, 6 (Winter 1947–48), 7, in which the chair is illustrated because of its plastic-based "webbing woven of Saran thread."

43. Risom believes that the government may have allowed Knoll to use standard woods such as beech, birch, and maple—known in the furniture trade as B/B/M—even during the war, because the furniture used in USO clubs had to be durable; interview between Jens Risom and Kate Carmel, September 15, 1989.

44. E. McKnight Kauffer, *Posters* (New York: Museum of Modern Art, 1937). Also see Mark Haworth-Booth, *E. McKnight Kauffer: A Designer and His Public* (London: Gordon Fraser, 1979), 85–86.

45. Monroe Wheeler, ed., *Britain at War* (New York: Museum of Modern Art, 1941). E. McKnight Kauffer's friend T. S. Eliot was one of the contributors to the catalogue's text.

46. For example, Alexander Calder's *Little Ball with Counterweight* (c. 1930) has an elliptically curved wire with a ball at each end; see Jean Lipman, *Calder's Universe* (1976; Philadelphia: Running Press in cooperation with the Whitney Museum of American Art, New York, 1989), 249. Kauffer undoubtedly saw works by Calder during his trips to Paris in the 1930s; see Haworth-Booth, *E. McKnight Kauffer*, 63.

47. Smithsonian Institution, National Museum of Design, Cooper-Hewitt Museum, New York, acc. no. 1963.39–271, gift of Marion Dorn. For another version of this design, see Haworth-Booth, *E. McKnight Kauffer*, plate 62.

48. Eliot F. Noyes, *Organic Design in Home Furnishings* (New York: Museum of Modern Art, 1941), 26.

49. Ibid., 9.

50. Much of the information presented here comes from interviews with the designer and is documented in *Eva Zeisel: Designer for Industry* (Montreal: Musée des Arts Décoratifs de Montréal, 1984), 32–36.

51. Louis Hellman had consulted Alfred Barr, Jr., on a previous occasion; see Alice Goldfarb Marquis, *Alfred H. Barr Jr., Missionary for the Modern* (Chicago: Contemporary Books, 1989), 194.

52. The design was published in "Textile Studies Assembled by Marianne Strengell Dusenbury," *Arts and Architecture*, 62 (July 1945), 28–29.

53. John and Marilyn Neuhart, and Ray Eames, *Eames Design: The Work of the Office of Charles and Ray Eames* (New York: Harry N. Abrams, 1989), 86–87.

54. *Domus*, 242 (January 1950), 22–25.

55. "International Competition for Low-Cost Furniture Design," *The Museum of Modern Art Bulletin*, 15 (January 1948), 13.

56. Letter from Davis Pratt to David A. Hanks, July 11, 1980; cited in David A. Hanks, *Innovative Furniture in America* (New York: Horizon Press, 1981), 106.

57. All of the winning designs were published in Edgar Kaufmann, jr., *Prize Designs for Modern Furniture from the International Competition for Low-Cost Furniture Design* (New York: Museum of Modern Art, 1950).

58. "The Herman Miller Collection" (1952), 102.

59. George Nelson, *Living Spaces* (New York: Whitney Publications, 1952), 23. Edgar Kaufmann, jr., "Eames and Chests," *Art News*, 49 (May 1950), 38, refers to "a crude construction commonly used for metal storage bins."

60. Letter from Ed Rossbach to Christa C. Mayer Thurman, August 24, 1987.

61. Color can be applied directly to the warp threads already stretched on the loom, but a protective barrier must be held under the warp threads in front of the beater while they are being painted. Only the short section between the beater and the front apron can be colored at one time, and the paint must dry before weaving can begin again. See Else Regensteiner, *The Art of Weaving* (West Chester, Pennsylvania: Schiffer Publishing Company, 1986), 167. In ikat dyeing, the pattern is tie-dyed in the threads before weaving is begun. Certain portions of the yarn (either warp or weft, or warp and weft) are wrapped to resist the dye. See Alfred Bühler, Eberhard Fischer, and Marie Louise Nabholz, *Indian Tie-Dyed Fabrics* (Ahmedabad: B. U. Balsari, 1980), 149.

62. Letter from Rossbach to Thurman, August 24, 1987.

63. Ibid.

64. Knorr shared the prize with German designer Georg Leowald; see Kaufmann, *Prize Designs for . . . Low-Cost Furniture Design*, 16. Much of the information presented here was gathered at interviews between Donald Knorr and Kate Carmel, March 14 and June 15, 1989.

65. Knoll Associates catalogue (1950), n.p.

66. Kaufmann, *Prize Designs for . . . Low-Cost Furniture Design*, 13.

67. Although she had moved her design studio in 1948 to New York, Dorothy Liebes retained a studio in San Francisco until 1952, and *Bon Bon* was probably produced there.

68. "Snapshot: Dorothy Wright Liebes, First Lady of the Loom," *Interiors*, 106 (July 1947), 86–91, 134, 136.

69. Ed Rossbach, "The Glitter and Glamour of Dorothy Liebes," *American Craft*, 42 (December 1982–January 1983), 9–12.

70. Michelle Murphy, "Trends in Woven Materials," *New York Times*, October 3, 1948.

71. Joan Hess Michel, "Dorothy Liebes' Design and Weaving," *American Artist*, 35 (April 1971), 79.

72. Robert J. Clark et al., *Design in America: The Cranbrook Vision 1925–1950* (New York: Harry N. Abrams in association with The Detroit Institute of Arts and The Metropolitan Museum of Art, 1983), 203. Much of the information presented here was gathered at an interview between Robert Sailors and Kate Carmel, June 9, 1989.

73. *Architectural Forum*, 94 (January 1951), 86.

74. Bernard Rudofsky, "Stoffe dattiloscritte di Rudofsky," *Domus*, 242 (January 1950), 23.

75. "Stoffe inventate ma non disegnate," *Domus*, 242 (January 1950), 24.

76. The letter, dated December 21, 1950, was in Bernard Rudofsky's possession. "Mon cher Rudofsky, Vos tissus imprimés avec des caractères d'imprimerie sont ravissants; ils sont amusants parce qu'ils se raccordent aux plus vieilles traditions . . . hindoues et que le modèle en est établi par des dactylos tapant sur des machines à écrire! Il ne reste plus qu'à avoir un pyjama avec cela ou une robe à donner à la première jeune fille que l'on rencontrera sur sa route. Amicalement à vous. LE CORBUSIER." (My dear Rudofsky, Your printed fabrics with typeface are delightful; they are amusing because they recall the oldest . . . Hindu traditions and [to think] the design is created by typists striking typewriters! All that remains is to use it for a pair of pajamas or a dress to give the first girl that you meet on the street. Best regards, LE CORBUSIER.)

77. Information on the dating of this model was kindly supplied by Annet van der Kley-Blekxtoon, Curator, Stichting Nationaal

Glasmuseum Leerdam, Leerdam.

78. Edgar Kaufmann, jr., *What Is Modern Design?* (New York: Museum of Modern Art, 1950), 23–26.

79. *Glass 1959* (Corning, New York: Corning Museum of Glass, 1959), 12–16, passim.

80. See, e.g., *The Modern Spirit—Glass from Finland* (Riihimäki: Suomen Lasimuseo, 1985), nos. 5 and 54. This glass was greenish in tint, just as the French glass of the period inevitably had pigmentation.

81. See Kaj Franck's designs for Iittala, model nos. 3225 and 3239 (the former illustrated in *The Modern Spirit*, no. 8), and also Tapio Wirkkala's designs for the same factory, model nos. 3234, 3235, and 3242. Although Marinot did not resume production after the war, other French craftsmen, such as André Thuret and Jean Sala, continued the art of *malfin*, or bubbled glass.

Streamlined Modern

82. The phenomenon apparently waits to be studied in depth in a scholarly way. There are a few preliminary studies available: e.g., Donald J. Bush, *The Streamlined Decade* (New York: George Braziller, 1975); Martin Greif, *Depression Modern: The Thirties Style in America* (New York: Universe Books, 1975).

83. Henry-Russell Hitchcock and Philip Johnson, *The International Style: Architecture since 1922* (New York: Museum of Modern Art, 1932), 65–66.

84. For a sense of how Streamlining was understood in terms of domestic interiors, see "Straight Lines and Streamline," *Arts and Decoration*, 40 (January 1934), 38ff.

85. Hitchcock and Johnson in *The International Style* criticized the rounded corner of the living room in an Innsbruck apartment house (p. 226) as not being "justified by function" or "necessary to the design." They criticized the rounded base of George Howe and William Lescaze's Philadelphia Savings Fund Society Building (p. 158) because it is "awkward" in relation to the rectangular tower. They criticized the rounded edges of a Japanese electrical laboratory (p. 228) because they "blur the effect of volume."

86. Philip Johnson in *Machine Art* (New York: Museum of Modern Art, 1934), n.p.: "Styling a commercial object gives it more 'eye-appeal' and therefore helps sales. Principles such as 'streamlining' often receive homage out of all proportion to their applicability."

87. Edgar Kaufmann, jr., "Two Decades of Interiors: Design, the Guiding Stars, 1940 and 1960," *Interiors*, 120 (November 1960), 178. In 1939 Alvar Aalto, who by then had traveled in the United States, spoke against the industrial designer and "this brash surface formalism, 'superficial streamlining.'" See Göran Schildt, *Alvar Aalto: The Decisive Years* (New York: Rizzoli, 1986), 180.

88. Edgar Kaufmann, jr., *What Is Modern Design?* (New York: Museum of Modern Art, 1950), 8. See also idem, "Borax, or the Chromium-plated Calf," *Architectural Review*, 104 (August 1948), 88–93.

89. Sheldon and Martha Cheney, *Art and the Machine* (New York and London: Whittlesey House, 1936).

90. László Moholy-Nagy, *Vision in Motion* (Chicago: Paul Theobold, 1969), 34, 52–54.

91. Russel Wright, quoted in Greif, *Depression Modern*, 43.

92. The Airline Chair Company was a fledgling business started by Kem Weber to manufacture the *Airline* chair. The extant correspondence in the designer's files ("*Airline* Chair," correspondence file, Kem Weber Archives, Architectural Drawings Collection, University of California, Santa Barbara) indicates that the company may have been little more than a name placed on the letterhead and in drafts of contracts with potential backers. Letters on company stationery and an unsigned, undated contract labeled "tentative agreement" between Weber and George R. V. Stegner (identified as a "manufacturer of fine fixtures and furniture") are to be found in the Weber Archives.

The example in the Stewart Collection is one of a pair bought directly from Weber by the architect Harwell Hamilton Harris for use in the Birtcher house, Los Angeles (1941–42), and can be seen *in situ* in a contemporary photograph (fig. 83).

93. Letter from Kem Weber to Lawrence Kocher, editor of *Architectural Record*, March 13, 1935. "*Airline* Chair," correspondence file, Kem Weber Archives.

94. Ibid.

95. Among the articles written about the chair were "Wrap It Up and Take It Home," *Retailing (Home Furnishings Edition)*, May 13, 1935, 12; "Airline Chair of Wood by Kem Weber," *Architectural Record*, 77 (May 1935), 311.

96. On June 27, 1935, Kem Weber wrote to a number of stores, companies, and individuals, stating that the *Airline* chair was not yet available but that they would be notified when orders were being accepted. The recipients of these letters included Bullock's, Barker Brothers, Bamberger's, Macy's, Moderne Furniture, and General Electric. Kem Weber received invitations from Grand Rapids Chair, Johnson Furniture (Grand Rapids), and Johnson Chair (Chicago), Baker Furniture, Koehler, Sikes, and Thonet to come and discuss his chair during a trip east scheduled for the summer of 1935. Weber also contacted Mueller Furniture, Kittinger, and Heywood-Wakefield, but none expressed interest.

97. The patent for the digital movement cited on the clock was granted on February 12, 1935.

98. Undated advertising brochure.

99. Bush, *The Streamlined Decade*, 64–67.

100. For a history of the jukebox, see Vincent Lynch and Bill Henkin, *Jukebox: The Golden Age* (Berkeley, California: Lancaster-Miller, 1981), 7–12.

101. The mechanism of the *Penny Phono* was invented by William F. Falkenberg with the help of Dr. Gordon Keith Woodward; see Scott C. Corbett, *An Illustrated Guide to the Recordings of Spike Jones* (Monrovia, California: Scott C. Corbett, 1989), 3; "New Type Phone and Record Introduced," *Coin Machine Journal*, 17 (August 1939), 45; *Presenting Penny Phono* (Hollywood: Cinematone Corporation, 1939).

102. I am indebted to Aileen Gaughan, of Walter Dorwin Teague Associates, for her help in providing this information.

103. Jean Puiforcat, quoted in Bevis Hillier, *Art Deco of the 20s and 30s* (New York: E. P. Dutton, 1968), 115. The golden section can be expressed algebraically as $a/b = b/a + b$ (the smaller is to the greater as the greater is to the sum of the two). The fractions $\frac{5}{8}$ and $\frac{13}{21}$ afford an approximate idea of this ratio.

104. Jean Puiforcat, quoted in Francoise de Bonneville, ed., *Jean Puiforcat* (Paris: Editions du Regard, 1986), 68.

105. Ibid., 54.

106. Jean Puiforcat, quoted in Kathryn B. Hiesinger and George H. Marcus, eds., *Design 1900–1940* (Philadelphia: Philadelphia Museum of Art, 1987), 40.

107. Bonneville, *Puiforcat*, 93.

108. The date of design and the attribution are established by drawings in the company archives; later variants (different in terms of size or monograms) are dated 1942. I am grateful to Ulf Jeppson of GuldsmedsAktieBolaget for his help. In recent times, the design of this object has often been attributed to Count Bernadotte; e.g., Hans Wichmann, *Industrial Design, Unikate und Serienerzeugnisse. Die Neue Sammlung, Ein neuer Museumstyp des 20. Jahrhunderts* (Munich: Prestel Verlag, 1985), 159; and sale catalogue, Christie's, London, April 15, 1987, no. 198.

109. See Claire Selkurt, "New Classicism: Design of the 1920s in Denmark," *Journal of Decorative and Propaganda Arts*, 4 (Spring 1987), 16–29.

110. The use of pewter may have been prompted by the scarcity of silver for luxury products during the war; see J. David Farmer, "Metalwork and Bookbinding," in Robert J. Clark et al., *Design in America: The Cranbrook Vision 1925–1950* (New York: Harry N. Abrams in association with The Detroit Institute of Arts and The Metropolitan Museum of Art, 1983), 166.

111. The drawing (D89.199.1) was formerly owned by Marguerite Kimball, financial secretary at the Cranbrook Academy of Art.

112. Bonneville, *Puiforcat*, 103.

113. See the catalogue of the sale, Sotheby, Parke-Bernet, New York, May 2, 1972, nos. 15–43.

114. See, for example, the *Norris* and *Prince* ceramic pitchers by the Hall China Company, illustrated in Harvey Duke, *Superior Quality: Hall China* (New York: ELO Books, 1977), 82–83. See also the *Fiesta* pitcher by the Homer Laughlin China Company, illustrated in Helen E. Stiles, *Pottery in the United States* (New York: E. P. Dutton, 1941), 78.

115. Melissa Gabardi, *Art Deco Jewellery 1920–1949* (Woodbridge, Suffolk: The Antique Collectors' Club, 1989), 209.

116. The resemblance between the bracelet made in New York and the bracelet made in Paris reminds us of the closeness of the various branches of the Cartier firm, despite their official separation.

Biomorphic Modern

117. It was not possible to consult J. V. Mundy, "Biomorphism" (Ph.D. diss., Courtauld Institute of Art, London, 1987). I am indebted to Gregory Gilbert for bringing the existence of this work to my attention.

118. László Moholy-Nagy discussed a similarly shaped table made at his Chicago school in terms of "a better placing of people around the table. . . ." See Moholy-Nagy, *Vision in Motion* (Chicago: Paul Theobold, 1969), 59. However, Christopher Wilk and W. Scott

Braznell brought to my attention an earlier tradition of such shaped worktables for metal-smiths; see John Culme, *Nineteenth-Century Silver* (London: Hamlyn, 1977), 122; also Alan Crawford, *C. R. Ashbee* (New Haven: Yale University Press, 1985), fig. 36.

119. Barbara Cartlidge, *Twentieth-Century Jewelry* (New York: Harry N. Abrams, 1985), 50, 54.

120. Cf. the very different type of Cubist-derived camouflage used for the "dazzle ships" in World War I, discussed and illustrated in Richard Cork, *Vorticism* (Los Angeles: University of California Press, 1976), vol. 2, 520–24.

121. Marcel Breuer, quoted in James and Katherine Morrow Ford, *Design of Modern Interiors* (New York: Architectural Book Publishing, 1942), 116. See Christopher Wilk, *Marcel Breuer: Furniture and Interiors* (New York: Museum of Modern Art, 1981), 135–59, for the development of such "free form" plywood furniture; also "New Pittsburgh Home Designed by Walter Gropius and Marcel Breuer," *Interiors*, 100 (April 1941), 16–21, for an especially Biomorphic design.

122. Jack Pritchard, *View from a Long Chair* (London: Routledge & Kegan Paul, 1984), passim.

123. Moholy-Nagy, *Vision in Motion*, 59, 67, 73, 84, 90, passim.

124. For example, see Robert Goldwater in association with René d'Harnoncourt, *Modern Art in Your Life* (New York: Museum of Modern Art, 1949), 27; Robert J. Clark et al., *Design in America: The Cranbrook Vision 1925–1950* (New York: Harry N. Abrams in association with The Detroit Institute of Arts and The Metropolitan Museum of Art, 1983), 128, 131; John and Marilyn Neuhart, and Ray Eames, *Eames Design: The Work of the Office of Charles and Ray Eames* (New York: Harry N. Abrams, 1989), 26, 28, 39–41, 45, 96.

125. Willy Rotzler, "Woher des Wegs? Wohin der weg?," *Form* (Cologne), 13 (1961), 9.

126. Although they did not marry until 1950, E. McKnight Kauffer and Marion Dorn lived together from 1924 on; see Mark Haworth-Booth, *E. McKnight Kauffer: A Designer and His Public* (London: Gordon Fraser, 1979), 37, 93. Kauffer and Dorn exhibited their rugs together in 1929; see "New Designs for Wilton Rugs by E. McK. Kauffer and Marion V. Dorn," *Creative Art*, 4 (January 1929), 35–39.

127. E. McKnight Kauffer, quoted in "New Designs for Wilton Rugs," 37.

128. Ibid., 38.

129. For the production and dating of these two vases, see *Alvar and Aino Aalto as Glass Designers* (Iittala: Iittalan Lasimuseo, 1988), nos. 39, 46.

130. I found especially helpful the information presented in Göran Schildt, *Alvar Aalto: The Decisive Years* (New York: Rizzoli, 1986), 136–39.

131. Ibid., 107–14.

132. Letter from Satu Grönstrand of Iittala Lasitehdas to David A. Hanks & Associates, August 22, 1989.

133. Interviews between Benjamin Baldwin and Alice Zrebiec, June 12, 1989, and between William Machado and Alice Zrebiec, June 12, 1989.

134. "Fabrics," *California Arts and Architecture*, 66 (October 1949), 25.

135. Interviews between Baldwin and Zrebiec and Machado and Zrebiec, June 12, 1989.

136. Toni Lesser Wolf, "Goldsmith, Silversmith, Art Smith," *Metalsmith*, 7 (Fall 1987), 22.

137. Art Smith, quoted in *Art Smith: Jewelry* (New York: Museum of Contemporary Crafts, 1969), n.p.

138. From 1946 to 1958, Margaret de Patta and her husband, Eugene Bielawski, conducted a limited production operation. De Patta created about sixty prototypes in silver from which rubber molds were made; the multiples were then cast. Except for a period of about one year only, when she employed an assistant, de Patta did all the casting and hand finishing, while Bielawski supervised every step of the production. When this production work was terminated, many of the pieces were preserved but in an unassembled state.

139. Robert Cardinale and Hazel Bray, "Margaret de Patta: Structure, Concepts and Design Sources," *Metalsmith*, 3 (Spring 1983), 12.

140. Margaret de Patta, quoting László Moholy-Nagy, in Yoshiko Uchida, *The Jewelry of Margaret de Patta: A Retrospective Exhibition* (Oakland, California: Oakland Museum, 1976), 15.

141. Erik Lassen, *Henning Koppel: En Mindeudstilling (A Commemorative Exhibition)* (Copenhagen: Kunstindustrimuseet, 1982), 13.

142. The technique used was basse-taille (low cut), in which the shape to be enameled is stamped into the cast silver form, at varying levels. Transparent enamel is then applied to the entire surface. The deeper areas create darker colors, as more enamel is used to fill these depressions.

143. The first model (no. 974), designed in 1947, is cited in the chronology of Henning Koppel's works in *Henning Koppel*, 19. The third (no. 992) and fourth (no. 1052) were designed in 1952 and 1956, respectively.

144. "For Your Information," *Interiors*, 125 (June 1966), 8.

145. For an informative account of the handworking procedure employed in a similar pitcher by Henning Koppel, see Arne Karlsen and Anker Tiedemann, *Made in Denmark* (Copenhagen: Jul. Gjellerup, 1960), 39–43.

146. The information presented here is documented in *Eva Zeisel: Designer for Industry* (Montreal: Musée des Arts Décoratifs de Montréal, 1984), 36–40.

147. Although there is some doubt about the date of Isamu Noguchi's chess table (see note 149), it was certainly not his first furniture design. It followed, both chronologically and stylistically, tables commissioned by A. Conger Goodyear (1939) and Philip Goodwin (c. 1941) and a table made first as an experimental plaster model (1940) and then later manufactured by the Herman Miller Furniture Co. (1947).

148. Isamu Noguchi, *A Sculptor's World* (New York: Harper and Row, 1968), 26.

149. A letter of October 21, 1986, from the artist's office to Christopher Wilk states that Isamu Noguchi recalls making the table around 1947; however, it was during January 1945 that the Julien Levy Gallery in New York held an exhibition entitled "Imagery of Chess" and it may have been for this occasion that Noguchi designed the table. See Julien Levy, *Memoir of an Art Gallery* (New York: G. P. Putnam's Sons, 1977), 310.

150. The letter referred to in note 149 states that the table was never manufactured. Yet it does appear in a 1950 catalogue of the Herman Miller Furniture Co., "The Herman Miller Collection, Furniture Designed by George Nelson, Charles Eames, Isamu Noguchi, Paul Laszlo," 50–51.

151. Giovanni Brino, *Carlo Mollino* (Milan: Idea Books, 1985), 44.

152. The provenance is established in a letter from Galleria Colombari Di Paola e Rossella Colombari, Milan, to David A. Hanks & Associates, June 18, 1990. For the project, see Brino, *Carlo Mollino*, 134–35. In addition to *Arabesco* tables in other interiors, Mollino designed a version to be mass-produced for the American market: "Across the Seas Collaboration for the New Singer Collection," *Interiors*, 111 (December 1951), 121–22, 125; also Brino, *Carlo Mollino*, 132–33.

153. Brino, *Carlo Mollino*, 124–27; "Casa verso la collina," *Domus*, 264–65 (December 1951), 16–22; Olga Gueft, "The Baroque Spirit in a Modern House," *Interiors*, 112 (December 1952), 88–91.

154. Peggy Guggenheim, ed., *Art of This Century* (New York: Art of This Century, 1942), 129, includes one painting by Leonor Fini, *The Shepherdesses of the Sphinxes*.

155. The material quoted here and elsewhere in this essay is from Helen Henley, "Improved Plastic Table Accessories Bid for Higher Social Recognition," *Christian Science Monitor*, October 21, 1947, 4.

156. Unless otherwise noted, all factual information in this entry is derived from interviews between Eva Zeisel and Christopher Wilk, December 8, 1987, and February 20, 1989.

157. Argentine designers Antonio Bonet, Juan Kurchan, and Jorge Ferrari-Hardoy created a nonfolding, cast-iron version of a camp chair around 1938. It was apparently first sold in the United States by the New York retailer Artek-Pascoe Inc. in its 1941 catalogue and by 1948 was distributed by Knoll Associates. Although quite different from Zeisel's chair, it nonetheless bears comparison. The various uses of Zeisel's chair were suggested by its availability in dining, lounge, or side-chair versions; see "Chair by Eva Zeisel Placed on Display," *New York Herald Tribune*, January 6, 1950.

158. Eva Zeisel worked on the chair's development with Hudson Fixtures, a metal workshop in New York, which manufactured a small quantity of chairs. These were sold through Richards Morgenthau of New York, a firm that also sold Zeisel's ceramic designs. Zeisel applied for a patent in 1949 and was granted one (2.574.367) in 1951.

159. The designation *Surrey* was given by Warner & Sons, which named all its jacquard-woven curtain fabrics after English counties and its lightweight dobby-woven fabrics after English villages.

160. Perhaps the best discussion of the involvement of Warner & Sons and Marianne Straub in this enterprise is given in Mary Schoeser, *Marianne Straub* (London: The Design Council, 1984), 84–86. See also Mary Banham and Bevis Hillier, eds., *A Tonic to the Nation, The Festival of Britain 1951* (London: Thames and Hudson, 1976), 60–61.

161. For example, articles promoting the same idea had appeared two years earlier: "DESIGN . . . 100,000,000 B.C.," *American Fabrics*, 2 (Spring 1947), 129; "Microcosmos," ibid., 4 (Fall 1947), 114–15.

162. Schoeser, *Marianne Straub*, 85–86. Her designs for woven textiles were nonrepresentational and, instead, explored inventive

combinations of materials, colors, and structure.

163. This model first appeared in two Iittala catalogues of 1952: "Taidelasi uutuudet 15.2.1952" (Iittala Museum Archives MK 13), n.p.; "Taidelasi, Konstglas, Art Glass 1952 Karhula-Iittala" (Iittala Museum Archives MK 15), 9. It was still listed in the 1959 catalogue "Karhula-Iittala 1.1.59" (Iittala Museum Archives PK 10), 3, but did not appear in the company's 1960 catalogue (Iittala Museum Archives PK 12).

164. Timo Sarpaneva, quoted in Kathryn B. Hiesinger and George H. Marcus, eds., *Design since 1945* (Philadelphia: Philadelphia Museum of Art, 1983), 98.

165. The vase appeared, perhaps for the first time, in a Kosta advertisement in *Form*, 49, no. 6 (1953), 197* (fig. 157); also *Form*, 49, no. 10 (1953), 274*. According to a letter from Maria Sjögren of Kosta Boda to Martin Eidelberg, September 27, 1989, both vases were in production for about ten years.

166. For example, see Göran Schildt, "Nutida Italienskt Konsthantverk," *Form*, 49, nos. 3–4 (1953), 62–66.

Modern Historicism

167. Edgar Kaufmann, jr., *What Is Modern Design?* (New York: Museum of Modern Art, 1950), 7.

168. See Wilhelm Lotz, "Ewige Formen—Neue Formen," *Die Form*, 6 (May 15, 1931), 161–66; W. Riezler, "Ewig—Zeitlos," ibid., 167–76; W. von Wersin, "Nochmals 'Ewige Formen,'" ibid. (July 15, 1931), 313–14.

169. Kaufmann, *What Is Modern Design?*, 7–8.

170. Henrik Sten Møller, *Tema Med Variationer, Hans J. Wegner's Møller* (Tønder: Sønderjyllands Kunstmuseum, 1979), 34–37. Letter from Hans Wegner to R. Craig Miller, June 21, 1988.

171. See Charles D. Gandy and Susan Zimmermann-Stidham, *Contemporary Classics: Furniture of the Masters* (New York: McGraw-Hill, 1981), 113.

172. E.g., "Rorstrand Sponsors Tableware Research," *Crockery and Glass Journal*, 152 (March 2, 1953), 48–49. For the Swedish archaeological expedition, see Nils Palmgren, Walter Steger, and Nils Sundius, *Sung Sherds* (Stockholm: Alqvist & Wiksell, 1963).

173. See Glenn Nelson, "Stalhane of Sweden," *Craft Horizons*, 22 (March–April 1962), 11–16.

174. Isamu Noguchi, *A Sculptor's World* (New York: Harper and Row, 1968), 27.

175. Interview with Isamu Noguchi in Eric Larrabee and Massimo Vignelli, *Knoll Design* (New York: Harry N. Abrams, 1981), 46. That the first lamp was aluminum was something Noguchi mentioned many times over the years; however, he failed to note its size and, apparently, photographs of it do not survive.

176. The model *H* shade was originally hung from the ceiling, but in 1962 Isamu Noguchi designed a base for it and turned the shade upside down so that it would fit on the base.

177. The story is recounted in an article that must have come from the artist or a press release: "Shapes of Light, Noguchi's New Akari Sculptures," *Interiors*, 128 (January 1969), 12. A description of the origins of Isamu Noguchi's paper lanterns written only a few years after they were conceived is given in Isamu Noguchi, "Japanese Akari Lamps," *Craft Horizons*, 14 (September–October 1954), 16–18.

178. Noguchi, "Japanese Akari Lamps," 18.

179. Isamu Noguchi, "Akari—Isamu Noguchi," *Arts and Architecture*, 72 (May 1955), 14, 31.

180. In those lamps designed after 1954, Isamu Noguchi departed from one of the main conventions of the Gifu lanterns. He eliminated the wooden rims *(wa)* used at the top and bottom edges and replaced them, in the case of the hanging lamps, with an internal, thin metal frame and, in the case of the standing lamps, with a set of flanges that affix to the top and bottom of the supporting rod. These elements prevent the lamps from collapsing, a feat that the thin bamboo framework alone could not achieve.

181. See "Shapes of Light," 12.

182. Information regarding these two models and their dates of production was kindly provided by Mirja-Kaisa Hipeli of the Arabia pottery in a letter to Martin Eidelberg, September 12, 1989. A vase in the *Branch* pattern (save that the leaves curve in the opposite direction), designed in 1942, is in the Museum of Applied Arts, Helsinki; see *Form Function Finland* (1988), 24. A bowl with the *Flower* design is illustrated in "Keramiikka," *Ornamo*, 13 (1949), 53.

183. See "Ceramiche," *Domus*, 17 (July 1939), 86; Mirja-Kaisa Hipeli, *Friedl Kjellberg* (Helsinki: Arabia Museum, 1989), figs. 7–21.

184. Soame Jenyns, *Later Chinese Porcelain: The Ch'ing Dynasty (1644–1912)* (London: Faber & Faber, 1951), 73, plate CIV, no. 1; William B. Honey, *The Ceramic Art of China and Other Countries of the Far East* (London: Faber & Faber, 1945), 156.

185. See, e.g., Garth Clark, "Leach in America: The 1950's," *Ceramic Arts*, 2 (Spring 1984), n.p.

186. The same ideas, in the same order, and thus seemingly from a press release, appear, e.g., in Arne Karlsen and Anker Tiedemann, *Made in Denmark* (Copenhagen: Jul. Gjellerup, 1960), 136; also in Erik Zahle, ed., *A Treasury of Scandinavian Design* (New York: Golden Press, 1961), 227. Ironically, in a photograph of her studio, the artist can be seen using this teapot in conjunction with handled cups (from the *Gemina* service); see Kataruna Dunér, "Två stengodsklassiker," *Form*, 61, no. 3 (1965), 165.

187. Gertrud Vasegaard used this combination twenty years earlier for pitchers and bowls whose forms were Western. See Erik Lassen, *En Københavnsk porcelaensfabriks historie* (Copenhagen: Nyt Nordisk Forlag, 1978), figs. 104, 105.

188. In addition to being singled out by the authors cited in note 186, it was selected by Finn Juhl for the 1968 exhibition held at the Victoria and Albert Museum "Two Centuries of Danish Design" (see Jennifer Hawkins Opie, *Scandinavia: Ceramics and Glass in the Twentieth Century* [London: Victoria and Albert Museum, 1989], 43); also see *Danskt 50. Tal* (Stockholm: Nationalmuseum, 1981), 29; David R. McFadden, ed., *Scandinavian Modern Design: 1880–1980* (New York: Harry N. Abrams, 1982), 43, 168; Kathryn B. Hiesinger and George H. Marcus, eds., *Design since 1945* (Philadelphia: Philadelphia Museum of Art, 1983), 114.

189. Although the company's promotional material claims that the object was designed in 1961, it was already available commercially by 1958. E.g., see "Rassegna domus," *Domus*, 343 (June 1958), n.p.

190. The ice bucket was initially made in two sizes; the 19 ½-inch-high model was discontinued in 1974. See "Jens Quistgaard" (Dansk International Designs, Ltd., c. 1982), 5.

191. Ibid., 7.

192. Jens Quistgaard, quoted in ibid., 6.

193. Ada Polak, *Modern Glass* (London: Faber & Faber, 1962), 54.

194. For the former, see Atillia Dorigato, *Ercole Barovier 1899–1974: Vetraio muranese* (Venice: Marsilio Editore, 1989), 38–41. For Venini, see, e.g., Rosa Barovier Mentasi et al., *Mille anni di arte del vetro a Venezia* (Venice: Albrizzi Editore, 1982), 310, no. 651.

195. Dorigato, *Ercole Barovier*, 77, no. 165. Interestingly, it was exhibited by the artist in 1951, the year that Venini introduced its *pezzato* wares.

196. Ibid., 101–4.

197. Ibid., 105.

198. Meyric C. Rogers, *Italy at Work: Her Renaissance in Design Today* (Rome: Compagnia Nazionale Artigiana, 1950), 34, illustrated; see also *Domus* 252–53 (November–December 1950), 58.

199. For a good summary of the technical aspects, see Harold Newman, *An Illustrated Dictionary of Glass* (London: Thames and Hudson, 1977), 330–31.

200. August Warnecke, *Kultur in Glas und Porzellan* (Hamburg: August Warnecke, 1965), 17, 34, 66–67, 72. Also, Paolo Venini's introduction in 1961 of the *Opalini* or *Cinesi* series of monochromatic vases with Orientalizing shapes can be seen as an attempt to achieve a conservative form of Modernism.

201. The date for the design of this chair is given as 1955 by Nathan H. Shapira, who had the help of Gio Ponti's daughters and the archives of Ponti's firm in preparing his chronology; Shapira, "The Expression of Gio Ponti," *Design Quarterly*, 69–70 (1967), 29. Other dates in the literature include: 1956, in Penny Sparke, *Design in Italy* (New York: Abbeville, 1988), 96; 1957, in Hiesinger and Marcus, *Design since 1945*, 133. The last is actually the date of production.

202. It was first published in "'Proposta per la casa' alla XI Triennale," *Domus*, 337 (December 1957), 33, 35; see also Pier Carlo Santini, *Gli Anni del design italiano: Ritratto di Cesare Cassina/The Years of Italian Design: A Portrait of Cesare Cassina* (Milan: Electa, 1981), 114. The chair was still in production in 1978; see Karl Mang, *History of Modern Furniture* (New York: Harry N. Abrams, 1978), 43.

203. "Sedie di Chiavari," *Domus*, 242 (January 1950), 46. See also "Sezione del mobile," *Domus*, 221 (July 1947), 60; "Dalla Mostra-Mercato di Firenze," *Domus*, 228 (September 1948), 30. For a history of the Chiavari chair, see Mang, *History of Modern Furniture*, 42–43.

204. See the Cassina advertisement in *Domus*, 259 (June 1951), n.p.

205. Gio Ponti, "Senza aggettivi," *Domus*, 268 (March 1952), 1, as translated in Centrokappa, *Il Design italiano degli anni '50* (Milan: IGIS, 1981), 296. This chair was first illustrated in *Domus*, 264–65 (December

1951), cover, 15. It was put into production in 1952; see *Domus*, 389 (February 1963), d/1030.

206. The name *Superleggera* was not introduced until 1957 with model 699. However, later authors have extended the name back to model 646; see, e.g., *Gio Ponti, Arte Applicata* (Milan: Centro Internazionale di Brera, 1987), no. 132.

207. Gio Ponti, quoted in the Cassina advertisement, *Domus*, 350 (January 1959), n.p.

208. See "'Proposta per la casa' alla XI Triennale," 33, 35; "La sedia 'superleggera' di Gio Ponti," *Domus*, 352 (March 1959), 44–45.

209. See the company's sales brochure "Figli di Amadeo Cassina 1967," n.p.

210. Gio Ponti frequently used these chairs in both his commercial and his domestic interiors. He also chose them for his own apartment. See "Una casa a pareti apribili," *Domus*, 334 (September 1957), 24–27.

211. See the Knoll advertisement in *Interiors*, 107 (December 1947), 13.

212. Letter from Marco Albini to Christine W. Laidlaw, June 9, 1989. Occasionally the design and production dates have been confused in recent literature. According to Vittorio Bonacina, Franco Albini later modified the design; see "La Produzione di Vittorio Bonacina," *Il Mobile italiano*, April 1958, before p. 10. The original chair is illustrated in *Domus*, 262 (October 1951), 2, and ibid., 276 (December 1952), 36. Albini's modification may have included the horizontal, interwoven strips at the top, which were first illustrated in ibid., 295 (June 1954), 50.

213. When the chair was first introduced, it was attributed to Franco Albini alone; see, e.g., *Domus*, 295 (June 1954), 50; also Franca Helg, ed., *Franco Albini, 1930–1970* (New York: Rizzoli, 1981), 144. Later, the name of Albini's partner, Franca Helg, was also included; see, e.g., Sparke, *Design in Italy*, 102. However, it would seem that Helg had no part in this design; letter from Marco Albini to Laidlaw, June 9, 1989. Helg did design several pieces of furniture for Vittorio Bonacina in 1959, including a table to match the *Margherita* chair.

214. Wicker furniture was popular in Italy; pieces were illustrated in *Domus*, 226 (January 1948), 34–35; ibid., 228 (September 1948), 30.

215. See "La produzione di Vittorio Bonacina," before p. 10.

216. Ibid.; letter from Albini to Laidlaw, June 9, 1989.

217. See the interior by Constantino Corsini and Giuliana Grossi, illustrated in *Domus*, 343 (June 1958), 38; also one by Sergio Mazza, illustrated in "Soggiorno notte e servisi in un nuovo appartamento," *Il Libro dell'arredamento*, 5 (1962), 1–7. Franco Albini and Franca Helg also used the chair in their interiors; see *Domus*, 348 (November 1958), 18–19.

218. Hans Wegner never named his chairs. As far as he knows, it was Finn Juhl who first used the name *Peacock*—in a lecture on furniture at the Museum of Arts and Crafts in Copenhagen; letter from Hans J. Wegner to Christine W. Laidlaw, September 6, 1989. The name was in general use by 1965; see Johan Møller Nielsen, *Wegner, en dansk møbelkunstner* (Copenhagen: Gyldendal, 1965), 101.

219. Hans Wegner, quoted in Hiesinger and Marcus, *Design since 1945*, 117.

220. Letter from Wegner to Laidlaw, September 6, 1989. Another variant of the Windsor chair was designed by Gunnar Eklöf for Nässjö Stolfabrik. Its back angle changes halfway up and cants backward, as if it were a Windsor version of Gio Ponti's *Leggera* chair; see *Form*, 48, no. 5 (1952), 23.

221. A slightly later armchair with a low, rounded back by Sonna Rosén for Nässjö Stolfabrik was compared to a peacock's tail in 1951. It was later imported into the United States as the *Sun Fan* chair; see *Form*, 47, no. 7 (1951), 166; *Interiors*, 116 (December 1956), 169.

222. Letter from Wegner to Laidlaw, September 6, 1989.

223. The cotton batting replaces the original but disintegrated foam-rubber pad that was removed during conservation in 1985.

224. "George Nelson 'Pretzel-Chair' ICF," *Domus*, 63 (March 1986), 61.

225. John Pile's authorship of the chair's design was first revealed in print in "George Nelson 'Pretzel-Chair' ICF," 61. During the 1950s it was far less common than today to credit the work of firm designers who were not partners.

226. In 1958 Edward J. Wormley replaced the original leather upholstery with a handwoven upholstery fabric designed by Henning Watterston.

227. According to the designer, the chair was one of a pair installed in the Dunbar Furniture Company's Los Angeles showroom; conversation between Edward J. Wormley and David A. Hanks, October 2, 1988. Although production began in 1947, the model was not included in a Dunbar catalogue until 1954; it was later included in "The Dunbar Book of Contemporary Furniture" (1956), 69.

228. Letter from Edward J. Wormley to Richard Riemerschmid, February 27, 1950. The 1950–52 correspondence between Wormley and Riemerschmid was published in Winfried Nerdinger, *Richard Riemerschmid, vom Jugendstil zum Werkbund, Werke und Dokumente* (Munich: Prestel Verlag, 1982), 532–33.

229. Kaufmann, *What Is Modern Design?*, 12.

230. Undated letter to David A. Hanks & Associates from Edward J. Wormley at the time Le Musée des Arts Décoratifs de Montréal acquired this chair in 1982. According to Wormley, he gave Richard Riemerschmid's original sketches and letter to the Museum of Modern Art, New York, but they cannot be located at present. The letter was published in Nerdinger, *Richard Riemerschmidt*, 532–33.

231. Telephone conversation between Wormley and Hanks, October 2, 1988.

232. See the illustrations of Wormley interiors with Tiffany lamps in Robert Koch, *Louis C. Tiffany, Rebel in Glass* (New York: Crown Publishers, 1964), 216–17.

233. The necklace probably dates not much before 1940 because the workmanship is far better than the examples from William Spratling's atelier of the 1930s, which tended to be rather crudely executed.

234. Jack Lenor Larsen, quoted in *Jack Lenor Larsen: 30 ans de création textile* (Paris: Musée des Arts Décoratifs, 1981), n.p.

235. Much of the information presented in this commentary comes from a series of telephone conversations between Coral Stephens and Kate Carmel in the spring of 1990.

236. *Jack Lenor Larsen*, n.p.

237. The circumstances of the commission and information concerning the development of the design were related in an interview between Ray Komai and Alice Zrebiec, August 31, 1989.

238. These materials and Peruvian linen are mentioned in William J. Hennessey, *Modern Furnishings for the Home* (New York: Reinhold Publishing, 1952), 272, and the information has been confirmed by the designer. Fiberglass is not cited.

Postwar Modernism

239. See *Compasso d'Oro 1954–1984* (Milan: Electa, 1985). The history of the Milan Triennales remains to be written, though some aspects are covered in Emilio Ambasz, ed., *Italy: The New Domestic Landscape* (New York: Museum of Modern Art in collaboration with Centro Di, Florence, 1972), 302–40.

240. *The Lunning Prize* (Stockholm: Nationalmuseum, 1986).

241. Eva Zeisel, "Registering a New Trend," *Everyday Art Quarterly*, 2 (Fall 1946), 1–2.

242. Henning Koppel, quoted in Arne Karlsen and Anker Tiedemann, *Made in Denmark* (Copenhagen: Jul. Gjellerup, 1960), 38–39.

243. Although the name *Kanttarelli* is consistently used, it does not figure in the Iittala official records, where only model numbers are used. That this was the name Tapio Wirkkala chose is confirmed by inscriptions on his three drawings of the vase now in the Iittala Museum Archives. One inscription, in the designer's own handwriting, says, *Sveitsilainen Sieni* (Swiss Mushroom), the other two, of uncertain authorship, say *Kanttarelli*.

244. The date of design is confirmed by the three drawings of 1947 in the Iittala Museum Archives, all of which seem to be preparatory studies for this vase, despite the fact that one was ex post facto labeled "Kanttarelli 1."

245. The model is first listed in an Iittala catalogue of 1948 "Koristehiottu-Ta Taidelasikokoelma" (Iittala Museum Archives MK 3), 4; also in another 1948 catalogue (Iittala Museum Archives MK 4), n.p. (last page). It was still listed in the 1960 catalogue "Karhula-Iittala 1.10.1960" (Iittala Museum Archives PK 12), 37. The company apparently issued no 1961 catalogue, and the model is not listed in the catalogue of the following year, "Karhula-Iittala 1.9.1962" (Iittala Museum Archives PK 14).

246. These differences in price are recorded in the catalogue "Karhula-Iittala 1954" (Iittala Museum Archives PK 3). The limited-edition vase, no. 3800, cost 16,000 markka, while the second version, no. 3280, cost only 3,400 markka.

247. Georg Jensen Inc. in New York was still selling Tapio Wirkkala's platters in 1954; see *Craft Horizons*, 14 (March–April 1954), 7.

248. For an informative contemporary account of the platters, see Annikki Toikka-Karnoven, "Plywood Sculpture: Tapio Wirkkala Uncovers a New Decorative Medium," *Craft Horizons*, 12 (September–October 1952), 10–13; also letter from Sami Wirkkala, the designer's son, to Christine W. Laidlaw, November 17, 1989. Martti Lindqvist also helped Wirkkala and his wife install the Finnish exhibition at the Milan IX Triennale in 1951; see *Tapio Wirkkala* (Helsinki: Finnish Society of Crafts and Design, 1981), 115–16.

249. *Tapio Wirkkala*, 18, 22–24. Some of the plywood pieces were also compared to a dragonfly's wing in contemporary reports; see, e.g., Lisa Licitra Ponti, "Le Invenzioni di Tapio Wirkkala," *Domus*, 266 (January 1952), 44.

250. "The Most Beautiful Object of 1951," *House Beautiful*, 94 (January 1952), 66–67. Also see Lisa Licitra Ponti, "Le Forme di Tapio Wirkkala," *Domus*, 256 (March 1951), 38–40; Edgar Kaufmann, jr., "The Wonderworks of Tapio Wirkkala," *Interiors*, 111 (November 1951), 94–99; Ponti, "Le Invenzioni di Tapio Wirkkala," 44–45; Ferdinand Aars, "To Finske Kunsthandverkere," *Bonytt*, 12 (April 1952), 64–65; *Tapio Wirkkala*, 23, 26, 121.

251. For Tapio Wirkkala's sculptures, see "Forme in legno di Tapio Wirkkala," *Domus*, 284 (February 1953), 41–44; "Fantasia Finlandia," *Interiors*, 113 (August 1953), 56–61; *Tapio Wirkkala*, 19, fig. 50.

252. Letter from Sami Wirkkala to Christine W. Laidlaw, January 1, 1990.

253. Annikki Toikka-Karnoven, "Design in Metal by Three Scandinavians," *Craft Horizons*, 15 (March–April 1955), 10–11.

254. Ibid.; "Finlandia, forme nuove per la Triennale," *Domus*, 298 (September 1954), 40–43; "La Finlandia alla Triennale," *Domus*, 300 (November 1954), 18–19. Not all of Tapio Wirkkala's vases were floral forms. One resembles Constantin Brancusi's early sculptures of birds; see Toikka-Karnoven, "Design in Metal," 11.

255. *Rosenthal, Hundert Jahre Porzellan* (Hanover: Kestner Museum, 1982), 96–99.

256. Brynner had originally used a synthetic spinel; illustrated in Irena Brynner, *Jewelry as an Art Form* (New York: Van Nostrand Reinhold, 1979), 15. Later she replaced it with the present stone.

257. Albert E. Elsen, *Modern European Sculpture 1918–1945: Unknown Beings and Other Realities* (New York: George Braziller in association with the Albright-Knox Art Gallery, 1979), 78.

258. Ibid.

259. Somewhat more conventional, silver-plated flatware was designed by Arne Jacobsen for the hotel snack bar; illustrated in *Studio Yearbook* (1961–62), 93.

260. The desk lamp and wall lamps can be seen in situ in "Arne Jacobsen, Immeuble de la S.A.S. à Copenhagen," *L'Architecture d'aujourd'hui*, 31 (March 1960), 61, 63; the floor-lamp version is illustrated in Tobias Faber, *Arne Jacobsen* (New York: Frederick A. Praeger, 1964), 156. All versions—for desk, wall, and floor—were subsequently put into general production by Louis Poulsen & Co.

261. It was still being described as in production in 1957; e.g., "Una Casa a pareti apribili," *Domus*, 334 (September 1957), 35. Argenteria Krupp was bought out by Sambonet of Milan, and precise production records are not obtainable at present.

262. Fraser's was the San Francisco store that imported and distributed this flatware in the United States.

263. Ada Louise Huxtable, "Stainless Comes to Dinner," *Industrial Design*, 1 (August 1954), 34.

264. Ibid., 32.

265. The tray is a replacement made by the designer especially for this set.

266. For an excellent account of Gio Ponti's viewpoint, see Sparke, *Design in Italy*, 78.

267. Bevis Hillier, *The Style of the Century 1900–1980* (New York: E. P. Dutton, 1983), 154.

268. Bruno Munari, quoted in Enrico Marelli, *Gli Argenti, Lino Sabattini* (Bregnano: Sabattini Argenteria, 1982), 3.

269. Letter from Guido A. Niest of Sabattini Argenteria to Toni L. Wolf, February 21, 1989.

270. Information regarding the model numbers, dates of design and production, and attributions has kindly been provided by Giuliana Tucci, Venini S.p.A. There are disparities between the company's records and documentation recorded elsewhere, and in certain instances we have relied on these other sources.

271. Leo Lionni, "Una Visita a Morandi," *Domus*, 319 (June 1956), 39–42.

272. On these decanters, see "Murano," *Domus*, 252–53 (November–December 1950), 58–59.

273. Tiny copper filings are traditionally used to make aventurine glass. The fact that larger pieces are included in Toni Zuccheri's bottle reflects the postwar interest in coarser textures; however, their expressive possibilities are restrained here by the smooth outer casing of clear glass. In fact, the Venini firm did not develop the idea further.

274. Massimo Vignelli's hanging lamps for Venini were being retailed in New York by mid-1955; see the Venini-Altamira advertisement in *Interiors*, 115 (August 1955), 119; also "Glass in Strict or Fanciful Form," ibid., 115 (September 1955), 142. Vignelli lamps with *fascia* decoration like those in the Stewart Collection are illustrated in "Venini vasi, Venini lampade," *Domus*, 314 (January 1956), 46.

275. Much of the information presented in this commentary comes from an interview between Massimo Vignelli and Martin Eidelberg, January 10, 1990.

276. See "Italia a New York," *Domus*, 298 (September 1954), 3–10.

277. For acknowledgment of Massimo Vignelli's participation, see "Venini vasi, Venini lampade," 45–48; also "Notizario domus," *Domus*, 318 (May 1956), n.p. For an attribution of the hanging fixtures to Paolo Venini alone see *Glass 1959* (Corning, New York: Corning Museum of Glass, 1959), 229–30. Also see *Venini Glass* (Washington, D.C.: Venini International, S.R.L., and Smithsonian Institution Traveling Exhibition Service, 1981), 15, where a different chronology is given.

278. Letter from Valeria Fantoni Borsani, the designer's daughter, to Christine W. Laidlaw, September 12, 1989.

279. See "Una Nuova poltrona," *Domus*, 318 (May 1956), 33–34 and the Tecno advertisement in the same issue, n.p.

280. Penny Sparke, *Design in Italy* (New York: Abbeville, 1988), 95.

281. Ibid., 92.

282. The first change was made before September 1959; see "Il Nuovo negozio 'Tecno' a Milano," *Domus*, 358 (September 1959), 41. The date of the second change is given in a letter from Borsani to Laidlaw, September 12, 1989. For an illustration of the later model, see Sparke, *Design in Italy*, 100.

283. *Jean Prouvé, Serge Mouille: Two Master Metalworkers* (New York and Paris: Antony de Lorenzo and Alan Christine Counourd, 1985), 65, 68.

284. It has been claimed that Timo Sarpaneva initiated his experiments in March 1954;

see *Form Finland (Suomalainen Muoto)* (Helsinki: Museum of Applied Arts, 1986), no. 45. However, the vase was listed in the Iittala 1954 catalogue (Iittala Museum Archives PK 3), and since it was presented at the Milan X Triennale that year as well, it seems likely that it was designed in 1953, as is also proposed in *The Modern Spirit—Glass from Finland* (Riihimäki: Suomen Lasimuseo, 1985), no. 81. Other vases in the series, such as the *Lancet*, were designed in 1952; see *The Modern Spirit*, no. 79.

285. *The Modern Spirit*, no. 81.

286. At some time after 1958 the decanter was reclassified as model no. 2501; see ibid., no. 82.

287. There is some confusion about the dating of these decanters. Only model nos. i-400 and i-401 are listed in the 1956 Iittala catalogue (Iittala Museum Archives MK 24). According to the Timo Sarpaneva model book in the same archives, the gray version of no. i-401 was terminated on February 26, 1960, and all the others were terminated in 1966. *The Modern Spirit* incorrectly claims (no. 82) that the no. i-401 decanter was produced between 1959 and 1965. The equally incorrect dates 1954–64 have been cited for the *i* series in *Form Finland*, no. 49.

288. It is perhaps significant that model no. i-403 does not appear in the Iittala catalogue for 1956 (Iittala Museum Archives MK 24). Since no catalogue seems to have been published in 1957, the first record of no. i-403 is in the 1958 catalogue, *Karhula-Iittala 1.9.1958* (MK 36). As the catalogue was published in January, the model must have been issued in the previous year.

289. Timo Sarpaneva, quoted in *Form Finland*, no. 49.

290. These decanters by Kaj Franck, Timo Sarpaneva, Carl-Harry Stålhane, and Henning Koppel were illustrated, respectively, in Érik Zahle, ed., *A Treasury of Scandinavian Design* (New York: Golden Press, 1961), fig. 209; *Studio Yearbook* (1962–63), 128; *Form*, 53, nos. 6–7 (1957), 141; and Erik Lassen, *En Københavnsk porcelaensfabriks historie* (Copenhagen: Nyt Nordisk Forlag, 1978), fig. 107.

291. *Studio Yearbook* (1959–60), 93.

292. Later reclassified as model no. 500.

293. Letter from Jarno Peltonen, former director of Taideteollisuusmuseo (Museum of Applied Arts), Helsinki, to the office of David A. Hanks & Associates, December 14, 1982, reporting on interviews between Kaj Franck and Kirsi Niemisto held on October 26 and November 2, 1982. The second decanter was model no. KF 1501 (later model 501); see *The Modern Spirit*, no. 18. For a view of both decanters on display at the Milan XI Triennale, see Vittoriano Viganò, "XIe Triennale de Milan," *Aujourd'hui: Art et architecture*, 15 (1957), 80–99.

294. The alternative Finnish names *Kremls Klockor* and *Kremlin Kellot* are given in Kerttu Niilonen, *Finskt glas* (Helsinki: Kustannusosakeyhtiö Tammi, 1966), 57; also *The Modern Spirit*, no. 18.

295. *Studio Yearbook* (1958–59), 101.

296. Zahle, *Treasury of Scandinavian Design*, fig. 210.

297. The date 1959 is cited in *Bohemian Glass* (London: Victoria and Albert Museum, 1965), no. 40. The carafe was perhaps first published by Jan Kotík, "Glass and Ceramics

in the Czechoslovak Stand at the XIIth Triennale in Milan," *Czechoslovak Glass Review*,
15 (November–December 1960), 9.

298. Adolf Matura, "Fostering the High Design
Standards of Glass Products," *Czechoslovak
Glass Review*, 14 (September–October
1959), 4.

299. Miroslav Mičko, "Czechoslovakia's Participation in the XIIth Triennale di Milano,"
Czechoslovak Glass Review, 16, no. 2 (1961),
44–45; see also Kotík, "Glass and Ceramics,"
9.

300. It is referred to as a lemonade set in *Bohemian
Glass*, no. 40; and in Robert J. Charleston,
"Bohemian Glass from the Museum of Indus-
trial Art in Prague Exhibition at the Victoria
and Albert Museum," *Apollo*, 81 (June
1965), 488. It is called a water set by Kotík,
"Glass and Ceramics," 4; and by Mičko,
"Czechoslovakia's Participation," 45.

301. On the dating of this service, see *Rosenthal,
Hundert Jahre Porzellan*, 90, 159 (a com-
pleted study of the coffeepot drawn by
Loewy's office and dated October 26, 1953).
Also see Shirley Howard, "Rosenthal-Block
Launches Classic Modern," *Crockery and
Glass Journal*, 155 (December 1954), 136.

302. Alberta C. Trimble, *Modern Porcelain* (New
York: Harper & Brothers, 1962), 172–73;
while this author presents much important
firsthand information, her account is not always reliable.

303. *Retailing Daily*, March 24, 1952. The many
forms and patterns were exhibited for the first
time at that year's Leipzig trade fair and were
ready for distribution in the United States by
July; see "Loewy Designs Modern Dinnerware Patterns for Rosenthal China," *Crockery
and Glass Journal*, 151 (July 1952), 71.

304. *Rosenthal, Hundert Jahre Porzellan*, 90. It
should be remembered that in 1950, when
Tapio Wirkkala was employed in Loewy's
New York office, work on the *2000* service was
still in progress and that Wirkkala's own ideas
were used for the *Finlandia* service (fig. 288).

305. Hubert Griemert, "Einfluss und Wachstum,"
Keramische Zeitschrift, 6 (1954), 392. Rosenthal tried to suggest that the ideas flowed in
the opposite direction by misdating Griemert's work to 1956; see *Rosenthal, Hundert
Jahre Porzellan*, 90. For the work of the
German ceramist, see Adalbert Klein, "Von
gestaltenden Handwerk zur Serien Produk-
tion der Werkform," *Keramische Zeitschrift*,
7 (1955), 387–90.

306. For the designs by Lucienne Day, see
"Rassegna domus," *Domus*, 361 (December
1959), n.p.

307. Letter from Torun Bülow-Hübe to Toni
Lesser Wolf, September 16, 1989. Torun
states that from 1948 to 1956 she maintained
her workshop in Sweden but stayed in France
for long periods of time, traveling with her
young children.

308. "The Silversmith of Biot," *Time*, September
1, 1961, 46.

309. Letter from Bülow-Hübe to Wolf, September
16, 1989.

310. Merette Bodelsen, *Sèvres-Copenhagen: Crystal Glazes and Stoneware at the Turn
of the Century* (Copenhagen: The Royal
Copenhagen Porcelain Manufactory, 1975),
76–77.

311. *Machine Art* (New York: Museum of Modern
Art, 1934), no. 381.

312. "Svezia, forme astratte," *Domus*, 230 (1948),
50.

313. "Stålhanes stengods," *Form*, 44, no. 3 (1948),
48.

314. In 1959 Hans Wegner noted that the *Round*
chair had required some seven years to perfect. He initially designed it for mass production, but after creating a number of versions
he decided that it had to be handcrafted. At
the same time, Wegner also outlined his
working method, from sketch to final production. See Marilyn Hoffman, "Danish Furniture," *Craft Horizons*, 19 (March–April
1959), 38.

315. An upholstered version with a padded leath-
er seat was developed in 1950 for the
American market. See Charles D. Gandy and
Susan Zimmermann-Stidham, *Contempo-
rary Classics: Furniture of the Masters* (New
York: McGraw-Hill, 1981), 120.

316. Caning on the crest rail was, however, still
available by special order; ibid. The example
in the Stewart Collection is one of the early
versions. It is also unusual in that three
strands of the seat caning extend down over
the wood rail on both the front and back. In
most versions this occurs only on the back of
the chair.

317. Other examples include a pedestal office
chair, model JH 502 (1955); a highly sculptural series with upholstered crest rails (1957–
61); a side chair with metal frame, model JH
701 (1965), and an armchair, model PP 55
armchair (1976).

318. Arne Karlsen and Anker Tiedemann, in
Zahle, *Treasury of Scandinavian Design*, 17.

319. The bowl and drawings for it appear in a
photograph of the designer published in *Interiors*, 110 (September 1950), 83. This would
invalidate Finn Juhl's belief, expressed in a
letter of April 30, 1987, to Jennifer Toher
[Teulié], that the bowl was designed in 1951.
A blueprint for this bowl dated 1951 was probably done after the initial design. The bowl is
dated 1949 in David R. McFadden, ed.,
Scandinavian Modern Design 1880–1980
(New York: Harry N. Abrams, 1982), 151; it is
dated 1950 in Kathryn B. Hiesinger and
George H. Marcus, eds., *Design since 1945*
(Philadelphia: Philadelphia Museum of Art,
1983), 200.

320. Letter from Juhl to Toher [Teulié], April 30,
1987.

321. Ibid.

322. Dates cited for the design and manufacture of
the *Ant* chair range from 1951 to 1953. In a
letter to R. Craig Miller, June 3, 1988, Bård
Henriksen of Fritz Hansen Møbler states that
mass production of the chair was begun in
1952.

323. Johan Pedersen, *Arkitekten Arne Jacobsen*
(Copenhagen: Udgivet, 1957), 90.

324. Tobias Faber, *Arne Jacobsen* (New York: Frederick A. Praeger, 1964), 67.

325. The idea of a "continuous" chair of one piece
and material goes back to Gerrit Rietveld's
experiments in the 1930s. His Z chair of 1934
(fig. 491) was an early "visual" realization, as
was Eero Saarinen's later *Pedestal* chair of
about 1955 (fig. 335).

326. The Biedermeier side chairs are in Heinrich
Kreisel, ed., *Die Kunst des deutschen Möbels*
(Munich: C. H. Beck, 1973), vol. 3, fig. 380.

327. Letter from the importer, George I. Tanier, to
David A. Hanks & Associates, August 14,
1989.

328. The model numbers of the *Swan* armchair
variants are: no. 3321 (settee), nos. 3320 and
3322 (fixed and adjustable pedestal), and no.
4325 (four-legged base).

329. Because there are no precise factory records,
the *Veckla* series is generally dated vaguely to
the 1950s. Model nos. 243 and 245 were
already advertised in 1950, presumably just
after having been put into production; see
Form, 46, no. 3 (1950), back cover. Undoubtedly, lower model numbers, such as 236, had
been designed by then as well. Indeed, no.
236 appears as an incidental accessory in photographs of an interior; *Form*, 47, nos. 4–5
(1951), 68–69.

330. It should be remembered that *Soft Forms* remained in production through the 1940s and
1950s, making it contemporary with *Veckla*,
although the patterns it bore, such as *Gray
Bands* (1945–69) and *Spaljé* (1942–52), obscured its likeness. See *Gustavsberg, 150 år*
(Stockholm: Nationalmuseum, 1975), 40,
nos. 198, 199.

331. Ibid., no. 203.

332. E.g., Astone Gasparetto, "Arte decorativa
alla XXV Biennale," *Domus*, 251 (October
1950), 38–39; "I Vetri italiani alla Triennale," ibid., 262 (October 1951), 27–29. The
model in the Stewart Collection is illustrated
on page 28.

333. For a series of photographs showing the
pezzato process at the Venini factory, see Bard
Clow, "Venetian Glass," *Craft Horizons*, 16
(July–August 1956), 41–43.

334. In 1950 Fulvio Bianconi and the Venini
workshop also introduced a series of black-
and-white glass figurines of commedia
dell'arte characters. Here, too, the designer's
inventions were based on earlier ideas, specifically, an eighteenth-century tradition of such
glass figurines, but because his forms were
highly stylized, the public was charmed into
seeing only innovation.

335. For illustrations of such bowls, see Suzette
Morton Zurcher, "Prestini, a Contemporary
Craftsman," *Craft Horizons*, 8 (November
1948), 24–25.

336. Letter from James Prestini to David A.
Hanks, February 28, 1986. Such later works
are illustrated in "Industrial design per la casa,
alla Triennale," *Domus*, 301 (December
1954), 57.

337. Letter from James Prestini to David A.
Hanks, September 25, 1986.

338. The history of the early development of *Tomorrow's Classic* dinnerware is based on interviews between Eva Zeisel and Martin
Eidelberg in 1983 and 1984.

339. An agreement between Eva Zeisel and
Jonathan Higgins (who subsequently formed
the Middlehurst China Company to distribute the line) was signed on August 10,
1951. The dinnerware was being shown by
the end of the year; see Ann Ruggles, "China
Plates That Snuggle in Your Lap," *New York
World-Telegram and Sun*, December 19,
1951, 18. It was not released commercially
until February 1952; see *Crockery and Glass
Journal*, 150 (January 1952), 50; "Merchandise Cues," *Interiors*, 111 (February 1952),
114. See also *Eva Zeisel: Designer for Industry* (Montreal: Musée des Arts Décoratifs de
Montréal, 1984), 71 n.65.

340. The borrowing went in the opposite direction
as well. The forms of *Tomorrow's Classic* were
used with little change by W. R. Midwinter,
Ltd., of Burslem, Stoke-on-Trent; see *Studio
Yearbook* (1955–56), AD142.

341. For the history of this project, see *Tapio Wirkkala*, 121–22. I am grateful to Otmar Siegl

and Bernd Fritz of Rosenthal for their help.

342. The inscriptions on the plates cite six grand prizes from the Milan Triennales. Wirkkala was awarded three such prizes at the 1951 exhibition and three more at the 1954 exhibition. He received a seventh grand prize at the 1960 Triennale; the fact that this seventh prize is not noted on the plate suggests that the plate was made before 1960.

343. For a more appropriate pattern, designed by Josef Gallitzin and called *Northland*, see *Studio Yearbook* (1958–59), 62.

344. Robert King, who has been credited with the design (Hiesinger and Marcus, *Design since 1945*, 157), was a draftsman and model maker on John Van Koert's staff. Much of the information presented in this essay comes from a series of conversations between John Van Koert and Toni Lesser Wolf in the spring of 1990.

345. The print department of this organization (Swiss Federation of Consumer Cooperative Societies), founded in 1910, was noted for its linoleum-cut prints during the 1950s. Armin Hofmann made many of them, primarily for the Basel Kunsthalle and the Gewerbemuseum.

346. Mary Schoeser and Celia Rufey, *English and American Textiles from 1790 to the Present* (London: Thames and Hudson, 1989), 205.

347. "Art, Architecture and Decoration Merge Ideally in Saarinen-Swanson Modern," *House and Garden*, 92 (October 1947), 152–57ff.

348. See "Drama of Decoration," *Arts and Decoration*, 42 (February 1935), 47.

349. In a letter of September 29, 1986, to David A. Hanks & Associates, Edison Price recalled that the lamp was designed in 1953. This date is confirmed by the lamp's initial publication: Lois Wagner, "The Glow and the Gleam of It All: A Review of New Lamps," *Interiors*, 113 (November 1953), 111. The date of 1948 cited in *High Styles: Twentieth Century American Design* (New York: Whitney Museum of Art in association with Summit Books, 1985), 215, is erroneous and perhaps is based on the date of completion of the architect's home in New Canaan, Connecticut.

350. "Philip Johnson Remembers Richard Kelly," *Lighting Design & Application*, 9 (June 1979), 49.

351. The candelabra lamp appears in interior views of the Johnson house published in articles after the house was completed; e.g., Arthur Drexler, "Architecture Opaque and Transparent," *Interiors*, 109 (October 1949), 90–101. Richard Kelly was responsible for the subtle lighting at Johnson's house, where glass walls disappeared at night as the landscape and trees were illuminated from both indoor and outdoor sources.

352. Interiors for which Philip Johnson chose the three-legged version of this lamp include the Richard S. Davis residence, illustrated in Olga Gueft, "Philip Johnson: Three Recent Works," *Interiors*, 113 (July 1954), 63; and a Madison, Connecticut, remodeling, published in "It's Time the Architect Got into the Act," *House and Home*, 6 (October 1954), 148.

353. A surviving blueprint from Edison Price, Inc., now in the files of David A. Hanks & Associates and probably intended for the later production, is dated March 31, 1967.

354. Microscopic analysis shows one warp: black rayon; five plain wefts: black cotton, black rayon, gold strips encased in polyester film; two bouclé wefts: gray rayon, white rayon.

355. I am grateful to J. L. Lowe, Jr., vice-president, Automotive Division of Chatham Manufacturing Company, for this information. See Chatham Manufacturing Company, "Our History: A Photographic Sketch" (1983); "Trends in Automobile Upholstery Fabrics," *American Fabrics*, 38 (Winter 1957), 70–71.

356. Correspondence between Marianne Strengell and Christa C. Mayer Thurman, May 1982.

357. Gerda Nyberg was a weaver from Pontiac, Michigan, who wove for Marianne Strengell for years. See Robert J. Clark et al., *Design in America: The Cranbrook Vision 1925–1950* (New York: Harry N. Abrams in association with The Detroit Institute of Arts and The Metropolitan Museum of Art, 1983), 197.

358. Dorothy Bryan, "Marianne Strengell's Approach to Design," *Handweaver and Craftsman*, 4 (Fall 1960), 29.

359. Jack Lenor Larsen, "Notes on Textile Designing for Mass Production," (M.F.A. thesis, Cranbrook Academy of Art, Bloomfield Hills, Michigan, 1951).

360. The handwoven version of *Remoulade* won the first award in the 1955 American Institute of Decorators Home Furnishings Design Competition: "AID Product Design Awards," *Interiors*, 114 (May 1955), 116. After that, the fabric, part of Larsen's Spice Garden Collection, was produced by Bolan Mills in Paterson, New Jersey, a franchised mill that Jack Lenor Larsen later bought and operated until the mid-1960s.

361. "Taproot: Jack Lenor Larsen with Susan Goldin," *Interweave* (Summer 1979), 19.

362. F. Schumacher & Company, "Schumacher's Taliesin Line of Decorative Fabrics and Wallpaper Designed by Frank Lloyd Wright" (1955), 24.

363. "Frank Lloyd Wright: His Contribution to the Beauty of American Life," *House Beautiful*, 98 (November 1955); interview of January 6, 1988, between John de Koven Hill, former architectural editor of *House Beautiful*, and Christa C. Mayer Thurman.

364. Interview between Hill and Thurman, January 6, 1988; also René Carrillo, "Recollections of Frank Lloyd Wright" (manuscript, Princeton, New Jersey, 1988), 1.

365. See correspondence on microfiche under "Wright," "Schumacher," and "Carrillo" at the Frank Lloyd Wright Memorial Foundation, Taliesin West, Scottsdale, Arizona.

366. A few of the original drawings for the Taliesin Line, executed by Frank Lloyd Wright's assistants, are in the Archives of American Art. There is none for *Design 104*, however.

367. The Taliesin Line fabrics ranged in price from $3.40 to $13.50 a yard. Frank Lloyd Wright's collection for the Heritage Hendredon furniture company followed in 1955. Karastan planned a series of carpets by Wright for the spring of 1956 but made only two samples.

368. The origins of the names *Antelope* and *Springbok* remain obscure, although they clearly refer to animals of the British Empire.

369. Hazel Conway, *Ernest Race* (London: The Design Council, 1982), 44–45. Some examples of the chair have painted brass feet; these are alleged to have been made for the Festival of Britain, but there is as yet no documentary confirmation of their provenance.

370. Ibid., 47.

371. The donor purchased the chair "in probably 1950"; letter from Muriel Kalis Newman to David A. Hanks, March 5, 1988.

372. See Eliot F. Noyes, *Organic Design in Home Furnishings* (New York: Museum of Modern Art, 1941), 12–17.

373. I am referring to the side chairs in wood (models LCW and DCW) and in metal (models LCM and DCM) initially made by the Evans Products Company and subsequently by the Herman Miller Furniture Co.

374. Perhaps the most famous designs in that decade for a three-dimensionally molded plastic chair are the sketches of conchoidal chairs by Ludwig Mies van der Rohe. See Ludwig Glaeser, *Ludwig Mies van der Rohe* (New York: Museum of Modern Art, 1977), 16, 76–85.

375. See "Designs for Postwar Living," *California Arts and Architecture*, 60 (August 1943), 23–33, 43. The house design was done in collaboration with Oliver Lundquist.

376. See "Modern Doesn't Pay, or Does It?," *Interiors*, 105 (March 1946), 66–74.

377. The photographs are in the Eero Saarinen Archives at Yale University, New Haven.

378. In an interview between Florence Knoll Bassett and R. Craig Miller, February 1, 1982, the designer noted that in the late 1940s and early 1950s the technology was so rudimentary that molded plastic required a bonding agent to achieve any rigidity; it was thus necessary to cover the resultant rough shells with foam-rubber padding and upholstery. The shells for the no. 70 chair were initially made by the Winner Manufacturing Company, Trenton, New Jersey, of fibers bonded with Paraplex P-43 resin. See "Chemistry Builds a Chair," *Rohm & Haas Reporter*, November–December 1951, 2–4. The first fiberglass chair to feature its natural surface was, of course, Charles and Ray Eames' model DAR armchair (fig. 309).

379. Edgar Kaufmann, jr., *Prize Designs for Modern Furniture from the International Competition for Low-Cost Furniture Design* (New York: Museum of Modern Art, 1950), 6, 10.

380. The caption on one of the drawings (ibid., 21) refers to a "coating over entire metal shell thick enough to cut down heat transfer and to dampen sound." The catalogue text nowhere mentions that the designs submitted were for metal. There is an early description mentioning the neoprene coating in Don Wallance, *Shaping America's Products* (New York: Reinhold Publishing, 1956), 180–81.

381. Although their manufacture is referred to in Edgar Kaufmann, jr., "Eames and Chests," *Art News*, 49 (May 1950), 38, the plastic chairs do not appear in the 1950 Herman Miller Furniture catalogue but only in the edition of 1952. As was often the case with the early production of Eames furniture, the manufacture of individual parts—in this case the molded seat units—was first undertaken and developed in cooperation with a local manufacturer and only later taken over by Herman Miller. A chair in the Stewart Collection (D83.137.1), which must have been manufactured before 1955, carries the label of Zenith Plastics Company, Gardenia, California, makers of the seat.

382. "Pure Design Research," *Architectural Forum*, 97 (September 1952), 145.

383. Eric Larrabee and Massimo Vignelli, *Knoll*

Design (New York: Harry N. Abrams, 1981), 68.

384. Bertoia left the Eames office disgruntled, feeling that he and other office members had not received credit for their work—which had been specifically promised by Charles Eames—at the time of the Museum of Modern Art's Eames retrospective in 1946. See ibid., 68–69. The undated interview with Bertoia in the Knoll Archive (kindly provided by Carol A. Kim of Knoll International) that forms the basis of the chapter in *Knoll Design* titled "Harry Bertoia, USA (Italy), Third Round" does not, in fact, discuss the completely open arrangement with Knoll implied in Larrabee and Vignelli's book, by which Bertoia could work on whatever project he wished, under no obligation to develop furniture.

385. "Pure Design Research," 145.

386. "Everything must be separated according to function"; Harry Bertoia, quoted in ibid., 146.

387. "Harry Bertoia," *Interiors*, 125 (November 1965), 154.

388. "The New Seat with a Neater Teeter," *Life*, February 6, 1956, 122, 125.

389. Larrabee and Vignelli, *Knoll Design*, 46; also a letter from the Isamu Noguchi studio to David A. Hanks, July 24, 1986.

390. "Knoll Index of Contemporary Design" (1954), 21–22.

391. *Design Quarterly*, 38 (1957), 13.

392. Letter from Noguchi studio to Hanks, July 24, 1986.

393. Inez Svenson, *Tryckta Tyger fran 30–tal till 80–tal* (Stockholm: Liber Forlag, 1984), 38.

394. The drawing is in the collection of Ka Markelius, wife of the designer. The collage is in the Nationalmuseum, Stockholm. Letter from Astrid Sampe to Christa C. Mayer Thurman, July 1988.

395. Illustrated in *Form*, 51, no. 2 (1955), 51*; ibid., 53, no. 5 (1957), 136.

396. From the artist's statement provided in his autobiographical sketch.

397. Clement Meadmore, *The Modern Chair: Classics in Production* (New York: Van Nostrand Reinhold, 1979), 118–21.

398. "New Color Philosophy at Knoll," *Interiors*, 118 (May 1959), 144.

399. "The Crème de la Crème: A.I.D.'s Citation of Merit Awards," *Interiors*, 118 (May 1959), 12.

400. Interview between Earl Pardon and Toni Lesser Wolf, February 2, 1988.

401. Ibid.

402. Statement by the artist in *Earl Pardon: Retrospective Exhibition* (Saratoga Springs, New York: Skidmore College Art Gallery, 1980), n.p.

403. Oppi Untracht, *Jewelry Concepts and Technology* (Garden City, New York: Doubleday & Co., 1982), 75. For the quarternary principle (which the tetrahedron symbolizes), see J. E. Cirlot, *A Dictionary of Symbols* (New York: Philosophical Library, 1962), 256, 319; Carl G. Jung, *Man and His Symbols* (New York: Dell Publishing, 1964), 59, 62, 214, 246, 266–72.

404. In the interview between Wolf and Pardon, February 2, 1988, the artist stated that to the best of his knowledge no other jeweler at that time was using enamel in such a limited way. He added that, in retrospect, the enamel dots should not have been there at all. In a later pendant (illustrated in *Ornament*, 10 [Au-

tumn 1986], 45), he relinquished the rigid geometry of the triangle, piercing the space frame with many more metal wires, arranged in an increasingly haphazard manner. This later pendant is a dense nest of gold pins, above which reside horizontal, square gold plates and multicolored beads. The beads act as a substitute for the enamel dots, and their placement at different heights reflects Pardon's earlier use of tetrahedrons of various sizes. Thus, despite a major stylistic shift, the artist never abandoned the idea of spatial puzzles.

405. In addition to such renderings, the portfolio has magazine articles on her interiors. A second portfolio compiled by Haraszty and now in the Stewart Collection (D88.178.2) has samples of the fabrics she designed for Knoll along with notices of the awards they won. Much of the material presented here is based on a telephone conversation between Eszter Haraszty and Christine W. Laidlaw, January 16, 1990; also an interview between Haraszty and Kate Carmel, May 1989.

406. "Knoll Associates: Drum Beaters for Modern," *Life*, March 2, 1953, 72–77.

407. "Epanouissement du mobilier moderne," *Maison & jardin*, 19 (February–March 1954), 38–42; "In casa di americani a Parigi," *Domus*, 296 (July 1954), 24–25; "Under a Paris Skylight," *Esquire*, 42 (August 1954), 61–64; "The Sound and the Fury," *Esquire*, 42 (November 1954), 14; Olga Gueft, "The Exhilarated World of Eszter Haraszty," *Interiors*, 115 (June 1956), 92–99.

408. Gueft, "The Exhilarated World of Eszter Haraszty," 93–94. Haraszty later used colors running through the spectrum in her own apartment in New York; see "La Casa di un'artista," *Domus*, 325 (December 1956), 15–20.

409. "A Sweeping Flat Roof Unites This Large and Complex Plan," *House and Home*, 7 (June 1955), 116–21. The ceramic panel on the back wall, by Rut Bryk, Tapio Wirkkala's wife, was exhibited at the Milan X Triennale in 1954; see "La Finlandia alla Triennale," *Domus*, 300 (November 1954), 22.

410. *Fibra* was first advertised in *Interiors*, 112 (May 1953), 21. It was made until at least 1965, since it is included in a Knoll Associates price list of that year.

411. Telephone conversation between Eszter Haraszty and Christine W. Laidlaw, August 29, 1989.

412. Telephone conversation between Haraszty and Laidlaw, January 16, 1990.

413. In the 1950s *Fibra* came in eight color ways; in 1965, six color combinations were available. See *Interiors*, 113 (September 1953), 96; Knoll Associates price list of 1965.

414. Interview between Eszter Haraszty and Kate Carmel, May 1989.

415. Ibid.; Terence Conran, *Printed Textile Design* (London and New York: Studio Publications, 1957), 54.

416. Aline Saarinen, ed., *Eero Saarinen on His Work* (New Haven: Yale University Press, 1962), 68.

417. Ibid.

418. The presence of the designer's full name on the goblet probably can be explained by the circumstances under which the goblet was acquired. The dealer-authors Ray and Lee Grover visited a great many glassblowers about 1970 and, when signatures were lacking on objects they acquired, had them added

in accordance with the taste of the art market. They published this goblet in their book *Contemporary Art Glass* (New York: Crown Publishers, 1975), plate 120, and sold it at Sotheby's, New York, February 17, 1984, no. 133. A more conventional factory signature can be seen on the second *Tulip* goblet in the Stewart Collection; the N signifies Nils Landberg, and the U signifies that it was worked freehand and without engraved decoration.

419. Illustrated on exhibit at Milan in *Form*, 53, nos. 6–7 (1957), 160.

420. E.g., *Glass 1959*, 287; Zahle, *Treasury of Scandinavian Design*, 184; Hiesinger and Marcus, *Design since 1945*, 107; McFadden, *Scandinavian Modern Design*, 6, 157.

421. Cf. Nils Landberg's wineglasses, illustrated in Geoffrey Beard, *International Modern Glass* (London: Barrie & Jenkins, 1976), 89.

422. Among the Swedish factories that produced imitations of the *Tulip* goblet are Alsterfors, Gullaskruf, Lindshammar, and Måleras; see *Form*, 55, no. 7 (1959), 445; ibid., nos. 8–9 (1959), 516; ibid., 56, nos. 3–4 (1960), 224; ibid., no. 6 (1960), 409. Bjørn Wiinblad designed one for Rosenthal; *Crockery and Glass Journal*, 169 (October 1961), 16. For examples from two American firms, Tiffin and Morgantown, see *Crockery and Glass Journal*, 168 (March 1, 1961), 2; ibid. (March 31, 1961), front cover; ibid. (June 1961), back cover.

423. See, e.g., Helmut Ricke and Ulrich Gronert, *Glas in Schweden, 1915–1960* (Munich: Prestel Verlag, 1986), 173, no. 276. Nils Landberg also designed a candlestick version of the *Tulip* goblet; see *Form*, 57, no. 6 (1961), 367.

Modern Pattern and Ornament

424. *Die Form Ohne Ornament* (Stuttgart: Deutsche Verlags-Anstalt, 1924). This show was at the core of the Museum of Modern Art's exhibition "Machine Art" of a decade later.

425. "Drama of Decoration," *Arts and Decoration*, 42 (February 1935), 47–49. Philip Johnson's radio-drama discussion with Mrs. Platt is discussed in part on page 23 above.

426. Edgar Kaufmann, jr., *What Is Modern Design?* (New York: Museum of Modern Art, 1950), 18. Almost as if in error, Kaufmann (29) included a chandelier by Paavo Tynell like the one in the Stewart Collection (fig. 391); he described it as "decorative" but made no further comment on its stylized ornament.

427. Walter Browder, "Good Design . . . as Far as It Goes," *Crockery and Glass Journal*, 152 (March 2, 1953), 5; Edgar Kaufmann, jr., "Letter to the Editor," ibid., 152 (April 1953), 66; Browder, "Really Good Design," ibid., 153 (August 1953), 5, 31.

428. It was held on November 4, 1953, and the panelists included Edgar Kaufmann, jr., designers Paul Mayer and Eva Zeisel, the philosopher Suzanne K. Langer, and the Home News editor of the *New York Times* Betty Pepis.

429. Robert Goldwater in association with René d'Harnoncourt, *Modern Art in Your Life* (New York: Museum of Modern Art, 1949).

430. In certain instances it was very successful, but in other cases, such as a textile that copies a Fernand Léger stained-glass window or an-

other that reproduces literal images of Picasso ceramic plates, replete with cast shadows, the concept and the final product are open to scrutiny.

431. Goldwater and d'Harnoncourt, *Modern Art in Your Life*, 5.

432. The tapestry is described in the accompanying exhibition catalogue, *Modern French Tapestries* (New York: Bignou Gallery, 1936) n.p. According to Anne Hamilton Sayre, "A World Premiere of Tapestries from Beauvais and Aubusson Designed by Modern Painters of Paris," *Art News*, 34 (April 4, 1936), 7, *Hommage à Mozart* was not on view, due to lack of space, but could be seen on request. In addition to other venues in the United States, including Chicago and San Francisco, the tapestries were also shown in Brussels, London, and Paris.

433. The model, an oil on canvas, is currently on loan from the Hillman Family Foundation to the Brooklyn Museum; see Maurice Laffaille, *Raoul Dufy: Catalogue raisonné de l'oeuvre peint* (Geneva: Editions Motte, 1977), vol. 4, 79, no. 1490. André Abdul Hak, *Oeuvres de Raoul Dufy: Collections de la Ville de Paris* (Paris: Musée d'Art Moderne de la Ville de Paris, 1976), 30, no. 55, lists Dufy's various paintings on this theme.

434. In addition to Sayre, "A World Premiere of Tapestries," articles whose authors championed the tapestries included Raymond Cogniat, "Tapisserie pour notre temps," *Art et décoration*, 66 (December 1937), 25–32; "Dr. Albert C. Barnes in 'An Epoch in Art History': A Recent Radio Address," *Art News*, 34 (May 23, 1936), 6; "France with Modernistic Tapestries Points Another Way to Serve Art," *Art Digest*, 10 (May 1, 1936), 8. Among the opposing critics were E. M. Benson, who was "not inclined to believe that Madame Cuttoli's efforts to revive the hand-loomed tapestry market will produce any lasting or fruitful results. If the tapestry is to play an important rôle in the art of tomorrow, this cannot be accomplished by separating the artist from the weaver, nor by ignoring the potentialities of the machine as a productive unit": "Modern French Tapestries at the Bignou Gallery," *American Magazine of Art*, 29 (May 1936), 328–30. The author of "Progress or Decadence," *Antiques*, 29 (June 1936), 262, contended, "If there is any eternal underlying principle in art it is that the nature of the material should control the character of the design and should be apparent in the completed work. Violation of this principle to demonstrate technical virtuosity achieves not art, but only a stunt performance." Mixed reviews of the tapestries were expressed in "Amazing Tapestries," *Art Digest*, 10 (April 15, 1936), 23; and "Modern French Tapestries at Messrs. Reid & Lefevres," *Apollo*, 25 (June 1937), 362.

435. The Churchill Lathrops, the original owners of this poster, traveled to France in the 1920s and 1930s and knew A. M. Cassandre personally. It was probably during one of their trips that the artist signed it, in the lower righthand corner.

436. A. M. Cassandre, quoted in André Salmon, ed., *Maîtres français de l'affiche* (1943), vol. 3, 15, as cited in Alan M. Fern, *Word and Image* (New York: Museum of Modern Art, 1968), 60.

437. For the general history of Picasso's involvement with ceramics, see Georges Ramié, *Pi-*

casso's Ceramics (New York: Viking Press, 1976); for the dating of the specific model in the Stewart Collection, see ibid., 277 (no. 681), 291. Also see Alain Ramié, *Picasso: Catalogue of the Edited Ceramic Works, 1947–1971* (Vallauris: Galerie Madoura, 1988), 51.

438. See "Picasso's Peace Poster," *Graphis*, 5, no. 28 (1949), 329. It should be remembered that Picasso had openly sided with the Communists in 1944, and although his art had been condemned by them in 1947 as bourgeois and decadent, he maintained his allegiance. In fact, the Communist mayor of Vallauris, engaged in a rivalry with the non-Communist mayor of Antibes, where Picasso resided, valued Picasso's endeavors in ceramics.

439. Picasso had designed a similar dove a year earlier without the burst of light; see Ramié, *Picasso's Ceramics*, 277 (no. 680).

440. For Centro Studio Pittori nell'Arte del Vetro and examples of its work, see Astone Gasparetto, *Il Vetro di Murano dalle origini ad oggi* (Venice: N. Pozza, 1958), 145, figs. 179–84; also Roberto Aloi, *Vetri d'oggi* (Milan: Ulrico Hoepli, 1955), 152–70; *Intérieurs 50* (Brussels: Immeuble Pierre Cardin, 1983), no. 138; *Die Fünfziger* (Munich: Museum Villa Stuck, 1984), no. 45. The project is not mentioned in the patron's brief autobiography, Peggy Guggenheim, *Confessions of an Art Addict* (New York: Macmillan, 1960), and it is barely referred to in Nicolas and Elena Calas, *The Peggy Guggenheim Collection of Modern Art* (New York: Harry N. Abrams, 1966), 14, though several examples of such glass can be seen in photographs of the Guggenheim home (figs. 1, 2, 5).

441. The glass industry had tried this type of collaboration prior to World War II. For example, the American glasshouse of Steuben had invited designs from Raoul Dufy, Isamu Noguchi, Jean Cocteau, Pavel Tchelitchev, and others; see *The Collection of Designs in Glass by Twenty-seven Contemporary Artists* (New York: Steuben Glass Inc., 1940).

442. "Picasso convertirà alla ceramica," *Domus*, 226 (1948), 24–25; Ennio Golfieri, "Le Ceramiche di Picasso al museo di Faenza," *Bolletino d'arte*, 37 (1952), 21–25.

443. For example, a vase with faces executed by Aureliano Toso reproduces a 1947 Picasso ceramic; see Aloi, *Vetri d'oggi*, 155; and Ramié, *Picasso's Ceramics*, fig. 252. Likewise, the figure of a woman holding a vase that was executed by Vetraio Ermanno Nason imitates another 1947 ceramic; see Aloi, *Vetri d'oggi*, 154; and Ramié, *Picasso's Ceramics*, figs. 266, 267.

444. Cf. Ramié, *Picasso's Ceramics*, figs. 584, 739. The closest parallel is, in fact, another glass vase by IVR di Mazegga, illustrated in *Die Fünfziger*, no. 45.

445. *Glaskunst aus Murano* (Basel: Gewerbemuseum, 1955); see also "Murano, vetri d'arte," *Domus*, 312 (November 1955), 37; "Fucina degli angeli," *Domus*, 327 (February 1957), 35.

446. For a statistical analysis of Italy's exportation of ceramics, see *Italian Ceramics* (Rome: Commercio Estero Istituto Centrale, 1954), 176.

447. The best study of Salvatore Meli's method is Joseph A. Pugliese, "Meli," *Craft Horizons*, 18 (November–December 1958), 29–31.

448. Although Meli had thrown on the wheel earlier in his career, he abandoned the process to

avoid the restraint it engendered. A transitional period in which some forms were still symmetrical and others, though thrown on the wheel, had asymmetrical sculptural appendages is recorded in a photograph in "Le Ceramiche italiane alla Triennale," *Domus*, 262 (October 1951), 23.

449. Pugliese, "Meli," 29.

450. Ibid., 30; Gian Carlo Polidori, "Salvatore Meli," in *Cinquanta ceramisti italiani 1952–57* (Milan: Associazione Nazionale degli Industriali della Ceramica e degli Abrasivi, 1957), 122.

451. Pugliese, "Meli," 29.

452. Letter from Gilbert Portanier to Martin Eidelberg, September 27, 1989.

453. Portanier, quoted in Jacques Wolgensinger, *Gilbert Portanier: Céramique* (Angoulême: Galerie Arts-Objets, 1988), n.p.

454. Telephone interview between Michele Wright, assistant to Christa C. Mayer Thurman, and Alexander S. Cochran, cousin of William F. Cochran Ewing, September 11, 1987. The rug could also be used as a wall hanging; see *Studio Yearbook*, 44 (1954–55), 49.

455. See Jack Cowart et al., *Henri Matisse Paper Cut-Outs* (Saint Louis: The Saint Louis Art Museum and The Detroit Institute of Arts, 1977), 204.

456. Alfred H. Barr, Jr., *Matisse—His Art and His Public* (New York: Museum of Modern Art, 1951), 279.

457. *Look*, October 24, 1950, 143.

458. James Thrall Soby, *Joan Miró* (New York: Museum of Modern Art, 1959), 118, 120. The barroom also had ashtrays, match covers, and paper coasters based on images from the painting.

459. "Great Art and Fashion Fabrics," *American Fabrics*, 35 (Winter 1955–56), 52–55; "New Fabrics Put Modern Art in Fashion," *Life*, November 14, 1955, 140–41; Bernice Fitz-Gibbon, "DepARTment Stores," *Art in America*, 64 (Spring 1956), 21.

460. Jean Lipman, *Calder's Universe* (1976; Philadelphia: Running Press in cooperation with the Whitney Museum of American Art, 1989), 334.

461. Ibid., 229, 270.

462. David Bourdon, *Calder/Mobilist/Ringmaster/Innovator* (New York: Macmillan, 1980), 49–51.

463. A *Piece of My Workshop* could be applied directly to a wall or hung like a scroll. See James Thrall Soby, "Mural-Scrolls," *Arts and Architecture*, 66 (April 1949), 26–28.

464. A redrawn version of this poster is illustrated in Paul Rand, *A Designer's Art* (New Haven: Yale University Press, 1985), 15.

465. Ibid., 14.

466. This information was kindly supplied by R. Roger Remington, project director, Graphic Design Archive on Videodisc, Rochester Institute of Technology. The design was illustrated in C. F. O. Clarke, "Alvin Lustig: Cover Designs," *Graphis*, 4, no. 23 (1948), 243, fig. E. This proves that it was used for the first edition of the book and that it should not be dated 1951, as in Bob Melson's article "Alvin Lustig: The Designer as Teacher," *Print*, 23 (January–February, 1969), 68.

467. The first edition appeared in 1948, the second in 1951. The third and latest edition appeared in 1962 and has gone through eleven printings.

468. "The Lavernes—Partners in Design," *Craft*

Horizons, 9 (Winter 1949), 14.

469. Not all were persuaded. Apropos of a similar Alvin Lustig design, one commentator wrote, "Lustig frequently amuses himself with symbols, such as the man and woman, dog, fish, moon, snake, star, and branch. Probably means something." See *Interiors*, 106 (September 1946), 69.

470. William J. Hennessey, *Modern Furnishings for the Home* (New York: Reinhold Publishing, 1952), 280.

471. *Progressive Architecture*, 35 (March 1954), 134.

472. The all-cotton fabric was *Imported Dreamspun* from Switzerland; the other was *Nubbin*. Beginning in 1959, *Seedy Weeds* was printed on *Imported Dreamspun* and *Spinnaker*, an American fabric made entirely of cotton. See Adler-Schnee Associates's "Wholesale Price Lists" for 1953, 1956, 1959, 1964, and 1965.

473. Heal's issued *Calyx* on linen and with its name in the selvage. Since this example is on a different material and the selvage mark lacks the English firm's name, it may well be an edition by Greef Fabrics.

474. James DeHolden Stone, "Curtains in the Breeze," *The Studio*, 145 (February 1953), 47.

475. For interesting comparisons between the designs and the finished vases, see Helmut Ricke and Ulrich Gronert, *Glas in Schweden 1915–1960* (Munich: Prestel Verlag, 1986), 144–45, 149, 152, 154, 158, 159. The design illustrated on page 159, on a vase dated c. 1950, is closely related to one of the vases in the Stewart Collection (D89.193.1).

476. Orrefors's engraved glass was executed on thin blanks until the 1930s, when much heavier bodies were favored, as in Vicke Lindstrand's vase of 1930 (fig. 372). Likewise, *Graal* glass—another cased technique, and a predecessor of *Ariel*—at first had thin walls but after 1930 took on a comparable heaviness.

477. See, e.g., Ricke and Gronert, *Glas in Schweden*, 139, no. 204.

478. The other three exhibitions were held in 1958, 1960, and 1966. Their archives are located in the Archives Nationales (Centre des Archives Contemporains de Fontainebleau, ref. 850025, boxes 39–67).

479. Willy Boesiger, *Le Corbusier* (New York: Praeger Publishers, 1972), 84.

480. "The Lavernes—Partners in Design," 12–14.

481. *Interiors*, 108 (March 1949), 21.

482. Interview between Erwine Laverne, David A. Hanks, and Jennifer Toher [Teulié], September 10, 1986.

483. "The Lavernes—Partners in Design," 13.

484. *Martha Graham: Sixteen Dances in Photographs by Barbara Morgan* (1941; reprint, Dobbs Ferry, New York: Morgan & Morgan, 1980), 125.

485. Interview between Ed Wiener and Toni Lesser Wolf, February 1988.

486. Ibid.

487. Shortly after it was made, Harry Bertoia gave this brooch to Marguerite Kimball, the financial secretary at the Cranbrook Academy of Art.

488. Alexander Calder occasionally riveted but never fused or soldered the metal.

489. J. David Farmer, "Metalwork and Bookbinding," in Robert J. Clark et al., *Design in America: The Cranbrook Vision 1925–1950* (New York: Harry N. Abrams in association with The Detroit Institute of Arts and The Metropolitan Museum of Art, 1983), 166.

490. The original blueprint for this design, in the collection of Irving Harper, is marked "Chronopak #4." The model numbers of the 4755 and 4756 clocks do not reflect the original numbers, which were *Chronopak #4* and *#1*, respectively; though they were designed earlier than the models with 2000 numbers, these clocks were later reclassified with 4000 numbers. The Howard Miller Clock Company has claimed that the 4755 clock was designed in 1949 and in production by 1950 (letter from Dev VanWoerkem to David A. Hanks, December 9, 1987); however, the clock may have been designed slightly earlier since a photograph of it, together with furniture designed by Isamu Noguchi for the Herman Miller Furniture Co., appeared in *Interiors*, 108 (March 1949), 132.

491. The original blueprint for this design, in the collection of Irving Harper, is marked "Chronopak #1" and dated December 1, 1947, with a notation that revisions were made on March 22 and May 18, 1948.

492. On the original blueprint for this design, in the collection of Irving Harper, this model is numbered 2213.

493. The original blueprint for this design, in the collection of Irving Harper, is dated March 31, 1954, and the model is labeled as *Cat's Cradle Wall Clock*. The clock is called *Spider Web* in *Furniture Forum*, 5, no. 2 (1954), section 4, 3.

494. In an advertisement this model is referred to as *The Kite Clock: Interiors*, 113 (September 1953), 128. An original blueprint for a *Diamond Portable* clock, dated December 9, 1953, in the collection of Irving Harper, shows *Kite* designed for desktop use.

495. Letter from Irving Harper to David A. Hanks, February 1, 1988. The *Chronopak* series of clocks was distributed nationally through the Richards Morgenthau Company.

496. Jay Doblin, *One Hundred Great Product Designs* (New York: Van Nostrand Reinhold, 1970), 77. Doblin recalls that the source of his information was George Nelson. According to Isamu Noguchi, he signed no formal agreement to be a consultant on the clock series and never acted in such a capacity; telephone conversation between Allen Wardwell, director of the Isamu Noguchi Garden Museum, Long Island City, New York, and David A. Hanks, November 30, 1988.

497. Arthur Drexler, "Calder: We Try to Keep Up with the Irrepressible Sculptor," *Interiors*, 109 (December 1949), 80–87.

498. George Nelson, "Planned Expansion," *Industrial Design*, 1 (February 1954), 108.

499. Letter from Helena Tynell, widow of the designer, to Toni Lesser Wolf, August 28, 1989.

500. According to Birgitta Treskog of AB Gustavsberg, for whose assistance in a number of ways I am grateful, a photograph of this vase in the company's archives is dated 1951. A closely related design appears on a similar vase illustrated in *Studio Yearbook* (1952–53), 63; the illustrations in this periodical are generally of objects made a year or two earlier.

501. His fabric of 1959, also called *Pleasure Garden*, is illustrated in *Stig Lindberg—formgivare* (Stockholm: Nationalmuseum, 1982), 32–33, no. 194.

502. The motif of the attentive listener can be linked to a Stig Lindberg fabric called *Pottery* (fig. 401).

503. Erik Wettergren, "Form and Colour at Gus-tavsberg," *Porslin*, 2 (1955), 101.

504. See, e.g., *Studio Yearbook* (1943–48), 109.

505. Kim Taylor, "Stig Lindberg," *Graphis*, 15 (July–August 1959), 311.

506. "Stig Lindberg, Designer," *Everyday Art Quarterly*, 23 (1952), 14–15.

507. The heavy tabletop was betrayed by the minimal nature of the functionalist frame. The top recently developed a longitudinal crack owing to insufficient support from beneath, necessitating the addition of metal braces in 1989.

508. Letter from Dan Klein of Christie's, London, to Jennifer Toher [Teulié], September 3, 1986.

509. Stanislav Libenský's work can be compared with the abstractions of Václav Spála. See *Filla, Gutfreund, Kupka øch Tjeckisk Kubism 1907–1927* (Prague: Nationalgalleriet øch Konsthanhtverksmuseet, 1983), 58–59.

510. Letter from Enrico Gregotti, general manager, Bossi, S.p.A., to Christine W. Laidlaw, August 31, 1989.

511. Letter from Fernand Léger to Enrico Gregotti, July 22, 1950. Léger said that the other fabric was "heavy and bad" ("lourd et mauvais").

512. Letter from Fernand Léger to Douglas Cooper, July 1949; see Douglas Cooper, *Fernand Léger et le nouvel espace* (Geneva and Paris: Edition des Trois Collines; and London: Lund, Humphries, 1949), 102.

513. The opposite wall of the room on the SS *Lucania* was covered with a mirror designed to extend visually the space of the room even further. See Gio Ponti, "Interni della 'Lucania,'" *Domus*, 287 (October 1953), 21–23.

514. Peter de Francia, *Fernand Léger* (New Haven: Yale University Press, 1983), 196–97.

515. Werner Schmalenbach, *Léger* (New York: Harry N. Abrams, 1976), opposite plate 40.

516. For a partial illustration of the window, see Luce Hoctin, "The Renaissance of Church Art in France," *Graphis*, 13 (May 1957), 231; for the artist's original drawing, see "Trying Abstraction on Fabrics," *Art News*, 54 (November 1955), 43. Also see C. C., "Great Art and Fashion Fabrics," *American Fabrics*, 35 (Winter 1955–56), 52–55; Fuller Fabrics advertisement, ibid., 32.

517. For the history of this project, see Lida Livingston, ed., *Dalí: A Study of His Art-in-Jewels—The Collection of the Owen Cheatham Foundation* (Greenwich, Connecticut: The Graphic Society, 1959). They were possibly crafted for Alemany & Ertman by New York jeweler Varian Deverne. In 1958, an expanded collection of Dalí jewels was purchased by the Owen Cheatham Foundation, which raised money for its religious and educational projects through exhibition loans to museums and other institutions. A group associated with the Terrot Moore Museum at Cadaqués, Spain, bought the collection in 1981, and in 1987 the jewels were sold to a Japanese foundation.

518. Ibid., 12.

519. For the jewelry with lips and eyes, see Livingston, *Dalí: A Study of His Art-in-Jewels*, 36–37, 46–47.

520. For Dalí's explanation of the motif, see ibid., 28. For other images of the cracked or pierced globe, see Robert Descharnes, *Salvador Dalí*, trans. Eleanor R. Morse (New York: Harry N. Abrams, 1984), 284; also Karin V. Maur et al., *Salvador Dalí* (Stuttgart: Verlag Gerd Hatje, 1989), 84.

521. For the mural and the *Vogue* cover, see Descharnes, *Salvador Dalí*, 39, 279, 299; one exemplar of *Le Roi Soleil* was sold at Hôtel Drouot-Richelieu, Paris, December 1, 1988, no. 4.

522. Descharnes, *Salvador Dalí*, 131; Daniel Abadie, *La Vie publique de Salvador Dalí* (Paris: Centre Georges Pompidou, Musée National d'Art Moderne, 1980), 97.

523. For some examples of Dalí's use of shellfish, see Abadie, *La Vie publique de Salvador Dalí*, 81, 98.

524. For Dalí's works satirizing Picasso, see Descharnes, *Salvador Dalí*, 244, 308.

525. Another section of this yardage in the Stewart Collection (D86.170.1c) has the printed mark "'Leaf Hands' by Salvador Dalí" in the selvage.

526. As stated in the advertising announcement released by Schiffer Prints in 1949; Library, Museum of Modern Art, New York, vertical file for textiles.

527. Textile manufacturers, such as Onondaga, had previously developed designs from the work of lesser-known artists; see "Painters' Prints," *Vogue*, January 1, 1947, 124ff.; also *Life*, April 21, 1947, 94–97.

528. "Schiffer's Superlative Stimulus," *Interiors*, 108 (July 1949), 136; "Fabrics," *California Arts and Architecture*, 66 (August 1949), 16.

529. Livingston, *Dalí: A Study of His Art-in-Jewels*, 34–35, 44–45.

530. Alvin Lustig, "Modern Printed Fabrics," *American Fabrics*, 20 (Winter 1951–52), 68, notes that Jean Mersel was designing for Ciro Sportswear using the fabrics of Salvador Dalí, Bernard Rudofsky, George Nelson, and Abel Sorensen.

531. Interviews between Barnaba Fornasetti, Piero's son and successor, and Christopher Wilk, May 10–12 and June 2, 1989. A rare published description of Piero Fornasetti's technique is in Gio Ponti, "Printed Furniture," *Graphis*, 8, no. 39 (1952), 78.

532. "Le Ceramiche italiane alla Triennale," *Domus*, 262 (October 1951), 18. The porcelains were from various factories: Ceramica di Bellote, Richard Ginori, Laveno, Eschenbach, Arzberg, Winterling, and Hutschenreuther; letter from Fornasetti S.r.l. to Martin Eidelberg, October 23, 1989.

533. For forty such variations on this theme of the face, see "Lavoro e divertimento di Fornasetti," *Domus*, 313 (December 1955), 51–54.

534. "Fornasetti a tavola," *Domus*, 285 (August 1953), 46; Gio Ponti, who was his important supporter as well as collaborator, also tried his hand at dining ensembles in which the plates surrealistically "disappeared," but the effect was nonetheless more architectural; see "Tavola in positivo-negativo," *Domus*, 289 (December 1953), 26–47.

535. "Fornasetti," *House and Garden*, 122 (August 1962), 77.

536. The phrase is taken directly from Kramer's own promotional flyer. See Mark Foley, "Sam Kramer: Fantastic Jewelry for People Who Are Slightly Mad," *Metalsmith*, 6 (Winter 1986), 11. The mushroom motif was used by Kramer as his trademark and was meant as a direct reference to the phallus.

537. Sam Kramer, "Gems in New Contexts," *Craft Horizons*, 12 (September–October 1952), 30–31.

538. Sarane Alexandrain, *Surrealist Art* (New York: Thames and Hudson, 1985), 150.

539. Ibid., 143.

540. For further discussion of this phenomenon, see Martin Battersby, *The Decorative Thirties* (New York: Walker, 1971), 129–98.

541. "Emprunt des Grands Barrages," *L'Echo de la presse*, July 20, 1951.

542. Interview between Giò Pomodoro and Luce Hoctin in *Giò Pomodoro* (Rome: Marlborough Galleria d'Arte, S.p.A., 1964), 4.

543. Enrichetta Ritter, "Pomodoro: The Jewelry of Arnaldo and Giò," *Craft Horizons*, 25 (July–August 1965), 10.

544. Interview between Pomodoro and Hoctin, 4.

545. Abraham Moles, "The Work of the Pomodoros and the Artifices of Perception," *Art International*, 3, no. 8 (1959), 71.

Expressionist Modern

546. Photographs of Voulkos at work are included in Conrad Brown, "Peter Voulkos," *Craft Horizons*, 16 (September–October 1956), 12–18. For several suites of photographs of Jackson Pollock performing, see Hans Namuth, *Pollock Painting* (New York: Agrinde Publications, 1980).

547. For Hicks's oeuvre, see Monique Lévi-Strauss, *Sheila Hicks* (Paris: Pierre Horay and Suzy Langlois, 1973). For Hesse's work, see Lucy R. Lippard, *Eva Hesse* (New York: New York University Press, 1976); Bill Barrette, *Eva Hesse, Sculpture* (New York: Timken Publishers, 1989). An interesting comparison could be made between Hicks's wall hanging for the Ford Foundation (1967) and Hesse's *Ring around Arosie* (1965), both of which use repeated spirals of wound fiber as their motif.

548. Robert Morris, "Anti Form," *Artforum*, 6 (April 1968), 33–35.

549. The stimulus of the ceramics of Picasso and Joan Miró was signaled early on in a seminal article: Rose Slivka, "The New Ceramic Presence," *Craft Horizons*, 21 (July–August 1961), 35.

550. Sam Hunter, *The Museum of Modern Art* (New York: Harry N. Abrams and the Museum of Modern Art, 1984), 445.

551. Letter from Ibram Lassaw to David A. Hanks, November 10, 1987.

552. Ibram Lassaw, quoted in Renée Sabatello Neu, *Jewelry by Contemporary Painters and Sculptors* (New York: Museum of Modern Art, 1967), n.p.

553. For the exhibition, see Henry-Russell Hitchcock, *Gaudí* (New York: Museum of Modern Art, 1957). Much of the information presented in this essay is based on interviews between Irena Brynner and Toni Lesser Wolf in the spring of 1989.

554. A very similar chair that preceded this one is now in the Detroit Institute of Arts: Davira S. Taragin, Edward S. Cooke, Jr., and Joseph Giovannini, *Furniture by Wendell Castle* (New York: Hudson Hills Press in association with the Detroit Institute of Arts, 1989), 17, 20–21.

555. *Young Americans 1962* (New York: Museum of Contemporary Crafts, 1962), 36, no. 36.

556. For a clear discussion of the emergence of fiber as a medium for sculpture, see Mildred Constantine and Jack Lenor Larsen, *Beyond Craft: The Art Fabric* (New York: Van Nostrand Reinhold, 1972).

557. Jasia Reichardt, *Magdalena Abakanowicz* (Chicago: Museum of Contemporary Art,

1982), 50.

558. Magdalena Abakanowicz, quoted in ibid., 48.

559. Ibid., 15.

560. In the case of the 1953 jar, the dry greenware was covered with wax resist, the drawing was scratched into the wax, and then a white slip was applied and rubbed into the incised lines. After the bisque firing, a red slip was applied. Voulkos also developed other variants of this etching-related process. See Rose Slivka, *Peter Voulkos, A Dialogue with Clay* (New York: New York Graphic Society in association with American Crafts Council, 1978), 10, 12–13.

561. For some of Peter Voulkos's own paintings, see ibid., 38, 57, plate 18.

562. Joseph Hurley, "Toshiko Takaezu, Ceramics of Serenity," *American Craft*, 39 (October–November 1979), 4–5; see also Joy Hakanson, "Another Look at Craft Exhibition," *Detroit News*, March 13, 1955.

563. "To Toshiko, symmetry is cold and mechanical, and she will deliberately *distort* a perfect form. She prefers to capture the essence of roundness; the idea of roundness; shapes that will give the illusion of fullness"; Susan E. Meyers, "The Pottery of Toshiko Takaezu," *American Artist*, 33 (February 1969), 42.

564. Arthur Drexler, "The Andersen Armchair," *MoMA* (Winter 1974–75), n.p., describes the process. This article was reprinted (without citing the source) with illustrations in *Aagaard Andersen* (Copenhagen: Jens Jorgen Thorsen, 1985), 20–23. See also "Upping the Nature of Materials," *Progressive Architecture*, 47 (March 1966), 173–75.

565. Gunnar Aagaard Andersen, "Furniture Reconsidered," *Mobilia*, 296–97 (1980), 89.

566. The Andersen chair was an object held in much affection by the director of the Museum of Modern Art's Department of Architecture and Design, Arthur Drexler, who often exhibited it and wrote about it with what one can only describe as considerable empathy.

567. Harvey Littleton, quoted in what is perhaps the best account of his early experimentation with glass: Dido Smith, "Offhand Glass Blowing," *Craft Horizons*, 24 (January–February 1964), 22–23, 53–54.

568. Harvey Littleton, "Glass by Erwin Eisch," *Craft Horizons*, 23 (May–June 1963), 14–17.

569. Smith, "Offhand Glass Blowing," 53–54. Interestingly, Peter Voulkos and Harvey Littleton had both participated in the 1959 American Craft Council's National Conference at Lake George, New York. Voulkos spoke and demonstrated at the wheel, while Littleton chaired a session devoted to glass.

570. Ibid., 54. The marbles were actually the glass matrix of fiberglass and were developed by Dominick Labino, then vice president and director of research for the Glass Fibers Division of Johns Mansville. The use of such marbles was intended also to get around the problem of exposing students to corrosive fumes.

571. *Woven Forms* (New York: Museum of Contemporary Crafts, 1963), 6.

572. Much of the information presented here derives from an interview between Sheila Hicks and Kate Carmel, December 22, 1989.

573. The Evolving Tapestry series was exhibited at the American Cultural Center in Paris in 1967–68. The brown group is now in the collection of the Museum of Modern Art, New York.

Beyond Modern

574. E.g., see Lawrence Alloway, *American Pop Art* (New York: Collier Books, 1974).

575. For a good overview, see Michael Auping, *Abstraction · Geometry · Painting: Selected Geometric Abstract Painting in America since 1945* (New York: Harry N. Abrams in association with the Albright-Knox Art Gallery, Buffalo, 1989).

576. Robert Venturi, "A Justification for a Pop Architecture," *Arts and Architecture*, 82 (April 1965), 22; idem, *Complexity and Contradiction in Architecture* (New York: Museum of Modern Art, 1966).

577. The following discussion of Guild House is based on the architect's own analysis in Robert Venturi, Denise Scott Brown, and Steven Izenour, *Learning from Las Vegas* (1972; Cambridge, Massachusetts: The MIT Press, 1977), 90–103.

578. For a discussion of Ettore Sottsass's stylistic evolution, see Penny Sparke, *Ettore Sottsass Jnr* (London: The Design Council, 1982), 20–46.

579. The popular name *Marshmallow* was apparently introduced at an early date; it appears on a blueprint in the collection of Irving Harper that is dated July 22, 1955.

580. The drawing in the Stewart Collection from Irving Harper (fig. 481) is dated June 3, 1954, with revisions dated February 7, 1955. An original blueprint in the collection of Irving Harper is dated July 22, 1955. The sofa was first published in "Pre-Market Furniture Introduction," *Interiors*, 115 (May 1956), 114.

581. Interview between Irving Harper and David A. Hanks, June 6, 1989.

582. "Design for the Designer: Three Interiors George Nelson Inhabits and Works In," *Interiors*, 117 (May 1958), 118–22.

583. Letter from George Nelson to David A. Hanks & Associates, October 14, 1981.

584. According to the donor, the lamp was purchased in 1966.

585. Friedrich Becker's first truly kinetic piece, which varied *automatically* with the random movements of the wearer, was done in 1964. See Karl Schollmayer, *Friedrich Becker: Schmuck, Silbergerät, Kinetische Objekte 1951–1983* (Düsseldorf: Kunstverein für die Rheinlande und Westfalen), n.p.

586. Barbara Cartlidge, *Twentieth-Century Jewelry* (New York: Harry N. Abrams, 1985), 109.

587. There has been confusion as to the proper manufacturer of the chair. Vitra, after discussions with Verner Panton, approached Herman Miller. The latter agreed to fund technical work on the design, and manufacture was a joint venture, with Vitra acting as a subcontractor. The chair was marketed under the Herman Miller name alone, as was typical of the joint ventures undertaken by Herman Miller and Vitra since 1957. From 1973 to 1975, Herman Miller manufactured the chair in the United States, while Vitra continued to produce it in Europe. This information was provided in letters from Linda Folland, of Herman Miller, Inc., to Christopher Wilk, October 12, 1989, and January 4, 1990; Rolf Jehlbaum also supplied information and on November 8, 1989, wrote a memo for an interview held on November 17, 1989, between Alexander von Vegesack of the Vitra Design Museum and Christopher Wilk.

588. Verner Panton's design represented a logical development of the single-piece molded seat pioneered by the Eameses, but its form has little to do with earlier, unsuccessful attempts at single-piece chairs, such as Robert Lewis and James Prestini's well-publicized single-piece chair developed for the Museum of Modern Art's competition for low-cost furniture; see Edgar Kaufmann, jr., *Prize Designs for Modern Furniture from the International Competition for Low-Cost Furniture Design* (New York: Museum of Modern Art, 1950), 44–47.

589. For a series of German single-piece chair designs by Helmut Bätzner, R. Reineman, and Walter Päpst, see *Form* (Cologne), 33 (March 1966), 13; ibid., 34 (June 1966), 70. An important design of 1961, mass-produced starting in 1966 by the Artemide firm, was Vico Magistretti's *Selene* stacking chair; see Emilio Ambasz, ed., *Italy: The New Domestic Landscape* (New York: Museum of Modern Art in collaboration with Centro Di, Florence, 1972), 41.

590. Much of the factual information presented here is derived from correspondence between Verner Panton and Christopher Wilk, May 8 and 28, June 5 and 8, 1989.

591. Letter from Panton to Wilk, June 8, 1989. The wood chair was designed for a competition sponsored by the WK Gesellschaft für Wohngestaltung mbH, an association of furniture dealers. The designer was dissatisfied with the chair's structure and its high cost of manufacture.

592. The mold was made by Dansk Acryl Teknik. Although Panton recalls starting discussions with Vitra in 1962–63, the first successful prototypes (molded from GFK Polyester, a fiberglass-reinforced plastic) were apparently made and published in 1967. Early production models were made from Baydur (alternatively described as PU-hardfoam) which was then lacquered. In 1970 the material was changed to BASF-brand Luran-S, a thermoplastic. The same material was used when the design was reproduced in the late 1980s by Horn Gmbh & Co. KG of Rudersberg, Germany. This information was provided in letters from Panton to Wilk, May 28 and June 8, 1989, and by the Vitra technical staff, as presented during the interview between von Vegesack and Wilk, November 17, 1989.

593. These had been preceded in 1966 by the production of Vico Magistretti's *Selene* stacking chair.

594. Arthur D. Bracegirdle's name is recorded on the design registration form (no. 942763), submitted July 15, 1969.

595. The design of *Eclipse* has previously been dated 1965; see Ambasz, *Italy: The New Domestic Landscape*, 59; however, a sketch of the lamp that shows preliminary planning stages (fig. 497) is dated 1966. It was illustrated in "Una Piccola lampada di Magistretti," *Domus*, 453 (August 1967), 33.

596. *Domus*, 384 (November 1961), 18.

597. "Una Nuova lampada da parete in vetro," *Domus*, 409 (December 1963), after p. 30.

598. A piano lamp with a shade that revolved around the light bulb was designed by K. J. Jucker at the Bauhaus in 1923; Hans M. Wingler, *The Bauhaus* (Cambridge, Massachusetts: The MIT Press, 1969), 314–15. A somewhat similar arrangement is seen in a table lamp by Stilnovo; "Rassegna domus," *Domus*, 313 (December 1955), n.p. However, both lacked Vico Magistretti's metaphor of an eclipse.

599. The *Eclipse* lamp is said to have been designed so that in addition to sitting on a table, it could be hung on a wall to be used for reading in bed; see *Domus*, 453 (August 1967), 33.

600. Ibid.

601. E. Sottsass, Jr., "Experience with Ceramics," *Domus*, 489 (August 1970), 56–57.

602. Ibid.

603. Sparke, *Ettore Sottsass Jnr*, 14, 15, 34–35.

604. "Elementi di arredamento: armadi, tavoli, specchi, ceramiche," *Domus*, 353 (April 1959), 39–43.

605. Letter from Ettore Sottsass to Christine W. Laidlaw, September 5, 1989.

606. Guia Sambonet, *Ettore Sottsass: Furniture and a Few Interiors* (Milan: Arnoldo Mondodori, 1985), 18, 36. This example of tower furniture was originally published in "La Casa con la bambina cinese," *Domus*, 406 (September 1963), 22–23.

607. Sparke, *Ettore Sottsass Jnr*, 40.

608. Ettore Sottsass, quoted in Max Bill and Ettore Sottsass, Jr., "Design and Theory: Two Points of View," in Kathryn B. Hiesinger and George H. Marcus, eds., *Design since 1945* (Philadelphia: Philadelphia Museum of Art, 1983), 3.

609. Ettore Sottsass, "Ettore Sottsass Jr: Mobili 1965," *Domus*, 433 (December 1965), 38, as translated in Sambonet, *Ettore Sottsass: Furniture*, 39.

610. Sottsass, "Ettore Sottsass Jr: Mobili 1965," 35–42. Another set of furniture was exhibited in 1967; see Tomasso Trini, "Ettore Sottsass Jr: Katalogo mobili 1966," *Domus*, 449 (April 1967), 37–45. The sketch (fig. 505) was first published in 1985; see Sambonet, *Ettore Sottsass: Furniture*, 40. Sottsass drew the production plan in March 1988. Some minor changes were introduced, especially in the horizontal drawers in the middle and the two central vertical posts at the top.

611. According to Fausto Abatinelli of Flos (telephone conversation with Christine W. Laidlaw, June 6, 1989), the lamp was put into production right after the design had been completed and was discontinued about 1978 because it became too expensive to produce. This lamp is discussed in Cara McCarty, *Mario Bellini, Designer* (New York: Museum of Modern Art, 1987), 54.

612. *Domus*, 303 (February 1955), 38.

613. Information in this essay was given by Grete Jalk to Christopher Wilk in a letter of August 3, 1989, and in a telephone interview, September 6, 1989.

614. The dish-shaped seats and backs of the Eameses' 1946 chairs (fig. 30) were widely imitated and, as in the 1962 Jalk chair, often put on somewhat inharmonious bases. A Danish example is Hans Wegner's *Skalstol* (Shell Chair) of about 1948, published in Johan Møller Nielsen, *Wegner, en dansk møbelkunstner* (Copenhagen: Gyldendal, 1965), 82.

615. Malitte was the name of the artist's third(?) wife (conversation between Roberto Matta and Luc d'Iberville-Moreau, director of Le Musée des Arts Décoratifs de Montréal, April 24, 1989). He also used her name for the title of a painting in 1962; see Francesco Arcangeli and Franco Solmi, *Sebastian Matta* (Bologna: Museo Civico, 1963), no. 28.

616. Conversation between Matta and d'Iberville-Moreau, April 24, 1989.

617. One of the first illustrations of *Malitte* shows

it in green with a yellow center. See "Eurodomus," *Domus*, 463 (June 1968), n.p.

618. Alain Sayag and Claude Schweisguth, eds., *Matta* (Paris: Centre Georges Pompidou, Musée National d'Art Moderne, 1985), 202–3. For Matta's sculpture, see *Matta: Skulpturen und Bilder* (Zurich: Gimpel & Hanover Galerie, 1964).

619. For *Sofo*, see *Domus*, 475 (June 1969), 29.

620. Information from the Marimekko records was kindly provided by Riitta Koljonen, manager of public relations, in a letter to Alice Zrebiec, September 12, 1989.

621. The designer's records indicate that his experiments began in 1965; letter from Anders Reihnér, AB Orrefors Glasbruk, to Kate Carmel, May 14, 1990. See also *Form*, 62, no. 6 (1966), 397; ibid., no. 9 (1966), 625. Much of the information presented here was obtained in an interview between Gunnar Cyrén and Martin Eidelberg, October 7, 1989.

622. To understand more clearly how Cyrén interpreted nature, one might look at the way the artist created exotic birds in silver. See Helena Dahlbäck Lutteman, "Gunnar Cyrén," in *Contemporary Swedish Design* (Stockholm: Nationalmuseum and Svensk Form, 1983), 25.

623. "Notiser," *Form*, 62, no. 6 (1966), 397.

624. Ray and Lee Grover, *Contemporary Art Glass* (New York: Crown Publishers, 1975), 118; David R. McFadden, ed., *Scandinavian Modern Design, 1880–1980* (New York: Harry N. Abrams, 1982), 190–91; *The Modern Spirit—Glass from Finland* (Riihimäki: Suomen Lasimuseo, 1985), figs. 23–24.

625. See especially a design that the Venini firm executed for Philips; illustrated in Dan Klein and Margaret Bishop, *Decorative Art 1880–1980* (Oxford: Phaidon and Christie's, 1986), 230–31.

626. In the same way, Kaj Franck's late series of bubbled-glass vases (see Grover, *Contemporary Art Glass*, 118, plate 85) can be seen as a reprise of an idea from 1947; but the early glass has a controlled mass of bubbles encased within a smooth contour, whereas the later work has burst bubbles covering the exterior and thus reflects the new taste for rougher, more aggressive surfaces.

627. There were other color ways as well. The 1965 Herman Miller, Inc., price list for fabrics also lists model no. 65012 in orange, magenta, and black on white and no. 65032 in gray green, raw umber, and ultramarine light on white.

628. The dating of this and the other *Palio* series textiles is based on information supplied in a letter from Linda Folland, of Herman Miller, Inc., to Christine W. Laidlaw, September 27, 1989.

629. Charles Lockwood, "A Perfectionist at Play," *Connoisseur*, 213 (January 1983), 92–99. For photographs by Charles Eames of Alexander Girard's house, see "A Santa Fè," *Domus*, 353 (April 1959), 49–51.

630. Ten of Siena's seventeen districts take part in any given race, and the winning district receives a silken banner called a *palio*, which has a painted image of the Virgin. The name means both the prize and the event. For a recent account of the Palio and the intrigues and ceremonies involved, see Lis Harris, "Annals of Intrigue (The Palio)," *The New Yorker*, June 5, 1989, 83–104.

631. Telephone conversation between Susan Girard, the designer's wife, and Christine W. Laidlaw, August 28, 1989.

632. Each of Alexander Girard's patterns came in several color ways. Although our examples have muted tones (*Palio* is black on grayish beige; *Palio 2* is goldenrod yellow on off white; and *Palio 6* is Aztec gold on natural), brighter colors were available: teal, blue, coral, peach, lavender, sea green, and bright yellow green, each combined with white or natural; see letter from Folland to Laidlaw, September 27, 1989.

633. Terence Conran, *Printed Textile Design* (London and New York: Studio Publications, 1957), 40; Jack Lenor Larsen, "Alexander Girard," in "Nelson, Eames, Girard, Propst: The Design Process at Herman Miller," *Design Quarterly*, 98–99 (1975), 31.

Biographies and Corporate Histories

Aalto, Hugo Alvar Henrik Born Kuortane, Finland, February 3, 1898; died Helsinki, May 11, 1976

Alvar Aalto's contributions to modern design are manifold: in addition to the domestic and civic architecture, including major industrial housing projects and city planning, he has deeply influenced the fields of furniture, lighting, and glass design.[1]

After completing architectural studies at Helsingen Teknillinen Korkeakoulu (Helsinki University of Technology) in 1921, Aalto designed simple frame pavilions for the Industrial Exposition at Tampere in 1922. The rusticism and classicism of these structures characterize much of Aalto's earliest work. Two years later Aalto married Aino Marsio, a qualified architect who worked jointly with her husband for twenty-five years.[2] Aalto's development followed a continuous progression, beginning with the classicism of such buildings as the Southwestern Agricultural Cooperative Building at Turku (1928). The Constructivist elements in his *Turun-Sanomat* newspaper building (1930) marked a break with traditionalism, and in the Paimio Sanatorium (1929–33) and the Municipal Library at Viipuri (1935), two landmark buildings, Aalto employed the International Style. Although ever a rationalist, Aalto remained concerned with the intimate aspects of designed environments. In his organic shaping and use of natural materials, already evident in the lecture hall at the Viipuri library and dramatically exploited in the Finnish Pavilion for the New York World's Fair (1939), Aalto created a highly original and freely expressive version of the Modernist style. The Museum of Modern Art in New York held an exhibition of Aalto's work in 1938, which helped establish his international reputation. In 1940 Aalto returned to the United States as professor of architecture at Boston's Massachusetts Institute of Technology. After the war Aalto completed a number of important commissions that included several civic buildings, notably, the House of Culture (1955–58) and the Finlandia Concert Hall (1964) in Helsinki and the Cultural Center (1963) in Wolfsburg, Germany.

Although Aalto was in the avant-garde when he experimented with tubular steel furniture in the 1920s, it was in the area of molded plywood that he made his greatest advancements. A molded plywood seat supported on a bent tubular frame was a transitional stage; the *Paimio* chair (1930–33) showed the fully developed solution: a sweeping, rounded form comprised of laminated birch sides bent into a continuous, closed curve. An equally important design is the laminated armchair of 1932, model no. 379, whose sides bend in an open curve to cantilever the seat and back. These and other designs, such as his L-leg stool and trolley cart, established a formal vocabulary for plywood furniture, and, through the Artek firm that Aalto and his associates founded, he disseminated it worldwide.

In his later furniture designs, Aalto refined the earlier work. Taking the L-leg as his basis, in 1947 he developed the Y-leg, which provided a functional and visual joining of horizontal and vertical planes. This, in turn, evolved into the fan leg, a form made more graceful by the vaultlike plane of striated laminates at the knee.

Aalto's glassware dates from 1932, when he and Aino competed in a Karhula-Iittala competition. The *Bölgeblick* and related series of pressed-glass tableware,

with its emphatic geometry of concentric rings and stepped sides, echoes the hard-edged geometry of Aalto's early architecture. The same aesthetic can be seen in the *Riihimäki Flower* set of stacked vases, which won a second prize in the 1933 competition sponsored by the Riihimäki glassworks. On the other hand, Alvar Aalto's winning series of vases with undulant walls, known as *Aalto* or *Savoy*, for a 1936 Karhula-Iittala competition is characteristic of the architect's later organic style.

Aalto humanized the International Style, and the validity of his vision is confirmed by the great esteem in which his architecture is still held and the continuous production of his furniture and glass designs.

MOR

Aarnio, Eero Born Helsinki, July 21, 1932

Aarnio is one of the architects and designers responsible for firmly establishing Finland in the international design market of the 1960s.

Aarnio was educated at the Taideteollisuuskeskuskoulu (School of Industrial Design) in Helsinki from 1954 to 1957. His early furniture designs conformed to the earlier twentieth-century Finnish practice of following the Finnish heritage of furniture making by staying close to traditional design procedures and focusing on native materials.

However, by the 1960s Aarnio was experimenting with plastics, making a major departure from the traditional forms that are structured with legs, backs, and joints, and he delighted in the vivid, chemical colorations of the synthetic material as opposed to the natural grain of wood. His exciting plastic creations, especially the *Ball* (1963–65), *Bubble* (1965), and *Pastilli* (1968) chairs, were widely photographed and publicized and came to characterize the nonconformist spirit of that time. Of balloon rotundity, scooped out or slightly flattened, they form a single unit of seat and base and can even create an enclosure.

In his own design practice in Helsinki, established in 1962, Aarnio has specialized in interior and furniture design and has also worked in other areas, especially graphic design and photography. His current interest lies in the potential of computer-aided design. Aarnio has been the recipient of many international design awards.

KC

Abakanowicz, Magdalena Born Falenty, Poland, June 20, 1930

The life and art of Magdalena Abakanowicz—one of Europe's most avant-garde fiber designers—have been deeply influenced by her experiences during World War II and life in postwar Eastern Europe.[3] During her professional training at the Academy of Fine Arts in Warsaw between 1950 and 1954 she was considered a rebellious and unconventional painting student, unwilling to accept the stylistic restrictions imposed by Socialist Realism. Her artistic maturation was stimulated by contact with the avant-garde artists grouped around the painter Heryk Stazewski, who familiarized her with Western artistic developments. Later in the 1950s she returned briefly to the Academy of Fine Arts to study weaving but left when the instruc-

tors insisted that she conform to conventional weaving methods.

Her international reputation commenced with her participation in the "1st International Biennial of Tapestry" in Lausanne in 1962 and a show of her work that same year in Paris. During the 1960s she began the series of loom-woven sculptures referred to as *Abakans*, starting with wall-hung reliefs and then progressing to monumental three-dimensional forms or arrangements in space. Enthusiastic response from the West ensured frequent exhibitions, and she has in the past three decades achieved international recognition for her sculptural environments, in which she employs mediums as diverse as burlap, bronze, wood, and stone. She has had more than sixty exhibitions in Europe, North and South America, Australia, and Japan, and her work is in major public collections throughout the world.

Abakanowicz lives and works in Warsaw, and she has been a professor at the Academy of Fine Arts in Poznan since 1965.

KC

Akari Associates A subsidiary of the Isamu Noguchi Foundation, Akari Associates is the coordinator and manager of worldwide sales of a line of electric lamps that the sculptor Isamu Noguchi began designing in 1951. Known as *Akari*, which in Japanese means *light*, these lighting fixtures were inspired by traditional Japanese paper lanterns. They are manufactured in Gifu, Japan, by Ozeki & Co., Ltd., a company founded in the nineteenth century that makes traditional festival lanterns used throughout Japan, in addition to those designed by Noguchi.

The early *Akari* production line, which consisted of relatively small-scale table models, was greatly expanded over the years. In 1962, Akari introduced standing lamps lit with fluorescent tubes, though the line was suspended by the end of that decade. Noguchi responded to the cheaper imitations that others soon produced by offering an even greater variety of shades in more complex shapes. In 1969 he conceived thirty new designs, which Akari marketed in signed, limited editions. Today, *Akari* lamps are available in more than sixty models, including some of the sculptor's earliest efforts as well as the most recent—pyramidal modules to cover an entire ceiling.

Akari Associates is located in Long Island City, New York. Akari-Gemini, an independent company founded in 1985 with headquarters in Santa Barbara, California, now distributes Akari lamps in North America. The sale of *Akari* lamps helps support the Isamu Noguchi Foundation.

MOR

Albini, Franco Born Robbiate (Como), Italy, October 17, 1905; died Milan, November 1, 1977

Like most Italian designers, Albini was trained as an architect, graduating from the Politecnico of Milan in 1929.[4] He worked in Gio Ponti's studio both before and after his graduation, until he set up his own studio in 1930. Albini turned away from Ponti's more traditional approach to design in the 1930s and joined the rationalist architects who designed interiors for the Milan

VI Triennale of 1936. He was one of the first Modernist Italian designers to achieve international recognition, and his work was widely imitated.

A man of many talents, Albini became one of Italy's major postwar architects, a city planner, a designer of furniture and interiors, consumer products, museum installations, and exhibitions. He was editor of the design periodical *Casabella* from 1945 to 1946 and taught interior architecture, decoration, and furniture design at the Istituto Universitario di Architettura, Venice, from 1949 to 1964 and then at the Politecnico in Milan.

In 1951 Albini started working with architect Franca Helg. Some of their best-known works are the restoration of the Museo di Palazzo Rosso in Genoa (1952–54), the Rinascente department store in Rome (1957–61), stations for the Milan subway system (1960–63, 1967–69), and the Snam office building, San Donato Milanese (1970–72). The firm was enlarged in the 1960s when Antonio Piva joined in 1962 and the architect's son Marco in 1965. The firm's work is known for the careful way in which it is fitted into its environment.

From the 1930s through the 1950s, Albini designed furniture for Knoll, Poggi, Bonacina, Arflex, Pirelli, Siemens, and Fontana Arte. His pieces, like the *Luisa* chair of 1955 or the *Tre Pezzi* chair of 1959 (both designed with Franca Helg), were noted for their spare, Modernist geometry. Although Albini and Helg designed two lamps for Sirrah and an armchair for Bonacina in 1968, Albini is said to have lost interest in designing individual objects toward the end of his career, supposedly because designing had become dominated by the connection between production and consumption.[5]

CWL

Alemany & Ertman, Inc.
The history of this New York City jewelry firm is somewhat obscure, despite the fame it has enjoyed as the producer of a series of spectacular jewels designed by Salvador Dalí.[6] One of the partners in the venture was the Argentinian-born diamond merchant Carlos B. Alemany, who apparently arrived in New York around 1948. The other partner, Charles Eric Ertman, was described as a Finnish shipping magnate; he was in New York by 1945, but his business activities are not known.

By 1948 the firm of Alemany & Ertman was established at 608 Fifth Avenue, adjacent to the jewelry district, and its principal business was in diamonds. Incorporated during the course of the next year, it moved its operation to 745 Fifth Avenue, just off Fifty-seventh Street, the home of many New York galleries. About this time it introduced the Dalí jewelry, as both unique *objets d'art* (which were bought by the Catherwood Foundation) and closely related designs produced in limited series. In each case, Alemany & Ertman acted as promoters and distributors, while the manufacture was left to professionals in the jewelry district.

The firm's name was reduced to Alemany & Co., Inc., about 1957, though Ertman was still listed in business at the same address for several years more. By 1964 Alemany had changed his declared specialization from diamonds to gemstones, and he also changed his place of business, to the fashionable St. Regis Hotel, where he remained until about 1988.

ME

Alexander Smith and Sons
The firm of Alexander Smith and Sons was one of the leading midnineteenth-century American carpet and rug manufacturers. Founded by Alexander Smith (1818–1878) in 1845, it was established at a small mill in West Farms, Bronx, New York. In 1849, Smith met Halcyon Skinner (1824–1900), a carpenter by trade and an inventor. Smith and Skinner worked on several inventions, all intended to speed up the weaving process for carpets and rugs. In 1855, the two conceived the idea of a power loom to weave Axminster, or tufted, carpets.[7]

After fires destroyed the West Farms plant in the early 1860s, Smith moved the company to Yonkers. During the mid-1870s, Alexander Smith became known nationally and internationally as a producer of quality carpets.[8]

During the following sixty years the company expanded steadily and was so successful that it had no need to shut its mills down during the Depression. At the end of World War II, the company celebrated its one-hundredth anniversary, and by then it was "the largest carpet manufacturer in the world."[9] Several walkouts and strikes occurred during the 1950s. The mill was moved to Greenville, Mississippi, but offices remained in New York City, and the firm merged on December 30, 1955, with Mohawk Carpet Mills.

CCMT

American Thermos Bottle Company
The American Thermos Bottle Company was founded by William B. Walker in 1907. Manufacturing began in Brooklyn, New York, and later expanded to Manhattan. By 1912, as growing sales demanded a new, larger facility, the company moved to Norwich, Connecticut, beginning production at the new plant in the spring of 1913. By 1920 the company expanded further, with plants in Japan and England. With the death of its founder in 1922, the company was reorganized the next year, followed by further expansion and consolidation. In 1925 it merged with the Icy-Hot Company of Cincinnati, Ohio.

Throughout the 1930s and the 1940s, new products were introduced, all related to insulated bottles and picnic kits. The 1950s was a decade of expansion into other fields through the acquisition of a producer of plastic wall tile and bathroom fixtures and also a manufacturer of picnic equipment. In 1956 the corporate name was changed to the American Thermos Products Company, reflecting the company's diversification. In 1960, the American Thermos Products Company merged with the King-Seeley Corporation under the name of the Thermos Division of the King-Seeley Thermos Company. During 1968 King-Seeley became a wholly owned subsidiary of Household Finance Corporation (now Household International). In 1982, King-Seeley Thermos Company merged with the Wallace Murray Company to form Household Manufacturing and it operated as a wholly owned subsidiary of Household Manufacturing. In 1986 the company merged yet again, with Structo, its sister division in Household Manufacturing, to form the Thermos Company. A recognized leader in vacuum and insulated products, it was composed of three divisions (Halsey Taylor, Structo, and Thermos) with manufacturing plants in Freeport, Illinois, and Batesville, Mississippi, and it employed over ten thousand people. In 1989 the Thermos Company was sold to Nippon Sanso K.K., a Japanese supplier of industrial gases, as well as other industrial and consumer products.

GS

A. Michelsen
A. Michelsen is one of Denmark's major silver companies.[10] It was founded in Copenhagen in 1841 by Anton Michelsen (1809–1877), who seven years later was appointed court jeweler. He was succeeded in 1877 by his son Carl (1853–1921). The firm made silver in traditional Danish styles, including Viking Revival, and the work it executed for the Danish court was copied from eighteenth-century pieces. Near the end of the century, Arnold Emil Krog, the painter whose Japanese-inspired designs had brought international fame to the Royal Copenhagen porcelain factory, convinced Carl Michelsen to produce designs in a more modern style. Michelsen commissioned designs from Krog, the painter Harald Slott-Møller, and the designer Thorvald Bindesbøll, among others, and this campaign resulted in a most successful showing at the Paris Exposition Universelle in 1900. Bindesbøll's designs, with their stylized, petallike motifs, are particularly distinctive.

The founder's grandson, Poul Michelsen (1881–1957), took control in 1921. Architect Kay Fisker designed much of the firm's silver in the 1920s. At its most interesting it is related to Scandinavia's Moderne classicism. Tellingly, Fisker's design for a pitcher (1927) suggests an analogy with one by Johan Rohde for Georg Jensen Silversmithy a few years earlier; indeed, in terms of design leadership, as Jensen's star rose, Michelsen's declined. In 1941 the firm celebrated its centenary with a competition, which led to commissioned designs from the architects Tove and Ev. Kindt Larsen as well as Ole Hagen.

Erik Herlow was Michelsen's major designer in the decades after World War II; although many of his works received critical attention, they were essentially conservative, with only a slight hint of the lyric freedom exhibited by other postwar silversmiths. A. Michelsen began to work in nonprecious metals such as silver plate. As a special commission it produced Arne Jacobsen's *AJ* flatware in stainless steel for the SAS Hotel (1957). Nanna Ditzel and Arje Griegst are among those who have contributed more recent designs. In 1969 A. Michelsen began collaborating with the Royal Copenhagen factory in the production of jewelry. Today the two firms, as well as Bing & Grøndahl and Georg Jensen, have been fused into one corporation, each with its separate operation, headed overall by Carlsberg Tuborg.

ME

Andersen, Gunnar Aagaard
Born Ordrup, Denmark, July 14, 1919; died Dronningmølle, Denmark, June 29, 1982.

Active as a painter, sculptor, architect, and designer, Gunnar Andersen studied at two Copenhagen institutions, Kunsthåndvaerkerskolen (School of Arts and Crafts) from 1936 to 1939 and Kongelige Danske Kunstakademi (Royal Danish Academy of Fine Arts) from 1940 to 1946, and at the Kungliga Konsthögskolan (Royal Academy Art School), Stockholm, from 1939 to 1940.[11] He made his artistic debut at the 1937 "Kunstnernes Efterårsudstilling" (Artists' Fall Exhibition) and thereafter continued to exhibit works inspired by natural forms and Asian textiles throughout Europe and in the United States, Israel, Venezuela, and Brazil.

Recognized for his keen and occasionally irreverent application of new styles, materials, and technologies, Andersen was as widely praised for modular paintings and sculptures with rearrangeable parts as he was for poured urethane foam chairs, a winding-pipeline heating unit installed at the Damgaard Textile Mille, and a system of seven pure colors devised for Unika-Vaev, which ultimately became a Danish standard for furniture fabrics. Graphic designs, most notably for the periodical *Mobilia*, book illustration, interior design, and light sculpture were among his other professional interests.

Both in his practice and in theory, which he communicated as a professor of painting at the Copenhagen Kunstakademi from 1972 to 1981, Andersen emphasized a thorough technical knowledge of materials and stressed that the most challenging aspect of design is to make creative use of the very qualities of a material that initially appear to provide the greatest limitations.[12]

MBF

Apelli & Varesio F. Apelli and L. Varesio had a small furniture-making company in Turin in the late 1940s and early 1950s. The firm is best known for making much of Carlo Mollino's bentwood furniture, using the cold-bending process for which Mollino received a patent in the 1940s. All of these pieces were made to order rather than mass-produced. Indeed, photographs of the Apelli & Varesio shop show men working by hand on several models of Mollino's furniture.[13]

CWL

Arabia Oy Finland's most important pottery, Arabia was founded in 1873 as a subsidiary of the Swedish Rörstrand pottery in order to gain access to the Finnish and Russian markets.[14] Molds for the forms, the printing plates for the decoration, and even the sale catalogues were brought from Sweden. Arabia's style was essentially a close imitation of English majolica and commercial transfer-printed china. Before the end of the century some of the majolica wares by Thure Oberg approached the style of Italian Art Nouveau, though the resemblance to Royal Copenhagen porcelains, with their naturalism and soft palette, was more evident in most of the factory's modern lines.

Arabia remained indebted to its Swedish owners and foreign competitors for a long time to come, but it gave indications of a growing independence. By the 1890s much of the technical work was being done in Finland; dinner services with Finnish scenes had been introduced; and, perhaps most significant, the *Fennia* and *Penna* series of 1902 were both decorated with specifically Finnish geometric designs and paralleled the nationalist movement visible at the Paris Exposition Universelle of 1900. The drive toward independence culminated in 1916, when the Arabia factory was purchased from Rörstrand by three Finnish businessmen.

The firm's work remained conservative, tied to past models and decoration, throughout most of the 1920s, though it showed some interesting experiments in crystalline and flambé glazes. From 1924 to 1927 ownership passed to German business interests, after which it returned to Finnish hands; as part of that transaction, Arabia gained a controlling interest in the Rörstrand factory until 1932. During the late 1920s and early 1930s the stable of Arabia artists began to take shape. Among them were Greta-Lisa Jäderholm, Austrianborn Friedl Holzer (Holzer-Kjellberg), and the Swedish artist Tyra Lundgren, who were joined in the 1930s by Toini Muona, Aune Siimes, Michael Schilkin, and Birger Kaipiainen. Commercial products still constituted a major portion of the business. In addition to dinnerware, sanitary wares became important commodities. Its first tunnel kiln, necessary for mass production, was completed by 1929 and was the largest in the world. By the mid-1930s Arabia reputedly had the greatest output of any European pottery, selling largely to South America, the Mediterranean, and the Near and Far East. While its art wares gained prizes at the Barcelona World's Fair in 1929 and the Milan V Triennale in 1933, Arabia could not be considered a leader in design.

It was only in the postwar years that Arabia's achievements became truly celebrated on an international scale. In 1945 Kaj Franck was hired as the chief designer, followed by Kaarina Alio and Ulla Procope. In 1947 Arabia was taken over by the Wärtsilä conglomerate. Concerted planning became an important part of its work. Franck's *Kilta* dinnerware (1952) typifies the highly successful modern designs that were introduced. The art wares were quite diverse—from the delicate porcelains of Kjellberg and Siimes to the reedlike, reduction-glazed vases of Muona to the rich pictorial images of Kaipiainen and Rut Bryk. In the 1960s it was decided that production wares should be anonymous, but the art wares have continued to display distinct personalities, as is shown by the strong forms and glazes of Kylikki Saimenhaara's vases and the sculptural forms of Taisto Kaasinen.

ME

Argenteria Krupp The corporate history of this Milanese firm is not public knowledge. Apparently owned by the Krupp von Essen family, it manufactured stainless steel flatware and holloware. Arthur von Essen sold the company's patents to the Milanese firm of Sambonet sometime around 1952, and the Krupp line is still marketed today by A.K. S.p.A., one of the two divisions of a holding company controlled by the Sambonet family.[15]

TLW

Arström, Folke Emanuel Born Bromma, Sweden, October 15, 1907

Folke Arström studied art in Stockholm, primarily at the Kungliga Tekniska Högskolan (Royal Institute of Technology) from 1927 to 1929, and then at the Kungliga Konsthögskolan (Royal Academy of Art School) from 1929 to 1936. At the start of his career he worked as a painter and graphic designer. He was employed at the Stockholm exhibition of 1930 and the following year did decorative painting in Linköping, including work for the Röda Kvarn cinema. He created posters and maps for the Statens Historika Museum in 1934 and decorative maps for other Swedish museums. Another of Arström's specialties is heraldic emblems. However, the major portion of his career has been devoted to industrial design, primarily using metals and, later, plastics. He worked with GuldsmedsAktieBolaget from 1935 to 1940 and with AB Gense Eskilstuna from 1940 to 1960, serving as artistic director. Among his other clients have been Skånska Ättiksfabriken, Primusfabrikerna, and Annebergfabrikerna. His work was awarded medals at the Milan Triennales from 1951 to 1960, and in 1961 he received the Gregor Paulsson trophy from the Svenska Slöjdföreningen for pioneering work in stainless steel and plastic.

GS

Artek OY Artek OY was founded on October 15, 1935, in Helsinki, with Nils-Gustav Hahl and Maire Gullichsen as partners and Alvar and Aino Aalto as principal shareholders. Artek's name, created by Aalto, was intended to suggest the union of art and technology. The firm was planned as "a centre for modern furniture and housefittings [and] exhibitions of art and industrial art."[16] The emphasis was on interior design projects for modern industrial and residential settings, as well as on public education through a gallery, reading room, and cultural publications—all underscoring an international exchange of ideas. During its early years the company indeed sold Moroccan carpets and Venini glassware, displayed Léger paintings and Calder sculptures, and sponsored a major show of French art. Yet from the beginning, its major source of income and identity was the wholesale and retail sales of Aalto's plywood furniture. International recognition came first from Great Britain and increased significantly as a result of popular exhibitions, including the world's fairs in Paris (1937) and New York (1939).

World War II and its aftermath, with its accompanying serious shortages of vital materials, adverse currency regulations, and import restrictions, interfered with Artek's operation throughout the early and mid-1940s. By 1947 the firm had recovered sufficiently to sell a significant amount of furniture in the United States. However, the ambitious cultural education program, once an integral part of the corporation, was ultimately dropped.

By the 1970s and 1980s, Artek's exports of Aalto furniture approached prewar levels in Sweden, the United States, Denmark, and Italy, while domestic sales became increasingly important, and new markets opened up in South America, Australia, and Japan. Now viewed as familiar modern classics rather than as the revolutionary forms that they were when first introduced, Aalto's plywood furniture continues to be marketed internationally by Artek. In addition, a design staff that includes Benaf Schulten, Sinikka Killinen, and Marja Pystynen is committed to new product development.

MBF

Artemide S.p.A. Studio Artemide, founded in Milan in 1960 by Ernesto Gismondi, manufactures home furnishings, but it is best known for its lamps. Gismondi, Sergio Mazza, Vico Magistretti, and Emma Schweinberger Gismondi were among those designing for Artemide in the 1960s. Some of the most famous lamps are Magistretti's *Eclipse* (1966), Richard Sapper's *Tizio* (1972), and Mario Bellini's *Area* (1975).

In addition, the company has made furniture, such as Mazza's steel bed (1963), since the early 1960s. Artemide was one of the first Italian firms to make plastic furniture, including Magistretti's *Selene* dining chair, designed in 1961 but not put into production until 1967, and Magistretti's *Studio 80* table, designed to be used with the chairs.

In recent years, the company has continued to feature the work of well-known designers. When Ettore Sottsass asked Gismondi to produce some lamps for Memphis, Gismondi decided to back the new group, becoming its president and majority stockholder in June 1981. Although the Memphis group has disbanded, Artemide still produces lamps by Memphis designers Michele de Lucchi, Carlo Forcolini, and Sottsass. Emilio Ambasz and Mario Botta are two designers who have also recently designed lamps for Artemide.

CWL

Arundell Clarke British by birth, Arundell Clarke returned to London in the early 1920s from service in the Indian Cavalry. He established a reputation as an innovative interior designer and became known as the owner of one of London's few shops devoted to modern furniture.[17] Arriving in New York in 1933 to work on the British Empire Building in the Rockefeller Center complex, he remained and established his own shop, Arundell Clarke Ltd., in that building. During the 1930s Clarke continued his interior design work in New York. By 1940 he was also manufacturing furniture of his own design and importing objects from abroad. He also tried his hand at fashion design[18] and gradually became involved in the home-textiles industry.

Beginning in 1947 Clarke managed Knoll's fabric showroom. After several years at Knoll, he again struck out on his own. When the new Arundell Clarke fabric showroom opened in 1952, Clarke was recognized as one of America's most "inspired . . . fabric impresarios."[19] His was one of a handful of American fabric houses willing to produce avant-garde designs, and these were created by Benjamin Baldwin, John Rombola, and Eszter Haraszty. He converted an Upper East Side town house into a theatrical display space with dramatically lit black or white rooms, accented by his collection of modern paintings and furnished with his seating designs. In this setting he presented his collection of silk-screen-printed fabrics as works of art. The company continued in business until 1969.

LN

Asko Finnternational
Since Asko's beginnings in 1918 as Lahden Puuseppätehdas (Lahti Carpentry Factory) in Lahti, Finland, the company has stood for Modernist functional furniture.[20] It became Finland's first mass-production furniture factory.

The firm was founded by Aukusti Avonius, who in the early 1930s changed the factory name to Asko and then prefixed the factory's name to his own surname. Asko-Avonius kept his sights on multipurpose furniture that addressed Scandinavia's new social issues and smaller housing units. In the 1930s Asko promoted the concept of the functionalist ensemble, manufacturing many suites of such furniture. At the same time, the firm's program of exportation began in earnest. During the war years Asko Factories Ltd. (its name as of January 1, 1940) was restricted by government rationing policies.

Postwar requirements spawned new techniques and new designs. In the early postwar years, many of Asko's home and office furnishings were based on Danish and Swedish models to meet market demands, but indigenous designs came to the fore in the 1950s, and Asko secured the services of Finland's top architectural designers. Ilmari Tapiovaara, who had designed curved, laminated wood furniture in the late 1930s, created foam-rubber-upholstered lounge chairs for Asko in the 1950s. *Askolette*, a foam-rubber-upholstered furniture collection, was designed by Ilmari Lappalainen and Olli Borg in 1954. In the mid-1950s Lappalainen created eighteen ergonomic chairs for Asko. Simultaneously, Borg designed lounge chairs with tubular steel frames as well as Asko's first sofa beds and sectional bookcases. Tapio Wirkkala worked free-lance for Asko during this decade. By 1956, when the Scandinavian Modern style was at its peak, Asko was Scandinavia's largest furniture factory.

Asko responded to the continued popularity of furniture suites in the 1960s, but these new models were softer and bigger. Eero Aarnio's upholstered fiberglass *Ball* chair was for the avant-garde public, while Esko Pajamies worked with birch and pine in a more conservative style, loosely based on rural Finnish designs. New impetus now came from foreign designers, such as Italy's Vico Magistretti and Germany's Gunter Renkel.

On Asko-Avonius's death in 1965, operations were merged into Asko Finnternational. Asko maintains stores in West Germany, Sweden, Belgium, France, and England and has two complete home furnishings department stores in Lahti and Jyvaskyla.

FTH

Baldwin, Benjamin
Born Montgomery, Alabama, March 29, 1913

While perhaps best known as an architect and designer of tranquil, uncluttered interiors, Benjamin Baldwin has also been widely recognized for his furniture and textile designs. He received a master of fine arts degree in architecture from Princeton University in 1938 and subsequently was awarded a scholarship to the Cranbrook Academy of Art. In the years immediately following, Baldwin was employed by Eliel and Eero Saarinen, and then he established an architectural partnership with Harry Weese. After service in the United States Navy from 1941 to 1945, he designed interiors and furniture for Skidmore, Owings and Merrill in New York City.

In 1948 Baldwin established Design Unit New York, his first independent atelier, where he designed textiles in association with William Machado and carried out remodeling projects notable for spare ornamentation and logical spatial organization. His proven ability to create elegant, aesthetically consistent environments within existing structures brought furniture and interior design commissions from distinguished architects, including Louis Kahn (Phillips Exeter Academy library and dining hall, Yale Center for British Art) and

Edward Larrabee Barnes (Museum of Fine Arts, Dallas).

Throughout his career, Baldwin's achievements have been lauded by critics and colleagues alike. He was made a charter member of the Interior Designers Hall of Fame in December 1985.

Baldwin, who now divides his time between home-studios in East Hampton, New York, and Sarasota, Florida, designs furniture for Jack Lenor Larsen and gardens for private clients.

MBF

Ballmer, Walter
Born Liestal, Switzerland, July 22, 1923

Originally a painter, Ballmer studied at Basel's Kunstgewerbeschule from 1940 to 1944 under Herman Eidenbenz. He then worked for the C. J. Bucher publishing house in Lucerne for two years before immigrating to Italy in 1947, when he began designing for the Boggeri Studio. Until the mid-1950s Ballmer free-lanced for large corporate clients such as Pirelli, Geigy, and Montecatini. In 1956 he became a staff graphic designer for the advertising department of Olivetti, manufacturer of office machines and office furniture, and because he remained in that position for twenty-five years, Olivetti is the corporation with which his work is most closely associated.

Ballmer's early training at the Kunstgewerbeschule familiarized him with the principles of the Bauhaus and with the Swiss graphic tradition practiced by such artists as Herbert Matter. Ballmer developed a progressively refined, minimalist system of visual communication to convey his clients' products.

While Ballmer's orientation has always been primarily toward the realm of graphic art, he has designed packaging, displays, and large decorative murals for Olivetti, as well as for other clients. In all areas of endeavor, he infuses meaning into a form, symbol, or word, developing an international visual language so necessary in our era of global corporations.

Ballmer also designed several international exhibitions to promote Olivetti's products. His best known were "Olivetti Style" (1961), "Olivetti Innovates" (1965), and "Olivetti Image" (1973); for the latter he received the Ljubljana Bio 5 gold medal.

Today, Ballmer maintains his own graphic design studio, Unidesign, in Milan.[21]

FTH

Basaldella, Mirko
Born Udine, Italy, September 28, 1910; died Cambridge, Massachusetts, November 24, 1969

Mirko Basaldella was Italy's best known and most imaginative midcentury sculptor, who created large-scale bronzes rich in surface texture. Like Joan Miró and Paul Klee, Mirko relied on a totemic idiom of mythological symbols for the modern era.

He and his artist brothers, Dino and Afro, were the sons of a housepainter. Mirko acquired his formal training in the art academies of Venice, Florence, and Monza. Working in the Milan studio of sculptor Arturo Martini from 1932 to 1934, Mirko developed a figurative idiom. He subsequently moved to Rome and began to exhibit his work.

As a result of a trip in 1937 to France, Mirko was exposed to Cubism, and he explored this style before permanently capitulating to abstraction. His first major abstract work is also one of his most important: the bronze gates and balustrades for the war memorial at the Ardeatine Caves in Rome (1949–50). In the 1950s, Mirko experimented with a variety of mediums—copper, cement, painted plaster, and bronze—to express his language of symbols, which often referred to archaic Italian or ethnographic sources. Surrealistic

animals and figures were often the subjects of his free-standing sculptures. Mirko also executed architectonic sculpture for the Food and Agriculture Organization Building (1951) in Rome, a project for which he also executed murals and mosaics.

From 1957 until his death, Mirko taught at Harvard's Carpenter Center for Visual Arts, first as a lecturer on design and later as director of the Design Workshop. Examples of his sculpture were placed on the Harvard campus, and he also continued to execute European commissions.

Mirko had solo shows in commercial galleries such as New York's M. Knoedler & Co., Inc. (1947, 1948, 1949) and Rome's Galleria Schneider (1954, 1958). In 1954 the Venice Biennale devoted an entire room to his work, and in 1955 he won the grand prize at the São Paulo Biennal. Mirko has been the subject of many posthumous exhibitions in Italy, most notably "La Fondazione Mirko per Firenze," held at the Palazzo Strozzi (1979).[22]

FTH

Bayer, Herbert
Born Haag am Hausruch, Austria, April 5, 1900; died Montecito, California, September 30, 1985

One of the seminal graphic designers of the twentieth century, Herbert Bayer carried the Bauhaus's aesthetic message to the world of commercial art in both Europe and America.[23]

Bayer had no formal art education. Apprenticed to architect and designer Georg Schmidthammer in nearby Linz, Bayer was exposed to the work of the Vienna Secession and the theories of the early Deutscher Werkbund. Bayer left for Darmstadt, Germany, in 1920 and worked as an architectural draftsman under Josef Margold at the Grand Duke Ernst Ludwig of Hesse's artists' colony.

Prompted by Wassily Kandinsky's treatise *Concerning the Spiritual in Art*, Bayer enrolled in the Bauhaus at Weimar in October 1921. He began in Kandinsky's mural-painting workshop and then branched out into other mediums, notably typography. During this period Bayer experimented with the aesthetics of prevalent contemporary movements, such as De Stijl, Constructivism, Dada, and Surrealism. In 1923 Bayer began a *Wanderjahr* in Italy. He returned to the Bauhaus's new Dessau facility in 1925 to become the first master of its typographic workshop. Bayer retained the Bauhaus's exclusive use of antielite, lowercase type in his personal signature.

In 1928 Bayer moved to Berlin, where he worked as art director of *German Vogue* and the Berlin branch of Dorland Studio, the prominent international advertising agency. His work, always solidly based on geometric relationships, had become increasingly Surrealistic by the late 1920s. He also introduced Bauhaus techniques of collage, photography, and photomontage to the world of commercial art.

With his close associate and friend Marcel Breuer, Bayer visited the United States in 1937 to attend a planning meeting with Walter Gropius and László Moholy-Nagy, who were organizing an exhibition on the Bauhaus for the Museum of Modern Art. Bayer was commissioned to design the exhibition and the layout of its monograph.[24]

Bayer immigrated to the United States the following year and lived in New York City until 1946. During this period, Bayer was consultant art director to John Wanamaker (1941–42) and J. Walter Thompson (1944) and art director of Dorland International (1944–46). Bayer became consultant designer to the Container Corporation of America in 1946 and moved to Aspen, Colorado. Container Corporation's chairman, Walter Paepcke, was committed to an alliance of art and business. To further this cause, he and Bayer forged the Aspen Institute for Humanistic Studies; its activities include an influential annual international design conference. In 1975 Bayer moved to Montecito, California, to act as a consultant for his other major corporate client, Atlantic Richfield, while continuing his personal work in painting, sculpture, and architecture.

Aside from Bayer's significant formal contributions, he was among the first to successfully bridge art and commerce.

FTH

Becker, Friedrich Born Ende bei Hagen, Germany, May 25, 1922

Friedrich Becker was a pioneer in the field of kinetic jewelry.[25] By utilizing geometrically patterned and permanently changing compositions made from precious metal and gemstones, Becker has interpreted in a wearable form the kinetic art created in Germany in the early 1960s, especially by the painters and sculptors in the Cero group: Heinz Mack, Gunther Uecker, and Otto Pena.

Becker trained as a mechanical fitter in Düsseldorf and studied aeronautical engineering in Thorn before serving an apprenticeship as a gold- and silversmith. He was a student at the Werkkunstschule in Düsseldorf, from which he graduated in 1951. He qualified for his master's degree and opened his own workshop in 1952. An influential teacher, he served as head of the Metal Design department in 1964 and director of studies and pedagogic director in 1970 at the Werkkunstschule, Düsseldorf, and was professor at the Fachhochschule, Düsseldorf, in 1970. He retired from teaching in 1982; however, he continues to create jewelry.

Although his output from the 1950s was often undulant and even Biomorphic in character, it became geometric and minimalist in the early 1960s. His mature work from the 1960s, 1970s, and 1980s is based on two main themes: variability and movement. In the former category, metal rods joined by articulated axles can be fixed in different positions by means of spring pressure. In the latter category, invisible micro ball bearings allow balanced weights, in the shapes of disks, bars, and cones, to move and rotate in opposite directions and at various angles and speeds, controlled solely by gravity and the random movements of the wearer.

Becker has received many distinctions and prizes, including the Bayerischer Staatspreis in 1959, the Staatspreis Nordrhein-Westfalen in 1965, and the Rosenthal Studiopreis in 1982. He had a solo exhibition at Goldsmiths' Hall in London in 1966 and a retrospective in 1984 at the Kunstverein für die Rheinlande und Westfalen in Düsseldorf.

TLW

Bellini, Mario Born Milan, February 1, 1935

Mario Bellini is one of Italy's leading industrial designers.[26] Trained as an architect, he graduated from the Politecnico in Milan in 1959. Unlike most Italian designers, Bellini did not start out as an architect designing furniture for his interiors but has been concerned with objects since the beginning of his career. Since 1963 he has served as chief industrial design consultant for Olivetti in Milan, designing typewriters, calculators, and desktop computers in sleek, sensuous forms with surfaces pleasant to the touch. He has also designed automobiles, household appliances, televisions, a camera for Fuji in Japan, tableware for Rosenthal, lamps for Artemide and Flos, and furniture for Cassina, C & B, and Poltrona Frau Italia. In the 1960s Bellini started designing large, blocky chairs, such as his 932 chair made by Cassina (1965), which departs from the traditional system of a frame and cushions, consisting instead of several blocks of foam covered with leather and belted together. Likewise, his *Chiara* lamp for Flos (1964) has no internal skeleton but is

made from a single sheet of steel. From the mid-1970s through the 1980s, he designed smaller chairs with rigid frames that were dressed by their covers, such as his *Cab* chair for Cassina (1976), whose leather cover zips up the legs like boots, and the *Figura* chair for Vitra (1979–84), whose cover is belted as if it were a dress.

In the late 1970s, while continuing to design objects, Bellini gradually turned to architecture, redesigning Milan's trade fair area and planning schools and housing. In 1986 he became editor-in-chief of *Domus*.

CWL

Bellmann, Hans Born Turgi, Switzerland, September 25, 1911

A committed Bauhaus practitioner, architect-designer Hans Bellmann found the best outlet for his work to be designing exclusively for the Zurich interior design and furniture manufacturer Wohnbedarf A.G.[27] The mission of this avant-garde firm, founded in July 1931 by Sigfried Giedion, architect Werner M. Moser, and entrepreneur Rudolf Graber, was to produce well-designed furniture at affordable prices.

Bellmann studied engineering drafting from 1927 to 1930 in Baden and then attended the Bauhaus in Dessau and Berlin from 1931 to 1933, where he studied under Ludwig Mies van der Rohe. From 1933 to 1934, Bellmann worked in Mies van der Rohe's studio. After stints in various Swiss architectural firms, he opened his own office in Zurich in 1946.

Bellmann was a member of the Schweizerischer Werkbund from 1947 to 1960. Like many of his Bauhaus-trained colleagues, he also taught, at Zurich's Kunstgewerbeschule and at the Basel Allgemeine Gewerbeschule, both from 1948 to 1954. In 1964 and 1965, he taught at Washington University, Seattle, and at Harvard University.

FTH

Bertoia, Arieto (Harry) Born San Lorenzo (Udine), Italy, March 10, 1915; died Bally, Pennsylvania, November 6, 1978

Harry Bertoia expressed himself with equal facility in both functional and nonfunctional idioms, in the worlds of handicrafts and industry, and in small-scale as well as monumental objects.[28]

Upon arriving in the United States in 1930, Bertoia lived with a brother in Detroit. He graduated from Cass Technical High School in 1936 and then attended the Art School of the Detroit Society of Arts and Crafts until 1937. He received a scholarship to the Cranbrook Academy of Art, a school that sought to integrate the philosophy of the Arts and Crafts movement with the realities of industrial design. Cranbrook proved a perfect haven for the young metal craftsman. He reopened a metal shop that had been closed since 1933 and began teaching full time. He also produced his own work, some of which was in a Streamlined style, while the remainder displayed a primitive whimsicality.

Due to the metal shortage caused by World War II, the metal-craft department suspended operations in 1943, and Bertoia was transferred to the graphics department; his monoprints of the 1940s register the influences of Kandinsky and Klee. In 1943 he married Brigitta Valentiner, whose father, William Valentiner, then director of the Detroit Institute of Arts, was a proponent of abstract art. A comparable move to hard-edged abstraction is evident in Bertoia's jewelry of the time.

Bertoia left Michigan in September 1943 to join Charles and Ray Eames in California, where he continued to make jewelry, exhibiting it with his graphics in New York and San Francisco from 1943 to 1947. The association between the Eameses and Bertoia ended because of contractual disagreements and also

because of the former's emphasis on wood and the latter's desire to concentrate on the use of metal in furniture production.

In 1946 Bertoia became a citizen of the United States. Because he began working for Knoll Associates, he moved to Bally, Pennsylvania, near the company's factory. He set up a studio in 1950, producing designs for metal furniture to be manufactured by Knoll. In 1952 the firm introduced the *Diamond* and *Bird* chairs, which utilized space-enclosing wire grids. Bertoia also began to design architectural and freestanding sculptures, some of them incorporating sound. One of his most important architectural commissions was a welded steel screen, made with tilted planes of surface-fused copper, nickel, and brass, for the Manufacturers Hanover Trust Co. in New York City in 1954, for which he won the gold medal of the Architectural League of New York. He was also awarded a gold medal from the American Institute of Architects in 1973, and in 1975 the American Academy of Letters conferred on him its Academy Institute Award.

TLW

Bianconi, Fulvio Born Padua, Italy, August 27, 1915

Fulvio Bianconi is celebrated as one of the leading Italian glass designers of the postwar years.[29] His family moved to Venice while he was still young, and he became involved with glass from an early age, working for a studio in Madonna dell'Orto. After the war he worked for the perfume manufacturer Gi. Vi. Emme, designing perfume bottles and advertising, even painting a mural for the company dining room. The turning point in Bianconi's career came in 1948 when he met Paolo Venini and began designing for his glasshouse. In the Venice Biennale that year, Venini presented a successful series of highly stylized, humorous figurines of commedia dell'arte characters designed by Bianconi. These were followed by other glass figures and perhaps one of the most popular conceits in postwar glass, the *Fazzoletto* (Handkerchief) vase. More substantial were Bianconi's anthropomorphic and Biomorphic vases, as well as his intensely chromatic *Pezzato* (Pieced) and *A spicchi* (Segmented) vases, many of which were shown to great acclaim at the Milan IX Triennale in 1951.

After 1951 Bianconi left Venini and took an independent path. Many of his glass designs were executed by other Venetian glasshouses, and he exhibited them in Milan, where he still resides. On occasion Bianconi has returned to Venini; in the mid-1950s he contributed to Venini's successful *Morandiane* series and designed the *Scozzese* (Scottish) vases, with bold plaids of caning. Beginning in the early 1960s, Bianconi also worked for Vitossi; one of their collaborations, a vase with spiral stripes, received an award at the Milan XIII Triennale of 1964. Two years later Bianconi returned to the Venini factory to create a series of *Informali* (Informal) vases.

Bianconi's work of the 1970s has been decidedly sculptural, such as a series of expressive heads and glass cubes with figures drawn in glass that are encased within—but all display a humor comparable to that seen in his glass and advertising material of a quarter-century earlier. One of Bianconi's most recent projects has involved working with glassmakers in Hersgswil, Switzerland.

ME

Bill, Max Born Winterthur, Switzerland, December 22, 1908

Interdisciplinary artist Max Bill was one of the formulators of the modern Swiss graphic-design movement that evolved in the late 1920s and the 1930s. Bill's essentially Constructivist style, with its strong emphasis on typography, became a model internationally for contemporary advertising.

Bill's approach to design consistently reflects the Bauhaus training that he received at Dessau from 1927 to 1929, following three years' study as a silversmith at the Zurich Kunstgewerbeschule. In those early years he experimented with Cubism and Dada, influences that he would later reject in favor of a highly theoretical, reductionist style.

In 1929 Bill returned to Zurich with the Bauhaus message. Committed to clarity of design based on geometric principles, Bill and other Swiss Constructivists put their aesthetics into practice in a series of type-oriented posters commissioned in the late 1920s and 1930s by Zurich's Kunstgewerbemuseum. Bill's work gained further acceptance in his designs for the Swiss pavilion at the Milan VI Triennale exhibition in 1936. In the 1940s Bill and his Zurich colleagues executed important commissions for the Swiss Ministry of the Interior.

Bill began to apply his theories to industrial design in 1944. He allied the moral and social impetus of Bauhaus teaching with mass production to express the machine-age aesthetic. "Mass production of consumer goods will, in future, be the criterion by which we judge the cultural level of a country."[30] Bill organized a "Gute Form" exhibition for the Schweizerische Werkbund at the Basel fair of 1949, which was very influential in the international market of consumer goods.

From 1951 to 1956, Bill was the first director of the newly created Hochschule für Gestaltung at Ulm, West Germany, which he also designed. The school's ideas were initially based on Bauhaus principles. Under Bill's guidance, the school provided rigorous artistic training and stressed the importance of the designer as a cultural interpreter.

Functionalism has dominated Bill's designs, as can be seen in his molded plywood chair of around 1950, manufactured by Horgen-Glarus. Perhaps his best-known design is the spartan-looking stainless steel and aluminum clock of 1957 manufactured by Junghaus.

For the past three decades, Bill has continued to apply his aesthetics in his Zurich studio, primarily in the fields of painting and sculpture. This work, while still based on geometric principles, is more organic and rooted in self-expression. However, his major and most original contribution to twentieth-century art is best summarized in his commercial graphic work.

FTH

Bing & Grøndahl
The first private porcelain manufactory in Denmark, Bing & Grøndahl was founded in 1853 by the brothers Herman and Jacob Bing, businessmen established in the capital, and Frederick Grøndahl, a modeler formerly employed at the Royal Copenhagen factory.[31] In 1895 it became a public stock company.

One of the firm's first successes was its copies of Bertel Thorvaldsen's Neoclassic sculpture, sometimes executed on a monumental scale. Until well into the 1890s much of its wares was Beaux-Arts in form and highly pictorial in decoration. A turning point was the *Heron* service (1886–88) designed by Pietro Krohn, a curious blend of Japanese and Rococo styles. Krohn's Japanese-based naturalism provided the key to evolving a modern style at Bing & Grøndahl, just as it did at its Scandinavian rivals, the Royal Copenhagen and Rörstrand factories. Although often overshadowed by its rivals, Bing & Grøndahl had its successes, notably a distinctive line of pierced, delicately rhythmical vases carved by Effie Hegerman-Lindencrone and a series with stylized floral motifs and geometric patterns paralleling the ceramics and silver of Thorvald Bindesbøll.

In the 1920s and 1930s Bing & Grøndahl's work resembled that of many northern European potteries. The style of prewar days prevailed in much of its por-

celains, though they displayed considerably less delicacy. It also turned to high-fired stoneware; noteworthy examples are the animal statues by Knud Kyhn (who also worked for the Royal Copenhagen factory, reminding us of the often close connection between the two firms) and the witty mythological subjects modeled by Jean René Gauguin (son of the painter). Although occasionally responding to the Modernist idea of simple forms, as in Ebbe Sadolin's dinner service of 1934, the firm's primary focus was on more traditional values.

In the postwar years Bing & Grøndahl maintained its older lines of wares, such as its blue and white decorated porcelains and figurative statues. More interesting was Gertrud Vasegaard's Orientalizing stoneware and her Chinese-inspired dinner and tea services in porcelain. In the 1960s and early 1970s, the silversmith Henning Koppel designed some fluent objects in porcelain, mostly derived from forms he had created in silver for Georg Jensen. Carl-Harry Stålhane, well known for his ceramics at the Royal Copenhagen factory, contributed some restrained designs for porcelain, as did Erik Magnussen. On the other hand, the humorous stoneware sculpture of Sten Lykke Madsen shows that the firm kept abreast of changing styles in a very different direction.

As in many of the northern European ceramic factories, the art studio at Bing & Grøndahl is maintained as a matter of prestige; it forms only a small part of the firm's operation, sustained by the more profitable production of dinnerware and commemorative plates, which are inevitably conservative in style and commercially oriented.

ME

Bitossi *see* Cav. G. Bitossi & Figli

Blattmann Metallwarenfabrik AG
Founded in 1838 in Wädenswil, Switzerland, this family-owned corporation recently celebrated its one-hundred-and-fiftieth anniversary as a manufacturer of metal products. While best known among design historians for the *Landi* chair, created in 1939 by Hans Coray, the firm is primarily a manufacturer of kitchenware and parts used by large-scale industrial enterprises. Beginning with the presidency of Ernst Blattmann (1954), the firm has adopted the trade names Caldor, TECA, and MEWA in its housewares division, MEWA in its helmet division, and MEWA and Minmetalswiss in its steel-furniture division.

MBF

Bojesen, Kay
Born Copenhagen, August 15, 1886; died Gentofte, Denmark, August 28, 1958

From the 1930s through the 1950s, the designer-craftsman Kay Bojesen created practical, appealing objects in both silver and wood for everyday use.[32] As one of Denmark's first functionalists, Bojesen employed rounded forms devoid of ornament and emphasized the special qualities intrinsic to his materials to achieve a personal version of the Modernist style.

Bojesen trained as a silversmith with Georg Jensen from 1907 to 1910 and in 1911 at the Fachschule für Edelmetallindustrie (Technical School for Precious Metals) in Schwäbisch-Gmünd. After briefly working as a craftsman in Paris, Bojesen returned to Copenhagen, where by 1913 he established his own workshop. By the late 1920s Bojesen rejected Jensen's decorative style in favor of the clean lines and smooth surfaces that characterized his work thereafter.

Of Bojesen's considerable silver output, which included flatware and hollowware, perhaps the most acclaimed was his archetypal cutlery designed in the 1930s. One of the first to experiment with the three-

pronged fork, he was continually refining his ideas for the shapes and angles of eating utensils. Simple flatware that he created in 1938 received a grand prize at the Milan IX Triennale in 1951; it was later slightly modified for production in stainless steel.

Bojesen's functional yet sensual approach to design is also evident in his wooden wares, all based on lathe-turned shapes. His classic spherical double salad bowl (1949), which was awarded a gold medal at the 1954 Milan X Triennale, exemplifies his sensitivity to proportion and surface. He was also internationally recognized for the amusing wooden toys that he began to make in 1935, the most famous of them a monkey, which was widely imitated.

Bojesen sought to promote acceptance of high-quality modern design, both through his own work and through Den Permanente, a Copenhagen exhibition and sales gallery that he conceived and opened in 1931. Among his numerous shows, both at home and abroad, was a solo exhibition in 1938 at Det Danske Kunstindustrimuseum in Copenhagen. In Bojesen's workshop, artisans crafted his designs as well as those of outside designers, among them Magnus Stephensen, Ole Wanscher, and Finn Juhl. Bojesen's workshop continues today, operated now by his son.

In addition to his workshop production, Bojesen designed ceramics for Bing & Grøndahl (1930–31) and stainless steel tableware for Motala Verkstad, Motala, Sweden, and the Universal Steel Co., Copenhagen.

LN

Bonacina & C. *see* Vittorio Bonacina & C.

Borsani, Osvaldo
Born Varedo, Italy, August 17, 1911; died Milan, April 16, 1985

Borsani came from a family of furniture manufacturers. He received his architectural degree from the Milan Politecnico in 1937. That year he and his brother, Fulgenzio, founded Arredamenti Borsani di Varedo. Osvaldo developed the designs and handled the production. He also designed their headquarters building in Milan (1951), showrooms in Paris and Rome (1968, 1969), and their two factory buildings (1962, 1970).[33]

Osvaldo's first designs were traditional ones in wood or metal, but in 1953 he started experimenting with metal, glass, and other materials. At the same time the brothers changed the firm's name to Tecno to express their new, high-tech approach. Many of Osvaldo's designs of the mid-1950s are for furniture that moves in some way. His divan D70 of 1954 opens to become a bed, the lounge chair P40 of 1955 has a hinged footrest and an adjustable seat and back, while the S88 chair of 1957 folds.

At first Osvaldo found it more satisfactory to make his own designs, but by the 1960s Tecno was also working with other architects and designers. In 1959 Osvaldo and Eugenio Gerli designed a new Tecno showroom in Milan with three floors of furniture visible through the glass facade. They designed the *Graphis* office system of modular furniture, introducing a new, all-white look to the office in 1968. Then in 1970 Osvaldo created an industrial design team for Tecno, the "Centro Progetti Tecno," consisting of himself, his daughter Valeria, her husband, Marco Fantoni, and others. This team has designed office furniture and multiple seating for auditoriums and airports.

CWL

Borské Sklo Glassworks, National Corp.
Borské Sklo, formed by a merger of Borské Sklárny, Borocrystal, and Umělécké Sklo in January 1953, was one of eight Czechoslovakian national corporations orga-

nized under the Chief Administration of Glass and Ceramics and is located in Bor, a region in the north where glass manufacture is concentrated. The corporation was part of the Communist regime's effort to centralize and modernize the Czechoslovakian household glass industry.[34] The corporate mission was to reestablish the competitive international position of Czechoslovakian glassware by attracting trained glass artists, establishing design and research laboratories, developing educational programs for trainees, and automating the manufacturing process where appropriate.

Between 1957 and 1959, René Roubíček became the manager of artistic development, Ladislav Oliva and Karl Wünsch were engaged as staff artists, and Pavel Hlava, Adolf Matura, Miulše Roubičková, Maria Stáhlíková, and others were employed as "external co-workers." The firm exhibited a variety of art and utilitarian wares at the 1958 Brussels World's Fair and went on to broaden its exposure with presentations in Europe, Asia, and North and South America.

By 1974 the Ministry of Industry had replaced Borské Sklo with a newly founded branch corporation at Nový Bor, known first as Užitkové Sklo (Household Glass), then as Crystalex.

MBF

Bossi, S.p.A. Bossi is a commercial textile company
in Cameri, near Novarra, Italy. The firm was founded in 1907 and has been growing slowly but steadily since, making textiles for clothes, upholstery, and other home decorative uses. In 1950 Enrico Gregotti, then one of the company's two general managers, commissioned Fernand Léger to design a fabric, but it was the only time the firm has been associated with a well-known artist or designer.[35]

CWL

Breuer, Marcel Lajos Born Pécs, Hungary, May
22, 1902; died New York, July 1, 1981

Architect Marcel Breuer studied and eventually taught at the Bauhaus, where he emerged as one of the most talented and original of the students.[36] In 1925, at the age of twenty-three, he arrived at one of the most stunning innovations in the history of design—the development of tubular steel furniture. While his famous tubular steel designs are today taken for granted, their impact on the architectural world of the late 1920s was profound. His furniture designs were first recognized and then widely imitated as the only furniture suitable for use in the daringly new Modernist architecture of the period.

In 1928, after three years as a teacher at the Bauhaus, Breuer resigned to establish his own architectural practice in Berlin, although a lack of commissions dictated that he spend the major portion of his time working on interior renovations, mostly of apartments, and furniture. His architecture existed only in project form until 1932, when, at the age of thirty, he built the Harnischmacher house in Wiesbaden.

During the following years, he traveled around Europe and the Mediterranean, continuing to design furniture, mainly in aluminum, and interiors, finally realizing (together with Alfred and Emil Roth) designs for the Doldertal apartment buildings in Zurich. In 1935, with the assistance of his friend and former teacher Walter Gropius, he immigrated to England, where he formed a partnership with F. R. S. Yorke and designed furniture for the Isokon Furniture Company. He also experimented with molded and cutout plywood furniture designs for Heal and Son and a number of private commissions.

In 1937 Breuer joined Gropius on the architecture faculty at Harvard University, and the two men also formed a partnership. As teachers, they influenced an

entire generation of architects through their teaching; as partners, until they separated in 1941, they produced many of the finest houses of the period. During these years, Breuer continued work on his cutout plywood furniture for, among others, Bryn Mawr College (1938), the Frank House in Pittsburgh (1939), the Pennsylvania pavilion at the 1939 New York World's Fair, the Geller House in Lawrence, New York (1945), and the Museum of Modern Art's "International Competition for Low-Cost Furniture Design" (1948). In 1949, after moving his office to New York City, he was commissioned by the Museum of Modern Art to design a house in its sculpture garden, an event that foreshadowed an increase in commissions.

During the 1950s, Breuer enlarged his New York office in response to a series of large public, institutional, and commercial commissions; the collaborative nature of his firm's work was acknowledged by the formation of Marcel Breuer Associates in 1957. At this time Breuer's aesthetic noticeably shifted: he became increasingly concerned with solidity and monumentality, specifically, with sculptural effects achieved by exploiting the structural possibilities of concrete. Among the best-known examples of his and his partners' later work are the Saint John's Abbey Complex in Collegeville, Minnesota (1953–68), the IBM Research Center in La Gaude, France (1960–61), and the Whitney Museum of American Art in New York City (1963–66). Breuer retired from active practice in 1976.

Marcel Breuer wanted to be remembered first and foremost as an architect rather than as a furniture designer. Yet his furniture was undeniably his most important and enduring achievement. His tubular steel chairs, in particular, remain among the most original and vital designs of our century, with a ubiquity, a continuing presence in our daily lives, to which few architectural designs could aspire.

CW

Brynner, Irena Born Vladivostok, Russia, December 1, 1917

Irena Brynner is known for sculptural, organic jewelry, mostly from highly textured or lacy cast gold elements combined often with unusual stones.[37] She has solved the functional problems of closure through original inventions, such as necklaces that loop around the neck and earrings that encircle the ear.

At the age of twelve, Brynner, a double cousin of the late actor Yul Brynner, left Vladivostok with her Russian mother and Swiss-Manchurian father and moved to Dairen, China, when the latter was appointed Swiss consul general there. In 1936 she attended college and art school in Lausanne, Switzerland, returning four years later to China, where she studied painting with several Manchurian artists. In 1946 she moved to San Francisco, where she explored academic sculpture with Michael Von Mayer. Two years later she met the sculptor Ralph Stackpole, who introduced her to the works of Miró, Picasso, and contemporary American artists.

Around this time Brynner saw a neckpiece by sculptor Claire Falkenstein that inspired her to try her hand at jewelry. Her early pieces showed a strong Bauhaus influence, derived via Margaret de Patta. After a brief apprenticeship with Carolyn Rosene, she worked with San Francisco jeweler Franz Bergman; in 1950 she attended adult education classes to learn technique. She set up her first studio at home and sold the jewelry at Casper's, a furniture store in San Francisco, and Nany's, a shop specializing in contemporary jewelry. Soon Georg Jensen was selling Brynner's jewelry in New York, and in 1956 she flew East to find additional outlets. After experiencing the stimulating atmosphere of New York, she decided to move there permanently in 1957, opening her own shop at 46 West Fifty-fifth Street in late 1958.

Brynner's style became far more baroque and textural after she moved to New York, due both to an exhibition of Antonio Gaudí's architecture at the Museum of Modern Art and to the fact that it was illegal to use an oxygen tank (needed for soldering) in a New York apartment. She turned to lost-wax casting, a technique well suited to textural effects.

In 1958 Brynner's jewelry was exhibited at the Brussels World's Fair and the following year at a solo exhibition at the Museum of Contemporary Crafts in New York. In 1972 she closed her New York shop and moved to Geneva, Switzerland, where she continued to work until 1984, when she returned to New York.

She has won several national and international awards, including a Diamonds International Award in 1971, and is the author of *Modern Jewelry—Design and Techniques* (1968) and *Jewelry as an Art Form* (1979). She is also an accomplished mezzo-soprano who sings traditional Russian music.

TLW

Bülow-Hübe, Vivianna Torun Born Malmö,
Sweden, December 4, 1927

Torun Bülow-Hübe's jewelry is revolutionary in its sensual form and the way that many of her designs use long, undulating strips of silver to trace the natural contours of the body as they twist asymmetrically around them. Made of hand-forged silver and semiprecious stones, her minimalist, linear sculptural pieces represent a radical departure from traditional jewelry.[38]

Torun completed her studies at the Konstfackskolan in Stockholm in 1948. Her career is divided into four periods, related to where she worked: Sweden (1948–56), France (1956–68), Germany (1968–78), and Indonesia (1978 to the present).

Between 1948 and 1956, because of her marriage to a French architect, Torun traveled back and forth between Sweden and France, maintaining workshops in both countries. She had her first exhibition in 1948 in Stockholm and opened her first workshop in that city in 1951. This first period is characterized by the use of inexpensive but beautiful materials such as wood, pebbles, rattan, and leather. In 1951 she was commissioned by Orrefors to create silver jewelry, which was exhibited in Sweden, Norway, Italy, and France.

In 1956 Torun moved to Paris and opened a workshop in her home. Two years later, in order to expand her operation, she relocated to Biot, on the French Riviera, and during this period she made some of her most innovative designs. She met Picasso while collecting pebbles on the beach there; he was so impressed with her work that he arranged for her to have a solo exhibition in Antibes in 1958. In 1967 Anders Hostrup-Pedersen, then the director of Georg Jensen Silversmithy in Copenhagen, invited Torun to design jewelry for the Danish company. Jensen took over her entire production, and she continues to make new designs for the firm; some of her best-known designs, such as the *Escargot* ring and *Eternity* bracelet (based on the Möbius strip), are still in production.

In 1968 Torun moved to Germany. In addition to her work as a jeweler, she designed porcelain and ceramics for Hutschenreuther AG, glassware for Glashütte Löhnberg, and leather handbags. In 1978 she relocated to Jakarta, Indonesia, where she maintains a workshop for the production of jewelry made from indigenous materials such as pure gold, opals, and agate from Java, and shells, mother-of-pearl, and buffalo horn from the South Seas.

Torun has received many awards, including the silver medal at the Milan X Triennale in 1954, the gold medal at the Milan XII Triennale in 1960, the Lunning Prize in 1960, and Sweden's Grand Prize for Artists in 1965.

TLW

Calder, Alexander Born Lawnton, Pennsylvania, July 22, 1898; died New York, November 11, 1976

One of the best-known sculptors of the twentieth century, Alexander Calder created an unusually varied yet coherent body of work.[39] His toys, animals, jewelry, and household objects were as important to him as his monumental works. His inventiveness led him to make wonders out of nothing—bits of wire, tin cans, glass shards.

Calder was the son and grandson of sculptors, and his mother was an accomplished painter. In 1919 he graduated from the Stevens Institute of Technology in Hoboken, New Jersey, with a degree in mechanical engineering, after which he traveled widely and held various engineering jobs. In 1923 he entered the Art Students League in New York, where he was influenced by the Ashcan school of painters. After holding several routine commercial illustrating jobs, Calder went to Paris in 1926. There, while working on sculpture, he began to make toylike animals of wood and wire for his own amusement. His meeting in 1930 with Piet Mondrian made him suddenly aware of the modern movement in painting, which influenced his work in the direction of the abstract. Among the other influential artists he met in Paris was Joan Miró, with whom he established a lasting friendship.

In the winter of 1931–32, Calder began to make motor-driven sculptures, but beginning in 1932, most of his mobiles relied only on air currents. In 1933 Calder exhibited nonmoving works that Jean Arp described as stabiles, a term that Calder continued to use. Calder moved toward increasing monumentality in his later works.

In the 1930s and 1940s, Calder's reputation expanded through annual exhibitions in Europe and the United States, climaxed by a solo exhibition at the Museum of Modern Art in New York City in 1943. During the 1960s his accomplishments were recognized through major exhibitions in Kassel, West Germany, at the Solomon R. Guggenheim Museum, New York, and the Musée d'Art Moderne de la Ville de Paris.

It was from 1933 to 1952 that Calder designed the bulk of his jewelry, created with an economy of means and a witty charm. Certain pieces were reminiscent of his sculptures and toys. Others were inspired by myriad sources: Eskimo, Navaho, African, Greek and Etruscan, and Moroccan. The first show devoted entirely to jewelry took place in 1938 at Alvar Aalto's Artek Gallery in Helsinki. His work was hailed universally and had a great liberating effect on postwar jewelry.

Calder's international recognition resulted in other nonsculptural commissions. In 1948 Calder's designs for murals were manufactured by the New York wallpaper firm Katzenbach and Warren. Calder also created textile designs in 1949 for Laverne Originals in New York, and in 1962 Pierre Baudouin commissioned nine small tapestries for Aubusson. *Une Floppée de Soleils*, a monumental tapestry measuring 8 by 20 feet, was commissioned by the IBM Corporation in 1973 for its corporate offices.

In the 1970s Calder's studio was at Saché, near Tours, where he designed his major stabiles and experimented with free-form drawings and paintings. Although Calder spent most of his time in France, he also maintained a home and studio in Roxbury, Connecticut.

MOR

Carl Hansen & Son A/S Carl Hansen (born 1883)

established in his native Odense, Denmark, in 1906 a cabinetmaking shop, which specialized in traditional, handmade tables and chairs for local clients.[40] Such vernacular-style furniture of beech and ash remained its mainstay until 1930, when Carl Hansen began producing furniture designed by Danish architects,

including a Windsor-style armchair designed by Frits Henningsen in 1935, which is still in production by the firm.

In 1949 Hans Wegner began designing chairs for the company; this productive collaboration lasted until 1966. Wegner's chairs had previously been handmade by Johannes Hansen; starting in 1950 Carl Hansen began mass-producing them. In the same year, Carl Hansen began exporting furniture to the United States, at first through retailers such as Zacho in Los Angeles and later through George Tanier, Frederik Lunning, and Georg Jensen Silversmithy in New York City.

Although Carl Hansen & Son is today the largest producer of Wegner chairs—supplying markets in Europe, the United States, and Japan—the company continues to work with other architects' designs, including the brightly colored, lacquered tables and chairs designed by leading Danish architect Bernt Peterson.

Carl Hansen & Son remains a family-owned business, currently under the direction of Jørgen Gerner Hansen, its founder's grandson. Today it employs twenty craftspeople, which by Danish standards makes it a medium-scale operation. Although the furniture is made in quantity by mass-production methods, the firm still emphasizes skillful woodworking traditions.

MOR

Carlu, Jean Born Bonnières-sur-Seine (Yvelines), France, May 3, 1900

The long career of this important French graphic artist included many poster designs.[41] As Jean Carlu spent thirteen years in the United States at the height of his artistic maturity, his style was influential on both sides of the Atlantic.

Born into a family of architects, he at first studied architecture, at Paris's École des Beaux-Arts. Carlu executed his first poster in 1917. The following year he lost his right arm in a tram accident. This tragedy prevented him from using architectural instruments, so he turned exclusively to graphic design.

Carlu introduced Cubism into poster design. He explored the movement's formal possibilities, as well as a system of visual symbols that he evolved after attending a Sorbonne lecture on the subject by Juan Gris. *Mon Savon*, Carlu's well-known poster of 1925, exemplifies the synthesis of these elements.

In the early 1930s Carlu became one of the first graphic artists to use photomontage in poster design. Not surprisingly, he applied the new technique in movie posters, but he found the force and realism it offered appropriate for product posters. He also designed three-dimensional metal posters. With the recurring threat of war in Europe, Carlu, a passionate anti-Nazi, formed the Office de Propagande Graphique pour la Paix with other like-minded colleagues in 1932. His *Pour le Désarmement des nations* poster of that year marks the beginning of a large body of posters concerned with war.

In the same year Carlu began to prepare for Paris's 1937 "Exposition Internationale des Arts et Techniques," for which he was director of the Pavillon de la Publicité Graphique et Lumineuse. This role led to his designing the Hall of Honor of the French pavilion at the 1939 New York World's Fair. Because he was handicapped and could not serve with the French forces, it was decided that he could best help the war effort by remaining and working in the United States. Carlu designed the first American defense poster of World War II, *Stop Hitler Now* (1940), and during the war Carlu regularly designed posters for the United States Office of War Information. His best-known war poster, distributed in factories nationwide, was *America's Answer Is Production* (1941).

Carlu remained in New York until 1953, designing for American clients such as Pan Am World Airways

and the New York subways, as well as for Perrier and Shell. Subsequent major commissions created from his Paris studio included advertising campaigns for Air France and Larousse. He retired in 1974.

FTH

Cartier For 140 years the house of Cartier has been

synonymous with the best in fine jewelry and *objets d'art*.[42] Founded in 1847 by Louis-François Cartier, a leading jewel merchant patronized by Princess Mathilde Bonaparte (cousin to the emperor), the firm passed in 1874 to his son Alfred, who after Napoléon III's fall put the company back on its feet by taking advantage of the discovery of diamond mines in South Africa. In 1898 Alfred's son Louis-Joseph joined Cartier as a partner, and in 1899 the firm moved to 13 Rue de la Paix, where it remains to this day.

In the early 1900s Cartier jewelry consisted of diamond-encrusted bows and swags recalling the style of Louis XVI. The *objets d'art* were quite similar to those of Fabergé in their employment of guilloché enamels, pavé diamonds, and carved semiprecious stones. Cartier is famous for its "mystery" clocks (introduced in 1913), whose diamond hands move freely around a translucent quartz face, showing no indication of any attachment to the mechanism.

In 1902 a branch was opened in London, run by Louis's brother Jacques, and in 1909 one was launched in New York, presided over by Pierre, another brother. In 1917 the New York store moved to the former Morton Plant mansion at the corner of Fifth Avenue and Fifty-second Street. The character of the Cartier style offered in each branch varied only slightly; the English variety was more restrained, while the American held more closely to its Parisian origins.[43]

Cartier's most original designs were perhaps produced in the 1920s and 1930s. In those two decades, its output was characterized by an opulent use of colored gemstones, enamel, and diamonds, often inventively combined with carved jade or coral Buddhas and elephants from India. Cartier was known for its opulent fantasies rather than the Cubist-inspired geometry of Jean Fouquet, Gérard Sandoz, and Raymond Templier, the firm's competitors at that time.

Louis Cartier retired in 1932, handing over the running of the *haute joaillerie* to Jeanne Toussaint, his "discreet friend" and artistic director, who had been responsible for the extraordinary success of the line of panther jewelry and whose influence was felt until her death in 1978. The Cartier style in the postwar period was characterized by natural images, both animal and vegetable, created with colored gemstones and textured gold.

In 1948 Louis's son, Claude Cartier, was appointed president of the New York branch. The Paris, London, and New York branches were sold to separate owners in the early 1960s, to be reunited in the 1970s by a group of investors who acquired control of the firm in 1972 and appointed Robert Hocq, a French industrialist, president. When Hocq died in 1979, control of the company passed to his daughter, Nathalie.

TLW

Cassandre, A. M. (pseudonym of Adolph Jean-Marie Mouron) Born Kharkov, Russia, January 24, 1901; died Paris, June 17, 1968

Cassandre was one of the most gifted, versatile, and influential poster artists of the twentieth century.[44] Born into an upper-middle-class French family living in Kharkov, capital of the Ukraine, Cassandre came to Paris in 1918. He studied art at the Académie de la Grande Chaumière and the Académie Julian, absorbing lessons that would have a lasting impact on his work. His first posters date from 1923 and bear his pseudonym, invented to preserve his name for an anticipated career as a painter. Cassandre was allied in the mid-1920s with three other leading graphic artists, Charles Loupot, Paul Colin, and Jean Carlu. They formed a group humorously called "Les Trois Mousquetaires" (The Three Musketeers), which, in turn, constituted the cornerstone of the Union des Artistes Modernes and French advertising art for two decades.

Cassandre's mature style emerged in the mid-1920s and is best summarized by his 1925 poster for the newspaper *L'Intransigeant*. In his commercial design Cassandre employed softer imagery than that used by his Bauhaus contemporaries. His streamlined, machine-age style was the perfect medium for advertising tourism, this pastime having recently become popular with the growing leisure class. From the late 1920s on, some of his most dramatic poster work was done for the great European express trains and steamship lines.

In 1930 Cassandre founded the Alliance Graphique with Charles Loupot and advertising mogul Maurice Moyrand, whom he met while working for the publisher Hachard. Cassandre and he had a long professional association. Around this time Cassandre began designing typefaces for the Peignot foundry. Throughout his career, he was committed to lettering and typography as important elements of design. One of his best-known advertising campaigns, begun in 1930, was for the wine-distribution firm Nicholas, for which he invented an appealing cartoon figure.

Surrealist tendencies became increasingly more apparent in Cassandre's work of the 1930s, and the imagery of his posters became more lyrical. However, designs for theater costumes and decor, as well as easel painting, began to take precedence over Cassandre's graphic work.

Between 1936 and 1939 Cassandre made some trips to the United States, where he worked for American firms and magazines. He executed covers for *Harper's Bazaar* until 1940. In 1936 the Museum of Modern Art held the first exhibition of his posters in America.[45] Consequently, Cassandre gained an international audience, and his style was widely imitated. Ironically, he stopped designing posters at this apogee in his career.

Cassandre pursued easel painting from 1940 until his death. His theater work reached its height during and just following World War II. He continued to design type, and his last typeface, never published, was posthumously named after him. Cassandre's lasting contribution was to establish France's graphic arts style, making it synonymous with sophistication, humor, and restraint.

Cassandre died, a suicide, in 1968.

FTH

Cassina S.p.A.
Cassina has long been one of the leading Italian furniture-making companies in the field of modern design. The family had been joiners since the 1750s, and in the twentieth century, it had moved into upholstered furniture as well. Umberto and Cesare Cassina founded Cassina Amedeo in Meda, near Milan, in 1927.[46] The name was changed to Figli di Amedeo Cassina in 1935, and before 1970 it changed again, to Cassina S.p.A.

At first Cassina was a small workshop making traditional furniture. As its business grew in the late 1930s, Cassina started to rationalize its workshops and adopt more mechanized production. In the 1940s it began to turn away from historical styles to more modern ones. Around 1950, it received large orders to furnish several Italian ocean liners, the SS *Andrea Doria* (partly designed by Gio Ponti), SS *Raffaello*, and SS *Michelangelo*. This spurred the firm to move into mass production. At the same time, instead of merely reacting to demand, it began to innovate by commissioning architects and designers.

Gio Ponti started working with Cassina in 1950 and was its most important designer for many years. Perhaps his best-known design was a lightweight chair based on the traditional Chiavari model. In the late 1950s and early 1960s Cassina produced couches, chairs, and tables designed by Ico Parisi, Carlo De Carli, Gianfranco Frattini, and Olli Mannermaa. Also in the 1950s Cassina started making furniture for Knoll, to be sold under the Knoll name.

By the mid-1960s Cassina was one of the leading Italian furniture makers, producing simple, Modernist chairs such as Vico Magistretti's 892 chair of 1963 and novel innovations such as Mario Bellini's 932/2 chair of 1964–65, made of polyurethane blocks belted together.

Cassina has maintained its position as a leading Italian producer of avant-garde furniture. Some of Cassina's more recent designs have been Bellini's *Cab* chair (1977), Magistretti's *Maralunga* chair (1979) and *Verandah* sofas (1984), and Gaetano Pesce's eccentric, Post-Modern *New York Sunrise* sofa (1980) and *Cannaregio* sofa (1987).

In addition, Cassina put several classic furniture designs of Le Corbusier, Charlotte Perriand, and Pierre Jeanneret into production in 1965, and in the 1970s it began adding classic pieces by Charles Rennie Mackintosh, Gerrit Rietveld, Erik Gunnar Asplund, and Frank Lloyd Wright.

CWL

Castiglioni, Achille
Born Milan, February 16, 1918

Achille Castiglioni is the youngest and only surviving member of a group of three brothers who, from the late 1930s on, created a wide range of design projects, including exhibitions, interiors, furniture, lighting, and industrial products.[47] The Castiglioni brothers have come to represent an important aspect of the postwar Italian design movement.

Characteristically, the brothers came out of an architectural background and flourished through the patronage of a number of forward-looking Italian manufacturing companies. Achille graduated from the Politecnico di Milan in 1944 and operated as a freelance designer in that city with both brothers until 1954 (the year of his brother Livio's death), with his brother Pier Giacomo until the latter died in 1968, and since that date, on his own.

Achille consistently demonstrated an extremely thoroughgoing attitude toward the design process, working on a range of goods that have offered radical new solutions to new problems. He takes his main inspiration from fine art. Echoing Marcel Duchamp's concept of the "ready-made," his stool for Zanotta borrows the seat from a tractor. The idea of "redesign" emerged from this approach; Castiglioni sees his role as an essentially evolutionary one, that of transforming the existing environment by reworking forms, images, and technologies.

In addition to working with a number of Italy's leading manufacturers—Flos, Zanotta, Brionvega, Cassina, and BBB Bonacina among them—Castiglioni has been involved since the 1950s with the organization of the Milan Triennales. Inevitably, he has received numerous awards, among them the Compasso d'Oro in 1955, 1960, 1962, 1964, 1967, and 1969. He has contributed significantly to design education in Italy and remains one of the giants of contemporary Italian design.

PS

Castle, Wendell
Born Emporia, Kansas, November 6, 1932

For the past three decades Wendell Castle has been the best-known American maker of contemporary art furniture who uses centuries-old skills of fine cabinetmaking.[48]

Castle trained as a metal and wood sculptor at the University of Kansas and moved to New York State in 1961. As a result of public acclaim for his sculptural furniture, within two years he became head of the woodworking department of the Rochester Institute of Technology. Although he was inspired by the fluent contours of postwar Scandinavian furniture, many of his first works were cagelike in form and spiky in silhouette, suggesting sculpture more than furniture. He then evolved simpler, more svelte forms, the most famous of which is his music stand (1963). He achieved some of his most dramatically shaped furniture using lamination, a technique that had interested him since he was a boy building model airplanes and which was used by sculptors in the 1950s. In 1969 he experimented with furniture made with painted, fiberglass-coated, reinforced plastic on metal stovepipe cones. He made price-conscious plastic furniture for production in 1969–70 for Beylerian Ltd. and Stendig Inc. that reflected contemporary Italian designs, such as his humorous, tooth-shaped *Molar* chair in the Pop mode.

Beginning in 1974, Castle used luxurious woods such as rosewood and zebrawood, which he inlaid with precious veneers or ivory, recalling the work of the great eighteenth-century French cabinetmakers and of Émile-Jacques Ruhlmann (whose forms are also echoed in Castle's most recent work). His consistently superlative craftsmanship is especially evident in his series of trompe-l'oeil furniture with carved Surrealistic wooden still lifes, begun in 1976 and continued into the 1980s, as well as in his current work, which has evolved within a historicizing, Post-Modernist context.

Castle maintained a school of woodworking from 1980 until 1987. It was absorbed by the Rochester Institute of Technology in 1987 and became part of the School for American Craftsmen. His shop is in a former soybean mill in Scottsville, New York. Since 1986 he has been an artist-in-residence at the Rochester Institute of Technology.

FTH

Castleton China, Inc.
The genesis of this company can be attributed to the disruption of European trade caused by World War II.[49] About 1939 the German manufactory Rosenthal Porzellan AG closed its United States distributor, the Rosenthal China Corporation. Louis E. Hellman, representative of the latter firm, contracted with the Shenango Pottery Company of New Castle, Pennsylvania, to produce the Rosenthal shapes,[50] and to do so he created Castleton China, Inc., with Shenango Pottery investing $25,000 in the new venture.

To promote the new company's wares, Hellman instituted a program of decorating Castleton dinnerware with transfer-printed copies of paintings by important artists of the American scene, including regionalists Paul Sample and Thomas Hart Benton and émigrés Marcel Vertès and Salvador Dalí. Hellman then approached the Museum of Modern Art, sponsor of the "Organic Design in Home Furnishings" competition of 1940–41, to find a designer for modern-style dinnerware. He was directed to the recently arrived émigré Eva Zeisel. An agreement was reached and she created a set in 1942–43, with the Museum of Modern Art acting as an arbiter of design. Due to wartime restrictions the dinnerware, baptized *Museum*, was not released until 1946, after a prestigious introductory exhibition at the Museum of Modern Art. The great fanfare and positive publicity gave Hellman the prestige he had been seeking.

However, Castleton China did not become an advocate of Modernist design. Succumbing to the pressure of the marketplace, it offered mostly traditional wares, and it subsequently issued even the *Museum* service with mundane, commercial patterns that countered the underlying principles of the original design. Emulating the earlier publicity campaign, the company issued the *Museum* service with some of Castleton's earlier, artist-designed prints as well as new reproductions after paintings by Picasso, Modigliani, and other artistic giants. Despite a national tour, the line made understandably few inroads.

In 1951, the very year that Rosenthal resumed operating an American subsidiary, Hellman withdrew from Castleton, Shenango Pottery purchasing all of his stock and thus gaining control of both manufacture and distribution. Castleton China continued to receive some prestigious commissions, such as gilt service plates for President Dwight D. Eisenhower in 1955 and a dinner service in 1968 for President Lyndon B. Johnson, but it did not surpass its American or, more significantly, its European and Oriental rivals.

In 1959 the control of Shenango Pottery, Castleton's parent company, passed to Sobiloff Brothers, and in 1968 the assets of Shenango, including Castleton, were sold by Sobiloff Brothers to Interpace Corporation, a diversified holding company with other interests in the ceramics industry. Some years later it was decided to phase out the production of fine dinnerware, and the Castleton China division was closed by 1976.

ME

Cav. G. Bitossi & Figli

In 1921 Guido Bitossi founded a pottery in Montelupo, a locale not far from Florence with a tradition for ceramic manufacture and the home of the Bitossi family of potters since the fifteenth century. At first it was a traditional artisanal workshop. After the death of its founder in 1937, the business passed into the hands of his children and became known as Cav. G. Bitossi & Figli. The business expanded considerably in the postwar years, when Bitossi, in addition to selling art wares, tiles, and sanitary wares, began producing raw materials for the ceramic industry. Under the artistic directorship of architect Aldo Londi since 1946, the pottery has produced traditional decorative objects and wares for Rosenthal Studio-Haus and, with its Hollywood Collection, produces the designs of Ettore Sottsass, Marco Zanini, and other leading designers.

In 1976 the firm was bought by Flavia Manifattura Ceramica Artistica S.p.A. The Gruppo Bitossi, as it is now known, comprises a complex series of divisions, each with a separate business function.

ME

Chatham Manufacturing Company

Originally the Elkin Woolen Mills, the company was founded in 1877 by Alexander Chatham and his brother-in-law, Thomas Lenoir Gwyn, at Big Elkin Creek, North Carolina. In 1890, Chatham acquired Gwyn's interest in the mill and renamed it the Chatham Manufacturing Company. The expanding company built near the Yadkin River in 1893, and by 1907 there was a branch plant in Winston-Salem, North Carolina; in 1916 a new plant was built in Elkin, the company's present site.

In 1936 the company made its first automobile upholstery fabric, for the Packard Motor Company. The Winston-Salem finishing plant was moved to Elkin in 1938–40. During World War II it produced mainly blankets, while the cloth department was discontinued for the duration of the war. Leaksville Mills, a blanket-manufacturing company, was acquired by Chatham Manufacturing Company in 1952. In 1972, the company introduced a "fiber-woven" process; it patented machines to produce fabric "directly from fiber, eliminating spinning and weaving processes."[51] An additional plant for woolen goods was opened in 1978 at Boonville, North Carolina.

Today, the company remains an important commercial firm, producing fabrics for the bedding industry and for the home-furnishing market as well as for the automotive industry. The Chatham family controlled the firm for five generations until 1987, when the company was bought by Northern Feather Ltd., a Danish firm.

CCMT

Christofle *see* Orfèvrerie Christofle

Cinematone Corporation

Cinematone was a jukebox manufacturer in Hollywood, California, founded in 1939.[52] It manufactured the *Penny Phono* invented by William F. Falkenberg, a man well known in the coin machine industry, with the help of Dr. Gordon Keith Woodward. The *Penny Phono*, available in both floor and counter models, held special slow-playing records with twenty songs, ten on a side. As a result, the *Penny Phono* did not need the elaborate record-changing mechanisms of conventional jukeboxes and, in theory, cost less to own and operate.

Cinematone's own music department, Cinematone Studios, provided the special records, and artists from nightclubs, movie studios, and radio networks took part in the Cinematone recording orchestra. Its most important band leader was the zany Spike Jones, who served as music director until February 1940. Cinematone Studios produced a new record each week until the company went out of business in 1942.

CWL

Clarke, Arundell *see* Arundell Clarke

Clover Box and Manufacturing Company

Established in 1918, the Clover Box and Manufacturing Company was involved in the production of plastics by the 1940s.[53] Located in the Bronx, New York, from 1942 to 1953, the company experimented with new technology, notably a process for shaping plastic objects that utilized vacuum pressure rather than molds. Its line of Plexiglas *Cloverware*, formed by this technique and introduced in 1947, was developed in conjunction with the designer Eva Zeisel.

By the early 1950s, plastics dominated Clover's production. When the company's president, Monroe L. Dinell (1890–1956, retired 1954), relocated the firm to Norwalk, Connecticut, in 1953, it was renamed Clover Plastic Contours, Inc. Its new facilities, consisting of eleven thousand square feet, were devoted to the manufacture and processing of plastic parts for various military and commercial uses.

LN

Colin, Jean

Born Paris, February 1, 1912; died Paris, August 6, 1982

Jean Colin was one of France's best-known midtwentieth-century graphic designers.[54] His work encompassed advertising art, book design, typography, and murals. He created more than four hundred posters for many corporations including Shell, Air France, Cinzano, Électricité de France, and the Société Nationale des Chemins de Fer (SNCF).

From 1930 to 1933, he studied graphic art at Paris's École Nationale Supérieure des Arts Décoratifs, under A. M. Cassandre and Jean Carlu. He returned to the school as a lecturer from 1951 to 1962.

Colin's work often juxtaposes the realism of photography with the fantasy of illustration to create visual surprises that attract the spectator. Generally, Jean

Colin's style was less decorative and more geometric than that of many of his French colleagues; his choice of lettering is always a pronounced aspect of the overall design.

Jean Colin participated in many international exhibitions. Featured in two American solo exhibitions—in New York in 1956 and in Philadelphia the following year—Colin also exhibited regularly in the Warsaw poster biennial from 1968 on. He was a founding member of the prestigious AGI (Alliance Graphique Internationale), for which he organized an exhibition at the Musée du Louvre in 1955. He won the Martini gold medal for the best French poster of 1959.

He lived in Bougival, a suburb of Paris, and worked as a design consultant until his death.

FTH

Colin, Paul

Born Nancy, France, June 27, 1892; died Nogent-sur-Marne, France, June 18, 1985

The career of Paul Colin, one of France's most prolific and important poster artists and stage designers, spanned nearly a century.[55] His graphic style flowered with the Jazz Age, with which it is most often associated, and from then on, Colin's characteristically humorous and economical designs were a dominant influence in the development of the French poster.

Paul Colin studied at the Écoles des Beaux-Arts of Nancy and Paris, where he moved in 1913 to begin his career as a painter. A costume designer as well as a stage designer of nearly eight hundred sets, Colin used the theater as a frequent theme in his posters. The year 1925 was a watershed for his art—as well as for the Art Deco style—beginning with a job at the Théâtre des Champs-Élysées. His poster for "La Revue Nègre," the American show that introduced Josephine Baker to Paris, brought him overnight success. Colin's totally stylized graphics embodied Jazz Age modernity and the era of the flapper. His frequent subjects were the black jazz musicians who took Paris by storm and Josephine Baker, wearing her celebrated skimpy costumes. His subsequent work was much in demand for theaters and music halls. Colin also did a large body of posters making public appeals, such as for war veterans and World War II charities.

In 1926 he founded the Paul Colin School, where he expounded his theories on graphic design, thereby influencing generations of French poster artists. While his posters show a strong Cubist influence, his paintings, often of nudes and still lifes, are freer in execution and are stylistically close to the work of Jules Pascin and Per Krohg. After World War II, although Colin remained busy and kept abreast of the various shifts in style, he did not maintain a position of leadership.

Colin's work was the subject of many European exhibitions. The Musée des Arts Décoratifs, Paris, had a retrospective of his work in 1949, as did the Sorbonne in 1982. Responding to this return to favor, Colin often reworked his earlier themes in the later part of his life.

FTH

Colombo, Cesare (Joe)

Born Milan, July 30, 1930; died Milan, July 30, 1971

This Italian designer worked on a wide range of projects, including interiors, exhibitions, furniture, and industrial products.[56] Like many of his contemporaries, he trained as an architect, at the Politecnico di Milan, but, unlike most of them, he also studied fine art, at the Accademia di Belle Arti di Brera e Liceo Artistico. His early career in Milan, in fact, was as a painter and sculptor, and it was not until 1955 that he opened his own office. In 1962 he began working as an industrial designer, in response to requests from manufacturers, and by the end of the decade he had worked with a number of leading firms, among them Kartell and O-Luce.

Joe Colombo's reputation as a designer is based, however, on a relatively small output. Among this, his plywood chair and his plastic chair for Kartell are outstanding items that show how he combined his skill as a sculptor with his knowledge of materials and technology. His furniture and light designs—notably his *Elda* armchair of 1963, his *Supercomfort* chair of the following year, and his *Alogena* lamp of 1970—all manifest a meticulous detail of form. On the other hand, Colombo never neglected the utilitarian aspect of his designs.

Shortly before his death in 1971, Colombo became interested in the Orient and published an article on "dynamic space" in Japanese design.[57] His work from the 1960s coincides with the moment when Italy achieved a worldwide reputation for its design; Colombo's highly minimal, controlled work was well respected abroad, helping to promote the Italian design movement internationally. He received numerous awards, among them a Compasso d'Oro for his *Spider* lamp in 1967 and the first Salone di Macchine e Attrezzature per l'Uffici (SMAU) prize for his *Boby* trolley in 1971.

PS

Copier, Andries Dirk Born Leerdam, the Netherlands, January 11, 1901

Through both his free-blown art glass and his mass-produced utilitarian glassware, Andries Copier gained an international reputation for himself and the Koninklijke Nederlandsche Glasfabriek Leerdam (Royal Leerdam Glass), with which he has been closely associated.[58]

After finishing elementary school, Copier joined Leerdam's etching department in 1914. While working there, he studied painting at De Middenstand (1915–18) and attended the Vakschool voor Typografie, Utrecht (1918–19). In 1921, after a brief stint of military duty, he became a draftsman in Leerdam's sales and design department. At the same time, he studied with graphic designer J. Jongert, first privately and then at the Academie voor Beeldende Kunsten en Technische Wetenschappen, Rotterdam.

Copier began designing glass and advertisements for Leerdam in 1922 and subsequently became involved in the installation of Leerdam's exhibitions. In 1924 he exhibited his first *Unica* pieces, unique forms inspired by historical models that gradually became progressively modern, with thick walls and simple shapes. Copier often employed an iridescent material and then developed a tin crackle in the glass, a process he used on many of his pieces from 1925 through the 1930s. Beginning in 1926, Copier designed *Serica* pieces as well, art glass of unlimited production that was usually based on successful *Unica* designs. Copier also designed mass-produced household ware. His early works, such as *Smeerwortel* (Comfrey, 1922–23), winner of a silver medal at the Paris "Exposition Internationale des Arts Décoratifs et Industriels Modernes" in 1925, were based on forms found in nature. Copier's subsequent works showed a more functionalist style, and by the late 1920s and 1930s the influence of De Stijl was evident. His *Gildeglass* (1930), designed in association with the Dutch wine merchants, became a standard both in the Netherlands and abroad.

Copier had become artistic director of Leerdam in 1927. In 1940, he helped found the Leerdamse Glasschool and served as its first head. In the later 1940s, when ornamentation prevailed, he produced some of his best art glass—thick-walled vases with figurative relief decoration. The number of Copier's designs diminished during the postwar era. While his asymmetrical *Unica* pieces of the 1950s were less successful, his *Gourmet* glasses won an award at the Milan XII

Triennale in 1960, and in 1958 his design for the Leerdam pavilion at the 1958 Brussels World's Fair won a grand prize.

Copier explored other avenues as well. He made designs for stained and sandblasted windows. In 1946 and again in 1958 he designed plastic dishes for KLM. During the 1950s and 1960s he designed dinner and coffee services for the German ceramic company Eschenbach.

Copier retired from Leerdam in 1971, only to begin working with glass again six years later, first in De Oude Horn, a studio in Acquoy, and since then with glass artists such as Lino Tagliapietra and Harvey Littleton. In 1988 he designed new *Unica* pieces for Leerdam.

LN

Coray, Hans Born Wald, Switzerland, June 9, 1907

Known primarily as the designer of the *Landi* chair, Hans Coray has pursued multiple interests. His scholarly studies were in the field of Romantic literature, for which he received a doctorate in 1929, and the following year he designed his first chair, out of metal wire. This dichotomy of interests persisted: Coray taught high school while continuing to work with metal, designing objects as diverse as lunch boxes and ski runners. Due to a skiing accident in 1932, he was obliged to spend the greater part of the 1930s resting, and he used the opportunity to delve into subjects such as graphology, astrology, psychology, and religion.

Coray emerged as a prominent designer at the 1939 "Landesaustellung" (Swiss National Exhibition) in Zurich, not only because of his aluminum *Landi* chair, which was used throughout the exposition, but also through his work on the interiors of various pavilions—those for the press, the aluminum and electrical industries, and the applied arts section of the chemical industry.

Over the course of the next half-century Coray remained multifaceted. A primary aspect of his career has been his work as a sculptor, primarily in metal, and a painter. Like his father before him, he also dealt in ethnographic art, between 1968 and 1973. Coray has always remained active in the world of design: creating jewelry in the early 1940s, handmade leather items in the early 1950s, and periodically returning to furniture. His chairs and tables from the early 1950s were sold through the progressive Swiss concern Wohnbedarf.

A retrospective exhibition of Coray's work was staged in 1986 in Zurich. It helped to bring together many aspects of his career, most of which have remained essentially unknown outside of his native country.[59]

ME

Cuttoli, Marie Bordes Born 1880; died 1973

Interested both in textiles and in contemporary painting, Marie Cuttoli bridged both arts to create an important artistic medium.[60]

Following her marriage in 1912 to Paul Cuttoli, an active politician and newspaper publisher in Algeria and later a senator from Algeria, she divided her time between Algeria and Paris.[61] Living in the North African cities of Constantine and Sétif, she discovered the beauty of the native craftsmanship and was instrumental in expanding the market for local work by adapting it to European tastes. She organized embroidery workshops that supplied Parisian couture houses and made an international success of carpet workshops that wove rugs in modern designs.

In Paris she was a friend of the avant-garde painters and an avid collector of their work. Through Jean Lurçat, whom she met in 1925, she became aware of the lack of creative contemporary models for tapestry and the economic depression at both Aubusson and Beauvais. At Lurçat's urging, Cuttoli invited the mas-

ters of the Paris school to design tapestries for her; Georges Rouault was the first to agree in 1928. Serving as "éditeur," she had their paintings woven into tapestries, primarily at the Aubusson ateliers of Delarbre, Simon, and Legoueix in the mid-1930s. These "easel tapestries," after the work of Pablo Picasso, Georges Braque, Raoul Dufy, Henri Matisse, and other prominent painters, premiered in 1936 to a mixed critical reception but captured the public's attention, paving the way for later, more significant artistic developments effected by Lurçat. Cuttoli continued in her role as "éditeur" after the war as well, having tapestries woven to the designs of other famous painters. An astute collector as well as a promoter of the arts, Cuttoli contributed to the intellectual and artistic life of France, her efforts recognized by honors conferred by the government.

AZ

Cyrén, Gunnar Born Gävle, Sweden, July 23, 1931

Gunnar Cyrén is known not only as an accomplished silversmith but also as a designer of glass. In bridging these two mediums he has achieved a rare feat.[62]

His first love was silver. This stems not from family tradition but, rather, chance: his skillful use of his hands brought the fourteen-year-old boy into an apprenticeship with a silversmith in his native town. He finished his apprenticeship at age twenty, and after serving in the military, he entered the Konstfackskolan in Stockholm. He completed studies there, as well as a summer's work in granulation with Elisabeth Treskow at the Kölner Werkschule, by 1956. Marriage, a brief stay in Stockholm, and work as a silversmith in Uppsala completed the first part of what might have been a traditional background for a young silversmith.

Then, in 1959, on the recommendation of the director of the Konstfackskolan, Cyrén received an appointment at the famed glasshouse of Orrefors. Mastering the new material directly on the site, he soon achieved prominence through exhibitions at Svensk Form in Stockholm in 1961 and 1963. He introduced opaque, brightly colored glass to the factory; the most famous of his works in this genre are his *Pop* glasses of 1966, the same year he won the prestigious Lunning Prize. In the late 1960s, he made a series of enameled glass bowls with humorously erotic scenes in a caricatural style. Though he rose to the position of artistic director at Orrefors and achieved international fame in the glass world, he temporarily abandoned the medium of glass.

In 1970 Cyrén settled back in Gävle and began designing in all mediums, especially plastic, for Dansk International. Despite the deleterious effects of the oil crisis and the fall of the American dollar, his *Gourmet* line was introduced in 1973. In 1975 Cyrén returned to his original calling, establishing a silversmith's studio and shop in Gävle. His work, whether based on natural or geometric forms, shows precision and finesse. In addition, he resumed work for Orrefors in 1976, but on a free-lance basis. He maintains this dual allegiance to silver and glass today.

ME

Dalí, Salvador Born Figueras, Spain, May 11, 1904; died Figueras, January 23, 1989

Salvador Dalí was one of the leading Surrealist painters and a master at publicizing himself.[63] Beginning in 1921 he studied at the Real Academia de Bellas Artes de San Fernando in Madrid. In Madrid he became friends with the poet Federico García Lorca and the filmmaker Luis Buñuel. His early works were reminiscent of the paintings of Pablo Picasso and Joan Miró. In 1929 he moved to Paris and became a member of the Surrealist artists and writers. There he studied the writings of Sigmund Freud and began probing the subconscious in his paintings with sharply focused, fragmentary images, irrationally combined. As in the best known of these works, such as *The Persistence of Memory* (1931) and *Soft Construction in Boiled Beans—Premonition of Civil War* (1936), they form a hallucinatory world of sexuality, horror, and decay. He developed what he called a "paranoiac-critical theory" with Freudian implications in his writings as well as in his paintings. Like Hegel, Dalí felt that painting built a bridge between his interior and exterior worlds. Dalí also collaborated with Buñuel in making two films, *Un Chien Andalou* (1929) and *L'Âge d'Or* (1931), which caused sensations because of their horrific aspects.

In the mid-1930s Dalí was at his peak, painting and creating Surrealist objects like *Venus de Milo with Drawers* (1936), made with Marcel Duchamp, and *Rainy Taxi* (1938), an abandoned vehicle with ivy growing on it in which he placed dummies of a driver and a hysterical woman. He disliked mechanical things and designed furniture from living forms. For the English collector Edward James, he created a sofa in the shape of Mae West's lips that was executed by Jean-Michel Frank (1936) and a telephone in the form of a lobster. Dalí's designs for couturière Elsa Schiaparelli, including a dress adorned with a lobster and a hat in the form of a shoe, were widely celebrated.

By the end of the 1930s Dalí was as renowned as an eccentric as he was as an artist. In 1939 André Breton, the self-appointed leader of the Surrealists, repudiated Dalí, partly because their forms of exhibitionism collided. Dalí came to the United States that year and stayed during World War II.

After the war, Dalí's style changed, as he turned to painting atomic particles and objects in the middle of disintegration, as well as large religious scenes. He was especially active as a designer during these years, as his powers as a painter began to wane. Manufacturers asked him to design a wide variety of goods: textiles, men's ties, greeting cards, and tiles. One major project was a set of jewelry for Alemany & Ertman, Inc. (c. 1948–50). He accepted so many of these commissions and charged such high fees that Breton called him "Avida Dollars," an anagram of Salvador Dali. In 1954 he returned to Spain, continuing to design and paint until he became too ill to work.

CWL

Dansk International Designs Ltd.
The Danish tableware firm was founded in 1954 by American entrepreneur Ted Nierenberg in response to the postwar life-style that emphasized simplicity, a style that was well suited to contemporary Scandinavian designs. Dansk produces glassware (mostly hand-blown), candle holders, dinnerware, wooden objects, silver plate, and stainless steel flatware and cookware. The Dansk coordinated line of tabletop products has been synonymous with Scandinavian modern style worldwide for more than three decades. All of Dansk's "premier designers," such as Jens Quistgaard and Gunnar Cyrén, are Scandinavian, but others, such as the American textile designer Jack Lenor Larsen, are also significant contributors to the Dansk line.

The strong craft tradition that survives in the Scandinavian countries is evident in Dansk products like Quistgaard's ovenproof *Flamestone* line (1957), inspired by the black-glazed peasant pottery of rural Denmark. Respect for materials is a Dansk credo, whether it be the teak of hand-turned bowls, the stainless steel of flatware, or the plastic of tabletop items. Since its inception, the firm has been committed to the postindustrial craft approach to tabletop design; there has been little stylistic evolution in Dansk's designs.

Dansk, whose headquarters are in Mount Kisco, New York, is a contract manufacturer. The firm has over one hundred factories throughout the world and sells its products worldwide. Some of its major outlets are its own discount stores, which proved so popular that new products were developed just for these stores. Since 1984, when Nierenberg sold the firm, it has been headed by D. Richard Ryan.

FTH

Day, Lucienne Conradi
Born Coulsdon, England, January 5, 1917

A free-lance designer in various mediums, Lucienne Day is perhaps best known for her textile patterns, particularly those furnishing fabrics manufactured by Heal and Son of London during her long collaboration with that firm.[64] Day received her education in London, first at the Croydon School of Art (1934–37), then at the Royal College of Art (1937–40). In 1942 she began teaching at the Beckenham School of Art; the same year, she married industrial designer Robin Day. Six years later, she went into private practice as a freelance designer, sometimes working with her husband.

Calyx, designed for the Festival of Britain of 1951 and Day's first major commission, introduced lively, stylized forms executed in a fresh color palette—elements characteristic of her style. Her extremely popular textile designs earned Day international recognition and many awards, including the gold medal at the Milan IX Triennale in 1951 and a grand prize in 1954. In addition to her work for Heal's, she also designed a variety of textiles, carpets, and wallpapers for Edinburgh Weavers, Tomkinson's Carpets, the Wilton Royal Carpet Factory Ltd., and John Lewis, as well as other European and American manufacturers.

In addition to her work with textiles, Day has designed china decorations for Rosenthal (1957–69) and served on the firm's jury for the selection of new designs (1960–68). She has acted as color consultant for industry and designed interiors for BOAC passenger aircraft. In 1963 the Royal Society of Arts named her a Royal Designer for Industry, and in 1987 she was the first woman to be elected master of the faculty, serving a two-year term.

More recently she has turned her attention to creating one-of-a-kind wall hangings composed of small squares of plain or shot silk stitched together by hand. Called "silk mosaics," they are abstract in style, architectural in reference, and indicative of Day's innate sense of successful color combinations.

AZ

De Patta, Margaret Strong Bielawski
Born Tacoma, Washington, March 18, 1903; died Oakland, California, March 19, 1964

Margaret de Patta's greatest innovations lay in her use of architectonic structuring, kinetics, and transparency in jewelry.[65]

Originally interested in painting, she studied at the Academy of Fine Arts in San Diego from 1921 to 1923, at the San Francisco School of Fine Arts from 1923 to 1925, and in 1926 at the Art Students League in New York City. In 1929 she returned to San Francisco and began to establish herself as a painter. At the same time, she hoped to make jewelry that exhibited the principles of modern art. She studied the rudiments of the craft with an Armenian artisan, Armin Hairenian. In 1935 she had her own workshop and by 1936 she was placing jewelry at Amberg-Hirth, a San Francisco craft store. Her designs of this period were based on ethnic types, inspired by pre-Columbian and Turkish models.

She attended a summer session at Mills College in Oakland in 1940, where she met László Moholy-Nagy. The basic tenets of Constructivism—the rigorous structuring of space by means of light, line, and color—had a profound effect on de Patta. She sought to translate these principles into the medium of jewelry. She attended Moholy-Nagy's School of Design in Chicago from 1940 to 1941 and began to evolve a visual vocabulary that included rectangular planes slicing space at oblique angles, real or implied movement of parts, translucency, transparency, and the effect of shadows cast by pierced disks and stainless steel screening. She experimented with optical effects such as magnification, reduction, and distortion as integral elements of the composition.

While at the "Chicago Bauhaus," she met and married Eugene Bielawski, who was teaching a design course there. He shared her belief in modern jewelry based on the principles of abstraction and three-dimensional structure. In 1941 she and Bielawski settled in the Bay Area, where she established a jewelry studio. By 1946 the demand for her handcrafted jewelry far outweighed the supply, whereupon she and her husband began a limited production operation, selling each piece for under fifty dollars. However, the business aspects eventually became too overwhelming, and in 1958 the Bielawskis abandoned manufacturing.

De Patta designed other objects besides jewelry: flatware, hollowware, and, for Edith Heath in Sausalito, ceramic vessels. She and her husband moved to Napa in 1951, where they unsuccessfully attempted to establish a school based on the philosophy of the Bauhaus. Eventually, they moved back to Oakland.

De Patta received many local and some national awards and honors. Her work was included in the American exhibit at the Brussels World's Fair in 1958. A retrospective exhibition of her work was staged by the Museum of Contemporary Crafts in New York in 1965, but she still has not received the international recognition that is due an innovative artist of her stature.

TLW

Dreyfuss, Henry
Born New York, March 2, 1904; died South Pasadena, California, October 5, 1972

Henry Dreyfuss was the youngest of the four leading American industrial designers who rose to fame in the late 1920s and early 1930s.[66] The other three were Raymond Loewy, Norman Bel Geddes, and Walter Dorwin Teague.

Dreyfuss's early career was in the theater. Initially an apprentice to industrial designer Norman Bel Geddes, he then designed sets, costumes, and lighting for the Strand Theater in New York and the Radio-Keith-Orpheum (R.K.O.) vaudeville chain. This experience, which lasted five years, proved invaluable in his work as an industrial designer.

In 1929, at the age of twenty-five, Dreyfuss established his own industrial design firm in New York. One of his first employees, Doris Marks, became his wife and business manager. His straightforward and unassuming manner appealed to businessmen and characterized his work, which, though in the Streamlined style, generally eschewed flashiness.

One of Dreyfuss's first clients, the Bell Telephone Laboratories, proved to be his most significant and longest lasting. His model no. 300 desk phone was introduced in 1937, and it remained the standard until 1949, when it was replaced by the classic model no. 500; in 1964 he introduced the sculptural *Trimline* phone. These projects exemplified his credo: "We bear in mind that the object being worked on is going to be ridden in, sat upon, looked at, talked into, activated, operated, or in some other way used by people individually or en masse."[67] This concern for what is now termed ergonomics is one of his most important contributions to the field of design.

The scope of Dreyfuss's firm was considerable. He placed his stamp on flyswatters, alarm clocks, thermos bottles, pens and pencils, typewriters, and magazine design. The firm has maintained long-standing consulting relationships with AT&T (beginning in 1930), John Deere & Company (1937), Hyster (1951), Polaroid (1961), and American Airlines (1963). Dreyfuss collaborated with architect Wallace K. Harrison in creating *Democracity*, the model city contained within the Perisphere at the New York World's Fair of 1939. A lifelong interest in symbols that could be understood universally led him to compile a *Symbols Sourcebook*, which was first published in 1972.

Some of his most successful designs were in the field of transportation. These include the complete redesign of the New York Central Railroad's *Mercury* (1936) and the *20th Century Limited* (1938), as well as airplane interiors for Pan Am, Lockheed, and American Airlines. Commencing in 1944, the Dreyfuss firm began one of the largest and most extensive of its projects for the American Export Lines. For a period of some seven years the firm was engaged in the overall design of the SS *Independence* and SS *Constitution*. Other significant architectural and interior design work included the corporate headquarters of the Bankers Trust Company in New York City (1962) and branch offices.

In 1969 Dreyfuss retired from the firm, which continues to the present as Henry Dreyfuss Associates.

GS

Dufy, Raoul Born Le Havre, France, June 3, 1877; died Forcalquier, France, March 23, 1953

One of the leading French painters to emerge from the Fauve movement, a style he carried to the mid-twentieth century, Raoul Dufy has come to be regarded as a minor master. His views of leisured society are often dismissed as "decorative"; in fact, a major portion of the painter's energy was devoted to the decorative arts.[68]

Dufy's early training was in Le Havre at the École des Beaux-Arts. In 1896 he went to Paris, where he attended the École des Beaux-Arts, and then, about 1904, he worked in a Post-Impressionist vein. After he came in contact with Henri Matisse and the Fauves in 1906, his palette became more intense and arbitrary, his draftsmanship more abrupt. He experimented briefly with Cubism through the mid-1910s, though he always maintained the visual integrity of the motif. By 1920 Dufy had established his mature style, a bold, calligraphic language, and the ground is often a staccato series of textured passages. Dufy's patches of intense color generally do not coincide with their respective objects in accordance with the artist's understanding that the perception of an object's color is retained longer than the sense of an object's contours.

Woodcuts that Dufy made for Guillaume Apollinaire's book of poems *Le Bestiaire* in 1909 represent a transition to the decorative arts. These intentionally naive prints in the tradition of *images d'Épinal* led to a commission from couturier Paul Poiret for notepapers, followed by commissions for various decorations. Poiret established a studio for Dufy where he could experiment with printing textiles for the couturier's dresses. In 1912 Dufy also began designing for Atuyer, Bianchini et Férier (soon to be Bianchini-Férier), a silk house in Lyons. While some patterns were geometric, the boldest were freely drawn florals and scenic motifs with bright Fauvist colors. By the time of the 1925 "Exposition Internationale des Arts Décoratifs et Industriels Modernes," Dufy's work typified the verve and wit of French decorative art at its most decorative and most modern.

Ceramics was another medium that attracted Dufy's talents. In 1923 Dufy was introduced to José Lloréns Artigas, a Catalan potter recently established in Paris, and they began a collaboration that lasted until the late 1930s. Artigas provided the forms and technical expertise and Dufy the decoration, which was in as bold a style as his paintings, with broad patches of color and incised lines.

Marie Cuttoli, who turned to many of the leading painters of the Paris school, commissioned a substantial number of models for large-scale tapestries and furniture upholstery from Dufy in the 1930s. For the 1937 Paris "Exposition Internationale des Arts et Techniques," the artist was chosen to create a mural for the Palais de la Lumière: a decoration of six hundred square meters, which was heralded as the largest painting ever produced. From 1930 to 1933 Dufy designed textiles for the New York firm of Onondaga, and the Corning Glass Works called upon him for designs to be engraved in 1938.

Dufy did not receive comparable commissions after the war, but his style of freely drawn figures and loosely associated patches of intense color became the foundation stones of so much postwar decoration that the power of Dufy's pictorial language remained truly influential.

ME

Dunbar Furniture Corporation of Indiana

This furniture company's beginnings were humble. In 1919, when business was slack at Riney Dunbar's Buggy Works in Linn Grove, Indiana, due to the rising popularity of the automobile, Aloysius Dunbar built a rocking chair for his wife. So many neighbors wanted one that he moved his nineteen employees and equipment to Berne, Indiana, and started producing furniture under the name of Dunbar Furniture, Inc., in 1919. A new plant was built in 1920, and the first showroom opened in 1927.

Edward J. Wormley came to the Dunbar firm in 1931 as director of design, and he designed all of the company's furniture for the next thirty-seven years. At first he turned out traditional pieces, mostly in the English or Early American style. Then he introduced unornamented and simplified traditional designs and, by the mid-1930s, designs influenced by Swedish Modern. In the late 1930s, Dunbar was manufacturing two separate lines: one modern, the other traditional.

During the war the company turned to government work, making wooden tail sections for airplanes. In 1946 the firm, then known as Dunbar Furniture Manufacturing Co., was back in full production. By 1950 it assumed its current name. Wormley averaged a hundred designs a year; the 150–piece Janus Collection (1957) was Dunbar's largest line. Each collection was offered as a nucleus for people making their own arrangements. Wormley's designs tended to be conservative, using rich materials and fine craftsmanship, and could be mixed with antiques or with furniture people already owned.[69] Although Dunbar continues to produce many of the older Wormley pieces, it has commissioned works from contemporary avant-garde designers. Michael Graves recently designed the Dorsey Collection of chairs and sofas, which reflect the Streamlined curves of the 1930s.

CWL

Eames, Charles Born Saint Louis, Missouri, June 17, 1907; died Saint Louis, August 21, 1978

Eames, Ray Kaiser Born Sacramento, California, December 15, 1913; died Los Angeles, August 21, 1988

The careers of Charles Eames and Ray Eames were extremely influential in the development of modern American design, encompassing not only furniture and architecture but also interior design, filmmaking, and exhibition design.[70]

Charles Eames began his career in architecture in 1924, studying at Washington University in Saint Louis, Missouri. He later twice established his own, short-lived firms, first in 1930 and again in 1935.

In 1938 he was awarded a fellowship to study architecture and design at the Cranbrook Academy of Art in Bloomfield Hills, Michigan, which precipitated a major turning point in his career. There he made friends with faculty member Eero Saarinen, son of architect Eliel Saarinen and director of Cranbrook. He also met Ray Kaiser, a painter and sculptor who had studied painting in New York City with Hans Hoffmann from 1933 to 1939, before going to Cranbrook. Eames and Kaiser married in 1941, and they embarked on a lifelong collaboration.

The Eameses' careers in furniture design began in 1940 with a competition sponsored by the Museum of Modern Art, "Organic Design in Home Furnishings," which was intended to foster attractive low-cost furniture and exploit new technological possibilities. Collaborating with Saarinen and assisted by Ray, Charles won first prize in two categories, one for modular furniture and the other for a molded plywood chair.

In 1941 the Eameses moved to California, where they worked for the United States Navy, developing molded plywood stretchers and splints; this work proved invaluable in evolving the processes and tools necessary to mass-produce their furniture designs. By 1946, the Eameses' design for a molded plywood side chair, model LCW, was ready for mass production by Herman Miller. Probably the single most influential postwar chair, it and other pieces were exhibited at the Museum of Modern Art in 1946, in a major show devoted to their work, which established their international status. A series would follow, each growing out of the preceding one, first in molded polyester, in 1949, then in aluminum, in 1958. In 1956 the Eameses introduced the now-classic lounge chair and ottoman of aluminum, rosewood, and leather. The Eameses' last furniture show at the Museum of Modern Art was in 1973.

Charles Eames's most significant architectural work was his own house in Pacific Palisades, California (1948–49). It is the most famous of a series of "Case Study" houses built under the sponsorship of *Arts and Architecture* magazine. Though constructed of standard prefabricated parts adapted to residential use, it reflects an almost Japanese aesthetic in its use of opaque and transparent panels in a Mondrian-like play of design. For all the seeming austerity of this industrialized exterior, the interior presented a different aspect, accented by walls painted in primary colors and enlivened by the extraordinary mélange of toys, dolls, pillows, and other objects that the Eameses enthusiastically collected. In 1978 the Eames house received the American Institute of Architects Twenty-five-Year Award.

Beginning in 1950, Charles and Ray Eames produced some fifty films. The first was a series on toys, but perhaps the best known is *Powers of Ten* (1968), made for the Commission of the College of Physics. Exhibitions, most often employing a time-line technique, were commissioned by institutions and corporations; these include "Mathematica" (1961), for IBM, and "The World of Franklin and Jefferson" (1975), created for the American Revolution Bicentennial Administration. The multimedia slide presentation was another Eames innovation. "Glimpses of the USA," a twelve-minute presentation employing some 2,200 images on seven screens, was presented at the American Exhibition at the Moscow World's Fair (1959). It is in the films and exhibitions that the hand of Ray Eames is said to be felt most vividly.

Throughout their long careers Charles and Ray Eames notably affected design. Their works became staples of residences, offices, schools, and airports throughout the United States and the world over.

GS

Edison Price, Inc., New York The firm Edison Price, Inc., was formed in 1952 in New York City to design and manufacture lighting devices for architects

and lighting consultants. Its founder, Edison Price, was the second generation of an American lighting dynasty: his father, William E. Price, founded Display Stage Lighting Company in 1917.[71] A mechanical wunderkind, young Price assisted the important designer Cleon Throckmorton in devising special effects in the early 1940s. During that time, Price invented a rear-projection light machine and helped Isamu Noguchi build sets for Martha Graham ballets. Through Noguchi, Price was introduced to the architectural innovator R. Buckminster Fuller.[72] Other Price developments of those early years include important devices still used today to manipulate and control difficult-to-reach lighting equipment in photography, film, and television studios.

Price's technical wizardry and familiarity with lenses, specular finishes, and manufacturing techniques gave rise to equipment capable of implementing the effects imagined by lighting designers. Edison Price and the fixtures designed by his company have had a decisive influence on the development of architectural lighting. Price also had a close working relationship with the lighting consultant Richard Kelly, famous for so many of the concepts and so much of the terminology employed in this field. Many of the most renowned architects and architectural firms of the past four decades, including Philip Johnson, Ludwig Mies van der Rohe, I. M. Pei, Louis Kahn, Marcel Breuer, and Skidmore, Owings and Merrill, have worked with Price.

KC

Edwin Raphael Company

Located in Holland, Michigan, the Edwin Raphael Company manufactured drapery fabrics and draperies. It specialized in creating screen-printed textiles intended for draperies for institutional usage and stage curtains. Among the designers who worked for the firm in the 1950s was Marianne Strengell. Edwin Raphael, president of the company, was a native Texan, and his company designed and executed the interior of President Lyndon B. Johnson's private plane.

The firm maintained a showroom in Chicago and marketed its goods nationwide. In 1962, ground was broken for a new twenty-thousand-square-foot plant in Holland to house the company's offices and design and manufacturing facilities, including three one-hundred-and-eighty-foot-long tables for large-scale screen printing.

LN

Ernst, Joseph Caspar (Jupp)

Born Paderborn, Germany, December 20, 1905; died 1987

Jupp Ernst's long association with the influential Kassel school of graphic art was primarily as a teacher of the subject at the renowned Staatliche Werkkunstschule in Kassel.[73]

Ernst was a free-lance graphic designer from 1929 to 1948 before becoming director of the Werkkunstschule at Wuppertal (1948–54). He collaborated as well in the Auto Union Bauhaus carpet factory (1937–55). In 1954, Ernst became director of the prestigious Kassel school, remaining in that capacity until 1969. He was head of the Drawing and Commercial Art departments and a lecturer in the latter.

Ernst was also concerned with three-dimensional design. From the early 1950s he was involved with launching a Council for Molding, and in 1951 he established an institute for industrial design at the Wuppertal Werkkunstschule. He served as an advisory member of the Federation of German Industry and was an editor of the design periodical *Form*, established in 1956 in Cologne.

Ernst was a very active organizer and participant in postwar German design circles. He represented German design at international conferences, and his work was exhibited internationally from 1959 until his retirement.

FTH

Firma Karl Mathsson

Karl Mathsson was a fourth-generation member of a family of cabinetmakers in Värnamo, Småland, in southern Sweden. He went into the family trade and established a furniture manufacturing firm, Firma Karl Mathsson, in Värnamo in 1920. The firm worked in Empire, Rococo, and other traditional styles. When Karl's son Bruno created innovative chair designs in the 1930s and 1940s, his father's shop made them to order. Although this was an expensive way of manufacturing furniture, the firm saved money by eliminating the dealer and selling directly to the customers. During these years, the company stopped producing its traditional wares and made only Bruno's designs.

Bruno became the manager of Firma Karl Mathsson in 1957. Then in 1978, DUX Industrier, which had been making some of Mathsson's metal furniture designs since 1966, took over the production of Firma Karl Mathsson, which was still making Bruno Mathsson's classic wooden designs.

CWL

Flos S.p.A.

In 1960 Dino Gavina, with the help of Cesare Cassina and others, formed Flos to produce lamps.[74] Both founders were important furniture manufacturers who wanted to produce lighting fixtures that would be appropriate for their furniture. The company was located in Merano, Italy, near the Austrian border, but in 1963 it moved to Nave, a suburb of Brescia, to be near the design center of Milan.

Flos has always made extremely modern, sometimes high-tech lamps. Its lamps were made of plastic, but in 1962 it branched out into metal, glass, and marble. The first designers were Tobia Scarpa and the Castiglioni brothers, Pier Giacomo and Achille. Perhaps the Castiglionis' most famous lamp of the 1960s is the Flos *Arco* lamp of 1962. Another prominent architect who produced designs for the firm was Mario Bellini, who created the *Chiara* lamp in 1964.

Flos expanded in the 1970s and 1980s, establishing European, American, and Japanese affiliates and acquiring Arteluce in 1974. Achille Castiglioni and Scarpa continued to design for the company during these years. Other designers were Paolo Rizzato in the 1970s and Bruno Gecchelin and Luciano Pagani in the 1980s.

Flos has kept its designs in production for many years: it is still making many of the Scarpa and Castiglioni lamps introduced in the 1960s and 1970s.

CWL

Fornasetti, Piero

Born Milan, November 10, 1913; died Milan, October 16, 1988

Piero Fornasetti was an artist who turned his considerable talents, particularly those as draftsman and printer, to the creation of decorative objects for daily use. Although the details of his life are occasionally clouded by the legacy of his own mythologizing, it appears that he studied at the Accademia di Belle Arti di Brera e Liceo Artistico, from which he was expelled, and later the Scuola Superiore d'Arte Applicato, Castello Sforzesco. Frustrated by the lack of classical training available, Fornasetti studied on his own, filling his library with handbooks on the history of crafts, treatises on design, and architectural pattern books. Thus he taught himself painting, engraving, printmaking, and other crafts. Unafraid of modern techniques, he also eventually developed new methods of printing on three-dimensional objects through photographic means.

As an artist developing during the 1930s, Fornasetti was influenced by the modern neoclassicism of the Novecento architects and painters, the classical Surrealism of Giorgio De Chirico and others, and by the designer who would become his chief promoter and collaborator, the architect and editor Gio Ponti. Early on, Fornasetti achieved fame through his engraving and lithography of illustrations and entire books after De Chirico, Marino Marini, Massimo Campigli, and Eugene Berman, among others. He continued producing books of his own drawings until his final years, often in an edition of one. Ultimately, it was his love of drawing and his skill as a draftsman that lay at the basis of all his work.

A group of printed scarves that Fornasetti made in 1940 first convinced Ponti to publish Fornasetti's work in *Domus*. His subsequent career as a designer through the 1940s and 1950s was devoted largely to the creation of a wide range of objects for the interior, the most famous of which were perhaps his ceramics and furniture. The objects—the porcelain blanks or wooden forms—were first manufactured by others, then Fornasetti decorated them with his secret, carefully guarded printing processes. He also designed complete interiors, the most famous being the ill-fated ocean liner SS *Andrea Doria*.

Fornasetti was a man of limitless energy and copious output. He slept very little and drew constantly throughout his entire life. He was also a difficult individual who, had he been willing to collaborate with manufacturers or license his designs, might have had greater commercial success, but his temperament did not allow for that. With few exceptions, he undertook the manufacturing and marketing of his products himself. A factory was established at his rambling Milan home, and from the 1940s until his death, he had either a wholesale showroom, a retail shop, or both in his native city. His firm was a commercial success in the 1950s and early 1960s, when Fornasetti products were retailed worldwide, but the period thereafter until the 1980s was a fallow one. His son Barnaba continues the family business, reproducing designs from throughout his father's career as well as introducing new products based on earlier designs.

CW

Franck, Kaj

Born Viipuri, Finland, November 9, 1911; died Santorini, Greece, September 26, 1989

One of Finland's most influential postwar industrial designers, Kaj Franck is best known for the timeless utilitarian ceramics and glassware, characteristically pure of form, that he designed for Oy Wärtsilä AB's companies, Arabia and Nuutajärvi-Notsjö.[75]

From 1929 to 1932 Franck studied furniture and interior design at the Taideteollinen Korkeakoulu (Central School of Industrial Design), Helsinki, where he began teaching in 1945. From 1960 to 1967 he served as art director there, and in 1973 he was appointed professor of art; he has also lectured widely. In Franck's early career, he designed lighting fixtures for Taito Oy (1933) and furniture for Te Ma Oy (1934–37), both in Helsinki, and textiles for the Associated Woolen Mills, Hyvinkää (1937–39). He sporadically designed interiors as well.

In 1945 Franck began his long association with the Arabia pottery, eventually becoming head of its design department (where he remained until 1960). His modular *Kilta* range (1952), inexpensive and colorful dinnerware composed of complementary rather than uniform pieces, revolutionized the industry.[76] Of similar conception, his mix-and-match set of enameled bowls won a grand prize at the 1957 Milan XI Triennale.

In 1946 Franck was cowinner (along with Tapio Wirkkala) of a glass competition sponsored by the Iittala glassworks, a distinction that led to his employment there until 1950. His designs for Iittala included clear crystal vessels enlivened with air bubbles or engraving. In 1951, Franck became artistic director of the Nuutajärvi-Notsjö glass factory (which had recently been purchased by Wärtsilä), a position he maintained until 1976. As at Arabia, Franck's leadership had a major impact on the artistic growth of the firm. His creativity is evidenced in his thin-walled soap bubbles (1951), the *Kremlin Bells* double decanters (1957), and small animal sculptures, such as the *Woodcock* (1954), infused with air bubbles and metallic inclusions. During the 1960s and 1970s, Franck's work for Nuutajärvi included filigree and pressed glass. His pioneering work during the 1950s brought him numerous awards, including a gold medal (1951) and honorable mention (1954) at the Milan Triennales, the Lunning Prize (1955), and the Compasso d'Oro (1957).

From 1968 to 1973 Franck served as art director of the Silicap group, Oy Wärtsilä. After his retirement from Wärtsilä in 1976, he continued to teach and maintained an independent practice, designing such objects as plastic tableware and flatware for Sarvis Oy (1979). A retrospective of Franck's work is planned by the Museum of Modern Art in New York for early 1992.

LN

Fritz Hansens Eft. AS

Fritz Hansen established a cabinetmaking shop in Copenhagen in 1872 that specialized in wood turning and producing frames in wood and iron for upholstered furniture.[77] In 1915 his son, Christian E. Hansen, invented a process for manufacturing bentwood chairs in the Thonet tradition, and during the 1920s the company capitalized on this process. When Christian's sons, Fritz and Søren, came into the firm in 1932, they moved it in a more modern direction. They began working with architects and designers to produce furniture with clean, functional lines. The company made then-seemingly modern but actually conservative wooden chairs by Kaare Klint, as well as avant-garde tubular steel chairs by Dutch designer Mart Stam. Hans Wegner designed his first *Chinese* chair for the firm in 1943–44.

After World War II the firm moved from bent to laminated wood. Its first model, the *Ax* chair of 1950 by Peter Hvidt and O. Mølgaard Nielsen, was influenced by the molded plywood fuselage of a Mosquito airplane. In 1950 Poul Kjaerholm also worked briefly for Fritz Hansens Eft., producing very bold prototypes that were not put into production at the time. Better known was the work of Arne Jacobsen, Fritz Hansen's leading designer until 1971; his *Ant* chair went into production in 1952, his *Egg* and *Swan* chairs in 1958. In 1968 Piet Hein and Bruno Mathsson designed a successful group of tables for Fritz Hansen. This was followed by Verner Panton's *Series 1.2.3* chairs in 1974.

The firm remained in the Hansen family for four generations. However, in 1979 it was bought by Skandinavisk Holding Company, and the offices were moved to a building near the factory in Allerød. In 1982 Fritz Hansens Eft. took over the production of much of Kjaerholm's furniture, including some of the models created for Fritz Hansens three decades earlier.

CWL

F. Schumacher & Company

Frederick Schumacher (1852–1912), a French textile representative for the firm Passavant et Cie, came to the United States in the early 1880s to establish a New York salesroom. When the New York enterprise was closed in 1889, Schumacher went into business for himself. He bought the Passavant merchandise in New York and established a staff, and, on August 1, 1889, F. Schumacher & Company began to operate.[78] Schumacher took on Paul Gadebusch (1865–1943) as a business partner in 1893, and his nephew Pierre Pozier (1880–1952) in 1899. He acquired his first mill space in the old Waverly Mill complex in Paterson, New Jersey, in 1895.

Schumacher & Company expanded steadily throughout the United States, and neither world war affected the company's development. By 1923, Schumacher & Company was introducing less costly, domestically printed designs that became known as Waverly fabrics, and in 1935, Waverly Fabrics became a separate division. A carpet subsidiary followed in 1939. Carrillo Fabrics and its owner, René Carrillo, joined the company in 1933 and became consolidated with the Schumacher firm in 1941.

Around 1925, Pozier commissioned major French designers Paul Follot, Edouard Bénédictus, E. A. Séguy, Henri Stéphany, and Paul Poiret to design for Schumacher. Soon he turned to a number of American designers who were experimenting with the newly invented synthetic Dupont fibers for automobile and airplane interiors. Notable among these were industrial designers Donald Deskey, Adolph Griven, and Ruth Reeves. Pozier also commissioned designs from other innovative artists, such as architect Joseph Urban and interior designer Dorothy Draper.

In 1946 the company moved its mill to Madison Avenue in Paterson, where it remained until 1950, when it relocated to its present site in Midland Park, New Jersey. Since World War II, Schumacher has issued numerous collections, such as the folk art-inspired Folly Cove Collection in 1947 and the historical-based Williamsburg Collection, Henry Ford Collection, and Farmers Museum Collection. Thus, the company reached a wide market and covered a broad spectrum, from opulence to simplicity.

CCMT

Fuller Fabrics Inc.

Founded in New York City by Daniel B. Fuller (born May 21, 1900; died August 16, 1977) in 1933 as a cotton-goods converter, this firm prepared yardage for apparel manufacturers by dyeing, printing, and chemically treating it. When the company was liquidated in 1935, Fuller joined Albert H. Vandam Company, where he organized the Fuller Fabrics department and became president of the firm after Vandam's death. In 1946, together with three associates from the Vandam Company, he founded a second cotton-converter firm, D. B. Fuller and Co., which was bought by J. P. Stevens & Co. in 1955 but continued to operate as an autonomous unit. During the 1950s and 1960s, roller and screen printing were carried out at D. B. Fuller and Co.'s plant in Easthampton, Massachusetts, while the design staff was located in New York City.[79]

Most of Fuller's cottons were printed with traditional patterns and were used by manufacturers such as White Stag and Jonathan Logan for women's sportswear. Fuller's advertising generally stressed the functional rather than the aesthetic qualities of its fabrics, but it aroused great public attention with its innovative Modern Master Print line of 1955—a marked departure from the conservative course of most of the midtown, high-volume fabric trade.

MBF

Gavina S.p.A.

Marcel Breuer called Dino Gavina "the most emotional and impulsive furniture manufacturer in the world."[80] In the late 1940s and 1950s the Dino Gavina company, located in Bologna, made hoods for jeeps, upholstered seats for railroad cars, and a few pieces of furniture. After Gavina met the designers Carlo Mollino, Carlo De Carli, and Pier Giacomo Castiglioni at the Milan X Triennale in 1954, he turned to making furniture. Since he considered himself a pioneer of antirationalism, he produced objects inspired by Marcel Duchamp's ready-mades, such as Castiglioni's *Cavalletto* (Sawhorse) trestle-table (1955), which moved a staple of the carpenter's shop into the domestic interior. He also produced designs by Franco Albini and Franca Helg.

In 1960 Gavina formed Gavina S.p.A. in Foligno as an offspring of his first company, with Carlo Scarpa as president; Scarpa also designed the Bologna showroom. Gavina S.p.A. made Achille and Pier Giacomo Castiglioni's *San Luca* chair (1960) and designs by Mario Bellini, Vico Magistretti, Marco Zanuso, and Tobia Scarpa. In 1962 Gavina S.p.A. started manufacturing Marcel Breuer's Bauhaus designs, the first time they had been made in mass production; in fact, it was Dino Gavina who gave the name *Wassily* (Kandinsky's first name) to one of Breuer's most famous designs.

In the mid-1960s Gavina S.p.A. began offering novel seating forms made from large polyurethane blocks—the *Malitte* system (1966) by Sebastian Matta, a longtime follower of Duchamp, and *Marcel, Raymond,* and *Suzanne* (all 1965), named in honor of Duchamp and two of his siblings, by Kazuhide Takahama.

In 1967 Dino Gavina sold the company to Knoll International and proceeded to set up the new firms of Simon International and Gemini to manufacture furniture.

CWL

George Nelson Associates *see* Nelson, George

Georg Jensen Silversmithy

The Georg Jensen style has varied widely in its eighty-seven-year history, yet it has always acknowledged current ideas. From the original flower and fruit motifs created by Georg Jensen himself to the sweeping curves of today's creations, the designs have remained abreast of contemporary Scandinavian styles.[81]

Having trained as a sculptor and, at age fourteen, been apprenticed to a goldsmith, Georg Arthur Jensen (1866–1935) opened his silversmithy in 1904 in Copenhagen. He began producing jewelry for two reasons: first, he had been encouraged by Det Danske Kunstindustrimuseum's earlier purchase of jewelry Jensen had created while working as foreman for metalsmith Mogens Ballin, and second, considerably less capital was needed to make small objects. Hatpins were the most popular item; Jensen carried more than one hundred different designs in silver with semiprecious stones, based upon flower and animal motifs and related in style to Lalique, albeit more symmetrical. His first hollowware design, the bulbous *Blossom* teapot with its ivory handle, dates from 1905 (*Blossom* pattern flatware was added in 1919), and in 1908 the *Continental* flatware pattern, reminiscent of Norwegian wooden peasant cutlery, was introduced. *Acorn*, the company's most consistently popular flatware pattern, was designed by Johan Rohde in 1915. Jensen and Rohde had met just before 1900 at the workshop of Mogens Ballin and began collaborating in 1903. They signed a formal contract in 1917 and were to maintain close professional ties until they both died in 1935.

A great many contributed to the company's designs. Harald Nielsen (1892–1977), Jensen's brother-in-law, joined the firm as a designer in 1909 and became chief administrator in 1935 and codirector about 1946. He influenced the firm's style in the 1920s, imbuing his hollowware and flatware with voluminous, stylized fruit and flower ornaments. He also worked in a progressive, geometric mode, exemplified by his *Pyramid* flatware, which was introduced in 1927. Swedish geometric simplicity entered the Jensen style after 1930, with the designs of Count Sigvard Bernadotte, whose classically inspired forms in a modernized eighteenth-century style were usually incised with fluting. Henry Pilstrup, with the firm since its beginning, became foreman of the jewelry workshop in 1918 and remained in that post until 1957. His designs tended toward the geometric and minimal, utilizing the clean lines of Modernism. Sculptor and engraver Arno Malinowski, active as a jewelry designer for the company from 1936 until 1965, created animal designs in the early 1940s that combined conventional Scandinavian motifs with a static, Modernist idiom.

The decade of the 1950s was a very prosperous and creative one for the firm, and the most important designer of that period was Henning Koppel, who joined the smithy in 1945 and designed bold new holloware, flatware (for example, *Caravel*, 1957) and jewelry with undulant, Biomorphic forms. Nanna Ditzel's jewelry of the 1950s and 1960s explored concavity and convexity in forms that seem to recall parts of the body. Torun Bülow-Hübe utilized lyric gestures in her curvilinear jewelry designs of the 1960s and 1970s.

Part of the success of Jensen's firm is due to its international scope. From 1909 to 1914, the Georg Jensen branch shop in Germany sold 90 percent of its output. In 1918, the shop in Paris was opened, followed by one in London in 1921. The New York outlet opened in 1924. Shops opened in Brussels and Barcelona in 1925 and 1935, respectively. Georg Jensen Silversmithy won the grand prix at the world exhibitions of 1910, 1915, 1925, 1929, and 1935. Koppel's designs won gold medals at the Milan Triennales of 1951, 1954, and 1957, and the firm's designers, including Ditzel, received additional medals in 1960.

In 1955 a traveling exhibition, "Fifty Years of Danish Silver," was organized to commemorate the silversmithy's golden anniversary, and in 1980 the firm was honored with an exhibition held at the Renwick Gallery, Washington, D.C.

Georg Jensen Silversmithy has kept in the forefront of modern design, but it has never abandoned its successful older designs, still producing them alongside its most contemporary offerings.

TLW

Girard, Alexander Born New York, May 24, 1907

Although American by birth, Alexander Girard was raised and educated in Florence, Italy, the son of an Italian father and an American mother. He wanted to become an architect, and a Florentine traveling scholarship enabled him to study at the Architectural Association in London, from which he graduated with honors in 1929. He opened his first architectural office in Florence in 1930, specializing in interiors and furnishings. Simultaneously, he pursued further studies at the Royal School of Architecture in Rome, graduating in 1931. Girard opened an office in New York in 1932 and also enrolled at New York University, graduating in 1935.[82]

After marrying Susan Needham, Girard moved to Detroit in 1937. By 1943, he was commissioned to design interiors for the Ford and Lincoln motor companies. Two years later Girard was appointed color consultant by the General Motors Research Center, and in 1952 he became design director of the Herman Miller textile division, and he is still associated with that firm today. He moved his office once more in 1953, this time to Santa Fe.

Girard concerned himself with all aspects of interiors, furniture, graphics, and industrial design. He has also been involved in a number of innovative museum installations.[83] A registered architect in New York, Michigan, Connecticut, and New Mexico, he designed various buildings ranging from homes to restaurants. Among his principal works are the Ford Motor Company offices, Dearborn, Michigan (1946); the Irwin Miller residence, in collaboration with Eero Saarinen, Columbus, Indiana (1955); La Fonda del

Sol restaurant, New York (1960); Herman Miller, Inc., Textiles and Objects Shops, New York (1961). He also redesigned all visual aspects for Braniff International, Dallas (1964); L'Étoile restaurant, Santa Fe (1966); and the building and site for the exhibition "El Encanto de un Pueblo" at the Hemisfair, San Antonio, Texas (1967–68).

In 1956, in collaboration with Charles Eames, Girard produced a film in Mexico entitled *Day of the Dead*. Girard has also written extensively. In 1968 he published *The Magic of a People—El Encanto de un Pueblo*, which stems from his interest in folk art.

His awards include a gold medal from the Barcelona World's Fair, 1929; awards from the Museum of Modern Art's "Good Design" fabric competition, 1946; the Governor's Award for Outstanding Contribution to Fine Arts in New Mexico, 1981; and a gold medal from the American Craft Council "for stimulating an international appreciation of Folk Art," 1985.

Girard's textiles are strong both in color and composition, clear to understand, clever and witty in context. Girard is little concerned about the fiber content or the construction of the fabric; the strength of his designs comes from the inspiration of his extensive collection of folk art, which displays strong colors like purple, shocking pink, and orange. To Girard, "color is sexy. It is playful. It disturbs."[84]

CCMT

Glaser, Milton Born New York, June 26, 1929

Milton Glaser was cofounder and president of Push Pin Studios, New York, a major design laboratory established in 1954 that codified and popularized the psychedelic art of the 1960s.[85]

Glaser attended Manhattan's High School of Music and Art before studying art at the Cooper Union, from which he graduated in 1951. He received a Fulbright scholarship and studied with Giorgio Morandi at the Accademia delle Belle Arti e Liceo Artistico, Bologna.

Glaser began to design posters in the mid-1960s, making many for the music and entertainment industries. His hallmark was the use of contrasting, strong, psychedelic colors, which created jarring optical effects. His bright, cheerful style was also deemed suitable for children: he illustrated children's books, designed a New York City toy store for Child Craft (1970), and designed the Sesame Place Play Park (1979). Also committed to adult education, he has taught at New York's School of Visual Arts since 1961 and at the Cooper Union since 1977.

The influential *Push Pin Graphic Magazine*, first published in 1957, was a forum for promoting his studio's avant-garde ideas; Glaser made many contributions to the magazine's design and layout. With *New York* magazine, which he started with Clay S. Felker in 1968, he established the archetype for other city magazines. In 1973 he redesigned *Paris Match*, literally overnight, and in 1977, *Esquire*.

Some of Glaser's most important architectural commissions have been for the food industry, such as the restaurant and observation deck of the World Trade Center in New York. Since 1978 he has been involved in the redesign of the Grand Union supermarket chain.

Glaser's work has appeared in many exhibitions, notably in four solo shows, including one at the Museum of Modern Art in 1975. He was voted into New York's prestigious Hall of Fame of the Art Directors Club and appeared on the cover of *Time* magazine in 1969, the year of the studio's fifteenth anniversary.

Glaser remained president of Push Pin Studios until 1974, three years before the firm was disbanded. Its work was very influential in the United States and abroad and was widely imitated. Today the staff of Milton Glaser Inc. works from a Manhattan town house, producing, as before, a wide range of commercial art.

FTH

GuldsmedsAktieBolaget GAB GuldsmedsAktie-

Bolaget GAB (Goldsmiths Company), a leading Scandinavian manufacturer of flatware made from silver, silver plate, and stainless steel, was founded in Stockholm in 1867.[86] Designer Jacob Ängman, a key figure in the development of modern Swedish silver, joined GAB in 1907 and was responsible for establishing the firm's reputation. His work during the 1920s, reminiscent of late eighteenth-century Swedish silver, was characterized by a spare ornamentation and the classicism typical of the period. Ängman remained at GAB as artistic director until his death in 1942, when he was succeeded by Sven-Arne Gillgren. Other artists of the 1930s and 1940s included Maja-Lisa Ohlsson, Just Andersen, Folke Arström, and Ture Jerkeman, some of whom produced work in the Streamlined style.

The 1960s was a period of considerable growth. In 1961 C. G. Hallberg of Stockholm was merged with GAB. In 1964 GAB merged with Gense (Gustav Eriksson NySilverfabrik in Eskilstuna, founded in 1856), a pioneer in the development of stainless steel tableware in the 1930s; with this merger GAB became the largest metalware-producing company in northern Europe. In 1978 Upsala-Ekeby AB took over GAB, and the following year its head office was moved to Eskilstuna. In 1986 the firm became a wholly owned subsidiary of Proventus Handels och Industri AB, belonging to the Proventus Group. Gillgren remained artistic director until 1975. Its current roster of designers includes Count Sigvard Bernadotte, Monica Backstrom, and Rolf Karlsson, and its products range from Bernadotte's restrained versions of traditional goblets and beakers to Karlsson's *Reflex* series of vases and candlesticks that are minimalist cubes with intriguingly irregular, highly polished, rippling surfaces.

GS

AB Gustavsberg The town of Gustavsberg, situated

on the island of Värmdö, near Stockholm, received its name after becoming the property of Gustaf Gabrielsson Oxenstierna in the midseventeenth century. He built a brickworks there, which served as the basis of a pottery works established in 1825.[87] The pottery looked to England for industrial expertise, importing English workers as well as English clays, the latter in such great quantity that Gustavsberg ran its own fleet of shipping vessels—hence the anchor mark that the factory still uses today as its emblem.

In addition to the wares one would expect of any commercial, nineteenth-century pottery, the Gustavsberg factory created Viking Revival vases and dinnerware in the National Romantic style of the 1870s, and, at the turn of the century, when Gunnar Wennerberg became artistic director, introduced Art Nouveau sgraffito wares. The factory entered an important new phase in 1917, when, through the influence of the Swedish Society of Industrial Design, it hired Wilhelm Kåge. Under his artistic direction the factory responded to the major stylistic currents of Modernism for the next quarter of a century, in both its art and functional wares. Kåge's work ranged from a decorative expressionism (*Worker's Service*, 1917) to a severe functionalism (*Praktika Service*, 1933), and, in his *Argenta* and *Farsta* wares, he skillfully blended ancient and Oriental styles with the Modernist mode of the thirties, as did many of his compatriots.

The deleterious effects of the Depression ultimately took their toll on the company, and in 1937 it was sold to KF Konsum (Swedish Cooperative Union and Wholesale Society). The plant was modernized, a division for sanitary wares was instituted, and, most important, the development of its artistic wares was encouraged, with the establishment of its Studio.

Aided by Sweden's neutrality, the pottery pressed forward even during the depths of World War II. Kåge's faience was painted in a style reminiscent of the School of Paris, his *Soft Forms* dinnerware (1940) explored asymmetry, and his *Surrea* series (1940), despite its name, was Cubist in inspiration. Kåge's protégé, Stig Lindberg, experimented with Biomorphism, while other ceramists in the Gustavsberg Studio went their separate ways, Berndt Friberg working in an Oriental-inspired manner, and Tyra Lundgren sculpting naturalistic forms.

In 1949 Lindberg succeeded Kåge as artistic director, and the factory embarked again on a program of artistic expansion. In addition to maintaining or updating older lines, Lindberg introduced exciting Biomorphic shapes and patterns in stoneware and painted faience, as well as in lines such as *Veckla* (1950) and *Pongo* (1953). Utilizing the rich resources of this industrial company, Lindberg employed new technology for his flameproof *Termagods* service (1955–58), created exciting designs for the plastics division, and devised large-scale ceramic and enameled steel murals.

After Lindberg's retirement in 1980, the position of art director was assumed by Karin Björquist. Much of the free tradition of Gustavsberg's Studio continues today, carried on by a younger generation of artists, including Anders Liljefors and Bengt Berglund. However, the ceramic production at Gustavsberg now constitutes less than 10 percent of the industrial company's overall operation.

ME

Hall China Company

Essentially a producer of commercial kitchen items, Hall China has a history that extends back almost a century.[88] Robert Hall had risen to become director of the East Liverpool Pottery Company, which was situated in the Ohio town of the same name. In 1901 five companies in that town, a center of a booming ceramics industry, merged to form the East Liverpool Potteries Company, but the venture proved unsuccessful, and in 1903 three companies split off again. Robert Hall bought his old plant and renamed it the Hall China Company. Its major products were sanitary wares and decorated dinnerware.

Robert Hall, Jr., succeeded as president upon the death of his father in 1904. During his tenure the firm developed a leadless, noncrazing glazed ware that greatly helped boost sales. The isolation of the United States from European factories during World War I also contributed to Hall China's establishment in the American market. It primarily produced institutional china, although there was a short-lived attempt to produce domestic dinnerware again. In 1920 it began to market teapots from its institutional line and found it such a profitable market that Hall became the world's largest manufacturer of teapots.

Hall's products were produced in a wide range of colors and used a great deal of overglaze gilt and decalcomania decoration. Although most of its designs are traditional and conservative, some of the Streamlined designs introduced in the later 1930s are quite striking. An important part of its production was geared to companies that used the ceramics as premiums. One of the most famous of these lines is the *Autumn Leaf* kitchen items, sponsored by the Jewel Tea Company; begun in 1933, it remained in continuous production for over forty years. In 1932 the company introduced kitchenware, and four years later, it tried its hand again at manufacturing dinnerware. Hall's other major type of product, refrigerator wares, was also created for other companies—first the handsomely Streamlined *Patrician* (1938) and *Emperor* (1939) lines for Westinghouse, then for Sears, Roebuck, Montgomery Ward, Hotpoint, and General Electric.

The products that Hall has made since World War II for the greater part continue the vein of conservatism evidenced earlier; many of its models and patterns remained before the war. The lines designed by Eva Zeisel, however, are an exception. The first was the

dinnerware *Tomorrow's Classic*, issued in 1951, whose rhythmic forms were a major innovation and whose decorative patterns were outspokenly fresh and modern. A great commercial success, it was touted as "America's fastest selling modern dinnerware." In 1954 Hall issued a line of Zeisel's kitchenware and in 1957 a second set of dinnerware, called *Century*.

ME

Hansen, Carl see Carl Hansen & Son A/S

Hansen, Fritz see Fritz Hansens Eft. AS

Hansen, Johannes see Johannes, Hansen as

Haraszty, Eszter Born Budapest, September 28, 1923

Eszter Haraszty is best known both as a colorist and for the fabrics that she designed for Knoll Associates in the 1950s.[89] She studied art history at the Magyar Kepdömüvészeti Föiskola (Hungarian Upper School for Paintings) in Budapest and did some textile designing while in school. After the war, faced with a shortage of materials, she painted designs on sheets and window shades. When the Communists took over Hungary in 1947, she was visiting her sister in Washington, D.C. Having decided to remain in the United States, she stayed in New York with the Marcel Breuers, friends of the family.

In 1949 Haraszty became director of textiles for Knoll. In 1950 she introduced *Transportation Cloth*, a pure linen industrial fabric, and *Knoll Stripes* (1951), designed for Marcel Breuer, the first patterned fabric he ever used. Her brightly colored, geometric designs received awards from the American Institute of Decorators and were included in the "Good Design" exhibitions of the Museum of Modern Art. At Knoll, she worked with a group of important European and American designers—including Marianne Strengell, Evelyn Hill, Angelo Testa, Stig Lindberg, Sven Markelius, and Astrid Sampe—who made the firm a leader in modern textiles.

Haraszty also served as Knoll's colorist, selecting colors and fabrics after Florence Knoll's Planning Unit had planned the interior and chosen the furniture. A brilliant colorist, she used vibrant colors to enliven the severe lines of the Knoll style. However, her relationship with Florence Knoll was not cordial, and after Hans Knoll was killed in 1955 and Florence Knoll assumed control of the firm, Haraszty left. Since then she has been a color consultant for IBM, interior design consultant for American President Lines, and a designer and color consultant for Victor Gruen Associates.

In 1960 Haraszty moved to California and subsequently designed domestic interiors for clients in Paris and the United States. She has also used her sensitivity to color in other fields—embroidery and gardening—and has written two books, *Needlepainting* (1974) and *Living with Flowers* (1980).

CWL

Heal and Son Ltd.

This important English home-furnishings manufacturer and retailer was begun in 1810 by John Harris Heal as a feather-dressing business in London.[90] In 1818 Heal established a mattress and feather-bed firm at Tottenham Court Road—the center of Victorian London's furniture trade—a few doors south of the company's present location. Over the next few decades the business expanded to include bedroom furniture. Through innovative billboard advertising, mail-order catalogues, and the introduction of room

settings, Heal and Son became one of London's largest suppliers of home furnishings.

Ambrose Heal, Jr., entered the family firm in 1893 and designed furniture for Heal and Son starting in 1896. His first catalogue (1898) showed designs in the Arts and Crafts manner. In 1905 the firm was converted from a partnership into a limited company, with Ambrose as managing director and, after his father died in 1913, as chairman. Although Heal and Son Ltd. offered expensive, handmade furniture, it also sold inexpensive, machine-made furniture, which reached a large market. In the 1930s, under the influence of its designers J. F. Johnson, Leonard Thoday, Arthur Greenwood, and others, Ambrose began to employ laminated woods and tubular steel. In addition to a successful range of inexpensive furniture designed by Greenwood and E. W. Shepherd, Heal's stocked furniture by Ludwig Mies van der Rohe and commissioned new designs from Marcel Breuer. It also began to develop a fabric department.

Regular furniture production ceased during World War II, while the company provided parachutes, protective clothing, bedding, and other military supplies. However, in 1946 Heal and Son was the largest exhibitor at the "Britain Can Make It" exhibition at the Victoria and Albert Museum, the first of many design shows held in London after the war. Heal's quickly gained prominence with award-winning designs such as Lucienne Day's textile *Calyx* (1951) and Clive Latimer and Robin Day's leaning storage system. Beginning in 1954, annual "New Design" exhibitions at Heal and Son served as showcases for the latest contemporary designs. Its CONtext collection of imported furniture, beginning in 1959, offered Verner Panton's chairs along with other Scandinavian designs. By 1960, Heal and Son fabrics had become so successful that a subsidiary, Heal's Fabrics, was created, producing important designs by Lucienne Day, Peter Hall, and others.

In 1984 Heal and Son was acquired by Terence Conran and continues today as Heal's, one of Conran's four chains of stores.

MOR

Herman Miller Furniture Co.

Since the 1930s, Herman Miller, Inc., has been one of the chief manufacturers of modern furniture in the United States. It is descended from the Star Furniture Company, which had been founded in 1905 in Zeeland, Michigan, by Herman Miller and others. Dirk Jan De Pree, who began working for that firm as a clerk in 1909, rose in rank to become its president in 1919, and he changed its name to Michigan Star Furniture Company. Convinced that the company could be better run, De Pree and his father-in-law, Herman Miller, bought 51 percent of the stock in 1923 and renamed the firm Herman Miller Furniture Co.[91] Miller supplied most of the cash and the name, while De Pree managed the business. The firm became Herman Miller, Inc., in 1969.

At first, the company made ostentatious furniture in historical-revival styles. Gilbert Rohde, who was hired as a designer in 1930, convinced De Pree, a devout Christian, that it was dishonest to make furniture that pretended to be something it was not and persuaded him to manufacture furniture in a Modernist vein.

After Rohde's death in 1944, George Nelson served as design consultant from 1946 until his death in 1986. He not only designed for the company himself, he worked with other designers as well. The firm produced Isamu Noguchi's Biomorphic coffee table (1947) and Charles and Ray Eames' early plywood furniture (the LCW chair and WFS screen) in the early 1940s, as well as their molded fiberglass chairs and wire furniture (the DAR chair and ETR table) in the 1950s and 1960s. In 1952 the firm expanded into fabric and

375

wallpaper, Alexander Girard serving as designer for that division into the 1970s. Girard's bright, geometric fabrics complemented the firm's furniture designs.

The Herman Miller Research Corporation was formed in 1960, headed by Robert Propst. Moving beyond the domestic sphere, Propst developed an Action Office system with details designed by Nelson. He then created a materials-management system for hospitals. These became Herman Miller's most commercially successful operations in the 1970s. However, it still produced furniture that remained in the vanguard of international design. Its designers in the 1960s and 1970s included Poul Kjaerholm, Fritz Haller, and Verner Panton, and their work ranged from Kjaerholm's refinements of traditional Modernist vocabulary to Panton's exciting plastic chair. One of Herman Miller's recent ventures is the Ethospace office system (1984), parts of which were designed by Geoff Hollington and Jean Beirise. Since the 1960s the Herman Miller firm has been represented internationally, and in 1990 it is still expanding its operations.

CWL

Hicks, Sheila Born Hastings, Nebraska, July 24, 1934

Sheila Hicks was a prime figure in the textile revolution of the 1960s, constantly exploring different techniques and materials, often derived from ethnic sources, to give new meaning and vitality to her medium and establishing it as an art form.[92]

As an undergraduate at Yale University (1954–57), she studied painting with Josef Albers and was influenced by his Constructivist theories of color and composition. She also came to know Anni Albers, the most important of the Bauhaus weavers. In 1957–58, she traveled in South America as a Fulbright scholar in painting and began to weave in the pre-Columbian tradition, experimenting with back-strap looms she made herself. Since then she has always carried a portable loom with her.

Hicks completed a master of fine arts degree in painting at Yale in 1959, writing her thesis on pre-Columbian textiles under Dr. George Kubler. Then, at the invitation of Matias Goeritz, she taught color and design at the Universidad Nacional Autonoma de Mejico, working with local weavers at the same time. She executed a series of *Hieroglyphs*—monochromatic, textured bas-reliefs in wool—and began finishing her work with intricately structured fringes. In 1961 she received her first commission, for bas-reliefs in hand-spun wool, from Mexican architect Luis Barragan, who became her mentor and remained so until his death in 1989. Around this time, Hicks began to explore the possibilities of freestanding, three-dimensional works, made on and off the loom.

In 1964 Hicks established a studio in Paris, L'Atelier des Grands-Augustins. Together with Claire Zeisler and Lenore Tawney, she gained international attention in an exhibition, "Gewebte Formen," at Zurich's Kunstgewerbemuseum. In that same year she cofounded an experimental workshop at Wuppertal, West Germany, taking advantage of its mechanized equipment to enlarge her format. A selection of her Wuppertal works was exhibited in northern Europe and in the showrooms of Artek, Knoll Associates, and Herman Miller.

Major commissions ensued, including works for the Ford Foundation Building in New York City (1967); the TWA terminal at Kennedy Airport, New York (1970); the Conference Center in Mecca (1976); King Saud University, Riyadh (1982–84); World Wide Plaza, New York (1989); and Bouygues S.A. corporate headquarters, Saint-Quentin-en-Yvelines, France (1990).

Ethnic influences contributed fanciful and complex design techniques to her art in the 1960s and 1970s. European references have permeated the work of the last ten years that was made in her later Paris studio, Atelier Cour de Rohan. She uses a rich mix of colors and materials and incorporates neon tubes, cords, Lurex, and synthetic and natural fibers of all kinds. In recent years she has returned to pure fibers of linen, silk, and hand-spun wool. Continually experimenting, she has recently completed a series of trompe-l'oeil *basse lisse* tapestries, as well as a series of airy woven miniatures for a 1988 exhibition at Merrin Gallery, New York City.

FTH

Hofmann, Armin Born Winterthur, Switzerland, June 29, 1920

Hofmann's poster work is representative of the postwar continuation of the influential Swiss school of graphic design, maintaining the disciplined tradition established by such artists as Herbert Matter and Max Bill.

Hofmann studied at the Zurich Kunstgewerbeschule, training ground for many of Switzerland's top designers. After working for several graphic design firms, he started his own in Basel in 1947 and began teaching at that city's Allgemeine Gewerbeschule. His commitment to the poster began around 1950.

Hofmann's bold graphic designs received early recognition in the United States, and he was sought after to train American artists. In 1955 he was invited to lecture at the Philadelphia College of Art. The following year he lectured at the International Design Conference at the Aspen Institute for Humanistic Studies and at Yale University's School of Art. Hofmann has taught at Yale ever since. Since 1980 he has served as director of the Yale Summer Program in Graphic Design in Brissago, Switzerland. He has also published on the subject, notably *Graphic Design Manual: Principles and Practice* (1966).

In a well-established Swiss tradition, Hofmann often incorporates photography into his designs to create dramatic, evocative posters with an extreme economy of means. Other effects are achieved using lithography or linocut. Hofmann's best-known poster designs are for cultural events. He has done many for performances and exhibitions at Basel's Basler Theatre, Kunsthalle, and Gewerbemuseum.

Hofmann's work was acknowledged by the Museum of Modern Art in New York with a retrospective exhibition in 1981.

FTH

Holzer-Kjellberg, Elfriede Amalie Adolfine (Friedl) Born Loeben, Austria, October 25, 1905

Although celebrated today for the purity of her Oriental-inspired, oxblood-glazed porcelains and delicately pierced rice-grain vessels, Friedl Holzer's early ceramics were grounded in a very different tradition.[93] She had trained at the Akademie für angewandte Kunst in Graz, where she learned the highly decorative and humorous mode of the Wiener Werkstätte that characterized much Austrian decorative art. In 1924, soon after graduation, she traveled to Finland and began working in the Arabia pottery. At first she continued in the Austrian mode, creating stylized figurines, masks, and vases with low-relief decoration. Her work received a certain acclaim at international expositions, winning a silver medal at Barcelona in 1929, a gold medal at Brussels in 1935, and a silver medal in Paris in 1937. In 1933 she married Erik Kjellberg, an engineer at Arabia.

During the 1930s, Kjellberg, like Toini Muona and other artists at the Arabia factory, was increasingly attracted to the beauty of Chinese Sung ware, and like her colleagues at other Scandinavian potteries, she began using high-fired stoneware as well as porcelain and experimenting with celadon, oxblood, and other exotic Eastern glazes. Her simple, geometric vases, enhanced only by brilliant chromatic passages, are closely tied to that era's search for undecorated form.

On the other hand, Kjellberg's most distinctive specialty was decorative ware based on an ornamental aspect of Oriental ceramic tradition: rice-grain porcelains. By 1942, after a decade of experimentation, she had evolved a successful system for producing these works, and Arabia established a special department with Kjellberg in charge. She created the master patterns—simple geometric or floral clusters—which were hand cut by assistants. Made on a relatively large scale, they remained a staple of the pottery through the postwar years; the division was closed only in 1974.[94]

In the 1950s Kjellberg occasionally attempted slightly sloped forms and clustered groups of vessels in a manner suggestive of Muona, but she remained essentially true to her earlier vision of Oriental-inspired pure forms, a vision that was rewarded with a gold medal at the Milan X Triennale in 1954 and the ceramics exhibition at Cannes in 1955. Even the few production pieces she created for Arabia suggest the restrained range of her work: the *FK* service (1953) has very simple forms, and the *Helmi* service (1969), with a band of rice-grain decoration, has forms partially based on Chinese covered bowls. This focused vision has been maintained in the work Kjellberg created even after she retired from the Arabia pottery in 1970.

ME

Howard Miller Clock Company The Howard Miller Clock Company, known for its postwar innovative clock designs, began in 1926 as the Herman Miller Clock Company in Zeeland, Michigan.[95] It was founded by Howard Miller (born c. 1905), who named it for his father, Herman Miller, general manager of Colonial Manufacturing, which produced grandfather clocks, also in Zeeland, and later cofounder of the now-famous Herman Miller Furniture Co. in the same city. Howard learned about making clocks from his father. He studied in Germany before starting his own firm to make cases for mantel clocks (throughout the years, the company has usually imported clock movements produced in the Black Forest area of Germany). During the Depression the firm was reorganized and assumed its present name. Howard Miller is still associated with the company, which is now run by his sons, Jack and Philip.

In 1939 the company introduced clocks of Modernist design at the New York World's Fair. Its focus was diverted during World War II, when it made antiaircraft covers for planes built by the Ford Motor Co. After the war, it produced a variety of products designed by George Nelson Associates, beginning in 1948 with a series of clocks without numbers, including the famous *Ball* clock. Among the other Nelson designs were the *Bubble* collection of lamps (c. 1952), which have a translucent plastic skin sprayed over a wire cage, fireplace accessories, weather vanes, and birdhouses.

Despite this Modernist interlude, during the 1950s and 1960s the company produced mainly traditional-style grandfather clocks. In the 1970s and 1980s it concentrated on smaller digital and alarm clocks. Most of its current models are traditional in design although some, such as the *Museum* clock by George Nathan Horwitt (1989), an enlarged version of his Movado watch, are more modern.

The company has expanded into making domestic furniture; in 1983 it bought the Hekman Furniture Co., and then in 1989 it introduced a line of wooden curio cabinets that are basically clock cases with shelves.

CWL

Iittala Lasitehdas Oy The Iittala glassworks was founded in 1881 by the Swedish master glassblower Petter Magnus Abrahamsson.[96] In 1917 Iittala was bought by A. Ahlström Oy, a conglomerate that two years earlier had bought the Karhula glassworks. The company henceforth became known as Karhula-Iittala, with the Karhula factory emphasizing machine production and the Iittala factory specializing in blown glass.

Iittala rose to prominence in the postwar period. One of its major designers was Kaj Franck, who conceived simple forms, often with a bubbly mass on the interior. However, he left in 1950. Ultimately more important were the contributions of Tapio Wirkkala, who created works that, while abstract and strongly sculptural, had a basis in natural forms. Wirkkala began his career in 1946 with a design that came to be synonymous with Scandinavian art glass: the famous *Kanttarelli* vase. In his early years at Iittala, Wirkkala worked exclusively in art glass. He has expressed many themes in his work, foremost among them a fascination with forms inspired by nature and the Finnish landscape. The motif of a single trapped air bubble is observed in the *Tokio* (1954) and *Marsalkansauva* (Marshal's Baton) vases, as well as the utilitarian *Tapio* (1954) glassware series, Wirkkala's first.

The arctic landscape played an important part in more than one series of works: art glass vases such as *Jaavuori* (Iceberg) and *Jaapala* (Ice Block) of 1950, with their fractured surfaces, and *Paadarin jää* (Paadar's Ice) of 1960, its undulating and rippling surface a poetic evocation of the changing patterns of melting ice. These mark a change in Wirkkala's aesthetic toward a more expressive, irregular surface texture and interior mass. In glassware there is the glistening *Ultima Thule* (1968) and *Pallas* (1984), table crystal that appeared shortly before the artist's death.

Timo Sarpaneva, trained as a graphic artist, became a designer for Iittala in 1950. He achieved immediate fame at the Milan X Triennale when both his sculptural vases *Lansetti II* (Lancet II), 1952, and *Orkidea* (Orchid), 1953, were awarded a grand prix. In the mid-1950s Sarpaneva developed a midrange glass series, culminating in 1956 with the *i* line of thin material in his preferred colors of bluish gray, greenish gray, and lilac, along with clear. Following Wirkkala's lead, he became preoccupied with textures. Working with charred wood molds, he evolved a series of sculptures about 1964 with barklike surface textures. This was then extended into vases with variegated surfaces and into mass-produced objects like candlesticks and glasses (1967–68). Sarpaneva, presently the firm's senior designer, ultimately returned to smoother, more geometric forms, as in his *Claritas* series (1983).

New designers include Valto Kokko, who joined the company in 1963, and Jorma Vennola, who has been with Iittala since 1975. Vennola has experimented in combining glass with other materials: the *Kaveri* (1979) series of wine goblets originally juxtaposed clear, colorless glass with multicolored plastic bases, and the *Paula* (1977) series is wrapped with steel handles. The firm's youngest designer is Mikko Karppanen, who joined Iittala in 1983.

In 1988 the company was merged with Nuutajärvi-Notsjö to form a new corporation: Iittala-Nuutajärvi Oy, which also includes the Humppila and Napapiiri glassworks.

GS

Isokon Furniture Company Isokon was established in 1931 by Jack Pritchard, his wife, Molly, and the architect Wells Coates "to promote building and furniture of strictly modern functional design" in England.[97] The name, derived from the term *isometric unit construction*, was first applied to the Isokon Flats (also called Lawn Road Flats, completed 1934), a modular concrete housing complex in Hampstead, which the Pritchards commissioned from Coates.

In 1935 Pritchard formed the Isokon Furniture Company to market well-designed furniture, made primarily of plywood.[98] Walter Gropius and Marcel Breuer, two Bauhaus émigrés who had recently taken up residence at the Lawn Road Flats, served, respectively, as controller of design and as designer until their departure for the United States in 1937. Breuer produced five bent-plywood furniture designs for the Isokon Furniture Company, most notably the *Long Chair* and a group of nesting tables.[99] With the assistance of Harry Mansell, Isokon's craftsman, these were put into production in 1937; they proved to be an artistic rather than a commercial success.

Isokon's progressive tradition was continued by Egon Riss, an expatriate Viennese architect who created several witty yet functional designs for the firm in 1939. A small book rack, the *Isokon Penguin Donkey*, was marketed through leaflets distributed in Penguin paperbacks. Although World War II interrupted production, a later version, the *Isokon Penguin Donkey Mark 2*, designed by Ernest Race in 1963, was produced in large quantities until 1980. Another Riss design, the *Bottleship*, was also adapted by Race in 1963; both *Donkey* and *Bottleship* were sold in knock-down form.

After a postwar hiatus, during which time Pritchard served as director of the Furniture Development Council (1949–62), Isokon resumed production in 1963, concentrating primarily on Breuer's *Long Chair* and the redesigned *Donkey*. Since its inception, the Isokon Furniture Company and Jack Pritchard have been synonymous with outstanding British design and the Modernist ideal of allying art and technology.

LN

Isola, Maija Born Riihimäki, Finland, March 15, 1927

Following her education in the textile department of the Taideteollinen Korkeakoulu (Central School of Industrial Design) in Helsinki (1946–49), Isola became one of the major creative forces at Printex, for which she designed printed textiles for interior furnishings from 1949 to 1960. Her designs for furnishing and dress fabrics have also been instrumental in shaping the look of the company's affiliate, Marimekko, from its inception in 1951 until recent years.[100]

Her first designs, inspired by African art Isola saw in Norway in 1949, were executed in brilliant-colored crayons and evolved into hand-brushed stripe patterns for Printex. Isola's work includes a detailed, decorative series in the mid- and late 1950s derived from botanical prints, the Ornamentti series of the late 1950s, based on the folk art of Slovakia, and another from the late 1960s and early 1970s based on peasant art from her native Karelia. However, her most celebrated works are probably the oversize geometrics that she first introduced in the mid-1960s that are like Color Field paintings. They have subsequently become synonymous with the name Marimekko.

A recognized force in contemporary textile design, Isola's work has been shown in numerous exhibitions in Europe, the United States, and Australia and has been acknowledged with many awards.

AZ

Jacobsen, Arne Born Copenhagen, February 11, 1902; died Copenhagen, March 24, 1971

Arne Jacobsen's introduction to the fields of design and architecture was as a craftsman, a training that instilled in him a lifelong respect for fine materials and details. He apprenticed initially as a mason at the Skolen for Brugskunst (School of Applied Arts) in Copenhagen from 1917 to 1924. This was followed by architectural studies from 1924 to 1927 at the Kongelige Danske Kunstakademi (Royal Danish Academy of Fine Arts), where he studied under Kay Fisker and Kaj Gottlob. Jacobsen spent the next three years in the office of the Copenhagen city architect, Poul Holsøe, and from 1930 he maintained a private practice.

Jacobsen's energies were devoted primarily to his architectural work; during the postwar years he was perhaps the most influential practitioner in Denmark.[101] He was not, however, an architect of the first rank, for he was basically an adapter—though an extremely skillful and sensitive one—of other artists' concepts.

In terms of the applied arts, Jacobsen's most important work was also produced in the postwar years, for which he was given the grand prize at both the Biennal de São Paulo, Brazil (1953), and the Milan XI Triennale of 1957.[102] He, along with Poul Kjaerholm and Verner Panton, represents one of three distinct schools in postwar Denmark—the industrial designers.[103] Industrialization in the furniture business did not really begin in Denmark until after the war, but by 1960 the craft tradition had been supplanted.[104] Jacobsen was a leader in the movement for mass production, the use of new industrial materials, and international marketing.

Jacobsen's chair designs for Fritz Hansens Eft. are among his most accomplished work. Following Charles and Ray Eames' experiments in the 1940s, and also influenced by Alvar Aalto's innovations, he produced a number of designs with molded plywood shells, most notably the *Ant* chair (no. 3100) of 1952 and the model no. 4130 side chair of 1955.

The sculptural chairs of Eero Saarinen were another major influence on Jacobsen. The Dane designed four such pieces with upholstered plastic shells in 1957 for the SAS Royal Hotel, and a number of these were subsequently mass-produced. A prototype for a plastic pedestal chair of 1968, which featured a highly sculptural shell, may now be perceived as his most arresting form in this manner.

Working for a number of Danish manufacturers during the 1950s and 1960s, Jacobsen also produced a wide range of furniture designs for both home and office: tables, sofas, desks, and sectional seating in both metal and wood. They were, however, less original than his chair designs for Fritz Hansen.

In terms of everyday objects, Jacobsen was equally prolific. Starting in the mid-1950s, he produced a large number of product designs, often to be accessories for his buildings. These pieces reflect two quite different vocabularies: one concerned with soft, sculptural shapes and a second group with hard-edged, geometric forms.[105] For an architectural designer like Jacobsen, though, such distilled objects may often be as revealing of large aesthetic concerns as his buildings.

RCM

Jalk, Grete Born Copenhagen, June 18, 1920

Trained as a cabinetmaker, Grete Jalk was one of several designers whose work brought international recognition to modern Danish furniture in the 1950s and 1960s.[106] Particularly evident in her chairs of bent, laminated wood are the qualities of economy and craftsmanship that distinguish Danish design.

After studying philosophy at the Københavns Universitet, Jalk trained as a cabinetmaker's apprentice from 1940 to 1943. From 1943 to 1946, she studied furniture design at Kunsthåndvaerker-og Kunstindustriskolen (Copenhagen High School of Arts, Crafts, and Industrial Design), where she later taught (1950–60), and at the Kongelige Danske Kunstakademi (Royal Danish Academy of Fine Arts). Subsequently, she drafted for several architectural firms in Sweden, Switzerland, and Denmark. Jalk began designing furniture in 1946, but it was not until 1954 that she established her own design office.

Although primarily known for her furniture, much of which was designed for Poul Jeppesen, Jalk successfully entered designs for wallpaper, printed textiles, and silver in competitions during the early 1950s and 1960s. Her silver toilet accessories won first prize in the Georg Jensen design competition for its fiftieth anniversary in 1955.

Jalk's furniture has been exhibited extensively in Scandinavia and Europe, both in group shows and solo exhibitions in London, Bern, and Zurich, and has received numerous awards. Since 1969, Jalk has served as exhibition designer for the Danish Ministry of Foreign Affairs. Her writings include *40 Years of Danish Furniture Design* and contributions to *Mobilia* (1956–74). Jalk now resides and works in Skodsborg, Denmark.

LN

Jensen, Georg *see* Georg Jensen Silversmithy

Johannes Hansen as Johannes Hansen as is a small
furniture firm best known today for its production of Hans Wegner's designs. This firm was started in 1915 when Johannes Hansen (1886–1961) opened a cabinetmaking shop in Søborg, near Copenhagen.[107] Hansen had served his apprenticeship in small country workshops and worked his way through Germany, Switzerland, and France as a journeyman carpenter. At first his firm made pieces designed by architects, since furniture designers as such did not yet exist. To encourage the development of Danish design, his firm took an active role in cooperatives promoting Danish arts and crafts, and from 1925 on, Hansen was one of the promoters of the annual exhibitions of the Copenhagen Cabinetmakers' Guild, which lasted until 1968.

Johannes Hansen began working with Wegner in 1940. For many years, the firm executed Wegner's designs for chairs by hand, while Wegner's machine-made furniture was produced by other shops. Their most famous collaborations were on the *Peacock* chair of 1949 and the *Round* and *Folding* chairs of 1951.

Johannes Hansen died in 1961, some years after he had retired. His youngest son, Poul, now runs the firm, and a third generation has recently become involved. The firm continues to produce Wegner's old designs as well as pieces by other designers, including steel furniture by Erik Krogh and Jørgen Høj.

CWL

Johnson, Philip Cortelyou Born Cleveland, July 8, 1906

Philip Johnson entered architecture circuitously; his earliest renown was as a historian and critic.[108] After studying classics and philosophy, he received a bachelor's degree from Harvard University in 1930. From 1932 to 1934 he acted as the Museum of Modern Art's first director of the newly established Department of Architecture. Johnson's reputation as a polemicist began with the seminal "International Exhibition of Modern Architecture," which he organized with Henry-Russell Hitchcock in 1932.

Johnson entered the Harvard Graduate School of Design in 1940, when he was thirty-four, earning his bachelor of architecture degree in 1943. He returned to his post at the Museum of Modern Art in 1949, as director of the Department of Architecture and Design, relinquishing it in 1954 to begin private practice. Johnson continued to promote the career of Ludwig Mies van der Rohe with a 1947 exhibition and an important monograph. He also served as associate architect with Mies on the Seagram Building in New York City (1954–58), an icon of the International Style. Johnson's most celebrated work is probably his own Glass House in New Canaan, Connecticut (1949), which is frankly indebted to the work of Mies.

Throughout the 1950s, Johnson executed a series of private residences, and in the early 1960s he was commissioned to design buildings for cultural institutions, among them the Munson-Williams-Proctor Institute in Utica, New York (1960); the Amon Carter Museum of Western Art in Fort Worth, Texas (1961); and the Sheldon Memorial Art Gallery for the University of Nebraska at Lincoln (1963). While still basically working in the International Style, he also exhibited a strong neoclassical bent and an interest in monumentality.

In 1967 Johnson formed a partnership with Chicago architect John Burgee, thereby inaugurating a new era in his career. The serrated corners of the Diversified Services Building in Minneapolis (1968–73) and the twin trapezoids and slanted tops of Pennzoil Place in Houston (1970–76) heralded a move away from the International Style "glass box" and reflected Johnson's interest in minimalist sculpture.

In 1978 Johnson was the recipient of numerous accolades, including the American Institute of Architects gold medal. Johnson's AT&T Building in New York City (1978–83) created a *succès de scandale*. More important, it made Post-Modernism acceptable as a mode for corporate skyscrapers and became the first of a string of controversial, historicizing towers; notable others were the Gothic PPG Place in Pittsburgh (1979–83); the well-received neo-Deco Transco Tower in Houston (1985); and the gabled 190 South LaSalle Street building in Chicago (1987).

Johnson has cut an elegant figure on the architectural scene for decades. Rarely an innovator, he has nevertheless exerted a tremendous influence. Irritating to diehard Modernists is the fact that his work has not followed a single, strict line of development. Age has not diminished his astute interest in the ideas of younger architects, as was evidenced by his exhibition "Deconstructivism" at the Museum of Modern Art (1988), which seemingly set yet another new direction for architecture.

GS

Juhl, Finn Born Copenhagen, January 30, 1912; died Copenhagen, May 17, 1989

Finn Juhl, one of Denmark's most influential designers of this century, was trained as an architect. From 1930 to 1934 he attended the Kongelige Danske Kunstakademi (Royal Danish Academy of Fine Arts), where he studied under Kay Fisker. For the next eleven years he worked in the office of the architect Vilhelm Lauritzens, though by 1937 he had begun his long collaboration with the cabinetmaker Niels Vodder. In 1944 Juhl became a teacher of interior design at the Frederiksberg Tekniske Skoler (School of Interior Design), a post he maintained until 1955. In 1945 Juhl opened his own office in Copenhagen.

Juhl has designed a wide range of industrial products,[109] but a considerable part of his career has been devoted to interior design and architecture. These commissions were remarkable neither for innovative form, structure, nor spatial conception, yet their elegance and simplicity came to represent Danish design in the 1950s. Juhl's preoccupation was more with color, texture, and furniture arrangements, which he handled with remarkable finesse.[110]

It is, however, as a furniture designer in the 1940s and 1950s that Juhl may claim to be an artist of the first rank.[111] He won some thirty-six prizes in competitions in Copenhagen during this period, as well as five gold medals at the Milan Triennales of 1954 and 1957. Juhl was recognized at that time as the leader of the "artist-designers" in Denmark after the war. He led the reaction against the earlier "functional and anonymous style" of Kaare Klint, urging instead a highly individualistic style with strong links between the fine and applied arts. He was fascinated with free-form sculpture, primitive art, and organic architecture and design. All of these influences were readily integrated into his work.

During the 1940s and early 1950s, Juhl created a series of seating designs—elegantly handcrafted by Niels Vodder—with articulated wooden frames supporting sculptural upholstered units; the series became the paradigm of the Scandinavian organic look. This was extended in a larger furniture series for Baker Furniture in the United States (1949–51). In 1953 Juhl designed sofas, chairs, and tables with metal frames for Bovirke, Denmark; these were followed in the late 1950s by a series of wooden pieces for mass production for France & Son, Denmark. One of Juhl's most interesting late designs, however, is a powerful geometric sofa (*Bo 117*) of around 1957 for Bovirke, which may now be seen as a harbinger of Post-Modernist design.

RCM

Kartell S.p.A. Kartell, founded in 1949 by Giulio
Castelli in Binasco, near Milan, was one of the first Italian companies to experiment with the manufacture of plastic goods.[112] In the 1950s it made a variety of attractive small housewares, designed by Gino Columbini: cups and saucers, serving utensils, dish drainers, and wastebaskets, all in bright colors. In 1956, Kartell started publishing *Qualità*, which, beginning as one of the first in-house magazines published in Italy, soon became a significant design magazine.

In the 1960s Kartell slowly began expanding its offerings, both in terms of the range and scale of the objects: first with lamps by Sergio Asti and Sergio Favre, as well as by Achille and Pier Giacomo Castiglioni, then with Marco Zanuso's and Richard Sapper's polyethylene stacking children's chairs (designed in 1961 but not produced in quantity until 1967), and also with Joe Colombo's full-size dining chair of 1965, made of stronger ABS plastic and molded in one piece. Kartell also began production in Easley, South Carolina, as well as in Binasco.

Among the other designers who have worked for Kartell are Alberto Rosselli, Gae Aulenti, and Anna Castelli Ferrieri, the last Kartell's artistic director for many years. Today Kartell makes armchairs, tables, shelving systems, and kitchen furnishing units as well as the small housewares that established its original and deserved reputation for well-designed plastics.

CWL

Kauffer, Edward McKnight Born Great Falls, Montana, December 14, 1890; died New York, October 22, 1954

E. McKnight Kauffer secured his reputation as a graphic artist with the stunning posters he designed in England between the two world wars.[113]

American by birth, he studied at the School of the Art Institute of Chicago and then at the Académie Moderne in Paris, with the financial backing of Professor Joseph McKnight, with whom he had studied in Chicago and whose name he adopted.

In 1915 Kauffer moved to London. He was a founding member in 1920 of Group X, an artist's group led by the Vorticist painter Wyndham Lewis. However, as his posters proved so much more successful, Kauffer soon gave up painting. Although he greatly admired the posters of Toulouse-Lautrec, his bold and striking designs of the early 1920s, such as *Winter Sales Are Best Reached by Underground* of 1924, were stylistically closer to the Vorticism of Lewis and of Edward Wadsworth. Kauffer's posters for the London Underground Railways, Shell-Mex, and British Petroleum were so renowned that he was considered one of the leading Modernist artists in England; one of his posters even decorated the Oxford rooms of Evelyn Waugh's fictional hero, Charles Ryder, in *Brideshead Revisited*.[114] By the mid-1930s Kauffer's posters came to reflect the odd juxtapositions and more lyrical lines of Surrealism, as found in the work of such artists as Man Ray, who shared Kauffer's studio in 1935.[115]

Kauffer loved books and illustrated many, including some by T. S. Eliot, his friend for many years. He also designed rugs, probably influenced by rug designer Marion Dorn, with whom he lived after separating from his first wife in 1923. Most of the rugs, for the Wilton Royal Carpet Factory, were in a Cubist vein, but several from the 1930s have Biomorphic forms.

In 1937 the Museum of Modern Art in New York gave Kauffer a solo exhibition of his posters.[116] The next year he was the first foreigner to be named Honorary Designer for Industry of the Royal Society of Arts in London. These events could be seen as marking the apogee of his career.

Fleeing World War II, Kauffer and Dorn moved to New York in 1940. Unfortunately, Kauffer's career suffered; he found it difficult to get commissions in the competitive New York market. Although he designed catalogue covers for the "Britain at War" and "Organic Design" exhibitions at the Museum of Modern Art in 1941 and created book jackets for Modern Library as well as posters for American Airlines until 1953, his strongest work was that done earlier while he was in England.

CWL

Kelly, Richard Born Zanesville, Ohio, September 22, 1910; died New York, July 10, 1977

Richard Kelly contributed significantly to midcentury architecture by inventing many of the forms and concepts of lighting that complemented the architect's intent.

Kelly displayed a youthful interest in stage setting and lighting effects while participating in high school dramatics.[117] He supported himself during and after his attendance at Columbia College (graduating in 1932) as an interior designer and merchandiser of his own designs, including lighting fixtures. These latter attracted the interest of the architectural community, which was beginning to recognize the difficulty of finding an electrical lighting system suited to the pure, clean forms of the Modernist idiom. In the 1930s Kelly acted as lighting consultant on a number of important projects, including the General Electric Exhibition House of 1935, Tiffany & Co., 1938, and the Masterpieces of Art Building at the New York World's Fair of 1939.

To extend his familiarity with architectural practice, Kelly enrolled in Yale University's School of Architecture, receiving a bachelor of architecture in 1944, and worked in several architectural firms. In 1947 he opened his own office as an architectural lighting consultant. Kelly employed his revolutionary concepts, such as "wall washing," to create subtle nuances and effects. His skill at enhancing and dramatizing buildings and interiors was greatly sought after, and he collaborated with many of the foremost Modernist American architects of his period, including Philip Johnson, Eero Saarinen, Ludwig Mies van der Rohe, Louis Kahn, and Gordon Bunshaft.

An effective and generous teacher, Kelly took an active role in educating architects and designers in the philosophy and methods of lighting design and was responsible for creating much of the basic terminology of contemporary lighting. He received numerous awards, chief among them the American Institute of Architects 1964 Collaborative Achievement in Architecture Award as one of the collaborators on the Seagram Building and the Four Seasons Restaurant.

KC

Knoll Associates, Inc. This international furniture manufacturer and distributor, founded in 1938 by Hans Knoll, has been associated since its inception with rational, Modernist furniture. Many of the greatest names in twentieth-century architecture and design have worked for Knoll, creating an integrated approach to interior design and forging the modern corporate image.[118]

Hans Knoll, born in Stuttgart, May 8, 1914, inherited a tradition of Modernist furniture. His father, Walter C. Knoll, made early Bauhaus and other avant-garde furniture in the family factory in Stuttgart. Like many Germans, Hans Knoll immigrated to the United States, in 1937. The following year he opened the Hans G. Knoll Furniture Company on East Seventy-second Street in New York City, using the design talent of recent émigrés. Jens Risom from Denmark designed Knoll's first chair in 1941; its clean, functional lines would become a hallmark of the firm. The early designs were executed in unpretentious birch, cherry, and walnut.

In 1943 Florence Shust (known as Shu), a Cranbrook Academy of Art graduate who had worked for Walter Gropius and Marcel Breuer in Boston, started working for Knoll. A 1945 commission for the design of Nelson Rockefeller's office at Rockefeller Plaza, executed by Florence and Hans, marked the company as designers for the corporate image. The following year the two married and formed Knoll Associates, Inc., a designation they maintained for the next thirteen years and which was celebrated in promotional materials and the corporate logo by Herbert Matter.

Although Knoll has always striven to create unified interiors, it established separate divisions, such as the Knoll Planning Unit, begun in 1945 and headed by Florence Knoll, who moved the company from a Scandinavian to a Bauhaus-oriented style. In 1948 Ludwig Mies van der Rohe gave Knoll the right to reproduce his famous 1929 *Barcelona* chair and ottoman, followed by the *Brno* chair and other works. Other early Knoll designers were Franco Albini, Hans Bellmann, Pierre Jeanneret, and Isamu Noguchi. A number of Cranbrook graduates worked for Knoll, including Eero Saarinen (the *Womb* chair of 1948 and *Pedestal* chairs and tables of 1956) and Harry Bertoia (wire furniture of the 1950s).

In 1947 the firm established a new division, Knoll Textiles. At first Marianne Strengell of the Cranbrook Academy served as a consultant, and Evelyn Hill directed the hand-weaving studio. From 1949 to 1955 Eszter Haraszty directed the division.

Florence Knoll assumed the presidency of the firm following her husband's untimely death in an automobile accident in 1955. Four years later, the firm was sold to Art Metal, Inc., a large manufacturer of traditional metal office furniture, and Florence Knoll became a consultant. She returned briefly to run the Planning Unit's last project—the interior of the CBS Building in New York—and then severed her ties.

In 1965 the company became a subsidiary of Walter E. Heller International, a Chicago-based financial company, and in 1967 Massimo Vignelli began designing its graphics. The following year Knoll acquired Dino Gavina's company and, along with it, its important repertoire of works by designers such as Marcel Breuer and Sebastian Matta. In response to the growing internationalism of its activities and stable of designers, the firm's name was changed yet again in 1969, to Knoll International, a designation that had been in use since 1951 for its European operation. It was acquired by General Felt Industries in 1977 and today is owned by one of the partners of General Felt, Marshall S. Cogan.

Office landscape systems became a Knoll hallmark. An early example is the open modular plan for the Connecticut General Life Insurance Company corporate headquarters in Hartford, Connecticut (1949–50). Among its later successes was the Stephens Open Office Furniture, first developed in wood for the Weyerhaeuser Company in 1973 by Bill Stephens, and the Andrew Morrison Office System.

While many Knoll designs of earlier decades are now accepted as classics, the firm continues to expand its offerings. Among the important contemporary contributors are Vico Magistretti, Angelo Mangiarotti, and Gae Aulenti. In recent years Knoll has offered furniture by Post-Modernist designers such as Robert Venturi and Ettore Sottsass.

Knoll International maintains a United States network of twenty-eight sales centers, supplemented by independent dealers. With an overseas headquarters in Paris, there are sales offices in eight European cities, and others worldwide. Interestingly, Knoll is perceived differently in the United States and in Europe: Americans use Knoll furniture primarily for offices, while Europeans use it in their homes.

FTH

Knorr, Donald Born Chicago, December 25, 1922

Because his university education was interrupted by wartime service in the United States Navy, architect Donald Knorr was unable to complete his professional training at the University of Illinois at Urbana-Champaign until 1947. At that point he decided to continue postgraduate studies at the Cranbrook Academy of Art in Bloomfield Hills, Michigan. Intending to concentrate on urban planning under Eliel Saarinen, he actually spent most of his time taking the many design courses available.

In late 1947 he joined Eero Saarinen's architectural office, where work was in progress on such major projects as the General Motors Research and Development Center. After hours, he worked with Saarinen on the development of furniture, particularly on the chairs model nos. 71 and 72 for Knoll Associates. Encouraged by the Saarinens, Knorr entered the Museum of Modern Art's "International Competition for Low-Cost Furniture Design" of 1948–50 and was one of two first-prize winners in the seating category. This design, subsequently manufactured by Knoll Associates, is perhaps Knorr's most celebrated work.

In 1949 Knorr and his wife, a Cranbrook-trained textile designer, moved to the San Francisco area, where he joined the local office of Skidmore, Owings and Merrill. He opened his own architectural practice, Don Knorr and Associates, in 1951 and then, from 1957 to 1976, was a partner in Knorr-Elliott Associates, also in San Francisco. He has achieved recognition in the northwest United States and Alaska for commercial and residential architecture. Since about 1970 he has been a partner in Lane-Knorr-Plunkett, a firm headquartered in Anchorage, Alaska. From 1976 to the present he has also maintained his own office in San Francisco, Don Knorr and Associates. Although he has continued to design furniture for his own projects, none has achieved the significance of the 1950 prize winner.

KC

Komai, Ray Born Los Angeles, October 25, 1918

Ray Komai's course of graphic art studies at the Art Center School in Los Angeles was interrupted by his internment in a camp for Japanese-Americans during World War II. After the war, Komai finished his studies and moved to New York, where in 1948 he opened a design office that specialized in advertising and related graphic-art design. From 1952 to 1960 Komai was associate art director for *Advertising Forum*, and from 1963 to 1976 he was a designer with the United States Information Agency, for which he designed cultural exhibitions in Germany, Austria, India, and Japan.

Occasionally Komai has turned his skills toward the field of decorative arts, including textile design. His design for a cover of *Interiors* magazine caught the attention of Erwine Laverne of Laverne Originals, who commissioned Komai to design drapery textiles for his firm. Janet Rosenblum Incorporated produced Komai's abstract patterned designs for upholstery and drapery fabrics from 1956 to 1967. According to Komai, these textile designs were inspired by the paintings of Paul Klee, Pablo Picasso and other Cubist painters, and by primitive art, notably tribal masks from Africa and New Guinea.

Advertising work for the J. G. Furniture Company led to Komai's designing tables and seating for this manufacturing company. His molded plywood chairs were influenced by an early interest in origami and by the furniture of Charles and Ray Eames. A molded plywood chair with a one-piece seat and slit back, designed by Komai in 1949, was selected for the Museum of Modern Art's "Good Design" exhibition of the following year.

MOR

N.V. Koninklijke Nederlandsche Glasfabriek

Leerdam A glass factory was founded in 1765 at Leerdam, near Rotterdam, that was the ultimate ancestor of the modern corporation Koninklijke Nederlandsche Glasfabriek Leerdam, or the Royal Dutch Glassworks. [119] During the nineteenth century the firm manufactured utilitarian bottles and table glass of generally undistinguished design. The appointment of P. M. Cochius as general director in 1912 ushered in an important new era. Spurred by the contemporary De Stijl movement, he turned to architects such as Karel Petrus Cornelis de Bazel, and later Hendrik Petrus Berlage, to produce modern designs. Cochius hired decorative artist Cornelis de Lorm, who began working for Leerdam in 1917, and ceramist Christiaan Johannes Lanooy made his first glass designs in 1919. Their table glass was characterized by simplicity of form and minimal decoration.

Joris Johannes Christiaan Lebeau, a painter and graphic artist, joined Leerdam in 1922. In addition to simple, mass-produced tableware, he also designed crackle and cameo glass. Andries Copier, Leerdam's preeminent artist, began his long association with Leerdam in 1914 at the age of thirteen. He rose in the ranks: by 1921 he oversaw the production of glassware designed by artists; in 1923 he became responsible for the aesthetic supervision of most glassware; finally, in 1927, he was made the general artistic director. About 1923, in association with Lebeau (who left in 1926), Copier initiated experiments that resulted in the *Unica* series of free-form pieces by various designers, though Copier himself was the principal designer for the *Unica* line. With these works Copier was to achieve international renown, beginning with a silver medal at the 1925 Paris "Exposition Internationale des Arts Décoratifs et Industriels Modernes." Around 1926 Copier developed the *Serica* pieces, a less costly complement to the *Unica* series. From 1929 to 1931, Frank Lloyd Wright produced sixteen designs, though none was to see commercial production.

In 1937 Leerdam merged with N.V. Vereenigde Glasfabrieken, the United Glassworks, which maintained plants at Maastricht and Schiedam. In 1940 Copier founded the Leerdamse Glasschool to teach glassblowing to its factory employees. It was soon expanded to include cold-glass decoration techniques such as cutting, engraving, and etching. Floris Meydam and Willem Heesen, graduates of the Leerdam Glass School, have contributed significantly to the contemporary renown of the firm. Meydam, now a chief designer, began at Leerdam in 1935 and produced his first *Unica* piece in 1951, at a time when Copier had become more involved as aesthetic director. Heesen entered the glass factory in 1945 and has been chief designer since 1967. He played an important role in the revival of diamond-point engraving, a technique for which the Dutch were famed in the eighteenth century.

Sybren Valkema, a teacher and artist of considerable technical skill, has been with Leerdam since 1943. In 1968 the Glasvormcentrum (Glass Form Center) was instituted to do experimental and development work. In 1969 he was responsible for the construction of the first studio kiln in Europe, at the Gerrit Rietveld Academie in Amsterdam.

GS

Koppel, Henning Born Copenhagen, May 8, 1918; died Copenhagen, June 27, 1981

Henning Koppel is best known for the dramatic and highly original metalwork he created for Georg Jensen Silversmithy. [120] His background included the study of drawing under Bizzie Høyer in Copenhagen (1935–36), and of stone sculpture, under Anker Hoffmann at the Kongelige Danske Kunstakademi (Royal Danish Academy of Fine Arts), also in Copenhagen (1936–37). In 1938 he went to Paris to study at the Académie Ranson, where he doubtless became familiar at firsthand with modern French painting and sculpture. During the war he took refuge in Stockholm, where from 1940 to 1945 he worked both as an assistant to the sculptor Carl Milles and as a jewelry designer under Estrid Ericson for the firm Svenskt Tenn.

When he returned to Copenhagen in 1945 and joined the Jensen firm, Koppel was a fully trained artist. Working primarily on small pieces of jewelry, he introduced highly sculptural forms with irregular, Biomorphic contours that broke with convention. In the late 1940s and 1950s, when silver was again more available, he turned to hollowware. His pitchers of 1948 and 1952, his fish platter of 1954, and his *Caravel* flatware of 1957 displayed bold forms and graceful curves.

Through the 1960s and 1970s, as Koppel continued to work with silver, he remained the master of subtly curved contours, although his forms were more elegantly refined and far less eccentric than before. In the 1970s he also designed silver sculpture, thus returning to his earlier training.

Although best remembered for his work at Jensen, Koppel worked for other firms as well. He designed several porcelain objects for Bing & Grøndahl in 1961, 1975, and 1978; lights and clocks for Louis Poulsen in 1967; and glass for Orrefors in 1971. His ability as a designer was recognized in numerous exhibitions and by many prizes: three gold medals at Milan Triennales (1951, 1954, 1957), the Lunning Prize (1953), and the International Design Award from the American Institute of Decorators (1963), among others.

DAH & JTT

Kosta Glasbruk Kosta, established in 1741, has the distinction of being the oldest surviving glassworks in Sweden. [121] Its name is an acronym formed from the names of its two founders, Anders Koskull and Georg Bogislaus Stael von Holstein. Its early production was of traditional drinking glasses, windowpanes, and chandeliers. From 1756 until the late nineteenth century it was owned by the Wickenberg family, but in 1875 it became a public stock company. It attracted international attention at the end of the nineteenth century when it began to produce cameo glass in imitation of the work of Émile Gallé, and it employed a number of prominent designers, including Alf Wallander and Gunnar Gunnarson Wennerberg.

In 1917, the program of the Svenska Slöjdföreningen (Swedish Society of Industrial Design), which encouraged companies throughout Sweden to hire artists as designers, infused the factory with a new vitality. Among those hired by Kosta were Edvin Ollers, a member of the artists' group known as the Optimists, and Edvard Stromberg. Ollers designed relatively simple forms, decorated with a simplified type of cameo work that recalls the contemporary production from the Daum factory of France.

In the 1920s and 1930s a number of new designers were added: Ewald Dahlskrog (also from the Optimists), Sten Branzell, Sven Erik Skawonius, Tyra Lundgren, and Elis Bergh, the latter serving as artistic director until 1950. The output of the Kosta factory between the two world wars was marked by the traditional Modernist canon of simple forms and clarity of glass. The vases from the later 1930s were increasingly thick and heavy, in accordance with the taste of the time. Occasionally the glass was engraved in the style of Scandinavian Moderne classicism or with Art Deco geometric motifs. The works of Skawonius and Lundgren from the late 1930s have deeply cut, angularly stylized motifs of fish, birds, and leaves. While Kosta's output between the two world wars was distinguished in its quality, it was not necessarily distinctive or original. Indeed, it was overshadowed by the achievements of the Orrefors factory, which, though newly founded, had outstripped Kosta in terms of artistic supremacy and technical innovation.

The hiring of Vicke Lindstrand in 1950 revivified the Kosta factory. Since Lindstrand had worked at Orrefors in the late 1930s, many of his designs for Kosta were based on ones previously initiated at Orrefors, and he also brought with him the *Ariel* and *Graal* techniques of working the glass. Lindstrand created forms that, in the typical postwar manner, are often gently asymmetric and have a lyric sense of line, often introduced into the mass of the glass as colored filaments or engraved on the surface. By the late 1950s Kosta had shifted back to greater symmetry.

Among the outstanding designers who worked for Kosta in the 1960s and 1970s are Mona Morales-Schildt and Ann and Göra Wärff, the former best known for her faceted polychrome *Ventana* series and the latter team for their humorous scenes in cameo glass—the two genres suggesting the diversity of approaches in modern glass and the ever-changing nature of Kosta's products.

In 1935 Erik Åfors, owner of the Åfors glassworks, bought 50 percent of Kosta's shares, and he later bought an additional 12 percent. Åfors also gained control of the Boda and Johansfors glassworks. These factories entered into a cooperative relationship in the 1960s, and since 1971 have been partners in the combine AB Åforsgruppen.

ME

Kramer, Sam Born Pittsburgh, November 22, 1913; died New York, June 9, 1964

Sam Kramer was a true Surrealist in both his work and his life. [122] He opened his own retail outlet in 1939 in New York City's Greenwich Village, where his shop was outrageous by even the most avant-garde standards. He made jewelry from unconventional gem materials, like small geodes, and from the oddest things, including teeth and meteorites. He shaped metal into equally unusual configurations that suggested erotic and anthropomorphic beings. His work encompassed Surrealism, Primitivism, and, finally, Abstract Expressionism.

Kramer's business promotion was equally bizarre. His advertising flyers, distributed by "Space Girls" clad in green tights and wearing green makeup, promised ". . . things to titillate the damnest ego—utter weirdities conceived in moments of semi-madness. . . ."

Little wonder, then, that the *New Yorker*, in 1942, published a notice about him entitled "Surrealistic Jeweler."[123]

He had attended the University of Pittsburgh School of Journalism. When his family moved to California during the Depression, he transferred to the University of Southern California, from which Kramer graduated in 1936. While there he took a jewelry course taught by ceramist Glen Lukens, a champion of the spontaneous in art.

In 1936, after a brief stint as a journalist in California, Kramer returned to Pittsburgh and worked for a manufacturing jeweler, learning the trade. In 1937 he and his wife, Carol, also a jeweler and often his co-worker, traveled to the Southwest to study Navaho jewelry. He came to New York in 1939, studied gemology at New York University, and opened his Eighth Street shop.

Although a cult developed around him among the postwar "beat generation," and although his emphasis on action and process aligned him with the most avant-garde New York art, Kramer did not receive national or international recognition commensurate with his genius during his lifetime. Recently, however, his contribution has been reevaluated, and he is today considered one of the most significant innovators of the post–World War II American studio jewelry movement.

TLW

Krupp *see* Argenteria Krupp

Kultakeskus Oy In 1918 several Finnish goldsmiths founded the firm Suomen Kultaseppien Keskus Oy (Center of Finnish Goldsmiths Co.) in Hämeenlinna. Soon thereafter its name was changed to Kultakeskus Oy (Gold Center Company). In 1962, because most of its hollowware and flatware was silver, the company name was changed to Hopeakeskus Oy (Silver Center Co.).

Kultakeskus Oy was also the name of a small goldsmith's shop in Helsinki that had been founded by Nestor Westerback in 1897 and made jewelry. In 1975 Hopeakeskus Oy merged with Kultakeskus Oy, keeping the former's offices in Hämeenlinna but taking the name of the latter firm. It produces both metalware and jewelry, using a full range of metals—gold, silver, platinum, alpacca, pewter, and bronze. The firm's current designer is Karl Laine.[124]

Outside of Finland, Kultakeskus is best remembered for the designs Tapio Wirkkala created for the company from 1951 to 1983, consisting of five complete sets of tableware and more than six hundred other objects, including jewelry. Many of Wirkkala's silver pieces are still in production today.

CWL

Landberg, Nils Born Västra Vingaker, Sweden, May 26, 1907

For four decades Nils Landberg served as one of Orrefors's chief glass artists, first as engraver and then as designer.

After attending the Konstindustrieskolen (formerly the School of Arts and Crafts) in Göteborg (1923–25), Landberg began his long association with Orrefors as a student at its newly established school of engraving (1925–27). He then studied briefly in France and Italy before returning to Orrefors, where he worked as an engraver and assistant to Edward Hald. He joined the company's design team in the mid-1930s. Landberg's engraved glass in this period was exhibited at the Paris "Exposition Internationale des Arts et Techniques" in 1937 and the New York World's Fair in 1939.

Landberg's engraved designs ranged from the representational to the abstract. His designs for graceful, elongated vessels in clear and subtly tinted glass produced in the 1950s explored the tensile limits of the material and demanded close collaboration between designer and technician. His series of fragile *Tulip* goblets of 1957, each blown in its entirety from a single two-toned mass, was awarded a gold medal at the Milan XI Triennale of 1957. His designs for functional tableware are equally refined. Landberg also designed lighting fixtures, including those for the SS *Stella Polaris* (1946), and ornamental windows and doors.

Landberg retired in 1972. A retrospective of his work, "Nils Landberg—The Orrefors Glass Artist," was mounted by the Orrefors Museum in 1986.

LN

Larsen, Jack Lenor Born Seattle, August 5, 1927

Jack Lenor Larsen initially studied architecture and furniture design at the University of Washington in Seattle until he took courses in weaving, the medium that was ultimately to play such a major part in his life. After interrupted studies in Seattle (University of Washington, 1945–47, 1948–50) and in Los Angeles (University of Southern California, Los Angeles City College, and Chouinard, 1947–48), he opened a weaving studio in Seattle in 1949. He completed his formal education in 1950–51 at the Cranbrook Academy of Art, Michigan, from which he received a master of fine arts. He then moved to New York City, organized a studio, and in 1953 established Jack Lenor Larsen incorporated. His knowledge of all phases of textile manufacturing stood him in good stead: his translations of these techniques into custom designs and, by 1956, into power-loom manufacturing established him as a leading textile designer.[125]

In 1958 he initiated Larsen Design Studio, with Win Anderson as president. Larsen became a consultant to the United States State Department on grass weaving in Taiwan and Vietnam and was codirector of the Fabric Design Department at the Philadelphia College of Art in 1959 and 1960. By 1968, he had opened offices of Jack Lenor Larsen International in Zurich, Stuttgart, and Paris. Larsen's empire continued to expand in the 1970s. Thaibok Fabrics Ltd., an American firm originally established in the 1940s in Bangkok, became part of the Larsen enterprise by 1972. Divisions for carpets and leather followed in 1973, and in 1976 Larsen established a furniture division as well. Among his recent projects are his tableware designs for Dansk International (1980) and his Terra Nova Collection for Mikasa and Martex (1985).

Many influences formed Larsen's artistic personality. Ed Rossbach, his teacher at the University of Washington, was the one to suggest Larsen study at Rossbach's alma mater, Cranbrook. Marianne Strengell, head of the Weaving Department at Cranbrook, with her involvement with industry and her "professionalism, speed and efficiency,"[126] prepared him for New York and its fast pace. In 1947, while still living in California, he met contemporary weaver Dorothy Liebes; their approaches differed profoundly, but they shared an unrestrained love for color and a bent toward experimentation with synthetic fibers. Other mentors were Edgar Kaufmann, jr., Edward J. Wormley, Edward Benesch, and Fran Merritt.

Extensive travel also had a profound effect on Larsen, who is always searching for new ideas. One need only think of his Indonesian Collection of 1959 or his African Collection of 1963, done in collaboration with Coral Stephens.

Larsen's accomplishments are well known, and countless exhibitions have included his textiles. In 1964 Larsen won the gold medal at the Milan XIII Triennale, and three honorary doctoral degrees were bestowed on him in 1981 and 1982. In addition to

giving many lectures and seminars, he has coauthored several major publications on the fiber medium.[127] Production centers and showrooms in thirty countries today maintain his international presence.

CCMT

Lassaw, Ibram Born Alexandria, Egypt, May 4, 1913

Ibram Lassaw's aim as a sculptor and jeweler has always been to render the spiritual substantive. Fused drips of molten bronze in the Abstract Expressionist manner represent for him the inner life of natural phenomena.

When he was eight years old his family left Egypt and moved to New York City. As a youngster, he took modeling classes at the Brooklyn Children's Museum. Although he furthered his studies at the academic Beaux Arts Institute of Design from 1930 to 1931 and later at the City College of New York, Lassaw became increasingly aware of avant-garde European sculpture through such publications as *Cahiers d'Art*. He was especially attracted to the Russian Constructivists, from whom he deviated, though, in his insistence on organic references even in his most abstract compositions. Julio Gonzalez was his greatest influence, inspiring him to abandon solid mass and open up his forms.

Lassaw began to experiment with open space, first by applying plaster to a wire armature but leaving areas of naked wire revealed. By the late 1930s, he was arranging chemically patinated Biomorphic metal shapes, cut from sheet metal and wire, in shadow boxes. The shadow boxes were eventually eliminated, and the flat, amorphous shapes evolved into clusters of molten, metal drips that had cooled. The resulting images were meant to represent the molecular structure of flowers and other natural phenomena.

Lassaw's mature work was foreshadowed by *Milky Way* (1950), which was created from bits of dripped plastic built up on a metal armature. Exhibited at the Whitney Museum of American Art in 1951 in "Abstract Painting and Sculpture in America," it displayed the artist's preoccupation with structures that grow and evolve in space. In his next phase he substituted plastic with alloys of chemically colored bronze, brass, and nickel, well exemplified by *The Clouds of Magellan*, a wall sculpture commissioned in 1953 for Philip Johnson's Connecticut guest house. These works spawned his experimental forays into the making of jewelry—an essential aspect of his oeuvre and one of great consequence for subsequent artisans.

Lassaw was one of the founding members of the American Abstract Artists in 1936 and president of the organization from 1946 to 1949. After World War II, he became involved with the New York Abstract Expressionist school, with which he has "profound affinities both of style and intellectual content . . . based on a shared sense of personal authenticity and existential truth, which are given definition in the act of creation."[128]

TLW

Laverne Originals When, in 1947, Estelle and Erwine Laverne won a first award from the American Institute of Decorators for the best printed fabric for that year, they were already a successful and well-known design team.[129]

Erwine Laverne, a native New Yorker (born March 1, 1909), had studied in the United States and in 1928 went abroad to continue his education.[130] While overseas, he won the gold medal at the 1929 international exposition in Brussels for his faux-marble paintings. Upon his return to New York in 1931, he enrolled in the Art Students League, where he studied with Kimon Nicolaides, Kuniyoshi, and Hans Hoffmann; in 1934 Laverne met his future wife there. Estelle Lester (born

New York, February 29, 1915) was a scholarship student who studied with Nicolaides, Kuniyoshi, Morris Kantor, William Zorach, and Hoffmann. They were married in 1934, and a partnership dedicated to merging the fine arts with applied design became their mission.

Simultaneously with their marriage, they established a wallpaper firm, Laverne Originals.[131] At first the Lavernes operated a showroom for giftware, but soon after they tried their hand at designing wallpapers, textiles, and furniture. From 1945 to 1947 the firm specialized in all three areas. In 1948 the name of the firm was changed to Laverne International to broaden the concept of its business and for reasons of prestige. Erwine Laverne applied his interest in marble and wood-grain patterning to his *Marbalia* series of wallpapers and fabrics. While some of their furniture designs are straightforwardly functional, paralleling postwar developments, their Lucite creations are as humorous as Estelle Laverne's textile designs.

The textile designs showed three distinctly different styles: his was organic, fluid, and abstract; hers, representational and humorous; the third style was geometric shapes conceived as linear, repeating patterns. The designs were silk-screened by the Lavernes themselves on natural and synthetic materials. To broaden the selection, the Lavernes introduced the Contempora Series during the later 1940s. Prominent contemporary artists and designers, such as Alexander Calder, Ray Komai, Alvin Lustig, Gyorgy Kepes, and Oscar Niemeyer, created designs for fabrics and wallpapers.

An impressive number of awards were bestowed on the Lavernes. The pace was set in 1948, when they received the American Fabrics Award from the Metropolitan Museum of Art and a Good Design Award from the Museum of Modern Art. Good Design awards followed in 1949, 1952, and 1953 for printed fabrics, wallcoverings, and furniture, respectively. They received first awards from the American Institute of Decorators in 1947, 1949, 1951, 1952, and 1957, as well as numerous citations.[132]

Due to Estelle Laverne's ill health, the business was closed during the course of 1964 and 1965, although some of the furniture, wallpapers, and textiles continued to be carried by a number of firms, and still are today.

CCMT

Leach, Bernard Howell Born Hong Kong, January 5, 1887; died Saint Ives, England, May 6, 1979

A man of many dicta, Bernard Leach's most remembered saying is "The pot is the man." His ceramics, known for their unassuming straightforwardness, strength, and respect of Eastern tradition, well summarize his life and work.[133]

Born of British parents, Leach spent his first decade in China and Japan, which set an indelible mark on him. He was educated in England and then studied art at the Slade School in London and learned etching from Frank Brangwyn. He returned to Japan in 1909 as an etcher, intending to support himself by teaching Japanese students this Western art, but a chance encounter with raku ceramics at a tea ceremony caused the roles to be reversed, and Leach became a student of the Orient.

Through his friends Kenkichi Tomimoto and Soestsu Yanagi and studies with Ogata Kenzan, the sixth generation of famous potters, and then Shoji Hamada, Leach absorbed Eastern principles. Although domiciled in Tokyo, he lived briefly in Peking and visited Korea. He made and exhibited porcelain and stoneware that were primarily in an Oriental mode, but he occasionally introduced Western themes.

In 1920 he, his family, and Hamada moved to England. Leach established a workshop at Saint Ives in Cornwall, in order to take advantage of the raw materials there and to associate himself with the old local tradition of British slipware. Most of his work, however, as well as his processes, his concern with textures and ash glazes, and even his climbing kiln, were in the Oriental tradition. In 1936 he opened a new studio at Skinner's Bridge, near Dartington Hall in Devon, where he taught with Pearl Buck, Aldous Huxley, and Mark Tobey—all of whom were concerned with a hybridization of cultures. He gave up slipware, having decided that stoneware suited better "the condition of modern life," but it was also symptomatic of his evergrowing fascination with the East. Throughout the 1920s and 1930s he traveled and exhibited in Japan, visiting or receiving visits from Hamada and Yanagi. He took on English pupils—Michael Cardew (1923), Katherine Pleydell Bouverie (1924), Nora Braden (1925)—and was joined in his work by his sons Michael and David, thus ensuring links to the next generation of British potters. In addition, Leach was a thoughtful author, publishing *A Potter's Outlook* (1928) and the very influential *A Potter's Book* (1940).

After World War II, Leach assumed a position of preeminence, due to the great abundance of his personal work and that of his studio, as well as to his influential writings. For almost three decades after the war, he continued to travel, exhibit, and lecture extensively, both in England and Japan, and made important trips to Scandinavia (1949) and the United States (1950). Besides those cited above, his writings include *A Potter's Portfolio* (1951), *A Potter in Japan* (1960), *A Potter's Work* (1967), and *Hamada: Potter* (1975). A major retrospective of his work was held at the Victoria and Albert Museum in 1977, some five years after Leach had been forced to stop working, a victim of blindness.

ME

Leerdam *see* Koninklijke Nederlandsche Glasfabriek Leerdam

Léger, Fernand Born Argentan, France, February 4, 1881; died Gife-sur-Yvette, France, August 17, 1955

Léger was one of the major French artists of the early part of this century.[134] He apprenticed with an architect in Caen and then attended classes at the École des Arts Décoratifs in Paris, the École des Beaux-Arts, and the more innovative Académie Julian. During the 1910s he became friendly with avant-garde artists and writers, among them Robert Delaunay, Guillaume Apollinaire, and Blaise Cendrars. While Pablo Picasso and Georges Braque were inventing Cubism, Léger developed his own variant, with fractured but solidly three-dimensional forms, as in *Nudes in a Forest* (1911). During the next few years his paintings became increasingly abstract, as in the *Contrasts of Forms* series.

Gassed while serving during World War I, he was invalided out of the French army. Although his portrayal of the fragmentation of urban life in *The City* (1919) was abstract, he soon returned to figurative painting. He became interested in the machine, painting an ideal world of precisely drawn, mechanical people, as in his *Three Women (Grand Déjeuner)* of 1921. In addition to painting, he worked with Cendrars on a film, *La Roue*, and designed sets and costumes for the ballet *La Création du monde* with a scenario by Cendrars and music by Darius Milhaud (1923). He also produced the film *Ballet mécanique* with Man Ray and others (1923–24).

In the mid-1920s, Léger was drawn to the Purism of Le Corbusier, and he painted murals for Le Corbusier's Pavillon de l'Esprit Nouveau at the "Exposition Internationale des Arts Décoratifs et Industriels Modernes" in 1925. In 1924 he established the Académie de l'Art

Moderne in Paris with Amédée Ozenfant. The school closed in 1939 because of World War II but was reopened as Atelier Fernand Léger by Nadia Khodasievitch, Léger's former pupil and later his second wife.

Léger spent the war in New York. Returning to France in 1945, he joined the Communist Party and campaigned for art that was accessible to the working class. His postwar paintings were mostly multifigured compositions of construction workers, circus performers, or picnickers, using simplified forms, bright colors, and heavy black outlines.

During these years, Léger received many commissions for decorative designs. In 1947 he designed mosaics for Notre-Dame-de-Toute-Grâce at Assy, and in 1949 he started designing ceramics, setting up his own ceramic studio the following year. He designed a tapestry and stained-glass windows for the church of the Sacré Coeur in Audincourt (1951), murals—including one for the United Nations (1952)—and theatrical sets and costumes. Most of his decorative designs were more abstract than his paintings.

The award of a grand prize at the Biennal de São Paulo in 1955, the very last year of his life, was a fitting climax for a prolific and well-respected painter, though perhaps his greatest works were those created early in his career.

CWL

Libenský, Stanislav Born Sezemice, Czechoslovakia, March 27, 1921

Together with his wife, Jaroslava Brychtová-Zahradniková (born July 8, 1924), Libenský became an eloquent advocate of the use of glass for artistic rather than functional purposes. He studied glassmaking and painting at the schools of glassmaking in Nový Bor and Železný Bród from 1937 to 1939. At Prague's secondary art school he studied with J. Holeček from 1939 to 1944, and, at the School of Applied Arts in the same city, with Joseph Kaplický, in the latter's studio, from 1944 until Libenský's graduation in 1950. It was with Kaplický that Libenský learned the importance of color, an element that became very prominent in his work. From 1945 to 1954 Libenský taught at Nový Bor, and he became a manager of artistic glassware at the factory attached to the school.[135] At the same time, he worked at Bor Studios as an artist, enameling glass with naturalistic and abstract designs.

While he was the director of the school of glassmaking at Železný Bród from 1954 to 1963, Libenský reached artistic and professional maturity. He and his wife began working together in 1955. Their first collaborative effort, the glass panel *Bird with Cherries* (1956–1958), maintained the figurative style of Libenský's earlier oeuvre[136] but moved toward abstraction in the fracturing of the forms and space by multicolored, irregular pieces of glass. At the 1958 Brussels World's Fair, a panel in a similar style won a grand prize. By 1961–62 the couple had executed their first large-scale glass sculpture, a stairway lattice balustrade for the International Hotel in Brno.

Beginning in 1963, when Libenský became the director of the School of Applied Arts in Prague, and continuing through the 1970s, Libenský increasingly addressed abstraction and scale, and he simplified his palette. During the mid-1960s, he and his wife continued working primarily on two-dimensional projects; by 1967 their work had developed into fully three-dimensional form, represented by their monumental sculpture in glass exhibited at the Montreal Expo '67.[137] By 1980 the couple was creating "glass environments," such as *Meteor, Flower, and Bird*, installed in the entrance of the Corning Museum of Glass in Corning, New York.[138] The spatial concepts explored in their objects paralleled those of many sculptors of the period, including Anthony Caro, an artist Libenský admired.[139]

Libenský's achievements are many, but he will be remembered most as a pioneer in the development of modern glass sculpture.

JTT

Lichtenstein, Roy Born New York, October 27, 1923

One of the core figures of the Pop art movement of the 1960s, Roy Lichtenstein first took up art as a hobby while he was attending the Franklin School on Manhattan's Upper West Side.[140] In 1940 he studied at the Art Students League with Reginald Marsh, whose subject matter—New York City street life—influenced his own. Lichtenstein continued his education at Ohio State University's School of Fine Arts and, after wartime military service, returned there to obtain a master of fine arts degree. He remained to teach until 1951. He then worked as an engineering draftsman in Cleveland.

He had his first solo show in New York at the Carlebach Gallery in 1951, and he made frequent trips to New York to exhibit his paintings, which were in the mainstream of the Abstract Expressionist movement.

He returned to teaching, at the New York State College of Education, Oswego, and then, from 1960 to 1963, at Douglass College of Rutgers University in New Jersey, not far from New York. During this latter period he frequented the Cedar Tavern on New York's University Place, where Jackson Pollock, Mark Rothko, Willem de Kooning, Franz Kline, and Barnett Newman often gathered.

His paintings reverted to representational imagery, his comic-strip frames first appearing in 1961, the year he joined Leo Castelli's gallery. Castelli also represented Andy Warhol, James Rosenquist, and Claes Oldenburg, and he promoted Pop art as an autonomous movement that reflected popular culture by translating commonplace images to a "high art" context. Lichtenstein's thematic subject matter of the 1960s ranged from sneakers and hot dogs to war and George Washington. He standardized these everyday icons in order to satirize them and strip away the "sacredness" of art. In his work of the late 1960s and 1970s he turned to the history of art for subjects, including ancient architecture and Art Deco, Cubism and Picasso, Purism, Surrealism, and Expressionism. The Solomon R. Guggenheim Museum in New York held a retrospective of his paintings in 1969.

Lichtenstein has worked in mediums other than painting: in addition to the posters he has produced since the early 1960s, he has transposed his two-dimensional symbols into sculpture and the decorative arts. The Castelli Gallery exhibited ceramics he made in 1965 in collaboration with Hui Ka-Kwong, a colleague from Douglass College. The Durable Dish Company manufactured six-piece place settings from Lichtenstein designs in 1966, and the artist designed a tea service for the Rosenthal firm that was issued in 1985.

In 1970 he was elected to the American Academy of Arts and Sciences. In that same year he moved to Long Island's art colony in Southampton; he continues to paint there and in his Manhattan studio.

FTH

Liebes Morin, Dorothy Wright Born Santa Rosa, California, October 14, 1899; died New York, September 20, 1972

Dorothy Liebes was first educated as a painter, receiving a bachelor's degree in art education from San José State Teachers College, and another in applied design from the University of California at Berkeley in 1923. From 1918 to 1929 she taught art in a number of public and private schools in California and New York City. Her first contact with textiles was in the summer of 1920 at Chicago's Hull House, where she studied weaving. Further studies included a year at the California School of Fine Arts in San Francisco[141] in 1925–26; by 1928 Liebes had also earned a master's degree in art education from Columbia University's Teachers College in New York. In 1929 she married Leon Liebes, a successful merchant, then went to Paris for a year to study textile design with French couturier Paul Rodier.

On her return to California in 1930, Liebes established her first weaving studio, on Powell Street in San Francisco. Her fabrics, all custom-designed, were in great demand because of their wide range of colors, their use of complementary colors, and their inclusion of unusual materials, especially Lurex, then a new glittery metallic yarn. She relocated her studio in San Francisco several times until 1948, when she and her design studio moved to New York.[142] That same year she married Relman Morin, a Pulitzer Prize–winning Associated Press special correspondent.

Her involvement with industry began in 1940 as designer and stylist for Goodall Fabrics Inc. of Sanford, Maine, an association she maintained until 1954. The Dobeckmun Company of Cleveland, known for its Lurex yarns, took on Liebes as a color stylist in 1946, and from then on she had unlimited access to the metallic yarns that she used so extensively. Other firms followed suit in hiring her.[143] One of her most enduring industrial relationships was with E. I. du Pont de Nemours and Company, which began in 1955 and lasted until the end of her life. She stated that the day she started working with synthetic fibers was one "of the most thrilling moments in my life."[144] She enjoyed the challenge of utilizing artificial fibers while preserving a handmade look and keeping prices reasonable.[145] As her involvement with the textile industry increased, custom production at her studio began to be affected, and in 1958 she terminated it altogether.

Dorothy Liebes's industrial endeavors were only a fraction of her activities: she lectured at universities, museums, and on radio and television and was actively involved with organizations like the American Craft Council, the Museum of Modern Art in New York, the San Francisco Museum of Art, and the Brooklyn Museum of Art's Design Division. In her lifetime she received over twenty international and national awards and participated in over one hundred exhibitions.[146]

CCMT

Lindberg, Frederick Sigurd (Stig) Born Umeå, Sweden, August 17, 1916; died San Felice Circeo, Italy, April 7, 1982

Known for his witty patterns and forms, Stig Lindberg was one of the major postwar Swedish designers.[147] His education was fairly traditional, first in Jönköping and then, from 1935 to 1937, at the Konstfackskolan in Stockholm. Between 1937 and 1940 he mostly worked under Wilhelm Kåge at the Gustavsberg factory; this was of crucial importance, diverting him from his intended career as a painter to one as a ceramist. He also studied briefly in Denmark and for six months at the Académie Colarossi in Paris, a period that he later claimed was "the cornerstone of his education as an artist."[148]

His early work at the Gustavsberg factory prior to 1940 shows a remarkable schism between a geometric, late Art Deco style and one using asymmetric, organic forms and decoration that presage postwar developments, the latter mode becoming the dominant one throughout the 1940s. Lindberg made his public debut at a group exhibition in the factory's Stockholm gallery in 1941 and gained international prominence after the war, when, in fact, his work became synonymous with the modern style of Scandinavia. From 1947 to 1949 he also designed glassware for the Målerås Glasbruk, and during this period he concurrently created richly patterned textiles for Nordiska Kompaniet and book illustrations, both of which were better suited to his pictorial gifts.

In 1949 he succeeded Wilhelm Kåge as artistic director of the Gustavsberg factory. Among the many new lines he introduced were the *Veckla* (1950) and *Pongo* (1953) wares and various dinnerwares, including *SA* and *Spisa* (1955). While it is easy to emphasize the playful eccentricity of his designs, it should also be remembered that Lindberg was in firm control of the technical and commercial aspects of the industry. He introduced the first flameproof dinnerware with his *Termagods* (1955–58), and he also designed for the company's new plastics division. He cleverly exploited the factory's physical plant in unexpected ways—for example, using the enameled-sink division to create a facility for large murals. Although he stepped down as artistic director in 1957, he continued to work for Gustavsberg, and from 1971 until 1980 he once again assumed his directorial position. During the interval between his two directorships, Lindberg pursued diverse outside activities, among them serving as senior lecturer in ceramics at the Konstfackskolan. In 1959 and 1960 he designed glassware for the Holmegaard factory, and in 1965 he lent his talents to the Kosta factory. He designed radio and television sets for Luna and playing cards for Swedish and British firms, as well as illustrating a considerable number of books.

His many achievements were well recognized in his lifetime, culminating in the award of the prestigious Prinz Eugen Medal in 1968. However, it was primarily his ceramics from the decade following World War II for which he will be best remembered, and the many prizes he received then—gold medals at the Milan Triennales of 1948 and 1957, grand prizes at the Triennales of 1951 and 1954, a gold medal at the Cannes ceramic exhibition in 1955—correspond to the apogee of his career.

ME

Lindstrand, Viktor Emanuel (Vicke) Born Göteborg, Sweden, November 27, 1904; died Småland, Sweden, May 7, 1983

The career of this internationally famous glass designer spanned almost a half-century and reveals in microcosmic form the evolution of avant-garde design both before and after World War II.[149]

When Vicke Lindstrand attended the Svenska Slöjdförenings Skola (School of the Swedish Society of Arts and Crafts) in his natal city from 1924 to 1927, his field of study was advertising, and, in fact, between 1922 and 1928 he worked as an illustrator and cartoonist for two local newspapers.

Only in 1928 did Lindstrand enter the field of decorative arts, joining the staff of Orrefors Glasbruk. His first designs, in the Moderne classicism that characterized Swedish style, received critical acclaim at the important Stockholm exhibition of 1930. Although slightly overshadowed by the work of the older Edward Hald and Simon Gates, Lindstrand's widely publicized vases, such as the *Shark Hunter*, became paradigms of Swedish modern glass. In addition, the artist received several major commissions, notably a window for the Swedish pavilion at the 1937 Paris exposition and a glass fountain for the 1939 New York World's Fair. Significantly, Lindstrand began exploring a softer style between 1935 and 1941, as can be seen in his *Graal* vases, where the fluent nudes suggest the rhythms of Matisse, and in his *Ariel* vases, where the forms of animals verge on the abstract.[150] Lindstrand left Orrefors in 1941. He had previously designed ceramics for Karlskrona Porslinsfabrik (1935–36), as had Orrefors artists Hald and Sven Erik Skawonius. In 1942 he returned to ceramics, assuming the duties of artistic director for the Upsala-Ekeby pottery, which, not coincidentally, had bought the Karlskrona works. Here his penchant for calligraphic, Matisse-like decor prevailed.[151]

Lindstrand returned to the glass industry in 1950, when he became artistic director at Kosta Glasbruk, a position he held until his retirement in 1973. His fertile imagination more than compensated for the simpler techniques at his disposal at the Kosta factory. Although some of his engraved pictorial designs strike a cloying note today, his bold, asymmetric forms and rhythmic use of internal threads of color are still exciting. In the latter half of the 1950s, he utilized a thicker crystal with equal freedom and success. Lindstrand's work was well published at the time, and he, together with Kosta, participated in all the major exhibitions. Yet, despite the vivacity and freshness of his designs, his work was not showered with the awards that some of his colleagues received. Time should rectify this neglect. He continued to work until his death at his glass studio in Åhus.

ME

Littell, Ross Born Hollywood, July 14, 1924

Ross Littell is known primarily as a textile and furniture designer.[152] He attended the Art Center School in Los Angeles on a scholarship and then served in the military from 1943 until 1946. In 1946 he enrolled at Pratt Institute in Brooklyn, New York, graduating in 1949 with honors in both graphics and industrial design.

Littell entered into a partnership with Pratt colleagues William Katavolos and Douglas Kelley in 1950. The three-man team worked for Laverne Originals, designing the Fifty-seventh Street showroom; a line of furniture, including the *T* chair; wallpapers; and fabrics. The fabrics received attention from the American Institute of Decorators (AID) and the Museum of Modern Art, New York, and were shown at the Milan X Triennale and the United States pavilion at the Brussels World's Fair of 1958.

In 1956 Littell opened his own studio, working as a free-lance designer and consultant for several firms, including Haviland. While in Italy in 1957, studying as a Fulbright scholar, Littell became interested in the microscopic structure of natural forms, and these investigations reinforced his determination to design patterns that combined arithmetical relationships, a balance of positive and negative fields, and a sense of rhythmic movement. One of his most successful designs, *Criss-Cross*, part of the collection he produced for Knoll Associates in 1959, was awarded an AID citation of merit.

Pursuing his interest in geometry, nature, and motion throughout the following decades, Littell collaborated with his wife, Inger Klingenberg, on a collection of Op art–influenced printed textiles and woven carpets for the Danish firm Unika Vaev in the 1960s. In the 1970s he independently produced a group of large-scale, incised-metal wall hangings that he called *luminars*. Most recently, he produced a collection of brightly colored upholstery fabrics, *African Vibes*, in collaboration with Finn Skodt for the Danish firm Kvadrat. Actively engaged in design research, Littell now lives and works in a rural Italian village near Lake Como.

MBF

Littleton, Harvey Kline Born Corning, New York, June 14, 1922

Harvey Littleton is generally regarded as the father of the modern studio glass movement.[153] As his father was the assistant director of research at the Corning Glass Works, the young boy grew up acquainted with the medium of glass. From 1939 to 1942 he studied at the University of Michigan, with an interest in industrial design, taking additional sculpture and

metalwork classes at the Cranbrook Academy of Art, Bloomfield Hills, Michigan, in 1941. Littleton saw service in World War II, and in 1945, while stationed in England, he studied ceramics at the Brighton School of Art with Nora Braden, a disciple of Bernard Leach.

Returning stateside, he completed a bachelor of design degree at the University of Michigan in 1947. Two years later, while a partner in an Ann Arbor design firm, he returned to Cranbrook to study ceramics with Maija Grotell and completed his master of fine arts degree in 1951, all the while teaching ceramics at the Toledo Museum of Art. From 1951 until 1977, he taught ceramics at the University of Wisconsin in Madison. His personal output was characterized by restrained, symmetrical stoneware forms with freely brushed strokes of slip or glaze. His position in the ceramics world grew steadily in the 1950s; he won a number of significant prizes and was active in establishing regional organizations.

The course of his career changed in 1957, when he spent eight months in Europe, much of the time in the glass factories at Murano and with Jean Sala in Paris. On his return to the United States he started experimenting, using a simple lead glass, which he melted in his own stoneware bowls. In 1961 he presented a paper to the American Craft Council on the possibility of glass as a studio medium. The turning point came in 1962 at experimental workshops held at the Toledo Museum of Art, at which Dominick Labino, research director for John S. Manville Fiber Glass, provided technical expertise. Littleton spent the summer in Europe, and German glass artist Erwin Eisch helped him see the expressive, liquid qualities of the medium. In the fall of 1962 Littleton began teaching glassblowing at the University of Wisconsin, introducing the material into the American university curriculum and initiating the American studio glass movement—events of great historical consequence for the medium of glass. His pedagogy is recorded in *Glassblowing: A Search for Form* (1971).

At first Littleton's work was highly expressionistic; the bubbles of glass were imploded, were exploded, had prunts added, or had trails of applied material irregularly wound around them. The forms gradually became simpler, and by the late 1960s the large blows of glass became sculptural loops, a theme Littleton then pursued through the next decades. Also he made bowls, each a different color and a graduated size, that were stacked concentrically to form, in effect, a sculpture. Alternately, tubes of bright color were fused and bent, gently twisted, or sliced at sharp angles. These tendencies toward regularity of form, polychromy, and large-scale sculpture offer an interesting parallel with American Color Field painting and minimalist sculpture.

In 1977 Littleton retired from teaching and established a studio in Spruce Pine, North Carolina, not far from the Penland School of Crafts, where he has continued to experiment not only with color and form but also with the technology of glass.

ME

Loewy, Raymond Born Paris, November 5, 1893; died Monte Carlo, July 14, 1986

Raymond Loewy was a flamboyant and versatile designer who created elegant, functional forms in many mediums from the 1920s to the 1980s.[154] He also helped establish the profession of industrial design in the United States. He was educated at the Université de Paris and received a degree in engineering from the École de Laneau in 1918, after serving in the French Army Corps of Engineers in World War I and receiving the Croix de Guerre four times.

In 1919 Loewy immigrated to New York, where he worked as a free-lance window designer for Saks Fifth

Avenue and Bonwit Teller as well as a fashion illustrator for *Vogue, Vanity Fair,* and *Harper's Bazaar.* He started his own industrial design firm in 1929 and made his reputation as a master of Streamlining. His first major success was the Gestetner duplicating machine (1929), followed by the *Hupmobile* car (1932), the *Coldspot* refrigerator for Sears, Roebuck & Company (1934), the furniture he exhibited at the Metropolitan Museum of Art (1934), and the bullet-shaped Pennsylvania Railroad S-1 locomotive (1937). By 1938, when he became an American citizen, he was recognized as one of the topmost industrial designers in the country.

After World War II, Loewy's designs became simpler, with long, gently curving arcs. His innovative Studebaker *Champion* (1947) incorporated the fenders into the body and had a long, low trunk; both front and back had projectile ends, causing people to joke that they could not tell if the car was coming or going. His principles of automotive design are beautifully summed up in the widely praised Studebaker *Avanti* (1962).

Loewy was also the master of corporate emblems and packaging, beginning with the Lucky Strike cigarette package (1942) and moving to such firms as Coca-Cola, Pepsodent, and the National Biscuit Company. In the 1960s he designed corporate logos for many firms, including British Petroleum, Shell (1967), and Exxon (1966). In addition, during the 1960s and 1970s, he worked for the United States government, designing Air Force One for President John F. Kennedy and the interiors of Skylab for NASA.

Loewy established a number of firms during the course of his long career. By 1939, he had offices in New York, Chicago, South Bend, São Paulo, and London. In 1944 he joined with four partners to form Raymond Loewy Associates. The Raymond Loewy Corporation was established in 1949 to deal with specialized architecture, and the Compagnie l'Esthétique Industrielle was created in 1953 with offices in Paris. In 1961 Raymond Loewy Associates was replaced by Raymond Loewy, William Snaith Inc., which in turn was superseded in 1975 by Raymond Loewy International, Inc., with offices in London and Paris. The latter office was closed in 1984.

CWL

Louis Poulsen & Co. A/S Although internationally celebrated today as a leading exponent of modern Scandinavian lighting, the firm began as the Copenhagen Direct Wine Import Company, established by Ludvig R. Poulsen in 1874.[155] During the early 1890s, when electric-power generators were first built in Denmark, Poulsen shifted to the sales of ceramic insulators, arc lamps, and plumbing materials. Ludvig's nephew, Louis Poulsen, took over the business in 1906, merging it with his own independent cork, fine china, glass, and silverware dealership. Two years later he moved the headquarters to its present location, still in Copenhagen. The company's name was changed to Louis Poulsen & Co. A/S in 1911 when Sophus Kaastrup-Olsen became a partner. Six years later Poulsen left the business, selling his share to Kaastrup-Olsen, but the name of the firm remained the same.

The new owner slowly phased out other products while increasing the sales of electrical equipment, and in 1924 he retained architect Poul Henningsen to develop a line of lighting fixtures. His *PH* lamps, first developed in 1927 and still in production, are among Poulsen's best-known products. They are characterized by a core of incandescent bulbs surrounded by concentric tiers of reflective metal bands. In the postwar years Poulsen manufactured designs by Arne Jacobsen, Verner Panton, and other well-known Scandinavian designers. The firm has also introduced the encapsulated fluorescent coil, the plastic grille, the strip-light ventilator, and both historical-revival and modern street lamps. The firm presently operates subsidiaries throughout Europe, as well as in the United States, Australia, and the Faroe Islands.

MBF

Lurçat, Jean Born Bruyère, France, July 1, 1892; died Saint-Paul-de-Vence, France, January 6, 1966

Although best known as the father of contemporary tapestry, Jean Lurçat was an accomplished artist in various mediums.[156] In 1912 he abandoned a medical career to study with Victor Prouvé in Nancy, later becoming a student of engraver Bernard Naudin and then an apprentice to fresco painter Jean-Pierre Lafitte. In his early career after World War I (in which he served in the infantry), Lurçat was a painter and decorative artist executing easel paintings, book illustrations, stage and costume designs, and frescoes. His personal style first reflected the influence of Cubism and later Surrealism. A world traveler himself, his work was exhibited internationally.

Lurçat's interest in textiles first manifested itself in 1917 with two designs, which were executed in petit point by his mother. After further exploring this medium, he became increasingly intrigued by tapestry. He designed for Marie Cuttoli (*L'Orage*, 1933), the Gobelins (*Les Illusions d'Icare*, 1936), and the independent Aubusson ateliers of Tabard, Goubely, Picaud, and others. His collaboration with François Tabard in 1937 and his viewing of the *Apocalypse* tapestries of Angers the following year sealed his fate. The rest of his productive career was primarily devoted to exploring the symbiotic relationship between tapestry weaving, architecture, and contemporary art.

Insisting that the proper role of tapestry is as monumental decoration integral with architecture, Lurçat freed the medium from its ties to easel painting and asserted the importance of designing cartoons to size, making them specifically for tapestry and ideally for a given site. Abhorring trompe-l'oeil effects in which weavers are obliged to capture the impression of the painter's brush, Lurçat proposed that the design be rendered in bold forms with few colors and woven in a coarse gauge to respect the two-dimensionality of the medium. In his own work Lurçat delved into the multiple meanings of images, developing a highly evocative repertoire of motifs which, on occasion, were further enhanced by poems written especially for his tapestries by such esteemed artists as Louis Aragon, Paul Éluard, and Tristan Tzara.

Lurçat's influence spread both through the impact of his work and his seminal writings. In addition to numerous articles, his theories were made known through *Le Travail dans la Tapisserie du Moyen Âge* (1947) (also appearing in other publications and in translated form as *Designing Tapestry*). The renaissance realized by Lurçat continues to manifest itself in successive generations of tapestry designs and weavers worldwide.

AZ

Lustig, Alvin Born Denver, February 8, 1915; died New York, December 4, 1955

During a brief but prolific career, graphic artist, architect, and industrial designer Alvin Lustig transformed American graphic design and typography. The most important early influence on Lustig was avantgarde European art, an interest that had been sparked by a teacher in his Los Angeles high school. A largely self-taught artist, Lustig acquired his smattering of formal education in a year at Los Angeles City College and a year at the Art Center School. He also spent three months with Frank Lloyd Wright at Taliesin West in 1935.

From 1936 to 1949 Lustig worked as a free-lance designer, primarily in Los Angeles. During this period

he also had his own typography and printing firm. Technical advances—mechanized typesetters, photoengraving, and high-speed presses—influenced his aesthetic, which recognized the industrialized nature of graphic design. Lustig also experimented with Surrealistic effects and sometimes incorporated photography into his work. In the late 1930s he worked for Ward Ritchie Press. Breaking all rules of traditional typography, Lustig's work for the company applied Bauhaus-inspired design principles.

Lustig came to New York City in the 1940s and frequented the studios of painters. As his widow remembered, "He always said the painters were the research scientists for him and he was turning [what he learned from them] into something practical."[157] He was director of visual research at *Look* magazine from 1944 to 1946, after which he returned to free-lance design on the West Coast. From 1944 to 1954 Lustig designed jackets for New Classics, a series of reprint books published by James Laughlin of New Directions Books; in a similar vein, he designed book jackets for Noonday Press.

Lustig perceived that the designer's role in society consisted of forming public taste and predicting trends. An influential teacher, lecturer, and writer, Lustig taught a graphic-design course at the avant-garde Black Mountain College in the summer of 1945 and also at the University of California, Southern California. During the 1950s, Lustig was visiting critic in design at Yale University. Lustig was committed to the alliance of fine and applied arts, stating, "You will find that the best design programs of art departments are always closely related to the best painting programs."[158]

Lustig worked in many different fields, including textiles and interiors. In the realm of architecture, he designed both commercial and residential buildings on the West Coast, including the Beverly Landau and the Beverly Carlton hotels. His furniture reflected the influence of Italian designers such as Franco Albini, whose work he knew from the pages of *Domus*.

Lustig suffered from a progressive disease that caused him to become totally blind by 1954. His work was acknowledged at an exhibition at the Museum of Modern Art that opened in October 1955, two months before his death.[159]

FTH

Machado, William Born Binghamton, New York, May 14, 1912

William Machado graduated from Hobart College, Geneva, New York, and attended the Harvard University Graduate School of Fine Arts. After military service from 1942 to 1946, he settled in New York and became associated with Benjamin Baldwin's atelier, Design Unit New York. The line of hand-printed fabrics produced by Baldwin and Machado in 1948 appeared in the first two "Good Design" shows held at the Museum of Modern Art in New York.

Machado remained associated with Baldwin through moves to Montgomery, Alabama, and Chicago. In 1957 he returned to Montgomery as an independent designer, working primarily as a consultant to architects. From 1965 to the present he has been involved in both furniture design and the renovation of residential and commercial spaces. His office is now located in New York City.

MBF

Madoura Pottery *see* Potterie Madoura

Magistretti, Ludvico (Vico) Born Milan, October 6, 1920

Vico Magistretti is one of the leading Italian designers of the postwar period.[160] After graduating from the

Politecnico in Milan in 1945, he worked first in his father's architectural office and then on his own as an architect and as an industrial, interior, and furniture designer. His architectural works have included a civic center for Campana, Argentina (1955); the Torre del Parco, an office building in Milan (1956); and country houses and city interiors.

Magistretti is best known for his furniture designs. His first furnishings were made for specific interiors. Then in 1960 he started designing furniture for Cassina, including his *Maralunga* chair, which won a Compasso d'Oro prize in 1979, and his *Sinbad* chair (1981), basically a horse blanket thrown over an upholstered base. He was one of the first Italians to design plastic furniture: his stackable, molded fiberglass *Selene* chair was designed in 1961 and was produced in bright colors by Artemide from 1966 on. Other plastic tables and chairs for Artemide followed, including the *Gaudí* chair (1979). Magistretti designed a number of lamps for Artemide, such as the *Eclipse* lamp (1966), and others for O-Luce. Some of his most recent designs are the *Pan Set* chair and dining table for Rosenthal Studio-Haus (1987) and the anodized-aluminum and plastic *Silver* chair for De Padova (1989), an office-style chair designed for use in the home.

CWL

Marimekko Oy Marimekko is perhaps Finland's best-known textile company. Its history is inextricably linked to that of its parent company, Printex, which Marimekko later eclipsed and absorbed in 1966.[161] Viljo Ratio founded Printex in 1949 for the production of printed textiles. Under the artistic supervision of Armi Ratia, the creative staff—which has included Maija Isola, Liisa Suvanto, and Vuokko Nurmesniemi—was given a free hand to respond to trends in art as well as social phenomena. The resulting printed cottons displayed fresh, often bold images, frequently in unconventional color combinations.

The potential uses for these extraordinary and experimental Printex fabrics, however, were not immediately evident to the consumer public. Therefore, in 1951 Armi Ratia established Marimekko, whose mandate was to demonstrate how these textiles could be used for home furnishings and clothing; the loose-fitting, comfortable, and informal Finnish *marimekko* ("Mary's dress") becoming a hallmark of the company. Printex fabrics and Marimekko fashions were introduced to a larger audience through the Brussels World's Fair of 1958, and the following year Benjamin Thompson, founder of Design Research in Cambridge, Massachusetts, brought the line to the United States. Partially due to pictorial coverage in *Life* magazine and the subsequent purchase of several dresses by Jacqueline Kennedy, Marimekko became extremely well known to the American public, which found the firm's products available through the increasing number of Design Research outlets.

A success in Europe and Asia, Marimekko is represented internationally in stores in more than twenty countries. It also sells wallpapers, tabletop items, bed linens, and related wares. In 1985, Marimekko was acquired by Amer Group Ltd., a Finnish multibusiness corporation.

AZ

Markelius, Sven Gottfrid (né Sven G. Jonsson) Born Stockholm, October 25, 1889; died Stockholm, February 24, 1972

Sven Markelius was a Swedish architect who concentrated on town planning.[162] He received his formal education in Stockholm, where he attended the Kungliga Tekniska Högskolan (Royal Institute of Technology, 1909–13) and Kungliga Akademien för de fria Konsterna (1913–15). Beginning in 1915 he also worked as an apprentice to Ragnar Oestberg, the prominent Swedish architect. One of the projects Markelius worked on was the east facade of Stockholm's town hall.

His first designs for buildings echoed the style of National Romanticism. His work became more Neoclassic during the late teens and, after he had encountered the work of Le Corbusier and the Bauhaus, more functional. He played an important part in the Stockholm exhibition of 1930. Markelius was among the first Swedish architects to introduce Modernism, not only in his own house in Stockholm in 1930 but also in the Hälsingborg concert hall of 1932. Markelius received international acclaim in 1939 as the architect of the Swedish pavilion for the New York World's Fair. The same year he was appointed chief of planning for the Royal Board of Building in Stockholm, a position he held until 1944. As city-planning director and head of the Stockholm Planning Office from 1944 to 1954, he developed the city plan for Stockholm. His brainchild was the "town sections," or satellite towns, planned to control the expansion of the capital.[163] The new suburbs and the renewal of the inner city well exemplified how the Swedish welfare state tackled the issues of housing and urban planning. After World War II, Markelius served on the United Nations Planning Board, the committee for the UNESCO Building in Paris, and on the UNESCO Arts Committee. He designed the Economic and Social Council Chamber for the United Nations Building in New York. Theater fascinated him throughout his life, and among his designs is the Stockholm city theater of 1960.

Markelius also taught at the Kungliga Tekniska Högskolan in Stockholm from 1918 to 1924 and again from 1937 to 1941. In 1949 he served as a visiting professor at Yale University, which presented him with the Howland Medal. Further awards include an honorary corresponding membership of the American Institute of Architects (1945) and the gold medal of the Royal Institute of British Architects (1962). He designed fabrics throughout his life, the first in the late 1940s for Nordiska Kompaniet. He also designed furniture, such as the stackable chairs for the Hälsingborg concert hall.

CCMT

Mathsson, Bruno Born Värnamo, Sweden, January 13, 1907; died Värnamo, August 17, 1988

Bruno Mathsson was an innovative Swedish designer of both furniture and architecture during the middle third of the century.[164] Descended from four generations of cabinetmakers from Värnamo, he served as an apprentice in the family workshop, Firma Karl Mathsson, from 1923 to 1931. In the early 1930s he was attracted to the functionalism of Marcel Breuer, Ludwig Mies van der Rohe, and Le Corbusier. Also, like Alvar Aalto, he was interested in laminated wood and experimented with different ways to bend it.

Between 1933 and 1936 he developed his first three chairs with laminated bentwood frames and webbed seats—the *Working Chair*, a lounge chair, and a reclining chair, all of which were produced by his father's firm after larger Swedish manufacturers refused them.

In the late 1940s and 1950s Mathsson designed houses with large plate-glass windows and heated floors, which were inspired by houses he had seen in the United States. This was a new type of housing in Sweden, and one that the Swedes were slow to accept. Appropriately, he also used glass to build a museum addition for Kosta Glasbruk in Småland, which one reviewer described as an ice-crystal palace.[165]

In 1957 Mathsson started managing Firma Karl Mathsson, although some of his designs of the 1960s were produced by other firms. In the early 1960s, he worked with mathematician Piet Hein, using Hein's

superellipse (a rounded rectangle) as the basis for a series of tables made by Fritz Hansens Eft. in Denmark. In the mid-1960s he designed the cloth and tubular-steel *Jetson* chair, the first of several of his metal chairs to be produced by DUX Industrier. DUX then took over Firma Karl Mathsson in 1978.

CWL

Mathsson, Karl see Firma Karl Mathsson

Matisse, Henri Born Le Cateau, Picardy, France, December 31, 1869; died Nice, November 3, 1954

Matisse is often regarded as the most important French painter of the twentieth century.[166] In around 1904 and 1905, he was one of an important group of painters who, under the influence of Post-Impressionism and African sculpture, developed a brilliantly colored, boldly executed style that came to be known as Fauvism. By the latter part of that decade his work emphasized ample, flat shapes and rhythmic movement. Always a masterful draftsman, Matisse was also fascinated by strong color, in part due to the influence of Near Eastern art and visits to North Africa. From those years come some of Matisse's most vivid and penetrating canvases, and throughout the 1920s and 1930s he remained the master of a sensual art. Matisse withdrew to Vence in the south of France in 1939, intending to retire from painting, but in fact he remained active to the very end of his life. Beginning in the mid-1940s, the encroaching paralysis of his hands led him to work with lavish colored collages of cut paper.

Designers were quick to recognize the decorative implications of Matisse's art, especially of the work from the 1930s through the 1950s. Yet Matisse himself did little in this regard. In 1907 he collaborated with André Methey to produce painted ceramic vases, plates, and tiles for Ambroise Vollard. But Matisse was better known for his activities as an illustrator and as a designer of theater decor, which included the sets for the Stravinsky-Diaghilev ballet *Le Chant du rossignol* (1920) and for *Rouge et noir* (1938).

Many of Matisse's major projects stem from the latter part of his career. In 1935 Marie Cuttoli commissioned him, along with many other leading painters of Paris, to design tapestries to be woven at Beauvais. He based his on a drawing he had made in Tahiti. In 1940 Corning Glass Works commissioned Matisse, along with other artists, to create designs to be engraved in glass. After the war Matisse was commissioned to design three tapestry cartoons: two were executed at the Beauvais factory in 1947, the third at the Gobelins factory in 1949. Matisse designed linen wall hangings and scarves for the London merchant A. Ascher, Inc., in 1947. In 1948 Alexander Smith of Yonkers, New York, engaged Matisse to design a rug, which was finally executed in 1951 under the title *Mimosa*, and in 1949 he designed a silk-screen mural for Katzenbach and Warren, Inc., of New York. In 1948 he was invited to collaborate with Fernand Léger, Jean Lurçat, Georges Braque, and Jacques Lipchitz in decorating the church Notre-Dame-de-Toute-Grâce at Assy. One of Matisse's most important projects, also undertaken when he was eighty, was the decorative scheme for the Dominican Chapel of the Rosary at Vence. Between 1948 and 1951 he designed tiled stations of the cross, leaded glass windows, the altar, altar furnishings, and liturgical vestments—all of which were widely celebrated at the time and deeply influential.

MOR

Matta Echaurren, Roberto Sebastian Born Santiago, Chile, November 11, 1911

Sebastian Matta studied architecture at the Pon-

tificia Universidad Católica de Chile, and he worked in the office of Le Corbusier in Paris in the mid-1930s.[167] Like many architects, he was uninterested in painting, but his attitude changed in 1937 when he met René Magritte, Pablo Picasso, and Joan Miró. That year he joined the Surrealists, and he exhibited his first drawings in 1938. At first, like Miró and André Masson, he was interested in automatism—painting without rational control by the mind—and his forms were vaguely organic. However, Marcel Duchamp was the most influential. Matta, like Duchamp, fused an interest in alchemy and cosmology in his paintings, as can be seen in his later painting *The Bachelors, Twenty Years After* (1964), a homage to the older artist. Over the years Matta developed a painting style dominated by spectral shapes in vast spaces that often pulsate with light.

In October 1939, Duchamp persuaded Matta and Yves Tanguy to come to New York to escape World War II. Matta's solo show at the Julien Levy Gallery in New York in 1940 electrified experimental American artists. He was one of several artists who helped bridge the gap between European Surrealism and what would become American Abstract Expressionism. In 1948 Matta returned to Europe, living in Rome and then in Paris and taking frequent trips to South America. That October he was expelled from the Surrealists, on the basis of what was termed intellectual disqualification and moral ignominy.

Although Matta continued to paint into the 1980s, he began to expand into different mediums in the late 1950s and early 1960s. In the late 1950s he started making metal sculpture reminiscent of the work of Alberto Giacometti and of Picasso's metal sculpture of the late 1930s. In the 1960s and 1970s, he designed several pieces of avant-garde furniture for Dino Gavina's firm, including *Malitte*, a set of seating furniture in puzzle form, and *MArgitta* (1970), a chair inspired by the work of Magritte. Also in the 1960s, he designed tapestries, which were woven by the Atelier Yvette Cauquil-Prince in France.

Matta became more politically involved in the late 1960s. In the 1970s exhibitions of his work were organized in Italy and Mexico to protest the Chilean junta that had overthrown Salvador Allende.

CWL

Matter, Herbert Born Engelborg, Switzerland, April 25, 1907; died Southampton, New York, May 8, 1984

In the 1930s, photographer and graphic designer Herbert Matter helped pioneer the use of photography in commercial art; indeed, Matter developed and specialized in photomontage.[168] This powerful and widely adopted technique crystallized the client's message into a simple, strong image and often introduced a Surrealist overtone.

From 1925 to 1927 Matter studied painting at Geneva's École des Beaux-Arts. He continued his studies in Paris at the Académie de l'Art Moderne with Fernand Léger and Amédée Ozenfant in 1928–29. During his Paris sojourn, from 1929 to 1932, he worked for the design firm Deverny et Peignot as a photographer and typographer. There he worked with A. M. Cassandre on posters and Le Corbusier on architecture and display.

In 1932 Matter designed an important series of photomontage posters for the Swiss National Tourist Office. Looking for further opportunities, he immigrated to New York in 1936, where, for the next decade, he worked as a free-lance photographer for leading magazines, such as *Vogue* and *Harper's Bazaar*, while also working for the most innovative advertising agencies. Matter was represented at the 1939 New York World's Fair in his design work for the Swiss and Corning Glass pavilions. From 1946 to 1957, Matter was a staff photographer for Condé Nast Publications. Throughout his career, his work was widely published in trade and art magazines. In 1949 he made a film, *The Works of Calder*, for the Museum of Modern Art, New York.

Matter's twenty-year collaboration with Knoll International as design and advertising consultant began in 1946. From 1950 on, he was a partner and vice president of Studio Associates, New York. He collaborated with Massimo Vignelli on the exhibition catalogue *Knoll au Louvre*.[169]

Matter was professor of photography at Yale University from 1952 to 1982, where he influenced three decades of young graphic designers. His own publications include a photographic book on compatriot artist Alberto Giacometti.[170] There have been many exhibitions of his work in American and European galleries and institutions. Often recognized by his peers, he was accepted into the Hall of Fame of the Art Directors Club in 1977.

FTH

Matura, Adolf Born Bystřice, Czechoslovakia, March 20, 1921; died Prague, January 14, 1979

Unlike many of his compatriot glassmakers, who focused on artistic glass, Matura concentrated on the production of functional household ware. He received his earliest training from 1938 to 1940 at the Specialized School of Glassmaking at Železný Bród, where he studied glass engraving and cutting under Ladislav Přenosil. From 1940 to 1945 he studied under K. Štipl at the School of Applied Arts in Prague. From 1945 on, Matura collaborated with Ludvika Smrčková, engraving his designs on her forms, while he continued his own independent work.

From 1951 to 1954, Matura worked at the Central Art Center for Glass and Fine Ceramics in Prague. Under the direction of K. Peroutka, he designed both pressed and cut functional glassware. While still working with engraved designs, he began to treat his vessels architectonically. In 1954 Matura was chosen to be the chief creative artist for the development of cut and pressed glass at the Central Art Center, a position he held until 1959. Two of his pieces exhibited in 1957 at the Milan XI Triennale reflected his divergent approaches: one vase, called *Blackthorns*, has a diamond-point engraved floral motif on a delicately curved form; the other consists of heavy clear and green glass with a strong geometric form.[171]

In 1959 Matura became chief creative artist in the glass department at the Institute for Interior and Fashion Design in Prague, a position he maintained until his death. In the early 1960s he created designs for Moser in Carlsbad that were distinguished for their simple, linear shapes, enlivened by bright color. The objects were praised because they respected Moser's traditional colors, but they included unusual optical effects of light refracting through the faceted surfaces of the vessels' thick walls.[172]

Although Matura continued to work in an architectonic style in the 1970s, he also passed through a decorative phase. Some pieces displayed motifs resembling flowers and faces, while others had festive arrangements of circles and diamonds. His pressed-glass dinnerware set of 1970–71 for the Rosice works, *Praha*, is the best example of this phase.[173]

An active member in the Czechoslovakian glass industry during the 1950s and 1960s, Matura was the president of the Creative Art Council for pressed glass in 1961, and in the 1960s he was a member of the Creative Art Council of the association of glassworks producing serviceable glass. It is in this latter division of the industry that he was best known. Matura participated in numerous international exhibitions, including the Brussels World's Fair (1958), the São Paulo

Biennal (1959), Moscow (1959), and the Milan XII Triennale (1960).

JTT

Michelsen *see* A. Michelsen

Mil-Art Company, Inc. Milton H. Schiffer, owner of Mil-Art Company, Inc., apparently manufactured needlepoint canvas during the early 1940s.[174] In 1945 he established Schiffer Prints as a division of Mil-Art and went into the printing of textiles for drapes and fabrics.[175]

One of Mil-Art's most important contributions was its Stimulus Collection of 1949, which offered thirty-six designs by six prominent architects and artists: Ray Eames, Salvador Dalí, George Nelson, Abel Sorensen, Bernard Rudofsky, and Edward J. Wormley. Each artist was responsible for six patterns. The trademark for the collection was a butterfly, symbolic of the concept of creation.[176]

According to telephone listings, the Mil-Art Company remained active until about 1963.

CCMT

Miller, Herman *see* Herman Miller Furniture Co.

Mirko *see* Basaldella, Mirko

Miller, Howard *see* Howard Miller Clock Company

Miró, Joan Born Montroig, Spain, April 20, 1893; died Palma de Majorca, December 25, 1983

Joan Miró, considered one of the masters of twentieth-century painting, is identified with the abstract Surrealist movement. His highly distinctive style, characterized by an iconography of imaginative symbols and a palette of flat, primary colors, was infused with fantasy and wit. Although the progressive Parisian art movements of the early twentieth century exerted a profound influence on Miró's art, an equally powerful force was the artist's Catalan heritage.[177]

The son of a goldsmith, Miró received his artistic training in Barcelona, from 1907 to 1910 at the Escuela de Bellas Artes under José Pasco and Modesto Urgell and then from 1912 to 1915 at Francisco Galí's progressive Academia Galí. In 1919, Miró made the first of many trips to Paris, where he began exhibiting his paintings. His association with the Surrealists there, especially during the mid-1920s, when his mature style was evolving, had a lasting impact on his work. Until the outbreak of World War II, Miró divided his time between France and Spain; after the war, he returned permanently to his native country. In 1956, Miró settled in Palma de Majorca, where he continued to work until his death.

While primarily recognized for his painting (he received the Carnegie International grand prize for painting in 1967), Miró successfully explored other mediums as well. From the late 1920s on, he produced numerous graphic works, especially lithographs, and was awarded the grand prize for graphic art at the 1954 Venice Biennale. Miró experimented with collage techniques and Surrealist "sculpture-objects" and executed many metal sculptures.

Beginning in 1944, ceramics accounted for much of Miró's artistic activity. In collaboration with his lifelong friend José Lloréns Artigas, he produced hundreds of ceramic sculptures and vases and several important

ceramic murals, including the monumental walls for the UNESCO headquarters in Paris (1958). Miró designed stage sets, too, including those for the Ballets Russes de Monte Carlo in 1926 and 1932, and stained-glass windows, for the Fondation Maeght in Saint-Paul-de-Vence (1978) and the Chapelle de Saint-Frambourg in Senlis (1979); he also collaborated with Josep Royo on a series of woven pieces in 1973.

LN

Mitchell, Peter Todd Born New York, February 16, 1924; died Sitges, Spain, February 28, 1988

The painter Peter Todd Mitchell's early years were spent in the sphere of the fashionable and the famous that surrounded his beautiful mother.[178] Her two marriages to Leonid Leonidoff, chief of Production at the Radio City Music Hall in New York, provided him with a lifelong taste for the theatrical. After pursuing art studies at Yale University School of Art and the Academia de Bellas Artes in Mexico City, Mitchell went to Paris, following his own inclination for Neoromantic painting.

Being handsome and well connected, he attracted the patronage of Jean Cocteau, who sponsored his first exhibition in Paris, at the Galerie Morihen in 1948. Connections in the world of haute couture led to commissions for printed textiles (1948) and into a career that was to support his aspiration as painter. Untrained in the mechanics of textile printing, he learned his trade working with the technicians of Bianchini-Férier. His fashion textiles for Norman Norell, Adele Simpson, and Claude Staron attracted the attention of the American home-furnishings companies, and by the early 1950s he was designing wallpapers and coordinated fabrics for the prestigious New York firm of Katzenbach and Warren. Commissions followed for a succession of distinguished firms, including Louis Bowen Inc., Scalamandre, and Walls Today.

After moving to more economical Spain in 1952, he was able to support his painting career by spending only half his time on commercial projects. Travels to Italy, North Africa, the Middle East, and India provided him with the decorative elements and architectural settings he loved to paint and from which he extracted details for murals and textiles. He frequently exhibited his paintings in Paris, London, and New York, but seems to have discontinued designing in the seventies after he began to collaborate with his mother on food and travel articles for *Gourmet* magazine, though he continued to paint.

KC

Molded Plywood Division, Evans Products Company In November 1942, Charles and Ray Eames and three colleagues established the Plyformed Wood Company in West Los Angeles to develop molded wood splints for the military and to work on other molded plywood products. On receiving its first contract from the United States Navy, the company moved to a larger factory and studio space in nearby Venice. Because navy payments lagged far behind the orders, cash-flow difficulties pushed Charles Eames to search for additional backing. In May 1943 he began discussions with Edward S. Evans, head of Evans Products Company, a Detroit-based manufacturer of industrial equipment, supplier of wood products, and owner of great fir wood forests, who was eager to find new uses for plywood. In October 1943, Evans bought the rights to produce and distribute Plyformed Wood Company's splints. The company was renamed the Molded Plywood Division and became a subsidiary of Evans Products Company, with the parent company holding the patents for the products developed.

In anticipation of the war's end, the Eameses and the Molded Plywood Division began applying their expertise to the development of low-cost, high-quality furniture made of bent plywood. Models of molded chairs, tables, and a storage system were produced in the fall of 1945, and Evans Products began to work on marketing and distribution—staging a press preview at the Barclay Hotel in New York in December 1945. The furniture was also shown in February 1946 at the Architectural League of New York and in March 1946 in a major exhibition of the Eameses' work at the Museum of Modern Art.

Mass production of some of the chairs began in the summer of 1946 in Venice. However, Evans Products was not comfortable with the prospect of distributing furniture. As of October 1946 the Herman Miller Furniture Co. of Zeeland, Michigan, gained the exclusive rights to market and distribute the plywood furniture. This came about a year after Edward S. Evans's death brought his son, Edward S. Evans, Jr., to the head of Evans Products. It was decided to consolidate all of the company's operations, including plywood molding, at a new plant in Grand Haven, Michigan. In April 1947 all production in Venice stopped, all the specially developed molding machinery was shipped east, the factory was shut down, and the division was dissolved. The distribution agreement between Evans Products and Herman Miller, Inc., continued for two years, when Herman Miller bought the manufacturing rights for the chairs from Evans Products.

KC

Mollino, Carlo Born Turin, May 6, 1905; died Turin, August 27, 1973

Carlo Mollino was the most daring Italian designer from the 1930s through the 1950s.[179] He was trained as an architect, receiving his diploma from the Università di Torino in 1931. After working with his engineer father, Enrico, from 1928 to 1931, he set up an independent practice. Mollino was active in many fields: as an urban planner, an architect, and a designer of interiors, furniture, and exhibitions. In addition, he was a photographer, avid filmgoer, skiing enthusiast, and race-car driver. He taught at the Politecnico in Turin from 1952 on; by 1968 he so rarely attended his own classes that he became one of the targets of student unrest.

Mollino did not like the architecture of the International Style, complaining that Ludwig Mies van der Rohe and others designed houses for "a world that does not exist, and that cannot exist except in some utopia."[180] He preferred a more organic architecture. His own buildings, influenced by the Turinese Baroque style and Art Nouveau, were forceful and expressive in the tradition of Antonio Gaudí, Antonio Sant'Elia, and Erich Mendelsohn. His best buildings, the offices of the Società Ippica Torinese in Turin (1937, demolished) and the Toboggan Lift Lodge at Lago Nero (1946), combined modern structural methods and materials with dramatic cantilevers and sweeping curves similar to those in contemporary works by Le Corbusier and Alvar Aalto.

Mollino started designing furniture in 1937. Unlike most Italian designers of the period, who were influenced by architecture, Mollino was more inspired by Surrealist painting and sculpture. In the Casa Miller in Turin (1938), a copy of one of Michelangelo's *Bound Slaves* served as a tabletop, while the Casa Devalle, also in Turin (1939), had mirrored walls to confuse the reading of space. During the 1940s and early 1950s Mollino designed apartments in Turin and their furnishings, including the Casa Minola (1944) and the Casa Orengo (1949).

In his furniture, Mollino was an innovator who experimented with plywood bent into eccentric shapes, and he patented a process for cold-bending plywood without a frame. He took the Streamlined contours of the 1930s and fused them with the Biomorphic lines of Jean Arp—though he claimed that the Baroque lines of his furniture were inspired by curving ski tracks.

In the mid-1950s Mollino turned away from furniture design and toward designing and driving race cars and airplanes; he drove an Osca 1100 of his own design in the Le Mans race in 1954. Mollino's return to architecture toward the end of his life was partly inspired by Carlo Graffi, with whom he worked intermittently from the late 1950s on. One of his most spectacular works was the Sala da ballo Lutrario in Turin (1959, with Alberto Bordogna), which, with its long, curved balconies and sweeping staircase, resembles an elaborate movie set.

His last major work was the interior of the Teatro Regio in Turin (1965–70), designed with Carlo Graffi. In typical Mollino fashion, he drew the plan of the theater so that it resembles the corseted torso of a woman.[181]

CWL

Mouron, Adolph Jean-Marie *see* Cassandre, A. M.

Müller-Munk, Peter Born Berlin, June 25, 1904; died Pittsburgh, March 13, 1967

For several decades one of America's foremost industrial designers, master silversmith Peter Müller-Munk brought an artisan's sensibility to modern industrial art.[182] Concerned with quality craft, space efficiency, and the appropriate combination of materials in machine-made products, Müller-Munk helped acquaint the American public with Modernism at its best.

After receiving a degree in the humanities from the Friedrich-Wilhelms Universität, Berlin, and training with the renowned German metalsmith Waldemar Raemisch at the Kunstgewerbeschule in Berlin, in 1926 Müller-Munk immigrated to New York, where for three years he designed silver for Tiffany & Company. Shortly thereafter he opened his own studio, first in New York and then in Chicago, and by 1930 he had entered the product-design field as well. During this period his utilitarian, superbly crafted silver designs were recognized and exhibited widely, among other places, at the "International Exposition of Art in Industry" at Macy's, New York (1928); "Contemporary American Design" (1928); and "Silver: An Exhibition of Contemporary American Designs by Manufacturers, Designers, and Craftsmen" (1937), the latter two at the Metropolitan Museum of Art.

In 1935, Müller-Munk, along with Donald Dohner and Robert Lepper, founded the first American degree-granting program in industrial art at Pittsburgh's Carnegie Institute of Technology. As associate professor there until 1944, and later in lectures elsewhere, he expounded his belief in a broad-based liberal-arts education for industrial designers; he himself epitomized the academic professional. He was active in the American Society of Industrial Designers and served as its president from 1954 to 1955. His advocacy of internationalism led to his becoming a founding member and the first president (1957–59) of the International Council of the Society of Industrial Designers (ICSID). His participation in a research project sponsored by the International Cooperation Administration of the United States State Department to promote indigenous design in developing nations took him to India, Turkey, and Israel (1955–60).

In 1945 he established Peter Müller-Munk Associates, a firm almost exclusively devoted to product design in its first decade. From its quarters in Pittsburgh, PMMA, as the company was commonly called, executed designs for a broad spectrum of American industries. Its products included home appliances, cameras, and commercial machinery for such clients as Westinghouse, U. S. Steel, and Bell & Howell. Müller-Munk's design for the waterfall-inspired blender for the Waring Mixer Corporation (1948) is a classic.

By 1966, PMMA was employing a staff of forty-four and had expanded its field of exhibition and transportation design. After Müller-Munk's death in 1967, the firm became increasingly involved in environmental and graphics design; it remained in business through 1983.

LN

Nathan-Garamond, Jacques Born Paris, March 26, 1910

After studying architecture and training as a graphic artist at Paris's École Nationale Supérieure des Arts Décoratifs, Jacques Nathan, as he was known, became most noted for his analytical approach to design.

Nathan began his career working for one of the leading French Art Deco interior designers, Paul Brandt. His earliest professional experience in typography and layout was from 1931 to 1933 for the periodical *L'Architecture d'aujourd'hui*, and later he was art director for the luxury magazine *Style*. Nathan created posters for product advertising and public-service campaigns; some of his earliest posters were done for the French Ministry of Education's Salon des Arts Ménagers. He participated in the Pavillon de la Publicité at the 1937 Paris "Exposition Internationale des Arts et Techniques." In addition to his work in posters and for magazines, he taught at the École Nationale Supérieure des Arts Décoratifs, Paris. Like the work of many of his contemporaries, Nathan's tightly constructed compositions were rooted in the teachings of the Bauhaus. Experiments with photomontage in the 1930s heightened Nathan's Surrealist tendencies.

After World War II, when he returned from deportation to Germany, he reopened his graphic-design studio, and in 1951 he resumed teaching. In the work of this period, a more evident Surrealism was combined with the prevalent linear dynamism of the 1950s to create a controlled sense of fantasy. Nathan's clients included UNESCO, Philips, Air France, SNCF, and Mazda. He also designed decorative panels for the 1958 Brussels World's Fair. Also in 1958 he won the Martini grand prize, and in 1963 the Martini gold medal. In 1988 the artist was the subject of a retrospective exhibit in Toulouse.[183]

FTH

Nelson, George Born Hartford, Connecticut, May 29, 1908; died New York, March 5, 1986

Trained as an architect at Yale University (1928–31), George Nelson also became a furniture designer, teacher, and writer. In 1932 he won the Prix de Rome in architecture for his Neoclassic design of an auditorium building,[184] and he then studied at the American Academy in Rome from 1932 to 1934. On his return to New York in 1935, he became an associate editor of the prestigious *Architectural Forum*, and from 1943 to 1944 he served as comanaging editor. This journal had a profound effect on him, as it showed the work of the International Style architects who were to influence his furniture and interior designs. In 1944 he was appointed head of the Fortune-Forum experimental department of Time, Inc., but remained with *Architectural Forum* as a consultant.

During an architectural partnership with William Hamby from 1936 to 1942, Nelson began his work as an industrial designer. Two highly influential products were created by Nelson's associates under his direction: the first was *Grass on Main Street* (1942), a proposal for the now-familiar pedestrian mall; the other was *Stor-*

agewall (1944), a combination storage unit and room divider, codesigned with Henry N. Wright.[185]

From 1946, when he became design director of the Herman Miller Furniture Co., a position he held until his death, Nelson and his staff produced a number of direct and functional designs, including the *Coconut* chair (1956), the *Sling* sofa (1964), the *Action Office* (1964), and the *Executive Office* (1971), as well as numerous clocks, lamps, textiles, and showroom interiors. In 1956 Nelson created the first pole system in the United States, *Omni*, designed for Aluminum Extrusions; this was a forerunner of his *Comprehensive Storage System*, designed for Herman Miller in 1958. One of Nelson's major contributions at Herman Miller was his employment of many young, talented designers, including Charles Eames and Alexander Girard. Others in Nelson's office who made significant contributions to furniture designs were Arthur J. Pulos and Irving Harper.

While continuing to work for Herman Miller, Nelson opened his own design firm, George Nelson Associates, in partnership with Gordon Chadwick, late in 1947. The firm's work included restaurants, shops, office interiors, the United States pavilion for the Moscow exhibition of 1959, as well as the Chrysler display and the Irish pavilion at the New York World's Fair of 1964. The firm closed in 1983.

Nelson is remembered as much as an author as a designer. Books such as *Tomorrow's House* (1945), *Problems of Design* (1957), and *How to See* (1977) reflect his pithiness, keen wit, and sensitive eye. He edited an important series of books in 1979 for the Whitney Library of Design, including *Chairs*, *Storage*, *Display*, and *Living Spaces*. In 1983 Nelson wrote "The Design Process" for the catalogue of the Philadelphia Museum of Art's "Design since 1945" show and designed the exhibition installation. In Nelson's work and prolific writings, his practical design theory is evident; his warmth and humanism tempered the extremes of modern design.[186]

DAH

Noguchi, Isamu Born Los Angeles, November 17, 1904; died New York, December 30, 1988

Isamu Noguchi was one of the leading American sculptors of this century.[187] Born of a Japanese father and an American mother, he was raised in both countries and remained bound to the traditions of both.

Taken to Japan, he was apprenticed briefly to a carpenter there in 1914 and then sent back to the United States in 1917 for schooling. After a short stint as a premedical student at Columbia University, he enrolled at the Leonardo da Vinci Art School in New York in 1924. In 1927 he went to Paris as a Guggenheim Fellow, where he worked as Constantin Brancusi's assistant for six months. Then in 1931–32 he traveled to the Far East, via Berlin and Moscow. He studied brush drawing in Peking as well as ceramics and gardens in Japan.

Noguchi's Japanese heritage surfaced in *The Queen* (1931), which was influenced by Japanese Haniwa terra-cotta tomb effigies. During the 1930s he made sculpture with muscular figures like those in the work of Diego Rivera and José Clemente Orozco. His major work of the 1930s was a bas-relief symbolizing freedom of the press for the Associated Press building at Rockefeller Center. He also made stage sets for Martha Graham who, along with R. Buckminster Fuller, was an important mentor for the young sculptor. These were followed by a series of Biomorphic sculptures made of thin slabs of marble interlocked to create a frame around interior spaces, as in *Kouros* (1947).

Noguchi's first furniture was a rosewood and glass table in the Biomorphic style (1939) designed for A. Conger Goodyear, president of the Museum of Modern Art. He followed this with a somewhat similar coffee table (1944) for Herman Miller Furniture Co., whose thin slabs are simpler versions of those used in his sculpture of the same period. Similarly, Noguchi's table lamp for Knoll Associates (c. 1945) grew out of his series of *Lunar* sculptures of the early 1940s. In 1951 Noguchi revisited Japan, where he designed his first *Akari* lamps as luminous, sculptural versions of traditional Japanese paper lanterns. He went on to design versions of *Akaris* for the next twenty-five years.

In the 1950s Noguchi began creating sculpture gardens, culminating in the Isamu Noguchi Garden Museum in Long Island City, which opened in 1985. Noguchi's interest in rough, primal stone had been stimulated by his study of Japanese gardens. He started using it for his sculpture, often making irregularly shaped, large pieces such as *Black Sun* (1969), whose hole recalls his earlier use of interior space. He worked with metal as well; in the Horace E. Dodge and Son Memorial Fountain in Detroit (1978), he combined his interest in light and water as both move over granite as well as stainless steel.

CWL

AB Nordiska Kompaniet AB Nordiska Kompaniet (known as NK) was founded in 1902, the merger of Stockholm's two largest retail companies, KM Lundberg and Joseph Leja. It was modeled after the department stores Harrod's in London, Au Louvre in Paris, Marshall Field in Chicago, and Wertheim in Berlin. In 1915, NK moved to Hamngatan, into a building by the architect Ferdinand Boberg. As the store grew physically over the years, other well-known architects became involved with the building, including Hans Asplund, Bengt Lindroos, Ragner Uppman, and Jan Larsson.[188] Over the decades NK expanded: today it operates department stores in Stockholm, Göteborg, and Malmö; fashion houses in Täby and Farsta; interior design divisions in Stockholm and Göteborg; and a subsidiary for real estate in Stockholm and Göteborg.

Since its inception, NK has addressed the issue of good design in furniture and other decorative arts and as it pertains to the environment and human beings. This can perhaps be best documented through the NK Textilkammare, which was established in 1936. The following year the company appointed Astrid Sampe (born May 27, 1909) as director of Textilkammare, a position she held until 1972.[189] Aside from directing the division, Sampe actively designed for the Textile Design Studio. In 1944–45 she began an association with textile printer Eric Ljungberg (1907–1983). In 1947, Ljungberg established his own company, Ljungbergs Textiltryck, in Floda, Sweden, and printed many of the textiles designed by NK's artists. Today, his firm continues under the direction of his son Lars.

One of NK's most publicized textile collections under Sampe's leadership was *Signerad textil* (Signed textiles). It featured designs by such well-known architects as Sven Markelius and Alvar Aalto and designers Olle Bonnier, Stig Lindberg, and The Svedberg. Today, AB Nordiska Kompaniet flourishes and continues to hire its own designers for exclusive merchandise. It reestablished its interior design division, NK Inredning AB, as an independent company in 1986.

CCMT

Nuutajärvi-Notsjö Nuutajärvi is the oldest surviving Finnish glassworks.[190] It was founded by Captain Jakob Wilhelm De Pont under the Swedish name Notsjö in 1793 in the town of Urjala, near Helsinki. Early production centered around window and bottle glass. Filigree and pressed glass was produced from the middle of the nineteenth century. The company was purchased in 1853 by Adolf Törngren, who created a more modern facility. Before going bankrupt in 1866, Törngren made Nuutajärvi the leading glassworks in Finland. By the turn of the century, the company was transformed into a private concern.

Nuutajärvi-Notsjö emerged on the international scene after World War II. Seeking to improve the quality of its products, Erik Lindqvist, manager of the firm during World War II, secured the services of designer Gunnel Nyman. During her brief stay (1946–48), Nyman created straightforward designs for household glass and art glass, such as the *Serpentine* vase of 1947, which are strong and sculptural. She often combined heavy glass with controlled air bubbles and contrasting forms encased within.

In 1949 the firm was turned into a joint stock company. However, in 1950 a fire forced the sale of the company to the industrial concern of Oy Wärtsilä AB, which also owned the Arabia pottery. Nuutajärvi then underwent a period of complete modernization under its new managing director, Gunnar Stahle.

From 1950 to 1976, Kaj Franck served as designer and art director, in addition to his responsibilities at Arabia (1945–60). The manufacture of bottle glass ceased, while household and art glass in colored glass was emphasized. Franck is noted primarily as a designer of markedly restrained, practical designs. A series of glass pitchers (1954) and double decanters (1958) artfully combine highly functional shapes with a wide array of colors. However, Franck also created art pieces such as *Soap Bubble*, *Fish*, and *Woodcock* of the early 1950s. Two years after Franck's arrival he was joined by Saara Hopea-Untracht, with whom he shared a close and sympathetic working relationship until her departure for the United States in 1960. Some of Franck's later works, such as his plaques with concentric rings of color (1965) and his bubbled glass vessels (1970), suggest a changed, less elegant and less subtle sense of form.

Oiva Toikka became the artistic director in 1963. His work, characterized by a certain exuberance and a Pop-inspired aesthetic, ranges from designs for mass production that are obviously derived from nature, such as the tableware patterns *Dewdrop* (1964) and *Peony* (1976), to the colorful and sculptural art ware *Lollipop Isle* (1969), which encases an assemblage of polychromatic objects within clear cubes. Current artists include Heikki Orvola, who uses colored and lustered glass; Kerttu Nurminen, who, along with Orvola, experiments with filigree techniques; and Markku Salo, who uses sandblasting to achieve a variety of surface patterning and specializes in enclosing the glass in wire frames.

In 1988 the company was merged with the Iittala glassworks to form Iittala-Nuutajärvi Oy.

GS

Nylund, Gunnar Born Paris, May 1, 1904

Throughout his long career, Gunnar Nylund designed both ceramics and glass for various Scandinavian companies, though he is best known as a ceramist at Rörstrand in Sweden.[191] Trained as an architect in Copenhagen (1923–25), he was influenced both by his father, the Finnish sculptor Felix Nylund, and his mother, a Danish ceramist. After working as a ceramist at Bing & Grøndahl from 1926 to 1928, he founded the short-lived (1929–30) stoneware workshop Nylund & Krebs Keramiske Vaerksted in Denmark with Nathalie Krebs, who subsequently established the Saxbo works. His work from this period exhibits a functionalist approach.

Nylund joined Rörstrand in 1930. Except for a brief hiatus during 1937 and 1938 when he was artistic director of Bing & Grøndahl, he was one of Rörstrand's leading designers until 1959. There Nylund worked primarily in richly glazed stoneware, though particularly in the 1930s he also favored chamotte ware with a rich, rough surface, and he designed more traditional dinnerware in porcelain. He employed a wide variety of styles, both historical and current. Some of his early stoneware vases resemble Chinese forms, but by the 1950s they were typically asymmetric, abstract pieces. Nylund is also noted for his stylized stoneware animal sculptures.

In addition to his work at Rörstrand, Nylund served as artistic director of the Strömbergshyttan glass factory, Sweden, from 1954 to 1957 and of the Nymølle Fajansfabrik, Nymølle, Denmark, from 1959 to 1963, after which he did free-lance design work for both Rörstrand and Strömbergshyttan. He established his own studio, Designia, in Malmö in 1971, concentrating on glass and working in metal as well; one of his metal commissions was a sculpture for the town square in Lidköping.

LN

Nyman, Gunnel Anita Gustafsson Born Turku, Finland, September 19, 1909; died Helsinki, October 7, 1948

Gunnel Nyman studied furniture design and interior decoration under Arttu Brummer at the Helsinki Taideteollinen Korkeakoulu (Central School of Industrial Design), from which she graduated in 1932.[192] Like her mentor, who was one of Finland's leading designers of glass between the wars, Nyman spent her career working in that industry. From 1930 until the end of her life (except for a brief period in 1932), she worked at Riihimäen Lasi. Her simple, geometric forms and interest in bubbled glass link her work closely with that of her teacher, Brummer. She concurrently held other positions. From 1932 until 1936 she designed lighting fixtures for Taito Oy, and from 1933 to 1937 she designed for Karhulan Lasitehdas. For Oy Boman she designed furniture (1936–38) whose heavy, curved forms typify Modernism just before the outbreak of war. Although not a well-known figure outside of Finland at that time, Nyman produced designs that received some attention abroad, most notably at the Paris Exposition of 1937, where she was awarded gold and silver medals.

Nyman enjoyed a brief moment of international prominence in the first years after World War II. While continuing to work at Riihimäki, she contributed designs to both the Nuutajärvi-Notsjö (1946–48) and Iittala (1946–47) factories. Her most celebrated works were in heavy crystal with twisted forms or were internally decorated with trapped air bubbles or colored filaments. She also designed furniture for Oy Idman (1946–48) with fluent forms that recall the innovations of Finn Juhl and other Scandinavian designers. By the time Nyman died at the age of thirty-nine, her work in glass was already of seminal importance, for many of her ideas continued to dominate Scandinavian glassmaking. Her interest in spiraling threads of color and bubbled glass was carried forward by many of the northern factories, and her predilection for natural forms, such as the calla lily and mussel shell, looked forward to many of the most important designs of her young countryman Tapio Wirkkala.

ME

Öhrström, Karl Edvin Born Burlöv, Sweden, August 22, 1906

Trained as a sculptor, Edvin Öhrström designed functional and decorative glass for AB Orrefors Glasbruk, where he worked from 1936 to 1957, and monumental public sculptures and windows as an independent artist.[193]

In Stockholm, Öhrström attended the Kungliga Tekniska Högskolen (Royal Institute of Technology) from 1925 to 1928 and then studied sculpture and graphics at the Kungliga Konsthögskolan (Royal Academy Art School) from 1928 to 1932. Until 1934 he pursued drawing studies in Paris at the Maison Wat-teau, the Académie Colarossi, and the Académie de l'Art Moderne under Fernand Léger.

During the two decades that Öhrström was associated with Orrefors, he worked on a part-time basis, two months a year. When he joined the staff in 1936, he advocated soft-edged forms. He introduced a technique for turning glass in a fluted wooden mold on a wheel, creating extremely thick-walled, hard-edged vessels with internal refractive rings. He created decorative designs to be engraved. Some of them with that typically Scandinavian Moderne classicism, such as *A Wish to the New Moon* (1942), are still in production. Öhrström is particularly noted for his ornamental vases in *Ariel* glass, a technique he helped develop in 1937 in which air bubbles trapped within several layers of clear and colored glass are manipulated to create decorative patterns. The reflective air pockets within the glass complement the solidity of Öhrström's forms. His first *Ariel* designs contained figural elements reminiscent of Léger and the Paris school, often in combination with abstract decorative passages. The early designs were exhibited to great acclaim at the Paris "Exposition Internationale des Arts et Techniques" in 1937 and the 1939 World's Fair in New York. A tendency toward zoomorphic forms in the manner of Joan Miró and Jean Arp became progressively more important in his postwar work. He also utilized the *Ariel* technique to produce geometric designs.

Throughout his career Öhrström has maintained a private studio, using technical help and space rented from the Lindshammer glassworks. Since leaving Orrefors in 1957, he has concentrated on sculpting in glass. The 120-foot-high glass and steel sculpture, *Vertical Accent* (1969), in Sergels Torg Square, Stockholm, is an impressive example of his public works.[194]

Öhrström's glass was the subject of an exhibition staged at the Malmö museum in 1968 and another, "Edvin Öhrström: Sculptural Designer at Orrefors 1936–57," held at the Orrefors Museum in 1987.

LN

Orfèvrerie Christofle Founded in 1830 by Joseph-Albert Bouilhet, a prominent Paris jeweler, and Charles Christofle, both Bouilhet's brother- and son-in-law, Société Orfèvrerie Christofle was the largest jewelry and silversmithing company in the French capital. In 1840 it made a decisive turn when it bought the patents to Henri de Ruolz's electroplating process. Later, before the midcentury, it established an agreement with the British firm of Elkington, whose patents proved superior. By midcentury, the firm became primarily identified with one product: electroplated silver.[195]

Because of its use of base metals, Christofle could produce opulent work at relatively moderate prices. On the other hand, it had the distinction of attracting distinguished clients: it furnished Napoleon III and Empress Eugénie with a huge service for the Tuileries palace and state railroad cars for Pope Pius IX, and it cast much of the sculpture that adorns the facade of Charles Garnier's Opéra in Paris. Christofle's ordinary wares might be relatively sober or, more often, elaborate, with historical or naturalistic decoration. In the 1880s, under the artistic direction of Émile Reiber, Christofle introduced the styles and techniques of the Near and Far East, including enameling and encrustations of colored metals. Another innovation was the electroplating of actual plants and animals. The sculptor Albert-Ernest Carrier-Belleuse provided Belle Époque–style sculpted models, and at the turn of the century Christofle produced Art Nouveau designs, some by Alphonse Mucha. The firm exhibited its tour-de-force creations at every major national and international exhibition and, from the gold medal it obtained at the London World's Fair of 1851 on, was frequently rewarded. Christofle had stores in many of the major European capitals and conducted a thriving business in the Near East and South America.

By the 1920s Christofle had assumed the tenets of the new decorative style: simplified geometric volumes and a restrained, modernistic classicism. Among its designers of this period were Luc Lanel, the team of Louis Süe and André Mare, Paul Follot, and the Dane Christian Fjerdingstad. Its pavilion at the 1925 "Exposition Internationale des Arts Décoratifs et Industriels Modernes," shared with Baccarat, was frequently cited with praise. Christofle expanded even further, opening subsidiary plants in Argentina, Switzerland, and Italy. One of its most famous commissions was the metalware for the SS *Normandie*.

Just before World War II, Christofle offered Gio Ponti's famous candlesticks of crossed horns and, after the war, his flatware. In the mid-1940s Christofle briefly experimented with pictorial designs by artists, including Marie Laurencin, Jean Cocteau, and Henry de Waroquier. In the early 1950s it produced some of Tapio Wirkkala's designs. A more concerted drive to establish a modern idiom was its creation of *Formes Nouvelles*, a line directed by Lino Sabattini at its Milan operation.

After one hundred and fifty years, the firm had grown to become the largest exporter of silverware worldwide. Despite the changes in style and the creation of new stores and factories, the firm (which became a joint stock company in 1930) is still controlled by members of the founding Bouilhet family. And its past history is inevitably linked with its present production: the flatware pattern *Baguette*, which it first introduced in 1861, is still in production and is reputedly the most commonly used in Europe. It recently reintroduced its SS *Normandie* accessories, and in 1987 it initiated a line of jewelry, thus returning to the firm's original craft.

ME

Orrefors Glasbruk AB The internationally celebrated glassworks of Orrefors is situated in the forested Swedish province of Småland. Founded as an ironworks in 1726, the company began producing bottle glass only in 1898.[196] After Johan Ekman bought the company in 1913 he recruited master glassblowers Gustav and Knut Bergqvist and other skilled technicians and began the production of cameo glass. However, it was the arrival of painters Simon Gate in 1916 and Edward Hald in 1917 that marked the emergence of Orrefors as an internationally significant artistic force. Soon after their arrival, the *Graal* technique was invented. An extension of the cameo process in which the cut design is reheated, cased, and blown further, it encouraged an expressionist tendency, and Gate and Hald employed it with great success. Their superb designs for engraved crystal, which combined Moderne abstraction with classicism, also catapulted Orrefors into international prominence. At the influential Paris "Exposition Internationale des Arts Décoratifs et Industriels Modernes" of 1925, Orrefors's elaborately engraved bravura pieces captivated critics.

In 1933 Hald assumed the reins of managing director, a position he retained until 1944. Keeping pace with stylistic changes, the glass became heavier. In some instances, the decoration was sparse, and the inherent refractive properties of the material were emphasized. In 1937 Edvin Öhrström, Vicke Lindstrand, and Gustav Bergqvist developed the *Ariel* technique, an extension of the cased *Graal* work in which air bubbles form a major element of the design.

Helped by the neutrality of Sweden during World War II, Orrefors maintained its tradition of artistic excellence and innovation. It continued to produce elaborately engraved glass and intricately worked *Graal* glass. While the style of the 1930s was retained for some of its older engraved models, most of the glasshouse's work was in a fluent, abstract postwar idiom. It also produced classicly simple forms that were light, softly contoured, and had minimal, if any, ornamentation. Nils Landberg, for example, created elongated, delicate shapes, as in his *Tulip* series, and Ingeborg Lundin, who specialized in pure forms, created *Apple*. The company and its artists were recipients of numerous prestigious awards. At the 1957 Milan Triennale, for example, these two artists were awarded gold medals, while Sven Palmquist received a grand prix for his *Fuga* bowls, made by spinning molten glass on an iron mold.

During the 1960s, the dynamic designs of Gunnar Cyrén, such as the heavy *Pop* goblets of 1966 with brightly colored opaque stems, injected a contemporary look into the firm's production. The late 1960s and the 1970s were yet another period of change. Recent designers include Eva England, known for her painterly renditions of *Graal* glass, and Olle Alberius, who also has worked with traditional Orrefors techniques. Newer artists are moving away from traditional functional shapes to more purely sculptural pieces. In 1988 Orrefors began producing an art glass collection of signed, limited-edition pieces.

Over the years Orrefors's designers, given a great amount of artistic autonomy, have excelled equally at the production of art and household glass. The company's plant at Sandvik (purchased in 1918) specializes in affordable, utilitarian glassware; a lighting division there was for many years under the direction of lighting designer Carl Fagerlund. A school in glassmaking techniques is maintained by the firm, and in 1957 the Orrefors Museum, designed by Bengt Gate (Simon's son), was established. In the 1970s Orrefors purchased the Alsterfors, Flygsfors, and Strömbergshyttan glasshouses, but by 1980 these subsidiaries were defunct.

LN

Panton, Verner Born Gamtofte, Denmark, February 13, 1926

As one of the most versatile contemporary industrial designers, Danish architect Verner Panton has created a broad range of products, including furniture, lighting, and textiles.[197]

Panton studied at the Ingeniør hojskolen, Odense Teknikum (Odense Technical School, 1944–47) and at the Kongelige Danske Kunstakademi (Royal Danish Academy of Fine Arts), Copenhagen (1947–51), before working as an associate with Arne Jacobsen (1950–52). In 1955, he established his own architectural and design office, based first in Denmark (1955–62), then France (1962), and finally in Binningen, Switzerland (1963 to the present).

Recognized particularly for his chairs, Panton has persistently explored the idea of the single-piece seating unit. While Panton's one-piece molded plastic stacking chair (1960) remains his most significant contribution to twentieth-century design, his cone chair (1958), with its frame of stainless steel wire, is another imaginative creation. Panton has consistently been recognized for his skillful exploitation of advances in technology and materials and for his unconventional use of form and color. Representative of his work for the lighting firm Louis Poulsen is the colorful, enameled-metal *Flower Pot* series (1968). In contrast to his fluid designs for other mediums, Panton's textiles are predominantly geometric, as, for example, the Victor Vasarely–inspired *Geometry I* for Unika-Vaev (1960).

In addition to his product designs, Panton's work includes numerous public interiors and the exhibition ships *Visiona I* and *II* for Bayer Chemical (Cologne, 1968 and 1970). Among his more noteworthy architectural commissions are the Cardboard house (Fyn, 1957) and the Spherical house (Copenhagen, 1960).

The recipient of many design prizes, including the International Design Award given by the American Institute of Decorators (1963, 1968, 1981), Panton's work was exhibited at the Musée des Arts Décoratifs, Paris, in 1969.

LN

Pardon, Earl Born Memphis, Tennessee, September 6, 1926, died Saratoga Springs, New York, May 4, 1991

Earl Pardon's most significant contribution has undoubtedly been made in the fields of studio jewelry and enameling, although throughout his forty-year career he has constantly worked as a painter and sculptor as well.

Pardon received a bachelor of fine arts in painting in 1951 from Memphis Academy of Art, where he also began his study of jewelry. He earned a master of fine arts, also in painting, from Syracuse University in 1959. The greatest influences on his art have come from Paul Cézanne, Pablo Picasso, and Oriental Zen painters.

In 1951 Pardon began teaching enameling and jewelry making at Skidmore College in Saratoga Springs, New York, where today he is a professor of art, having served a period as chairman of the art department from 1968 to 1977. Pardon's jewelry is characterized by an emphasis on color, which he achieved through the use of free-form enamel shapes in the 1950s and 1960s, colored stone, bead, and metal assemblages in the 1970s, and combined abalone shell and riveted enamel plaques in the 1980s.

Pardon took a one-year leave of absence from Skidmore in 1954 to become assistant director of design at Towle Silversmiths in Newburyport, Massachusetts. While there he designed flatware and hollowware, introducing enameling into Towle's line. His *Contempora House* flatware pattern was decorated with enamel buttons.

In 1959 Pardon was commissioned by the Museum of Contemporary Crafts in New York to execute a wall sculpture for its exhibition "Enamels," which traced the history of that medium, and in 1960 he created a sculptural screen made of brass, copper, bronze, and nickel for the corporate headquarters of the Prudential Life Insurance Co. in Newark, New Jersey.

Pardon has participated in numerous group and solo exhibitions, mostly in the United States, including a retrospective exhibition at the Art Gallery of Skidmore College in 1980.[198]

TLW

Picasso, Pablo Ruiz y Born Málaga, October 25, 1881; died Cannes, April 8, 1973

Pablo Picasso holds the distinction of being widely regarded as the single most important artist of the first half of the twentieth century—and, some would argue, of the entire century.[199] His career, with the various phases through which his art evolved, suggests the restless history of twentieth-century art itself.

Picasso's first training was with his father, a drawing teacher, and he then pursued formal studies in Barcelona. Alternating between Paris and Barcelona from 1900 to 1904, he settled in the French capital by 1904. After a series of tentative experiments in various styles, he entered his Blue and Rose periods (1901–6), which emphasized expressiveness and drawing. Beginning in 1907 he became engrossed with the work of Paul Cézanne and African art, and made major breakthroughs with his colleague Georges Braque in creating Analytic and Synthetic Cubism and introducing the collage technique.

After World War I Picasso entered a momentary classicizing phase, but this was soon succeeded in the 1920s by the resurgence of an expressive idiom. He was often allied with the Surrealists, but he did not abandon many of his Cubist inventions. These diverse elements were fused with a dynamic power and expressive draftsmanship. From the *Guernica* of 1937, an acknowledged masterpiece of this century, to his later variations in the 1950s on Eugène Delacroix's *Women of Algeria* and Diego Velázquez's *Las Meninas*, Picasso's art remained dynamic and idiosyncratic—and much praised, often debated, and frequently imitated.

Though he remained in Paris during the German occupation during World War II, Picasso moved to the south of France immediately thereafter, settling first in Antibes (1946), then at Vallauris (1947), and finally in Cannes (1955). By the time of his death, he was a venerated old master of modern painting, his art and his life well known to an admiring public.

A protean creator, Picasso excelled in many mediums. His etchings, lithographs, and linocuts are major contributions to the history of the print. His hundreds of posters are, likewise, a notable achievement. Picasso put his hand to sculpture, creating an important body of works in the middle of his career and an equally important series of flat and folded metal sculpture in the 1960s. His stage sets and costumes in the late 1910s and 1920s, such as those for the Jean Cocteau-Erik Satie-Sergei Diaghilev ballet *Parade*, were major artistic statements.

Even if Picasso had not been involved with traditional categories of the decorative arts, his influence would be adjudged profound, since the sheer power of his pictorial imagery swayed many midcentury textile designers, potters, glassmakers, and jewelers. Actually, Picasso was involved with the decorative arts in the latter part of his career, after World War II. Undoubtedly the most important undertaking was his work in ceramics. A chance encounter with Suzanne and Georges Ramié at the Potterie Madoura in 1946 led the following year to an intense involvement that extended over the next two-and-a-half decades, during which time Picasso created over two thousand examples, some unique, most put into serial production. These works, at least at first, had a revolutionary impact.

Picasso also tried his hand at glass, creating models to be executed in Murano as part of entrepreneur Egidio Constantini's *Fucina degli angeli* project, supported by Peggy Guggenheim, in the early 1950s. Also not immune to Picasso's inquiry was the world of jewelry. A visit to a dentist in 1952 sparked his interest in gold and dental equipment; this chance encounter resulted in a single pendant. Then, starting in 1956, he made nineteen designs that he commissioned French goldsmith François Hugo to execute as silver platters and gold medallions. They were produced in a small edition but were not released until 1967.

Picasso was involved in a number of other projects in the decorative arts. In the 1950s, for example, some fifty of his paintings were transformed into Jean Crotti's and Roger Malherbe's *Gemmaux* glass mosaics. Picasso's designs were occasionally translated into textiles, rugs, and tapestries. The abundance of these projects, some authorized, some not, have created an unfavorable aura about Picasso's general relation with the decorative arts. When he was directly involved, as in the case of ceramics, the collaboration proved fruitful and influential. The further removed the artist was, the more uninspired the results were, and the more clouded the issue has become.

ME

Polaroid Corporation The Polaroid Corporation was formed in 1937 to acquire the assets of Edwin Land's and George Wheelwright III's interests in the field of light polarization and to develop this field technically and commercially.[200] Early applications of

light polarizers included microscopes, polariscopes, and camera filters. Sunglass lenses, nonglare automobile headlights, and desk lamps were among the company's first products on the commercial market. Throughout its history Polaroid, based in Cambridge, Massachusetts, has been associated with distinguished designers and artists such as Walter Dorwin Teague, Charles Eames, and Ansel Adams.

Fusing polarizers with photography, Polaroid developed the Vectograph technique for three-dimensional pictures in 1940. It was used extensively for aerial reconnaissance surveys during World War II. Polarizing filters and nonpolarizing colored filters for use in gunsights, periscopes, and binoculars were among the many specialized applications produced for the war effort.

In 1944 Polaroid began researching a one-step photographic system, which resulted in the model no. 95 camera (1948), the first of its kind. Over the next decades Polaroid continued its development of instant-photography products, offering increasingly lower-priced cameras with greater technical competence.

In more recent years, the company entered the sonar and fiber optics industries and since 1984 has offered video and personal computer products. Polaroid became the largest software duplicator in the world with the formation in 1987 of a new subsidiary called Media Duplication Services Ltd.

MOR

Pomodoro, Giorgio (Giò) Born Onciano di Pesaro, Italy, November 17, 1930

Giò Pomodoro, most famous for his sensual metal sculptural reliefs, also created an expressive body of jewelry by his own hand—a rare accomplishment among most so-called artist-jewelers, who usually leave the craftsmanship to others. He viewed jewelry as miniature sculpture, replete with all the qualities of important monumental work.

Originally trained as a painter and graphic artist, Pomodoro began in 1950 to fabricate small silver reliefs and jewelry. He was inspired by Surrealist art, and his philosophical sympathies ran to Franz Kafka, Ezra Pound, Guillaume Apollinaire, and the poetry of Paul Éluard and W. H. Auden. In 1952–53 he lived in Florence, where he was exposed to Action Painting at the Galleria Numero. He began to execute assemblages of iron and stone and automatic drawings. In 1954 he went to Milan, where he was active in an art group linked to the French movement Tachisme.[201] That same year he exhibited his sculpture for the first time in a solo show at Galleria Numero and showed jewelry at the Milan X Triennale.

At the Venice Biennale in 1956, Pomodoro first saw the work of Jackson Pollock, whose Abstract Expressionist paintings, along with those of Franz Kline, had a lasting effect on him. He began to create assemblage sculptures out of different materials—wood, textiles, paper, bits of trees, plaster—as well as negative reliefs in clay that were preoccupied with growth, multiplication, and gesture.[202] These led to rounded, cast-bronze sculptural reliefs, whose surfaces undulated organically with light and shadow.

Pomodoro's work in jewelry, begun before his sculpture, greatly influenced his larger work.[203] Created mostly for the Marlborough Galleria d'Arte, Rome, and private commissions, it was inspired by Mediterranean cultures and by Byzantine, medieval, and Renaissance jewelry. Then, as now, it paralleled the main elements in his sculptural reliefs; for example, the tension between figure and ground was explored by the contrast of red and white gold, precious and semi-precious stones, and the opposition of smooth and roughened textures.

In 1959 Pomodoro won the prize for sculpture at the Paris Biennale and, in 1962, the Bright Prize for sculpture at the Venice Biennale. In the early 1960s, he and his brother, Arnaldo, encouraged several leading painters, sculptors, and architects to design jewelry, much of it eventually made at the GEM Montebello Laboratory in Milan, a jewelry workshop begun in 1967 by their brother-in-law Gian Carlo Montebello.

TLW

Ponti, Giovanni (Gio) Born Milan, November 18, 1891; died Milan, September 15, 1979

Gio Ponti was one of the most important Italian architects and designers of the century. In addition, he was an extremely influential spokesman for the Modernist cause, both as a writer and as a professor on the architecture faculty at the Milan Politecnico from 1936 to 1961.[204]

After serving in the Italian army in World War I, Ponti received his diploma in architecture from the Politecnico in 1921. From 1923 to 1930 he designed ceramics for Richard Ginori, where his father-in-law worked.[205] His decorations were lighthearted, tinged with classicizing and Surrealist elements. This blend of the traditional and modern was typical of much of his work.

In 1928 Ponti founded the magazine Domus, one of the most important and widely read international magazines of design; he served as its editor until 1941 and again from 1948 until his death in 1979. He also wrote several books on architecture.[206] He directed the second, third, and fourth Biennale Exhibitions of Decorative Arts at Monza and then in 1933 helped move the exhibition to Milan in order to enlarge it. The Milan Triennale became the primary international showcase for modern design in the decades after World War II.

In 1952 Ponti joined with Antonio Fornaroli and Alberto Rosselli to form an architectural firm, Studio Ponti-Fornaroli-Rosselli, which was active until 1976. Their best-known work is the Pirelli building (1956) in Milan, designed with Pier Luigi Nervi and Arturo Danusso as engineering consultants; in this structure, Ponti moved away from the anonymous block of the Miesian skyscraper by tapering its ends and defining the roof. Ponti's last major building was the Denver Art Museum of 1972, designed with James Sudler.

Ponti was in the forefront of the postwar Italian design revival. He designed a wide variety of objects with sleek, curving lines: an espresso machine for La Pavoni in 1949, plumbing for Ideal Standard and stainless steel flatware for Krupp in the 1940s and 1950s, and brightly colored glassware for Venini in the 1940s and 1950s. He also designed interiors for Italian ships, including the ill-fated SS Andrea Doria. Some of Ponti's most important furniture was designed for Cassina, Knoll, Arflex, and Tecno in the 1950s and 1960s. His furniture designs tend to be light, with elegant, spare lines and tapering legs. As in his Leggera chair, Ponti created a modern style by using traditional elements in a new way. Around 1950 he collaborated with Piero Fornasetti, who supplied elaborate decorations for Ponti's interiors and furniture.

CWL

Portanier, Gilbert Born Cannes, September 28, 1926

Like many ceramists, Portanier started out as a painter.[207] As a child, he was spared some of the upheaval of World War II because his father, a Provençal magistrate, held posts in the Midi and Monaco. In 1945, after the young Portanier finished his secondary education, he set off for Paris and the École des Beaux-Arts to study painting and—to satisfy his father—architecture. In the French capital he became associated with the Surrealist circle of André Breton and François Picabia, as well as with Pablo Picasso, Ossip Zadkine, and Jean-Paul Sartre. Because his mother was Belgian, he spent a brief period in 1947 in Brussels, where he met René Magritte and Pierre Alechinsky, among others, and had his first solo exhibition of his paintings.

Portanier's career took a major turn during a 1948 vacation on the Côte d'Azur. After visiting Picasso in Vallauris, he and two friends became so interested in ceramics that they decided to stay and learn the medium. They opened a studio, Le Triptyque, and, while the others eventually moved on, Portanier remained. By 1953 he had begun to establish his reputation as a potter. He received a silver medal at the Brussels World's Fair of 1958, showed some eighty pieces alongside the ceramic work of Picasso and Fernand Léger at the Hamburg Museum für Kunst und Gewerbe, and moved into the Vallauris pottery where he still works today, fittingly, on the Rue des Potiers (Potters' Street).

Picasso's influence marked much of Portanier's work from the 1950s and 1960s, showing mainly in the style of Portanier's draftmanship, but he did not outrightly imitate Picasso's ceramics. In the mid-1960s Portanier began working in ceramic sculpture as well. He developed a series of enamels for use on pottery, and he experimented briefly with limited editions. In recent years his painting style has become more expressionistic and through the 1980s he has focused on thematic concerns, like masks, music, chess, and conversation.

Portanier has won many awards throughout his career, such as grand prizes at the Faenza international ceramics exhibition (1966) and the Vallauris Biennale (1982). He has exhibited widely throughout France, elsewhere in Europe, and in the United States, but his greatest audience has been in Germany. Accordingly, it was the Hamburg Museum für Kunst und Gewerbe that gave him a major retrospective in 1985.

ME

Potterie Madoura Madoura is the pseudonym used by French potter Suzanne Ramié (born 1905). She studied at the École des Beaux-Arts in Lyons and then traveled to Vallauris in 1936 to study ceramics at the Atelier du Plan. After the war, she and her husband, Georges, established the Atelier de Vallauris, which traded under the name Madoura. There she made rustic earthenware, some in traditional local styles. She produced unique pieces and limited editions, which included fountains, lamps, wall panels, and furniture plaques.

The Madoura pottery achieved international renown through its association with Pablo Picasso. In 1946 Picasso visited an exhibition of Vallauris potters organized by Madoura. Invited to the studio, he made a few objects, which he left to be fired. He returned the following summer and then began working with ceramics in earnest. At times he used the traditional shapes furnished by Madoura; at other times he manipulated them to create more unorthodox forms. Picasso's inventions were occasionally presented as unique objects, but more often were produced in limited or unlimited series, the Madoura staff cleverly imitating Picasso's manner. By 1948 Picasso had established himself in a villa in the hills outside Vallauris to which he returned periodically until 1955, when he moved to Cannes. However, he still continued to make pottery, sending the pieces to Madoura for firing.

GS

Poulsen, Louis see Louis Poulsen & Co. A/S

Pratt, Davis J. Born Marion, Indiana, June 27, 1917; died Gainesville, Florida, January 20, 1987

A writer, teacher, and designer, Davis Pratt studied at the University of Chicago and László Moholy-Nagy's

School of Design in Chicago prior to serving in the armed forces during World War II.[208] In 1951 and 1952, Pratt designed school equipment for the Welsh Manufacturing Company in Chicago. Later, with Harold Cohen, he cofounded Designers in Production, a Chicago-based firm that designed and manufactured chairs, tables, storage furniture, and other household furnishings.

In 1948, while an instructor in product design at the (renamed) Institute of Design, Pratt designed a chair made with an inflatable inner tube, which was a co-winner of the second prize for seating with Charles and Ray Eames' entry in the Museum of Modern Art's "International Competition for Low-Cost Furniture Design" in 1948. Pratt's dissatisfaction with the complexity of spring-and-pad upholstery and his striving for low-cost, portable forms later led to designs of spun-nylon tubular covers over steel frames for lounge chairs and other household furniture. Many of these designs were commercially produced by Designers in Production during its operation from 1952 to 1957. Beginning in 1957, Pratt lectured in design at the University of Southern Illinois at Carbondale and conducted design research projects, notably one on Japanese design education in 1964.

MOR

Prestini, James Born Waterford, Connecticut, January 13, 1908

Prestini's interest in crafts derived from his childhood experiences of making utilitarian objects under the supervision of his father, a skilled stonecutter and craftsman. In 1930, he received a degree in mechanical engineering from Yale University's Sheffield Scientific School; in 1932 he graduated from Yale's School of Education. While teaching mathematics at Lake Forest Academy in Lake Forest, Illinois, from 1933 to 1942, Prestini began making the subtle, lathe-turned wooden bowls that he continued to create until 1953.

In 1938 Prestini served an internship at the University of Stockholm, where he worked with Carl Malmsten as an apprentice furniture designer and craftsman. Then, inspired by László Moholy-Nagy's book *The New Vision*, in 1939 he enrolled in the Chicago School of Design, where he also held a position as instructor of design, from 1939 to 1946. In the Bauhaus tradition, Prestini, as craftsman, and Moholy-Nagy, as artist, taught the foundation course together. Prestini taught again from 1952 to 1953, when Serge Chermayeff was director.

From 1943 to 1953 Prestini worked as a research engineer at the Armour Research Foundation at the Illinois Institute of Technology in Chicago. Receiving a grant from the Museum of Modern Art, New York, for the "International Competition for Low-Cost Furniture Design" in 1948, Prestini, in collaboration with Robert Lewis and the Armour Research Foundation, prepared an innovative design for a molded, one-piece lounge chair made of resin-impregnated wood fiber. This experimental chair, suggested in part by Ludwig Mies van der Rohe's sketches for conchoidal-form chairs, was not put into production, but the team won the special $2,500 prize for the best research report.[209]

In 1950 an exhibition of Prestini's work in wood was held at the Museum of Modern Art, and a monograph was published, gaining the artist public recognition.[210] In 1953 he helped to organize Knoll International, Italy, and, while abroad from 1953 to 1956, he experimented with bent plywood to make bowls approached as pure form in wood rather than as functional objects. These led to sculptural works made from elements of standard structural steel.[211]

Represented in numerous museums and private collections, Prestini's work in wood is highly regarded and has influenced other American artisans in wood. His wood objects and steel sculptures have been awarded

prestigious prizes, including the Diploma d'Onore at the Milan X Triennale (1954) and the Diploma di Collaborazione at the XV Triennale, a Ford Foundation fellowship in 1962–63, and a Guggenheim fellowship in 1972–73. Since 1956 he has disseminated his principles of craft as a basis for design at the University of California, Berkeley, in the Department of Architecture's Design Laboratory, which he created.

DAH

Price, Edison see Edison Price, Inc.

Prouvé, Jean Born Paris, April 8, 1901; died Nancy, France, March 22, 1984

Flexibility by means of changeable prefabricated elements was the hallmark of French architect Jean Prouvé's work. His many innovative public and private buildings and furniture designs were executed in the most technically advanced twentieth-century materials, generally metal. His style, embodying an engineer's approach to design, remained consistently geometric and functional throughout his career.

At the turn of the century, his father, painter and engraver Victor Prouvé, was one of the leaders of the craft-oriented School of Nancy, as was Jean's godfather, Émile Gallé. Jean, however, preferred machinery to craft, yet when his proposed career in engineering was interrupted by World War I, he became an iron craftsman, one of Nancy's specialties, opening his own studio in 1923. He also taught ironworking at Nancy's École Supérieure. One of his early commissions (1925) was for avant-garde lighting fixtures, grilles, and storefronts for the architect Robert Mallet-Stevens.

Ateliers Jean Prouvé, founded in 1931, became known for its architectural innovations. For the Buc Air-Club near Versailles, Prouvé designed the first curtain wall (1936), an external nonsupporting wall of prefabricated modules. His radically functional approach to architecture was applied to postwar mass-housing projects. In 1944 he opened an experimental factory at Maxéville, near Nancy, where he also executed furniture designs. He began a period of collaboration with Le Corbusier, Pierre Jeanneret, and Charlotte Perriand on a variety of design projects, including prefabricated postwar housing in Marseilles and the staircases and kitchens of the Cité Radieuse.

Prouvé designed furniture from 1924 on and found "no difference between the building of furniture and the building of a house; materials, calculations, and sketches are exactly the same."[212] His prewar furniture was industrial in appearance, having a pared-down, mechanical orientation. In 1954 Prouvé left the Maxéville factory and began to work in Paris. Two years later he founded Les Constructions to continue the execution of his furniture. Designed for mass production, Prouvé's postwar furniture had sleek, Moderne lines and a more aesthetic appeal than his earlier work. It was represented by Galerie Steph Simon of Paris from 1947 to 1963.

Prouvé's later architectural collaborations include Paris's UNESCO Building, the Paris Communist Party Headquarters, the Perrache train station in Lyons, and the Forum des Halles in Paris. His awards include the Auguste Perret Prize of the International Union of Architects (1963) and a first prize in architecture awarded by the City of Paris (1982). Prouvé served as president of the jury of the Centre Pompidou, Paris. He was given a retrospective exhibition of his architectural and engineering designs at the Institut Français d'Architecture in 1983.[213]

FTH

Puiforcat, Jean Born Paris, August 5, 1897; died Paris, October 20, 1945

Jean Puiforcat's obsession with "divine" proportions,

his adherence to Modernism, and his use of weighty silver, often in combination with other rich materials, set a standard for French luxury goods between the two world wars.[214]

Born into a silversmithing dynasty, Puiforcat eventually surpassed the tradition of luxury items that his father, Louis-Victor, had initiated around 1900. Jean began an apprenticeship in the family business after his return from World War I, at the age of seventeen. Passionately interested in sculpture and a devout admirer of Aristide Maillol, he studied with Louis-Aimé LeJeune, learning to master volume and to design in abstract forms. His contributions to the 1925 Paris exposition epitomized the trend toward purity of form and unadorned surfaces.

In 1929, Puiforcat, along with Gérard Sandoz, Raymond Templier, Jean Fouquet, Nicolas and Jean Luce, Le Corbusier, Charlotte Perriand, Pierre Jeanneret, and others, founded the Union des Artistes Modernes, whose first exhibition took place in the spring of 1930 and whose work emphasized an economy of line and plain surfaces. The UAM's guiding principle was that form should derive from function. The aesthetic high point of Puiforcat's career came in 1937, at the "Exposition Internationale des Arts et Techniques," where an entire pavilion was devoted to both his secular and liturgical work, which was mostly based on circular forms and the golden section.

Deploring the rise of Fascism in Europe, Puiforcat and his Cuban wife, Marta (née Estevez), sailed for Cuba, where they remained for six months. However, they settled in Mexico because of its silver mines and opulent natural vegetation; these, and the indigenous Aztec motifs, were to influence his ensuing output. In 1942 he opened a silversmithy in Mexico. Most of the work was exported to the United States, where it was sold exclusively through John Rubel.

Horrified by the breakdown of European civilization, Puiforcat decided to remain permanently in Mexico, even after World War II ended. However, he became ill on a voyage to France to settle some business affairs and died two days after his arrival in Paris.

TLW

Quistgaard, Jens Harald Born Copenhagen, April 23, 1919

One of Scandinavia's best-known designers in the decorative arts, Jens Quistgaard is most noted for transposing the standards and appearance of traditional crafts to mass-produced design, notably for Dansk International Designs, Ltd.[215]

Wood carving was one of the first craft disciplines Quistgaard learned, probably from his sculptor father, Harald Quistgaard, who was a professor of sculpture at Copenhagen's Kongelige Danske Kunstakademi.

Jens Quistgaard apprenticed at the Georg Jensen Silversmithy, and after the war he became a free-lance designer. The multidisciplined Quistgaard has turned his hand from wood and glass to cast-iron cookware and stainless steel flatware as well as stoneware. His work, rooted in the organic and traditional crafts of Denmark, has been inspired by Viking ship hulls, wagons, carts, and peasant pottery.

Quistgaard began his design career with Dansk in 1954, working with American entrepreneur Ted Nierenberg, and for thirty years he was its leading—often the only—designer. His *Fjord* steel and teak flatware, teak bowls and ice buckets, and enameled steel *Kobenstyle* cookware for Dansk typify the clean-line elegance of his designs. Quistgaard won the Lunning Prize in 1954, the fiftieth anniversary competition for the Georg Jensen Silversmithy, and the Scandinavian Award and is a six-time winner at the Milan Triennales.

Quistgaard presently maintains a studio in Copenhagen's old section and an eighteenth-century farmhouse on the southern Danish coast. His designs for various European and American companies still encompass a diverse range of products: jewelry, cast-iron stoves, furniture, and architecture.

FTH

Race, Ernest Born Newcastle-upon-Tyne, England, October 16, 1913; died London, January 22, 1964

Ernest Race is one of the few twentieth-century British designers to achieve international recognition.[216] Throughout his career he remained committed to using novel materials and innovative construction techniques, although he maintained a degree of conservatism in the forms of his furniture.

After attending St. Paul's School in London, Race trained as an interior designer from 1932 to 1935 at the Bartlett School of Architecture, London University, and then worked as a draftsman from 1936 to 1937 for Troughton and Young, manufacturers of lighting fixtures. From 1937 to 1939, after a trip to India, he operated a shop in London that marketed textiles of his own design that were handwoven in India, as well as some modern English furniture.

Race's professional career as a furniture designer began in 1945, when he entered into partnership with J. W. Noel Jordan to form Ernest Race Ltd.[217] Due to the postwar shortage of wood, the firm's early productions employed alternative materials, like metal; noteworthy are Race's cast-aluminum *BA3* chair (1946) and his steel-rod designs, especially the *Springbok* and *Antelope* chairs, designed for the Festival of Britain in 1951. During the 1950s, when the firm was particularly active in the contract furniture market, Race turned to plywood. His ingeniously foldable and stackable *Neptune* deck chair for the Orient Line (1953), made with only two molds, exemplifies Race's lifelong devotion to the solution of design problems.

In 1961 the company changed its name to Race Furniture Ltd., but Race resigned in 1962.[218] Afterward he served as consultant designer to Cintique and Isokon Furniture Company. Among Race's numerous distinctions were his election as Royal Designer for Industry (1953), and gold and silver medals at the 1954 Milan X Triennale.

LN

Rand, Paul Born New York, August 15, 1915

Paul Rand studied art at Pratt Institute, Parsons School of Design, and later (1939) at the Art Students League with the newly arrived German painter George Grosz. At the same time, he began his career in commercial art. From 1932 to 1934 he worked for the studio of New York industrial designer George Switzer. By 1938, at the age of twenty-three, he was art director of *Esquire-Coronet* and *Apparel Arts*, where he revolutionized magazine illustration with a fresh approach. By applying the aesthetic principles of the Bauhaus and avant-garde European art, Rand regenerated American advertising art by the late 1930s.

Rand then began his outstanding work in the field of corporate and product identification. An early example is his well-known adaptation of A. M. Cassandre's famous Dubonnet man for the firm's American advertising campaign, which began in 1941. Using humorous visual puns, always simple and with an unusual twist, Rand began to develop a language of symbols to create visual communication, which became the hallmark of his style. To stimulate interest further, he often employed collage and montage.

From 1941 to 1954 Rand was advertising art director for the large and prestigious Weintraub Agency in New York. He developed a tight, shorthand style of design that was specifically integrated with the copy, and this was widely adapted throughout the industry. Rand

stated, "To realize the production of modern advertising and industrial art in terms of functional-aesthetic perfection is to realize the oneness of art and living."[219] From the 1950s on, Rand was commissioned to design many corporate trademarks and promotional materials. His clients included IBM, Westinghouse, United Parcel Service, the American Broadcasting Company, and Cummins Engine.

A dedicated theoretician, Rand published his philosophy in many articles on the graphic arts. He further broadcast his ideas by teaching at Pratt Institute (1946), Cooper Union, the Advertising Guild, and, from 1956 on, at the Yale University School of Architecture. His many design awards attest to a national and international reputation, and he was elected to the Hall of Fame of the Art Directors Club, New York, in 1972.

His important personal art collection at his home in Weston, Connecticut, including folk art as well as works by Jean Arp, Paul Klee, Le Corbusier, Fernand Léger, and El Lissitsky, reflects some of the sources of influence on his art.

FTH

Raphael, Edwin see Edwin Raphael Company

Raymond Loewy Associates see Loewy, Raymond

Red Lion Furniture Company The Red Lion Furniture Company, founded by S. S. Sechrist in 1907, was the first such industry in Red Lion, Pennsylvania, a town some eight miles southeast of York,[220] although other furniture companies were soon established there.

The Red Lion Furniture Company specialized in the manufacture of bedroom and dining-room furniture. By 1913 the allied Red Lion Table Company, which also manufactured bedroom and dining-room suites and specialized in *Tu-way* tables, was established. In 1917 the Red Lion Cabinet Company was formed, though actual production did not begin until 1920. The plant of the Red Lion Furniture Company was expanded in 1919 and again in 1926, indications of an apparently thriving business. In response to the advent of radio in the early 1920s, a new plant devoted exclusively to the production of radio cabinets was built in 1930; its principal clients were companies such as Atwater Kent and Philco. In 1941 the Red Lion Furniture Company was selected by the Museum of Modern Art, New York, to produce Charles Eames and Eero Saarinen's prize-winning designs for modular furniture.

It would seem that after the upheavals of World War II, the company did not resume the manufacture of domestic furniture. By the late 1940s, the Red Lion Furniture Company was producing more than three thousand radio and television cabinets per day and employed twelve hundred workers. Except for the period from 1942 to 1945, when the company was engaged in defense production, it continued to produce radio and then television cabinets until 1959, when the plant was closed.

GS

Red Wing Potteries, Inc. This pottery, located in Red Wing, Minnesota, along the banks of the Mississippi, was established in 1878 under the name of Red Wing Stoneware Company.[221] It was a commercial company from its inception, producing utilitarian farm and domestic objects. Two brothers, John H. and H. S. Rich, reorganized the company in 1882. In 1894 it joined the Minnesota Stoneware Company and the North Star Stoneware Company to create the Union Stoneware Company to sell their products, leaving

their manufactories separate and independent. In 1906 the firm merged with the Minnesota Stoneware Company to form the Red Wing Union Stoneware Company. The new company also absorbed the North Star Stoneware Company.

E. S. Hoyt, who became manager of the Red Wing Stoneware Company in 1891, helped the firm overcome the dwindling farm market for stoneware during the 1920s. It began to make flower pots and produce a commercialized form of art pottery. In addition to various lines produced under Red Wing's own name, from about 1933 to 1938 it made art pottery for George Rumrill, an Arkansas distributor, which was sold under the name Rum Rill. Red Wing also began making dinnerware in the 1930s, including a multicolored *Gypsy Trail* line. In 1936 the firm changed its name from Red Wing Union Stoneware Company to Red Wing Potteries, Inc. By the 1940s, the importance of art pottery was subordinated to dinnerware, which became the company's staple. In 1947 the manufacture of all stoneware ceased.

In 1945, then-company president H. H. Varney asked industrial designer Eva Zeisel to create an informal dinnerware service, resulting in the *Town and Country* service, released commercially in 1947. Another industrial designer, Belle Kogan, also worked for Red Wing occasionally. However, the firm's dominant artist was Charles Murphy, who came to Red Wing from the ceramic center in East Liverpool, Ohio, and served as its chief designer from the 1940s through the 1960s.

Like many commercial American potteries in the postwar era, Red Wing faced serious competition from cheaper overseas rivals. Once a prosperous concern, it was run with ever-increasing losses from 1955 to 1958. Under R. A. Gilmer it tried diversification by producing new casual china in 1959 and in 1964 began manufacturing restaurant and hotel dinnerware. However, on June 1, 1967, the employees struck over wages. This, coupled with marginal profits and foreign competition, resulted in a decision by the shareholders to liquidate the company on August 24, 1967.

GS

Revere Copper and Brass Incorporated In 1801 American patriot-silversmith Paul Revere turned entrepreneur and founded the country's first copper-rolling mill in Canton, Massachusetts. He established a fledgling industry that expanded with the country's growth, due primarily to the burgeoning needs of the military and the ship-building industry. By the closing decades of the nineteenth century, inventions such as the telephone, electrical devices, and, later, the automobile opened new markets for copper goods. The Revere Copper Company merged in 1900 with the Taunton Copper Company and the New Bedford Copper Company to form the Taunton-New Bedford Copper Company. Further consolidation occurred in 1928, with the incorporation of this company with five others—the Baltimore Copper Mills, the Michigan Copper and Brass Company, the Dallas Brass and Copper Company, the Higgins Brass and Manufacturing Company, and the Rome Brass and Copper Company. In 1929 the new conglomerate became known as Revere Copper and Brass Incorporated.[222]

During the 1930s, Revere Copper and Brass pioneered a distinctive line of giftware, much of which was designed by America's leading industrial designers, such as Norman Bel Geddes, Frederick Priess, and Peter Müller-Munk.[223] Revere is also noted for its production of cooking utensils. Its most successful product line, copper-clad stainless steel *Revere Ware*, designed by W. Archibald Welden, was introduced to the public in 1939. It achieved instant success, and its classic design has remained relatively unchanged.

During World War II, the company's factories were converted to the war effort, but afterward Revere enjoyed a period of considerable expansion. One of its new plants, in Clinton, Illinois (established 1950), gradually became the company's centralized, then sole facility. It currently produces and distributes the full line of *Revere Ware*. In 1988, the Revere Ware Corporation was purchased by the Corning Glass Works, of which it is now a subsidiary.

LN

Richards Morgenthau & Company

Richards Morgenthau & Company, also known as Raymor, was the largest wholesale distributor of modern home accessories in the United States until the early 1980s, when the company was disbanded.[224] Founded in 1941 by Irving Richards, the New York–based firm evolved out of Russel Wright Accessories, with which Richards had been associated as business partner since 1935. Wright's *American Modern* dinnerware remained a staple of the company for many years, still accounting for approximately one-third of its business in 1954.

An enthusiastic supporter of good contemporary design and a pioneer in its promotion, Richards partially attributed the firm's accomplishments to the accurate targeting of the upper middle class, rather than the most affluent segment of American society, as a fertile market for contemporary design. In addition, Richards Morgenthau & Company maintained an informed, motivated sales force throughout the country that represented only Raymor's products.

Because of his knowledge of the field and his inherent sense of style, Richards succeeded in attracting to his firm the top names in contemporary design and marketing their goods successfully. Although initially he represented exclusively Russel Wright's wares, Richards soon branched out to include the work of major American designers in the 1940s: Gilbert Rohde, Paul Frankl, Donald Deskey, Walter Dorwin Teague, Charles and Ray Eames, Walter von Nessen, Henry Dreyfuss, Peter Müller-Munk, Eva Zeisel, George Nelson, and Paul McComb. In addition to distributing goods designed and manufactured elsewhere, Raymor sold lighting fixtures and decorative objects made in its own factory in Union City, New Jersey; from 1947 on, Irving Richards was responsible for designing much of the firm's production in ceramics and glassware.

During the 1950s and 1960s, when the company began importing and promoting an increasing proportion of foreign merchandise, Richards Morgenthau was a significant force in the dissemination of Scandinavian and Italian design. Although it originally concentrated on decorative objects, in the mid-1950s the company entered the furniture market. Richards traveled extensively and became acquainted with the major Continental designers. Consequently, Raymor represented the work of some of the best names in modern European design: Tapio Wirkkala, Arne Jacobsen, Finn Juhl, Hans Wegner, Ettore Sottsass, John Mascheroni, Aldo Londi, Paolo Venini, and Marcello Fantoni, to name a few.[225] During its four decades, Richards Morgenthau was distinguished by its steadfast faith in contemporary design and its ability to market it.

LN

Rietveld, Gerrit Thomas

Born Utrecht, the Netherlands, June 24, 1888; died Utrecht, June 25, 1964

The architecture and furniture designs that Gerrit Rietveld pioneered in the 1920s and 1930s have become icons of Modernism.[226] Spatially and technically innovative, Rietveld's work has exerted a profound influence on his contemporaries and later twentieth-century designers.

After an apprenticeship in his father's cabinetmaking shop from 1899 to 1906, Rietveld worked as a draftsman in a jewelry firm. He operated an independent cabinetmaking shop in Utrecht from 1911 to 1919, during which time he studied architecture with P. J. Klaarhamer. Throughout his career, Rietveld was involved in the design of buildings, interiors, and furniture.

While a member of De Stijl from 1919 to 1931, Rietveld took into three dimensions the Neoplastic principles of rectangularity and reliance on primary colors that defined that group; most exemplary are his *Red and Blue* chair (1918) and the Schroeder House, Utrecht (1924), his most significant architectural commission. In 1923, Rietveld displayed his *Berlin* chair, more a piece of sculpture than a functional object, at the Bauhaus exhibition in Weimar. His fiberboard *Birza* chair (1927) was the first created from a single sheet of material. Among Rietveld's other notable designs are a structurally innovative lighting fixture (1920) and his Z or *Zig-Zag* chair (1934), the latter perhaps his most revolutionary chair design.

Adhering to the philosophy that art should be available to all, Rietveld constructed most of his furniture from readily available, inexpensive wood products. His crate furniture (1934), sold in knockdown form by Metz & Company, which manufactured and marketed many of Rietveld's furniture designs, particularly conformed to that ideal.

In contrast to these early angular designs in wood, for which Rietveld is most recognized, the later work exhibits a softer aesthetic and the use of other materials. Rietveld experimented with metal as early as 1927, employing tubular steel for a chair frame, and in 1942 he designed a chair of stamped aluminum.

In 1928 Rietveld was one of the founding members of CIAM (Congrès Internationaux d'Architecture Moderne). As his career progressed, Rietveld increasingly turned his attention to architecture. During the 1950s and 1960s, when his earlier contributions began to receive international recognition, Rietveld saw his practice expand both in magnitude and scale. In 1961 he formed a partnership with two young architects, J. Van Dillen and J. Van Tricht. Their commission for the interior of the Steltman Jeweller's Shop (The Hague, 1963) resulted in Rietveld's last furniture designs.

Most of Rietveld's furniture was executed by his cabinetmaker, G. A. van de Groenekan, from 1917 until 1971. At that time, the rights were bought by Cassina of Milan, which continues to reproduce Rietveld's landmark designs.

LN

Risom, Jens

Born Copenhagen, May 6, 1916

Jens Risom studied furniture and interior design at Kunsthåndvaerkerskolen in Copenhagen, where Kaare Klint taught him to value simplicity and utility.[227] After working in the architectural office of Ernst Kuhn in the Danish capital, Risom went to the United States in 1939 to study and decided to remain in New York.

At first Risom was a free-lance designer, designing textiles for Dan Cooper, Inc., and interiors for a model home in Rockefeller Center that *Collier's* magazine had commissioned from Edward D. Stone. In 1941 he met Hans Knoll; they traveled around the country together visiting modern architects, and then Risom designed for Knoll fifteen pieces—chairs, tables, cabinets—with a Scandinavian sense of modernity.

After serving in the United States Army, Risom formed Jens Risom Design, Inc., in 1946, one of a very few companies in this country specializing in modern furniture at that time. Risom was always the sole designer, working on both furniture and textiles, which continued to be Scandinavian Modern in spirit. His work tended to be subtly rather than aggressively modern, with simple shapes and clearly articulated parts, and it was known for being well crafted and durable. During the mid-1950s he advertised his domestic furniture with strikingly uncluttered images by fashion photographer Richard Avedon.[228] By the 1960s, he began to concentrate on office furniture. His philosophy, based on his wartime experience, was that well-planned, well-designed equipment does a better job than a copy or a partial updating of something old.[229]

After Dictaphone bought Risom Design in 1970, Risom stayed on as chief executive for another three years. Since then he has headed his own free-lance design service, Design Control, in New Canaan, Connecticut.

CWL

Rörstrands Porslinfabrik AB

The oldest and most important Swedish porcelain factory, the Rörstrand firm has managed to keep in the forefront of changing styles throughout the centuries.[230] It was founded as a private company with royal support in 1726 in the Rörstrand Castle in Stockholm, and initially produced faience in the Delft style. By 1783, when it bought the rival Marieberg factory, it was producing creamware. It remained without local competition until the founding of the Gustavsberg factory in 1827, and until the middle of the nineteenth century it produced only stoneware. In 1867 it was incorporated as Rörstrand Aktiebolag, and its range of wares was expanded to include stoneware, majolica, and various porcelain bodies. An indication of the company's growth is the size of its staff: about one hundred workers in 1760, double that number by 1850, and about one thousand by 1900.

Rörstrand rose to international prominence only at the end of the nineteenth century. In 1895 Alf Wallander joined the company, becoming art director three years later. Inspired by developments in Paris, both by Japoniste-derived images of nature and by the Art Nouveau style, Wallander and his staff created delicately sculpted and painted porcelain vases and dinnerware that were universally acclaimed and imitated.

The next major phase of Rörstrand's development occurred in 1917, when, through the efforts of the Svenska Slöjdföreningen, Edward Hald was hired as a free-lance designer for the earthenware division. His first works were expressionist, linear patterns, which paralleled the work of Wilhelm Kåge at the Gustavsberg factory, and some Fauve-inspired figurative designs. Hald continued to work for Rörstrand until 1929, and others on the staff included Tyra Lundgren. In 1926 the Rörstrand factory was moved to Göteborg, and control of the company passed to the Arabia pottery, a Finnish concern that Rörstrand had originally created and controlled until 1917.

Gunnar Nylund was appointed art director of Rörstrand in 1931; his work included heavily textured chamotte ware with carved geometric motifs, picturesque animal sculptures, and, at the opposite extreme, functional objects of simplicity. In 1932, after Arabia ceded control, the Rörstrand factory acquired AB Lidköpings Porslinfabrik and seven years later transferred the entire Rörstrand operation to the Lidköping facility.

Due to Sweden's neutrality during World War II, the plant continued in operation; its wares ranged from the tranquil beauty of Nylund's Oriental-inspired stoneware to the boldly painted decoration of Isaac Grünewald. It was only after the war that the Rörstrand factory regained the ascendant position it had held at the turn of the century. The elegantly tapered, mat-glazed stoneware vases by Nylund and Carl-Harry Stålhane garnered much praise, and Hertha Bengston's *Blå Eld* (Blue Fire) dinnerware showed comparable attenuated forms. A considerable amount of Rörstrand's wares, such as Nylund's *Abstrakt* series, was decorated with typical postwar geometric patterns or with stylized folksy patterns, such as Marianne Westman's *Mon Amie* service (1951). Signs of a later, changed aesthetic are evident in the disproportioned *Pop* range designed by Inger Persson (1968) and the inventively complex geometric forms and patterns of Rolf Sinnemark, which were introduced in the mid-1980s.

The ownership of the Rörstrand company has changed several times in the past decades. In 1964 it was acquired by Upsala-Ekeby AB, and in 1983 the Rörstrand company was bought by Arabia, which had become part of the Wärtsilä conglomerate. Then in 1988, a year after Arabia bought AB Gustavsberg, the two Swedish potteries were joined to form Rörstrands-Gustavsberg AB.

ME

Rosenthal Porzellan AG This firm began when

Philipp Rosenthal returned to his native Germany in 1879 after having worked with a porcelain importer in Detroit, Michigan. Following in the family tradition — his father had owned a porcelain factory in Werl — he created Philipp Rosenthal & Co. in Erkersreuth, whose principal activity was the decoration of porcelain blanks procured from nearby factories.[231] As the business flourished, the company moved to Selb, built its own porcelain factory, and began manufacturing in 1891, followed by another factory in Kronach six years later.

Rosenthal's earliest wares were generally florid in form and decoration and often aped commercial competitors, such as Haviland & Co. At the turn of the century it imitated the softly colored pictorialism of the Scandinavian porcelain firms, and was visibly swayed by the Art Nouveau style and the more geometric tendencies of German Jugendstil. It exhibited widely and won a gold medal at the Paris Exposition Universelle of 1900.

Rosenthal fostered its artistic aspirations by supporting the newly founded (1908) Königliche Fachschule in Selb, which was directed by Fritz Klee; by establishing in 1910 a special Kunstabteilung (Art Department) at Rosenthal; and by producing figurines in the spirit of the Royal Copenhagen factory. While affected during and after World War I by the restrictions of raw materials and the difficulties of international commerce, Rosenthal rebounded in the 1920s. The number of new buildings established at Selb and the previous purchase of Thomas & Ens' facility in Marktredwitz are outward indications of its success. It transferred its main offices to Berlin in 1920 and established showrooms in major capitals.

The company's wares were marked by the eccentricities of the modernistic style then current in German decorative art. The highly exaggerated figures sculpted by Gerhard Schliepstein and the painted decoration of Tono Zoelch typify the best of the firm's production in this vein. Although some designs, such as the *Daphne* dinnerware by Wilhelm Wagenfeld (1937), responded to the Modernist concern for simplicity, this was not a major aspect of the firm's work.

Concurrent with the rise of the Nazis, Philipp Rosenthal left control of the firm in 1934, and its main office was moved back to Selb. With the outbreak of war, production was geared to simple household items and Germany's war effort.

In the postwar years, as West Germany's economy recovered, the Rosenthal firm also revived. Starting in 1950 it was again headed by a member of the founding family, Philip Rosenthal, Jr., who oversaw a process of expansion as the firm bought additional factories and gained markets in businesses around the world.

Stylistically, Rosenthal followed the postwar tendency toward elongated geometric forms, expressed beautifully in the *Oval* mocha service of Rudolf Lunghard (1951), while the urge toward Biomorphism was exhibited in the forms of Beate Kuhn, Hans Wohlrab, and Fritz Heidenreich. About 1952 Rosenthal embarked on a new program of commissioning works from internationally famous designers, hoping to capitalize on the designers' reputations and thus gain access to the markets of their respective countries. Among those employed were Raymond Loewy and Tapio Wirkkala. In addition to its traditional medium of porcelain, Rosenthal expanded its operation to include complementary glassware (it had already bought several glass factories over the past decades). A new business, DOMUS GmbH, was founded in 1960 to produce flatware, lighting fixtures, small furniture, and gift accessories, and the first Rosenthal Studio-Haus retail stores were opened. In 1961 a new designation, Studio-Linie, was created for its modern porcelains, and new commissions for functional items and sculpture were given over the course of the next decades, some to older contributors such as Wirkkala, but also to Timo Sarpaneva, Bjorn Wiinblad, Walter Gropius, Henry Moore, Niki de Saint-Phalle, Salvador Dalí, and Victor Vasarely.

Rosenthal's corporate history, especially since World War I, has involved the frequent purchase and sale of many factories as well as changes in corporate structure and name. In 1969 the various branches were reorganized into several different companies, only to be reorganized once again in 1974 into Rosenthal Glas und Porzellan AG. The name of Rosenthal has remained a constant element, and equally constant, despite the inevitable concessions to the pressure of the marketplace, has been its involvement with forward-looking design.

ME

Rossbach, Charles Edmund (Ed) Born Chicago, January 2, 1914

One of the leading figures in midcentury American weaving, Ed Rossbach received his bachelor of arts degree in 1940 from the University of Washington in Seattle, where he had majored in painting and design.[232] A master's degree in art education from Columbia University's Teachers College, New York, followed in 1941. His career as a seventh-grade teacher in Puyallup, Washington, was short-lived, as he was drafted into the army in 1942. After the war, he enrolled on the GI Bill at the Cranbrook Academy of Art, Bloomfield Hills, Michigan, in 1946, where he majored in ceramics and weaving. Although Marianne Strengell headed the Department of Weaving and Textile Design, Rossbach acknowledges that the greater influence came from Robert Sailors, her assistant director. Rossbach graduated with a master of fine arts in 1947. He returned to the University of Washington that year and began teaching. In 1950 he married the California artist Katherine Westphal, and they settled in Berkeley, where he became a professor of design at the University of California. His impact as a teacher for twenty-nine years has been of tremendous importance in the fiber field.

Rossbach is guided by a thorough technical knowledge of the materials at hand — including their limitations. His weaving uses subtle colorations, often a monochromatic color scheme. His experimental textile work led in 1976 to a series of art pieces he called "silk brocades," including *Homage to Boris Kroll*, *Mickey Mouse*, and a *Mad Ludwig* series. In several of these, he included photographic images. His work continues to be innovative and experimental. His baskets incorporate unconventional substances, such as vinyl, rice paper, lacquer, newsprint, feathers, and plastic bags.

Rossbach's devotion to his students left no time for commission work. He did, however, participate in national and international exhibitions. From 1946 to 1954, he was always included in the trend-setting annual "International Textile Exhibition" at the University of North Carolina at Greensboro, and the Museum of Contemporary Crafts in New York has shown his work since 1956. His work was seen abroad in, among other venues, the United States pavilion at the Brussels World's Fair (1958) and the Milan XIII Triennale (1964). In 1990 the Textile Museum in Washington, D.C., held a retrospective of his work.

Rossbach has authored a number of books[233] and, most recently, has written a series of important articles on the hand-weaving movement in the United States during the 1940s.[234]

CCMT

Rudofsky, Bernard Born Vienna, April 13, 1905; died New York, March 12, 1988

Bernard Rudofsky was educated in his native Vienna, where he attended the Technische Universität Wein from 1922 to 1928 and received a master's degree in architecture and engineering, followed by a doctorate in technical science in 1931. From 1932 to 1938, Rudofsky practiced architecture in Milan and Naples and served as editor and art director for *Domus*. From 1938 to 1941 he worked in São Paulo. He visited the United States in 1935, and, after winning an inter-American design competition, he returned in 1941 at the invitation of the Museum of Modern Art. At that time he decided to establish his residence and office in New York, and he subsequently became an American citizen and a licensed architect. However, because of the war, he felt that the opportunity to practice was lost and that he was beyond the point of resuming that aspect of his career.

Rudofsky's connection with the Museum of Modern Art developed into a long relationship. From 1944 to 1945, Rudofsky served as the museum's director of apparel research. He was also guest director of major exhibitions, such as "Are Clothes Modern?" (1944), "Textiles U.S.A." (1956), and "Architecture without Architects" (1964), an exhibition that toured for eleven years. From 1961 to 1965 Rudofsky was consultant to the museum's Department of Architecture and Design. Concurrently, he worked on design magazines. In 1943, he was associate editor and art director for *New Pencil Points* (known today as *Progressive Architecture*), and from 1946 to 1949, he was the editorial and art director for *Interiors*.[235]

Rudofsky's teaching career included a Bemis Visiting Lectureship at Massachusetts Institute of Technology in Boston (1956–57) and a research professorship at Waseda University in Tokyo (1958–60). At Yale University, New Haven, he was visiting critic in 1961, then visiting professor of art in 1965–66. He held a guest professorship in 1975 at the Kongelige Danske Kunstakademi (Royal Danish Academy of Fine Arts) in Copenhagen.

Rudofsky has received Fulbright scholarships (1958 and 1959), a Ford Foundation grant (1963), Guggenheim fellowships (1963, 1964, and 1971), and National Endowment for the Arts research grants (1978, 1981, and 1982). Writing in English, German, and Italian, he authored nine books.[236] In 1980 he became scholar-in-residence at the Cooper-Hewitt Museum, New York, for the exhibition "Now I Lay Me Down to Eat," and in 1985, at the invitation of the Indian government, he conducted research and design work in preparation for the "Golden Eye" exhibition, also at the Cooper-Hewitt.

In addition to being an architect, designer, teacher, scholar, editor, and author, Rudofsky was a social commentator whose varied interests brought him in contact with a myriad of subjects. Rudofsky looked upon himself as a cosmopolitan being with only "air roots," as he once said, "like some jungle plant."[237]

CCMT

Saarinen, Eero Born Kirkkonummi, Finland, August 20, 1910; died Ann Arbor, Michigan, September 1, 1961

Throughout his brief career Eero Saarinen consistently employed a reductivist yet rhythmic approach to his architectural and furniture designs. His use of the technology of new materials and his lyrical sense of line and proportion encapsulate the architectural style of the postwar era.[238]

Eero Saarinen immigrated to the United States in 1923 with his father, Finnish architect Eliel Saarinen, who helped establish and became president of the Cranbrook Academy of Art in Bloomfield Hills, Michigan. His mother, Louise (Loja) Gesellius, was widely regarded for her textile designs. From 1929 to 1933 Eero Saarinen designed furniture for the adjacent Kingswood School for Girls, designed by his father. Eero then studied sculpture at the Académie de la Grande Chaumière, Paris (1930–31), and earned a bachelor of fine arts degree from the Yale School of Architecture, graduating in 1934. After living in Finland for two years he returned to Michigan and worked in his father's office. As can be seen in the bentwood furniture he designed for the Kleinhans Music Hall in Buffalo, New York, he had been swayed by Alvar Aalto's progressive work.

From 1939 to 1942 Saarinen worked as an assistant in the Department of Architecture at Cranbrook, where he formed a close relationship with Charles Eames. The two men collaborated on furniture and houses. They won two first prizes in the 1940 Museum of Modern Art "Organic Design in Home Furnishings" contest, one for seating—introducing the seminally important idea of a three-dimensionally molded shell—and the other for modular furniture.

Eero Saarinen had known Florence Schust Knoll when she attended Kingswood School and the Cranbrook Academy in the early 1930s, and she later interested him in designing furniture for Knoll Associates. In 1943, Eero Saarinen designed his first chair, of bent plywood, for Knoll Associates, for whom he would design his best-known furniture, including the model no. 70 lounge chair (1946–48), the first fiberglass chair to be mass-produced in the United States.

Eero continued to work in his father's office, which from 1944 to 1947 was known as Saarinen, Swanson and Saarinen, and then, from 1947 to 1950, was known as Saarinen, Saarinen and Associates. In 1950 Saarinen established his own firm, called Eero Saarinen and Associates, in Bloomfield Hills; it included designer Kevin Roche and partner John Dinkeloo. Saarinen rose to great prominence in the last decade of his brief life, during which time his major architectural designs were executed. These include the TWA terminal at Kennedy Airport (1956–62), the CBS headquarters building, New York (1960–64), an auditorium and chapel at Massachusetts Institute of Technology (1953–56), and Dulles International Airport, Washington, D.C. (1958–62). The strongly sculptural and expressive character of his architecture is reflected in his furniture designs as well, most notably in the *Pedestal* series of chairs and tables designed for Knoll (1955–57). His death at the age of fifty-one cut short one of the most accomplished and promising careers of the Modernist movement.

FTH

Sabattini, Lino Born Correggio, Italy, September 23, 1923

Lino Sabattini regards the fabrication of useful objects as a creative act; he stresses design over problems of production and emphasizes aesthetics over the limitations of industrial production.[239]

His parents moved the family during World War II, and, having attended only elementary school, Sabattini took a job in a Como shop selling brass knickknacks. When he was fourteen years old he happened on a copy of *Domus*, Gio Ponti's influential magazine of architecture and design, which "became his textbook, his Academy of Fine Arts, and his correspondence school."[240] A few years later, he made the acquaintance of the displaced German potter Rolando Hettner, who lived like a hermit on the shore of Lake Como. Hettner's independent, artistic sensibility greatly affected Sabattini.

At age thirty, Sabattini left the constrictions of the commercial brass shop and moved to Milan, where he set up a metalworking studio in a small basement. Ponti admired the voluminously bulging forms of Sabattini's work, such as the *Boule* teapot of 1950, and subsequently published photographs of these designs in *Domus*. He also helped the artist to exhibit in the Milan Triennales from 1954 to 1969, supported several solo exhibitions, and encouraged Sabattini to publish his designs in important reviews.

From 1956 to 1963 Sabattini was director of a new line—*Formes nouvelles*—for Christofle, the French manufacturers of electroplated silver, which had a plant in Milan. However, his modern designs met with great resistance, and his preference for hand-forming went counter to Christofle's use of mass-production techniques. In 1964 Sabattini left Milan and returned to Como, where he opened his own silversmithy, with about twenty-five apprentices. This company is still in operation.

Over the years Sabattini has won twenty gold medals, including a gold medal from the international fair of Munich in 1962 and the Sole d'Oro at the international exhibition of silver in San Remo in 1965. His *San Remo* coffee service received an award at the Milan XI Triennale in 1957.

TLW

Sailors, Robert D. Born Grand Rapids, Michigan, May 23, 1919

A graduate of Olivet College and the School of the Art Institute of Chicago (bachelor of arts degree, 1939), Sailors developed an interest in weaving during a 1941 summer program at the Cranbrook Academy of Art.[241] Returning to Cranbrook in 1942, he completed a master's degree under Marianne Strengell and from June 1944 until December 1946 served as assistant director and instructor in the weaving department.

In 1947 Sailors established his own studio in Bitely, Michigan, eventually producing both hand- and power-loom-woven textiles that were distributed through showrooms in eight major American cities. As the studio prospered, Sailors invited two former students and another professional weaver into partnership, and the studio eventually employed twenty-three people. Sailors was among the first to incorporate unusual materials, such as bamboo and wood slats, into drapery textiles. His greatest commercial success was with bamboo-slatted shades produced for rapidly expanding restaurant chains such as Big Boy.

In 1962 Sailors reduced the scale of his business and moved home and studio to Belmont, Michigan, where as sole proprietor he concentrated on hand-loomed fabrics. He moved again in 1974 to Cortez, Florida; primarily working alone, he continues to produce woven shades and textiles for numerous restaurant chains. Ever experimental, he incorporates unusual materials such as jute, aluminum stripping, and plant materials into his textiles and rugs.

KC

Sarpaneva, Timo Tapani Born Helsinki, October 31, 1926

One of the most laureated Finnish designers in the postwar period, Timo Sarpaneva has worked in many mediums, though it is his contributions to the Finnish glass and textile industries for which he is best known.[242]

Under Arttu Brummer, he studied graphic design at the Taideteollinen Korkeakoulu (Central School of Industrial Design), graduating in 1948, just as Finland emerged from the hardships of the war. His design for a vase with engraved lines in the manner of Tapio Wirkkala's *Kanttarelli* vase won a second prize in a 1949 contest sponsored by the Iittala glassworks, and he began working for the company the following year, mainly designing posters and other graphics. Like the prize-winning embroideries he exhibited at the Milan IX Triennale in 1951, his images have a spidery quality of line, reminiscent of Paul Klee's paintings and Wirkkala's graphic designs. Sarpaneva's first important creations in glass for Iittala, such as the *Devil's Churn* series (1950), are Biomorphic in form. By 1952 he had begun a series of elegantly tapered vases with internal pockets of air created by steam; one of these, the *Lancet*, was awarded a grand prize at the Milan X Triennale, and another, the *Orchid*, was named "The Most Beautiful Design Object of the Year" by *House Beautiful* in 1954. He ingeniously extended the steam-blowing process to the *i* series of two-tone colored objects, which won a grand prize at the Milan XI Triennale in 1957.

Sarpaneva turned his attention to textile design in 1955, creating for Porin Puuvilla Oy in Pori a successful series of woven, primarily striped patterns in a new spectrum of color ways. He remained with this company as artistic director until 1966, and from 1964 to 1972 he also worked for the Kinnasand textile mill in Sweden. Between 1960 and 1972 he designed a series of limited-edition rya rugs for Villayhtymä Oy, Helsinki; their combination of knotted tufts and machine-set weft demonstrates the ingenious way that Sarpaneva allied handicraft with industrial processes.

The cast-iron cookware that Sarpaneva designed for W. Rosenlew & Co. in Pori in 1960 received a silver medal at the Milan XII Triennale in 1960 and the American Institute of Decorators (AID) award in 1963. Also for Rosenlew, he designed plasticized shelf-lining paper and wrapping paper that were printed with several colors simultaneously on a rotary press. Here, too, Sarpaneva's inventiveness was rewarded with an AID award, in 1969, and a Eurostar from the European Packing Federation in Vienna in 1965.

All the while, Sarpaneva continued to design glass for the Iittala works. In 1963 and 1964 the designer used discarded, charred wooden molds to create highly textured glass sculptures. In addition to these unique pieces, Sarpaneva used the process in his *Finlandia* range of drinking glasses and vessels for serial production; he even exhibited the charred molds themselves as wood sculpture. Most of Sarpaneva's work from 1965 to 1990 has been far simpler and more geometric: door handles for Primo Oy in Malmi (1964), the *Suomi* porcelain tableware and stainless steel flatware for Rosenthal (1974), *Jumo* (1978) and *Claritas* (1984) glass for Iittala.

Throughout his career, Sarpaneva worked on installation designs for international exhibitions, including the Finnish stand at the "H-55" exhibition at Hälsingborg in 1955, the Milan XI Triennale in 1957, and Expo '67 in Montreal in 1967, as well as the many exhibitions of his own work. The wide range of his activity suggests the versatility and success of this designer.

ME

Scarpa, Carlo Born Vicenza, Italy, June 2, 1906; died Sendai, Japan, November 28, 1978

Carlo Scarpa, one of Italy's most important mid-twentieth-century architects, is often categorized as a poet-architect.[243]

He graduated from the Accademia di Belle Arti in Venice in 1926. His early style was academic, but he soon abandoned it in favor of the International Style. His works of the 1920s and 1930s, many left as unrealized projects, show the rationalist simplicity of Adolf Loos and Ludwig Mies van der Rohe as well as Robert Mallet-Stevens. Scarpa also taught at the Istituto Universitario di Architettura, Venice, from 1933 on, giving classes in life and technical drawing as well as in decoration.

It was only in the postwar years that Scarpa received attention for his architecture, and by then his style had changed considerably. Le Corbusier's influence was manifest in his handling of external volumes, and the emphatic influence of Frank Lloyd Wright could be seen in the architect's use of materials and space, as well as in the repeated geometric ornamentation, all of which contributed to a richer, more complex structure. The edifices actually executed are surprisingly few: for example, the Veritti house, Udine (1955–56); the Zentner house, Zurich (1964); additions to the Canova museum, Possagno (1956–57); stores for Olivetti, Venice (1957), and Gavina, Bologna (1961). His complex drawings and the many important installations he designed—especially for the Venice Biennales from 1942 until 1972 and twelve major art exhibitions—also helped establish his reputation. After becoming a professor of interior design in 1952 at the Istituto Universitario di Architettura, Scarpa taught the architecture of interior design and architectural composition. The award of the Olivetti National Prize for Architecture in 1955 registered the formal recognition of his significance. In late works, such as the Brion Cemetery in San Vito d'Altivo (1970), the sense of scale, volume, and ornament suggest parallels with the rise of Post-Modernism.

In the early part of his career, Scarpa designed for Vetri Soffiati Muranesi Cappellin Venini & C., and when that firm was dissolved in 1925 he went over to Cappellin's new firm, Maestri Vetrai Muranesi Cappellin & C. He stayed there until 1932, and when Cappellin's firm went bankrupt, he rejoined Venini, assuming the position of artistic director. Unlike the fantasy-laden creations of his Venetian colleagues, Scarpa chose regular forms with simple volumes, paralleling the vocabulary of his architecture. He became immersed in the technical aspects of the glassworks and is credited with Venini's revival of *murrine* glass (1938). He designed the *Tessuto* series (1940), with its complex patterns of canes, and the *Battuto* series, with a ground surface resembling beaten metal (1940). Among Scarpa's last works for Venini were the *A fili* and *Pennellate* series (1942), in which irregular splashes of colored glass are wound around simple shapes. Though he left the Venini firm in 1947, he collaborated with it on subsequent occasions, such as the "Italia '61" exhibition in Turin.

From the beginning, Scarpa designed furniture and small accessories for himself and his clients, but this aspect of his work became significant only in the latter part of his career. His early designs have simple structures in accord with the International Style. Through Scarpa's association with Dino Gavina, several designs were put into production in the late 1960s and early 1970s by Gavina's later company, Simon International, but with significant changes. For example, a steel table Scarpa designed for the Zentner house with an ebony and ivory top was issued by Simon with a simple glass top. Several examples of furniture that Scarpa had designed for himself in the 1930s were produced by Bernini in the 1970s. Scarpa's flatware for the American firm Reed and Barton (1959) was later modified for his client Cleto Munari and then was produced in 1976 by Rossi and Arcandi, a firm that also produced Scarpa's designs for silver trays and compotes.

ME

Schiffer Prints *see* Mil-Art Company, Inc.

Schnee, Ruth Adler Born Frankfurt am Main, May 13, 1923

Ruth Adler spent her childhood in Düsseldorf, to which the family had moved in 1929 at the suggestion of the painter Paul Klee, a good family friend. Klee and the architect Emil Fahrenkamp taught the young girl the basics of painting and drawing;[244] she also had the benefit of her mother's training at the Bauhaus. Ruth Adler attended the Bluecher Schule (1934) and the Mueller Lyzeum (1935), both in Düsseldorf, and LaRamée (1936) in Lausanne.

After immigrating to the United States, Adler settled in Detroit, where she attended Cass Technical High School (1939–42) and developed a keen interest in design and fashion illustration. She won a full scholarship to attend the Rhode Island School of Design, where she completed her bachelor of fine arts in 1945. She spent the summer of 1944 on a fellowship at Harvard University's Graduate School of Architecture and Design, where she studied with Walter Gropius. Adler went to the Cranbrook Academy of Art on scholarship and graduated with a master of fine arts in 1946, having majored in design. She spent the summer in New York as an assistant at Raymond Loewy Associates. In the fall of 1946 she taught design courses at Michigan State College.

In 1947, her winning entry in the *Chicago Tribune's* competition "Better Rooms for Better Living" included a rendering of a patterned curtain fabric; it caught the eye of the firm Naess and Murphy, which gave Adler her first order.[245] She established herself as a fabric designer in Detroit that same year. During this initial period, she received prestigious awards from the American Institute of Decorators, one in 1947 for *Slits and Slats*, and two in 1948, for *Strata* and *Central Park South*, respectively.[246] She used both a linear style, as in *Seedy Weeds*, and one with interlocking patterns of abstract shapes, as in *Cuneiforms*. Occasionally she used the two together, as in *Lazy Leaves*.

In 1948 she married Edward (Ed) C. Schnee, a Yale graduate who was trained in business administration; they formed a partnership known as Adler-Schnee Associates. She designed, he printed, and together they operated in the Detroit area from 1949 to 1977. The shop carried their textiles, along with an inventory of well-designed European and American items, ranging from kitchen appliances and furniture to graphic and folk art.[247]

As Ruth Adler Schnee's responsibilities toward the retail business, her family, and her involvement with interior designing grew, she gave less time to textile design, and by the early 1960s she had given it up entirely.[248] The shop continued to operate under the Schnees' leadership until 1977, when they sold the business. After two years, it was dissolved. In 1979, they established themselves as Schnee and Schnee, specializing in aspects of interior design; Ruth Adler Schnee functioned as the designer, with Ed Schnee as her "detail man."[249]

CCMT

Schumacher & Company *see* F. Schumacher & Company

Seguso, Archimede Born Murano, Italy, December 17, 1909

Archimede Seguso, one of Murano's twentieth-century masters, was descended from a family that has been renowned for its glassmaking skills since the fifteenth century.[250] By the age of thirteen he was blowing glass, and by sixteen he had mastered the technical aspects of the art. In 1929, using a small furnace in the fireplace of his home, he began producing his own small objects. With others, including his father, Antonio, and Napoleone Barovier, Archimede was a

founding member of Seguso Vetri d'Arte in 1934 and served as its master glassblower, executing the designs of Flavio Poli as well as his own. After a long period of illness in the 1940s, he formed his own company in 1947, Vetreria Archimede Seguso, for which he has since produced art and table glass to his own and others' designs.

Seguso's postwar work has made him one of the most respected master glassblowers in Venice. He is most noted for his work in the traditional Venetian latticino glass and its variations. Using the technique of "evolved filigraine," he created works such as the *Merletto* (Lace) and *Piume* (Feather) vases in the 1950s, some of which were exhibited at the Venice Biennales and which are considered to be among his best.

Seguso's versatility is evident in the wide range of objects he has produced, from tabletop items and portrait busts to massive sculptures and elaborate chandeliers. His recent work includes two series of limited-edition multicolored vessels. A retrospective of his work was held at the Museum of Venetian Art in Otaru, Japan, in 1990.

LN

Smith, Alexander, and Sons *see* Alexander Smith and Sons

Smith, Arthur (Art) Born New York, October 28, 1917; died New York, February 20, 1982

Jeweler Art Smith combined a taste for East African artistic expressions and a Biomorphic formal vocabulary with a sense of drama.[251] He believed that true jewelry is always comprised of three basic elements: materials, space, and the human body—which he considered an armature for jewelry.

His father was a black militant, an officer in the radical Marcus Garvey movement of the early 1900s. Smith himself wanted to be an artist and received a scholarship to Cooper Union in 1942. There he was encouraged to study architecture, because jobs were readily available to minority applicants in the nondiscriminatory civil service. Although structural forms excited him, mathematics eluded him, so he concentrated on three-dimensional sculptural constructions in a variety of mediums. He graduated in 1946.

In the early 1940s he had taken a part-time job as crafts supervisor at the Children's Aid Society in Harlem. There he met Winifred Mason, a black craftswoman who assembled jewelry from scraps of copper and brass. He accepted a job in her Greenwich Village store and remained with her for several years. He learned the rudiments of metalsmithing from Mason, but for the rest, he was a self-taught metalsmith.

About 1946 Art Smith opened his own shop and studio on Cornelia Street in Little Italy, but racial prejudice forced him to move back to the more liberal atmosphere of Greenwich Village. By 1948, when he opened his shop at 140 West Fourth Street, his reputation as an innovative designer was widespread, due mostly to his participation in the second national exhibition of contemporary jewelry at the Walker Art Center in Minneapolis in 1948.[252]

Although Smith's work was bought by a variety of customers, his most noteworthy commissions include jewelry designed for the black dance companies run by Tally Beatty, Pearl Primus, and Claude Marchant; a brooch presented to Eleanor Roosevelt by the Peekskill NAACP; and a pair of cuff links for Duke Ellington. The Museum of Contemporary Crafts honored him with a solo show in 1969.

TLW

Soinne et Kni Soinne et Kni was a Helsinki firm, founded in 1930, that was known for its fabrication of

an especially strong, laminated wood for airplane propellers.[253] It subjected glued veneers to high pressure to form wood blocks that were more durable and attractive than ordinary plywood.

In the late 1940s the firm was owned by a friend of Tapio Wirkkala. When the designer visited the factory and saw its laminate product, he was reminded of the natural growth rings of a tree and was inspired to experiment with the material. The first products—wooden platters and bowls—were carved by Martti Lindqvist, a skilled craftsman who later carved Wirkkala's large, elaborate wooden sculptures from the same laminated material. Wirkkala's creations were the only design objects produced by Soinne et Kni.

The firm went out of business in 1972.

CWL

Sottsass, Ettore Born Innsbruck, Austria, September 14, 1917

Since his graduation from the Politecnico of Turin in 1939, architect-designer Ettore Sottsass has pursued a consistent career as Italy's leading radical designer, constantly challenging the status quo and proposing daring new forms and images for the objects of the everyday environment.[254]

Sottsass's father had been an architect in the rationalist tradition; Ettore was trained in the same tradition but after World War II sought to move away from that highly functional approach toward a more spontaneous creation of objects. Inspired by the fine arts—especially painting and sculpture—he searched for a prerational basis for design that would renew the language of the discipline and create a new relationship between objects and their users. This search benefited from trips abroad, particularly to the United States and India, where Sottsass saw objects within alternative cultures, which affected him greatly.

After little more than a decade as a free-lance interior designer in Milan, Sottsass became the chief consultant designer for Olivetti's electronics division in 1957. This gave him a secure basis from which to experiment with his more personal projects; thus, the early 1960s saw the emergence of radical designs for furniture and ceramics, including his Pop art-inspired wardrobes designed for Poltronova and exhibited in Milan in prototype form in 1966 and his *Yantra* and *Tantra* ceramic series.

Sottsass was an acknowledged leader in the world of Italian Anti-Design; in the mid-1960s, a number of younger architects looked to his work as inspiration for the "alternative" projects that were rapidly earning for Italy a new reputation for design radicalism. His rejection of functionalism as a basis for design practice stimulated a widespread shift away from this movement on the part of a large number of Italian architect-designers; inevitably, Sottsass became a figurehead for these new manifestations.

Through the 1960s, Sottsass continued to work simultaneously for Olivetti and on small-scale personal researches, and by the end of the decade his ideas were beginning to show in the typewriters and office furniture for that prestigious company. The 1970s represented a less prolific period in terms of output, but it served, nonetheless, as a period of consolidation, during which Sottsass reassessed his direction as a designer. Besides designing objects and environments, Sottsass has also written extensively—mainly for *Domus*—and lectured widely.

In 1981, along with a group of younger designers who worked with him in a number of different capacities, Sottsass launched the Memphis furniture collection in Milan. For the first time he became almost a household name, and the world focused on Milan as the home of Post-Modernism. Although the furniture looked extremely provocative and radical, it was, in fact, a continuation of Sottsass's work of the 1950s and

1960s. His career represents, therefore, a highly consistent path.

Sottsass continues to work for Olivetti, and he runs an architectural and design office in Milan with a group of younger partners.

PS

Spratling, William Born Sonyea, New York, September 22, 1900; died Iguala, Mexico, August 7, 1967

American architect William Spratling was fundamentally responsible for resuscitating the silver industry in Taxco, Mexico.[255] He fostered an interest in ancient Mexican motifs, which led to a renaissance in the design of Mexican silver jewelry and hollowware.

In 1915 Spratling studied at the Art Students League in New York and in 1917 he entered the School of Architecture, Aubern University, in Aubern, Alabama, graduating in 1921. From 1921 to 1929 he was adjunct professor of architecture at Tulane University in New Orleans. In 1926 he went to Mexico to study Spanish colonial architecture.

During his subsequent trips to Mexico in the late 1920s he became friends with artists Diego Rivera, Miguel Covarrubias, and David Siqueiros. Their idiosyncratic styles, which defined the nature of modern Mexican painting, influenced Spratling immeasurably. He moved to Taxco in 1929, at first to write a lighthearted account of everyday life in a Mexican village,[256] and he stayed on indefinitely. In 1931 he established a workshop, La Aduana, in an old customs house, where he designed jewelry, hollowware, and flatware based on pre-Columbian and colonial Hispanic ornament. He encouraged the revival of the silver-mining industry in the region, and imported traditional goldsmiths from Iguala.

Tourists loved the silver jewelry and other objects, which were often set with local stones, including amethyst, Mexican jade, and obsidian. The shop was expanded in 1934 and renamed Taller de las Delicias (Shop of Delights). During World War II, when European imports were cut off, American department stores turned to Spratling for his wares.

In 1945, after accepting outside investments, the name of the company was changed to Spratling y Artisanos. However, this venture was a failure and was dissolved later that year. In 1947 Spratling set up another shop, Taxco-el-Viejo. In 1948, at the request of the United States Department of the Interior, Spratling attempted a silver-working project with Alaskan Eskimos, using designs and materials native to that region, which in turn affected his own work.

After Spratling's death, Alberto Ulrich, an old friend, bought the company from Spratling's employees, who had inherited it. Known as Sucesores de William Spratling, S.A., it is reportedly operated the same way Spratling had run it, as both a workshop and retail establishment.

TLW

Stålhane, Carl-Harry Born Mariestad, Sweden, December 15, 1920; died Lidköping, Sweden, April 11, 1990

After studying sculpture with Ossip Zadkine at the Académie Colarossi in Paris, the nineteen-year-old Carl-Harry Stålhane joined the staff of the Rörstrand factory in 1939.[257] For the next several years he worked as an assistant to Isaac Grünewald, known for his Fauve-inspired painted decoration. By 1948, when Stålhane first achieved international attention, his work was quite unlike that of his mentors. He had created a series of slender, symmetrical vessels enriched only by muted tones of mat glazes—Orientalizing vessels distended with a lyric grace. Stålhane also produced a series called *Abstrakt*, with patterns of overlaid triangles and other geometric configurations typical of the postwar period. In addition to art ware, he contrib-

uted designs for functional dinnerware, notably the *SB*, *Blanca*, and *Vieta* services. Stålhane's work was acclaimed, receiving a gold medal at the Milan X Triennale in 1954 and an honorable mention at the next Triennale, as well as an International Design Award from the American Institute of Decorators.

In the 1960s Stålhane's work took a turn toward the expressive. Whereas some of his earlier vases had lightly incised lines, the incisions now became deeper and scarred the surfaces. The forms were asymmetrical and aggressive, going beyond the sculptural to become sculpture. He also produced some classically rounded forms, but these were on a monumental scale. While still employed at Rörstrand, he also taught ceramics from 1963 to 1971 at the Konstindustriskolen in Göteborg. In 1973 Stålhane left Rörstrand and established his own studio, Designhuset, in Lidköping, with Kent Ericsson assisting him.

ME

Stephens, Coral Barnes Born Johannesburg, South Africa, February 9, 1910

Without benefit of formal training as a designer or weaver, Coral Stephens has been the producer of what Jack Lenor Larsen called ". . . the most luxurious drapery material of the western world. . . ."[258] She achieved this by developing textiles using hand-spun yarn whose textures are impossible to duplicate with machine-processed yarn.

Early in her marriage, when confronted with the need to curtain a large expanse of window in her home, she commissioned the students of a mission school that did hand-weaving to execute a drapery to her design. Then in 1947, after moving to her new home on her husband's new forestry plantation in Swaziland, she was again confronted with vast windows and was disappointed to find the mission school closed. After a discouraging attempt at weaving the necessary fabric herself, she was approached by a school-trained Xhosa woman, Sylvia Mantenga from the Transkei, who was able to execute the textile designs in hand-spun mohair.

As friends and visitors began to request similiar textiles, the need to establish a formal business became apparent, and Stephens set up a company in 1952. She extended her employment of Sylvia Mantenga, who dyed the materials, set up the looms, and did all the weaving. As their commissions increased over the next ten years, Sylvia Mantenga employed local Swazi women and taught them to weave.

In 1990 the Coral Stephens workshop had eighteen looms and gave full-time employment to fifty-nine weavers, dyers, bobbin winders, and helpers; two hundred local women work part time at home as spinners. Ten looms produce drapery and upholstery fabrics and eight produce rugs. All these products are made of mohair imported from Lesotho. The largest market for these products has been South Africa and the United States, followed by Germany, Australia, and Great Britain. Advertising and marketing have been purposely restricted to prevent this cottage industry from growing beyond the control of Stephens and her daughter Jane, a trained textile designer who has immersed herself in her mother's craft.

KC

Steubenville Pottery Company The Steubenville Pottery Company was formed on November 17, 1879, in Steubenville, Ohio, in association with the English potter A. B. Beck, to produce ironstone and white ware.[259] Nearby East Liverpool, Ohio, which offered deposits of fine clay as well as proximity to the Ohio River and railroad transportation, attracted many immigrant English potters. By 1840 there were some fifty stoneware potteries in Ohio.

Early in its history Steubenville developed *Canton China*, semivitreous, opaque, cream-colored, and light in weight, which was made into vases, jardinieres, and toilet seats with various decorations or left plain. In 1881 the firm was incorporated, with W. B. Donaldson as president of the board of directors. The firm grew steadily through the turn of the century. By 1910 the company was in the hands of the Wintwringer family, which retained control until the pottery was closed.

The firm's most famous product was Russel Wright's *American Modern* of 1939, for which the then-bankrupt pottery revived its operation. Another prominent Steubenville line was the *Woodfield* leaf pattern. In 1959, the pottery ceased operations, a victim of labor costs and more competitive Japanese imports. The buildings were then sold to Barium Chemicals Inc. of Canonsburg, Pennsylvania. The Canonsburg Pottery purchased the Steubenville molds, manufactured some of the patterns, and continued to use the Steubenville name.

GS

Straub, Marianne Born Amriswil, Switzerland, September 23, 1909

Her long career combined weaving, industrial design, and teaching. Straub is among the rare few who blend a thorough understanding of loom technology with a constantly changing, original vision of design.[260] Her formal introduction to weaving was at the Kunstgewerbeschule in Zurich (1928–31) and to textile machinery at a local mill in Amriswil. Barred because of her gender from the Swiss Seidenwebschule, she left for England and attended Bradford Technical College (1932–33) instead. Her nine months (1933–34) at Gospels, Ethel Mairet's hand-weaving studio at Ditchling, was a complementary experience, during which she experimented with natural dyeing and hand spinning.

The majority of Straub's designs were intended to be widely produced and were often marketed without credit to the designer. From 1934 to 1937, while a designer for the Rural Industries Bureau, she helped rejuvenate the flagging Welsh woolen mills by providing updated ideas for fabrics. As head designer for Helios (1937–49), a division of Barlow and Jones, she was in charge of both printed and woven textiles, introducing furnishing fabrics that were innovative in their variety of yarns despite wartime restrictions. When Warner & Sons acquired Helios in 1950 and moved the dobby looms to Braintree, Essex, Straub established her studio there, continuing as a prolific designer until her retirement in 1970. From 1964 until the early 1970s she was also associated with Tamesa Fabrics, founded by Isabel Tisdall, and for which she designed sophisticated dobby-woven textiles particularly favored by architects.

Straub has remained an active influence on industrial design through her teaching and lectures. She currently resides in Cambridge, England.

AZ

Strengell, Marianne Dusenbury Hammarstrom Born Helsinki, May 24, 1909

Marianne Strengell graduated in 1929 from the Atheneum in Helsinki. She worked for Svenska Slöjdföreningen (Swedish Society of Industrial Design) in Stockholm, assisting in preparations for the Stockholm exposition of 1930. She then returned to Helsinki and was appointed art director of AB Hemflit-Kotiahkeruus Oy, a firm that featured exclusive lines of rugs, drapery, and upholstery fabrics.[261] Strengell maintained this association until 1936. From 1934 to 1936 she was also co-owner of the Helsinki firm of Koti-

Hemmet, which specialized in the designing of interiors, furniture, and textiles.

In the fall of 1936, Strengell took her first trip to the United States. In February 1937, she went to the Cranbrook Academy of Art, Bloomfield Hills, Michigan, where her first position was that of instructor of weaving, costume, and textile design, under Loja Saarinen. When Loja Saarinen retired in 1942, Strengell succeeded her.

Strengell continued to act in many other capacities besides teaching. In the early 1950s, she was appointed advisor for textiles for the International Cooperation Administration to Japan and the Philippines. The United Nations Technical Assistance Administration made her a consultant for textiles in the Far East. In the United States, she designed automobile fabrics for Chatham Manufacturing Company (1954–60) and was associated with architectural firms such as Skidmore, Owings and Merrill and Eero Saarinen and Associates and General Motors' "Motorama" (1958–60). She was also involved with industrial designers Raymond Loewy, Russel Wright, and the Saarinen-Swanson Group. A straightforward fabric designer who strives for quality, Strengell is primarily concerned with texture and a full range of colors; she willingly mixes natural and synthetic fibers in order to achieve the effects she seeks. She has designed some pictorial images for silk-screen printings,[262] but most of her work, including rugs and bedspreads, has been woven.[263]

Throughout her life, Strengell has exhibited actively, beginning with the international exhibitions in Barcelona (1929), Antwerp (1932), Milan (1933), Brussels (1934), Paris (1937), New York (1939), and San Francisco (1939–40). She won silver medals at the Antwerp and Milan exhibitions and bronze medals in Barcelona and Brussels. The "Organic Design in Home Furnishings" exhibition of 1940–41 at the Museum of Modern Art recognized her with an honorary mention.[264]

After her retirement from Cranbrook in 1961, Strengell became an advisor for the government of Jamaica in 1966, followed in 1967 by involvement with the International Labor Office for the United Nations in the same country. In 1968 she set up a weaving cottage-industry plan with the Appalachian Program.

For the last twenty-five years Strengell has resided in Wellfleet, Massachusetts, sharing studio space with her husband, Olav Hammarstrom. Although Strengell took up photography in the late 1960s, she has continued to work with textiles, on a commission basis.

CCMT

Swanson, Eva Lisa (Pipsan) Saarinen Born Kirkkonummi, Finland, March 31, 1905; died Bloomfield Hills, Michigan, October 23, 1979

Pipsan Saarinen was the daughter of Eliel and Loja Gesellius Saarinen.[265] After studying weaving, fabric design, metalwork, and ceramics at the Atheneum, Helsinki, and Helsingen Yliopisto (University of Helsinki) from 1921 to 1923, she moved with her family to the United States in 1923, ending up at the Cranbrook Academy of Art in Bloomfield Hills in 1925. The next year she married Robert F. Swanson, an architect. She was involved in the design of the Kingswood School, Cranbrook (1929–31), including the auditorium ceiling with aluminum reflectors and silver decoration. In 1929 she and her husband conceived the *Flexible Home Arrangements*, a line of thirty-two pieces of basic furniture to be produced by the Johnson Furniture Company that was planned in conjunction with other accessories. At the same time that she was running a contemporary interior design division during the mid-1930s as part of her husband's architectural firm, she taught costume design, batik design, and contemporary interior design at the Cranbrook Academy of Art.

Pipsan was a partner in the firm of Saarinen, Swanson and Saarinen, with her father, husband, and brother Eero, from 1944 to 1947. She designed the interiors of their buildings, including the General Motors Technical Center and the Milwaukee Cultural Center (1944–47). Then in 1947 she and her husband formed Swanson Associates and designed schools, hospitals, banks, and other institutions. By 1947 Benjamin Baldwin, Marianne Strengell, Lydia Winston, Charles Dusenbury, and other Cranbrook designers joined Pipsan and Robert in what became the Saarinen-Swanson Group, essentially a rejuvenation of the earlier *Flexible Home Arrangements* scheme. They presented a line that included furniture, carpets, fabrics, lamps, vases, and ceramic sculptures.[266] The furniture was Scandinavian in style with birch veneers. Pipsan designed fabrics with textures or geometric patterns in tranquil colors, preferring subtle color combinations. She designed fabrics for Edwin Raphael from 1952 to 1962 and carpets for E. T. Barwick Mills from 1957 to 1976. She created domestic interiors as well in the late 1950s. She exhibited frequently, was the recipient of numerous awards from the design community, and in 1972 was made an honorary member of the American Institute of Architects in recognition of her distinguished career as an interior designer.

CWL

Tabard Frères & Soeurs From 1637 until its closing

in 1983, the Tabard atelier of Aubusson produced fine, hand-woven tapestry. Under the directorship and influence of François Tabard (born Aubusson, France, April 14, 1902; died Aubusson, April 14, 1969),[267] the atelier broke with the lingering trend to reproduce earlier tapestries; instead, it actively set out to weave the designs of contemporary painters. In 1937 Tabard met Jean Lurcat, and the two subsequently worked together to revitalize the failing tapestry industry, not only introducing new models but also developing better cooperation between weaver and designer, including the use of color-numbered rather than painted cartoons, a limited palette based on the colors of the dyed yarns, and a coarse texture—innovations that also proved economically sound.

The production of the atelier was not limited to tapestries after cartoons by Lurçat but included weavings after designs by Raoul Dufy, Fernand Léger, Marc Saint-Saëns, Jean Arp, Mathieu Matégot, Victor Vasarely, and many others. After the death of François Tabard, the work was carried on by his brother Paul and his sisters Clémence and Marie-Antoinette.

Through his many writings, Tabard not only promoted tapestry, he also demystified the complexities of tapestry weaving, while demonstrating its potential and possibilities.[268]

AZ

Taito Oy Paavo Tynell and four equal investors

founded this metalwork firm in Helsinki in 1918.[269] During the 1920s and early 1930s a youthful staff working under Tynell's supervision designed a varied range of articles, including ceremonial swords and a bronze door for the Parliament building in Helsinki. By the mid-1930s the company was known primarily for its lighting fixtures, which were austere in their sparse use of ornament and thus consistent with the emerging International Style.

By 1940, Taito's staff had grown to more than 150 and its headquarters, while remaining in Helsinki, was moved twice. Although most of the firm's workers were eventually conscripted, Tynell was able to carry on during the course of World War II. He inventively employed wood, paper, and glass in lamp designs of the war period, using metal only to fulfill military contracts. After the war, Finland's active copper mines enabled Taito to manufacture brass fixtures. By the end of the decade these were available on the domestic and international markets.

In 1953 the firm was bought out by the Finnish conglomerate Idman Osakeyhtiö. Tynell was retained as the chief designer for the lighting division, and his work, most of it commissioned by architects, continued to be labeled Taito. In 1955 Taito executed the lighting for the office of the secretary general of the United Nations. When Tynell retired, in 1963, Idman Osakeyhtiö fully absorbed the lighting division.

MBF

Takaezu, Toshiko Born Pepeekeo, Hawaii, June 17, 1922

Eschewing many of the stylistic and ideological byways that have plagued the design and craft communities, Toshiko Takaezu has steadfastly created vases of great volume, deep color, and striking beauty.[270]

By 1951, when she entered the Cranbrook Academy of Art in Bloomfield Hills, Michigan, she was already something of an accomplished ceramist. She had studied technique at the Honolulu Academy of Art and as a nonmatriculated student under Claude Horan at the University of Hawaii. Several of her pieces had been accepted at the prestigious ceramic exhibitions in Syracuse, New York, and Wichita, Kansas, and Takaezu had already been teaching the craft herself. Once at Cranbrook, she found her mentor in Maija Grotell, with whom she studied until graduation in 1954. Although Takaezu also studied weaving with Marianne Strengell and sculpture with William McVey, and throughout her career has continued to weave and occasionally sculpt, it was Grotell's teaching—through deed as much as word—that deeply influenced her.

Takaezu's early works are marked by a distinct Orientalizing tendency, which was due as much to her Japanese-Hawaiian heritage as to the influence of Bernard Leach and his circle. At this point in her development she used muted ash glazes and calligraphic decoration on small bowls, teapots, and similar forms. An important turning point occurred when she upended a teapot and created a spouted vase. From this emerged a series of vessels, many multispouted, which, although thrown on the wheel, were paddled into asymmetrical forms. She also experimented with stacking the thrown spheres vertically, resulting in the *Tamarind* series. By the late 1950s Takaezu had begun to return to simpler forms—gently deflated, asymmetrical spheres, often with very small necks or minuscule openings, and endowed with bursts of brilliant color. Her glazed plates were rightly likened to landscapes.

During the course of her evolution, Takaezu supported herself by teaching. While at Cranbrook she taught at the Flint Institute of Art from 1952 to 1953, at Cranbrook Academy summer school from 1954 to 1956, and with Harvey Littleton at the University of Wisconsin in 1954 and 1955. She traveled to Japan in 1955, ostensibly to learn to make tea bowls but also to explore her ethnic roots, and then she returned to the Midwest. Settling in Cleveland in 1956, she taught at the Institute of Art there until 1966, with a leave in 1958–59 to revisit Hawaii and teach at the Honolulu Academy of Art. In 1966 she moved to New Jersey to take a position in the Creative Arts Program at Princeton University. She has lectured widely and since 1975 has maintained a studio in Quakertown, New Jersey.

By the mid-1960s Takaezu's formal vocabulary became crystallized. The growing simplicity and reductive nature of her vessels culminated in a series of large—often two feet in diameter—closed, globular shapes called *Moon Pots*. An alternate form was the *Ceramic Forest*—cylindrical vessels, often five or six feet in height, and rounded at the top. In their simplicity lies a certain majesty, and in their resonant glazes a poetry of color. Running throughout Takaezu's work is

a restrained, Zen-like mysticism, as in the variable groupings of the *Ceramic Forest* and in the inclusion of bits of clay inside a vessel that can create sound but remain unseen.

ME

Tawney, Lenore Born Lorain, Ohio, May 10, 1925

The career of fiber artist Lenore Tawney is permeated by her interest in mysticism.[271] Raised a Roman Catholic, she later sought inspiration in ethnic cultures, including American and Asian Indian, and in the mystical writings of Saint John of the Cross and Erich Neumann. Accordingly, her works invite deep religious contemplation.

As a student at the School of the Art Institute of Chicago (1946–48), Tawney studied sculpture with Alexander Archipenko and weaving with Marli Ehrman. She then moved to Paris and from there began a spiritual quest that took her first to Africa and the Near East. In 1954 she studied tapestry weaving with Martta Taipale, one of Finland's important weavers, at the Penland School of Crafts in North Carolina, which led to her own experiments on the loom. Her first weavings were innovative transparent linear weaves with exposed warps.

When Tawney moved to New York in 1957, she established herself in the first of a long series of lofts; her friends and neighbors included painters Jack Youngerman, Robert Indiana, and Agnes Martin, and she has remained close with ceramist Toshiko Takaezu, an artist who shares her interest in mysticism. In the early New York years she studied gauze weaving with Lili Blumenar, and, taking fetishistic pre-Columbian textiles as her models, she began tying shells and feathers into her fringes. In an entirely different vein, she made mixed-medium postcard collages—influenced by Kurt Schwitters's *Merz* collages and Joseph Cornell's boxes—with pebbles, feathers, and other natural materials. These postcards were actually sent in the mail.

As her work increased in size, Tawney broke away from the rectangular format of the loom. She created revolutionary three-dimensional woven forms that approach sculpture in concept, shaped by means of a reed, of her invention, that has an open top, permitting threads to be moved in or out. By the end of the 1960s she began her important *Cloud Formations*, public artworks two stories high, one of which was commissioned in 1978 by the General Services Administration in Santa Rosa, California. Composed of thousands of separate linen threads, they resemble cloudbursts of rain. In recent years Tawney has put weaving aside, concentrating on assemblages of natural matter and written texts in poetic constructions.

The artist has maintained her distance from the public, but her intensely private art has nevertheless been featured in major exhibitions, notably a traveling retrospective organized by the American Craft Museum.

FTH

Teague, Walter Dorwin Born Decatur, Indiana, December 18, 1883; died Flemington, New Jersey, December 5, 1960

One of the first industrial designers in America and an early exponent of Streamlining, Teague remained in the forefront of design in the postwar years as well.[272] According to him, the appropriate aesthetic appearance for the machine age "... must be built in and not applied; has nothing to do with decoration; is essentially a look of efficiency, competence, stability, durability, simplicity, and honesty, revealed with grace and charm."[273] These design ideals remained consistent throughout his career, as did his faith in modern technology and his belief that form follows function.

From 1903 to 1907, Teague studied nights at New York's Art Students League. One of his first jobs involved lettering and illustration for mail-order catalogues. Teague worked for Calkins and Holdin and another New York advertising agency before opening his own office, which catered to a clientele consisting primarily of advertising agencies and publishers, in 1911. He popularized the use of decorative borders—subsequently known as "Teague borders"—to frame advertisements.

Teague underwent a design catharsis, which he dated precisely to July 30, 1926. He went to Europe, where he studied Le Corbusier's work, and, from that time, devoted himself exclusively to the new field of industrial design. He later advanced his theories in a book, *Design This Day: The Technique of Order in the Machine Age*, published in 1940.

The rise of Teague's career coincided with the rise of post-Depression sales; he is best known for the application of his design principles to domestic objects. Because Teague's career touched many major corporations—Ford Motors, U.S. Steel, Corning Glass, and National Cash Register, to name but a few—his stylistic approach entered the mainstream of American life. Perhaps Teague's most popular early design, for the Eastman Kodak Company, was a molded plastic camera called the *Baby Brownie*, produced from 1934 to 1941 for a total of over 3.5 million. His revolutionary midcentury designs ranged from Scripto pens (1954–55) and Schaefer Beer cans (1957) to interiors of Boeing 707 airplanes (1956). The holder of many design awards, Teague was also the founder (1940) and first president of the American Society of Industrial Designers. He was president of the American Institute of Graphic Arts from 1951 to 1953. Throughout his career Teague also designed many architectural projects, such as the United States Air Force Academy in Colorado Springs.

His New York design firm has been known as Walter Dorwin Teague Associates since 1951. The firm became a managing directorship after Teague's death and was incorporated in 1967. It specializes in the design of products, packaging, graphics, interiors, transportation conveyances and systems, and visual communications, maintaining offices in Washington State, California, Arizona, Tennessee, Massachusetts, and Washington, D.C.

FTH

Tecno S.p.A. In 1927 Gaetano Borsani founded Atelier di Varedo, a firm that made traditional furniture by hand. In 1937 his sons, Osvaldo and Fulgenzio, opened Arredamenti Borsani di Varedo in Milan. Fulgenzio was in charge of the business, while Osvaldo developed the designs and handled production. Although they started out making wooden furniture, in 1953 they changed the firm's name to Tecno and began to produce high-tech furniture designed by Osvaldo. These pieces were made of steel with foam rubber upholstery and looked more like industrial goods than traditional home furniture. The first Tecno exhibit, at the Milan X Triennale in 1954, featured Osvaldo's D70 divan-bed. His P40 lounge chair and adjustable tables and beds followed.[274]

At first Osvaldo did most of the designing, but by the 1960s Tecno was also working with other architects and designers. Carlo De Carli's armchair with a spring-steel-supported back won the grand prize at the Milan XII Triennale in 1960. Eugenio Gerli designed tables and chairs for Tecno during the 1960s, and Gio Ponti designed a bed and a child's writing desk. In 1970 Osvaldo established the Centro Progetti Tecno for design, which is now headed by his son-in-law, Marco Fantoni. In the 1970s and 1980s Tecno expanded into molded plastic furniture for large-scale projects while continuing to produce furniture by name designers for business and domestic use, such as the *Nomos* desk series (1986) by Norman Foster Associates.

The Borsani family remains closely tied to Tecno: Fulgenzio is chairman, and Osvaldo's daughter, Valeria Fantoni Borsani, is vice president.

Testa, Angelo Born Springfield, Massachusetts, August 15, 1921; died Springfield, August 13, 1984

Angelo Testa was the son of Italian immigrants.[275] His primary schooling was in Springfield, Massachusetts, where he was born. Then he went to New York and enrolled in the New York School of Fine and Applied Arts. In 1939 he began attending the University of Chicago to study archaeology. However, he soon transferred to the Institute of Design, where he studied under László Moholy-Nagy, Gyorgy Kepes, and George F. Keck. In 1945 Testa became the first graduate of the Institute.

Although he painted and sculpted throughout his life, it was in the field of textile design that he left his greatest mark. His involvement in textiles began in 1942, with the pattern *Little Men*, a class assignment for a silk-screen project at the Institute of Design. In 1947 he established Angelo Testa and Company in Chicago, a firm that remained in business throughout Testa's lifetime. An exponent of Bauhaus principles, Testa experimented with the loom, and his patterns were translated into affordable, machine-woven goods. Far more numerous, though, were his printed designs, which were always silk-screened onto either white or natural grounds. He used only cotton or linen, never synthetic fabrics. His greatest interest was furnishing textiles, but he also designed clothing materials, carpets, and patterns for paper and plastic manufacturers.[276]

Throughout his career, his design vocabulary was primarily linear and geometric. Though Testa was lauded by contemporary architects, designers, and decorators, traditionalists frowned on his patterns. His honors include two Good Design awards from the Museum of Modern Art, for *Furrows* in 1945 and for *Banda-Duo* in 1950; an American Institute of Decorators award in 1947; and Philadelphia Print Club awards in 1946 and 1947.

His textile designing and production continued through 1960, *Poco* being one of his last commercial lines. Toward the end of his life he was still painting and creating large outdoor sculptures, as well as weaving and designing. He was also a prolific writer for *Look*, *The Christian Science Monitor*, and other periodicals.

Torun *see* Bülow-Hübe, Vivianna Torun

Towle Manufacturing Co. Silversmiths Towle

Silversmiths is one of the oldest table-silver concerns in the United States. Its origins can be traced to the shop founded in 1690 by William Moulton of Newburyport, Massachusetts, and carrying his name. Business continued under successive generations of Moultons until 1857, when the company passed to two former apprentices, Anthony F. Towle and William P. Jones, and was renamed Towle & Jones. From 1873 to 1880 Anthony F. Towle and his son, Edward F., engaged in business as A. F. Towle & Son. In 1882 the firm became the Towle Manufacturing Co. Silversmiths, the name by which it is still known today.

Although it is a firm rooted in traditional styling, producing mostly ornate, heavily oxidized sterling silver flatware and hollowware, it has occasionally explored modern design currents. The company brought out wares with restrained Art Nouveau–type curves around 1900 but immediately returned to a grandly festooned Victorian mode. In the 1920s and 1930s, it offered some simplified designs based on the Cubist principles of Art Deco, but again it reverted to the traditional.

In the postwar period John Van Koert served as product design director, from 1948 to about 1952, and Earl Pardon was assistant director of design from 1954 to 1955. Both designers updated the firm's approach by introducing modern styles such as Biomorphism and minimalist geometric. Today the company produces wares in silver, silver plate, stainless steel, and pewter—all in essentially traditional style.

Tynell, Paavo Born Helsinki, January 25, 1890; died Tuusula, Finland, September 13, 1973

Paavo Tynell was a pioneer in the field of Finnish lighting fixtures.[277] His innovative combinations of brass and glass gave his chandeliers and lamps a richness and elegance that belied the relative simplicity of their components.

Trained as a metalsmith at the Taideteollinen Korkeakoulu (Central School of Industrial Design) in Helsinki, Tynell taught metalwork there from 1917 until 1923. In 1918 he established Taito Oy, where he produced a wide range of metal articles, from ceremonial swords to the huge bronze doors in the Parliament building in Helsinki.

In the 1920s and 1930s he employed many young designers, such as Gunnel Nyman, Kaj Franck, and Alvar Aalto, who were later to gain international reputations. By the 1940s his company produced lighting fixtures, made from wood, paper, and glass, designed by Tynell himself. In the postwar period most of his lamps were made of brass alone or brass combined with glass. Many of these were decorative, with motifs adapted from flora, fauna, and natural phenomena such as snowflakes, and took the shape of several pendant units in mobilelike formations or clusters of glass shades affixed to brass stems. In 1948 Taito began exporting lamps to the United States, where they were enthusiastically accepted. They were sold through a Finnish-owned company, Finland House, in New York.

The outbreak of the Korean War in 1950 and the subsequent international recession curtailed exportation. This factor, along with additional domestic problems, caused Taito Oy to merge with the metalworks subsidiary of the conglomerate Idman Osakeyhtiö (Taito Oy's major shareholder and wholesaler). Tynell differed philosophically with the larger company but remained on as chief designer for the lighting division. At the same time, he designed lighting on a free-lance basis for international firms until he retired in 1963. The fixtures designed by Tynell for Idman continued to be marked with the Taito label.

Tynell was chairman of the Finnish Society of Decorative Artists, Ornamo, from 1926 to 1929 and again from 1936 to 1945. He received many awards, both in Finland and abroad, and received the Ornamo golden badge of honor (along with Alvar Aalto) in 1961.

Van Koert, John Born Saint Paul, Minnesota, June 30, 1912

John Van Koert, best known for his work in silver, has also designed furniture and exhibitions.[278] He graduated from the University of Wisconsin at Milwaukee in 1934, received a master's degree from Columbia University in 1935, and taught art and metalsmithing (especially lost-wax casting) in the late 1930s at the University of Wisconsin at Madison. After World War II, he worked for Henry Dreyfuss and then designed jewelry for Harry Winston.

In 1948, John Withers, the forward-looking general manager of Towle Manufacturing Co. Silversmiths, hired Van Koert to develop a progressive line of flatware and hollowware for the tradition-bound silver firm. Amid some controversy within the company, Van Koert conceived *Contour*, which, although aggressively promoted, was not well received by the public. Van Koert was also credited with "Knife/Fork/Spoon," a traveling exhibition organized by the Walker Art Center and sponsored by Towle.

After his association with Towle ended around 1952, Van Koert was appointed American director of "Design in Scandinavia," a traveling exhibition organized to promote Scandinavian design. In about 1957 Van Koert was retained by International Silver to set up worldwide juried competitions. Encouraged by furniture designer Edward J. Wormley, Van Koert began designing furniture in 1955. Among the companies he designed for in the 1950s and 1960s were Dunbar, Drexel, and Heywood-Wakefield.

Vasegaard, Gertrud Hjorth Born Rønne, Denmark, February 2, 1913

For a half-century, Gertrud Vasegaard has steadfastly created ceramics of simplicity, strength, and restrained Oriental quality.[279]

Born into a family of potters, the artist worked from age thirteen to seventeen as a decorator in the L. Hjorths Terracottafabrik, the pottery founded in 1859 by her grandfather in Rønne on the island of Bornholm. From 1930 to 1932 she studied ceramics at the Kunsthåndvaerkerskolen (School of Arts and Crafts) in Copenhagen and subsequently worked in the studios of the renowned Axel Salto and Bode Willumsen, as well as with the potter Olga Jensen.

She returned to Bornholm in 1933 and established a pottery with her sister Lisbet Hjorth (later Munch-Petersen) in Gudhjem, making mostly functional earthenware utensils. In 1935 she married the artist Sigurd Vasegaard. Three years later, with her husband and daughter, Myre, she moved to Holkadalen, where she established an independent studio.

Immediately after the war, when fuel and materials were scarce, Vasegaard received a welcome offer to join Bing & Grøndahl. She worked in its Copenhagen factory during the winter months, returning to her own studio for the remainder of the year until 1948, when she began working full time at Bing & Grøndahl. While maintaining her early preference for simple forms and restrained geometric decoration, she employed the company's high-fired stoneware. Instead of using Bing & Grøndahl's customary mat glazes, she employed vitreous glazes and explored the use of underglaze blue. Her restrained forms and decoration, limited palette, and indebtedness to Oriental traditions put her work in good stead with the overall taste of postwar design. Her favored motifs included an allover scale pattern, concentric diamonds, and small, foliated scrolls. In addition to her studio work, she designed three dinnerware sets, *Gemma* and *Gemina* (both 1959–61) and *Capella* (1975), and a tea set (1955–57) for mass production—all of which continued her Orientalizing aesthetic and her interest in restrained ornament.

In 1959 Vasegaard joined forces with her daughter and the chemical expert Aksel Rode from Bing & Grøndahl to establish a pottery studio in Allégade in Frederiksberg. Here she continues to pursue her earlier interests. Her contemporary work evidences a slightly freer brushwork and concern with texture and a preference for more polygonal forms and certain stepped motifs, as well as the same mastery and subtlety that have marked the artist's work throughout her long career.

ME

Venini S.p.A.

The Venini name has dominated Italian glassmaking for more than half a century; its technical innovations and bright colors have set a standard of excellence.[280]

In 1921 Paolo Venini (1895–1959), a Milanese lawyer, Giacomo Cappellin, a Venetian antiques dealer from a Como family of glassblowers, and Andrea Rioda, a Venetian glassmaker, joined forces; their company was incorporated in 1924 under the name Vetri Soffiati Muranesi Venini Cappellin & C. One of its successes was the line of *soffiati classici* vases based on ones seen in the works of Renaissance painters such as Veronese, Holbein, and Caravaggio. In 1925, the firm was awarded a grand prix at the Paris "Exposition Internationale des Arts Décoratifs et Industriels Modernes," but the partnership was terminated.

Paolo Venini took sole control under the new appellation Vetri Soffiati Muranesi Venini & C. Napoleone Martinuzzi, the newly appointed art director, followed his leanings as a sculptor by initiating a series of humorous animals and potted plants in *pulegoso* (bubbled) glass; perhaps the most fantastic was the stylized, lifesize statue of Josephine Baker. Under Martinuzzi's tenure, which lasted until 1931, the Venini firm made chandeliers, fountains, and leaded-glass windows, architectural commissions that formed an important part of the company business. The firm invited the Milanese architects Gio Ponti, Tomaso Buzzi, and Lanci Marelli to contribute designs. Ponti's works, such as the *Esagonali* (Hexagonal) glasses (1933), were generally architectural, whereas Buzzi's tended toward Neoromanticism.

The architect Carlo Scarpa, who had begun designing for the glassworks in its early years, returned in 1932 as artistic director and instituted many interesting innovations, such as the *Corroso* (Corroded) series with acid-treated surfaces. Scarpa also revived many of the older techniques of Venetian glassmaking, but he recast them in a modern mode. Among his most important achievements was the revival of the *filigrano* technique, using threads of glass canes, and his *Murrine* bowls made of fused slices of cane in imitation of ancient Roman glass. Among the outside artists who worked at Venini was the Swedish ceramist Tyra Lundgren, who in 1938 created a charming series of leaf-shaped dishes and birds.

At first World War II only restricted the firm's activities. In 1942 Scarpa introduced the *Pennellati* (Pennant) series of vessels with freely applied threads of color and *Battuto* (Beaten) vases with wheel-ground surfaces. Finally the war caused the factory to close in 1943. When it reopened in 1946, it assumed a dominant position in Murano. Gio Ponti continued to create new designs, including a series of bottles with anthropomorphic shapes, many multicolored and using the *in calmo* technique of joining different, partially shaped sections while still in a molten state. Some of these were modified for the *Morandiane* series of 1956, named after Giorgio Morandi's still life paintings. Fulvio Bianconi joined the firm in 1948 and made many important contributions—commedia dell'arte and other figures, the much-celebrated *Fazzoletti* (Handkerchief) bowls, and the *Pezzati* (Pieced) vases of fused sections of glass. In the early 1950s he also designed some Biomorphic vases and fluidly stylized figural bottles. In 1953 Massimo Vignelli began working for the Venini firm, conceiving an important series of desk and hanging lamps.

Behind this long listing of designers and designs stood the figure of Paolo Venini, who oversaw the firm's operations, worked closely with his designers, and adapted their ideas. After his death in July 1959, control passed to his widow, Ginette, and his son-in-law Ludovico de Santillana. They maintained the same bright palette and technical virtuosity and continued to invite outside artists.

Tobia Scarpa, son of Carlo, began working at Venini in 1959, creating the *Occhi* (Eyes) series, an extension of the *murrine* technique that endows the vases with a colored grid. In 1961 and 1962, the American Thomas Stearns initiated some strikingly handsome vessels on Venetian themes, such as his *Facciate di Venezia* (Facades of Venice), but his dark colors met with disfavor. Tapio Wirkkala came to work in 1966 (and again in 1970 and 1972), using Venini's by-then standard techniques but adapting them to tightly composed structures. Venini has also been host to American studio glass artists, beginning with Dale Chihuly in 1968, James Carpenter, and, more recently, Toots Zynsky.

In 1972 a fire destroyed the office building and much archival material, but reconstruction was completed by 1974. The continuity of family control was assured when Laura de Santillana, Paolo Venini's granddaughter, entered the firm in 1976. The following year, Sergio Biliotto, former owner of the Flos lighting company, and Aldo Tongana came into the firm as partners. The V-Linea glassworks, founded in 1965 by Ludovico de Santillana and Biliotto to utilize semiautomatic means of production, was coordinated with the Venini organization.

Throughout its history the Venini firm has exhibited regularly at the Venice Biennale and the Monza and Milan Triennales as well as at major world's fairs, garnering too many honors to be enumerated. While it continues to explore new ideas, it has survived so many interim shifts in taste that it has now put back into production many of its old models from the 1940s through the 1960s—models that have become recognized as classics of midtwentieth-century glassmaking.

ME

Vignelli, Massimo
Born Milan, January 10, 1931

Massimo Vignelli and his wife, Lella, are a design team whose work reflects their architectural training.[281] Massimo attended the Accademia di Belle Arti di Brera e Liceo Artistico, the Politecnico in Milan, and the Istituto Universitario di Architettura in Venice until 1957. During the mid-1950s Massimo designed a number of glass lamps for Venini. In 1957 he married Lella Valle (born Udine, August 13, 1934) and they left for the United States, Massimo working as a product designer for a Boston silversmith and Lella attending Massachusetts Institute of Technology's School of Architecture. A year later they moved to Chicago, where he taught at the Institute of Design and she worked in the interior design department of Skidmore, Owings and Merrill. After a few years they returned to Italy and, in 1960, established their own architecture and design firm. Lella received her doctorate from the Istituto Universitario di Architettura in Venice in 1962.

In 1965 Massimo founded Unimark International with a group of American designers; the firm had offices in New York, Chicago, and Milan. An opening in the New York office caused them to return to the United States in 1966, and though they planned to remain only a year or two, they stayed on permanently. At first they hoped to help transform society through design, but they realized that, in fact, society changes design.[282]

In 1971 they left Unimark and established Vignelli Associates to design corporate-identity programs, graphics, books, exhibits, and interiors, and in 1978

they set up Vignelli Designs to design furniture. The Vignellis are known for stylish, geometric, and functional-looking designs. Some of their most important work has been in graphics: they designed printed matter for Knoll in the 1960s and 1970s and logos for American Airlines in 1967 and Bloomingdale's in 1972. They have designed magazines and books for Rizzoli International and others. They often use the grid system for their books, as in the Audubon Society *Field Guides*. In addition, they have designed plastic tableware for ARPE and Heller since 1964; interiors for Saint Peter's Church, New York, in 1975; the *Handkerchief* chair of steel for Knoll in the 1980s; and their own offices in 1985–86, with a decor based on a grid system similar to that used in their book designs.

CWL

Vittorio Bonacina & C.

The Bonacina family has been associated with rattan for a century: Giovanni Bonacina, who had worked for rush and wicker furniture manufacturers in Germany, Austria, and Holland, established his own firm in Lurago d'Erba (Como), Italy, in 1889. First the company made wicker suitcases and trunks, and then chairs in the new Liberty Style. In the following decades it made furniture with Art Deco motifs.

After World War II, Giovanni's son Vittorio inherited the firm and was able to import rush and rattan from the Orient again. He started working with architects as designers in 1950, when Franco Albini designed two rattan chairs for the 1951 Milan IX Triennale—the *Margherita* chair for La Rinascente and the *Gala* chair for L'Enapi. The former is still in production. Designs were commissioned from other modern architects: Albini's partner, Franca Helg, designed several rattan pieces in the late 1950s, including a circular table to match the *Margherita* chair. By 1963 Bonacina was making furniture designed by such architects as Albini, Helg, Sergio Asti, Gian Franco Frattini, Vittorio Gregotti, and the firm of Meneghetti & Stoppino.[283] The firm expanded its range of high-style wicker and rush furniture in a bold new direction in 1972 when it made Ettore Sottsass's *Mickey Mouse* table. Other noted designers for Bonacina in the 1970s and the 1980s are Gae Aulenti and Renzo Mongiardino.

Although Vittorio Bonacina is now mostly retired, the firm remains in the family; his son, Mario, designed many of the more recent models. The furniture is still made largely by hand.

CWL

Vodder, Niels
Born Holsted, Denmark, November 10, 1892; died Allerød, Denmark, November 2, 1982

Niels Vodder began his cabinetmaking apprenticeship in a Holsted workshop and completed it in 1912 in Copenhagen. After serving two years in the Danish Engineer Regiment, he began employment as a journeyman, working throughout Europe. In 1915, after achieving the status of master artisan in shops in Cologne and Hamburg, he returned to work in Copenhagen. Three years later he took over the shop where he had completed his training.[284]

After several years of fabricating only Vodder's designs, the shop began to execute work for architects Arne Jacobsen and Mogens Volenen. Finn Juhl's well-known association with Vodder extended from 1936 until the late 1950s. The seating furniture that resulted from these combined efforts was internationally recognized for the high quality of its design and its artisanal skill. Between 1927 and 1957, Vodder furniture was exhibited almost annually in the Copenhagen Cabinetmakers' Guild exhibitions. His work was awarded the honorable mention and gold medal in both the 1951 and 1957 Milan Triennales. Niels Vodder closed his workshop in the early 1970s.

MBF

Voulkos, Peter Born Bozeman, Montana, January 29, 1924

Through the ceramics he created in the 1950s and 1960s, Peter Voulkos revolutionized American studio pottery, transforming it into an expressive art of great scale and dynamism.

After high school, he worked in Portland, Oregon, from 1941 to 1942, casting and welding fittings for Liberty Ships. During the latter part of World War II, he served in the air force. He attended Montana State University under the GI Bill of Rights, majoring in art. Although his primary interest was painting, a required course in ceramics under Frances Senska turned him to ceramics and sculpture. He then attended the California College of Arts and Crafts in Oakland from 1950 to 1952, receiving a master of fine arts in sculpture.

While Voulkos was still an undergraduate, his ceramics began to receive local and national recognition. His work was marked by forms of simple volumes and large scale, often bearing diminutive spouts or spooled lids (his thesis was on lidded jars), and generally decorated with thinly scratched, stylized figures reminiscent of those found in the work of Joan Miró and Pablo Picasso.

In 1952 Voulkos returned to Bozeman where, with ceramist Rudy Autio, he established a studio at the Archie Bray Foundation. Shoji Hamada and Bernard Leach were among the visitors that first year. A significant turning point was his three weeks of teaching at Black Mountain College near Asheville, North Carolina, and a subsequent stay in New York City; this put him in contact with the most avant-garde artists, many of whom were associated with Abstract Expressionism and related movements. The result of this experience was soon apparent. In Los Angeles, where he headed the ceramics department at the Otis Art Institute, Voulkos created forms that were still larger in scale and that he handled with a distinctive brutality: surfaces were slashed, clay slabs were applied in a collagelike fashion, slips and glazes were dripped freely, pots were stacked or juxtaposed with dynamic bravura. Voulkos's receipt of a gold medal at the 1955 Cannes international exhibition of ceramics suggests his growing world status. His importance in terms of the evolution of American pottery is suggested by the number of prominent ceramists who were then his pupils: Paul Soldner, Michael Frimkess, John Mason, Kenneth Price, Jerry Rothman, and Henry Takemoto.

In 1959 Voulkos began teaching at the University of California at Berkeley, where his students included yet another nucleus of soon-to-be famous ceramists: Robert Arneson, Clayton Bailey, James Melchert, Ron Nagle, Marilyn Levine, and Richard Shaw. Voulkos's work was marked by an ever-increasing manipulation of form and bold oppositions of volumes. His vases were highly sculptural, and many of his works were, in fact, sculpture. *Black Bulerias* won the Musée Rodin prize at the first Paris Biennale in 1959. An exhibition of his paintings and ceramic sculpture was held at the Museum of Modern Art in New York in 1960, and though it at first attracted little critical acclaim except in the craft world, Voulkos actively pursued his goals. He turned to bronze casting that year, ultimately achieving a vastness of scale that had not been possible with clay.

It was not until 1968 that Voulkos returned to ceramics in earnest, creating forms of a simpler monumentality: generally, they are composed of cylindrical volumes stacked in a vertical alignment, many of them covered with a somber black glaze. The other major form that has absorbed his attention is the large plate.

Often of epic proportions, this may be pierced and fractured—even split and glued with epoxy.

Disdainful of the ceramist's traditional concerns—such as clay bodies and special glaze formulas—Voulkos has always emphasized experimentation and activity. His frequent public demonstrations for students and at conferences, as much as his works themselves, embody the liberating force that he has given to the medium of clay. Winner of many awards, he was given a major retrospective exhibition by the American Craft Council in 1978.[285]

ME

Warner & Sons Limited
Since the early eighteenth century the Warner family has been involved with the production of fine textiles in England and has been particularly associated with silk weaving.[286] For the first five generations, beginning with William Warner (died 1712), they were scarlet dyers in Spitalfields and then in Old Ford. The origins of the company are closely tied to the activities of Benjamin Warner (1799–1839), a Jacquard engineer at Bethnal Green, and more specifically to those of his son, Benjamin (1828–1908). The latter continued the family business and expanded it to include designing, through acquisition in 1857 of the firm of the French designer Alphonse Burnier. Warner entered into a series of successive partnerships: with William Folliott (1867–1869), Charles Sillett (1870–1874), and Wager Charles Ramm (1870–1891). Warner & Ramm's small silk-weaving factory moved from Old Ford to Hollybush Gardens in Bethnal Green, with an office and showroom in Newgate Street. Although the firm produced primarily furnishing silks, it occasionally manufactured dress silks, and from 1874 on sold printed cottons, cretonnes, and chintzes.

Warner bought out Ramm in 1891 and brought his sons, Alfred (1856–1939) and Frank (1862–1930), into the business, which was renamed Warner & Sons. In 1894 the company acquired Daniel Walters & Sons, the largest English firm producing figured silks of equal quality. Warner transferred its looms to Walters's former site in Braintree. In 1921 Cloudesley Warner (1894–1928), son of Frank, was taken into the partnership, and he modernized the machinery and methods. Seven years later Warner & Sons Limited was formed.

The firm presented impressive displays of its lines in international exhibitions from the 1870s on, particularly in the years before and after World War I. Its range of silks included both reproductions of earlier styles and more contemporary modes: Japonisme as represented by designs of E. W. Godwin and Bruce Talbert in the 1870s and Art Nouveau.

Warner & Sons was a wholesale distributor for its own textiles as well as for bought-in fabrics that they secured from other manufacturers. The expansion of the firm continued in various directions throughout the twentieth century. An attempt to establish a Paris office, Société des Fabriques Textiles Warner S.A., lasted from 1922 until 1926. In 1927 the firm acquired Dartford Print Works, which specialized in hand-block printing and, later, screen printing, but this subsidiary was divested after World War II. More advantageous was the takeover in 1950 of Helios Ltd., including the looms, plant, and the rights to the innovative designs of Marianne Straub, which led subsequently to the direct employment of the talented designer herself. The firm's other important postwar designers were Alec Hunter, Theo Moorman, and Frank Davies.

As part of its growing emphasis on printed fabrics, Warner & Sons Ltd. became formally associated with Greeff Fabrics Inc. of New York in 1955 and obtained the right to print Greeff's designs in Britain. In 1964 a reciprocal arrangement was instituted whereby the two companies distributed the other's products in their own countries and established markets. Then in 1970

Warner & Sons was sold to Greeff Fabrics, which was a subsidiary of Simmons Company. In turn, Simmons was sold to Gulf and Western Industries Inc. in 1978. Ownership of Warner & Sons was transferred directly to Gulf and Western Industries in 1980, but five years later the latter company sold both Warner & Sons and Greeff to Wickes Companies, Inc. In October 1987 the name of the firm was changed to Warner Fabrics plc.

AZ

Weber, Karl Emanuel Martin (Kem) Born Berlin, November 14, 1889; died Santa Barbara, California, January 31, 1963

One of the best-known industrial designers on the West Coast of the United States in the 1920s and the 1930s, Kem Weber had a sleek Streamlined style that epitomized the burgeoning culture of California.[287]

Weber's training was in cabinetry under the tutelage of Eduard Schultz, a royal cabinetmaker in Potsdam. In 1908 he entered the Unterichtanstalt des Kunstgewerbemuseums (School of the Decorative Arts Museum) in Berlin, studying primarily with Bruno Paul. By the time Weber graduated in 1912, he had already worked on several of his master's projects and had supervised the construction of the German portion of the World's Fair held in 1910 in Brussels. In 1914 Weber helped design the German section for the "Panama-Pacific International Exposition" in San Francisco of 1915 and was sent there to supervise its construction. However, the worsening political situation prevented its execution, and Weber found himself stranded in California, unable to return to his native country due to the outbreak of the war.

During the war Weber held a variety of positions, many not concerned with design. After the war he moved to Santa Barbara, where he taught art, and then opened a design studio where he fashioned interiors, primarily in the Spanish Colonial style, executed furniture and other accessories, and produced architectural designs that suggest Egyptian, Minoan, and Mayan architecture at the same time that they acknowledge the tenets of European Modernism. In 1921 he moved to Los Angeles and began working for Barker Brothers, soon rising to the position of art director for that firm. All of his work—furniture, shop interiors, and packaging—displays the witty, angular style of European modernistic decoration; after becoming a United States citizen in 1924, Weber traveled to Europe the following year.

In 1927 Weber resigned as art director at Barker Brothers (though he continued to work for that firm) and opened his own industrial design studio in Hollywood. Weber's architectural commissions, such as the Sommer and Kaufmann shoe store in San Francisco (1929) and the Friedman residence in Banning (1928–29), are closely allied with the International Style, but they contain highly decorative passages. The project for a new school edifice (1934–35, with students from the Los Angeles Art Center School—where he taught from 1931 until 1941) suggests the sweeping thrust of Erich Mendelsohn's architecture. He designed small-scale objects for the Burbank silversmith Porter Blanchard and for Friedman Silver of New York (1928–29), generally with hard-edged geometric forms, while the clocks he created for Lawson Time of Alhambra (1934) have chic Streamlined forms. He occasionally tried the skyscraper style of Paul Frankl, with whom he was friends, but more often turned to the Streamlined style, as in his plywood *Airline* chair (1934–35). Some of his furniture for Barker Brothers and various commercial firms, such as the Lloyd Manufacturing Co. of Menominee, Michigan (1934), uses the international language of tubular steel but with flamboyant curves and without the austerity of a Marcel Breuer or Ludwig Mies van der Rohe.

During World War II Weber worked on a defense housing project and a system of prefabricated housing for the Douglas Fir Plywood Association of Tacoma. In 1945 he moved back to Santa Barbara, establishing a studio in his home. He essentially abandoned industrial design and for the next decade concentrated on architectural projects. Many of the private homes he designed in this period, like his own, left behind the International Style in plan and returned to traditional materials such as wood, brick, and fieldstone. They looked unquestionably modern but in the more informal style of the postwar years.

ME

Wegner, Hans Jorgensen Born Tønder, South Jutland, Denmark, April 2, 1914

Hans Wegner began his design career at the age of fourteen as an apprentice to a local cabinetmaker.[288] By 1932 he had become a journeyman, and he spent the next four years as a cabinetmaker. Dissatisfied with merely executing the designs of others, however, Wegner began studies in 1936 at the Teknologisk Institut (Institute of Technology) in Copenhagen. In the following year, he transferred to the Kunsthåndvaerkerskolen (School of Arts and Crafts) where he studied under O. Mølgaard Nielsen.

Wegner's design career began in 1938, when he accepted a position in the office of Arne Jacobsen and Eric Møller.[289] In 1943 he opened his own studio in Århus but after the war, in 1946, moved to Ordrup, Copenhagen. There he worked for two years in the architectural office of Palle Suenson and lectured at the Kunsthåndvaerkerskolen until 1953.

Wegner emerged as a mature designer in the late 1940s with a small series of chair forms that were first shown at the annual Cabinetmakers' Guild exhibitions. These remarkable designs established Hans Wegner at the age of thirty-three as the next leader of the craftsmen-designers—that is, as Kaare Klint's successor. This group became one of three distinct schools centered in Copenhagen in the postwar years, when Denmark emerged as the major center for Scandinavian furniture design. Wegner's contribution—indeed, his aesthetic achievement—was his modern reworking of the traditional wooden chair, whether hand- or machine-made. As an artist of the first rank, he provided at midcentury a viable alternative to Modernist industrial design. In recognition of these achievements, he was honored with the Lunning Prize in 1951.

Wegner's first notable design was the *Peacock* (model no. JH 550) armchair of 1947, which was clearly inspired by Windsor forms. Its light-colored, attenuated wooden frame, featuring a natural finish, marked a major shift in Danish furniture design.[290] This was followed some two years later by Wegner's folding chair (model no. JH 512), which reflected the Danish preoccupation with perfecting vernacular, collapsible furniture. It was, however, Wegner's famous *Round* chair (model no. JH 501), also introduced in 1949, that was perhaps his most memorable form. For more than a quarter of a century the Dane has modified and adapted it in a multitude of materials and models; a side chair of 1952 (model no. JH 505) remains one of the most successful variants. Wegner's other archetypal design in 1949 was for a wide, low lounge chair, influenced by Eero Saarinen's *Womb* chair of 1946–48. Wegner created a number of variants with molded plywood shells,[291] as well as one with a metal frame and string upholstery (model no. GE 225) in 1950. Perhaps the most pleasing example is the model no. JH 46 lounge chair of 1960—a bold, sculptural piece with a metal base.

Wegner's forte, however, remains the wooden chair with minimal upholstery, which he perfected with superb craftsmanship. When he worked in industrial design during the 1950s and 1960s, his large-scale forms, such as case pieces, upholstered furniture, and office systems, though they explored new technology with metal and molded plywood, were rarely as original or even altogether successful.[292] Despite its somewhat limited parameters, Hans Wegner's contribution to modern design has been significant.

RCM

Wiener, Edward (Ed) Born New York, July 10, 1918

Jeweler Ed Wiener has always insisted on change, believing that designers must create objects in response to new modes.[293] His work, from its beginnings in 1946 to the present, has familiar motifs, such as spirals or ovoids, fish and figures, but they are always updated stylistically and reworked with new materials and techniques.

Wiener apprenticed in his father's butcher shop, but during World War II he discovered an aptitude for manual skills while working on a radio assembly line. Inspired by seaside motifs experienced on a 1944 summer trip to Provincetown, Massachusetts, and also by Calderesque neoprimitive shapes, he began to make jewelry. In 1945 he enrolled in a general craft course at Columbia University, the only formal jewelry training he was to have. He then set up a studio in his home and began his professional career by fashioning monogram pins out of silver wire.

Attracted by Provincetown's bohemian atmosphere, Wiener opened his first shop there (shared with a sandalmaker) in the summer of 1946. He sold Mexican jewelry, handbags, and belts, as well as his own jewelry, and received much support from the artists who frequented his shop. Encouraged, he and his wife Doris[294] returned to New York in the fall of 1946 to open their first New York studio, on Second Avenue and Second Street. In the winter of 1947, Wiener opened a store, Arts and Ends, on West Fifty-fifth Street, close to the Museum of Modern Art. Most of his clients were artists, art teachers, and collectors of modern art. In 1953 he moved his store to West Fifty-third Street, even closer to the museum. Until 1958, he maintained a second shop downtown in Greenwich Village, another focus for modern jewelry.

In the mid-1960s, after visits to the medieval Musée de Cluny in Paris and the gem-cutting centers in Jaipur, India, Wiener was inspired to work in textured gold and to incorporate stones. He began to regard jewelry not only as adornment but also as amulets. Byzantine jewelry especially fascinated him, because of its formal compromise between European and Asian styles. He continued working in this current and, for the decade from 1971 until 1981, maintained a shop at Fifty-seventh Street and Madison Avenue. Now in his seventies, he is still making jewelry in a studio on East Twentieth Street and is involved in what he terms "the great reprise," his resurrection of forms and motifs he first used in his jewelry of the 1940s and 1950s. His work was the subject of a 1988 retrospective exhibition.

TLW

Wilton Royal Carpet Factory Ltd. Wilton is the successor to what is probably the oldest carpet-making factory in England.[295] Its oldest building dates back to 1655, when the first weavers were making tapestrylike carpets. In the eighteenth century, a local lord, the eighth earl of Pembroke, decided to upgrade the quality of the carpets, and to do so he smuggled two expert weavers out of France in empty wine barrels. They developed the Wilton weave, the first high-pile carpet to be machine-woven on a loom in England, in 1740. By 1791 there were three firms at Wilton making tapestries and carpets.

After Napoleon's defeat at Waterloo, the importation of Continental goods almost drove the carpet factories in Wilton out of business. But in 1835 Messrs. Blackmore and Son purchased the premises now used by Wilton Royal Carpet Factory and brought in looms for making hand-knotted carpets and weavers from Axminster. The carpets they produced were typical mid-Victorian florals in Persian, French, or Italian styles. One of the six exhibited in the Great Exhibition of 1851 was lent by Queen Victoria, suggesting the level of patronage. The carpet, seventy feet long and thirty-five feet wide, that Wilton wove in 1859 was claimed to be the largest carpet ever made. Power looms were introduced during the 1860s and 1870s.

In the 1870s the firm was bought by Yates & Wills, later known as Yates & Co. Around 1880, before setting up his own manufactory, William Morris designed some rugs for Yates. In the 1890s Pardoe Yates managed the firm. In 1905 it went bankrupt, supposedly because company money had been squandered by Yates on riotous living.

In order to save the jobs of the workers, the earls of Pembroke and Radnor formed the present company by private subscription that same year. The factory received its first Royal Warrant sometime between 1905 and 1910, and then the factory became known as Wilton Royal. After the triumph of French design at the "Exposition des Arts Décoratifs et Industriels Modernes" in Paris in 1925, Wilton started producing modern-style carpets as well as the more traditional designs that constituted the major portion of its business. During the 1930s carpets woven on hand looms were made to the progressive designs of E. McKnight Kauffer, Marion Dorn, and others.

After World War II the Modernist movement in British carpets, especially at Royal Wilton, languished, and in 1958 the company sold its hand looms to make room for more power machinery.

CWL

Wirkkala, Tapio Born Hanko, Finland, June 2, 1915; died Esbo, Finland, May 19, 1985

Wirkkala, Finland's most important postwar designer, received his early training at the Taideteollinen Korkeakoulu (Central School of Industrial Design) in Helsinki from 1933 to 1936.[296] After completing his military service he began a career in advertising. In 1944 he married Rut Bryk, a ceramic designer then working at the Arabia factory. His prize-winning entries for Iittala glasswork's design contest in 1946 won him a position with that company, and his *Kanttarelli* vases and engraved designs quickly brought him to public attention. In that same year he triumphed in a Bank of Finland competition to design new currency. In 1950 the trays of laminated wood he designed for Soinne et Kni were voted "the most beautiful object of the year" by the American Institute of Decorators. In his works he established an aesthetic that, though alluding to organic forms, was based on complex geometric forms and striated lines that recall Constructivist sculpture. His installations of the Finnish display at an industrial arts exhibition in Zurich in 1951 and at the Milan IX Triennale brought him still further acclaim: at the latter exhibition he was awarded three grand prizes. His international reputation was by now secure.

The decade from 1950 to 1960 marked the apogee of Wirkkala's organic style, characterized by fluent forms in glass, wood, and metal derived from leaves, eggs, polar ice blocks, and other natural motifs. In addition to designing, he served from 1951 to 1954 as art director of the Taideteollinen Korkeakoulu. He then left to work for six months with Raymond Loewy Associates in New York. Although he returned to his native land, he maintained his international contacts, beginning in 1956 a fruitful association with Rosenthal of Germany, including participation in the latter's DOMUS design team. Among the many exhibitions of industrial art that he designed were the Milan X Triennale in 1954 and the Brussels World's Fair of 1958. He continued to garner prizes at these events, including three grand prizes at the 1954 Triennale and a grand prize and gold medal at the XII Triennale in 1960.

Throughout the last twenty-five years of his career, Wirkkala worked with unabated diversity, for which he continued to receive recognition. The basic precepts of his approach to design did not change, but he manifested a marked preference for a simpler geometry. In addition to creating new designs for Iittala, he traveled to Venice in 1965 and began a collaboration with Venini. His association with Rosenthal resulted in new designs for porcelain, glass, and stainless steel. He designed similar types of objects for Finnish firms, as well as electric lamps and bulbs, knives, smoking pipes, and camping equipment. He also installed several important exhibitions of Finnish decorative arts. His most notable awards of the period are the five gold medals he won at the Faenza ceramics design competitions between 1963 and 1973. A major retrospective exhibition of Wirkkala's career was prepared in 1981 by the Finnish Society of Crafts and Design and circulated in Europe and the Americas.

ME

Wormley, Edward J. Born Oswego, Illinois, December 31, 1907

As chief designer and director of design for the Dunbar Furniture Company from 1931 to 1970, Wormley became known for his conservative adaptations of modern design and his prolific output.[297] Following his studies at the School of the Art Institute of Chicago from 1926 to 1927, Wormley worked in the design studios of Marshall Field in that city (1927–30) and Berkey and Gay in Grand Rapids, Michigan (1930), before going to Dunbar in Berne, Indiana, in 1931. That year Wormley traveled to London, Berlin, and Paris, visiting the offices of both Le Corbusier and Émile-Jacques Ruhlmann, which evinces something of the eclecticism that remained integral to his art.

During World War II, from 1942 to 1944, Wormley was in Washington, D.C., to head the Furniture Unit of the Office of Price Administration. He maintained his affiliation with Dunbar after the war, but in 1945 he also opened his own office in New York for designing interiors for residential and corporate clients. His postwar designs show an appreciation of the work of Scandinavian designers such as Finn Juhl, whom he visited in 1951. Wormley designed lamps for Lightolier, furniture for Drexel, and a series of cabinets for RCA, as well as carpets for Alexander Smith and Sons and textiles for Schiffer Prints. In both 1951 and 1952, his work was included in the "Good Design" exhibitions at the Museum of Modern Art, and in 1964 one of his chairs was exhibited in the Milan XIII Triennale. In 1960 he became a Fellow of the Association of Interior Designers. Although he closed his office in 1967, he continued as a consultant to Dunbar until 1970, when he retired to Weston, Connecticut.

Wormley's style over the years was consistent and recognizable, characterized by its sympathy with traditional design. He invented metal parts and frames to create stronger and less costly products, and his understanding of woodworking machinery helped him design well-crafted modern furniture in keeping with market needs.[298] Wormley's approach was that of an interior designer who never believed any individual piece of furniture to be more important than the interior as a whole. Edgar Kaufmann, jr., aptly described this approach by saying Wormley's furniture had "good manners."[299]

DAH

Wright, Frank Lloyd Born Richland Center, Wisconsin, June 8, 1867; died Phoenix, April 9, 1959

More than any other American, Frank Lloyd Wright helped to shape the history of modern architecture.[300] He developed a concept of an organic architecture to which he adhered throughout his career, requiring that all the furnishings of his houses express the spirit of the architectural whole. The scale, proportions, and materials of his furniture were calculated to create an effect of freedom and harmony.

In 1893 Wright established an independent architectural practice, and from then until his first trip to Europe in 1909–10, his Prairie School style took form. The low, horizontal lines that characterize this style developed slowly, beginning with the H. Harley Bradley residence in Kankakee, Illinois (1893), and the Ward Willits House in Highland Park, Illinois (1901), and culminating in the Frederick G. Robie House in Chicago and the Avery Coonley House in Riverside, Illinois, both of 1908. He designed furnishings that were integral to their architectural surroundings. A strong geometric quality, fidelity to natural materials, and adaptability to machine production characterize Wright's furniture designs throughout his career.

In 1908 Wright traveled to Europe to assist with the first major European publication of his work, *Ausgeführte Bauten und Entwürfe*, published by Wasmuth in Berlin. This trip is often seen as a major turning point in Wright's life and work. It established his fame in Europe, and Wright in turn was influenced by European—especially Viennese—design. On his return to the United States, the architect received several important commissions, including the Avery Coonley Playhouse in Riverside, Illinois (1912), and the Midway Gardens in Chicago (1914).

The character of Wright's Prairie furniture began to change after he returned from Europe in 1910; this is apparent in the furniture for Taliesin at Spring Green, Wisconsin (1911), and the Little House in Wayzata, Minnesota (1913). The darker-stained furniture of the Prairie years was replaced by unstained oak furniture that was lighter in color; the horizontal molding was abandoned; and the terminals of the vertical elements were eliminated. Forms became more straightforward and severely geometric.

In the mid-1930s, after a half-century of prolific architectural practice, Wright—in his late sixties—displayed a renewed creativity, as is evident in the Edgar J. Kaufmann residence, in Ohiopyle, Pennsylvania (1935); the S. C. Johnson Administration Building in Racine, Wisconsin (1936); and the inexpensive Usonian houses, which were introduced at this time. Ideally, a Usonian house and its furnishings were completed—both inside and out—in one operation, with all unnecessary materials and labor eliminated. Most furniture was built into the walls and was simple enough to be constructed on site by millworkers or by the homeowners themselves.

During the 1940s and 1950s, when Wright designed furniture for luxury houses, he followed his original principles of simplicity and the use of natural materials, occasionally adapting earlier designs. Wright's major endeavors in commercial design were the mass-produced furniture for Heritage-Henredon Furniture Company and fabrics and wallpapers for F. Schumacher & Company, put on the market about 1955.

DAH & JTT

Wright, Russel Born Lebanon, Ohio, April 3, 1904; died New York, December 21, 1976

A leading champion of Modernist design from the 1930s through the 1950s, Russel Wright tempered its dogmatic aspects by favoring a soft style, harmonizing it with traditional forms and creating for a casual lifestyle.[301]

Wright's emphasis on simplicity can perhaps be traced to his childhood: his father was a Quaker and their home had Mission-style furniture. He studied briefly at the Cincinnati Academy of Art in 1920 and then for a year at the Art Students League in New York. At Princeton University and in the summers, he worked in theatrical groups and assisted Norman Bel Geddes, who was then a stage designer. In 1924 he became an assistant to costume and set designer Aline Bernstein, a formative influence on his early career, and held other theatrical posts.

In 1927 Wright met Mary Small Einstein, a sculpture student from a wealthy, socially prominent family. They married, and following her advice, he left the theater to become a designer. His first works were witty and decorative, such as caricature masks of personalities and aluminum animals stylized in the manner of the Hagenauer Werkstätte of Vienna, that were sold through the New York shop of Rena Rosenthal. He then began producing a line of spun-aluminum household items—tea sets, pitchers, cocktail shakers, bun warmers—geometric in form, that he endowed with a purposefulness of function. These objects were destined for an urban, servantless America that entertained informally. Wright branched out into larger ventures, creating radios for the Wurlitzer Company, metal accessories for the Chase Brass and Copper Company, furniture for the Heywood-Wakefield Company, and a suite of furniture produced by Conant Ball Co. for R. H. Macy of New York. These designs display a gradual shift from the Streamlining of the Wurlitzer radio and the understated Cubist elements of the Heywood-Wakefield furniture to a traditionalism in the furniture for Macy's due to the use of solid maplewood, overlapping, butted joints, and even a homely clumsiness.

In 1935 Russel Wright, his wife, Mary, and Irving Richards, a designer and businessman, formed a partnership, Russel Wright Associates. One of their first ventures—and ultimately the great success of Wright's career—was the dinner service *American Modern*, designed in 1937 but not put into production until two years later. As part of the designer's growing promotion of a native, less European form of Modernism, Wright promoted a scheme called the American Way, which included his works and those of important American industrial designers. Its lofty ideals could not survive initial marketing problems and the wartime restrictions, and it folded.

In the postwar era, Wright remained concerned with the same issues as before. He developed further pieces for his *American Modern* dinnerware, which continued to be sold until 1957, and complementary glassware, table linens, and stainless steel flatware. He created another successful dinnerware set, *Casual China*, this for the Iroquois China Company, several sets in melamine plastic, and the *Easier Living* collection for the Statton Furniture Co. These and many other commissions suggest the well-established nature of Russel Wright's reputation as a leading designer. They all emphasized the casual American life-style (as did the book he and his wife coauthored, *A Guide to Easier Living*, 1951), and they all bore a family resemblance to the forms and colors he had established in the 1930s. Occasionally he tried newer ideas, as in the metal folding chairs and tables (1950) and school furniture (1955) for Shwayder Brothers. He also did packaging design, fabric and vinyl lines, and some interiors. But none of his postwar work equaled the artistic or commercial success of his earlier career, and except for a few scattered works in the 1960s, Wright was essentially retired. His wife had died in 1952 and Wright spent an increasing amount of time and energy on his country home, Dragon Rock in Garrison, New York, which was completed in 1961.

ME

Zeisel, Eva Polanyi Stricker Born Budapest, November 11, 1906

Eva Zeisel's long career as a designer for the ceramics industry and the progression of styles she employed reflect the history of twentieth-century avant-garde design, a history in which she often played a leading role.[302]

One of three children in a wealthy, intellectual family, Zeisel was raised in both Budapest and Vienna. She was trained by a traditional potter. Her early studio work and designs she created at the Kispester factory (1926) blended Hungarian folk art and humorous elements in the style of the Wiener Werkstätte.

Working in Germany at the Scramberger Majolika Fabrik in the late 1920s brought about a dramatic change in her career. Zeisel left handicraft for serial production, and her forms became geometric and hard-edged, in response to the new International Style. In 1930 she moved to Berlin and worked briefly for Christian Karstens. Then in 1932 she left for the Soviet Union, like other members of her family and friends, including the German physicist Alexander Weissberg, whom she married there. Despite the economic plight of that country, she found employment designing first for the Lomonosov factory in Leningrad (1932–34) and then the Dulevo factory (1934–36), rising to the position of art director of the China and Glass Industry of the Russian Republic. She was then caught in the Stalinist purges and imprisoned for almost a year and a half. She returned to Hungary but was soon forced to flee, this time from the Nazis. In England she married Hans Zeisel, a sociologist she had known in Berlin, and the couple immigrated to the United States.

Eva Zeisel arrived in New York in 1938 and gradually gained a position in the American ceramic industry. In 1939 she began teaching at Pratt Institute in Brooklyn and occasionally spoke and wrote articles on industrial design, all of which contributed to her career. The major turning point was a commission to create a dinner service for Castleton China in which the Museum of Modern Art acted as sponsor. Designed in 1942–43 but not put into production until after the war, *Museum* dinnerware was promoted as the first Modernist porcelain dinnerware in the United States. Its simplicity and formal elegance, its balance of austere geometry with subtle curves, were warmly praised by all critics.

In the postwar years Zeisel became increasingly concerned with curved forms. Her informal, particolored *Town and Country* for Red Wing Potteries (c. 1946) has elements that are asymmetrically flared and others that are zoomorphic. A third set produced by Hall China under the name *Tomorrow's Classic* was more insistently rhythmic than *Museum* but less eccentric than *Town and Country*, and it proved a great commercial success.

The late 1940s and early 1950s were her halcyon years. Zeisel received numerous commissions for tabletop services and kitchenware around the United States, and she also designed glass, plastic, and metal items—all marked by a fluidity of volume and what she termed a "lyric line." In 1953 she gave up her teaching post at Pratt Institute and moved to Chicago with her husband, though by the following year she was maintaining residences in both Chicago and New York. Most of her subsequent creations in the late 1950s were done for foreign concerns: Rosenthal (West Germany), Mancioli (Italy), and Noritake (Japan). Much of her work of this period remained at the design stage and did not go into production. Her last major American commission was a line of informal dinnerware for the Hyalyn Porcelain Company of Hickory, North Carolina (1963). By the mid-1960s, Zeisel was essentially in retirement. In 1983 she received a grant from the National Endowment for the Arts and returned to her native Hungary, working both in the Kispester-Granit and Zsolnay factories. The following year a retrospective exhibition of her work began touring North America and then Europe.

ME

Biographical Notes

1. The most extensive biography of Aalto is by Göran Schildt: *Alvar Aalto: The Early Years* (New York: Rizzoli, 1984); *Alvar Aalto: The Decisive Years* (1986). Other perceptive works are Juhani Pallasmaa, ed., *Alvar Aalto Furniture* (Helsinki: Museum of Finnish Architecture, 1985); and *Alvar and Aino Aalto as Glass Designers* (Helsinki: Iittala-Nuutajärvi Oy, 1988).

2. Following the death of Aino in 1949, Alvar Aalto married Elissa Makiniemi, also an architect.

3. The basic study on the artist is *Magdalena Abakanowicz* (New York: Abbeville, 1982).

4. The basic studies of the designer's work are Franca Helg, ed., *Franco Albini, 1930–1970* (New York: Rizzoli, 1981); and Stephen Leet, ed., *Franco Albini: Architecture and Design* (New York: Princeton Architectural Press, 1989).

5. Vittorio Gregotti, "Italian Design, 1940–1971," in Emilio Ambasz, ed., *Italy: The New Domestic Landscape* (New York: Museum of Modern Art, 1972), 333.

6. The history of the firm presented here is based primarily on data from Manhattan telephone directories. It has not been possible to question Carlos Alemany.

7. H. A. Harvey and Raymond D. McGill, *National Cyclopaedia of American Biography* (New York: James T. White & Company, 1971), vol. 5, 300–301.

8. Rosalie Flynn, Anne Macko, and Joe Rusik, *In the Mill* (Yonkers, New York: Hudson River Museum, 1987), 7–8.

9. Ibid., 9.

10. For a partial history of A. Michelsen, see Esbjørn Hiort, *Modern Danish Silver* (London: A. Zwemmer, 1954).

11. The most complete, current source of information regarding this artist is Jens Jorgen Thorsen, *Aagaard Andersen* (Copenhagen: Statens Museum for Kunst, 1982).

12. Gunnar Aagaard Andersen, "Furniture Reconsidered," *Mobilia*, 296–97 (1980) 89, 104.

13. The photographs of the Apelli & Varesi shop are illustrated in Giovanni Brino, *Carlo Mollino* (Milan: Idea Books, 1985), 56–57.

14. A basic history of the Arabia firm is found in the special centenary issue of the parent company's *Ceramics and Glass*, nos. 1–2 (1973).

15. Information on this firm was obtained from Eugene Paceleo of Sambonet, New York, and from an undated company brochure, "Silver: A Family Matter."

16. Pekka Suhonen, *Artek: 1935–1985* (Helsinki: Taideteollisuusmuseo, 1985), 14. In addition to this valuable catalogue, see Göran Schildt, *Alvar Aalto: The Decisive Years* (New York: Rizzoli, 1986), 121–28, for a clear presentation of the Artek period.

17. For a brief sketch of Arundell Clarke's early career, see Olga Gueft, "Clarke Plots a Journey into Light," *Interiors*, 111 (June 1952), 124–27.

18. See "Expert Tailoring in Slacks Is Urged," *New York Times*, March 14, 1945.

19. Gueft, "Clarke Plots a Journey into Light," 126.

20. The most complete source on Asko is Riitta Miestamo, *Suomalaisen huonekalun muotoja sisätö/The Form and Substance of Finnish Furniture* (Lahti: Askon Säätiö, 1981).

21. For a survey of Ballmer's work, see Glauco Felici, "Walter Ballmer," *Graphis*, 35 (January–February 1980), 326–39.

22. The catalogue of this exhibition provides the best discussion of Mirko Basaldella's work.

23. The basic studies on the designer are Arthur A. Cohen, *Herbert Bayer: The Complete Work* (Cambridge, Massachusetts: The MIT Press, 1984); and Gwen Finkel Chanzit, *Herbert Bayer and Modernist Design in America* (Ann Arbor, Michigan: UMI Research Press, 1987).

24. Herbert Bayer, Walter and Ise Gropius, eds., *Bauhaus 1919–1928* (New York: Museum of Modern Art, 1938).

25. For an excellent account of the jeweler's career, see Karl Schollmayer, *Friedrich Becker: Schmuck, Silbergerät, Kinetische Objekte 1951–1983* (Düsseldorf: Kunstverein für die Rheinlande und Westfalen, 1984).

26. The major source for Bellini is Cara McCarty, *Mario Bellini, Designer* (New York: Museum of Modern Art, 1987).

27. For Bellmann's career, see Edward Plüss, ed., *Künstler Lexikon der Schweiz, XX. Jahrhundert* (Frauenfeld: Verlag Huber & Co., 1958–67), vol. 1, 69.

28. On Bertoia, see Robert J. Clark et al., *Design in America: The Cranbrook Vision 1925–1950* (New York: Harry N. Abrams in association with The Detroit Institute of Arts and The Metropolitan Museum of Art, 1983), 163, 268; also June Kompass Nelson, *Harry Bertoia, Sculptor* (Detroit: Wayne State University Press, 1970).

29. Aspects of Bianconi's career are considered in Franco Deboni, *I vetri Venini* (n.p.: Umberto Allemandi & C., 1988), 52, figs. 89–125, 139; Carlo Dinelli, "Advertising Art in Italy," *Graphis*, 6, no. 33 (1950), 426–51; and Leonardo Sinisgalli, "Graphic Art in Italian House Organs," *Graphis*, 14, no. 80 (1958), 482–99.

30. Max Bill, "Beauty from Function and as Function," *Idea* 53 (1953), xi. Among the many studies on the artist are Margit Staber, *Max Bill* (Saint Gall: Erker Verlag, 1971); and Eduard Hüttinger, *Max Bill* (New York: Rizzoli, 1978).

31. The history of Bing & Grøndahl and its wares is recorded by Erik Lassen, *En Københavnsk porcelaensfabriks historie* (Copenhagen: Nyt Nordisk Forlag, 1978).

32. For Bojesen's work, see Erik Zahle, ed., *A Treasury of Scandinavian Design* (New York: Golden Press, 1961), 12–13, 102, 127, 252; Edgar Kaufmann, jr., "Kay Bojesen: Tableware to Toys," *Interiors*, 112 (February 1953), 64–67; and Esbjørn Hiort, *Modern Danish Silver* (London: A. Zwemmer, 1954), 8, 16, 25, 37, 42–47.

33. Much of the information on Borsani presented here was provided in a letter from his daughter, Valeria Fantoni Borsani, to Christine W. Laidlaw, July 3, 1989.

34. For a history of the firm, see *Bohemian Glass: The History of Bohemian Glass and the Present at the Crystalex Branch Corporation, Nový Bor* (Nový Bor: Crystalex Branch Corporation, 1985).

35. Letter from Enrico Gregotti to Christine W. Laidlaw, August 31, 1989.

36. For an overview of Breuer's career, see Cranston Jones, *Marcel Breuer: Buildings and Projects, 1921–1961* (New York: Frederick A. Praeger, 1962); and Christopher Wilk, *Marcel Breuer: Furniture and Interiors* (New York: Museum of Modern Art, 1981).

37. Much of the information about the artist presented here comes from interviews between Irena Brynner and Toni Lesser Wolf, 1988.

38. Much of the information about the artist presented here comes from an interview between Torun and Toni Lesser Wolf, February 1989, and from subsequent correspondence that year.

39. Alexander Calder, *An Autobiography with Pictures* (New York: Pantheon, 1966), affords perhaps the best picture of the artist as an individual. Daniel Marchesseau's catalogue *The Intimate World of Alexander Calder* (Paris: Solange Thierry Editeur, 1989, distributed New York: Harry N. Abrams, 1990) extensively treats Calder's smaller sculptures, toys, and jewelry.

40. Thanks are due Jørgen Gerner Hansen, who reported on the history of the firm Carl Hansen & Son in letters to David A. Hanks & Associates, February 7 and September 4 and 27, 1990.

41. The best survey of the designer's career is *Retrospective Jean Carlu* (Paris: Musée de la Publicité, 1980).

42. For an excellent account of the firm, see Hans Nadelhoffer, *Cartier, Jewelers Extraordinary* (New York: Harry N. Abrams, 1984).

43. Ibid., 43.

44. For the most complete study of the artist, see Henri Mouron, *A. M. Cassandre* (New York: Rizzoli, 1985).

45. See the catalogue *Posters by Cassandre* (New York: Museum of Modern Art, 1936).

46. The most important source for Cassina's history is Pier Carlo Santini, *Gli Anni del design italiano: Ritratto di Cesare Cassina/The Years of Italian Design: A Portrait of Cesare Cassina* (Milan: Electa, 1981).

47. The most complete study of the artist is Paolo Ferrari, *Achille Castiglioni* (Milan: Electa, 1984).

48. On the artist's career, see Davira S. Taragin, Edward S. Cooke, Jr., and Joseph Giovannini, *Furniture by Wendell Castle* (New York: Hudson Hills Press in association with the Detroit Institute of Arts, 1989); also Wendell Castle and David Edman, *The Wendell Castle Book of Wood Lamination* (New York: Van Nostrand Reinhold, 1980).

49. For the history of Castleton China, see Lois Lehner, *Lehner's Encyclopedia of U.S. Marks on Pottery, Porcelain & Clay* (Paducah, Kentucky: Collector Books, 1988), 419–24.

50. Shenango had already been under contract since 1936 with the Theodore Haviland Company of Limoges to produce its models for the American market.

51. For the company's history, see "Our History: A Photographic Sketch" (Elkin, North Carolina: Chatham Manufacturing Company, 1983).

52. For information on Cinematone, see Scott C. Corbett, *An Illustrated Guide to the Recordings of Spike Jones* (Monrovia, California: Scott C. Corbett, 1989), 1–6; "New Type Phone and Record Introduced," *Coin Machine Journal*, 17 (August 1939), 45; "Cinematone Building Record Library," ibid., 17 (September 1939), 34; "Builds Tune Library," ibid., 18 (February 1940), 51.

53. Some aspects of the firm's history are discussed in "Clover Plastic Contours Inc. Moves to Connecticut," *New York Times*, May 3, 1953, section 3, 6.

54. For Colin, see W. H. Allner, *Graphis*, 2 (January–February 1946), 106–9; Raymond Cogniat, "Jean Colin," *Graphis*, 8 (May–June 1952), 96–105.

55. It has not been possible to consult the monograph by Alain Weill and Jack Rennert, *Paul Colin Affichiste* (Paris: Éditions Denoël, 1989).

56. For the designer's work, see Ignazia Favata, *Joe Colombo and Italian Design of the '60s* (London: Thames and Hudson, 1988).

57. Joe Colombo, *Spazio dinamico*, vol. 3, *Orientamenti moderni nell'edilizia-appartamenti* (Milan: Edizioni Over, 1972).

58. For a full account of the artist's career, see Reino Liefkes, *Copier: Glasontwerper/Glaskunstenaar (Glass Designer/Glass Artist)* (Amsterdam: SDU Uitgeverij, 1990).

59. *Hans Coray—Künstler und Entwerfer* (Zurich: Museum für Gestaltung/Kunstgewerbemuseum, 1986).

60. Accounts of Cuttoli's life and contributions are given in "The Cuttoli Tapestry," *Réalités*, 197 (October 1959), 64–69; Madeleine Jarry, *La Tapisserie: Art du XXème siècle* (Fribourg: Office du Livre, 1974), 76–77; *Teppiche von Arp, Bissière, Calder, Ernst, Vieira da Silva, Klee, Laurens, Léger, Miró, Picasso* (Basel: Galerie Beyeler, 1961); *Collection Marie Cuttoli, Henri Lauglier, Paris* (Basel: Galerie Beyeler, 1970); Amédée Carriat, *Dictionnaire bio-bibliographique des auteurs du pays creusois* (Guéret: Société des Sciences Naturelles et Archéologiques de la Creuse, 1971), vol. 7, 528.

61. For her husband's career, see Roman d'Amat, ed., *Dictionnaire de biographie française* (Paris: Librairie Letouzey et Ané, 1960), vol. 9, 1431.

62. Much of the data presented here was obtained in an interview between Gunnar Cyrén and Martin Eidelberg, October 7, 1989. For brief appreciations of Cyrén's work, see Helena Dahlbäck Lutteman, "Gunnar Cyrén," in *Contemporary Swedish Design* (Stockholm: Nationalmuseum and Svensk Form, 1983), 24–27; and *The Lunning Prize* (Stockholm: Nationalmuseum, 1986), 166–69.

63. Some of the major recent books about Dalí are Robert Descharnes, *Dalí*, trans. Eleanor R. Morse (New York: Harry N. Abrams, 1984); Karin V. Maur et al., *Salvador Dalí* (Stuttgart: Verlag Gerd Hatje, 1989); Daniel Abadie, *La Vie publique de Salvador Dalí* (Paris: Centre Georges Pompidou, Musée National d'Art Moderne, 1980).

64. For additional information, see Ann Lee Morgan, ed., *Contemporary Designers* (London: St. James Press, 1985), 140–41; "Lucienne and Robert Day," *Arts Review*, April 29, 1983, 230.

65. The best studies of the artist's career are Yoshiko Uchida, *The Jewelry of Margaret de Patta: A Retrospective Exhibition* (Oakland, California: Oakland Museum, 1976); Robert Cardinale and Hazel Bray, "Margaret de Patta: Structure, Concepts and Design Sources," *Metalsmith*, 3 (Spring 1983), 11–15.

66. On Dreyfuss, see Henry Dreyfuss, *Designing for People* (New York: Simon and Schuster, 1955); and idem, *The Measure of Man: Human Factors in Design* (New York: Whitney Library of Design, 1959). A largely pictorial series was privately printed for the designer's firm: *Ten Years of Industrial Design 1929–1939* (1939); *A Record of Industrial Designs, 1929 through 1946* (1946); *Industrial Design—a Progress Report, 1929–1952* (1952); *Industrial Design—a Pictorial Accounting, 1929–1957* (1957); and *Industrial Design, Volume 5* (1964).

67. Dreyfuss, *Designing for People*, title page.

68. The standard references for Raoul Dufy's paintings are: Maurice Laffaille, *Raoul Dufy: Catalogue raisonné de l'oeuvre peint*, 4 vols. (Geneva: Editions Motte, 1972–77); and Fanny Guillon-Laffaille, *Raoul Dufy: Catalogue raisonné des aquarelles, gouaches et pastels* (Paris: Louis Carré, 1981–82). The best overall treatment of the artist's decorative art is in *Raoul Dufy* (London: Arts Council of Great Britain, 1983).

69. Edward Wormley, quoted in C. Ray Smith, "Edward Wormley," *Interior Design*, 58 (January 1987), 253.

70. For extensive surveys of the Eameses' careers, see John and Marilyn Neuhart and Ray Eames, *Eames Design: The Work of the Office of Charles and Ray Eames* (New York: Harry N. Abrams, 1989); Arthur Drexler, *Charles Eames: Furniture from the Design Collection* (New York: Museum of Modern Art, 1973).

71. The most useful account of Price's background is Stanley Abercrombie, "Edison Price: His Name Is No Accident," *Lichtberucht*, 8 (September 1979), 2–6.

72. The *Tensegrity* mast temporarily raised in the garden of the Museum of Modern Art, New York, for the R. Buckminster Fuller show in 1959 was fabricated in Edison Price's studio and owed much to his ingenuity; see "Lighting Consultants," *Industrial Design*, 10 (June 1963), 40.

73. In 1971 this institution was absorbed by the Gesamthochschule, Kassel.

74. According to information supplied in a letter from Robert Mongiardini of Flos to Christine W. Laidlaw, June 1, 1989, Dino Gavina, Cesare

Cassina, and Sergio Biliotti started discussing the formation of Flos in 1959 and founded the company in 1960. A founding date of 1959 was also given in "Per chi deve scegliere lampade di serie," *Domus*, 411 (February 1964), d/191–94. Virgilio Vercelloni said that discussions took place in 1961 and the company was founded in 1962; see Virgilio Vercelloni, *The Adventure of Design: Gavina*, trans. Antony Shugaar (New York: Rizzoli, 1989), 45–46.

75. For Kaj Franck's career, see Eeva Siltavuori, "A Dream of a Timeless Object: Kaj Franck's Pioneering Work in Finnish Design," *Form Function Finland* (March 1987), 38–45; *The Modern Spirit—Glass from Finland* (Riihimäki: Suomen Lasimuseo, 1985); and Ann Lee Morgan, ed., *Contemporary Designers* (London: St. James Press, 1985), 201–2.

76. Originally made in earthenware, the series was reissued in stoneware in 1981 under the name *Teema*.

77. The major source on Fritz Hansens Eft. is Svend Erik Møller, "100 Fritz Hansen 1872–1972," *Mobilia*, 206 (September 1972), n.p.

78. Much of the information presented here is derived from material in F. Schumacher & Company, New York, Centennial Research Archives.

79. Vinnie (Mrs. William) Fuller Fish kindly provided information about her father's firm, Fuller Fabrics. For further information, see "D. B. Fuller to Retire as Vice-President at Stevens May 21," *Daily News Record*, February 17, 1961; also "Hear Stevens Seeks Control of D. B. Fuller," *Women's Wear Daily*, July 11, 1955.

80. Marcel Breuer, as quoted in Virgilio Vercelloni, *The Adventure of Design: Gavina*, trans. Antony Shugaar (New York: Rizzoli, 1989), 15. This book is the main source on Gavina S.p.A. See also Centrokappa, *Il Design italiano degli anni '50* (Milan: IGIS, 1981), 82.

81. The best history of the company is *Georg Jensen Silversmithy: 77 Artists, 75 Years* (Washington, D.C.: Renwick Gallery of the National Collection of Fine Arts, 1980). See also Jørgen E. R. Møller, *Georg Jensen: The Danish Silversmith* (Copenhagen: Georg Jensen & Wendel A/S, 1985).

82. Much of the information presented on Alexander Girard is derived from correspondence between Susan Girard, the designer's wife, and Christa C. Mayer Thurman, August 28 and September 4, 1986, and from the designer's résumé.

83. Among the most important were "Interiors Exhibition," Italian Pavilion, Barcelona, 1929; "Exhibition for Modern Living," Detroit Institute of Arts, 1949; "Textiles and Ornamental Arts of India," Museum of Modern Art, New York, 1955; and "Multiple Visions: A Common Bond," Museum of International Folk Art, Santa Fe, 1982.

84. Elizabeth Tallent, "On Buying Folk Art: Alexander Girard's Advice to Travellers," *Architectural Digest*, 43 (June 1986), 37.

85. For further information on the artist, see Peter Mayer, ed., *Milton Glaser: Graphic Design* (New York: Overlook Press, 1973); also *The Milton Glaser Poster Book* (New York: Crown Publishers, 1977).

86. Thanks are due to Ulf Jeppson and Charlotte Celsing of GAB for providing information about this company.

87. For a brief history of the firm, see *Gustavsberg 150 år* (Stockholm: Nationalmuseum, 1975).

88. For an overview of Hall China's products, see Harvey Duke, *Superior Quality: Hall China* (New York: ELO Books, 1977); idem, *Hall 2* (New York: ELO Books, 1985).

89. Much of the information presented here is based on an interview between Eszter Haraszty and Kate Carmel, May 1989, and conversations between Haraszty and Christine W. Laidlaw, September 1989, and January 16 and September 4, 1990.

90. For a short history of Heal and Son Ltd., see Susanna Goodden, *A History of Heal's* (London: Lund, Humphries, 1984).

91. The principal sources of information on this company's history are Ralph Caplan, *The Design of Herman Miller* (New York: Watson-Guptill, 1976); and "Nelson, Eames, Girard, Propst: The Design Process at Herman Miller," *Design Quarterly*, 98–99 (1975), 1–64. In 1989 Herman Miller donated archival material and many examples of its furniture to the Henry Ford Museum and Greenfield Village in Dearborn, Michigan.

92. The artist's work has been discussed eloquently by Monique Lévi-Strauss in *Sheila Hicks* (Paris: Pierre Horay and Suzy Langlois, 1973), and in *Sheila Hicks* (Paris: Adam Biro, forthcoming).

93. For an overview of the ceramist's work, see Mirja-Kaisa Hipeli, *Friedl Kjellberg* (Helsinki: Arabia Museum, 1989), a book issued to coincide with a retrospective of her work staged at the Kappalaisen talossa, Porvoo.

94. Although Arabia reintroduced rice-grain work a decade later, it is of a different sort than that made under Kjellberg's direction.

95. See Steve Kaskovich, "Changing Times: Howard Miller Clock Co.'s Prosperity Spans Generations," *Detroit News*, October 30, 1989.

96. For an overview of the Iittala factory's history and products, see *The Modern Spirit—Glass from Finland* (Riihimäki: Suomen Lasimuseo, 1985).

97. For the history of Isokon and its principal founder, see Jack Pritchard, *View from a Long Chair* (London: Routledge & Kegan Paul, 1984); also *Isokon* (Newcastle-upon-Tyne: University of Newcastle, Hatton Gallery, 1980).

98. Pritchard's bias toward plywood derived from his ten-year employment (1925–35) with the Estonian firm Venesta Plywood Company. Before it became the Isokon Furniture Company, Isokon sold plywood furniture designed by Pritchard and Coates as well as by other companies, such as The Makers of Simple Furniture.

99. Breuer also designed the Isobar, the restaurant and social center at the Flats.

100. For accounts of Isola's career, see Amer Group Ltd., *Phenomenon Marimekko* (Espoo, Finland: Amer Group Ltd., 1986), 118–19; Susanne Frennberg, "Maija Isola," *Form*, 59, no. 6 (1963), 344–49.

101. For Jacobsen's architectural career, see Tobias Faber, *Arne Jacobsen* (New York: Frederick A. Praeger, 1964); Johan Pedersen, *Arkitekten Arne Jacobsen* (Copenhagen: Udgivet, 1957); and Poul Erik Skriver and Ellen Waade, *Arne Jacobsen* (Copenhagen: Danish Bicentennial Committee, 1976).

102. Perhaps his first decorative design of note was a series of textiles based on watercolors of Danish flora. These were done with his wife, Jonna, a textile printer, while they were living in exile in Sweden from 1943 to 1945. See Edgar Kaufmann, jr., "Danish Linens for the Sun," *Art News*, 48 (April 1949), 41, 61.

103. The other two groups were the "craftsmen-designers," represented by Hans Wegner and Børge Mogensen, and the "artist-designers," exemplified by Finn Juhl.

104. Erik Zahle, ed., *A Treasury of Scandinavian Design* (New York: Golden Press, 1961), 18–20.

105. Examples of the first group are door hardware for Carl Petersen, glassware for the SAS Royal Hotel, Copenhagen, and flatware for A. Michelsen. Examples of the second groups are his designs for textiles for the SAS Royal Hotel, kitchen fixtures for I. P. Lund, lighting for Louis Poulsen & Co., and the *Cylinda* line of holloware for Stelton.

106. For Grete Jalk's work, see *Profession: Designer* (Copenhagen: Danish Design Council, 1989).

107. The early history of Johannes Hansen is given in a letter from Poul Hansen to Christine W. Laidlaw, September 11, 1989. See also Johan Møller Nielsen, *Wegner, en dansk møbelkunstner* (Copenhagen: Gyldendal, 1965), 119–22, 129–31.

108. For an overview of Johnson's career, see John M. Jacobus, Jr., *Philip Johnson* (New York: George Braziller, 1962); Robert A. M. Stern, ed., *Philip Johnson, Writings* (New York: Oxford University Press, 1979); and Carleton Knight III and Robert A. Stern, eds., *Philip Johnson/John Burgee: Architecture 1979–1985* (New York: Rizzoli, 1985).

109. Juhl designed glassware for Georg Jensen, ceramics for Bing & Grøndahl, and wooden bowls for Kay Bojesen. His appliances include refrigerators for General Electric, typewriters for IBM, as well as appliances, lighting, and carpets for Unika-Vaev.

110. Among Juhl's most notable interiors were the Bing & Grøndahl showroom, Copenhagen (1946); the Baker Furniture showroom, Grand Rapids (1950); the second "Good Design" exhibition sponsored by the Museum of Modern Art, Chicago and New York (1951); a room for the Nordenfjeldske Kunstindustrimuseum, Trondheim, Norway (1952); the Trusteeship Council Chamber in the Conference Building at the United Nations, New York (1952); and the exhibition "The Arts of Denmark" at the Metropolitan Museum of Art, New York (1960).

111. For Juhl's furniture designs, see Finn Juhl, "Danish Furniture Design," *Architects' Year Book*, 3 (1949), 134–40; Finn Juhl, "Den 'Riktige' Form," *Bonytt*, 10 (January 1950), 4–7; Bent Salicath, "Finn Juhl and Danish Furniture," *Architects' Year Book*, 6 (1955), 137–56; and "Juhl Furniture, Baker's Grand Rapids Galleries," *Interiors*, 111 (November 1951), 84–94.

112. The best, though cursory, history of Kartell S.p.A. is Centrokappa, *Il Design italiano degli anni '50* (Milan: IGIS, 1981), 242, 306–7.

113. The best coverage of the designer's career is Mark Haworth-Booth, *E. McKnight Kauffer: A Designer and His Public* (London: Gordon Fraser, 1979).

114. Ibid., 33. Ryder also had a copy of Lytton Strachey's *Eminent Victorians*—possibly the edition with Kauffer's book jacket.

115. It was through Kauffer that Man Ray got the commissions to photograph T. S. Eliot, Virginia Woolf, and Aldous Huxley; see Haworth-Booth, *E. McKnight Kauffer*, 62–63.

116. See E. McKnight Kauffer, *Posters* (New York: Museum of Modern Art, 1937). The introduction was written by Aldous Huxley.

117. For Kelly's career, see Der Scutt, "Richard Kelly 1910–1977—A Personal Memento," *Lighting Design & Application*, 9 (October 1979), 56–58; also Richard Kelly, "Biographical Outline," November 10, 1955.

118. For further information on this company, see Eric Larrabee and Massimo Vignelli, *Knoll Design* (New York: Harry N. Abrams, 1981); and *Knoll au Louvre* (Paris: Musée des Arts Décoratifs, 1972).

119. On Koninklijke Nederlandsche Glasfabriek Leerdam, see Reino Liefkes, *Copier: Glasontwerper/Glaskunstenaar (Glass Designer/Glass Artist)* (Amsterdam: SDU Uitgeverij, 1990); A.

van der Kley-Blekxtoon, *Leerdam Glas 1878–1930* (Lochem-Gent: Tijdstroom, 1984); and *Leerdam Unica: 50 Jahre Modernes Niederlandisches Glas* (Düsseldorf: Kunstmuseum, 1977).

120. For the most thorough discussions of Koppel's career, see Viggo Sten Møller, *Henning Koppel* (Copenhagen: Rhodos, 1965); and Erik Lassen, *Henning Koppel: En mindeudstilling (A Commemorative Exhibition)* (Copenhagen: Kunstindustrimuseet, 1982).

121. One of the best overviews of Kosta's modern production is in Helmut Ricke and Ulrich Gronert, *Glas in Schweden 1915–1960* (Munich: Prestel Verlag, 1986), 186–228, 289–90.

122. Mark Foley, "Sam Kramer: Fantastic Jewelry for People Who Are Slightly Mad," *Metalsmith*, 6 (Winter 1986), 10–17.

123. "Surrealistic Jeweler," *The New Yorker*, January 3, 1942, 11–12.

124. The history of Kultakeskus Oy is based on information contained in a letter from Pirta Syrjänen of Kultakeskus Oy to Christine W. Laidlaw, May 9, 1990.

125. For more detailed information on the designer, see *Jack Lenor Larsen: 30 ans de création textile* (Paris: Musée des arts décoratifs, 1981); also Robert J. Clark et al., *Design in America: The Cranbrook Vision 1925–1950* (New York: Harry N. Abrams in association with The Detroit Institute of Arts and The Metropolitan Museum of Art, 1983), 271.

126. "Taproot: Jack Lenor Larsen with Susan Goldin," *Interweave*, 4 (Summer 1979), 18–24, 57.

127. Jack Lenor Larsen, Alfred Bühler, and Bronwen and Barrett Solyom, *The Dyer's Art: Ikat, Batik, Plangi* (New York: Van Nostrand Reinhold, 1971); Jack Lenor Larsen and Mildred Constantine, *Beyond Craft: The Art Fabric* (New York: Van Nostrand Reinhold, 1972); Jack Lenor Larsen and Mildred Constantine, *The Art Fabric: Mainstream* (New York: Van Nostrand Reinhold, 1981); Jack Lenor Larsen and Betty Freudenheim, *Interlacing: The Elemental Fabric* (Tokyo: Kodansha International, 1986); and Jack Lenor Larsen, *Material Wealth: Living with Luxurious Fabrics* (New York: Abbeville Press, 1989).

128. Sam Hunter, *The Sculpture of Ibram Lassaw* (Detroit: Gertrude Kasle Gallery, 1968); for an overview of the sculptor's career, see also Nancy Gale Heller, "The Sculpture of Ibram Lassaw" (Ph.D. diss., Rutgers University, 1982).

129. "AID Prize Winning Interior Designs," *Design*, 49 (February 1948), 18. The fabric that won the award was called *Atmosphere no. 1*, one in a series of designs called *Atmospherics*. Some of the information presented in this essay comes from an interview between Erwine Laverne and Kate Carmel, August 17, 1988.

130. "The Lavernes—Partners in Design," *Craft Horizons*, 9 (Winter 1949), 14.

131. "The Levities of Laverne," *Interiors*, 111 (March 1952), 114.

132. "Fabric and Wallcovering: Illustrated Wholesale Price List" (January 1961).

133. For a good overview of the ceramist's career, see Carol Hogben, ed., *The Art of Bernard Leach* (London: Faber and Faber, 1978). Also see the artist's illuminating autobiographical account: Bernard Leach, *Beyond East and West* (New York: Watson-Guptil Publications, 1978).

134. There is an extensive bibliography on Léger. Some recent works are: Bernadette Contensou, ed., *Léger et l'esprit moderne* (Paris: Musée d'Art Moderne de la Ville de Paris, 1982); Peter de Francia, *Fernand Léger* (New Haven and London: Yale University Press, 1983); Christopher Green, *Léger and the Avant-Garde* (New Haven: Yale University Press, 1983); Nicholas Serota, ed., *Fernand Léger: The Later Years* (Munich: Prestel Verlag, 1987); and Werner Schmalenbach, *Fernand Léger*, trans. Robert Allen and James Emmons (New York: Harry N. Abrams, 1975).

135. Libenský, along with Václav Platek, Karel Hrodek, and Josef Hospodka, took over the management of Umlĕcke Sklo (Artistic Glassware) at Nový Bor. See *Czechoslovakian Glass: 1350–1980* (New York: Dover Publications for The Corning Museum of Glass, 1981), 45.

136. This style continued to at least 1960; see "Sculptural Glass by Zuzana Pešatová," *Czechoslovak Glass Review*, 16, no. 1 (1961), 10–11.

137. See, for example, *The Sun of Centuries*, *Blue Concretion*, and *Crystal Column*, illustrated in William Warmus, "The Art of Libenský and Brychtová," *New Glass Review*, 6 (1985), 36–37.

138. For an illustration, see Durk Valkema, "Czechoslovakian Glass: 1350–1980," *American Craft*, 41 (August-September 1981), 44.

139. Warmus, "The Art of Libenský and Brychtová," 37.

140. The basic studies of the artist are Diane Waldman, *Roy Lichtenstein* (New York: Harry N. Abrams, 1971); Jack Cowart, *Roy Lichtenstein: 1970–1980* (New York: Hudson Hills Press in association with The Saint Louis Art Museum, 1981); and Laurence Alloway, *Roy Lichtenstein* (New York: Abbeville, 1983).

141. The California School of Fine Arts is today known as the San Francisco Art Institute.

142. The production studio remained in San Francisco until 1952 when it, too, moved to New York.

143. For a complete listing of her industrial clients, see *Dorothy Liebes Retrospective* (New York: Museum of Contemporary Crafts, 1970), 35.

144. Ibid., 4.

145. Liebes experimented with Orlon acrylic, nylon, rayon, Antron, Nemex, and Qiana nylon.

146. *Dorothy Liebes Retrospective*, 34–35.

147. The most complete overview of the designer's career is the exhibition catalogue *Stig Lindberg—formgivare* (Stockholm: Nationalmuseum, 1982). Also see Dag Widman, *Stig Lindberg—Swedish Artist and Designer* (Stockholm: Nordisk Rotogravyr, 1962); *Gustavsberg, 150 år* (Stockholm: Nationalmuseum, 1975).

148. Arthur Hald, "Stig Lindberg," *Graphis*, 6, no. 30 (1950), 149.

149. For a selection of Lindstrand's glass, see Helmut Ricke and Ulrich Gronert, *Glas in Schweden, 1915–1960* (Munich: Prestel Verlag, 1986), 113–20, 135–39, 212–27, passim.

150. Gregor Paulsson, ed., *Modernt svenskt glas* (Stockholm, 1943), figs. 46, 54. The importance of this type of Biomorphic design just before the war needs to be emphasized; Eero Saarinen and his first wife bought one such example on their honeymoon.

151. Helena Dahlbäck Lutteman, *Svensk 1900–tals–keramik* (Västerås: ICA Bokförlag, 1985), 118.

152. Much of the information presented here comes from biographical material kindly provided by the designer. Also informative is Aase Holm, "Ross Littell," *Living Architecture*, 8 (1989) 98–105.

153. For an account of the artist's career, see Joan Falconer Byrd, *Harvey K. Littleton: A Retrospective Exhibition* (Atlanta: High Museum of Art, 1984).

154. The most complete works about Loewy are *The Designs of Raymond Loewy* (Washington, D.C.: Renwick Gallery of the National Collection of Fine Arts, 1975); and Raymond Loewy, *Industrial Design* (London and Woodstock, New York: Overlook Press, 1979).

155. Data for this corporate history were kindly provided by Howard G. Cohen, president of Poulsen Lighting Co., Inc., Miami, Florida.

156. There is an extensive bibliography on Jean Lurçat. See Claude Roy, *Jean Lurçat* (Geneva: Pierre Cailleur, 1956); *Tapisseries de Jean Lurçat 1939–1957* (Belvès: Pierre Vorms, 1957); and, particularly, Amédée Carriat, *Dictionnaire bio-bibliographique des auteurs du pays creusois* (Guéret: Société des Sciences Naturelles et Archéologiques de la Creuse, 1967), vol. 4, 322–24.

157. Interview between Elaine Lustig Cohen, Jennifer Toher [Teulié], and Martin Eidelberg on June 20, 1986.

158. Holland R. Melson, Jr., *The Collected Writings of Alvin Lustig* (New Haven: Holland R. Melson, Jr., 1958), 21.

159. *Two Graphic Designers: Alvin Lustig and Bruno Munari* (New York: Museum of Modern Art, 1955).

160. For more information on Magistretti, see Ann Lee Morgan, ed., *Contemporary Designers* (London: St. James Press, 1985), 381–82.

161. For more information on the company, see Amer Group Ltd., *Phenomenon Marimekko* (Espoo, Finland: Amer Group Ltd., 1986); Ulf Hård af Segerstad, *Modern Finnish Design* (New York: Praeger Publishers, 1969), 45–46, 60; Erik Kruskopf, "Cottons with Character," in *Designed in Finland* (Helsinki: Finnish Foreign Trade Association, 1964), 26–27; *The Marimekko Story* (Helsinki: Marimekko Oy, 1964).

162. In 1921 the designer changed his surname from Jonsson to Markelius, as he wanted a less common one, and Mark was the name of a Swedish farm where his great-grandfather had been working; telephone conversations in July 1988 with Helene Hernmarck, the architect's niece, and correspondence with Eva Rudberg, architect and author of a forthcoming monograph on the architect. For the best survey of Markelius's work, see Reginald R. Isaacs's entry, "Markelius," in *The Macmillan Encyclopedia of Architects* (New York: Macmillan, 1982), vol. 3, 107.

163. Olga Gueft, "Arneberg, Juhl, and Markelius: Unodious Comparisons at the UN," *Interiors*, 111 (July 1952), 46–47.

164. The most complete studies of Mathsson are Carl E. Christiansson, "Bruno Mathsson: Furniture, Structures, Ideas," *Design Quarterly*, 65 (1966), 5–31; Elias Cornell, "Bruno Mathsson och Tiden," *Arkitektur*, 3 (March 1967), 103–13.

165. Olga Gueft, "A New Hall for Glass in Småland," *Interiors*, 115 (October 1955), 92–97.

166. For an excellent analysis of the artist's career, see Alfred H. Barr, Jr., *Matisse: His Art and His Public* (1951; New York: Museum of Modern Art, 1974); more recent works that include Matisse's decorative art are Pierre Schneider, *Matisse* (New York: Rizzoli, 1984); and Pierre Schneider and Tamara Preaud, eds., *Henri Matisse: Exposition du centenaire* (Paris: Grand Palais, 1970).

167. Good sources of information on Matta are *Matta* (Paris: Centre Georges Pompidou, Musée National d'Art Moderne, 1985); *Matta Cogitum* (London: Arts Council of Great Britain, Hayward Gallery, 1977); *Matta: Skulpturen und Bilder* (Zurich: Gimpel & Hanover Galerie, 1964); *Tapisseries de Chagall, Matta, Klee, Picasso: Atelier Yvette Cauquil-Prince* (Paris: Galerie Verrière, 1971).

168. For his work, see *Herbert Matter: A Retrospective* (New Haven: Yale University, School of Art, A & A Gallery, 1978).

169. *Knoll au Louvre* (Paris: Musée des Arts Déco-

ratifs, 1972).

170. Mercedes Matter, *Alberto Giacometti*, photographed by Herbert Matter (New York: Harry N. Abrams, c. 1978).

171. For an illustration of *Blackthorns*, see *Czechoslovakian Glass 1350–1980* (New York: Dover Publications for The Corning Museum of Glass, 1981), 108. For illustrations of the crystal and green glass vase, see "Czechoslovak Glass at the Milan Triennale," *Czechoslovak Glass Review*, 13, no. 1 (1958), 30; also *Undicesima Triennale di Milano* (Milan: 1957), cxxiii.

172. Ivo Digrin, "Traditional and Contemporary," *Czechoslovak Glass Review*, 16, no. 2 (1961), 56; Andrea Bohmannová, "New Designs by Adolf Matura of the Moser Glassworks," *Czechoslovak Glass Review*, 17, no. 7 (1962), 209.

173. For illustrations, see Alena Adlerová, "An Exhibition of Pressed Glass," *Glass Review*, 38 (November 1983), 5; Dušan Sindelář, "Tschechoslowakisches Glas—Das Glas gehört in der Tschecho," *Bildende Kunst*, 24, no. 2 (1976), 70; and *Sklár a Keramik*, 21, no. 8 (1971), 29.

174. New York City (Manhattan) Telephone Directory, 1941.

175. Ibid., 1949. Alvin Lustig, "Modern Printed Fabrics," *American Fabrics*, 20 (Winter 1951–52), 61–72; also advertisements in *Interiors*, 109 (August 1949), 57; ibid. (September 1949), 66; ibid. (October 1949), 58; ibid. (November 1949), 52; ibid. (December 1949), 113; and ibid. (January 1950), 70.

176. Telephone interview on January 11, 1989, between L. Anton Maix, formerly national distributing agent for Schiffer Prints, and Christa C. Mayer Thurman.

177. The literature on Miró is voluminous. For an appraisal of his work before 1961, see Jacques Dupin, *Joan Miró: His Life and Work* (New York: Harry N. Abrams, 1962); for an updated bibliography and excellent chronology, refer to *Joan Miró: A Retrospective* (New York: Solomon R. Guggenheim Museum, 1987). See also Michel Leiris, ed., *Joan Miró: Lithographs*, 4 vols. (New York: Tudor Publishing, 1972–81); *Miró, Artigas: Ceramics* (New York: Pierre Matisse Gallery, 1963); and *Sobreteixims* (New York: Pierre Matisse Gallery, 1973).

178. The information about Mitchell that is presented here is based on papers in the artist's archives, now in the possession of Priscilla Cunningham, Hampton Bays, New York.

179. The standard biography of Mollino is Giovanni Brino, *Carlo Mollino* (Milan: Idea Books, 1985).

180. Carlo Mollino, "Utopia e ambientazione II," *Domus*, 238 (1949), 25.

181. Brino, *Carlo Mollino*, 42.

182. For information on Müller-Munk, see Ann Lee Morgan, ed., *Contemporary Designers* (London: St. James Press, 1985), 441; also Arthur J. Pulos, *The American Design Adventure 1940–1975* (Cambridge, Massachusetts: The MIT Press, 1988), 44–45, 143, 166–67, 216–17, 302–5. Early articles by Müller-Munk himself include: "Handwrought Silver," *Charm*, 9 (April 1928), 38–39, 81–83; "Machine-Hand," *Creative Art*, 5 (October 1929), 709–12.

183. *Jacques Nathan-Garamond: Affiches* (Toulouse: Centre Municipal de l'Affiche, de la Carte Postale et de l'Art Graphique, 1988).

184. George Nelson, "Biographical Sketch: Winning a Design for an Auditorium Building," *Pencil Points*, 13 (June 1932), 428.

185. George Nelson and Henry N. Wright, "Storagewall," *Architectural Forum*, 81 (November 1944), 82–92.

186. George Nelson, "Styling Organization and Design," *California Arts and Architecture*, 64 (August 1947), 24.

187. For more on Noguchi, see Sam Hunter, *Isamu Noguchi* (New York: Abbeville, 1978); Nancy Grove and Diane Botnick, *The Sculpture of Isamu Noguchi, 1924–1979: A Catalogue* (New York: Garland, 1980); and Isamu Noguchi, *A Sculptor's World* (New York: Harper and Row, 1968).

188. Nordiska Kompaniet AB, "NK—Tradition under Renewal, Aktiebolaget Nordiska Kompaniet" (1985); also the company's annual report for 1986; and Nordiska Kompaniet AB, "Facts about Nordiska Kompaniet" (1987).

189. *Astrid Sampe—Swedish Industrial Textiles* (Stockholm: Nationalmuseum, 1984).

190. Some sense of Nuutajärvi's production is conveyed in *The Modern Spirit—Glass from Finland* (Riihimäki: Suomen Lasimuseo, 1985). It has not been possible to consult Vilho Annala, *Notsjö Glasbruk 1793–1943* (Helsinki, 1943).

191. For Nylund, see Bo Lagercrantz, *Modern Swedish Ceramics* (Stockholm: Lindqvists Publishing, 1950); Nils G. Wollin, "Keramikern Gunnar Nylund," *Domus*, 4 (January 1933), 15–19.

192. For the designer's career, see *Gunnel Nyman* (Riihimäki: Suomen Lasimuseo, 1987).

193. For a survey of the designer's work, see *Edvin Öhrström* (Småländ: Orrefors Museum, 1987); also see Ann Marie Herlitz-Gezelius, *Orrefors: A Swedish Glassplant* (Stockholm: Atlantis Publishers, 1984); J. A. Vincent, "A New Northern Light: Orrefors' Ohrstrom," *Interiors*, 112 (April 1953), 94–98.

194. See Bengt Larnker, "Work of Art or Architectural Accent?," *Avis* (1978–79), 15–25.

195. The most complete history of the firm is Henri Bouilhet, *Christofle 1830–1980; 150 ans d'orfèvrerie* (Paris: Chêne/Hachette, 1981).

196. For the history of the Orrefors company and its products, see particularly Ann Marie Herlitz-Gezelius, *Orrefors: A Swedish Glassplant* (Stockholm: Atlantis Publishers, 1984); also see Helmut Ricke and Ulrich Gronert, *Glas in Schweden 1915–1960* (Munich: Prestel Verlag, 1986), 19–40, 48–185, 272–88.

197. Panton has been the subject of numerous articles; for a synopsis and extensive pre-1983 bibliography, see Ann Lee Morgan, ed., *Contemporary Designers* (London: St. James Press, 1985), 469–71.

198. *Earl Pardon: Retrospective Exhibition* (Saratoga Springs, New York: Art Gallery, Skidmore College, 1980).

199. The literature on Picasso as a painter and printmaker is too immense to cite here. The best survey of his postwar involvement with the decorative arts is *Pablo Picasso: Maler, Grafiker, Bildhauer, Keramiker, Dichter* (Ingelheim am Rhein: n.p., 1981). See also these specialized studies: Georges Ramié, *Picasso's Ceramics* (New York: Viking Press, 1976); Alain Ramié, *Picasso: Catalogue of the Edited Ceramic Works, 1947–1971* (Vallauris: Galerie Madoura, 1988).

200. For the history of this corporation, see Deborah Gallin, *Polaroid Corporation* (Cambridge, Massachusetts: Access Press, 1989); Peter C. Wensberg, *Land's Polaroid: A Company and the Man Who Invented It* (Boston: Houghton Mifflin, 1987).

201. This European art movement of the late 1940s and 1950s propounded the use of the splash, blot, drip, and other spontaneous, calligraphic gestures in painting.

202. *Giò Pomodoro* (Rome: Marlborough Galleria d'Arte, 1964), 3b.

203. Willy Rotzler, "Arnaldo et Giò Pomodoro et le phénomène du bijou," *Ring des Arts*, 3 (Christmas 1962), 17–21.

204. For further information on the architect and designer, see Nathan H. Shapira, "The Expression of Gio Ponti," *Design Quarterly*, 69–70 (1967), 2–72; 28/78 *Architettura: Cinquante anni di architettura italiana dal 1928 al 1978* (Milan: Palazzo delle Stelline, 1979), 166–77; *Gio Ponti, Arte Applicata* (Milan: Centro Internazionale di Brera, 1987). It has not been possible to consult Lisa Licitra Ponti, *Gio Ponti: The Complete Work* (Cambridge, Massachusetts: The MIT Press, 1990).

205. For Ponti's ceramics, see *Gio Ponti: Ceramiche 1923–1930, le opere del Museo Ginori di Doccia* (Milan: Electa, 1983).

206. They include Gio Ponti, *Amate l'architettura* (Genoa, 1957), translated under the title *In Praise of Architecture* (New York: F. W. Dodge, 1960).

207. For the designer's career, see Jacques Wolgensinger, *Gilbert Portanier, Céramique* (Angoulême: Galerie Arts-Objets, 1988); Gisela Reineking von Bock and Carl-Wolfgang Schümann, *Sammlung Gertrud und Dr. Karl Funke-Kaiser; Keramik von Historismus bis zür Gegenwart* (Cologne: Kunstgewerbemuseum, 1975), 134, 352–60.

208. The information regarding Davis Pratt is based on interviews between Elsa Kula, the designer's widow, and Marc O. Rabun, October 23, 1989, and material from the artist's archive.

209. Edgar Kaufmann, jr., *Prize Designs for Modern Furniture from the International Competition for Low-Cost Furniture Design* (New York: Museum of Modern Art, 1950), 44–47. Much of the information presented here is based on the designer's résumé sent to David A. Hanks, February 28, 1986.

210. Edgar Kaufmann, jr., *Prestini's Art in Wood* (New York: Pocahontas Press, 1950).

211. See *James Prestini: Sculpture from Structural Steel Elements* (San Francisco: San Francisco Museum of Art, 1969).

212. Christine Counourd and Alan Paris, *Jean Prouvé, Serge Mouille: Two Master Metalworkers* (New York and Paris: Antony de Lorenzo and Alan Christine Counourd, 1985), 35.

213. Dominique Clayssen, *Jean Prouvé: L'Idée constructive* (Paris: Dunod, 1983).

214. The best study of this artist is Françoise de Bonneville, ed., *Jean Puiforcat* (Paris: Éditions du Regard, 1986).

215. For further information on Quistgaard, see *The Lunning Prize* (Stockholm: Nationalmuseum, 1986), 62–65.

216. For the career of the designer, see Hazel Conway, *Ernest Race* (London: The Design Council, 1982); also Gillian Naylor, "Ernest Race," in *Design*, 184 (April 1964), 54–55.

217. J. W. Noel Jordan (1907–1974), who owned a light engineering company, was interested in diversifying his postwar production and recognized the possibility of adapting engineering methods to furniture manufacturing; he served as managing director of the new company, while Race was director and chief designer. Their initial challenge was to produce furniture in compliance with the Utility Furniture Scheme that was then operational in Great Britain.

218. Race Furniture Ltd. presently supplies an international market with theater and courtroom seating, a specialty of its contract furniture business that stems from designs that Ernest Race introduced in 1957.

219. Paul Rand, *Thoughts on Design* (New York: Wittenborn, Schultz, c. 1947), 2. On Rand, see also idem, *A Designer's Art* (New Haven: Yale Univer-

sity Press, 1985).

220. For a history of the Red Lion Furniture Company, see C. M. Ehehalt, ed., *Pictorial Souvenir: The Borough of Red Lion, York County, Pennsylvania, Golden Jubilee, 1880–1930* (n.p.: Historical Society of York County, 1930).

221. For the history of Red Wing Potteries, see Lyndon C. Viel, *The Clay Giants: The Stoneware of Red Wing, Goodhue County, Minnesota*, 2 vols. (Des Moines: Wallace-Homestead Book, 1977, 1980); "Red Wing Is 75 Years Old," *Crockery and Glass Journal*, 151 (November 1952), 64; Lois Lehner, *Lehner's Encyclopedia of U.S. Marks on Pottery, Porcelain & Clay* (Paducah, Kentucky: Collector Books, 1988), 365–67.

222. For the history of the firm, see "The Spirit of Paul Revere: A Glorious Heritage for American Industry" (New York: Revere Copper and Brass Incorporated, 1973); "Paul Revere: Pioneer Industrialist" (New York: Revere Copper and Brass Incorporated, 1951); "Listen America . . ." (New York: Revere Copper and Brass Incorporated, 1970); "Revere Ware Corporation Celebrates the 50th Anniversary of Copper Clad Cookware" (Clinton, Illinois: Revere Ware Corporation, 1989).

223. For the gift line, see "Gifts by Revere, 1936" (Rome, New York: Revere Copper and Brass Incorporated, 1935).

224. The names Raymor and Richards Morgenthau & Company—the latter entity was not formed until 1947—were apparently used interchangeably. In actuality, Raymor was the design and importing division, while Richards Morgenthau was the sales branch and parent company. The latter name derived from Irving Richards's partnership with Eugene Morgenthau, originally a sales representative, whose main responsibility was managing the manufacturing plant; the two men had worked together since about 1937. See "Raymor," *Industrial Design*, 1 (February 1954), 124–27. The archives of the company are at Pratt Institute, New York. Much of the information presented here is based on an interview between Irving Richards and Kate Carmel, March 29, 1988.

225. See, for example, Ettore Sottsass, "Disegno italiano per l'America," *Domus*, 310 (September 1955), 46–47.

226. For the two aspects of the designer's work, see Theodore M. Brown, *The Work of G. Rietveld, Architect* (Utrecht: A. W. Bruna & Zoon, 1958); and Daniele Baroni, *Gerrit Thomas Rietveld: Furniture* (Woodbury, New York: Barron's, 1978).

227. For more information about Jens Risom, see Ann Lee Morgan, ed., *Contemporary Designers* (London: St. James Press, 1985), 512–13.

228. See, for example, *Interiors*, 113 (May 1954), 77; ibid., 116 (February 1957), 108.

229. Jens Risom in *Furniture Forum*, 10 (Spring 1959), n.p.

230. For the history of the Rörstrand factory, see Helena Dahlbäck Lutteman, *Svensk 1900–tals–keramik* (Västerås: ICA Bokförlag, 1985), 202 and passim; Jennifer Hawkins Opie, *Scandinavia: Ceramics and Glass in the Twentieth Century* (London: Victoria and Albert Museum, 1989), 105–23, 178.

231. A good, though by no means critical, overview of the company's history is *Rosenthal, Hundert Jahre Porzellan* (Hanover: Kestner-Museum, 1982).

232. For the artist's career, see the publication issued in conjunction with the retrospective exhibition of his career: Ann Pollard Rowe and Rebecca A. T. Stevens, eds., *Ed Rossbach: 40 Years of Exploration and Innovation in Fiber Art* (Asheville, North Carolina: Lark Books in association with the Textile Museum, 1990).

233. *Making Marionettes* (New York: Harcourt, Brace, 1938); *Baskets as Textile Art* (New York: Van Nostrand Reinhold, 1973); *The New Basketry* (New York: Van Nostrand Reinhold, 1976); *The Art of Paisley* (New York: Van Nostrand Reinhold, 1980).

234. This series appeared in *American Craft*: "Fiber in the Forties," 42 (October–November 1982), 15–19; "The Glitter and Glamour of Dorothy Liebes," 42 (December 1982–January 1983), 8–12; "Mary Atwater and the Revival of American Traditional Weaving," 43 (April–May 1983), 22–26; "In the Bauhaus Mode: Anni Albers," 43 (December 1983–January 1984), 7–11; "Marianne Strengell," 44 (April-May 1984), 8–11.

235. Much of the information presented here comes from Rudofsky's résumé; from obituaries in the *New York Times*, March 13, 1988, and the *Chicago Tribune*, March 16, 1988; from *Umriss*, 5 (March–April 1986), 3–27; and from an interview between Berta Rudofsky, the designer's widow, and Christa C. Mayer Thurman, January 25, 1989.

236. See Mary Vance, *Bernard Rudofsky: A Bibliography* (Monticello, Illinois: Vance Bibliographies, 1981).

237. Rudofsky, quoted in Peter Noever, "Umriss—Gespräch mit Bernard Rudofsky," *Umriss*, 5 (March–April 1986), 22.

238. For an overview of the American career of Eero Saarinen, as well as of his father, Eliel, and the rest of the family, see Robert J. Clark et al., *Design in America: The Cranbrook Vision 1925–1950* (New York: Harry N. Abrams in association with The Detroit Institute of Arts and The Metropolitan Museum of Art, 1983); also see Aline Saarinen, ed., *Eero Saarinen on His Own Work* (New Haven: Yale University Press, 1962).

239. The major study of Sabattini's career is Enrico Marelli, *Lino Sabattini: Suggestione e funzione, Intimations on Craftsmanship* (Mariano Comense: Edizioni Metron, 1979).

240. Ibid., 3.

241. The information presented here derives in part from interviews between Robert Sailors, David A. Hanks, and Kate Carmel, September 22, 1987, subsequent correspondence, and an interview between Sailors and Carmel, June 20, 1989; for further information, see Robert J. Clark et al., *Design in America: The Cranbrook Vision 1925–1950* (New York: Harry N. Abrams in association with The Detroit Institute of Arts and The Metropolitan Museum of Art, 1983), 275.

242. An overview of the designer's career, though by no means complete or critical, is given in Kaj Kalin, *Sarpaneva*, trans. Diana Tullberg (n.p.: Otava, 1986).

243. There are a number of major studies on the architect, including: Francesco Dal Co and Giuseppi Mazzariol, *Carlo Scarpa; the Complete Works*, trans. Richard Sadleir (New York: Rizzoli, 1985); and Maria Antonietta Crippa, *Carlo Scarpa* (Cambridge, Massachusetts: The MIT Press, 1986).

244. Gerry A. Turner, "Hand-Screened Textiles," *Design*, 51 (February 1950), 20.

245. *Interiors*, 106 (July 1947), 126; and letter from Ruth Adler Schnee to Christa C. Mayer Thurman, August 29, 1987.

246. *New Retailing Home Furnishings*, 18 (February 12, 1947), 8; *Greenwich House News*, 1 (April 1949), 1.

247. Letter from Ruth Adler Schnee to Christa C. Mayer Thurman, August 27, 1987, and the Schnees' résumé. The Schnees were also familiar with stores such as Georg Jensen Inc. (New York), Lott-Nagle (Philadelphia), and Garth Andrews (Bath, Ohio); the 1949 exhibition "Design for Living" at the Detroit Institute of Arts also had a tremendous impact on the young couple.

248. Her old designs were still carried by the shop, however. The last price list for textiles dates from 1965.

249. "Ruth and Ed Schnee, Connoisseurs of the Classic," *Detroit Free Press*, March 23, 1985.

250. On Archimede Seguso, see Madeleine Johnson Saravalle, "Glass in the Blood," *Connoisseur*, 220 (August 1990), 94–95. For information on the Seguso family, refer to "Archimede Seguso compie ottant'anni," *Rivista della stazione sperimentale del vetro*, 19 (July–August 1989), 305–6.

251. For an account of his career, see Toni Lesser Wolf, "Goldsmith, Silversmith, Art Smith," *Metalsmith*, 7 (Fall 1987), 20–25. In 1989 Camille Billops, director of the Archives of Black American Cultural History, New York, showed the author of this biography an old photograph of twenty-five brooches by Art Smith that were based on the Swahili alphabet. There are other references to African culture in his work.

252. This information was obtained at interviews for the Archives of American Art between Art Smith and Paul Cummings, held on August 24 and 31, 1971.

253. Soinne et Kni's history was apparently never recorded. The information given here is derived from letters from Sami Wirkkala, son of the designer Tapio Wirkkala, to Christine W. Laidlaw, November 17, 1989, and January 29, 1990.

254. For a more extended discussion of the artist, see Penny Sparke, *Ettore Sottsass Jnr* (London: The Design Council, 1982); Federica di Castro, ed., *Sottsass Scrapbook* (Milan: Casabella, 1976).

255. For an excellent account of the artist, see William Spratling, *File on Spratling: An Autobiography* (Boston and Toronto: Little, Brown, 1967).

256. *Little Mexico* (New York: Jonathan Cake and Harrison Smith, 1932).

257. For information about Stålhane, see Helena Dahlbäck Lutteman, *Svensk 1900–tals–keramik* (Västerås: ICA Bokförlag, 1985), passim; Glenn Nelson, "Stalhane of Sweden," *Craft Horizons*, 22 (March–April, 1962), 11–16; Ulf Hård af Segerstad, "Keramiska urladdningar," *Form*, 61, no. 6 (1965), 369–73.

258. The information presented here comes from a 1985 Coral Stephens Ltd. promotional brochure and from conversations between Coral Stephens and Kate Carmel in the fall of 1990.

259. For the history of the Steubenville firm, see Lois Lehner, *Lehner's Encyclopedia of U.S. Marks on Pottery, Porcelain & Clay* (Paducah, Kentucky: Collector Books, 1988), 446–47.

260. For the extensive biographical information on Straub, see Marigold Coleman, "A Weaver's Life," *Crafts*, 32 (May–June 1978), 38–43; Mary Schoeser, *Marianne Straub* (London: The Design Council, 1984); and Tanya Harrod, "Sources of Inspiration," *Crafts*, 97 (March–April 1989), 32–33.

261. Hemflit-Kotiahkeruus Oy was taken over by Marianne Strengell's mother, an interior designer, around 1877 to provide employment for the needy near Lovisa. See "Marianne Strengell and Hemflit," *Heimkultur*, March 1937.

262. *Shooting Stars* (1947) was designed for Knoll Associates; see *Art News*, 46 (May 1947), 36.

263. She has designed woven fabrics for Fieldcrest, Inc., from 1963 to the present.

264. For a more detailed listing of exhibitions of the artist's work, consult Robert J. Clark et al., *Design*

in America: The Cranbrook Vision 1925–1950 (New York: Harry N. Abrams in association with The Detroit Institute of Arts and The Metropolitan Museum of Art, 1983), 276.

265. The main source for Pipsan Swanson is Robert J. Clark et al., *Design in America: The Cranbrook Vision 1925–1950* (New York: Harry N. Abrams in association with The Detroit Institute of Arts and The Metropolitan Museum of Art, 1983), 188–89, 273–74.

266. Designs of the Saarinen-Swanson Group are shown in "Art, Architecture and Decoration Merge Ideally in Saarinen-Swanson Modern," *House and Garden*, 92 (October 1947), 152–55, 221ff.

267. For additional information about François Tabard and his atelier, see Amédée Carriat, *Dictionnaire bio-bibliographique des auteurs du pays creusois* (Guéret: Société des Sciences Naturelles et Archéologiques de la Creuse), vol. 7, 519–20, 528.

268. One of Tabard's best-known texts is an explication of the weaver's art first published in the technical section of Joseph Jobé, ed., *Grand Livre de la Tapisserie* (Lausanne: Edita, 1965); this explication, a standard reference, was translated and published in English in *The Art of Tapestry* (London: Thames and Hudson, 1965), 225–64.

269. The investors were E. O. Ehrström, F. Nykänen, G. Serlachius, and Emil Vikström. Helena Tynell, Paavo Tynell's widow, kindly provided historical information on Taito.

270. There is no study of the artist's entire career. For an appreciation, see Joseph Hurley, "Toshiko Takaezu, Ceramics of Serenity," *American Craft*, 39 (October–November 1979), 2–9. See also the ceramist's essay in John Coyne, ed., *The Penland School of Crafts Book of Pottery* (Indianapolis: Bobbs-Merrill, 1975), 138–55.

271. For a comprehensive study of this artist's work, see Kathleen Nugent Mangan, ed., *Lenore Tawney* (New York: Rizzoli, 1990).

272. For pertinent summaries of Teague's work and theories, see Jeffrey L. Meikle, "Celebrated Streamliners: Industrial Designers of the 1930s," *AIA Journal*, 72 (December 1983), 48–55.

273. Walter Dorwin Teague, quoted in Kenneth Reid, "Walter Dorwin Teague: Master of Design," *Pencil Points*, 18 (September 1937), 554.

274. For a brief history of Tecno, see Centrokappa, *Il Design italiano degli anni '50* (Milan: IGIS, 1981), 69, 304. Some of the information presented here was supplied in a letter from Valeria Fantoni Borsani, Osvaldo's daughter, to Christine W. Laidlaw, July 3, 1989.

275. The basic study of the artist's work and life is *Angelo Testa, 40 Years as a Designer, Painter, Weaver* (Chicago: University of Illinois Press, 1983). Additional information presented in this biography comes from the résumé provided by the artist and an interview between Angelo Testa and Christa C. Mayer Thurman, May 1982.

276. Among his major clients were Knoll Associates, Greeff Fabrics, Herman Miller Furniture Co., V'Soske, Edward Field, Everfast, F. Schumacher & Company, and Forester Textile Mills.

277. Much of the information presented here was provided by Helena Tynell, the designer's widow. For an excellent account of Tynell's career, see Oppi Untracht, *Saara Hopea-Untracht, Life and Work* (Porvoo: Werner Söderström, 1988), 35–36.

278. Much of the information presented here was furnished in conversations between John Van Koert and Toni Lesser Wolf in the spring of 1990.

279. For an account of the ceramist's career, see Vibeke Woldbye, *Gertrud Vasegaard, Keramiske Arbejder 1930–1984* (Holstebro: Kunstmuseum, 1985).

280. The most comprehensive history of the firm published thus far is Franco Deboni, *I Vetri Venini* (Turin: Umberto Allemandi, 1989); see also *Venini Glass* (Washington, D.C.: Smithsonian Institution and Venini International, S.R.L., 1981).

281. On their achievements, see *Design: Vignelli* (New York: Rizzoli, 1981); Stephen Kliment, "The Vignellis—Profile of a Design Team," *Designers' Choice '81* (Industrial Design, 1981), 6–12; Linda Lehrer, "Back to Basics," *Continental Profiles*, 3 (March 1990), 28–29, 50–53.

282. Kliment, "The Vignellis," 6, 8.

283. "Per chi deve scegliere mobile di serie: in giunco," *Domus*, 405 (August 1963), d/147; Vittorio Bonacina advertisement, *Domus*, 402 (May 1963), n.p.

284. Niels Vodder's biography was kindly provided by Vibeke Thogersen of the Niels J. Vodder Company in Vedbaek, Denmark, a firm run by the cabinetmaker's grandson that specializes in furniture designed by the elder Vodder.

285. Published concurrently was Rose Slivka, *Peter Voulkos: A Dialogue with Clay* (New York: New York Graphic Society in association with American Crafts Council, 1978).

286. For a detailed history of the company, see Sir Ernest Goodale, *Weaving and the Warners 1879–1970* (Leigh-on-Sea: F. Lewis, 1971); and Hester Bury, *A Choice of Design 1859–1980: Fabrics by Warner & Sons Limited* (London: Warner & Sons, c. 1981).

287. The basic, but still preliminary, study of the designer's work remains David Gebhard and Harriette von Breton, *Kem Weber: The Moderne in Southern California, 1920 through 1941* (Santa Barbara: University of California, 1969).

288. On the designer, see Henrik Sten Møller, *Teme Med Variationer, Hans J. Wegner's Møbler* (Tønder: Sønderjyllands Kunstmuseum, 1979); and Johan Møller Nielsen, *Wegner, en dansk møbelkunster* (Copenhagen: Gyldendal, 1965).

289. Wegner was responsible for some of the furniture for the Town Hall in Århus (1937–42).

290. Both Wegner and Børge Mogensen were leaders in this craftsman movement in the 1940s. They reacted against the popular taste for "highly polished, imitation mahogany" and heavy, upholstered furniture. Mogensen and Wegner were, in fact, among the few trained furniture designers— rather than architects—to collaborate with the cabinetmakers' guild during this period. See Erik Zahle, ed., *A Treasury of Scandinavian Design* (New York: Golden Press, 1961), 16.

291. One of the earliest such designs was a little-known entry for the "International Competition for Low-Cost Furniture Design," held at the Museum of Modern Art in 1948. See Edgar Kaufmann, jr., *Prize Designs for Modern Furniture from the International Competition for Low-Cost Furniture Design* (New York: Museum of Modern Art, 1950), 71.

292. Wegner's handmade furniture is executed by Johannes Hansen. Industrial production is handled by a consortium: Carl Hansen & Son, Odense (chairs); Andreas Tuck, Odense (tables); Ry-møbler, Central Jutland (storage units); Getama, West Jutland (upholstered furniture, beds); and AP Stolen, Copenhagen (exclusive upholstered furniture). See Nielsen, *Wegner*, 126.

293. For the jeweler's career, see Toni Lesser Wolf, "The Arts and Ends of Ed Wiener," *Metalsmith*, 8 (Summer 1988), 26–31; also *Jewelry by Ed Wiener* (New York: Fifty/50, 1988).

294. Doris Wiener worked briefly with her husband, until the early 1950s.

295. For a history of Wilton, see C. E. C. Tattersall and S. Reed, *A History of British Carpets* (1934; Leigh-on-Sea: F. Lewis, 1966), 128–31; and Jennifer Weardon, "Europe," in David Black, ed., *The Macmillan Atlas of Rugs and Carpets* (New York: Macmillan, 1985), 214–21.

296. For Wirkkala's career, see *Tapio Wirkkala* (Helsinki: Finnish Society of Crafts and Design, 1981).

297. The biographical information on Wormley given here is based on an interview between Edward J. Wormley and David A. Hanks, March 19, 1988. See also Edgar Kaufmann, jr., "Edward Wormley: 30 Years of Design," *Interior Design*, 32 (March 1961), 190; and C. Ray Smith, "Edward Wormley," *Interior Design*, 58 (January 1987), 250.

298. Edward J. Wormley, "Design in Relation to Living . . . a Challenge," *Craft Horizons*, 8 (February 1948), 17.

299. Edward J. Wormley, "Two Decades of Interiors: Reminiscences of a Survivor," *Interiors*, 120 (November 1960), 195.

300. For Wright's life and work, see Robert C. Twombly, *Frank Lloyd Wright: An Interpretive Biography* (New York: Harper and Row, 1973); Henry-Russell Hitchcock, *In the Nature of Materials* (1942, New York: Da Capo Press, 1973); David A. Hanks, *The Decorative Designs of Frank Lloyd Wright* (New York: E.P. Dutton, 1979).

301. For a brief survey of the designer's career, see William J. Hennessey, *Russel Wright, American Designer* (Cambridge, Massachusetts: The MIT Press, 1983).

302. For an overview of Zeisel's career, see *Eva Zeisel: Designer for Industry* (Montreal: Musée des Arts Décoratifs de Montréal, 1984).

Additional Caption Information

15. Laminated birch, molded plywood, lacquered; 26 × 23¾ × 34⅞ inches (66 × 60.5 × 88.5 cm)
19. Solid and laminated birch; 17¼ × 13¾ inches (43.8 × 34.9 cm)
24. Aluminum bars with support of wooden slats; 29 × 21¾ × 31 inches (71.1 × 55.2 × 78.7 cm)
27. Photographs and ink drawings; 20 × 30 inches (50.8 × 76.2 cm)
29. Molded plywood with metal rod; 28 × 30⅛ × 31 inches (71.1 × 76.5 × 80.8 cm)
39. Oil on canvas; 44 × 36.5 inches (111.8 × 92.7 cm)
43. Oil on incised Plexiglas, mounted in wood rails 1 inch from white plywood background; Plexiglas: 24¾ inches (63 cm) × bottom, 25⅞ inches (65.9 cm) × top, 26¼ inches (66.7 cm)
52. Lithograph printed in color; 30 × 45 inches (76.2 × 101.6 cm)
74. Borocilicate glass; left to right: 14⅝ inches high × 9⅓ inches diameter (37.2 × 24 cm); 17 inches high × 4 inches diameter (18 × 10 cm); 8½ inches high × 5⅛ inches diameter (21.5 × 13 cm); 5⅝ inches high × 3¼ inches diameter (14.3 × 8.2 cm)
75. Gray glass; 9⁹⁄₁₆ inches high × 9⅞ inches diameter (11.6 × 25.1 cm)
102. Spun, soldered, and hand-engraved sterling silver; 43⅔ inches high (17.2 cm)
106. Silver; urn: 14¼ inches high (36.2 cm); tray: 18 inches diameter (45.7 cm)
110. Painted wood relief; 34 × 23⅛ × 2⅜ inches (86.2 × 58.5 × 6 cm)
112. Original plaster; 19½ × 18¾ × 25½ inches (49.5 × 47.6 × 64.7 cm)
143. Pink Georgia marble, slate base; about 9 feet 9 inches high; base: 34⅛ inches high (86.6 cm) × 42 inches wide (106.7 cm)
266. Oak and cane; 30 inches high (76.2 cm)
345. Oil on canvas; 6 feet 1¼ inches × 55 inches (185.5 × 139.7 cm)
369. Tempera on canvas mounted on wood; 27¼ × 20⅝ inches (69.3 × 52.4 cm)
379. Oil on canvas; 8 feet 6½ inches × 12 feet 9½ inches (259.7 × 390.1 cm)
385. Wood, wire; 31 inches wide (78.7 cm)
409. Oil on canvas; 44 × 50⅛ inches (111.8 × 127.3 cm)
411. Oil on canvas; 9½ × 13 inches (24.1 × 33 cm)
432. Sterling silver, 14-karat gold, ivory, horn, taxidermy eye, coral tourmaline, garnet, cast and fabricated; 4¾ × 2¼ × ¾ inches (12.1 × 57.2 × 1.9 cm)
434. Pen and ink and wash; 9⅜ × 12½ inches (23.8 × 31.7 cm)
442. White and yellow gold; 6¾ inches (17.5 cm)
475. Copper metallic enamel and pencil on canvas; 99⅜ × 99¼ inches (252.4 × 252.1 cm)
504. Offset lithograph; 38 × 24⅝ inches (96.5 × 62.7 cm)

Photograph Credits

Our grateful thanks to the photographers, organizations, and individuals for providing material and kindly permitting its reproduction. All references are to figure numbers:

Courtesy of *American Craft* (formerly *Craft Horizons*), published by the American Craft Council, New York (October 1954), 169, (March–April 1955), 221, (September–October 1956), 443, (July–August 1960), 466; Collection of the American Craft Museum, New York, 432; Gift of Aileen Osborn Walsh, 456; Gift of Mr. and Mrs. Adam Gostomski, 457; Grete Aagaard Andersen, Helebaek, Denmark, 462, 463, 464; © Wayne Andrews/ESTO, Mamaroneck, N.Y. All rights reserved, 62; *Architect's Yearbook*, London (1955), 268; *Architectural Forum*, New York (January 1951), 70, (September 1952), 315; David Arky, New York, 471, 473; Copyright 1990 ARS N.Y.: ADAGP, 357, 360, 402, COSMOPRESS, 111, SPADEM, 339, 347, 348, 377, SPADEM/ ADAGP, 430; Art Centrum, Prague, 405, 407; Artemide S.p.A. Milan, 498; *Art et Décoration*, Paris (April 1932), 107; *Arts and Architecture*, New York (April 1949), 361; *Arts and Decoration*, Paris (January 1935), 12; Atlantis Verlag, Zurich: *Landesaustellung* Catalogue, 1939, 44; B. T. Batsford, Ltd, London: Dorothy Todd and Raymond Mortimer, *The New Interior Decoration* (1929), 120; Bauhaus-Archiv, Berlin, 41; By permission of Edith Luytens Bel Geddes, Hudson, N.Y., Executrix of the Bel Geddes Estate, 81; Benaki Museum, Athens, 451; Brigitta Bertoia, Barto, Pa., 383; Eugene Bielawski, San Francisco, 224; Bildarchiv Preussischer Kulturbesitz, Berlin, 7; James P. Blair, Washington, D.C., 9; Breda Fucine, Milan, 118; Rudolph Burckhardt, New York, 448; The Busch-Reisinger Museum, Harvard University, Cambridge, Mass., 39, Bayer Archives, 41; Cartier Archives, Paris, 109; Francesc Català-Roca, Barcelona, 452; Centre Georges Pompidou, Paris, 517; *Click* Magazine (September 1942), 415, 418; Cranbrook Academy of Art Museum, Bloomfield Hills, Mich., 106; Copyright 1990 DEMART PRO ARTE/ARS N.Y., 375, 419, 420; Denver Art Museum, Herbert Bayer Collection and Archive, 341, 342; The Design Council, London, 305, 306; *Deutsche Kunst und Dekoration*, Berlin (1899), 198; *Domus*, Milan (July 1939), 172, (May 1956), 246, 247, (May 1948), 208, (September 1948), 185, (November 1949), 186, 478, (January 1950), 72, (June 1950), 215, (November–December 1950), 241, (March 1952), 187, (October 1953), 410, (October 1957), 257, (April 1960), 262, (September 1963), 504, (April 1967), 497, (August 1967), 496, (November 1968), 510; © The Eames Office 1990, 31, 61, 310, 311; Editions du Regard, Paris: Anne Bony, *Les Années 40* (1985), 3, Françoise de Bonnevil, *Jean Puiforcat* (1986), 98, 105; Finlands Glasmuseum, Riihimäki, Finland, 77, 78, 214; The Finnish Society of Crafts and Design, Helsinki: *Catalogue: Tapio Wirkkala* (1981), 217; Fontana Arte S.p.A., Milan: Penny Sparke, *Design in Italy* (1988), 321; Barry Friedman Limited, New York, 491; Fritz Hansen, Copenhagen, 275, 276, 278; Gebrüder Thonet GmbH, Frankenberg/F.R. Germany, 196; Georg Jensen Museum, Copenhagen, 102, 136, 137, 139; Glashutte Valentin Eisch KG, Bayer Wald, Germany, 467; Richard P. Goodbody, New York, dust jacket: all objects except Teague lamp, frontispiece: all objects except Philip Johnson/Richard Kelly lamp, 16, 20, 25, 26, 30, 35, 36, 38, 40, 42, 46, 48, 50, 54, 55, 58, 59, 60, 64, 67, 68, 69, 71, 73, 76, 79, 87, 91, 94, 97, 100, 103, 104, 122, 124, 127, 128, 129, 131, 133, 134, 135, 140, 141, 148, 149, 152, 155, 161, 166, 170, 171, 174, 175, 177, 184, 188, 189, 190, 192, 194, 197, 200, 204, 206, 211, 216, 219, 220, 223, 225, 229, 232, 234, 235, 236, 238, 243, 248, 250, 251, 254, 259, 263, 265, 269, 270, 271, 273, 277, 280, 285, 286, 287, 288, 289, 291, 292, 295, 296, 297, 300, 301, 303, 304, 309, 313, 314, 320, 323, 325, 328, 331, 333, 336, 338, 340, 349, 351, 352, 356, 359, 362, 363, 365, 367, 368, 370, 371, 374, 376, 378, 381, 386, 387, 389, 390, 391, 394, 395, 396, 397, 401, 403, 404, 412, 414, 417, 422, 423, 424, 425, 426, 427, 428, 429, 434, 435, 436, 437, 438, 440, 449, 453, 458, 461, 468, 470, 484, 487, 492, 493, 494, 499, 500, 502, 508, 509, 514, 515, 516, 518, 519, 521, 524, 525, 530, back of dust jacket; © Görlich–Istituto Geografico De Agostini S.p.A., Novara, Italy: Marc Lavrillier, *50 Designers dal 1950 al 1975* (1978), 511; Pedro Guerrero, New Canaan, Conn., 302; AB Gustavsberg, Gustavsberg, Sweden, 279, 282, 400; Courtesy of *Harper's Bazaar*, New York, 439; Harwell Hamilton Harris, Raleigh, N.C., 83; Mrs. Wallace K. Harrison, Seal Harbor, Me., 364; Sheila Hicks, New York, 473; Hirshhorn Museum and Sculpture Garden, Smithsonian Institution, Washington, D.C., 475; Ulrico Hoepli, Milan: Roberto Alli, *Mobili Tipo* (1956), 245; Holt, Rinehart and Winston, Inc. (HRW College), Orlando, Fla.: Shirley E. Held, *Weaving* (1973), 334; *House and Garden*, Condé Nast Publications, New York (January 1926), 11; Idea Books Edizioni, Milan: Giovanni Brino, *Carlo Mollino: Architettura Come Autobiografia* (1985), 146, Ignazia Favata, *Joe Colombo and Italian Design of the Sixties*, published by the M.I.T. Press, Cambridge, Mass., 488; Iittala Glassworks, Iittala, Finland, 123, 156, 213, 249, 252; *The Illustrated London News*, London (August 28, 1943), 212; *Industrial Design*, New York (August 1954), 230, 231; *Interiors*, New York (May 1948), 205, (July 1949), 22, (December 1949), 421, (January 1950), 366, (March 1952), 167, (December 1952), 147, (August 1953), 218, (June 1956), 330; Interprint Solna Rotogravyr, Solna, Sweden, 399; Istituto Poligrafico dello Stato, Rome, 181; Grete Jalk, Skodsborg, Denmark, 512, 513; Philip Johnson, New York, 298; *Keramische Zeitschrift* (1955), 258; Mrs. Frederick Kiesler, New York, 114, 116; Knoll International, New York, 65, 66, 318; Kodansha International, Tokyo: Kazuko Koizumi, *Traditional Japanese Furniture* (1986), 168; Kunstmuseums Düsseldorf,

372; Kunstverein für die Rheinlande und Westfalen, Düsseldorf, Germany, 484, 485, 486; Ibram Lassaw, Southampton, N.Y., 448; Schecter Lee, New York, frontispiece: Philip Johnson/Richard Kelly lamp, 84, 96, 108, 125, 130, 138, 142, 144, 145, 160, 261, 283, 284, 299, 307, 326, 337, 350, 373, 384, 431, 450, 454, 455, 459, 460, 465, 503; *Life* Picture Service, New York, 317; © Stig Lindberg/BUS, Stockholm, 281; Little, Brown and Company, Boston: New York Graphic Society, *Dali: A Study of His Art in Jewels* (1959), 413, 416; Madame Jean Lurçat, Paris, 395; Pekka Mäkinen, Kuopio, Finland, 393; Marimekko Oy, Helsinki, 520; Mathsson International, Värnamo, Sweden, 21, 49; Mark Meachem, Teca Cay, S.C., dust jacket: Teague lamp, 18, 19, 23, 28, 32, 63, 93, 199, 228, 316, 324, 480, 483; Fausto Melotti, Milan, 237; Metropolitan Museum of Art, New York, Purchase, Fletcher Fund, 1953, 143; Floris Meydam, 255; G. Meyer, Pforzheim, Germany, 442; Jean Michelon, Paris, 472; Lancaster Miller, Berkeley, Calif.: Vincent Lynch and Bill Hemkin, *Jukebox: The Golden Age* (1980), 90; Robert Miller Gallery, New York, 445; The M.I.T. Press, Cambridge, Mass.: Mary Emma Harris, *The Arts at Black Mountain College* (n.d.), 327; Arnoldo Mondadori Editore S.p.A., Milan: Guia Sambonet, *Ettore Sottsass: Mobili e Qualche Arredamento* (1985), p. 40, 505; Barbara Morgan, Dobbs Ferry, N.Y., 380; Museum of Decorative Art, Copenhagen, 162, 264; Museum of Finnish Architecture, Helsinki, 13; Museum of Modern Art, New York, 14, 15, 17, 19, 24, 27, 29, 51, 52, 53, 74, 75, 110, 112, 266, 310, 345, 369, 379, 409, 411, 434, 504, Page 21 from *Prize Designs for Modern Furniture*, by Edgar Kaufmann, Jr. Copyright 1950, 310, Page 27 from *Organic Design in Home Furnishings*, by Eliot F. Noyes. Copyright 1941, 53; Masato Nakagawa, 327; Hans Namuth, New York, 444; The National Geographic Society, Washington, D.C.: *This England* (1960), p. 40, 9; Trustees of the National Museums of Scotland, Edinburgh, 180; Michio Noguchi, Courtesy of the Isamu Noguchi Foundation, Inc., New York, 165; Ing. C. Olivetti & C., S.p.A., Direzione Design, Milan, 242; A.B. Orrefors Glasbruk, Orrefors, Sweden, 158; Penn Central Corporation, Cincinnati, 80; Perls Galleries, New York, 382; Philadelphia Museum of Art, 294; Photo Researchers, New York, Mark Shaw Estate, 358; Polaroid Corporate Archives, Rochester, N.Y., 92; Giò Pomodoro, Milan, 441; Princeton University Press, Princeton, N.J.: Gertrude Coor, *Neroccio de' Landi* (1961), 343; Puiforcat-Orfèvre, S.A., Paris, 99; The Queens Museum, New York, 5, 6; Rheinisches Bildarchiv, Cologne, 56; RHODOS, Copenhagen, 226; Rijksmuseum, Amsterdam, 176; Giles Rivest, Montreal, Château Defresne, Mr. and Mrs. David M. Stewart, 33, 34, 37, 45, 47, 164, 178, 244, 256, 312, 329, 332, 335, 344, 346, 355, 388, 406, 408, 489, 495, 506, 523, 527, 528, 529; Rizzoli International Publications, New York: Gören Schildt, *Alvar Aalto: The Decisive Years*

(1986), p. 80, 115, p. 268, 126, Franca Helg et al., *Franco Albini, 1930–1970* (1979), p. 144, 191, p. 130, 193, Ann Ward, *Rings Through the Ages* (1981), p. 37, 451; Cervin Robinson, New York, 89; Röhsska Museum, Göteborg, Sweden, 392; Royal Institute of British Architects, London, Photograph Collection, 121; William K. Sacco, West Haven, Conn., 201; Schmuckmuseum Pforzheim, Pforzheim, Germany, 442; Louis Schwankenberg, 462, 463, 464; The Seattle Art Museum, 182; Karen Sebiri, New York, 433; John Selbing, Orrefors, Sweden, 158; Photography by Morton Shand, courtesy of the Museum of Modern Art, New York, 14; Solomon R. Guggenheim Museum, New York, 43; Sotheby's, New York, 163; Sovfoto, New York, 10; Statens Konstmuseer, Stockholm, 281; Coral Stephens, Piggs Peak, Swaziland, 203; Ezra Stoller © ESTO, Mamaroneck, N.Y., 117, 207, 210; Studio Chevojon, Paris, 4; *Studio Yearbook*, London, 25, 76, 233, 253, 293; Copyright 1990 SUCCESSION H. MATISSE/ARS N.Y., 320; Swedish Museum of Architecture, Stockholm, 322; Swedish Society of Crafts and Design, Stockholm, 157, 159, 398, 446, 522; The Harry S. Truman Library, Independence, Mo., 8; United States Department of the Interior, Bureau of Reclamation, Boulder City, Nev., 2; University of California, Santa Barbara, Calif., Architectural Drawing Collection, University Art Museum, 85, 86, 88; Reprinted by permission of the University of Texas Press, Austin: from Mary L. Davis and Greta Pack, *Mexican Jewelry* © 1963 by the authors, and by permission of Margarita Figueroa, 202; UPI/Bettman, New York, 1; Venini S.p.A., Venice, 183, 240; Venturi, Rauch and Scott Brown, Philadelphia, Pa., 476, 477; By courtesy of the Board of Trustees of the Victoria and Albert Museum, London, 119, 173, 179, 447; V. Vigano, Milan, 227; Viking Press, New York: Reproduced from *Calder's Universe* by Jean Lipman (1980), p. 229, 385; Vitra Design Museum, Weil am Rhein, Germany, 490; Niels Vodder, Vedbaek, Denmark, 267; Warner Fabrics, London, 153, 154; Washington University Gallery of Art, Saint Louis, Mo., 364; William Watkins, Philadelphia, 477; Whitney Museum of American Art, New York, 479; Wycombe Chair Museum, High Wycombe, England, 195; Yale University Archives, New Haven, 308; Eva Zeisel Archives, New York, 150, 151.

415

Index

421